SETON HALL UNIVERSITY

RJ506.M4 C58   MAIN

Communicative and cognitive abil

3 3073 00265442 2

D1372342

Communicative and Cognitive Abilities— Early Behavioral Assessment

Proceedings of the conference, Early Behavioral Assessment of the Communicative and Cognitive Abilities of the Developmentally Disabled, held at Orcas Island, Washington in May 1976.

Jointly sponsored by the National Institute of Child Health and Human Development of the United States Public Health Services and the Child Development and Mental Retardation Center, University of Washington, Seattle, Washington.

NICHD—Mental Retardation Research Centers Series

COMMUNICATIVE AND COGNITIVE ABILITIES— EARLY BEHAVIORAL ASSESSMENT

Edited by

Fred D. Minifie, Ph.D.
Professor, Department of Speech and Hearing Sciences
Child Development and Mental Retardation Center
University of Washington
Seattle, Washington 98195
and

Lyle L. Lloyd, Ph.D.
Chairman, Special Education Section
Purdue University
West Lafayette, Indiana 47907

University Park Press
Baltimore

SETON HALL UNIVERSITY
McLAUGHLIN LIBRARY
SO. ORANGE, N. J.

RJ
506
M4
C58

UNIVERSITY PARK PRESS
International Publishers in Science and Medicine
233 East Redwood Street
Baltimore, Maryland 21202

Copyright © 1978 by University Park Press

Typeset by The American Graphic Arts Corporation
Manufactured in the United States of America by
Universal Lithographers, Inc.,
and The Optic Bindery Incorporated.

All rights, including that of translation into other languages, reserved.
Photomechanical reproduction (photocopy, microcopy) of this book
or parts thereof without special permission of the publisher is prohibited.

Library of Congress Cataloging in Publication Data
Main entry under title:

Communicative and cognitive abilities.

(NICHD-Mental retardation research centers series)
Proceedings of a conference held at Orcas Island, Wash.,
May 1976; sponsored by the National Institute
of Child Health and Human Development.
Includes index.
1. Mentally handicapped children—Testing—
Congresses.   2. Cognition in children—Testing—
Congresses.   3. Interpersonal communication—

Congresses.   I. Minifie, Fred D.   II. Lloyd, Lyle L.
III. United States. National Institute of Child Health and
Human Development.   IV. Series: United States. National Institute of
Child Health and Human Development. NICHD-
Mental retardation research centers series.
[DNLM: 1. Communication—In infancy and childhood—
Congresses.   2. Mental retardation—In infancy and
childhood—Congresses.   3. Cognition—In infancy
and childhood—Congresses.   4. Language development—
Congresses. WS107.5.C6 C734 1976]
RJ506.M4C58   618.9´28´588075   78-5910
ISBN 0-8391-1235-1

Contents

Origins of Syntax, Semantics, and Pragmatics

Implications for Intervention

Conference Contributors and Participants

Dr. George Allen
Dental Research Center
University of North Carolina
Chapel Hill, North Carolina 27514

*****Martin S. Banks, Ph.D.**
Department of Psychology
The University of Texas at Austin
Austin, Texas 78712

Michael J. Begab, Ph.D.
Mental Retardation Program
National Institute of Child Health
    and Human Development
Bethesda, Maryland 20014

*****Melissa Bowerman, Ph.D.**
Bureau of Child Research and
Department of Linguistics
University of Kansas
Lawrence, Kansas 66045

Jennifer Buchwald, Ph.D.
Neuropsychiatric Institute
The Center for the Health Sciences
University of California at Los Angeles
760 Westwood Plaza
Los Angeles, California 90024

*****Earl Butterfield, Ph.D.**
Kansas Center for Mental Retardation and
    Human Development
Ralph L. Smith MR Research Center
University of Kansas Medical Center
Kansas City, Kansas 66103

George Cairnes, Ph.D.
Ralph L. Smith Mental Retardation
    Research Unit
University of Kansas Medical Center
Lawrence, Kansas 66044

*****Frances A. Campbell, Ph.D.**
Frank Porter Graham Child Development
    Center
University of North Carolina
Chapel Hill, North Carolina 27514

Robert Carpenter, Ph.D.
Communications Disorders
Child Development and Mental Retardation
    Center
University of Washington
Seattle, Washington 98195

Truman Coggins, R.A.
Communications Disorders
Child Development and Mental Retardation
    Center
University of Washington
Seattle, Washington 98195

Nancy Cook, Ph.D.
Child Language Acquisition Study
Child Development and Mental Retardation
    Center
University of Washington
Seattle, Washington 98195

*****David Crystal, Ph.D.**
Department of Linguistic Science
University of Reading
Whiteknights
Reading RG6 2AA England

*****Philip S. Dale, Ph.D.**
Department of Psychology
University of Washington
Seattle, Washington 98195

*Denotes conference contributors.

*Jill G. deVilliers, Ph.D.
Department of Psychology and Social
  Relations
William James Hall
33 Kirkland St.
Harvard University
Cambridge, Massachusetts 02138

*Peter A. deVilliers, Ph.D.
Department of Psychology and Social
  Relations
William James Hall
33 Kirkland St.
Harvard University
Cambridge, Massachusetts 02138

*Linda Doherty, M.A.
Department of Communication Disorders
2299 Sheridan Rd.
Northwestern University
Evanston, Illinois 60201

*Marcia Dunn, M.A.
Department of Human Development
130 Haworth
The University of Kansas
Lawrence, Kansas 66045

*Rebecca E. Eilers, Ph.D.
University of Miami
Mailman Center for Child Development
P.O. Box 520006
Miami, Florida 33152

*Joseph F. Fagan, III, Ph.D.
Department of Psychology
Case Western Reserve University
Cleveland, Ohio 44106

*Dale C. Farran, Ph.D.
Frank Porter Graham Child Development
  Center
University of North Carolina
Chapel Hill, North Carolina 27514

*Charles A. Ferguson, Ph.D.
Department of Linguistics
Stanford University
Stanford, California 94305

*Neal W. Finkelstein, Ph.D.
Frank Porter Graham Child Development
  Center
University of North Carolina
Chapel Hill, North Carolina 27514

*Macalyne Fristoe, Ph.D.
Department of Audiology and Speech
  Sciences
Purdue University
West Lafayette, Indiana 47907

Dedre Gentner, Ph.D.
Assistant Professor of Psychology
Developmental Psychology Program
Guthrie Hall NI-25
University of Washington
Seattle, Washington 98195

*Edwin K. Hammer, Ph.D.
School of Human Development
The University of Texas at Dallas
Dallas, Texas 75235

*Frances Degen Horowitz, Ph.D.
Department of Human Development
130 Haworth
The University of Kansas
Lawrence, Kansas 66045

Nancy Jackson, Ph.D.
Developmental Psychology
Guthrie Hall NI-25
University of Washington
Seattle, Washington 98195

Crystal Kaiser, Ph.D.
Special Education Department
Keene State College
University of New Hampshire
229 Maine
Keene, New Hampshire 03431

*Barbara K. Keogh, Ph.D.
Professor of Education
Moore Hall
University of California
Los Angeles, California 90024

F. X. Calvin Knobeloch, Ph.D.
Communicative Disorders Section
Biological Sciences Research Center
Division for Disorders of Development and
  Learning
Child Development Research Institute
University of North Carolina at Chapel Hill
Chapel Hill, North Carolina 27514

*Claire B. Kopp, Ph.D.
Department of Education
University of California
Los Angeles, California 90024

*Patricia K. Kuhl, Ph.D.
Department of Speech and Hearing
  Sciences
Child Development and Mental Retardation
  Center
University of Washington
Seattle, Washington 98195

Lewis A. Leavitt, M.D.
Infant Development Section
Waisman Center on Mental Retardation
  and Human Development
2605 Marsh Lane
University of Wisconsin
Madison, Wisconsin 53706

*Lyle L. Lloyd, Ph.D.
Special Education Section
Purdue University
West Lafayette, Indiana 47907

*Edgar L. Lowell, Ph.D.
John Tracy Clinic
806 West Adams Blvd.
Los Angeles, California 90007

*Marilyn O. Lowell, M.A.
Neuropsychiatric Institute
University of California, Los Angeles
760 Westwood Plaza C8-692
Los Angeles, California 90024

*Andrew N. Meltzoff, Ph.D.
Child Development and Mental Retardation
  Center and
Department of Psychiatry and Behavioral
  Sciences
University of Washington
Seattle, Washington 98195

*Fred D. Minifie, Ph.D.
Department of Speech and Hearing
  Sciences
Child Development and Retardation Center
University of Washington
Seattle, Washington 98195

John Mick Moore, M.A.
Child Language Acquisition Study
Child Development and Mental Retardation
  Center
University of Washington
Seattle, Washington 98195

*M. Keith Moore, M.S.
Child Development and Mental Retardation
  Center
University of Washington
Seattle, Washington 98195

*Philip A. Morse, Ph.D.
Department of Psychology
University of Wisconsin
Madison, Wisconsin 53706

Kevin Murphy, Ph.D.
The Audiology Unit
Royal Berkshire Hospital
Reading, England

Rita Naremore, Ph.D.
Speech and Hearing Center
Indiana University
Bloomington, Indiana 47401

*Katherine Nelson, Ph.D.
Ph.D. Program in Psychology
The Graduate School and University Center
  of the City University of New York
33 West West 42 St.
New York, New York 10036

*D. Kimbrough Oller, Ph.D.
Speech and Hearing Division
Mailman Center for Child Development
University of Miami
P.O. Box 520006
Miami, Florida 33152

*Anne D. Pick, Ph.D.
Institute of Child Development
University of Minnesota
Minneapolis, Minnesota 55455

*Craig T. Ramey, Ph.D.
Frank Porter Graham Child Development
  Center
University of North Carolina
Chapel Hill, North Carolina 27514

Jane A. Rieke, Ph.D.
Communication Programs
Experimental Education Unit
Child Development and Mental Retardation
  Center
University of Washington
Seattle, Washington 98195

*Philip Salapatek, Ph.D.
Institute of Child Development
University of Minnesota
51 East River Rd.
Minneapolis, Minnesota 55455

*Keith G. Scott, Ph.D.
Mailman Center for Child Development
University of Miami
P.O. Box 520006
Miami, Florida 33152

Bruce L. Smith, Ph.D.
Child Language Acquisition Study
Child Development and Mental Retardation
  Center
University of Washington
Seattle, Washington 98195

David Sparks, Ph.D.
Department of Speech and Hearing
  Sciences
Parrington Annex II
University of Washington
Seattle, Washington 98195

*Linda Swisher, Ph.D.
Department of Speech and Hearing
  Sciences
University of Arizona
Tucson, Arizona 85721

Dr. Gerald Turkewitz
Albert Einstein College of Medicine
Yeshiva University
1300 Morris Park Avenue
Bronx, New York 10461

*Wesley R. Wilson, Ph.D.
Department of Speech and Hearing
  Sciences
Child Development and Mental Retardation
  Center
University of Washington
Seattle, Washington 98195

*Ronald S. Wilson, Ph.D.
Child Development Unit
School of Medicine
University of Louisville
511 South Floyd St.
Louisville, Kentucky 40202

Foreword

The term mental retardation includes individuals with a very wide range of abilities and disabilities, spanning a spectrum from total dependency to near normality. By definition, these individuals share common attributes of low measured intelligence and a coexisting impairment in adaptive behavior. Underlying and contributing to these impairments are deficiencies in language and communicative skills.

The importance of the relationship between communicative and cognitive abilities can hardly be overstated. Children with intellectual deficits, whatever the etiology or severity of the condition, generally evidence delay in or nonacquisition of speech or language development. The absence of such skills, or other more rudimentary forms of communication, make learning or adaptation to environmental demands virtually impossible. In the human condition it may well be an indispensable element for continued cognitive growth. It is critical, therefore, that deficits be diagnosed early and intervention strategies applied.

The relationship of cognition and communication is not unidirectional. Just as intelligence has impacts on language acquisition and facility, so do communication deficits deriving from inadequacies of sensory inputs—as in blindness or deafness—affect cognition. Children develop cognitively and socially through mediated learning experiences, i.e., the interpretation by adults of meaningful events, objects, and relationships in their environment. Clearly, such mediation cannot take place without some method for communication, verbal or nonverbal.

The importance of communication research for understanding and modifying retarded performance is being increasingly recognized by behavioral scientists. The research, much of it conducted with normal infants and children, but relevant nevertheless, has addressed highly diverse and complex issues and phenomena. These have included infant speech perception and processing, concepts underlying language acquisition, receptive and expressive language relationships, and language structure and language training, to name but a few. More recently, generated in part by the successful use of symbolic representations with chimpanzees, investigators have turned their attention to the development of nonspeech communication systems for severely and profoundly retarded persons.

The proliferation of knowledge from these related studies promises to advance concepts and theory in child development and to significantly impact on the learning and adaptive capabilities of retarded persons. To realize this promise, it is essential that scientists be afforded a forum for the continuous exchange of information; that newly reported findings be subjected to careful scrutiny, and that emerging knowledge be rigorously compiled, analyzed, synthesized, and disseminated. These processes must of necessity be an integral part of our national effort to combat mental retardation.

In keeping with its focal responsibilities for research in mental retardation, the NICHD in 1971 launched the first in a projected seminar series on different aspects of this pressing national problem. The series was conceived as a co-sponsorship arrangement with specific mental retardation research centers, selected for their special interest or scientific expertise in a given content area. These centers, twelve in number and geographically located in various universities, constitute the nation's primary resource for research in mental retardation and related aspects of human development.

The University of Washington, Child Development and Mental Retardation Center served as host and co-sponsor for the conference from which this book is compiled. Their history of productive and far-ranging research on many dimensions of cognitive and communicative abilities makes them a particularly good selection for this role.

The first topic selected for this series was "Language of the Mentally Retarded," an indication of the crucial importance with which this area of research was regarded. The current volume—eighth in the series—despite the range of possible alternative topics, focuses once more on the language or communication theme.

The relatively short time interval between these two conferences speaks eloquently to progress in the field and complexity of the issues. This treatise and other recent publications offer no final solutions to the remediation of communication deficits in the mentally retarded. Neither does it provide complete understanding of the interrelationship and interdependence of cognitive and communicative abilities.

Nevertheless, this book represents a significant step forward toward helping the retarded, through the development of communication skills, to a fuller realization of life's opportunities and benefits.

Michael J. Begab

Preface

The conference from which this book was written was the result of cooperation between the National Institute of Child Health and Human Development and the Child Development and Mental Retardation Center at the University of Washington. The conference was designed to tackle one of the most complex and difficult problems facing child development specialists—that of assessing the relation between cognitive development and communicative development in normal and impaired populations of children. A variety of disciplines is represented among the contributors to this volume, since individual scientists attempting to understand this relationship are often frustrated and overwhelmed because of the need to extend their knowledge far beyond the bounds of the scientific discipline within which they find themselves. In one sense, child development specialists have found themselves approaching the understanding of the developmentally disabled child in much the same way that the seven blind men approached the elephant, each from a different perspective, each seeing only a small portion of the entire animal, and each responding to the information from his own discipline as if it represented the entire truth about the nature of the problem.

We should acknowledge at the outset of this volume that the knowledge base about the relations between communicative and cognitive development is only beginning to be put together. We see but the dim outlines of the issues that need to be addressed in order to fully understand the relations. Perhaps a much more appropriate analogy is offered by the Greek scholar, Plato, in his Allegory of the Cave. Plato described a number of persons seated side by side and facing the back of a cave. They were lifelong prisoners chained in such a way that their heads would only face the back of the cave. Behind them was an inclined path on which human figures walked back and forth, and behind the path was a huge fire that projected shadows of the human figures on the back of the cave. The prisoners, who were chained and spent their lives only looking at the back of the cave, thought that the shadows they saw on the back wall were reality. When one of the prisoners finally escaped and saw what the reality was, and came back and explained it to the other prisoners, none would believe because their experience and knowledge caused them to view the shadows as reality. In much the same way, present scholars constrained by the limited focus of their own disciplinary provincialism have begun to describe the small slices of reality they have observed in looking at communicative and cognitive abilities of the developing child.

The conference held on Orcas Island in Puget Sound during May, 1976 was designed to bring together groups of experts in the assessment of sensory abilities, memory, sensorimotor and cognitive development, developmental phonology, persons knowledgeable in the nature of syntactic, semantic, and pragmatic aspects of communicative development, and persons with substantial background in early intervention with children possessing communicative or cognitive delays. As will be seen from the reading of this book, the conference was not so much a shadow show as it was a broadening of knowledge regarding the types of assessment and intervention strategies being employed by other specialists in child development fields.

This volume provides a current review of the issues and strategies being employed in the assessment of, and intervention with, children with communicative and cognitive handicaps. One of the greatest difficulties encountered by child development specialists is deciding when and where to intervene with a child who has a communicative or cognitive delay. In large measure this difficulty is related to the pervasive lack of information about how to assess such delays and how to chart progress in communicative and cognitive development. It is hoped that one of the by-products of the publication of this volume will be the stimulation of professionals in several different disciplines to undertake the establishment of adequate data bases for assessing children with communicative and cognitive delays. The time has come for large scale studies of the communicative and cognitive abilities of many of the handicapped populations: mentally retarded, hearing impaired, visually impaired, neuromotor impairments, etc.

The first section of this book deals with current information on assessment. Scott's chapter critically reviews the advantages and disadvantages of high risk registers as a means of facilitating early identification of children with communicative and cognitive impairments. Even if screening instruments were available to allow for the efficient identification of children suspected of having communicative and cognitive delays, more detailed assessment of intelligence may need to be handled with care. Horowitz and Dunn argue that traditional testing instruments do not assess the parameters relevant to a child's growing communicative and cognitive skills. They call for an enlightened view of intelligence testing in their chapter— suggesting that assessing children's performances on behaviors more closely related to the everyday world of the child would provide a better means of assessing intellectual abilities.

W. Wilson and Salapatek and Banks provide very comprehensive chapters dealing with sensory assessment of children with auditory and visual impairments, respectively. These chapters not only review the current literature, but critically evaluate the assessment strategies being employed, and point directions for future research.

The second section reviews issues related to memory, sensorimotor development, and cognitive development through the use of: 1) children's attentional responses to visual stimuli of varying levels of novelty (Fagan), 2) the Bayley Scale of infant development (R. Wilson), and 3) children's performances on imitation and object permanence tasks requiring different levels of cognitive development (Moore and Meltzoff).

The third section deals with the processes through which young infants acquire the ability to produce and perceive differences among the speech sounds of their developing language system. Morse discusses infant speech perception, which is followed by Kuhl's comparison of the perceptual responses of human infants to speech and speech-like stimuli to those of primates and chinchillas to similar stimuli. The development of meaningful utterances and the impact upon such development by the interactions the young child has with the caregivers in his environment is highlighted in the fourth section. Collectively, the chapters by deVilliers and deVilliers, Bowerman, Ramey et al., and Nelson provide a comprehensive tutorial of the issues related to the pragmatics of communication and their impact on early child language development.

The final section of the book deals with the implications of basic research on communicative and cognitive development for professionals engaged in early intervention. The chapters by Lowell and Lowell, Hammer, and Doherty and Swisher describe current assessment and intervention technologies being employed with auditorily handicapped, visually impaired, and autistic children. The chapter by Keogh and Kopp provides a critical look at what needs to be done when moving from assessment to intervention with persons with communicative or cognitive delays.

The major papers in each of the four sections are primarily the product of the authors indicated, however, each paper was enhanced by the interaction with the other contributors, including several conference participants named in the list of contributors who are not identified with any given papers. In addition to the major papers in each section, discussion summaries were prepared by Dale, Eilers, Fristoe, Oller, and Pick. These five discussions provide a summary of the major points in each section, some interrelations of the various papers, participants' reactions to the various papers, and to some of the authors' own post-conference reflections. The book concludes with a final summary by Earl Butterfield, which provides an overview of some of the major issues and interrelationships of the conference as a whole.

Five people in particular deserve recognition and thanks: Tali Ott, who was responsible for coordinating the conference schedule, and Mick Moore, who supervised the use of audio-visual equipment at the conference. Without them the conference would not have run so smoothly. The services of Mary Johnson Kern, secretary of NIH, are also appreciated. Her contributions helped greatly in the success of the conference and the resultant book. Finally, a special thanks to Ellen Smock and Connie Long for their careful attention to bibliographical detail and consistency.

For many professionals, this book may well serve as the first multidisciplinary look at the realities of assessment and intervention with developmentally delayed populations. The main theme at the conference was that we are only beginning—but it is a *good* beginning.

Fred D. Minifie
Lyle L. Lloyd

Communicative and Cognitive Abilities—Early Behavioral Assessment

EARLY ASSESSMENT

The Rationale and Methodological Considerations Underlying Early Cognitive and Behavioral Assessment

Keith G. Scott

This paper addresses three basic questions: What is the need to assess early development? Who are the children that should be assessed? What are the problems in making early assessments? The rest of the volume addresses questions concerning the abilities and behaviors that we seek to measure, how these measurements are made, and how they are applied.

Early assessment of cognitive behavior is a new and exciting prospect for behavioral science. Its utility will ultimately center on three simple questions: Does it work? How much does it cost? Can we (this society) afford it? The answers to these questions are complex, and they lie at the intersection of scientific, ethical, educational, and economic concerns. A decade ago, most of us would have attempted to restrict our concerns to the scientific sector. The climate of research support makes this position no longer reasonable. In any case, such a restriction makes neither clinical nor economic sense in this mission-oriented area for the study of human development. It is clear that assessment and early intervention must be conjointly planned activities, and that their impact on society should be carefully studied.

THE NEED TO ASSESS EARLY DEVELOPMENT

Early assessment is one component of a general model of health care that aims to prevent handicaps that will interfere with health, development, and education. If it were to succeed, then all individuals born in our society would enter the mainstream of general well being. Prevention is thus viewed as a process of attenuation of risk for, and of, handicapping conditions.

3

The general prevention model has two components. The *primary prevention* component attempts to eliminate genetic errors and to eliminate obstetric complications so that infants are alive, well, and normal at birth. A postnatal care component attempts to further minimize infant mortality and enhance the health and developmental status of the newborn. Primary prevention is already immersed in a network of increasing scientific, ethical, and economic concerns. Genetic counseling and genetic screening have acquired an increased scientific base, but they are beset with questions of individual freedom and cost effectiveness (National Academy of Sciences, 1975). Improvements in perinatal care have reduced infant mortality (Chase, 1974) with the development of intensive care units. However, there are now serious concerns about the quality of survival of very low birth weight infants (less than 1500 grams), and issues of cost-benefit are at issue in competition for the health care dollars. The area of primary prevention is more developed than that of secondary prevention. However, the fiscal and ethical concerns that are now of large issue for primary prevention have close parallels to what will develop in the field of secondary prevention. The previously referred to report, *Genetic Screening* (National Academy of Sciences, 1975), contains much pertinent information.

Secondary prevention is concerned with ameliorating and managing preexisting or adventitious conditions, so that they do not become significant handicaps that will preclude an individual from entering the mainstream of society. Most behavioral and educational techniques are included in this rubric. Again, we have witnessed an increased concern about both ethical and monetary considerations associated with classification of children (Hobbs, 1975a,b,c) and with the benefits that may result from the intervention that will follow (Bronfenbrenner, 1974).

The role of early assessment is to detect infants and children who show early evidence of handicapping conditions, so that intervention or treatment can be arranged while it is most likely to be effective. In health care, the wisdom of taking action to prevent or ameliorate disease as soon as it can be detected is an almost accepted a priori. However, in behavioral intervention, the efficacy of early detection and intervention is not so generally acknowledged. Most studies have shown short-term gains in performance following early intervention (Stanley, 1973). However, the long-term prognosis of children with developmental delays can only be answered in prospective studies that follow a pattern of assessment as it relates to intervention, with the psychological educational and socioeconomic sequellae spelled out by following individuals through young adulthood. In studying the results of early assessment, studies that fail to follow infants at least through the first and second grades are unlikely to be very convincing. What needs to be said clearly is that the benefits of assessment and intervention have not been clearly demonstrated, although the outlook is not entirely bleak (Bronfenbrenner, 1974).

General statements about the efficacy of early intervention, such as those made earlier, may be inappropriate because they do not distinguish various models of detection and secondary prevention. The author would like to suggest three such models and consider their implications for systems for classifying children, choice of intervention (curriculum) content, form of intervention structure, choice of measures for evaluation and measurement of outcome, and conclusions about the efficacy of intervention.

Diagnosis Treatment Model

The *diagnosis-treatment model* is the first and oldest. It is medical in its origin, and is tied to the conception of a disease entity that, following identification, can be cured or managed by a prescribed treatment. The value of early identification in this framework is unlikely to be seriously questioned, because many disease entities are progressive and are likely to produce damage to related parts of the human biological structure. The treatment of congenital cretinism and phenylketonuria (PKU) are notable examples. The model has difficulty dealing with conditions that cannot be described by a specific syndrome, but rather represent aberrations in normal development. Although a condition may interfere with normal progress in school, it might not be precisely identified. Thus, there has been a serious question whether minimal brain dysfunction (MBD) is really a disease entity that may be appropriately treated by medical procedures (Schmitt, 1975).

The diagnosis-treatment model classifies children in terms of disease entities. The content of intervention is a prescribed course of medical treatment that is specific, generally well-understood, or at least accessible to systematic studies of extent, duration, and effectiveness. The measures of benefit from diagnosis and treatment are the removal or control of symptoms so that a syndrome can be judged no longer present, or at least controlled. Recovery is thus reasonably definable, and early intervention is most often effective.

The previous paragraph oversimplifies and minimizes the problems of medical research. It serves, however, as a useful general description. In general, the diagnosis-treatment model is highly appropriate in dealing with ailments that are already present, rather than as a basis for planning health maintenance. From a research point of view, it leads to the study of diseases and syndromes rather than normal development. It thus tends to be more appropriate in studying severe, rather than mild, handicaps.

Ability-Enrichment Model

The second model is the *ability-enrichment model*. This model is tied to the statistical conception of normality as described by the Gaussian distribution. The incidence of mental retardation has been overpredicted, based on these considerations (Mercer, 1973). For the environmentalist, prevention consists of identifying individuals who score low on some population trait, such as intelligence, and then providing a stimulating environment to elevate performance. This is postulated to initiate a chain from early identification to early stimulation, that has sequellae in educational and socioeconomic status. Because low performance on many psychomotor abilities is correlated with low socioeconomic status (Bloom, 1964; Hunt, 1961), the position has developed that cultural deprivation is a condition regularly associated with low performance on measures of ability. This position has been attacked as a myth (Ginsburg, 1972). The value of compensatory education has also been attacked (Jensen, 1969), but others (Kamin, 1974) have suggested that most of the data are at best questionable and are often methodologically flawed.

The ideas surrounding the ability-enrichment model have led to widespread social programs, such as Head Start, that seem to be relatively permanent parts of the national scene, and that are reviewed in detail elsewhere (Horowitz and Paden, 1973). It is interesting to note that this program has progressed from being generally oriented toward ability enrichment to having a more general health or educational maintenance role.

The systems of classifying children in the ability-enrichment model have most typically involved performance on a standardized test. For example, individuals below certain cut-off scores have been classified as borderline, mildly, moderately, or severely retarded. Although notions of social adaptations have been included, they are frequently very highly correlated with the ability scores, and are therefore not as independent as they sound in a written description. The model, with its implied ties to deprivation, or the need for enrichment, has not had specific content. Different investigators have had very different ideas concerning the nature and content of intervention material. The range of structure of intervention material has been wide, and only rarely (Karnes, 1969; Miller and Dyer, 1975) has an attempt been made to compare programs. The choice of measure for evaluation of outcome has tended to rely heavily on the same psychometric devices used to identify and classify. A number of major methodological problems result from this fact. They include: mean regression, motivational differences between experimental families who remain active in a program and controls but who do not have the same degree of self-selection, and the relation among pre-test measures, post-test measures, and the curriculum content. The ability-enrichment theorist is attempting to change a trait or ability, rather than to just promote learning. Thus, a program that uses the Stanford-Binet as a test-retest instrument should not use the Binet materials in curriculum content. The extreme case is clear. What is not so clear is when curriculum material is similar enough to the test materials to produce increased performance from generalized learning rather than from the training of abilities. The positions of the trait theorist and the learning and transfer theorist are paradoxical. According to the learning and transfer position, transfer of training is likely to occur under conditions where the similarities of stimulus and response are greatest to those present during training. The enrichment of traits can call for almost any environmental stimulation, such as a mobile on a crib, to produce an increase in a trait.

A more recently developed position for ability theory attempts to establish aptitude by treatment interactions. Thus, an interaction between type of instruction or curriculum content and a classification based on a trait profile is postulated. So far as this author is aware, this theory has not been systematically applied in early intervention research (see Berliner and Cahen, 1973; Snow, 1974).

It is clear that programs associated with the ability-enrichment model generally produce short-term increments in performance. The data on long-term sequellae in terms of psychological educational sequellae are either absent or unconvincing. A result is that the evidence that there are direct benefits from the measurement of abilities and the resultant intervention has been cast in grave doubt (Bronfenbrenner, 1974).

Assessment-Intervention Model

The *assessment-intervention model* is based on the idea that an individual achieves specific behaviors or skills that can be described either in a developmental sequence or in terms of a task analysis, and that these skills and their prerequisites can be assessed and then changed by a structured training experience. The thrust in the intervention field to develop this model has come from a number of diverse, and in their theoretical foundations, sometimes opposed, directions. On one hand, behavioral management techniques have emphasized skill analysis, developmentally defined goals, and criterion referenced curriculum material. On the other hand, from psycholinguistics and cognitive development, comes a literature that presents the general hierarchical model of cognitive prerequisites leading to the stages of language learning and cognition. What these very different theoretical origins share is a distrust of traits and quotients and a desire to explicate sequence and order. Their marriage may seem unlikely when it is considered that one has its origins in techniques of training and the other in the content of knowledge, but their common bonds are clear. This combination has found application in intervention research (Bricker and Bricker, 1974). Other workers (e.g., Karnes, 1975) are also basing intervention programs on developmentally based and referenced analyses.

Within the assessment-intervention model, early detection consists of identifying early delays in normal development. These delays are seen as part of a pattern or sequence of cognitive skills. The work of Piaget is of major interest in this connection and an important set of experimental scales are now available (Uzgiris and Hunt, 1975). Rather than classifying children with respect to age norms, what becomes important is to place the individual at his developmental stage. Thus, if the child is either advanced or delayed, a point of entry and a content for the curriculum materials is defined. There is, therefore, a close relationship between assessment and curriculum content. Such a model is generally appropriate for a wide variety of developmentally based tasks, such as the cognitive prerequisites of language, or for a task that might be task analyzed, like early reading. The measure of the outcome of intervention is the progress on the task or skill. In the short term, this is the immediate acquisition of a component, and on the long term, it is the rapidity and final level of development that is achieved. There are already some experimental applications of the model (Paraskevopoulos and Hunt, 1971) to the study of rearing differences. The assessment-intervention model is too new to be evaluated in terms of the efficacy of intervention. Just as the diagnosis-treatment model is the logical outcome of medical practice, and just as the ability-enrichment model stems from psychometrics, so the assessment-intervention model is a systematic position for developmental psychology.

POPULATIONS IN NEED OF ASSESSMENT

A brief review of the outcome populations from newborn nursery care provides a useful framework to discuss the need for early assessment and to consider questions concerning the relationship between screening and more in depth levels of assessment.

The infants born in a hospital providing comprehensive newborn care may be classified as follows:

1. *Infants from the Normal Nursery.* These children have healthy parents, normal gestation, uncomplicated delivery, and are of normal birth weight.

Furthermore, they have no detectable physical, metabolic, or neurological deficits. Such children constitute 90% of all births. (The incidence and population estimates given here and in the rest of this paper are not available from any single source. In some instances, they are based on excellent data, e.g., Mercer, 1973; in others, they are based on studies aimed to demonstrate quality of outcome, rather than incidence, e.g., Rubin, Rosenblatt, and Barlow, 1973. However, in most cases, several independent sources are available and they represent reasonable gross estimates.)

Subsequently, because of metabolic disease or other unknown etiological causes, about 0.1% of them will show marked developmental anomalies and will be classified as severely retarded (Smith and Simons, 1975). These developmental problems are not discernable at birth, and detection usually results from a medical examination.

By the time the normal infants have reached second grade, 15–20% of them will have been referred to a school psychologist, social worker, or speech therapist for some problem that significantly interferes with normal progress in school. This group of children is commonly not identified as having any handicap before first grade.

2. *Infants from Intensive Care Units.*   Infants from such facilities have a number of distinct problems that sometimes overlap. The majority of them are of low birth weight (90%). They may also be critically ill and/or suffer from respiratory distress. They are separated from their mothers for a prolonged period in isolettes, and are typically deprived totally of normal love, warmth, and vestibular stimulation. The mother is usually deprived of all interaction with her baby, possibly resulting in frustration and deconditioning. The babies are commonly kept in the hospital for periods of one to four months. Within this group, it is useful to distinguish two subgroups:

a. *Handicapped Infants.*   These are infants who are damaged because of congenital defects, birth trauma, or functional deficits in the neonatal period. These comprise 0.2% of all infants. Examples are those suffering from severe sensory handicaps, genetic disorders such as Down's Syndrome, or neurological deficits such as paralysis or spasticity. These infants have clinically obvious signs of relatively permanent handicapping conditions, and are reliably diagnosed by the attending neonatologist. They are the largest group of children who will be classified as severely or profoundly retarded. While good epidemiologic data is not available, it would seem that about 66% of the severely handicapped are diagnosed following medical examinations in the nursery or during early infancy.

b. *High Risk Infants.*   These infants have received intensive care as a result of medical complications, but at the time of discharge from intensive care they have no clinically obvious handicaps. They have been typically classified as high risk infants. These children comprise about 9–10% of all births. Prospective studies show that by school age, the incidence of some handicapping condition that interferes with normal progress in school, ranging from mild speech disorders to a need for special class placement, is about 30–35% (see Rubin, Rosenblatt and Barlow, 1973; Weiner, 1968).

It has been supposed that both the cost of screening and the time required for early identification of handicapping conditions could be reduced by the use of registers of "high risk," with "high risk" defined by the requirement of intensive care during the neonatal period. This does not seem realistic when the above incidences are translated into population figures. Of 10,000 infants, approximately 1,000 (10%) will need intensive care. (The percentages given in the parentheses in this section are of the total population.) Of these infants from intensive care, 20 (0.2%) will be classified as severely handicapped before discharge. Another 300 infants (3%) from intensive care will need some special services during their early school years. Considering the 9,000 who receive normal nursery services, 10 (0.1%) will subsequently fail to develop normally and will be diagnosed as severely handicapped. The severely handicapped are then this 10 and the 20 from intensive care, who together make up 0.3% of infants. Of the 9,000 normal nursery infants, 1,350 (15%) will be referred for some problem that significantly interferes with normal progress in school. When mild handicaps are considered, although the incidence is twice as high in high risk infants, the absolute numbers in the population will be 300 from intensive care versus 1350 from the normal nursery. It follows that a register of "high risk," consisting of infants who have received intensive care, would falsely eliminate the majority of children who will have mild handicapping conditions. Given that the majority of mild and moderate handicaps could only be detected by screening the general population of infants, and that many handicaps are not detected until school age (Rubin et al, 1973; Weiner, 1968; Werner, Bierman, and French, 1971), an attractive case can be made for the general screening of *all* infants for behavioral or cognitive handicaps. There are, however, other reasons to suggest that this may be unwise, at least at this time.

THE METHODOLOGICAL PROBLEMS OF ASSESSMENT

At present, widespread early screening or developmental assessment cannot be advocated on the grounds that data are not available to indicate the benefits that would be accrued, the costs involved, or the ethical implications of these problems. Involved in developing this basic core of information are a number of problems that are now considered.

The Problem of What to Measure

In deciding what behavioral processes should be assessed early, we are most likely going to look at some process, trait, or skill that will later prove significant for education of psychosocial sequellae in the individual's life. The relationship between cognitive and behavioral processes in infancy and these same processes in later life is a complex one that is not well understood. McCall, Hogarty, and Hurlburt (1972) have presented some data on the relationship between sensorimotor development and later IQ. Wachs (1975) has added further data of this kind. These attempts are important and all too rare. However, they reflect the lack of communication between the research in early cognition and the interventionist. In deciding what to measure, the first question is: What is it that one aims to detect early—some symptoms that might detect a disease entity? low status on an intellectual trait that might reflect a need for environmental stimulation? a significant delay in development that calls for a program of intervention? These are only some of the possible questions.

At the heart of this matter is the fact that we have inadequate data describing the course of normal development. Although theory has its role, it has too often led American researchers on child development down minor garden paths, resulting in the accumulation of masses of trivial data.

An additional major concern is that there are two appropriate criterion reference groups against which an infant's performance might be assessed. The term "mental retardation" assumes the theoretical position that the so-called "retarded child" suffers from a developmental delay, or a "deficit," rather than from a "defect." One position originally advanced by Dingman and Tarjan (1960) in this country, and presented most conspicuously by Zigler (1967), supposes that there are, in fact, two distributions as shown in Figure 1, an "organic" and a "familial-genetic" group of children. The epidemiologic data presented by Mercer (1973) support this position.

The data presented in the previous section on population of infants cast some light on the issue of what we are trying to detect. There seem to be two groups of infants who are not being detected until they present gross problems. The first is the

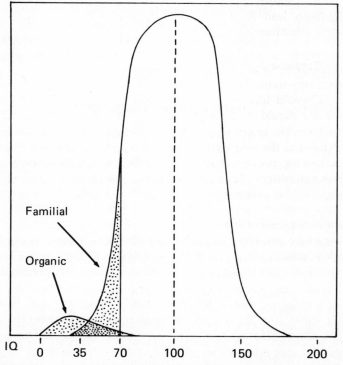

Figure 1.   The incidence of mental retardation diagrammed to show the two distributions that have been postulated. The figure is based on one presented by Zigler (1967).

group of children who seem normal at birth, but subsequently fail to develop and are classified as severely retarded, usually following medical diagnosis. It was estimated that they comprise about 0.1% of the population. They have either inborn errors of metabolism that are often autosomally recessive, such as severe galactosemia, Hurler's syndrome, or retardation of unknown etiology that may include CNS dysfunction, such as spasticity, hypertonia, or seizures. These children suffer from some clear physiological deficit. The second group consists of those children either from intensive care or from the normal nursery, who are healthy on discharge, but who will subsequently be found to have handicaps that significantly interfere with normal progress in school. The available data suggest that this group may include 20% of all school-age children. Most of them have some specific handicaps, often called learning disabilities, that are presently described largely from a trait perspective with instruments such as the Illinois Test of Psycholinguistic Abilities (Kirk, McCarthy, and Kirk, 1968; Paraskevopoulos and Kirk, 1969). Although widely used in educational practice, this approach is open to serious methodological questions and should be considered experimental (Hammill and Larsen, 1974; Wepman, Cruickshank, Deutsch, Morency, and Strother, 1975; Ysseldyke and Salvia, 1974).

An assessment or screening program could legitimately be aimed at either or both of these populations. The selection of process and measures will depend on intent. To advocate early screening or assessment, other than as a subject for research, without a sound theoretical and empirical basis as to what should be measured, will likely lead to mislabeling with attendant ethical problems, and an inability to assess effectiveness and benefits.

The Problem of Response Availability

Infants possess a very limited response repertoire. Thus, even if the experimenter has decided what he would like to assess, he must now try to decide what index or dependent measure should be used. A measure that is appropriate with a neonate will often be unsuitable at three months, six months, or indeed at any later age. When this is related to the previous section, it becomes clear that we are attempting to assess a developing process that is itself indexed by a developing and perhaps interactive response system. Thus, the involuntary looking so fruitfully utilized by Fagan (1978) in studying infant memory, becomes a voluntary strategy at a later age (Vurpillot, 1968). Furthermore, this choice of response has significant implications for the usefulness of an assessment procedure in applied or clinical settings, and as is shown later, when we consider the problem of access and accessor, results in issues that involve effectiveness, costs, and professional ethics.

Three general, but not totally discreet, classes of response systems are available:

1. *Reflexive or automatic behaviors that change as a function of stimulus input.* Such behaviors include visual fixation, heart rate, electrophysiological measures such as evoked potentials, and non-nutritive sucking. These techniques, in the main, have developed out of techniques used in experimental psychology. These behaviors are available very early and do no require that the experimenter obtain reinforcement control of the infant's response system.

2. *Behaviors that require reinforcement control of a response system by the experimenter.* These techniques are derived from operant methodology and seem to be useful from about five months on, and include the Tangible Reinforcement in Operant Conditioning Audiometry (TROCA) of Fulton and Lloyd (1969) and the recently introduced Visually Reinforced Infant Speech Discrimination (VRISD) technique (Eilers, Wilson, and Moore, 1977). These procedures have the advantages of precise control, parsimony of response in many applications, and simplified parallels with adult measures.

3. *Behaviors that occur in naturalistic settings.* Such behaviors include dyadic interactions between mothers and infants, observation of free interactive play between young children, and other nonlaboratory situations. The disciplinary thrust here comes from ethology and the conception of the "ethogram," a species-specific pattern of biologically adaptive behavior such as that which occurs in imprinting or mating. An example is the observation of feeding and behavior in the immediate postpartum days (e.g., Klaus, Jerauld, Kreger, McAlpine, Steffa, and Kennell, 1972; Thoman, Leiderman, and Olson, 1972). This procedure has the advantage of looking at a behavior that is critically important for early biological adaptation. Any disruption may be critical, and therefore may be particularly diagnostic. Also, if naturalistic observation is seen as a potentially valuable technique, then looking at critical interactions and situations provides some limits on the length of observation.

The Problem of Access and the Accessor

The choice of response measure and, indeed, the entire testing protocol, depends on what access is available to the infant, be it newborn, nursery, day care, home, or pediatrician's office. Clearly, a technique requiring electrophysiological recording in a screened room is unlikely for a home visit. On the other hand, a technique that requires an hour of a professional pediatrician's time in completing a mass screening examination is impractical on grounds of cost. Although at first the research effort in early assessment will be addressed to what process to measure with what response, the questions of where the procedure will be used and by what professional will rapidly become an issue. As Hobbs (1975a,b,c) points out, "Each professional group has a claim on part of the vocabulary of exceptionality. Thus, categories and labels function in part as boundary markers for professions, as definers of territory, as trademarks of the guilds. One can confidently predict a substantial measure of objection from professional groups to any proposed modification of classification systems, because the process could result in a redefinition of professional boundaries" (p. 27).

Problems of Validity

Early assessment and screening scales or instruments must ultimately be validated against some criterion in order to demonstrate their effectiveness. Very often psychometric devices have found their way into widespread use well in advance of any demonstrated utility. Clearly, this mistake should be avoided in early assessment. Depending on the use of a device, different kinds of validity will be of major concern. Following the major types of validity introduced by Cronbach (1949), one might distinguish among the following:

1. *Concurrent Validity.* Concurrent validity is of concern when, as the result of a testing procedure, an immediate estimate of current behavioral, intellectual, or developmental status will be made and used either to classify infants or as a starting point in arranging for intervention. Examples of concurrent validity data are inter-test correlations and comparisons between different methods of estimating the development of object permanence (e.g., Kramer, Hill, and Cohen, 1975). The experimental effort required here is only modest compared to other problems of validity.

2. *Predictive Validity.* Predictive validity is required if we wish to enable measures obtained at one age to be predictive of status at another age. Ultimately one might hope to predict status in adulthood from infant performance. This seems remote, and the prediction of performance in the early elementary school from infant status might be a more reasonable goal. It should be noted that at risk registers require sound data on predictive validity and that they should not be constructed in its absence. The experimental effort required to achieve predictive validity is large. Only well-run prospective (longitudinal) studies can provide such data. In themselves, such studies are frought with many difficulties, because of the many effects that one might expect to be associated with recent changes in intensive care medicine. Fortunately, a literature of the design of such studies is emerging (e.g., Goulet, Hay, and Barclay, 1974; Wilson, 1975).

3. *Construct Validity* Essentially, construct validity requires that a series of behaviors correlate with one another so that to some extent they measure the same thing. This is clearly the major validity problem for early assessment because it requires that we understand how some infant behavior is related to child behavior, and ultimately to adult behavior. The description of the patterning of behavior from birth through adulthood is the ultimate task of developmental psychology and will certainly not be completed during the lifetime of the participants of this conference. In the meantime, experimental effort that starts in infancy, or perhaps better still, during pregnancy, and relates a number of demographic, medical, behavioral, and educational facts about the child as he progresses through the early years of school, seems appropriate. As our measures and techniques develop, these studies will need to be repeated. As yet, to propose a large scale life-span study would seem premature.

Problems of Reliability and Correct Ascertainment

Assessment devices, to the extent that they are valid and reliable, make appropriate measurements. The problem of reliability is to determine the extent that errors of measurement lead to correct or incorrect decisions. The situation is diagrammed in Figure 2. Written in the cells are the terms used in psychometrics to describe the resulting written assignment of subjects. In medical procedures, a person who is

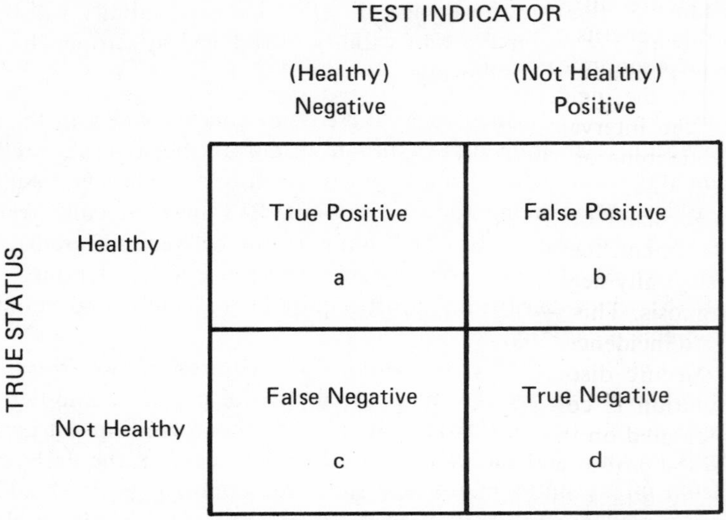

TEST INDICATOR

	(Healthy) Negative	(Not Healthy) Positive
Healthy	True Positive a	False Positive b
Not Healthy	False Negative c	True Negative d

TRUE STATUS

Figure 2.   The relationship between status of an infant as indicated by a test and the infant's true status, diagrammed to show the frequency of appropriate and inappropriate assignment. The terms and symbols are further discussed in the text.

actually healthy should obtain a negative test result, and it is usual to talk of the specificity or the proportion of healthy subjects with a negative test (a) when the test is administered to all the healthy subjects in a population ($a + b$). *Sensitivity* is the fraction of not healthy persons so recognized by a test (d) among those who are not healthy ($c + d$). The "cost" factor is the result of errors ($b + c$). The total cost of errors is $(b + c)/(a + b + c + d)$. Sufficient reliability data should be achieved before initiating mass screening, so that cutoffs can be selected that minimize the total cost. A clinical device that is used for making decisions about classification should have a very high reliability.

Problems of Cost Effectiveness and Benefit

The economic costs of an assessment should include not only the actual administration of the device, but all related administrative and overhead costs. The *effectiveness* of an assessment is the extent to which it achieves some defined goal such as correct identification of an infant with a disorder. The cost-effectiveness of an early assessment program would be the cost of all the assessments required to detect a child with a disorder. Consider PKU, which occurs in one out of 15,000–16,000 infants. Each PKU tests cost about three dollars. The cost of a detection is therefore approximately $45,000. As can be seen, if costs of tests are high or incidence low, the cost-effectiveness figure can become enormous, and beyond the resources of any health delivery system. To estimate the *benefits* of a procedure, data must be obtained on the good achieved. To achieve good, one must provide treatment or intervention following assessment. Thus, a benefit estimate requires that a treatment or intervention program be available that can be cost accounted and evaluated. This is obviously more difficult than simply considering effectiveness. It is generally agreed that the benefits of a social and medical service should outweigh the costs.

The basic economics of assessment center on these three factors: the cost of an individual test, the incidence of the condition we wish to detect, and the cost and outcome of the intervention. It would seem from our limited knowledge of early behavioral screening or assessment that we are not, at this time, in a position to estimate these factors.

Although behavioral research cannot answer questions about the cost-benefits of early assessment, there are some important strategic issues for research that seem to be almost totally neglected in any clinical discipline concerned with behavioral or sensory diagnosis. This issue centers on the cost-effectiveness question, particularly as it relates to incidence.

Most specific disorders occur with a relatively low incidence rate when the entire population is considered. Because the expense of an assessment is appropriately calculated on the cost of identifying a positive case from all cases tested, it follows that the cost-effectiveness will be high. There are two possible strategies that can be used to attack this incidence problem. One is to construct registers of high risk based on familial, demographic, or any clinically observable symptoms, and to test only these individuals on the grounds that from them will come the majority of those with the condition in question. It has been argued that "high risk," defined by treatment in an intensive care unit, does not adequately meet this requirement. The other strategy is to determine conditions of very low risk and not to test individuals who meet these established criteria. In some instances, this latter procedure may be quite simple. For instance, a large school system screened *all* the first grade children for learning disabilities, in an attempt to achieve early detection of the reading problems that were a major concern in middle school. The process took seven months, by which time approximately 30% of the children were reading above grade level. These children were at extremely low risk, and no case of learning disabilities was detected among them. The example seems absurd, but in most local and state services, routinue batteries of tests are required before any placement. Furthermore, interdisciplinary graduate training for professionals in many university-affiliated retardation centers is based on an in depth model that requires all disciplines do a "work-up" on each child. Typically, this is based on a battery of psychological, sensory, and educational tests, plus a nutritional interview, a social work case study, and a medical examination. When such a process is studied, it becomes clear that for many patients, the incidence of some problems can be judged to be extremely low, and certain procedures judged to be unjustifiable on a cost/incidence basis (Smith and Simons, 1975).

The statistical properties of registers of risk are well understood (Alberman and Goldstein, 1970). Coupled with data reviewed here, this leads to the conclusion that it is unlikely that registers can be refined to detect more than a fraction of the individuals who suffer from a handicap unless precise etiological links are established between particular events in the neonatal period and specific handicapping conditions. Such information is not presently available for any handicapping condition such as severe hearing loss, where multiple etiological patterns are involved. Where a very low rate of detection is present, typically where health maintenance services are poor, the detection rate may be markedly increased by the use of risk registers, but the general rule that this will not lead to detection of the majority of individuals with handicaps is likely to apply. There is marked danger, because these facts are badly understood, that screening programs aimed at particular problems and populations will consume the majority of time and effort in the expectation that the majority of handicaps will be prevented or detected.

Ethical Problems of Screening and Assessment

When children are screened or assessed, they are typically classified so that in some way they are assigned to an intervention or labeled to define eligibility or placement. There are serious concerns that this labeling stigmatizes the child so as to influence self-perception or the perception of others. Thus, the process of labeling may have severe consequences, even when it is substantially correct. In addition, the efficacy of the programs provided following classification or labeling, such as institutionalization or special class placement, is open to serious question. The material related to the above issues is extensively reviewed by Hobbs (1975a,b,c). Clearly, there are ethical concerns of a major nature surrounding the output of any system that assesses children.

One way of approaching the criteria for an ideal assessment system is to define the characteristics or safeguards that would make it ethically sound. One approach to this is in terms of the individual who will be the observer (assessor). Firth (1952) has provided a framework that presents criteria for an "ideal observer." From the point of view of ethical theory, such a position presupposes that absolute ethical criteria are possible, that from these a disposition can be made such that an observer would always act the same way under certain specifiable conditions, and that these conditions can be stated objectively in the sense that it need not be true that subjectively anyone has experienced any specific situation or set of conditions.

The ideal ethical observer has five characteristics that are discussed below in relationship to early assessment:

1. *Omniscience.* This characteristic requires that the observer has all the relevant facts. Thus, for example, a screening program should be introduced with a knowledge of the benefits to be gained. An assessment technique should be employed with a knowledge of its reliability and the incidence and consequence of the resultant misclassifications. It is clear that classification schemes for exceptional children have classified and placed children in special classes and institutions without the relevant facts about consequences.

2. *Omnipercipient.* This characteristic requires that the assessor be able to imagine the feelings of all parties concerned. For example, the assessor should be able to imagine the effects on parents and siblings, as well as on the infant as he grows older, of advising that an infant is permanently handicapped. In the past, parents have been counseled to institutionalize children, with little appreciation of how acute their feelings have been. Subsequently, when professional opinions changed, they were encouraged to deinstitutionalize the same child

with equally acute feelings about the errors they had been led to make. The feelings of individuals and their families when a handicapping condition is detected are often acute. The assessor should be able to imagine these feelings.

3. *Dispassion.* Characteristically, the assessor should be free from strong feelings. Thus, while he must have the relevant facts, be able to imagine the feelings of his clients, and be free of self-interest, he should not act out of aversion or sympathy. Strong emotional involvement by the assessor will likely impede adequate consideration of the facts and hazards. The appropriate role is that of the dispassionate problem solver, who can imagine the emotions experienced by the assessee and family, but who is not himself emotionally involved.

4. *Disinterest.* This characteristic requires that the assessor be free from self-interest so that he makes decisions that maximize the interests of his clients. Thus, the assessor should not be trying to promote a particular theoretical framework, a type of therapy, or protect some professional role.

5. *Consistent.* The assessor characteristically should use generalizable ethical principles in making his decisions that are applicable in other similar situations. It may not be possible to codify what is right and wrong, but an attempt should be made to spell out what principles underlie the decisions that are made.

The ideals set forth for the assessor above are in a sense abstract and perhaps difficult to apply in an individual case. However, they may become valuable guidelines, and may be used to ensure that the interest and feelings of the assessees are protected in the face of professional interest and disinterest. The principals demand that we have more information than has typically been available when new services are introduced for children.

This section on the problems of early assessment is meant to be cautionary. There are substantial issues relating to choice of measures, availability of responses in the infant, who controls and where access to the infant will be obtained, the immediate and predictive validity of the measures obtained, the reliability of measures, the cost of assessment, and finally, ethical concerns that need attention before any widespread programs of service should be introduced. It is an area where interdisciplinary research is a must and where intervention and service must be built on knowledge about behavior, professional roles, outcome, and cost.

SOME SUGGESTIONS FOR NEW PROGRAMS

The discussion of the problems that surround early assessment, presented above, may be destructive without a suggestion of meaningful first steps. This section opens with a presentation of what does not seem justified by the state of knowledge. First, a national screening program, as suggested by Meier (1973), is simply not appropriate at this time, nor may it ever be appropriate. It should be noted that, in general, maintenance programs and screening programs are contraindicated. An effective maintenance system is based on effective and early identification of problems as part of its regular program. To the extent that it is successful, there will be a low incidence of undetected conditions, and the incidence in a screened population is thus predicted to be very low. This means that a screening program instituted following an effective maintenance will display an unfavorable cost-effectiveness ratio. Hobbs (1975a) argues convincingly that screening is a poor substitute for an adequate health maintenance system. However, Hobbs goes on to argue that "until such time as comprehensive diagnostic and treatment programs can be provided, it would appear sensible to continue early screening programs, inadequate as they may seem to be, and to invest in research to improve them" (p. 97). The position suggested by the analysis in the present paper is that *any* assessment that is not directly related to an intervention program is unlikely to be justifiable in terms of methodology, benefit, cost, or the ethical concerns that arise. Screening or assessment are unlikely to be beneficial other than as part of a general educational maintenance model. The provision of special services outside such a model will inevitably result in the labeling of children as those with problems. Screening is appropriate only as a research topic in the present situation.

An assessment-intervention model of early childhood education that starts with parent training, that has patterns of behavior as criterion referenced by development sequence, and that studies children who have received intensive care is suggested as a research model. Essentially such a model would be based on knowledge both about normal development and about handicapping conditions. Such a model could possess the following advantages:

1. The problems of labeling and classification would be minimized in a framework that aimed to promote development from its current stage.
2. The problems of concurrent validity and reliability would be minimized, because errors should be self-evident and correctable within the training sequence employed.
3. There would be a framework of information on which to structure, guide, and evaluate intervention programs.
4. A theoretical base from the study of developmental psychology could be developed to provide an understanding of the patterning of skills that will allow longer term prediction. The predictive validity of infant assessments will only be moved from its current, largely correlational status to a theoretical framework as construct validity is built in a developmental framework.
5. Such a model allows for a clear, logical, and theoretical relationship to be stated between preassessment measures, intervention context, and post-assessment measures.

Careful prospective studies are called for that follow infants longitudinally from birth through the first few grades. By this time, most handicaps have appeared. Studies of this sort that include research both on assessment and on intervention as part of a package should play a major role in the future.

REFERENCES

Alberman, E. D., and Goldstein, H. 1970. The "at risk" register: A statistical evaluation. Br. J. Prev. Soc. Med. 24: 129–135.

Berliner, D. C., and Cahen, L. S. 1973. Trait-treatment interactions and learning. In F. N. Kerlinger (ed.), Review of Research in Education. Peacock, Itasca, Illinois.

Bloom, B. S. 1964. Stability and Change in Human Characteristics. John Wiley, New York.

Bricker, W. A., and Bricker, D. D. 1974. An early language training strategy. In R. Schiefelbusch & L. Lloyd (eds.), Language Perspectives: Acquisition, Retardation, and Intervention. University Park Press, Baltimore.

Bronfenbrenner, U. 1974. A report on longitudinal evaluations of preschool programs, Volume II: Is early intervention effective? Department of Health, Education and Welfare, No. OHD74-25.

Chase, H. C. 1974. Perinatal mortality: Overview and current trends. In R. E. L. Nesbitt (ed.), Clinics in Perinatology, Vol. I, Symposium on Perinatal Medicine Today. W. B. Saunders Company, Philadelphia.

Cronbach, L. J. 1949. Essentials of Psychological Testing. Harper and Brothers, New York.

Dingman, H. F., and Tarjan, G. 1960. Mental retardation and the normal distribution curve. Am. J. Ment. Def. 64: 991–994.

Eilers, R. E., Wilson, W. R., and Moore, J. M. 1977. Developmental changes in speech discrimination in infants. J. Sp. Hear. Res. 20(4):766–780.

Firth, R. 1952. Ethical absolutism and the ideal observer. Philos. Phenomenol. Res. 12: 317–345.

Fulton, R. T., and Lloyd, L. 1969. Audiometry for the Retard with Implications for the Difficult to Test. Waverley Press, Inc., Baltimore.

Ginsburg, H. 1972. The Myth of the Deprived Child: Poor Children's Intellect and Education. Prentice-Hall, Inc., Englewood Cliffs, New Jersey.

Goulet, L. R., Hay, C. M., and Barclay, C. R. 1974. Sequential analysis and developmental research methods: Descriptions of a cyclical phenomenon. Psychiatr. Bull. 81: 517–521.

Hammill, D. D., and Larsen, S. C. 1974. The effectiveness of psycholinguistic training. Except. Child. 41: 5–14.

Hobbs, N. 1975a. The futures of children. Jossey-Bass Publishers, San Francisco.

Hobbs, N. 1975b. Issues in the Classification of Children, Vol. 1. Jossey-Bass Publishers, San Francisco.

Hobbs, N. 1975c. Issues in the Classification of Children, Vol. 2. Jossey-Bass Publishers, San Francisco.

Horowitz, F. D., and Paden, L. Y. 1973. The effectiveness of environmental intervention programs. In B. M. Caldwell and H. N. Ricciuti (eds.), Review of Child Development Research, Vol. 3. pp. 331–402. University of Chicago Press, Chicago.

Hunt, J. McV. 1961. Intelligence and Experience. Ronald Press, New York.

Jensen, A. R. 1969. How much can we boost IQ and scholastic achievement? Harvard Educ. Rev. 39: 2.

Kamin, L. J. 1974. The Science and Politics of IQ. John Wiley and Sons, New York.

Karnes, M. B. 1969. Research and development program on preschool disadvantaged children: Final report. U.S. Office of Education, Washington, D.C.

Karnes, M. B. 1975. Precise early education of children with handicaps (PEECH). In J. H. Stock, J. Dewborg, L. L. Wnek, and E. A. Schneck (eds.), Selection and Validation of Model Early Childhood Education Projects. Battelle Columbus Laboratories, Columbus, Ohio.

Kirk, S. A., McCarthy, J. J., and Kirk, W. D. 1968. The Illinois Test of Psycholinguistic Abilities. Rev. ed. University of Illinois Press, Urbana, Illinois.

Klaus, M., Jerauld, R., Kreger, N., McAlpine, W., Steffa, M., and Kennell, J. H. 1972. Maternal attachment: Importance of the first post-partum days. New Engl. J. of Med. 286: 240.

Kramer, J. A., Hill, K. T., and Cohen, L. B. 1975. Infants' development of object permanence: A refined methodology and new evidence for Piaget's hypothesized ordinality. Child Dev. 46: 149–155.

McCall, R. B., Hogarty, P. S., and Hurlburt, N. 1972. Transitions in infant sensorimotor development and the prediction of childhood IQ. Am. Psychol. 27: 728–748.

Meier, J. 1973. Screening and assessment of young children at developmental risk. In the President's Committee on Mental Retardation. Publication No. (05) 73-90, 1-188. Department of Health, Education and Welfare, Washington, D.C.

Mercer, J. 1973. The myth of a 3% prevalence. In R. K. Eyman, C. E. Meyers, and G. Tarjan (eds.), Sociobehavioral Studies in Mental Retardation. Monogr. Am. Assoc. Mental Def. No. 1.

Miller, L. B., and Dyer, J. L. 1975. Four preschool programs: Their dimensions and effects. Monogr. Soc. Res. Child Dev. Vol. 40, no. 162.

National Academy of Sciences. 1975. Genetic Screening. National Academy of Sciences, Washington, D.C.

Paraskevopoulos, J., and Hunt, J. McV. 1971. Object construction and imitation under different conditions of rearing. J. Genet. Psychol. 119: 301–321.

Paraskevopoulos, J., and Kirk, S. A. 1969. The Development and Psychometric Characteristics of the Revised Illinois Test of Psycholinguistic Abilities. University of Illinois Press, Urbana, Illinois.

Rubin, R., Rosenblatt, C., and Barlow, B. 1973. Psychological and educational sequelae of prematurity. J. Pediatr. 52: 352–363.

Schmitt, B. D. 1975. The minimal brain dysfunction myth. Am. J. Dis. Child. 129: 1313–1318.

Smith, D. W., and Simons, F. E. R. 1975. Rational diagnostic evaluation of the child with mental deficiency. Am. J. Dis. Child. 129: 1285–1290.

Snow, R. E. 1974. Representative and quasi-representative designs for research on teaching. Rev. Educat. Res. 44: 265–291.

Stanley, J. C. 1973. Compensatory education for children ages two to eight: Recent studies of educational intervention. Proceedings of the Second Annual Hyman Blumberg Symposium on Research in Early Childhood Education. The Johns Hopkins University Press, Baltimore.

Thoman, E., Leiderman, P., and Olson, J. 1972. Neonate-mother interaction during breastfeeding. Dev. Psychol. 6: 110–118.

Uzgiris, I. C., and Hunt, J. McV. 1975. Assessment in Infancy: Ordinal Scales of Psychological Development. University of Illinois Press, Urbana, Illinois.

Vurpillot, E. 1968. The development of scanning strategies and their relation to visual differentiation. J. Exp. Child Psychol. 6: 632–650.

Wachs, T. D. 1975. Relation of infants' performance on Piaget scales between twelve and twenty-four months and their Stanford-Binet performance at thirty-one months. Child Dev. 46: 929–935.

Weiner, G. 1968. Long-term study of prematures: Summary of published findings. ERIC Document 43389, Computer Microfilm.

Wepman, J. M., Cruickshank, W. M., Deutsch, C. P., Morency, A., and Strother, C. R. 1975. Learning disabilities. In N. Hobbs (ed.), Issues in the Classification of Children, Vol. 1. Jossey-Bass Publishers, San Francisco.

Werner, E. E., Bierman, J. M., and French, F. E. 1971. The Children of Kauai. University of Hawaii Press, Honolulu.

Wilson, R. S. 1975. Analysis of developmental data: Comparison among alternative methods. Dev. Psychol. 11: 676–680.

Ysseldyke, J. E., and Salvia, J. 1974. Diagnostic-prescriptive teaching: Two models. Except. Child. 41: 181–185.

Zigler, E. 1967. Familial mental retardation: A continuing dilemma. Science 155: 292–298.

Infant Intelligence Testing

Frances Degen Horowitz and Marcia Dunn

DEFINING AND TESTING INTELLIGENCE

An underlying premise of this paper is that infant intelligence testing is a dubious topic for inclusion in a forum devoted to "Early Behavioral Assessment of the Communicative and Cognitive Abilities of the Developmentally Disabled." The quest for a stable measure of infant intelligence can be thought of as at best misguided and at worst misleading. In the sections that follow, an attempt is made to present this position and to suggest how some other approaches to the assessment of infant behavior and developmental progress may prove to be much more fruitful than intelligence testing during infancy.

The term "intelligence" is a positivistic nightmare. It carries with it all the colloquial baggage of excess meaning while at the same time having the definity of a number. All psychologists can recite the chant "Intelligence is what intelligence tests test," but is it true? The term "intelligence" and the concept of being intelligent are too firmly rooted in our everyday language to be confined to a numerical index. If only Binet and Terman and others had eschewed the use of "intelligence" and had invented a totally new term or had been at least more literal, as is the term behavioral quotient (BQ).

Unfortunately, however, we are to this day arguing fixity of intelligence, modifiability of intelligence, and the proper domain of the behaviors to be assessed for estimating intelligence. Even the question "Intelligence for what?" remains unanswered—survival in a jungle? social interaction? academic performance? creative behavior? job success? happiness? Even the continuum from profoundly retarded to genius is hardly an internally consistent metric. One need only to observe the institutionalized retarded child with a measured mental age of five and compare that child with a normal five-year-old to know that the child classified as retarded and the normal child, said to be equal in mental age, have mainly in common that they both passed and failed items on a test, which resulted in the same ratio of performance to age; otherwise, they do not resemble each other at all. "The 20th-century technological society's stratification device has become the intelligence test. As such, the intelligence test rests more upon its function for distribution of wealth than to its scientific merit" (Lewis, 1976, p. 16). Lewis's indictment may seem a bit harsh, but intelligence as a concept and intelligence testing as a technique or a tool have been under steady and heavy attack in the last twenty years.

In tracing the history of infant intelligence testing, authors invariably take us back to Galton, Cattell, and Binet, citing the now well-known events that resulted in the development of performance tests in 1905 to identify the children in the Paris school system who might most benefit from special educational opportunities. Next came the American standardization by Terman in 1916, which was followed by the first attempt to provide for an assessment of intelligence in early infancy in the 1920s, and finally came Gesell's "Developmental Schedules," Shirley's tests for the first two years, Buhler's "Baby tests," and Bayley's "California First Year Mental Scale" (Brooks and Weinraub, 1976). Neither Shirley nor Gesell considered their scales to be tests of intelligence, and as early as 1933 Bayley noted how little predictability there was between "behavior growth of the early months of infant development . . . to the later development of intelligence" (Brooks and Weinraub, 1976, p. 34). Table 1 provides a list of infant intelligence (development) tests currently in use or available.

The controversy of the 1920s and the 1930s centered on the question of whether or not intelligence was "fixed" and what degree of influence was exerted by the envi-

Table 1.   Some current infant assessment techniques

Name of test and reference	Age range
Bayley Scales of Infant Development (Bayley, 1969)	1 month–36 months
Neonatal Behavioral Assessment Scale (Brazelton, 1973)	0–1 month
Cattell Infant Intelligence Scale (Cattell, 1940)	2 months–36 months
Albert Einstein Scales of Sensori Motor Development (Escolona and Corman, 1969)	4 months–22 months
Denver Developmental Screening Tests (Frankenburg and Dodds, 1968)	1 month–6 years
Gesell Developmental Schedule (Gesell and Amatruda, 1954, 1962)	1 month–6 years
Northwestern Intelligence Tests (Gilliland, 1949, 1951)	1 month–9 months
Griffiths Scale of Mental Development (Griffiths, 1954)	2 weeks–24 months
Neurological Examination of the Full Term Newborn Infant (Prechtl and Beintema, 1964)	Newborn
Graham-Rosenblith Behavioral Examination of the Neonate (Rosenblith and Graham, 1961)	0–1 month
Infant Psychological Development Scales (Uzgiris and Hunt, 1975)	1 month–24 months

ronment on development; the intelligence test was the criterion measure. If an early measure of intelligence could be shown to be correlated to a later measure of intelligence, the argument for a fixed IQ would be strengthened. However, by 1955 Bayley was able to report that a review of the findings indicated that there was no relationship between early and later measures. She observed: "These findings give little hope to our being able to measure a stable and predictable intellectual factor in the very young . . ." (p. 807). Many reasons have been advanced to explain the failure to find strong correlations between early and later measures of intelligence: inherent instability of the infant; the changing nature of the behaviors sampled in intelligence tests across different ages, an intrinsic discontinuity between early and later development; and insufficiency in the testing technique, to be remedied, eventually, by the development of better tests.

For almost two decades, during the 1940s and 1950s, the matter seemingly rested at an impasse. Then several things happened: Americans discovered Piaget and they rediscovered the infant as an organism for study (Flavell, 1963; Lipsitt, 1963); the nature-nurture controversy was reopened in the academic world (Hunt, 1961); and child development and developmental psychology became inextricably related to social and political intervention programs aimed at young children (Horowitz and Paden, 1973). The shaping and modifiability of intelligence at once became the focus of discussion and argument, and intelligence testing again became the criterion tool. Let us look at each of these in turn and relate them to an analysis of how we might best proceed in our attempts to understand how development occurs, and in our attempts, how we can prevent developmental disabilities.

THE BASIC ISSUES

Piaget and the Competent Infant

We are indebted to Piaget for the entry of "sensorimotor intelligence" into our lexicon of terms to describe infant development. As a result of Piaget's observations, we have come to appreciate that infants are in intense concourse with the environment, and that the topography and nature of this concourse undergoes a series of systematic changes. The result is that we have a description of a sequence of interaction patterns that seems to be, in its broad outlines, typical of all normal infants. Requiring approximately the first two years of life for passage through the sequence, these patterns of interaction progress from the relatively limited response repertoire of the newborn infant to the active manipulation of environmental stimuli, and to the increasingly complex abilities of the infant to keep track of environmental events and objects. The sensorimotor period ends when the infant acquires language and begins to use a symbolic system.

Piaget's descriptions have stimulated an enormous amount of research of infant behavior and have irretrievably changed our perception of the infant organism. In contrast to our thinking of the infant as being helpless and largely reflexive in its response repertoire, we have come to see the infant as displaying a complex and constantly changing behavioral repertoire that marks the infant as a competent organism (Appleton, Clifton, and Goldberg, 1975; Stone, Smith, and Murphy, 1973).

During the decade of the 1960s, partially as a result of Piaget's influence, a number of experimental laboratories were established in this country. They were, and continue to be, devoted to the experimental analysis of infant perceptual and cognitive abilities and to the study of learning in infants.

As a result of these efforts, we know that infants discriminate a wide variety of stimuli, showing patterns of habituation and dishabituation to subtle stimulus cues, and that they can learn complex associations. In fact, as soon as someone observes that young infants *cannot* do something, it seems that someone comes along and demonstrates, with an improved or new technique, that they *can* do it. Many of the substantive aspects of these observations are the subjects of the other papers being prepared for this conference.

Not only have we necessarily become sensitized to a much richer behavioral repertoire as characteristic of the infant, but it has become obvious that we really have available to us a much more extensive response repertoire from which to choose in making a behavioral assessment of infants. Brooks and Weinraub (1976) report that five recent tests have been developed to measure sensorimotor development alone. Perhaps the most dramatic illustration of the development of more comprehensive and complex assessment techniques for looking at infant behavior is the Neonatal Behavioral Assessment Scale (Brazelton, 1973). This scale can be administered to newborn infants from the first day of life through about the end of the first month of life. The present test yields a score for 27 different items, in addition to the usual panoply of items related to newborn reflexes. The Neonatal Behavioral Assessment Scale assesses the infant's behavior in several different states and samples habituation to repeated stimulation, orientation to animate and inanimate visual and auditory stimulation, responses to mild stress, and state control abilities. Compare this to the paucity of items for newborn infants in the very early infant tests, or even to the totally reflex oriented neurological assessment of Prechtl and Beintema (1964).

One of the most impressive aspects of the assessment of newborn behavior using the Neonatal Behavioral Assessment Scale is the range of individual differences to be observed right after birth. We have been used to thinking that individual differences are either shaped by the environment or that they emerge in the course of development. The analyses of behavioral individuality (Escalona, 1968; Thomas, Birch, Chess, Hertzig, and Korn, 1963), and more recently the exploration of the effect of the infant upon caregivers (Lewis and Rosenblum, 1974), are fully consonant with the observations one makes about individual differences in using the Neonatal Behavioral Assessment Scale. Anyone who has used the Neonatal Behavioral Assessment Scale extensively, with its nine point scales for 27 different items, finds the scoring of the Bayley Scales of Infant Development a frustrating experience. One has the immediate sense that a great deal of information is being ignored when one scores the Bayley on a simple pass-fail basis.

Although one might say that the decade of the 1960s was impressive for the explosion of our knowledge about the abilities of infants during the first two years of life, the decade of the 1970s may be remembered for the renewed dawning of our concern for individual differences. It may provide a crucial key to the early identification of infants for whom the developmental course will not be normal. It is almost paradoxical that the overall result of the research of these two decades may lead to a greater appreciation for the role of both nature and nurture in the development of the human infant.

Nature-Nurture—And? Or?

The brief allusion to the early controversy over the relative influence of natural endowment and environmental forces in shaping the development of the child belies the emotional zeal that was invested in the argument by the proponents of one or the other position. Indeed, the earliest studies of infant conditioning were in service of an attempt to settle the question. If newborn infants could be conditioned, then this would be seen as evidence for the ability of the learning paradigm to account for development. Watson's famous challenge to form an infant to any social role was not mere bravado, but an expression of the passionate belief that the basic control over developmental outcome lay almost entirely in the hands of the primary caregivers (Watson, 1924). On the other side came the counter-challenge of how one might explain the regularity of developmental sequence and the impressive degree of individual consistency with regard to rate of development (Gesell, 1954). As noted earlier, one of the central kingpins in the argument was the stability of the IQ and the predictability of early to later IQ.

The initial and continuing indicators that neither stability nor prediction were being found were not seen by the proponents of the preponderant role of heredity as a counter-evidence for their position. Rather, the results became the signal to find the reasons that would explain the data while preserving the central role of hereditary and biological control of developmental outcome. Even the dramatic findings of Skeels and his colleagues (Skeels and Dye, 1939; Skeels, Updegraff, Wellman, and Williams, 1938) were not sufficient to dissuade those who believed the hereditary position. Their research, which demonstrated remarkable changes in developmental status with a change in environments, was so methodologically flawed that is was vulnerable to even the mildest critique. By the 1940s, with the evidence of the previous two decades for a perspective, the argument was declared a "draw" with a final appeal to common sense: Development is influenced by both nature and nurture and it was implausible that the effects of one could ever be fully isolated for the purpose of evaluation. Perhaps only a world war provided sufficient distraction for the issue to be sidelined.

In 1961, Hunt published his book *Intelligence and Experience*. He brought together all of the research literature bearing upon the question and tried to introduce some theoretical perspectives. The two theoretical perspectives involved Piaget's conception of the infant development and Hebb's proposals about the role of early perceptual stimulation on later learning. The conclusion strongly favored the role of environment as being the predominant factor in the development of intelligence. In that same year, Yarrow (1961) and Casler (1961) published reviews of the literature that strongly complimented Hunt's analysis by suggesting that perceptual stimulation in early infancy was an important component in affecting early development.

What was not immediately obvious was the potentially inherent conflict between accepting a Piagetian description of the regularity of early development while implicating environment as the controlling element in the outcome of intellectual development. Piaget's position, sans ideological commitment, is simply that the physical environment that is present for all infants is a sufficient environment for the development of sensorimotor intelligence, and that the infant is largely his own mediator of the concourse between the self and the environment, thus *discovering* how the world works and elaborating the behavioral repertoire to encompass the stimulation potential of the environment. In accepting the notion of the human organism as having evolved to a point of being evolutionarily preadapted to a particular sequence of behavioral development in infancy, Scarr-Salapatek (1976) recently stated the issue most strongly when she said: "I would argue that human infants have built-in biases to acquire certain kinds of intelligent behaviors that are consonant with primate evolutionary history, that these biases are programmed by the epigenotype, and that human environments guarantee the development of these behaviors through the provision of material objects that are assimilated to them" (p. 179). "All non-defective infants reared in natural human environments achieve all the sensori-motor skills that Piaget has described" (p. 185). "For the development of sensori-motor skills, nearly any natural human environment will suffice to produce criterion-level performance" (p. 186). Thus, Scarr-Salapatek and others have removed the nature-nurture controversy from the learning-maturation arena to the genetic versus environmental control arena.

One need only read the opening reviews of the February, 1976 issue of *Contemporary Psychology* to realize that we have recaptured the emotionality of the nature-nurture issue in the present-day controversy over the genetic versus environmental influence on IQ. Richard Lewontin and Sandra Scarr-Salapatek take entirely opposite points of view regarding the analysis presented by Leon Kamin in his book, *The Science and Politics of IQ* (1974). Kamin questions the data base that led Jensen (1969) and then Herrnstein (1973) to conclude that environmental intervention programs could not change intelligence in any profound manner, and that intelligence was largely accounted for by genetic factors. Lewontin thanked Kamin for his service to the field; Scarr-Salapatek scored him for his disservice to the serious discussion of the basis for intelligence.

Because the period of infancy is assumed to reflect environmental impact at its minimum, in comparison with later periods of development, the assessment of infant intelligence seemed, originally, to be the most promising strategy for providing evidence on the relative importance of genetic factors and environmental factors. In a discussion of an evolutionary perspective on infant intelligence, Scarr-Salapatek (1976) came to the conclusions noted previously: the human infant is evolutionarily preadapted to the achievement of all aspects of sensorimotor intelligence; although individual differences in rates of sensorimotor intelligence cannot be attributed to either genetic or environmental factors, at present such differences "are relatively unimportant variations on a strong primate theme" (p. 194). The implication is also that there is an inherent discontinuity between infant intelligence and later intellectual level—one of the earliest explanations offered by mental testers for the lack of predictability from early to later intelligence assessments. McCall (1976) employs a somewhat similar strategy in his analysis of mental development and intelligence testing of infants. McCall sees the lack of predictability in IQ from infancy to later childhood as an indication that "mental performance undergoes major qualitative shifts during the first few years of life" (p. 106), and that this changing *qualitative* nature of mental performance might imply that there are changes in the environmental and genetic determinants of mental performance over the period of infancy. McCall proposes that we adopt an entirely different strategy for looking at infant mental development:

> Assuming the infant tests are reliable samples of a significant portion of the infant's behavioral repertoire, it might be profitable to explore the test protocols for the purpose of describing such qualitative transitions in the development of mental behavior. If these transitions are marked, the determinants of one type of behavior at one age may be quite different from the determinants of another type of behavior at a developmentally distant age, and there may not be a sizeable correlation between precocity at one age and precocity at quite another age (p. 112).

The interest in predictability, in relative continuity, and in relative discontinuity are questions for science and academic debate. However, when we are dealing with human development, and particularly with child development, the answers to these questions have social and political implications. The imperative to action and to treatment is strong—sometimes enlisting dual motivations within the same individuals, at other times characterizing different movements among different groups or professions. More and more, however, the developmental scientist has found it increasingly difficult to be totally divorced from the questions of treatment and application. Like the medical doctor of old, asked to prescribe treatment with an imperfect knowledge of the basic mechanisms of disease, we are asked to respond to human needs without a base of substantial knowledge. The child who cannot learn today cannot be stored away until we have made scientific progress. Therefore, testing and assessment have served as dual tools—criteria measurements for scientific inquiry and evaluating devices for diagnosis and treatment.

The question, in its most powerfully proposed form, becomes one in which a choice must be made: Is the greater proportion of intelligence fixed by genetic factors or by environmental factors? Is the "heritability" as high as 0.80, or much lower? If one believes in a high heritability of "intelligence," then assessment becomes a tool for identifying individuals who might most benefit from an environment suited to the intelligence levels as they are assessed. If one does not accept the relatively high heritability estimate for intelligence, then assessment becomes a tool for evaluating individuals within different environments, and it becomes a criterion tool for evaluating environmental manipulations. Most of the intervention research has been based on the latter choice; some of the prediction research has been based on the former; some of the research on infant intelligence straddles the middle ground between the two points of view.

Assessment, Prediction, and Intervention

The newborn baby is assessed immediately after birth by the Apgar rating. The Apgar score, devised by Virginia Apgar, is based on rating of 0 (absent), 1 (fair), or 2 (good) on each of five characteristics. An infant rated good (2) on all five characteristics earns a score of 10 (the best score possible). The five characteristics are: appearance (color), pulse (heart rate), grimace (reflex to stimulation), activity (muscle tone), and respiration (respiratory rate).

This neonatal evaluation is made at one, five, and sometimes 10 minutes after birth. Based on five indicators of physiological functioning, it identifies infants who need immediate special care. It is a gross screening device for alerting physicians and nurses to the infant's birth condition. The typical newborn infant in an American hospital next receives a pediatric examination during the first 24 hours. During this examination, gross abnormalities may be identified. Most infants are evaluated as normal. If the course of recovery from birth is normal, the infant is dismissed from the hospital and goes home. Some of these infants continue to progress normally, but others do not. Infants whose recovery course is not normal in the first days are sometimes flagged for special care or are designated as "at risk" for normal development. Some of these infants continue to show an abnormal developmental course; others progress normally. One of the major questions toward which research has been pointed is: How early can we identify infants who will not exhibit normal development? Efforts to answer this question have ranged from the gross and relatively inexpensive strategy of asking parents questions about development milestones (e.g., Schmitt and Erickson, 1973) to more refined strategies of assessment of particular characteristics such as head circumference (e.g., Nelson and Deubschberger, 1970), or to the assessment of multiple predictor factors (e.g., Caputo and Taub, 1974; Ireton, Thwing, and Graven, 1970). The major outcome criterion has been performance on an intelligence test.

The assignment of the infant to a risk category at birth, because of prenatal or perinatal complications and/or functional problems in the first few days of life, is not a sure predictor of later developmental disability. A review of the extensive research on risk infants by Sameroff and Chandler (1975) resulted in a conclusion that implicated the importance of socioeconomic and familial factors: "The environment appears to have the potential of minimizing or maximizing such early developmental difficulties. High socio-economic status dissipates the effects of such perinatal complications as anoxia or low birth-weight. Poor social environmental conditions tend to amplify the effects of such early complication " (p. 236). Parmelee and Haber (1973) also concluded that cumulative scores or multiple criteria clusters of prenatal, perinatal, postnatal, and early infancy factors are better predictors of developmental outcome in later childhood than any one of these factors taken independently.

It has, in fact, been the case that the most successful identification and amelioration of developmental delay has come from the use of multiple indicators for targeting individual infants, and from the employment of intensive treatment programs aimed at preventing developmental delay. Although intervention is not the focus of this paper (see "Implications for Intervention," this volume), it is important to note that the most dramatic changes in developmental outcome have resulted from the most intensive treatment programs aimed at infants selected by the use of multiple criteria (Horowitz and Paden, 1973). The most widely known of these programs is the Milwaukee project, in which control-experimental differences at five and one-half years of age are of a magnitude of over 20 IQ points in a population of infants who were all slightly above normal at one year (Heber and Garber, 1975), but whose parents were within the low-normal and retarded range for intelligence.

The problem that presently faces those of us who are interested in the prevention of developmental delay is not a question of prediction, or even one of treatment or intervention. We could take the risk indicators (Meier, 1975, lists 34 of them to be taken into account from pre-conception to one month postnatal age) and institute a massive intervention program (á la the Milwaukee project), and in that large and expensive net probably prevent a fair amount of developmental delay, using the IQ as our major criterion measure. Is this practical? Are we likely to do it? Does the model rest too heavily on gross indicators and a traditional approach to evaluating developmental outcome? These authors believe so, and next suggest an alternate approach for consideration.

INDIVIDUAL DIFFERENCES AND ENVIRONMENTAL STIMULATION

Let us, for the moment, begin again, and take a somewhat different tack on the problem. The newborn infant is capable of learning simple associations (Siqueland and Lipsitt, 1966), of inhibiting responding to repetitive stimulation (Friedman, 1972), and of attending selectively to different stimuli (Cohen and Salapatek, 1975). Individual differences in newborn behavior seem to play an important role in the infant's interaction with the environment (Osofsky and Danzger, 1974). With regard to individual differences, there has been a recent accumulation of data that assign such differences an increasingly salient role in our evaluation of human infants (Lewis and Rosenblum, 1974).

There have also been several theoretical discussions concerning the role of individual differences in determining developmental outcome. Escalona (1968), Thomas et al. (1963), and others have speculated about the possible importance of matching characteristics of environmental stimulation with characteristics of individual children as being central to fostering normal development. In several articles and chapters, Horowitz (1965, 1968, 1969, 1976) has also dicussed the possibility that normal developmental outcome may partially depend on how successfully the infant's behavior elicits environmental stimulation from the environment, and how successful contingent environmental stimulation is in providing reinforcement for the infant's behavior. It is possible to derive two hypotheses from these speculations: Some infants have behavioral repertoires that are more successful in eliciting stimulation from the environment—particularly the social environment—than others, and "successful" caregiving is more likely to occur when caregivers are flexible in adjusting their behaviors to "match" the individual characteristics of the infants with whom they are interacting. Any serious test of these hypotheses would require reliable measures of individual differences and of environmental stimulation.

The difficulty we presently face is that we are only beginning to develop reliable measurement techniques that encompass the complexity of the interaction being described. On the environmental side we have extensive evidence that single environmental events presented contingently in controlled laboratory situations can functionally affect single responses in infants. We have additional evidence that infants respond to a wide variety of stimuli in the environment and that they process the information in these stimuli in various ways. However, how do we calibrate the stimulation that occurs in the complex flow of the natural environment? Bradley and Caldwell (1976) published a study of early home environment and changes in mental test performance in children from 6 to 36 months. Using a combination of interview and observation, the authors derived a measure of the quality of stimulation found in the home. They were able to demonstrate that this quality of stimulation is related to whether or not the change in mental test performance between 6 and 36 months is in an increasing or decreasing direction, or whether the performance is stable. They found that: "Mothers whose infants improve in mental test performance not only encourage and challenge the child to develop new skills but also provide the child with the kinds of play materials needed for development. By contrast, parents whose children decline in performance do a less adequate job of helping their infants organize the environment" (p. 96).

Using a much more complex observational system, and not relying at all on parent reports, Yarrow, Rubenstein, and Pedersen (1975) found that the level and variety of social stimulation in the home was positively correlated with infant functioning at five and one-half months using the Bayley Scales and some measures derived from the Bayley Scales.

Both the Bradley and Caldwell study and the Yarrow et al. study contribute important advances in our measurement of complex environmental stimulation. What they do not do is provide us with a finer analysis of the role of the infant's characteristics in the infant-environment interaction process. They do not provide us with a finer analysis of the infant's contribution to the interaction. It would seem that this is not an easy matter. In Lewis and Rosenblum's volume, *The Effect of the Infant on its Caregiver* (1974), there are eight articles on human infants; only three attempt to isolate the specific characteristics of the infant in the interaction. One looks at the gross effects of a blind infant on a caregiver (Fraiberg, 1974), and the other two are concerned with such factors as state, level of arousal, and sex (Korner, 1974), and with sleep organization in the premature (Dreyfus-Brisac, 1974). In an article on the variability of growth and maturity in the newborn, Tanner (1974) noted: "Whether . . . variations in size, shape, and maturity have an effect on the infant's caregiver we do not at present know; but clearly they may have" (p. 77). In a study of premature infants, Rubin, Rosenblatt, and Barlow (1973) concluded that low birth weight, rather than gestational age, was the major correlate of subsequent psychological and educational impairment. It is interesting to speculate that low birth weight is a stimulus dimension of the infant to which a caregiver may respond, and that gestational age is a less obvious stimulus dimension for a caregiver.

As was noted earlier, the Bayley Scales of Infant Development do not, in their present standardized form, offer us an evaluation of individual differences on dimensions that might be most functional in affecting the infant's interaction with the environment. Whether or not a child can do something may be only one factor in affecting environmental response to the child. The style with which he or she does it, the time it takes, the smoothness of the action, and the degree to which the child's behavior is reinforcing to the caregiver may be equally or more important at certain points on the interactive continuum.

There is one study that does attempt a finer analysis of the effect of the infant's behavior on the interaction with a caregiver. Osofsky and Danzger (1974) attempted to show that newborn infants whose behavior was more alert on the Neonatal Behavioral Assessment Scale looked more at their mothers during a subsequent feeding; infants who were more sensitive to certain types of stimulation seemed to elicit more of such stimulation from their mothers. However, the relationships were less strong and direct than one might have wished, and it is possible that the neonatal measurement technique itself needs further refining.

We have recently been working on refining the scoring procedure used with the Neonatal Behavioral Assessment Scale, and if we are successful, it will have some important implications for influencing the direction of infant assessment. The present Neonatal Behavioral Assessment Scale can be administered in about 30 minutes and requires about 5 to 10 minutes for scoring. In using the scale, an examiner can assess a wide range of newborn infant behaviors. In addition to typical newborn reflex behavior, the Scale attempts to assess the infant's ability to inhibit responding, to attend to auditory and visual stimuli, to be consoled, to self-quiet, and to react to mildly aversive stimulation. The scoring procedure differs from many of our standard psychometric techniques in that the examiner is trained to administer the technique in such a way as to try to elicit the best behavior of which the infant is capable and to score the infant on that best performance only. For example, if an infant usually fixates and does not follow an inanimate object when it is presented during the exam, but on *one* occasion turns his head to follow the object, the scoring for the item is based on the one occasion when the head turned to follow the object. Extensive experience in testing the newborn infant and in scoring using the Neonatal Behavioral Assessment Scale has convinced these authors that the current scoring procedure ignores some potentially important information about the "typical" response of the infant. It may well be that scoring the infant for typical as well as best response will prove to be much more informative than using the best performance alone.

Consider for a moment some of the possibilities that such a scoring approach might open to us. Infant A and Infant B are typically unresponsive, but with great effort the examiner can get the infants to be responsive; Infant C and Infant D are typically very responsive, and perform at their best levels during most of the exam. Infant A goes home to a persistent, achievement oriented mother who works extensively to get her baby to respond to her; Infant B goes home to a relaxed, somewhat nonachievement oriented mother who does not persist if the infant does not respond; Infant C goes home to a mother that is persistent and achievement oriented, and

Infant D goes home to a mother that is not persistent and achievement oriented. If we were to identify the infant in this group about whom we might be most concerned with regard to subsequent developmental outcome, we would choose Infant B—typically unresponsive, going into an environment that will not necessarily persist in eliciting the infant's behavior. The rationale is obvious. What is also obvious is that any "early" identification of an infant at risk for developmental delay requires an assessment of both the infant and the environment in order to target the combination that might most benefit from an intervention program.

During this last year we have been working on the development of a reliable supplementary scoring system for selected items on the Neonatal Behavioral Assessment Scale and are about to embark on a program of research aimed at assessment of individual behavioral differences and of environmental stimulation in a population of infants who have been medically classified as normal, and in a population of infants who have been medically classified as at risk. We believe that this strategy may prove to be more informative than the traditional strategies employed in infant assessment and studies of developmental outcome. The identification of infant-environmental matches that result in developmental delay could lead to the design of specific intervention strategies aimed at aiding caregivers in adjusting their interactive styles to the characteristics of the infant in such a way as to maximize eliciting, maintaining, and reinforcing behaviors thought to be significant for normal developmental progress.

The implications for infant assessment and for "intelligence testing" are potentially profound. If assessment is being used to describe infant functioning, preferred measures might include typical as well as best behavior, dimensions of the style of functioning, as well as other parameters of information processing strategies that infants employ. After all, it is quite possible that our most fruitful approach to understanding infant development and the prevention of developmental delay lies in an analysis that views the infant as a processor of environmental information who, in the exercise of processing strategies, functionally affects the amount, kind, duration, and timing of stimulus information made available to him or her. This point of view requires us to revise our infant intelligence measures in such a way as to allow us to assess whether a developmental milestone has been achieved, and at the same time to assess the manner in which the infant behaves—which in turn, is a stimulus variable in the interactive environment.

We sometimes have a greater appreciation for intellectual and cognitive style among adults than among children. Perhaps we have done less IQ testing of adults. We certainly do not assess developmental milestones in adulthood (mostly because we do not know which, if any, milestones should be assessed). Standard infant and child intelligence testing has perhaps blinded us to a more functional analysis of development, and thus has prevented us from devising measurement tools that will best serve both our scientific and applied interests.

SOME CONCLUSIONS

Perhaps the most basic question we can ask is: Why do we test an infant? Some infant intelligence tests were designed in the hope that they might enable an early assessment of intelligence that would be predictive of later intelligence. Other infant tests were designed to provide current estimates of developmental progress. Whether one assumes that all nondefective infants achieve everything possible in the first two years of life, or that there are qualitative changes in what we call intelligence between the first two years and later years, most of the present infant assessment tools are not thought to be predictive of later intelligence, except in the very gross instances of extreme retardation, which is easily detectable in early infancy.

Yet, the case is that the spectrum of individual differences does not narrow and disappear, and that children seemingly normal at birth grow into children with a variety of difficulties in learning, communicating, and behaving. Some show significant developmental delays. If we could develop a finer grained analysis of early development, we might increase our understanding of how development happens, and we might also provide the basis for assessments to dictate systematic intervention in order to prevent developmental problems. It is possible to contend that our developmental analyses are, at the present time, too simpleminded to attain these goals. Our assessment techniques are extremely gross, and even our hypotheses about relationships between early and later functioning are not very complex. As was pointed our earlier, we have made some progress on the matter of seeing the infant as a more complex and more competent organism then before. We still think of development in relatively simple ways, however. We still think within single systems.

Language development is one area where we have made great strides in recent years, but it is possible that we have yet to glimpse the full complexity of the system. For example, suppose we are interested in the precursors to superior language development, superior meaning the ability to use complex language at an abstract and symbolic level. Language development in this dimension is more than the number of words in a vocabulary, or sentence length. Early language development measured in terms of early receptive language ability or in terms of vocabulary, sentence length, or type-token ratio might provide some prediction of superior language skills at a later age. However, it is quite possible that any such prediction might be better made using some nonlanguage behaviors like ability to track informational transformations, ability to detect imbedded auditory and/or visual clues, and the development of humor. Large correlational and factor analytic studies sometimes attempt to catch such relationships with a broad-meshed net, but the nature of the correlations or the degree of the loadings is rarely so clear-cut as to result in a sense of confidence that one has indeed unraveled a rational skein in the fabric of development. Yet, if we are going to take the animal literature seriously on early stimulation, and if we are going to believe the results of the Milwaukee project, it is clear that some aspects of early experience, if not our present measures of development, do relate to later developmental functioning. For this reason, it seems imperative that we abandon the notion of infant intelligence testing and adopt a strategy for infant assessment that is a sufficient match for the complexity of the events that fully describe development and behavior during infancy. Not only might such a strategy yield a fuller understanding of the continuities between early and later development, but it might provide us with criterion measures that also tell us when and how to intervene, so as to produce discontinuities by preventing an otherwise set course of development from occurring. Among the important ingredients of such an approach are complex measures of individual differences, finer analyses of the information processing systems available to the infant, and the adoption of complex hypothetical models tracing later complex behaviors to possibly unlikely origins. Many of the papers presented in this volume have as their topics current research areas on infant functioning, and can provide the data base necessary for this kind of approach.

The time is past the point of writing any more articles on the limits and usefulness of infant intelligence tests; we should not be doing more studies that cast broad networks of variables, hoping to catch a substantial correlation over two points in time. Rather, we should be delving into the underlying mechanisms of systems and their interactions and looking for functional relationships between individual differences in these systems and environmental stimulation. We have begun to fully appreciate the complexity of the phenomena with which we are dealing; we ought, now, to try to ask the right questions.

REFERENCES

Appleton, T., Clifton, R., and Goldberg, S. 1975. The development of behavioral competence in infancy. In F. D. Horowitz (ed.), Review of Child Development Research, Vol. 4, pp. 101–182. University of Chicago Press, Chicago.

Bayley, N. 1955. On the growth of intelligence. Am. Psychol. 10: 805–818.

Bayley, N. 1969. Bayley Scales of Infant Development. The Psychological Corporation, New York.

Bradley, R. H., and Caldwell, B. M. 1976. Early home environments and changes in mental test performance in children from 6 to 36 months. Dev. Psychol. 12: 93–97.

Brazelton, T. B. 1973. Neonatal Behavioral Assessment Scale. William Heinemann Medical Books, London.

Brooks, J., and Weinraub, M. 1976. A history of infant intelligence testing. In M. Lewis (ed.), Origins of Intelligence, pp. 19–58. Plenum Press, New York.

Caputo, D. V., and Taub, H. B. 1974. An evaluation of various parameters of maturity at birth as predictors of development at one year of life. Percep. Mot. Skills 39: 631–652.

Casler, L. A. 1961. Maternal deprivation: A critical review of the literature. Monogr. Soc. Res. Child Dev. Vol. 26, no. 80.

Cattell, P. 1966. The Measurement of Intelligence of Infants and Young Children. The Psychological Corporation, New York.

Cohen, L. B., and Salapatek, P. 1975. Infant Perception: From Sensation to Cognition, Vols. I and II. Academic Press, New York.

Dreyfus-Brisac, C. 1974. Organization of sleep in prematures: Implications for caretaking. In M. Lewis and L. Rosenblum (eds.), The Effect of the Infant on Its Caregiver, pp. 123–140, Wiley Interscience, New York.

Escalona, S. 1968. The Roots of Individuality. Aldine Publishing Co., Chicago, Illinois.

Escalona, S. K., and Corman, H. 1969. Albert Einstein Scales of Sensorimotor Development. Albert Einstein College of Medicine of Yeshiva University, New York.

Flavell, J. 1963. The Developmental Psychology of Jean Piaget. Van Nostrand, Princeton, New Jersey.

Fraiberg, S. 1974. Blind infants and their mothers: An examination of the sign system. In M. Lewis and L. Rosenblum (eds.), The Effect of the Infant on Its Caregiver, pp. 215–232. Wiley-Interscience, New York.

Frankenburg, W. K., and Dodds, J. B. 1968. Denver Developmental Screening Test. University of Colorado Press, Denver.

Friedman, S. 1972. Newborn visual attention to repeated exposure of redundant vs. "novel" targets. Percept. Psychophys. 12: 291–294.

Gesell, A. 1954. The ontogenesis of infant behavior. In L. Carmichael (ed.), Manual of Child Psychology. Wiley, New York.

Gesell, A., and Armatruda, C. S. 1954. Developmental Diagnosis. Paul B. Holber, Inc., New York.

Gilliland, A. R. 1951. The Northwestern Intelligence Tests for Infants. Houghton Mifflin, Boston.

Griffiths, R. 1954. The Abilities of Babies. University of London Press, Ltd., London.

Heber, R., and Garber, H. 1975. The milwaukee project. In B. Z. Friedlander, G. M. Sterritt, and G. E. Kirk (eds.), Exceptional Infant. Vol. 3: Assessment and Intervention, pp. 399–433, Brunner/Mazel, New York.

Herrnstein, R. I. 1973. I.Q. in the meritocracy. Little, Brown, Boston.

Horowitz, F. D. 1965. Theories of arousal and retardation potential. Ment. Retard. 3: 20–23.

Horowitz, F. D. 1968. Infant learning and development: Retrospect and prospect. Merrill-Palmer Quart. 14: 101–120.

Horowitz, F. D. 1969. Learning, developmental research, and individual differences. In L. P. Lipsitt and H. W. Reese (eds.), Advances in Child Development and Behavior, Vol. 4, pp. 84–126. Academic Press, New York.

Horowitz, F. D. 1976. Directions for parenting. In E. J. Mash, L. A. Hamerlynck, and L. C. Handy (eds.), Behavior Modification and Families, pp. 7–33, Brunner/Mazel, Inc. New York.

Horowitz, F. D., and Paden, L. Y. 1973. The effectiveness of environmental intervention programs. In B. M. Caldwell and H. N. Ricciuti (eds.), Review of Child Development Research, Vol. 3, pp. 331–402. University of Chicago Press, Chicago.

Hunt, J. McV. 1961. Intelligence and Experience. Ronald Press, New York.

Ireton, H., Thwing, E., and Graven, H. 1970. Infant mental development and neurological status, family socioeconomic status, and intelligence at age 4. Child Dev. 41: 937–945.

Jensen, A. R. 1969. How much can we boost I.Q. and scholastic achievement? Harvard Educ. Rev. 39: 1–123.

Kamin, Leon. 1974. The Science and Politics of I.Q. Lawrence Erlbaum Associates, Inc., New York.

Korner, Anneliese. 1974. The effect of the infant's state, level of arousal, sex and ontogenetic stage on the caregiver. In M. Lewis and L. Rosenblum (eds.), The Effect of the Infant on its Caregiver, pp. 105–122. Wiley-Interscience, New York.

Lewis, M. (ed.). 1976. Origins of Intelligence. Plenum Press, New York.

Lewis, M. and Rosenblum, L. A. 1974. The Effect of the Infant on Its Caregiver. Wiley-Interscience, New York.

Lipsitt, L. 1963. Learning in the first year of life. In C. C. Spiker and L. P. Lipsitt (eds.), Advances in Child Development and Behavior. Academic Press, New York.

McCall, R. 1976. Toward an epigenetic conception of mental development in the first three years of life. In M. Lewis (ed.), Origins of Intelligence, pp. 97–122. Plenum Press, New York.

Meier, J. H. 1975. Screening, assessment, and intervention for young children at developmental risk. In B. Z. Friedlander, G. M. Sterritt, and G. E. Kirk (eds.), Exceptional Infant. Vol. 3: Assessment and Intervention, pp. 605–650. Brunner/Mazel, New York.

Nelson, K. B., and Deubschberger, J. 1970. Head size at one year as a predictor of 4 year I.Q. Dev. Med. Child Neurol. 12: 487–495.

Osofsky, J. D., and Danzger, B. 1974. Relationships between neonatal characteristics and mother-infant interaction. Dev. Psychol. 10: 124–130.

Parmelee, A. H., and Haber, A. 1973. Who is the "risk infant"? Clin. Obstetr. Gyn. 16: 376–387.

Prechtl, H., and Beintema, D. 1964. The Neurological Examination of the Full Term Newborn Infant. William Heinemann Books, London.

Rosenblith, J. D., and Graham, F. K. 1961. Behavioral Examination of the Neonate as Modified by Rosenblith from Graham. Brown Duplicating Service, Providence, Rhode Island.

Rubin, R. A., Rosenblatt, R., and Barlow, B. 1973. Psychological and Educational Sequelae of Prematurity. Pediatrics 52: 352.

Sameroff, A., and Chandler, M. 1975. Reproductive risk and the continuum of caretaking casualty. In F. D. Horowitz (ed.), Review of Child Development Research, Vol. 4, pp. 197–244. University of Chicago Press, Chicago, Illinois.

Scarr-Salapatek, S. 1976. An evolutionary perspective on infant intelligence species patterns and individual variations. In M. Lewis (ed.), Origins of Intelligence, pp. 165–197. Plenum Press, New York.

Schmitt, R., and Erickson, M. 1973. Early predictors of mental retardation. Ment. Retard. 16: 27–29.

Siqueland, E., and Lipsitt, L. P. 1966. Conditioned head-turning behavior in the newborn. J. Exp. Child Psychol. 3: 356–376.

Skeels, H. M., and Dye, H. B. 1939. A study of the effects of differential stimulation on mentally retarded children. Proceed. Addr. Am. Assoc. Ment. Def. 44: 114–136.

Skeels, H. M., Updegraff, R., Wellman, B. L., and Williams, H. M. 1938. A study of environmental stimulation: An orphanage preschool project. Univ. Iowa Stud. Child Welfare 15, No. 4.

Stone, J., Smith, H., and Murphy, L. 1973. The Competent Infant. Basic Books, New York.

Tanner, J. M. 1974. Variability of growth and maturity in newborn infants. In M. Lewis and L. Rosenblum (eds.), The Effect of the Infant on Its Caregiver, pp. 77–104, Wiley-Interscience, New York.

Thomas, A., Birch, H. G., Chess, S., Hertzig, M. E., and Korn, S. 1963. Behavioral Individuality in Early Childhood. New York University Press, New York.

Uzgiris, I. C. and Hunt, J. McV. 1966. An Instrument for Assessing Infant Psychological Development. Psychological Development Laboratories, University of Illinois.

Watson, J. B. 1924. Behaviorism. W. W. Norton, New York.

Yarrow, L. J. 1961. Maternal deprivation: Toward an empirical and conceptual re-evaluation. Psycholog. Bull. 58: 459–490.

Yarrow, L. J., Rubenstein, J. L., and Pedersen, F. A. 1975. Infant and Environment. John Wiley and Sons, New York.

Behavioral Assessment of Auditory Function in Infants

Wesley R. Wilson

The assessment of auditory function in infants has received increasing attention during the past decade. The result of this attention is viewed by some as having provided considerable improvement in the clinical assessment of hearing impairment in infants. Other critics are less kind, and feel that much of the work has been poorly conceived, poorly executed, and of little or no value to the hard-of-hearing. As with most arguments of this type, truth rests somewhere in between. This observer feels, however, that reasonable strides forward have been made during the past several years and that as the newly developed information and modified methodologies are moved into clinical practice on a wide basis, the field of auditory assessment of infants will have been advanced considerably. Perhaps Eisenberg (1976) best captures the essence of this argument when she points out that studies of infants' hearing have moved from a point of being pioneer efforts, 15 years ago, to a point of being rather commonplace now, with the results of these experiments serving to reflect "a progression from total to relative ignorance" (p. 157).

The purposes of this chapter are to: 1) detail some of the issues surrounding the topic of early assessment of auditory function in infants, 2) describe briefly the methodologies available for such assessment currently in use, 3) describe in detail recent modifications to existing test procedures and proposed new paradigms for auditory assessment of infants, with particular emphasis on their clinical utility, 4) consider the available data on application of these procedures to both normal and developmentally disabled populations, and 5) propose a test battery that presently may serve to provide useful information in the clinical evaluation of auditory function of infants.

Certain assumptions have been made in the preparation of this chapter. First, it is assumed that clinical assessment of hearing in infants is a desirable process, even given our present state of ignorance-knowledge. Although clinician and researcher alike may be uncomfortable with the many voids in our knowledge concerning audi-

This work has been supported by a contract from the National Institute of Child Health and Human Development (HD 3-2793) entitled "An Investigation of Certain Relationships Between Hearing Impairment and Language Disability."

tory abilities of infants, the parents of a hard-of-hearing infant would have little sympathy for a position that suggested any delay in assessment and intervention for their baby while the field attempted to produce final definitive answers on these matters.

The second assumption underlying the development of this chapter is that the focus should be on infants (birth to two years), with the greatest emphasis on birth to 12 months. Implicit in this assumption is the thesis that early intervention, particularly insofar as amplification is concerned, is advantageous and a desirable goal, *provided adequate assessment occurs.*

A third assumption is that the term "assessment" describes some manner of detailed evaluation and description of abilities, and must be differentiated from "screening." The purpose of screening procedures is to define a subgroup of a total population that needs more detailed study (assessment). The more detailed study should facilitate appropriate intervention, complimented by continued assessment. The results of screening evaluations usually do not allow appropriate intervention if the best potential assessment is not completed as an intermediary step. (A case in point is the indiscriminate placement of hearing aids on infants following neonatal screening.)

The final assumption is that the terms researcher, clinician—or even researcher, assessor, and intervenor—do not necessarily reflect different persons; in fact, from the point of view of the developmentally disabled, some of the most important advances have occurred when these roles were merged into a team effort or were assumed by the same person. Thus, although the terms are used to denote specific *roles* throughout the chapter, the roles are not presumed to represent totally separate fields of endeavor.

ISSUES IN INFANT AUDITORY ASSESSMENT

Issue 1. The Infant: An Active Receptor of Sound

In 1975, Cairns and Butterfield developed the argument that auditory assessment of infants must recognize a new view of infants as active receptors of auditory information, who, if given the chance, will interact with and control their auditory environment. With the explosion of information in the area of infant speech perception developed with the high amplitude sucking (HAS) and heart rate (HR) paradigms, there can no longer be any argument regarding whether or not the infant is an active receptor of sound, because the evidence is overwhelming on that point (see Morse, this volume, for a detailed review).

In the clinical assessment of audition, historical precedent has favored behavioral observation procedures[1] without reinforcement, because of the lack of

---

[1] The terms *behavioral audiometry* and *electrophysiologic audiometry* have taken on limited, specific meanings in the field of audiology; to ensure a common point of reference, they are used in this chapter as defined below:

1. *Behavioral audiometry* refers to auditory assessment procedures that involve the monitoring of a "voluntary" or overt response on the part of the infant. Reinforcement may or may not be included.

alternative methodologies. Thus, many clinicians continue to view the young infant as being passively involved with his environment because their methodology favors such a notion. In the behavioral approaches, this myth has led to detailed procedures for calibrating the signal precisely, attempting to calibrate the observer precisely, attempting to define the state of the infant as rigorously as possible, and then interpreting the results in terms of threshold values for the infant. Likewise, the emphasis on electrophysiologic procedures has often been the result of a quest to reduce the infant to a nonparticipatory piece of "equipment" that is part of a calibrated circuit that the tester can then maintain. One might wonder if many audiologists would not prefer dealing with infants who came from the "factory" with a detailed list of specifications, or better yet, a graphic printout of his auditory abilities, so that the audiologist could then check the calibration of the infant much as he maintains the calibration of other pieces of equipment in his circuit.

This issue is important to the topic of early behavioral assessment of auditory abilities, both in terms of development and transmittal of information. During the next few years, the change in view of infant auditory potential must be effectively communicated and moved into clinical practice along with the necessary data base to support this assertion. This issue is closely interrelated with the next issue, that of focus on measurement of sensitivity.

Issue 2. Focus on Hearing Sensitivity in Assessment of Infants

In the hearing assessment of adults, the audiologist devotes substantial time to the determination of both air-conduction and bone-conduction hearing sensitivity, based on a medical model of disease. As audiologists have approached the assessment of infants in a clinical setting, the presumption has often been that the primary focus should be on hearing sensitivity. In fact, much of the literature is devoted to discussions of methodologies for determining hearing sensitivity in infants with greater precision. The point of this argument is not to minimize the information available in such assessment, but rather to say that a view of auditory function as being tied predominantly to sensitivity is totally inappropriate. We need only remind ourselves that central lesions of the auditory system will not manifest themselves in changes in peripheral hearing sensitivity to realize one serious error in such a focus. Again, methodological constraints come into play. Later in the chapter we point to potential modifications of existing procedures that allow the audiologist to assess higher auditory function than that of sensitivity only. Furthermore, one need only to look again at the literature available in infant speech perception to realize that the infant possesses substantially greater auditory abilities than our measurement procedures have assumed.

For example, "behavioral observation audiometry" involves an observer who "scores" the infant's overt responses to auditory stimuli.

2. *Electrophysiologic audiometry* refers to auditory assessment procedures that involve electrophysiologic monitoring of either autonomic nervous system reflex activity to sound or direct recording of the bioelectric correlates of the original acoustic signal at various stations along the auditory nervous system. Response averaging may be included.

Issue 3. Methodological Differences Between Data
Collection in a Research Setting and in a Clinical Setting

The researcher in the area of infant audition is often willing to accept a methodology that is inefficient both in terms of subject drop-out rate and in terms of the time necessary to develop a single data point. For example, in the HAS paradigm, as used in the area of infant speech perception, the reported subject drop-out rate is often 40% or higher (Cairns and Butterfield, 1975); likewise, the procedure makes use of a treatment-by-groups design. On the other hand, because failure to respond is usually the variable of interest in auditory assessment, the clinician is forced to look for a paradigm that works on all infants and that will allow for a number of data points to be developed on each individual. Also, efficiency, in terms of number of visits required to complete assessment, cost of instrumentation, and sophistication required for response judgment, are important factors to the clinician.

The two methods used predominantly by researchers in the area of infant speech perception—HAS paradigm and HR paradigm—have not been adopted for clinical use, and the primary procedure used by most clinicians for infants under 12 months—behavioral observation audiometry (BOA)—did not lend itself to the types of discrimination paradigms required by the researchers, or the clinicians for that matter. Two problems are created: 1) norms developed by researchers cannot be applied to clinical populations at present, and 2) the inefficiency of the methodologies used by researchers restricts their use in collecting data on specific disordered populations that would serve to strengthen the theoretic interpretation of the results on normals. The cost and difficulty involved in collecting matched subjects for a treatment-by-groups design would be prohibitive with certain disordered populations (e.g., hard-of-hearing).

Issue 4. Comparison of Data Developed with
Behavioral Procedures not Employing Reinforcement to
Data Developed with Procedures Employing Reinforcement

BOA procedures, without reinforcement, have provided the primary data base for the clinical assessment procedures used with infants. Even within apparently similar procedures, differences in "normative" values have been noted. For example, Northern and Downs (1974), in comparing their Auditory Behavior Index to one developed by Murphy (1961), reported that their population showed less mature response levels as a function of age than did Murphy's. As another example, the thresholds developed for speech by Northern and Downs (1974) differ substantially from those reported by Thompson and Weber (1974). Likewise, the data developed using BOA procedures without reinforcement show considerable differences when compared to data developed using operant procedures. For example, in terms of threshold, both Northern and Downs (1974) and Thompson and Weber (1974) report an improvement in level of response as a function of age from birth through 21 months. In threshold data developed with an operant procedure (Wilson, Moore, and Thompson, 1976) no such pronounced shift was noted. Although the test-retest reliability figures of the operant procedures suggest much less variability in sample norms, and the thresholds obtained come much closer to approximating norms for older children (Eisele, Berry, and Shriner, 1975; Fulton, Gorzycki, and Hull, 1977; Wilson and Decker, 1976; Wilson et al., 1976), cross clinic data are not yet available, necessitating the cautionary note that even with such procedures, each clinic must at present develop its own norms.

Issue 5. Assessment Procedures for Determining Higher Order Function in the Auditory System

The BOA procedures have used scales of expected response, ranging from the reflex activity of the neonate to the localization of an older infant, as one means of charting development of the auditory system. Thus, proponents of this methodology would argue that any operant procedure would remove or seriously reduce the ability to make such judgments, because a single response is isolated for reinforcement. An alternative means of attempting to demonstrate central auditory function is suggested later in this chapter. Briefly, modeled on knowledge of the adult system, certan integrative tasks can be placed in the operant discrimination paradigm, thereby allowing the potential for direct assessment of higher order function.

In summary, these issues suggest that the field of infant auditory assessment is undergoing a change focusing primarily on methodologies. The demonstration that the infant possesses a highly developed auditory system and can actively react with sound invites such methodological changes, and suggests that the next few years should allow us to improve substantially our data base relative to auditory functioning in infants, if only we allow the infant to demonstrate meaningful ways of assessing such function.

ASSESSMENT OF SENSORY FUNCTION: AUDITORY

Before considering specific methodologies for assessment of auditory function, it may be helpful to consider briefly the system being assessed. Knowledge concerning the structure and function of the developing auditory system is incomplete. For the reader interested in more complete reviews on this topic, see Hecox (1975) or Eisenberg (1976).

Development of the Auditory System

Fetal Period The cochlea is first to develop; it reaches adult configuration early in the third fetal month (Timiras, 1972). The middle ear and cochlea reach full adult size by the fifth fetal month; likewise, cochlear function can be demonstrated (Elliott and Elliott, 1964; Nakai, 1970). The tympanic antrum develops late in the fetal period, and the mastoid air cells begin development during fetal life but complete their formation after birth (Moore, 1973). According to Faulkner (1966), auditory nerve fibers begin to myelinate during the sixth fetal month. Information as to whether or not the auditory cortex is completely medulated in a full term baby differs by source (Eisenberg, 1976; Hecox, 1975).

A number of investigators have indicated that the fetus is responsive to auditory signals (e.g., Dwornicka, Jasienska, Smolarz, and Wawryk, 1964; Johansson, Wedenberg, and Westin, 1964; Murphy and Smyth, 1962), although Bench and Vass (1970) report conflicting results. Bench (1970) feels that it remains to be demonstrated conclusively that the human fetus responds to sound before birth.

Early Infancy

State Factors Researchers who have spent most of their time working with neonates strongly emphasize the necessity of defining both state factors and environmental factors (Bench, 1970; Eisenberg, Griffin, Coursin, and Hunter, 1964). State is usually categorized on numerical scales (3 to 7 point) ranging from deep sleep to full wakefulness (Eisenberg, 1976). The effect of state is that the middle states allow generally better response ratios than do states at either extreme (deep sleep or full wakefulness). However, certain stimulus parameters interact with this finding (e.g., frequency—Eisenberg et al., 1964). Eisenberg (1976) also recommends that environmental factors be held constant, and specifically suggests for assessment of neonates that temperature be maintained at 78 to 82° Fahrenheit, humidity be maintained at 50%, and that indirect lighting be maintained with a constant diffusion.

Signal Factors Eisenberg (1976), in an extensive review of the effects of signal parameters, concludes that band width per se is probably not a critical determinant of auditory function during early life, although infants do respond more effectively to noise bands than to pure tones; that little information is available relative to short duration signals; for longer duration signals, the number of responses to signals increases more or less directly with duration in the range between 300 msec and 5 sec, although signal durations of 1 sec or more are clinically adequate for most kinds of infant studies. In terms of frequency, she concludes that low and high frequency signals have differential functional properties, with low frequency signals serving to soothe the infant and high frequency signals serving to distress the infant, and that signals in the carrier range for speech are more effective. In terms of signal rise and decay time, she reports rapid rise times to be associated with defense reflexes and slow rise times to be associated with orienting responses. Finally, relative to intensity, she reports that the neonate very likely has auditory sensitivity at birth that approximates values for adults, with the exception that a conductive loss of 35 to 40 dB seems to be present in all neonates for a few days. Recent data by Keith (1973, 1975), collected by means of impedance measurements, may contradict the assertion of conductive loss in neonates and is suggestive of good middle-ear function; however, more data are needed, including both impedance studies and otomicroscopy. Suprathreshold signals will produce more responses and intense auditory stimuli tend to increase body tension in crying babies. Finally, Eisenberg (1976) states that "most newborns, including premature infants and those with known abnormalities of the CNS . . . can discriminate sound on the basis of numerous acoustic variables" (p. 116).

Response Factors   The expected response in these infant behavioral procedures ranges from reflexive activity, including eye widening, eye blink, or arousal from sleep, up through direct localization of sound, first horizontally to the side and later to the side and down (Conway and Shallop, 1975; Murphy, 1961; Northern and Downs, 1974; Shallop, 1974). These investigators describe the expected responses in terms of general age of development. Movement from the general reflexive reactions (e.g., arousal) to localization following a sound is considered to reflect development in the auditory system. Infants who do not move through these stages are often defined as presenting an auditory developmental age commensurate with their response level.

As previously noted, Northern and Downs (1974) go on to describe the levels of signal that are required for such responses. The levels of signal are highest for the early developmental stages and decrease as the infant grows older. However, as previously noted, there are reasonably wide differences between predictive scales of this type, and large individual differences have also been noted in clinical use (Thompson and Weber, 1974).

In summary, we should again note that this information has been developed with observational procedures that have not included active participation on the part of the infant. To what extent this data base will change as a function of a movement to methodologies that include the infant more actively is not known at this time. However, the preliminary indications from clinical assessment procedures would suggest that substantial changes will occur.

Identification of Auditory Problems

Although the primary focus of this paper is on assessment, the process of identification must be considered as a prerequisite to assessment. Obviously, detailed assessment cannot be carried out on each infant within a society. The problem, then, is one of finding an effective means of identifying those infants in need of more detailed study with a cost-efficient system. Within the area of hearing, two procedures—neonatal screening and "at-risk" registries—have been applied.

Neonatal Screening   Neonatal screening developed in this country from two distinct bases: 1) the assertion of proponents that such procedures were feasible (e.g., Downs and Sterritt, 1964, 1967; Griffiths, 1964; Reddell and Calvert, 1969), and 2) the fact that in our health and educational system, the neonatal period was the only time when the total population was considered to be available for screening procedures, before school age. The screening procedures involved monitoring of changes in state following presentation of signals of high intensity—often in excess of 90 dB SPL. As reviewed elsewhere (see *Conference on Newborn Hearing Screening,* 1971), the extremely low yield of such programs, coupled with the fact that many of the infants identified by testing would also have been identified by some means of an "at-risk" register, led to the suggestion that a high-risk population should be identified by prenatal history and postnatal physical assessment. Specifically, the Joint Committee on Infant Hearing Screening (with representatives from the American Speech and Hearing Association, the American Academy of

Ophthalmology and Otolaryngology, and the American Academy of Pediatrics) developed a statement adopted by all three organizations, as follows:

> The Committee recommends that, since no satisfactory technique is yet established that will permit hearing screening of all newborns, infants AT RISK for hearing impairment should be identified by means of history and physical examination. These children should be tested and followed-up as hereafter described:
>
> I. The criterion for identifying a newborn as AT RISK for hearing impairment is the presence of one or more of the following:
>   A. History of hereditary childhood hearing impairment.
>   B. Rubella or other nonbacterial intrauterine fetal infection (e.g., cytomegalovirus infections, Herpes infection).
>   C. Defects of ear, nose, or throat. Malformed, low-set or absent pinnae; cleft lip or palate (including submucous cleft); any residual abnormality of the otorhinolaryngeal system.
>   D. Birthweight less than 1500 grams.
>   E. Bilirubin level greater than 20 mg/100 ml serum.
> II. Infants falling in this category should be referred for an in-depth audiological evaluation of hearing during their first two months of life and, even if hearing appears to be normal, should receive regular hearing evaluations thereafter at office or well-baby clinics. Regular evaluation is important since familial hearing impairment is not necessarily present at birth but may develop at an uncertain period of time later (1972).

The efficacy of the high-risk registry approach is not yet fully known. However, a limited number of studies do apply. Feinmesser and Bauberger-Tell (1971) reported that 20% of the population fell in an all-inclusive register of at-risk criteria for all difficulties and that this register identified 17 of 22 ultimately deaf children. However, they conclude that the "high-risk" register is of limited value because in part of the high number requiring follow up. Mencher (1974) saw 10,000 infants and was able to follow up 80% at regular intervals for two years. Of the nine babies eventually found to have confirmed auditory impairment, two had passed both behavioral screening and a high-risk classification. Five would have been detected by a high-risk register (same as above) and seven were identified by behavioral screening. He concluded that both behavioral screening and a high-risk register are necessary. Ehrlich, Shapiro, Kimball, and Huttner (1973) evaluated the communication skills in five-year-old children who had presented high-risk neonatal histories. Their findings included the fact that despite normal intelligence test results, 54% of the children needed special help. Respiratory distress, abnormal birth weight, and gestational age were the best predictors of disability. Significant hearing loss was found in 2.5% of their sample. The most commonly impaired functions were auditory discrimination in noise or quiet, auditory memory, visual figure ground discrimination, and visual memory.

There is no doubt that we must continue to focus on developing means of identifying infants who are in need of assessment. An alternative to those already suggested involves instrumental monitoring of the responsiveness of infants to sound stimulation over time. Simmons and Russ (1974) have suggested an automated system that includes a signal source (92 dB "sound level" at crib), motion-detecting transducers mounted on multiple cribs, and a response chart that reads the output of the motion-detecting transducers from each of the cribs as well as encoding the test presentation intervals. Their data indicated that the failure rate for the procedure has ranged from 14% to 6.2% (the change reflects development of the procedure and redefinition of pass-fail criteria); of the babies who failed the screening and were followed up, 4% had a moderate to severe hearing loss.

This procedure is automated and takes advantage of multiple test presentations spread widely throughout the infant's stay in the nursery. Machine scoring of results should be possible. One weakness in the procedure seems to rest in the signal level needed in the high noise levels of the nursery, which would preclude more sensitive identification of mild-to-moderate losses. Also, the cost factor involved in setting up such instrumentation in all hospital nurseries seems prohibitive. On the other hand, application of this procedure, on a portable basis, for high-risk infants might be possible. Murphy (personal communication) has described a similar apparatus with multiple channel readout for more definitive auditory assessment of infants.

In summary, procedures for identifying hearing impairment in infants have not been adopted widely in this country. Methodological considerations have restricted the procedures to definition of severe-to-profound losses only. The return from high-risk registers may be more valuable, particularly from the point of view of total communicative skills, than are the returns from neonatal screening procedures that focus only on reflex response to very high intensity sounds. It is fair to conclude, however, that no systematic means of identifying neonates with either mild-to-moderate hearing problems and/or central auditory deficits is on the immediate horizon, at least in terms of application to the total population of infants. If an appropriate means of scheduling all children for identification procedures at six months of age could be developed in this country, the tests available should offer substantially better results in terms of both identification of mild-to-moderate hearing losses, and in terms of definition of difficulties in auditory functioning.

Behavioral Assessment of Auditory Thresholds

Behavioral assessment of auditory thresholds in infants is based on observation of overt responses to controlled auditory signals. The two general approaches that have been employed clinically may be differentiated by whether or not reinforcement has been employed. Until recently, procedures involving some form of instrumental conditioning were restricted in use to infants over 12 months of age.

For infants under 12 months of age, audiologists have usually resorted to BOA, in which no conditioning is employed. A number of investigators have pointed out shortcomings in this procedure; for example, Ling, Ling, and Doehring (1970) and Weber (1969) have shown that it may be difficult to control observer bias; Moore, Thompson, and Thompson (1975) demonstrated that the infant may quickly habituate to the signal, making it difficult to determine whether absence of response is attributable to habituation or hearing loss; and Thompson and Weber (1974) found that the thresholds obtained vary widely across a group of presumed normal hearing infants. Thus, BOA serves best as an initial screening procedure to determine levels for further testing.

Based in part on the shortcomings of BOA, several investigators recently have explored the application of operant conditioning procedures to the assessment of hearing sensitivity in infants under 12 months (Fulton et al., 1975; Wilson and Decker, 1977; Wilson et al., 1976). In such procedures, the use of reinforcement is designed to strengthen an easily monitored single response mode, to keep the infant in an aroused or motivated state, thereby allowing more precise estimation of ability, and to reduce the habituation found in BOA by allowing the infant to actively interact with his environment.

Two types of operant procedures have been used. The first method involves an operant discrimination paradigm in which the auditory stimulus functions as a signal that reward is available, and the second makes use of conjugate reinforcement of operant responding to auditory stimuli. In this paradigm, the intensity of a continuously available reinforcing stimulus varies as a function of the rate of response. The essential difference between the two paradigms is that in the conjugate procedure, the stimulus is a consequence of the response and must in itself have reinforcing value to the infant. In the discrimination paradigm, definition of reinforcer is not confined to the category of stimuli under study and it may be possible to utilize a more potent reinforcer (Cairns and Butterfield, 1975). Although both paradigms are clearly an assessment of auditory function, one would seem more appropriate for determining preference type data and the other more appropriate for discrimination data. Because auditory threshold determination is seen as a discrimination task (presence or absence of signal), it is the discrimination paradigm that has been explored for that purpose.

Operant Discrimination Paradigm Within the operant discrimination paradigm, several different response modes have been explored—head turn, bar press, and leg swing. Likewise, different forms of reinforcement have been used—visual and edibles. However, the two procedures that have been used clinically for assessing the hearing sensitivity of infants have involved the head-turn response with visual reinforcement—called visual reinforcement audiometry (VRA)[2]—and the bar-press response with either edible reinforcement or visual reinforcement. When edibles (or other tangibles) have been used as reinforcers, the procedure has been called tangible reinforcement operant conditioning audiometry (TROCA), and when a visual reinforcer has been used, it is called VROCA (after Lloyd, 1966).

Visual Reinforcement Audiometry The use of VRA procedures for assessment of hearing sensitivity in infants and young children has been suggested by a number of authors (Haug, Baccaro, and Guilford, 1967; Liden and Kankkunen, 1969; Motta, Facchini, and D'Auria, 1970; Suzuki and Ogiba, 1960, 1961; Suzuki, Ogiba, and Takei, 1972; Tyberghein and Forrez, 1971; Warren, 1972). Generally, the lower age limit for application of this procedure was considered to be 12 months, although Haug et al. reported clinical success with a small number of infants in the 5 to 12 month range. In the original COR procedure, as described by Suzuki and Ogiba

---

[2] The VRA procedure has also been called Conditioned Orientation Reflex Audiometry, or COR after Suzuki and Ogiba, 1960; however, because we have used this procedure with individuals who do not initially show a reflex behavior to sound, we prefer the acronym VRA describing simply the reinforcement used and implying the head-turn response.

(1960), no attempt had been made to determine the relative effectiveness of different types of visual reinforcers to be employed.

In the first of a series of studies on this test procedure, Moore et al. (1975) investigated the auditory localization behavior of infants as a function of type of reinforcement using four conditions: 1) no reinforcement, 2) social reinforcement (a smile, verbal praise and/or pat on shoulder), 3) simple visual reinforcement (a blinking light), and 4) complex visual reinforcement (an animated toy). Forty-eight infants between the ages of 12 and 18 months served as subjects, meeting selection criteria that were designed to exclude possible cases of hearing loss. A complex noise was used as the auditory signal based on the previous work of Thompson and Thompson (1972), who demonstrated it to be more effective than pure tones in eliciting auditory responses from infants. All signal presentations were at a level of 70 dB SPL. Each subject received 30 stimuli and 10 control trials. The response interval was 4 sec, starting at stimulus onset, and any response had to be a clear turning of the head in the direction of the loudspeaker. Finally, both the examiner and the assistant had to score the behavior as a response in order for it to be counted.

Figure 1 shows cumulative responses of the four groups in blocks of stimulus trials. The results demonstrated that the complex visual reinforcement—an ani-

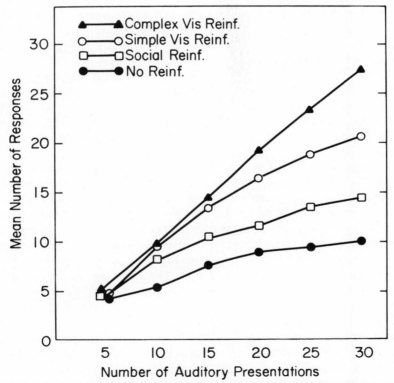

Figure 1.   Cumulative mean responses in blocks of stimulus trials for four reinforcement conditions—N = 12 infants (12–18 months of age) in each group (from Moore, Thompson, and Thompson, 1975).

mated toy—resulted in significantly more localization responses than the simple visual reinforcement—a flashing light. The light resulted in significantly more responses than social reinforcement, which resulted in significantly more responses than the no-reinforcement condition. Note that the complex visual reinforcement group continued to show a high rate of response over the full 30 presentations. For example, subjects in this group averaged eight responses to the last 10 stimulus presentations.

Two other findings were of importance. First, subjects randomly looked toward the sound source only 4.8% of the time when no auditory stimulus was present, based on the control trials, allowing the conclusion that random behavior was not a major factor in the number of positive responses obtained during test trials. Second, inter-judge reliability was high, with agreement occurring 99% of the time. The results of this study indicated that auditory localization behavior in 12- to 18-month-old infants is influenced by the type of reinforcement employed, and that the relationship is very systematic. Furthermore, it raised the question of whether or not the same procedure might be applicable to infants under 12 months of age, because the animated toy used in the procedure was considerably more effective than the types of visual reinforcers that had been used in previous VRA and COR procedures.

In the second study in this series (Moore, Wilson, and Thompson, 1977), we were interested in looking at the auditory localization responses of infants under 12 months of age, and we selected two conditions—no reinforcement and complex visual reinforcement—based on the results of the first study. Using the same paradigm, 60 infants between the ages of 4 and 11 months served as subjects, selected on the same criteria used in the previous study. The 60 infants were divided into two equal groups matched by age. One half received complex visual reinforcement, while the other half received no reinforcement and served as the control group. The experimental and control groups were then further divided into three age divisions for analysis—four-months-old, five- and six-months-old, and seven- to eleven-months-old.

Figure 2 illustrates the mean number of responses compared to the number of presentations for the seven- to eleven-month-old subjects. They responded at a significantly higher rate when visual reinforcement was used. Also, within the design paradigm of 30 presentations, no habituation of the response was noted. Figure 3 is organized in the same way and presents data for the five- and six-month-old infants. Again, the results are similar: a high rate of response with visual reinforcement and no clear evidence of habituation of response. Figure 4, also organized in the same manner, presents the data for four-month-olds. The actual age of the infants in this category ranged from three months, sixteen days to four months, fifteen days. As is readily apparent, the animated toy does not serve a reinforcement function for this age group.

The findings of this study suggest that the head-turn response, reinforced with an animated toy, may be used with infants five months of age and older. The range of responses, grouping all infants five months of age and above, was from 17 to 30. Thus, even the child giving the fewest responses was responding at a much higher rate than the mean rate for the nonreinforcement condition.

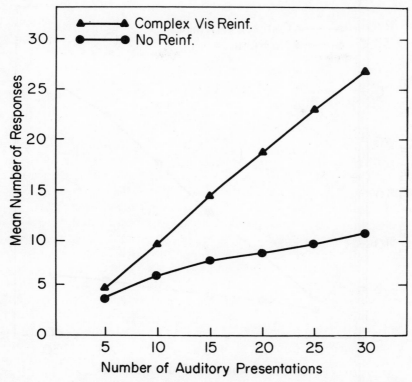

Figure 2. Cumulative mean responses in blocks of stimulus trials as a function of visual reinforcement and age—N = 10 infants (7–11 months of age) in each group (from Moore, Wilson, and Thompson, 1977).

These data indicate that a complex visual stimulus can be used to reinforce localization behavior of infants as young as approximately five months of age, in this paradigm. Of further interest, from the point of view of clinical assessment, is that the fewest number of responses of any subject five months of age or older in the experimental group was 17, which may be compared to the mean number of responses in the control groups of 5.5 for the five- to six-month-old control group and 10.7 for the seven- to eleven-month-old control group.

While the previous work by Moore et al. (1975) had demonstrated that a complex visual reinforcer was effective in significantly increasing the number of localization responses that infants 12 months of age and older would make to a suprathreshold auditory signal, the data in this study extend this finding downward in age to a level of five months. Below that age, the paradigm as presently consti-tuted is ineffective. The implications for clinical assessment are twofold: 1) the lower age limit for this operant conditioning approach is well below the age of 12 months, as suggested by Suzuki and Ogiba (1960, 1961) and Motta et al. (1970), and 2) the difference in number of single category responses that an infant will provide is substantial when an appropriate reinforcer is employed. Furthermore, the response-

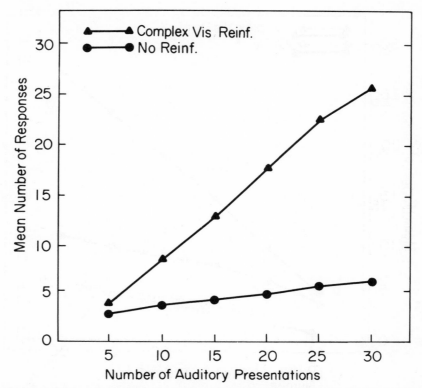

Figure 3.   Cumulative mean responses in blocks of stimulus trials as a function of visual reinforcement and age—N = 10 infants five and six months of age in each group (from Moore, Wilson, and Thompson, 1977).

to-stimulus functions (Figures 1 and 2) illustrate that the responses of the five- to eleven-month-old experimental subjects had not begun to habituate within the 30 presentations of this study. Had there been more trials, it is likely that there would have been even a greater difference between the control and experimental groups. The clinician desiring to assess an infant's response to more than a very limited number of auditory presentations would find these differences important.

The third study in this series, Wilson et al. (1976), was concerned with the auditory thresholds that could be developed by the VRA method. The response and response scoring procedures and use of control intervals were the same as for the previous studies, as was the subject selection procedure. Ninety infants between 5 and 18 months of age were divided into groups of 15 according to age. Threshold measurement, using a complex-noise signal, involved starting at 0 dB SPL and ascending in 20 dB steps until the first response occurred. After a second positive response, threshold sampling began using a protocol of attenuating the signal 20 dB after each positive response, and increasing it 10 dB after each failure to respond. Threshold was defined as the lowest presentation level at which the infant responded at least three times out of six. All results are reported in dB SPL using a 10 dB measurement interval.

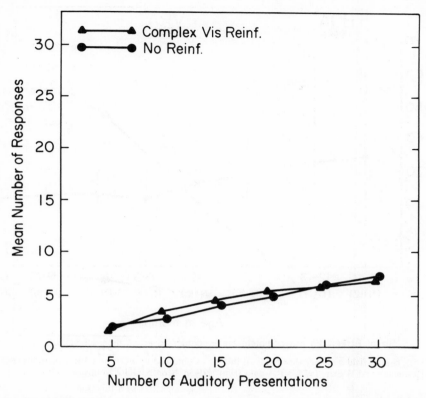

Figure 4.   Cumulative mean responses in blocks of stimulus trials as a function of visual reinforcement and age—N = 10 infants four months of age in each group (from Moore, Wilson, and Thompson, 1977).

Figure 5 presents the thresholds obtained by VRA, as a function of age, and provides comparative data from BOA procedures (Thompson and Weber, 1974). As can be noted, the mean response levels improved slightly with age, ranging from 21 dB to 29 dB SPL. The 10th and 90th percentile points were 20 and 40 dB SPL for the five-month-olds, and 20 and 30 dB SPL for the 6- to 18-month-olds. Compared to thresholds obtained by BOA for the same ages (from Thompson and Weber, 1974), the VRA thresholds are significantly better. Even more importantly, for infants six months old and above, the range between the 10th and 90th percentile is reduced from the 45 to 50 dB reported on BOA to 10 dB (or one measurement step) for the VRA procedure used in this study. Of further interest, from the point of view of clinical applicability, is that a total of 94 infants were tested to complete the sample reported. The data of three infants were not considered valid because of more than one false-positive response during the control intervals. (The average number of control intervals was 4.6 and the average number of false-positive responses was 0.37.) All but one infant six months of age or older yielded thresholds in one visit, with the exception requiring two visits. Sixty percent of the five-month-olds yielded threshold in one visit, while 40% did not complete the testing, usually because they began to cry. The average test-session duration was 10 minutes.

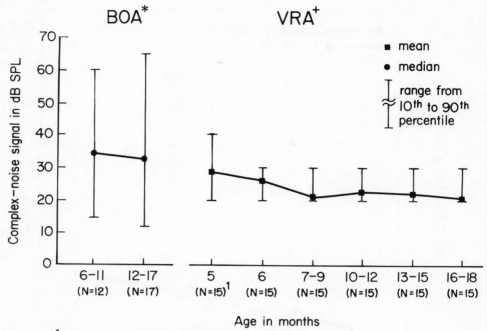

Figure 5.   Sound-field auditory thresholds of infants as obtained by BOA and VRA methods (BOA data from Thompson and Weber, 1974; VRA data from Wilson, Moore, and Thompson, 1976).

To determine the test-retest reliability of VRA with infants, 19 of the original subjects were reevaluated two to five months after the initial evaluation, using the same procedure. The test-retest comparison indicated that eight subjects had thresholds that were 10 dB better than the first evaluation; 10 subject's thresholds remained the same; and one subject had a threshold 10 dB poorer on the second evaluation. Thus, test-retest reliability was plus or minus one measurement step.

Clinical implications of this third study are substantial: 1) it has demonstrated that the thresholds obtained from infants are very close to those obtained for adults in the same situation, 2) even more importantly, the range of thresholds for the population of presumed normal hearing infants was very small, indicating that the values obtained can serve a usable function as clinical norms, a finding in direct contrast to the very wide dispersion demonstrated for BOA procedures, and 3) the procedure is economical of time and highly applicable to infants six months of age and older. At present, we use this procedure as the initial test for all clinical cases of appropriate age. We sample the infant's response either to speech or complex noise, and high- and low-pass filtered versions of either. This allows us to determine sound-field hearing sensitivity for a broad-band signal, as well as for a low-frequency emphasis signal and a high-frequency emphasis signal, to provide prediction of slope or pattern of loss when present. Clinically, we have used this procedure in air-conduction earphone measurements and bone-conduction measurements, and at present are involved in collection of normative data (Moore, Wilson, Lillis, and Talbott, 1976). Our interest in exploring earphone measurements with this procedure rests not only in our desire to develop air-conduction earphone thresholds, but also in being able to provide greater signal specificity for more detailed evaluation of suprathreshold auditory function.

TROCA and VROCA Procedures   The basic operant discrimination paradigm used in these procedures involves a bar-press response coupled with either edible or visual reinforcement. A number of reviews of these procedures, as applied to older difficult-to-test populations is available (e.g., Fulton, 1974; Fulton and Lloyd, 1975). This basic information is not repeated here.

In 1968, Lloyd, Spradlin, and Reid described the use of TROCA with three normal infants (7, 15, and 18 months of age) as a part of their report on the use of the procedure with profoundly retarded subjects. During the past year, two studies have looked at the usefulness of the procedure with infants (Fulton et al., 1975; Wilson and Decker, 1977).

Fulton et al. (1975) studied 12 children between 9 and 25 months of age, with a median age of 12 months. They attempted to develop earphone thresholds for pure-tone signals at the standard audiometric test frequencies. They obtained auditory measures with 7 of the original 12 subjects. Of the 5 subjects not tested, 2 were withdrawn by their parents, and the other 3 had not developed stimulus-response control training after 23 to 24 sessions. For the seven subjects who successfully completed the training procedures, screening procedures were carried out on two at a hearing level of 15 dB, and threshold assessment was completed on the remaining five. Threshold data per se are not provided in the report; the test-retest threshold differences were predominantly 5 dB or less, with only 7.6% exceeding 10 dB. Although the subjects for whom successful measurement was completed were all 12 months of age or older, the importance of this study rests in the fact that they have demonstrated that standard air-conduction test procedures, using earphones, can be successfully applied to infants. Furthermore, it raises the question of whether or not further discriminate auditory assessments could be completed once the infant is brought under stimulus control using the rigorous training program of Fulton et al. (1975). For example, Fulton (1974) has demonstrated that once profoundly retarded individuals are brought under stimulus control on the same training program, it is possible to complete SISI testing, Threshold Tone Decay testing, and other basic psychoacoustic paradigms related to frequency and intensity DL.

The second study, using both TROCA and VROCA procedures (Wilson and Decker, 1977), also looked at auditory thresholds of infants. Thirty-two infants between the ages of 7 and 20 months were seen using either type of reinforcer, as determined by the infant's preference. Suprathreshold auditory presentations, coupled with timeouts following false-positive responses, were used to bring the infant under stimulus control, defined as three successive HITS without an intervening false positive. Threshold was determined by a bracketing procedure using 10 dB measurement steps. The signals were warbled pure tones of 0.5, 1, 2, and 4 kHz, presented in a sound field.

Thresholds (average of the four frequencies) for the 26 infants brought under stimulus control ranged from 20 to 30 dB SPL; division of the sample into three age groups showed no differences in threshold as a function of age. Multiple test sessions were required (mean = 4). The procedure was successful with 64% of the infants under 12 months of age, and with 82% of those 13 to 20 months of age. The threshold values obtained with the TROCA/VROCA procedure are directly comparable to those obtained by VRA procedures.

In terms of clinical utility, the TROCA/VROCA procedures are more time consuming than the VRA procedure, as evidenced by a mean of 11.4 sessions for earphone testing (Fulton et al., 1975) and a mean of 4 sessions for sound-field testing (Wilson and Decker, 1976). However, at least for older infants and young children, the TROCA/VROCA procedures do allow for continued resampling of a child's auditory abilities in multiple test sessions. Our experience has been that once an infant is brought under stimulus control, he can be brought back on a number of occasions and be tested immediately.

Behavioral Assessment of Suprathreshold Auditory Abilities

Operant Discrimination Paradigm   Although the HAS procedure falls under this category, it is not discussed here because of its lack of clinical applicability as presently used. A modification of the VRA procedure has been used by Eilers, Wilson, and Moore (1977) to address the issue of developmental change in speech discrimination. This operant technique was developed to achieve the following goals: 1) to be applicable to a large proportion of infants tested, 2) to be time-efficient, 3) to be capable of testing a single child's discrimination, 4) to be capable of evaluating multiple speech contrasts for each infant tested, 5) to be applicable across a wide age range, and 6) to employ a reinforcer that is independent from the stimuli to be discriminated. In the Visually Reinforced Infant Speech Discrimination Paradigm (VRISD), infants are presented with one member of a contrastive stimulus pair at the rate of one syllable per second at 50 dB SPL. While the infant is entertained at midline, the speech stimulus is changed during a 4-sec interval. The infant is reinforced for a head turn at the change in signal by the activation of an animated toy. Initially, the *figure* stimulus is presented at a higher intensity than the *ground* stimulus. Once the infant has demonstrated responses to the intensity and/or speech signal difference, the intensities are equated. Each infant is then presented with three experimental and three control trials; to reach significance, the infant must respond appropriately five out of six times. Although the results of this procedure will be discussed elsewhere in this volume in terms of their import to the speech discrimination literature, it is important to note that the VRISD paradigm provided individual data on 90% of the infants tested on as many as 10 speech contrasts in as few as three 20-minute sessions.

These results suggest that for infants six months of age and older, it is possible to measure speech discrimination as evidenced by ability to differentiate between two contrastive speech stimuli on an individual subject basis. Although no data are yet available concerning the applicability of this procedure to disordered populations, the possibilities are exciting. For example, because this discrimination procedure does not require the receptive language abilities of most tests of auditory discrimination for children, testing of discrimination function can begin at a much younger age in the infant suspected of developmental disability. Furthermore, as more information about the discrimination abilities of normal infants is available, it will be possible to determine auditory discrimination developmental level for infants suggested of being delayed. Finally, the procedure may allow more detailed assessment of function of amplification systems, because a discriminative response to the speech signal is available through this paradigm. Although each of these possible uses is highly speculative at this time, it would appear that a breakthrough has occurred in developing a procedure for early assessment of auditory functioning.

Conjugate Reinforcement Paradigm As noted earlier, the conjugate procedures use the response to control the stimulus. The stimulus serves also as the reinforcer. This procedure has been used successfully by Friedlander (1969) in what he has called "The Play Test Technique." Cairns and Butterfield (1975) have suggested that manipulations of acoustic characteristics of the speech stimulus could be used to determine the infant's auditory abilities using this preference procedure.

More recently, Eisele et al. (1975) have used infant sucking rate to control the intensity change of a Bekesy-type audiometer. Testing 105 neonates, 100 responded to three pulsed pure-tone signals (1, 2, and 4 kHz) with highly consistent response levels. Although follow-up data are not fully available on the five infants who did not respond, one was found to have middle-ear effusions and another has a family history of deafness. Thus, the test may offer advantages for screening of sensitivity, although the task is clearly a suprathreshold procedure. Modifications in signal used could provide valuable data on neonatal auditory preferences.

Application to Developmentally Disabled Populations

Although operant test procedures were initially developed for use with the low-functioning child (Bricker and Bricker, 1969; Fulton, 1974; Lloyd et al., 1968), few reports on its use with infants and young children are available. Warren (1972) studied 25 high risk and 25 normal infants 12 to 24 months of age using VRA procedures, and found her procedure successful with 92% of the normals and 76% of the at risk infants. The two groups did not differ significantly in number of trials necessary to condition each.

Greenberg, Wilson, Moore, and Thompson (1977) studied 46 Down's Syndrome subjects between the ages of six months and six years. The diagnosis of Down's Syndrome was based on chromosomal tests, and all the infants and young children were reported on a questionnaire to be in good physical health. Twenty-five of the subjects were also administered the Bayley Scales of Infant Development (BSID).

VRA test procedures, as previously described, were used. Each subject was required to respond to two out of three presentations at either a 50 or 70 dB SPL conditioning level. If the subject failed to satisfy an initial conditioning criterion, an attempt was made to teach the turning response. If consistent responses occurred within a maximum of 10 teaching trials, the original test procedure was again attempted. For 25 subjects, the BSID was administered by a trained psychometrician during a separate session that fell within two weeks of the audiometric testing.

The results were: 1) many (68%) of the young Down's Syndrome subjects initially oriented toward a visual reinforcer in the presence of an auditory stimulus, 2) only a few (23%) of the subjects who did not initially orient could be taught to respond, 3) of the children who initially oriented or were taught to respond, thresholds were obtained on a large number (81%) in one visit, and 4) consistency of response could be systematically related to those infants and young children above ten months mental age equivalent as determined by the BSID. In addition, the results of the VRA procedure implied a higher incidence of hearing loss in the Down's Syndrome subjects than might be expected in the normal population. Finally, although not the primary purpose of the study, tentative norms may be considered for application of this specific VRA procedure to young Down's Syndrome clients. The data obtained revealed a threshold range of 30 to 60 dB SPL, a mean value of 40 dB SPL, and a mode of 30 dB SPL.

TEST BATTERY—INFANT AUDITORY ASSESSMENT

We have focused on recent developments in the area of behavioral assessment of auditory function in infants. Certainly, as noted, progress has been made; it is now possible to test reliably the auditory sensitivity of infants six months and older. Likewise, it is possible to measure one aspect of speech discrimination for the same population. Finally, the measurement of auditory preferences of neonates and infants is possible, at least to a limited extent. Further methodological developments, coupled with better "human engineering," should provide for even more exciting advances in these areas in the near future.

However, behavioral assessment of auditory function cannot be considered to comprise the complete test battery. The information available to the assessor from the group of tests known as impedance audiometry is essential in a complete test battery. Because the focus of this conference has been on behavioral procedures, we have not developed the topic of impedance audiometry with neonates and infants; suffice it to say, however, that an extensive literature does exist and these procedures are fully applicable to neonates and infants (see Jerger, 1975; Keith, 1973, 1975; Margolis and Popelka, 1975).[3] Likewise, recent developments in the area of auditory evoked response (AER) audiometry, and particularly in the brainstem evoked response (BER) audiometry promise greater potential for this procedure (see Davis, 1976; Hecox and Galambos, 1974) in defining specifically the state of the peripheral auditory system.

However, in terms of cost and efficiency factors, behavioral procedures coupled with impedance procedures are preferred. A preliminary test battery consisting of

---

[3] Between the time this chapter was written (1976) and publication (1978) several reports have challenged the validity of *normal* findings on impedance audiometry— specifically tympanometry—in infants under six months of age (e.g., Balkany and Zarnoch, 1978; Paradise, Smith, and Bluestone, 1976). *Abnormal* results were shown to be diagnostically significant.

VRA and impedance measurement can easily be accomplished on infants six months of age and older in less than one hour and on a single visit. The impedance testing can predict the status of the middle ear and predict threshold; the VRA procedure, if satisfactorily completed by the infant, determines threshold and denotes development of auditory function by the presence of a learned response.

TOWARD THE FUTURE

In spite of these recent advances, we must remain awed by our collective ignorance concerning auditory function in infants. Perhaps the brightest comment on the developments of the past few years is that we have started to break down the inertia of the past as many more persons are attempting to understand auditory function in a dynamic sense as it relates to speech perception. Perhaps some of this work has moved out of the research laboratory and into the clinical laboratory for more detailed study. If so, the field of clinical assessment of auditory function of infants may truly be advancing.

ACKNOWLEDGMENTS

Major contributions to much of the work reported on in this paper have been provided by Marie Thompson, Gary Thompson, Bruce Weber, Rebecca Eilers, Newell Decker, and particularly John Mick Moore, colleagues at the Child Development and Mental Retardation Center, University of Washington.

REFERENCES

Balkany, T. J., and Zarnoch, J. M. 1978. Impedance tympanometry in infants. Audiol. Hear. Ed. 4: 17.

Bench, J. 1970. Some methodological problems and techniques in infant audiometry. Biomed. Eng. 5: 12–14.

Bench, R. J., and Vass, A. 1970. Fetal audiometry. Lancet 1: 91–92.

Bricker, D. D., and Bricker, W. A. 1969. A programmed approach to operant audiometry for low-functioning children. J. Speech Hear. Disord. 34: 312–320.

Cairns, G. F., and Butterfield, E. C. 1975. Assessing infants' auditory functioning. In B. Z. Friedlander, G. M. Sterritt, and G. E., Kirk (eds.), Exceptional Infant. Vol. III. Brunner/Mazel, Inc, New York.

Conference on Newborn Hearing Screening, Proceedings Summary and Recommendations. 1971. U.S. Public Health Service and California State Department of Public Health, San Francisco.

Conway, S., and Shallop, J. K. 1975. Sound localization abilities of infants using the Murphy chair. Paper presented at Asha Convention, November, Washington, D.C.

Davis, H. 1976. Principles of electric response audiometry. Ann. Otol. Rhinol. Laryngol. 85(suppl. 28): 1–96.

Downs, M. P., and Sterritt, G. M. 1964. Identification audiometry for neonates: A preliminary report. J. Aud. Res. 4: 69–80.

Downs, M. P., and Sterritt, G. M. 1967. A guide to newborn and infant hearing screening programs. Arch. Otolaryngol. 85: 15–22.

Dwornicka, B., Jasienska, A., Smolarz, W., and Wawryk, R. 1964. Attempt of determining the fetal reaction to acoustic stimulation. Acta Otolaryngol. 57: 571–574.

Ehrlich, C. H., Shapiro, E., Kimball, B. D., and Huttner, M. 1973. Communication skills in five-year-old children with high-risk neonatal histories. J. Speech Hear. Res. 16: 522–529.

Eilers, R. E., Wilson, W. R., and Moore, J. M. 1977. Developmental changes in speech discrimination in infants. J. Speech Hear. Res. 20: 766–780.

Eisele, W. A., Berry, R. C., and Shriner, T. H. 1975. Infant sucking response patterns as a conjugate function of changes in the sound pressure level of auditory stimuli. J. Speech Hear. Res. 18: 296–307.

Eisenberg, R. B. 1976. Auditory Competence in Early Life: The Roots of Communicative Behavior. University Park Press, Baltimore.

Eisenberg, R. B., Griffin, E. J., Coursin, D. B., and Hunter, M. A. 1964. Auditory behavior in the human neonate: A preliminary report. J. Speech Hear. Res. 7: 245–269.

Elliott, G. B., and Elliott, K. A. 1964. Some pathological, radiological and clinical implications of the precocious development of the human ear. Laryngoscope 74: 1160–1171.

Falkner, F. (ed.). 1966. Human Development. W. B. Saunders Co., Philadelphia.

Feinmesser, M., and Bauberger-Tell, L. 1971. Evaluation of methods for detecting hearing impairment in infancy and early childhood. In Conference on Newborn Hearing Screening, Proceedings Summary and Recommendations, pp. 119–125. U.S. Public Health Service and California State Department of Public Health, San Francisco.

Friedlander, B. Z. 1969. Automated Playtest systems for evaluating infant's and young children's selective listening to natural sounds and language. Scientific exhibit, Asha Convention, November, Chicago.

Fulton, R. T. (ed.). 1974. Auditory Stimulus-Response Control. University Park Press, Baltimore.

Fulton, R. T., Gorzycki, P. A., and Hull, W. L. 1975. Hearing assessment with young children. J. Speech Hear. Dis. 40: 397–404.

Fulton, R. T., and Lloyd, L. L. (eds.). 1975. Auditory Assessment of the Difficult-to-Test. Williams and Wilkins, Baltimore.

Greenberg, D. B., Wilson, W. R., Moore, J. M., and Thompson, G. 1977. Visual reinforcement audiometry (VRA) with young Down's syndrome children. Submitted for publication.

Griffiths, C. 1964. The reliability of screening neo-nates with the hearometer. Paper presented at the 7th International Congress of Audiology, Copenhagen, Denmark.

Haug, O., Baccaro, P., and Guilford, F. R. 1967. A pure-tone audiogram on the infant: The PIWI technique. Arch. Otolaryngol. 86: 435–440.

Hecox, K. 1975. Electrophysiological correlates of human auditory development. In L. B. Cohen and P. Salapatek (eds.), Infant Perception: From Sensation to Cognition. Vol. II. Academic Press, New York.

Hecox, K., and Galambos, R. 1974. Brain stem auditory evoked responses in human infants and adults. Arch. Otolaryngol. 99: 30–33.

Jerger, J. (ed.). 1975. Handbook of Clinical Impedance Audiometry. Morgan Press, New York.

Johansson, B., Wedenberg, E., and Westin, B. 1964. Measurement of tone response by the human foetus. Acta Otolaryngol. 57: 188–192.

Joint Committee on Infant Hearing Screening. 1972. Supplementary Statement on Infant Hearing Screening, July 1. Also appears in Asha 16: 160 (1974).

Keith, R. W. 1973. Impedance audiometry with neonates. Arch Otolaryngol. 97: 465–467.

Keith, R. W. 1975. Middle ear function in neonates. Arch. Otolaryngol. 101: 376–379.

Liden, G., and Kankkunen, A. 1969. Visual reinforcement audiometry. Acta Otolaryngol. 67: 281–292.

Ling, D., Ling, A. H., and Doehring, D. G. 1970. Stimulus, response, and observer variables in the auditory screening of newborn infants. J. Speech Hear. Res. 13: 9–18.

Lloyd, L. L. 1966. Behavioral audiometry viewed as an operant procedure. J. Speech Hear. Dis. 31: 128–136.

Lloyd, L. L., Spradlin, J. E., and Reid, M. J. 1968. An operant audiometric procedure for difficult-to-test patients. J. Speech Hear. Disord. 33: 236–245.

Margolis, R. H., and Popelka, G. R. 1975. Static and dynamic acoustic impedance measurements in infant ears. J. Speech Hear. Res. 18: 435–443.

Mencher, G. T. 1974. A program for neonatal hearing screening. Audiology 13: 495–500.

Moore, J. M., Thompson, G., and Thompson, M. 1975. Auditory localization of infants as a function of reinforcement conditions. J. Speech Hear. Dis. 40: 29–34.

Moore, J. M., Wilson, W. R., Lillis, K. E., and Talbott, S. A. 1976. Earphone auditory thresholds of infants utilizing visual reinforcement audiometry (VRA). Exhibit presented at Asha Convention, November, Houston.

Moore, J. M., Wilson, W. R., and Thompson, G. 1977. Visual reinforcement of head-turn responses in infants under 12 months of age. J. Speech Hear. Dis. 42: 328–334.

Moore, K. L. 1973. The Developing Human: Clinically Oriented Embryology. W. B. Saunders Co., Philadelphia.

Motta, G., Facchini, G. M., and D'Auria, E. 1970. Objective conditioned-reflex audiometry in children. Acta Otolaryngol. Suppl. 273: 1–49.

Murphy, K. P. 1961. Development of hearing in babies. Hearing News November: 9–11.

Murphy, K. P., and Smyth, C. N. 1962. Response of foetus to auditory stimulation. Lancet 1: 972–973.

Nakai, Y. 1970. An electron microscopic study of the human fetus cochlea. Pract. Oto-rhinolaryngol. 32: 257–267.

Northern, J. L., and Downs, M. P. 1974. Hearing in Children. The Williams and Wilkins Co., Baltimore.

Paradise, J. L., Smith, C. G., and Bluestone, C. D. 1976. Tympanometric detection of middle ear effusion in infants and young children. Pediatrics 58: 198–210.

Redell, R. C., and Calvert, D. R. 1969. Factors in screening hearing of the newborn. J. Aud. Res. 3: 278–289.

Shallop, J. K. 1974. The assessment of hearing in young children with the Murphy chair. Paper presented at Asha Convention, November, Las Vegas.

Simmons, F. B., and Russ, F. N. 1974. Automated newborn hearing screening, the crib-o-gram. Arch. Otolaryngol. 100: 1–7.

Suzuki, T., and Ogiba, Y. 1960. A technique of pure tone audiometry for children under three years of age: Conditioned orientation reflex (C.O.R.) audiometry. Rev. Laryngol. 81: 33–45.

Suzuki, T., and Ogiba, Y. 1961. Conditioned orientation reflex audiometry. Arch. Otolaryngol. 74: 192–198.

Suzuki, T., Ogiba, Y., and Takei, T. 1972. Basic properties of conditioned orientation reflex audiometry. Minerva Otorinolaringol. 22: 181–186.

Thompson, M., and Thompson, G. 1972. Response of infants and young children as a function of auditory stimuli and test methods. J. Speech Hear. Res. 15: 699–707.

Thompson, G., and Weber, B. A. 1974. Responses of infants and young children to behavior observation audiometry (BOA). J. Speech Hear. Disord. 39: 140–147.

Timiras, P. S. 1972. Developmental Physiology and Aging. The Macmillan Co., New York.

Tyberghein, J., and Forrez, G. 1971. Objective (E.R.A.) and subjective (C.O.R.) audiometry in the infant. Acta Otolaryngol. 71: 249–252.

Warren, V. G. 1972. A comparative study of the auditory responses of normal and "at-risk" infants from twelve to twenty-four months of age using COR audiometry. Unpublished doctoral dissertation, University of Southern California, Los Angeles.

Weber, B. A. 1969. Validation of observer judgments in behavioral observation audiometry. J. Speech Hear. Disord. 34: 350–355.

Wilson, W. R., and Decker, N. T. 1977. Auditory thresholds of infants using operant audiometry with tangible and/or visual reinforcement. Submitted for publication.

Wilson, W. R., Moore, J. M., and Thompson, G. 1976. Sound-field auditory thresholds of infants utilizing visual reinforcement audiometry (VRA). Paper presented at Asha Convention, November, Houston.

Infant Sensory Assessment: Vision

Philip Salapatek, Martin S. Banks

The vision of human adults significantly depends on the visual input received early in life. Several ocular abnormalities that alter visual input have now been studied: strabismus (Banks, Aslin, and Letson, 1975; Hohmann and Creutzfeldt, 1975), cataracts (Gstalder and Green, 1971), astigmatism (Mitchell, Freeman, Millodot, and Haegerstrom, 1973), myopia (Fiorentini and Maffei, 1976), and eye-patching (Awaya, Miyake, Amaizumi, Shiose, Kanda, and Komuro, 1973). It has been found that the presence of these abnormalities during infancy and early childhood is correlated with deficits in subsequent adult vision even if the ocular abnormality is eventually corrected. The clinical implications of these findings are profound. Given the early susceptibility of the developing visual system, the diagnosis and treatment of visual dysfunction in infancy is now considered imperative. The recent experimental push to determine the visual capabilites of the normal human infant reflects this.

This chapter describes the visual and oculomotor capabilities characteristic of normal human infants. Included in the discussion are: 1) sensorimotor mechanisms such as accommodation of the lens, pupillary response, and eye and head movements, and 2) processing of basic stimulus attributes such as intensity, wavelength pattern, and depth. Clinical implications of research concerning these capabilities is suggested where reasonable. Many exciting topics concerning infant visual development, such as the perception of faces, object and event perception, and visual memory, are not discussed here because these topics are treated elsewhere in this volume (see chapters by Fagan, Horowitz and Dunn, Moore and Meltzoff, Wilson). The ambitious reader who wishes to further pursue the material that is presented in this chapter may consult a number of valuable sources (Bond, 1972; Bornstein, in press; Dobson and Teller, in press; Fantz, Fagan, and Miranda, 1975; Gibson, 1969; Haith, in press; Haith and Campos, 1977; Harter, Deaton, and Odom, 1976;

Funds allowing the completion of this chapter were provided by the following grants: HD-07317 to the first author; HD-01136 to the Institute of Child Development, University of Minnesota; and NSF-P2BI389 to The Center for Research in Human Learning, University of Minnesota.

Hershenson, 1967, 1970; Karmel and Maisel, 1975; Kessen, Haith, and Salapatek, 1970; Maurer, 1975; Peiper, 1963; Salapatek, 1975; Sokol, 1976; Spears and Hohle, 1967; Thomas, 1973).

TECHNIQUES OF MEASUREMENT

One of the most notable features of infant research during the past 15 years has been the application of increasingly sophisticated techniques to investigate early visual capabilities. Several psychophysiological techniques, including the electroretinogram (ERG), the visually-evoked cortical potential (VEP), electrooculography (EOG), optokinetic nystagmus (OKN) and corneal photography have been successfully applied to the study of visual development (Maurer, 1975). In addition to these sophisticated response measures, the psychophysical procedures applied to infant visual preference have correspondingly increased in rigor (Atkinson, Braddick, and Moar, 1977b; Banks and Salapatek, 1976; Teller, Morse, Borton, and Regal, 1974; Thomas, 1973). A variety of applications of these various techniques are presented in different sections of this chapter. Clearly, infant visual assessment in the future will rely heavily on a number of these psychophysiological and psychophysical techniques.

ANATOMICAL FACTORS

There is a wealth of information on the developmental visual anatomy of nonhuman mammals. However, ethical considerations have severely limited the acquisition of detailed, normative information in humans. Barber (1955), Haith (in press), Mann (1964), Maurer (1975), Salapatek (1975), and Scammon and Wilmer (1950) provide summaries of the existing human data. In general, there is at least quantitative development in most structures of the visual system during the first few months after birth. The bulbus (eyeball) grows considerably (Scammon and Wilmer, 1950). Changes in size, curvature, and relative positions of the cornea, lens, and retina occur. The retina itself undergoes considerable change postnatally. Rods and cones are distinguishable 15 weeks before birth, but cones within the central retina (the predecessor of the fovea) do not attain adult-like dimensions until at least four months after birth (Barber, 1955; Hollenberg and Spira, 1973; Mann, 1964). The macula is distinguishable at birth, but is quite immature in comparison to the adult macula. Cones within this retinal region are less densely packed than in the adult. The nuclei of retinal ganglion, amacrine, and bipolar cells, which have begun to migrate toward their adult positions in the parafovea or periphery, still overlay the eventual fovea. By four months, the packing density of central retinal cones is nearly adult-like and the ganglion, amacrine, and bipolar cells have migrated from the central macula, creating the so-called "foveal pit."

Considerable postnatal anatomical development occurs in the ascending visual pathways as well. The neonatal optic nerve is thinner than the adult. Myelinization of the nerve is not complete until at least one month of age (Maurer, 1975). The lateral geniculate nucleus (LGN) differentiates well before birth, but cell size within it changes significantly postnatally (Hickey, 1977). Cell size and arborization (among other factors) increase dramatically in the visual cortex (Conel, 1939, 1941, 1947, 1951, 1955, 1959, 1963; Larroche, 1966; Rabinowicz, 1964; Schade, Meeter and van Groeningen, 1962; Yakovlev and LeCours, 1967). Figure 1 illustrates this change in area 17 of the cortex. Presumably, postnatal growth of the visual cortex is manifest in visual behavior and, thus, may in part underlie some of the behavioral transitions observed in the first months of life.

Anatomical studies with kittens and monkeys indicate that visual deprivation significantly influences the growth of the eyeball (Wiesel and Raviola, 1977; Wilson and Sherman, 1977), cell size in the adult LGN (Wiesel and Hubel, 1963a), and connectivity in the visual cortex (Hubel, Wiesel, and LeVay, 1976). There is no evidence thus far that deprivation disturbs retinal development in any way, however (von Noorden, 1973). There are no existing data demonstrating similar anatomical effects in humans with histories of abnormal visual experience.

OCULOMOTOR COMPONENTS

Many components of the visual system must be coordinated to allow the mature human to direct and maintain visual fixation on particular parts of the environment. Localization of targets onto the most sensitive part of the retina—the fovea—is accomplished by the saccadic and vergence eye movement systems and the head movement system. Maintaining a stationary stimulus on the fovea while the head is moving is accomplished in part by the primitive vestibular eye movement system. Maintenance of a moving target in central vision while the head is stationary involves the smooth pursuit system. The state of each of these eye movement systems in the infant is herein described, as well as the state of the pupillary system, which is primarily involved in regulating the amount of light entering the eye, and the accommodative system, which is responsible for ocular adjustments to maintain sharpness of the retinal image.

Eye Movements

Saccadic Eye Movements A saccadic eye movement is a sudden change in fixation from one visual object to another. The saccadic system is thus used to relocate targets in the peripheral visual field onto the fovea for fine pattern analysis. In the adult, saccadic eye movements are very rapid (up to 800°/sec), and accurate (only a 10% error in the first saccade to a target) (Alpern, 1969b, 1971). Saccades are also ballistic; that is, once a saccadic eye movement has been initiated, it continues to its computed endpoint without significant further correction.

Saccadic-like eye movements are observed in both sleeping and awake newborns and even blind infants. They have been observed both as part of vestibular and optokinetic nystagmus (cf. Peiper, 1963; Schulman, 1973), and as part of the localization of peripheral targets (Aslin and Salapatek, 1975; Harris and Macfarlane, 1974; Macfarlane, Harris, and Barnes, 1976; Salapatek, 1975; Tronick, 1972; Tronick and Clanton, 1971). The likelihood of an infant executing a saccade to a peripheral target is: 1) greatest if the target is the only stimulus in the field,

Newborn   Three-month-old

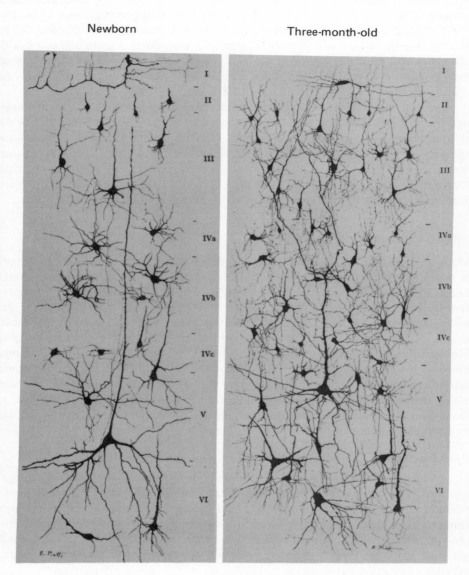

Figure 1.   Neuronal structure of the visual cortex of newborn and three-month-old humans. Drawings from Golgi-Cox preparations of the striate cortex. Left: Section from a human newborn. Right: Section from a three-month-old human infant. Cell size, length of axons, and arborization (among other parameters) seem to increase markedly from birth to three months. Roman numerals refer to cortical layers that also become more distinctive during this period. [Adapted from J. L. Conel, *The postnatal development of the cerebral cortex Vol. 1, Vol. 3.* Cambridge, Massachusetts: Harvard University Press. © 1939, 1947 by Harvard University Press.

2) greatest if the target is presented along the horizontal axis of the visual field, and 3) greater to more distant targets for two-month-olds than for neonates.

Of particular interest is the finding that the form of saccades is distinctive in young infants. The first saccade to a peripheral target does not necessarily move the line of sight 90% of the distance to the target, as it would in an adult (Aslin and Salapatek, 1975). Often a series of saccades, roughly equal in amplitude, are executed until the target is reached (Figure 2). Thus, the infant's line of sight "skips" toward the target. The number and magnitude of skips seems to increase with target distance. This unusual state of affairs persists until at least two months of age. Beyond that age there is no exact description of saccadic localization. Aslin and Salapatek (1975) have speculated that the dramatic undershooting of the infant saccadic system might in part be the result of the programming of, but failure to execute, directionally-appropriate head movements in conjunction with programmed and executed saccades.

The saccadic eye movement system, therefore, is sufficiently developed at birth to allow the neonate to localize stimuli of interest onto the central retina. The system, nonetheless, is somewhat immature. The effective visual field for the elicita-

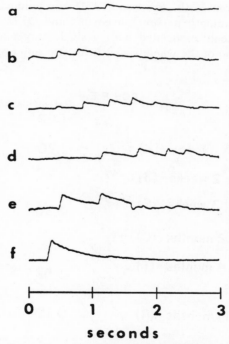

Figure 2.   Examples of typical infant and adult electrooculographic (EOG) recordings of saccades during localization of a peripheral target: (a) a single saccade to a target 10° in the periphery, (b) a double saccade to a target at 20°, (c) a triple saccade to a target at 30°, (d) a quadruple saccade to a target at 40°, (e) a double saccade to a target at 30° followed by a return movement, (f) example of an adult saccade to a target at 30°. Time marks represent seconds after target onset. From Aslin and Salapatek, 1975.

tion of saccades, and the form of the movement once elicited, are not adult-like. Observations of saccades in older infants are needed to describe the transition from infantile to adult-like movements.

Visual Pursuit Eye Movements   Smooth pursuit eye movements are those in which the velocity and direction of eye movements match the velocity and direction of a moving stimulus. In contrast to saccadic movements, pursuit movements are smoothly executed and slow (Alpern, 1969b; Robinson, 1968).

Newborns do not execute smooth pursuit movements to a moving target. In general, it seems that horizontal pursuit movements are observed at earlier ages than are vertical, but there is disagreement on the age at which pursuit movements, horizontal or vertical, first appear (Beasley, 1933a,b; Guernsey, 1929; Jones, 1926; Morgan and Morgan, 1944; Wolff, 1959). One study by Dayton and Jones (1964) used EOG to record eye movements in young infants. They report that smooth horizontal pursuit is generally not present before two months of age. Between birth and two months, "pursuit" movements consist of a jerky series of saccadic refixations of the moving target. The jerkiness of these movements decreases across at least the first year, as illustrated in Figure 3.

It is interesting to note, on the other hand, that smooth pursuit components of OKN are present from birth. Bronson (1974) has pointed out that the eliciting stimulus for typical smooth pursuit movements and OKN differ. Smooth pursuit concerns eye movements associated with a single target and OKN—movements associated with motion of the whole visual field. Bronson argues that the newborn's

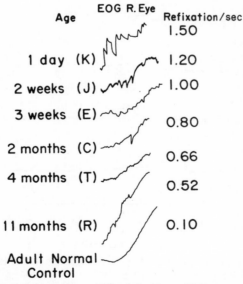

Figure 3.   Typical EOG records of pursuit eye movements at different ages. Pursuit movements were elicited by a small target moving horizontally from left to right. Average numbers of refixations per second, provided by figures on the right, decreased with age, indicating smoother pursuit. From Dayton and Jones, 1964. *Neurology 14*: 1152–1156.

ability to perform pursuit movements in OKN implies that neural centers involved in processing whole-field motion develop earlier than centers that process the movement of discrete targets on a stationary background.

Vergence Eye Movements   Vergence eye movements are those in which the eyes move in opposite directions (convergence or divergence) such that the lines of sight of both eyes are directed toward the same point in space (Alpern, 1969b; Robinson, 1968). They are important for binocular fusion and stereopsis. Vergence movements typically occur in conjunction with pursuit and saccadic movements, but different neurological centers control the three types of movements.

Until recently, studies of infant vergence concluded that the vergence system is not functional before 8 to 12 weeks of age (Ling, 1942; Maurer, 1974; McGinnis, 1930; Wickelgren, 1967). These studies, which used corneal photography to record eye position, reported that young infants generally do not exhibit sufficient convergence to targets at different distances. In other words, errors of divergence were observed, implying that young infants could not perform appropriate vergence movements. This error of divergence may be more apparent than real, however. Slater and Findlay (1972a,b) have argued that the error is an experimental artifact resulting from difficulty in estimating the line of sight (visual axis) from photographs of the pupil and corneal reflections of the reference lights that are used in corneal photography (see also Maurer, 1975; Salapatek, Haith, Maurer, and Kessen, 1972). This difficulty results from the fact that an eye's visual axis and optic axis (the line that bisects the center of the cornea, pupil, and lens) are not generally coincident. In fact, the angle between these two axes is approximately 8.5° in the neonate, which results in an apparent divergent strabismus.

Slater and Findlay (1975) used corneal photography to measure changes in newborn's vergence for targets at three distances. Because the 8.5° error remains constant for all vergence angles, the use of change scores allowed them to adequately assess vergence capabilities. They observed appropriate adjustments in vergence for stationary targets presented at two of the three distances. Aslin (1977) also used corneal photography and observed at least some convergence and divergence in one-month-olds to nonstationary, approaching, and receding targets. Aslin observed reasonably accurate vergence movements to such targets in three-month-olds. Figure 4 illustrates the major findings of this study.

Infants do not seem to perform appropriate saccadic refixation and vergence movements when a wedge prism is placed in front of one eye until about six months of age (Aslin, 1977; Parks, 1966).

In summary, more recent experiments indicate that neonates are able to perform vergence eye movements in correspondence with changes in target distance. It does not seem, however, that the infant vergence system is comparable to the adult until at least three to six months of age. The vergence system before this age is slower, less consistent, and less accurate than the adult system. Furthermore, the adequate stimulus for vergence may differ before six months. The implications of these findings for fusion and stereopsis are discussed later.

Vestibular Control of Eye Movements   The line of sight of the eye tends to be maintained on particular points in the environment despite changes in head position.

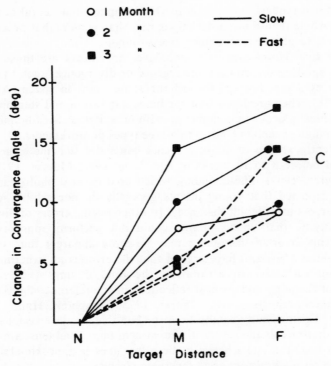

Figure 4.   Mean changes in convergence angle to a target moving in depth, in one-, two-, and three-month-old infants. Each point (at *M* and *F*) represents the change in convergence angle relative to convergence at the near target distance, *N*. *M* and *F* represent the mid and far target distances, respectively. *C* represents the change in convergence angle needed to maintain binocular fixation as the target moves from nearpoint, *N*, to farpoint, *F*. Change needed to maintain fixation from nearpoint to midpoint, *M*, was 11°, but is not indicated in the figure. From Aslin, 1977. *Journal of Experimental Child Psychology* 23: 141.

Reflex eye movements in response to changes in head position are termed static or stato-kinetic reflexes (Alpern, 1969b). These reflexes depend on vestibular function.

There are several different forms of these reflexes in adults. The static reflex of counterrolling of the eyes occurs if the head is tilted to the side. Stato-kinetic reflexes are typically elicited by angular rotation of the head and/or body. For example, nystagmus (smooth movements followed by saccadic refixations) occurs when the body is rotated around the vertical or horizontal axes whether the eyes are open or not. Compensatory eye movements that maintain the line of sight on particular points in space occur when the head (or head and body) is slowly moved. That these movements are qualitatively different from pursuit movements to moving targets was demonstrated by Robinson (1968).

Static and stato-kinetic reflex eye movements are generally present at birth (Peiper, 1963). The prewired nature of these movements is exemplified by Peiper's observation of them in blind infants. Compensatory eye movements are in fact reliable enough in normal young infants that they have been used to calibrate eye movement recording systems (Tronick and Clanton, 1971).

Eye-Head Coordination   Adults execute saccades to peripheral targets or pursuit movements to moving targets whether the head is restrained or not (Alpern, 1969b). Under normal conditions, in which both the eyes and head are free to move, most saccadic localizations of targets 10° or more from the line of sight involve the integrated programming of eye and head movements (Gresty, 1974). Thus, to localize a target at 30°, for example, eye and head movements are jointly programmed. A number of factors may affect the latency and duration of eye and head movements, but generally there is significant overlap of movement. In other words, head movements are initiated before the termination of the corresponding eye movements.

Several investigators have reported some conjunction of eye and head movements during the first months of life (e.g., Brazelton, Scholl, and Robey, 1966; Tronick and Clanton, 1971). However, from birth to two months of age there seems to be considerable variability within and between infants in the actual execution of appropriate head movements in conjunction with saccadic eye movements. Indeed, Aslin and Salapatek (1975) have suggested that young infants' saccades generally cover a small percentage of the distance to peripheral targets because appropriate eye and head movements are programmed, but only the eye movement component is actually executed. Parallel data regarding the conjuction of head movements with the smooth pursuit system are unavailable at this time. However, the smooth pursuit system itself is generally immature at this early age.

One might suspect that variable eye-head coordination during active looking is attributable to a lack of neuromuscular control of head movement. However, even newborns exhibit a good deal of head movement as part of the response pattern in a wide variety of reflexes, such as rooting, crying, suffocating, and the avoidance of intense odors (Peiper, 1963; Rieser, Yonas, and Wikner, 1976). What seems to be lacking is precise, voluntary coordination of head movements with eye movements in a variety of bodily postures. In this sense, the development of eye-head coordination is similar to the development of voluntary reaching. However, unlike voluntary reaching, there are no detailed published descriptions of its full development.

Optokinetic Nystagmus (OKN)   The rhythmic eye movements elicited by a continuously moving visual field constitute optokinetic nystagmus (OKN). OKN can be elicited either by moving the visual field before a stationary observer or by moving the observer before a stationary field (Alpern, 1969b). OKN to a moving field of vertical stripes has been observed in premature, term, and older infants (Dayton, Jones, Aiu, Rawson, Steele, and Rose, 1964b; Enoch and Rabinowicz, 1976; Fantz, Ordy, and Udelf, 1962; Gorman, Cogan, and Gellis, 1957, 1959). The Dayton et al. OKN apparatus is shown in Figure 5, and their records of typical newborn OKN response in Figure 6. By varying the width of the stripes, one can use OKN to estimate visual acuity in newborns and young infants.

Pupillary Response

The pupil is the variable aperture of the eye. It serves three primary functions: 1) partial regulation of the amount of light entering the eye, 2) increasing the depth of focus of the eye by decreasing the aperture of the optical system, and 3) reducing chromatic and spherical aberration of the optics of the eye (particularly in bright

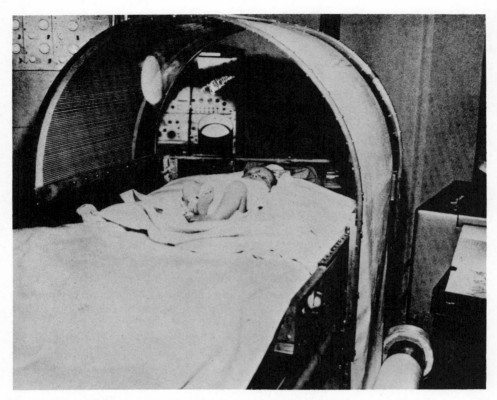

Figure 5.   Apparatus used by Dayton et al. (1964b) to elicit OKN in infants. To elicit OKN the vertical stripes shown are moved horizontally past the subject's eyes. EOG electrodes are placed on the sides of the infant's eyes to record OKN. From Dayton, Jones, Aiu, Rawson, Steele, and Rose. *Archives of Ophthalmology* © 1964, *71*: 867.

light for which pupil diameter is minimal) (Lowenstein and Loewenfeld, 1969). Changes in emotional state (autonomic activity) and in thought processes can also affect pupil diameter (Fitzgerald, 1968; Lowenstein and Loewenfeld, 1969).

Pupillary reaction to light is present in premature as well as in term infants, but it is more sluggish in younger infants (see Kessen et al., 1970, p. 348; Peiper, 1963, pp. 55–57 for summaries of published infant studies). The pupillary reaction is consensual from birth. There has been little investigation of the actual relationship between pupil size and light intensity in infants (Munsinger and Banks, 1974). Salapatek, Bechtold, and Bergman (1977) have recently examined this relationship, however, in one- and two-month-old infants (Figure 7). They found that average pupil diameter decreased by nearly 2mm as luminance was increased from a very dim to a very bright value (a range of 3 log units). Although there is considerable sluggishness and variability in the pupillary response, especially in one-month-olds, absolute pupil diameter by two months is not very different than adult diameters at any given luminance.

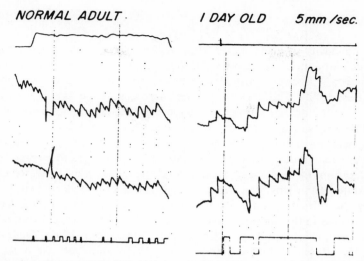

Figure 6.   Typical EOG records of newborn and adult OKN. The record on the left shows the EOG for each eye of an adult in the apparatus. The record on the right is from a one-day-old infant under the same conditions. Adapted from Dayton et al. 1964b. *Archives of Ophthalmology* © 1964, *71*: 868.

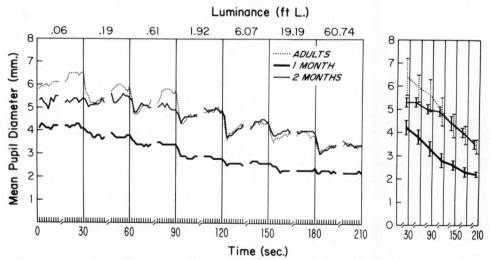

Figure 7.   Mean pupil diameter as a function of luminance in one-month-olds, two-month-olds, and adults. Each subject was presented with the same series of seven luminance levels (0.06 to 60.74 ftL in 0.5 log unit steps). Each luminance level was presented for 30 sec, following 10 min of dark adaptation. Left: Mean pupil diameter averaged sec by sec. Right: Mean pupil diameter averaged across the final 10 sec of each luminance level. From Salapatek, Bechtold, and Bergman, 1977.

Visual Accommodation

In adults, the clarity of visual input from objects at various distances is ensured by continual adjustment of the optics of the eye. This adjustment, termed "visual accommodation," is accomplished by changes in the shape of the lens (Alpern, 1969a; Toates, 1972). The curvature of the surfaces of the lens is greater for near vision than it is for distant vision; in other words, the refractive power of the lens is greatest while the eye is accommodated for viewing near objects.

Two aspects of infant accommodation are discussed: first, the refractive state of the eye when accommodation is relaxed; and second, changes in refractive state during active fixation. By use of certain solutions, the ciliary muscle, which controls the refractive state of the lens, can be weakened, and accommodation thereby relaxed. In this way the refractive state of the lens at rest can be determined. Retinoscopic studies performed in this manner have suggested that the average newborn is about 2 diopters hyperopic (far-sighted) (Cook and Glasscock, 1951; Duke-Elder and Abrams, 1970; Patel, Natarajan, and Abreu, 1970) and that this hyperopic error decreases during infancy and early childhood (Millodot, 1972). The hyperopic error may be more apparent than real, however. Glickstein and Millodot (1970) have described a measurement error in the direction of hyperopia inherent in retinoscopy. The magnitude of this measurement error is inversely proportional to the axial length of the eye. Because the axial length of the newborn eye is only about two-thirds the length of the adult eye, the measurement error should decrease with age.

Two experiments have assessed the infant's ability to accommodate during active fixation of targets at different distances (Haynes, White, and Held, 1965; White and Zolot, cited in White, 1971). Of course, these experiments were conducted without accommodation-relaxing solutions. It was found that infants two months of age and younger were unable to appropriately accommodate to various target distances. Figure 8 shows the average accommodative performance for the various age groups. Slopes of zero represent perfect accommodation, and slopes of one, no accommodative ability. Haynes et al. further report that in infants one month of age or less, the focal distance of the eye (distance to which the eye is accommodated) seems to be fixed at about 20 cm. Given this, one would expect one-month visual acuity to fall dramatically for distant targets. The acuity of one-month-olds, however, does not seem to change with target distance (Fantz et al., 1962; Salapatek, Bechtold, and Bushnell, 1976). This finding of no acuity differences as a function of distance implies that infants are in fact able to at least partially accommodate to distant objects and that earlier studies underestimate infant accommodation.

It is possible that the stimulus Haynes et al. (1965) and White and Zolot (cited in White, 1971) used was not an effective accommodative stimulus. A relatively small visual target, constant in physical size, was used for all stimulus distances. Therefore, the visual angle and intensity (total retinal flux) of the target decreased with increase in distance. Banks (1978) has repeated these studies using a stimulus whose visual angle (30° × 30°) and luminance were constant across stimulus dis-

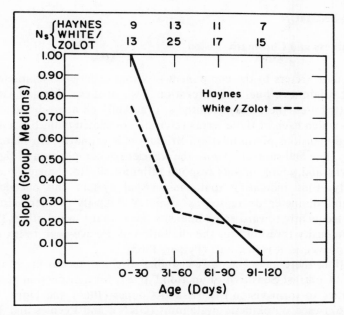

Figure 8.   Median slopes relating accommodation to target distance for infants of different ages in the Haynes et al. (1965) and White and Zolot (cited in White, 1971) studies. A slope of 1.00 indicates no change in accommodation when target distance is varied. A slope of 0 indicates that changes in accommodation correlate perfectly with changes in target distance. Intermediate values for slope indicate some, but not perfect, change in accommodation with change in target distance. From White, 1971.

tances. The target itself was a high-contrast, random checkerboard. Banks observed adult-like, appropriate accommodative changes in the large majority of the two- and three-month-olds, and many of the one-month-olds. His data, therefore, suggest that Haynes et al. and White and Zolot have underestimated the age at which infant accommodative flexibility approaches that of adults. Presumably, the small target, constant in physical size across distances, used by the other investigators was in fact not as effective an accommodative stimulus as the one Banks used. Stimulus parameters such as intensity, contrast, patterning, and overall size influence the accuracy and flexibility of accommodation in adults (Campbell, 1954; Charman and Tucker, 1977), so the same undoubtedly holds true for infants as well.

Another important consideration for the study of infant accommodation is visual acuity. There seems to be an intimate relationship between acuity and accommodative ability in adults. Persons with low acuity in one eye (unilateral amblyopia) do not accurately accommodate to stimuli presented to that eye alone (Wood and Tomlinson, 1975). Salapatek et al. (1976) and Banks (1978) have suggested that a similar relationship obtains in infancy: the development of accommodation during early infancy necessarily depends on the development of acute vision, which allows the detection of blur or focusing errors.

SENSORY FUNCTION

Color: Brightness and Chromatic Vision

The term "color" refers to the component of visual experience characterized by the attributes of brightness, hue, and saturation. Two of these, hue and saturation, are chromatic attributes; the other, brightness, is actually an achromatic attribute. The attributes to which each of these terms refer are correlated with, but not isomorphic to, physical dimensions of stimulation. Brightness is primarily correlated with stimulus intensity, hue and saturation with the wavelength composition of the stimulus.

Newborns and young infants respond differentially to changes in overall stimulus intensity, thus indicating that their visual system can encode brightness. Neonate pupil diameter decreases as stimulus intensity is increased. Newborns orient more frequently toward some intensity levels that toward others (Hershenson, 1964). The intensity threshold for the elicitation of the eye-neck reflex is a function of adaptation level, as it is in adults (Peiper, 1963).

In addition, there have been a few studies of simultaneous brightness discrimination. (See "Contrast Sensitivity Function," p. 87, for a discussion of the relevance of these studies to form vision.) Doris and Cooper (1966) and Doris, Casper, and Poresky (1967) used optokinetic nystagmus (OKN), and Peeples and Teller (1975) used preferential looking, to measure two-month-olds' ability to respond to an intensity increment upon a uniform background. All three experiments found reasonably high sensitivity to such increments. Peeples and Teller observed differential responding to stripes that differed from background intensity by only 0.04 log units, or about 10%. These data show that by two months, infants can discriminate small differences in intensity, but their capability is still far below that of adults who can discriminate intensity differences as small as one-third percent under similar conditions (Campbell and Robson, 1968).

Brightness in adults is not perfectly correlated with stimulus intensity. This is largely because the adult visual system is not equally sensitive to different wavelengths of light; in other words, equally intense lights of different wavelengths do not generally seem equally bright. Functions relating sensitivity to stimulus wavelength are called spectral-sensitivity functions. Two examples of such functions are shown in Figure 9. One, the photopic spectral-sensitivity function, depicts sensitivity for vision at daylight intensity levels, which is subserved by cones. The other, the scotopic spectral-sensitivity function, depicts sensitivity for vision at low intensity levels and reflects rod functioning. Although cones alone are responsible for chromatic vision, it may be seen from Figure 9 that both rods and cones are differentially sensitive to lights of different wavelengths.

Early attempts to determine spectral-sensitivity functions in neonates showed that the general form of each function is similar to that of the adult function (Peiper, 1927, 1963; Pratt, Nelson, and Sun, 1930; Smith, 1936; Trincker and Trincker, 1955). They provided some evidence for different functions under scotopic and photopic conditions, suggesting early functioning of both rods and cones. Unfortunately, each of these studies was flawed in one way or another. They have

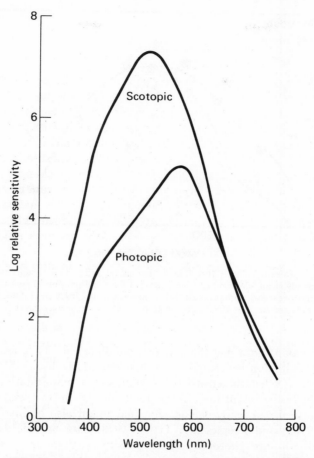

Figure 9.   Adult photopic and scotopic spectral-sensitivity functions. From Kaufman, 1974.

been summarized and criticized in a number of papers (Bornstein, in press; Dobson, 1976a; Peeples and Teller, 1975; Schaller, 1975).

Recently, two experiments have provided more rigorous estimates of infant photopic spectral sensitivity. Peeples and Teller (1978) used a preferential looking paradigm to measure spectral sensitivity in two-month-olds. They presented chromatic stripes on a white background, and varied the intensity of the stripes until threshold responding was obtained. Dobson (1976b) recorded the VEP to a variety of wavelengths in two-month-olds. She varied the light intensity at each wavelength to find the intensity necessary to elicit a criterion response. Figure 10 shows Dobson's averaged photopic spectral-sensitivity function for five two-month-olds. Teller and Peeples's two-month function is substantially in agreement with the one shown. Figure 10 also shows an adult spectral-sensitivity function determined using the VEP, and another function determined from psychophysical measurements. It seems that the two-month and the adult spectral-sensitivity functions are similar for wave-

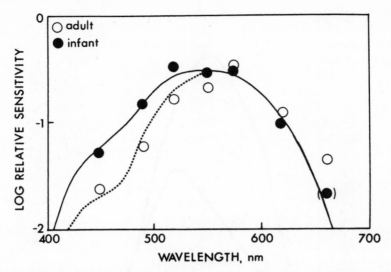

Figure 10.   Median spectral-sensitivity functions for five infant and two adult subjects. For comparison, Wald's (1945) psychophysically-determined foveal (dashed line) and parafoveal (solid line) functions are also plotted. The parafoveal function has been shifted upward by 0.4 log unit to coincide with the foveal function at wavelengths greater than 550 nm. From Dobson, 1976a. *Vision Research 16*: 372.

lengths greater than 550 nm, but that the two-month sensitivity function is relatively higher than the adults' for wavelengths less than 550 nm. Dobson (1976a) argues that the greater short-wavelength sensitivity of infants is a manifestation of less dense macular pigment in the infant than in the adult. Bornstein (in press) lists other factors, such as corneal and lenticular density, that might also be involved. Although the Dobson (1976a) and Peeples and Teller (1978) data provide dependable estimates of two-month-olds' photopic spectral sensitivity, there are to date no data of similar rigor on different infant age groups, infant scotopic spectral sensitivity, nor absolute thresholds for either photopic or scotopic vision.

The fact that the young infant's photopic sensitivity function is similar to the adult's suggests the possibility of the early appearance of adult-like chromatic vision. Of course, this finding alone is not sufficient evidence. To demonstrate the presence of early chromatic vision, one must demonstrate that infants can discriminate visual stimuli on the basis of hue alone. To do so, one must be able to equate the brightness of stimuli on the basis of spectral-sensitivity functions or, alternatively, randomly vary brightness during the experiment so that brightness is an irrelevant dimension on which to base discrimination.

A number of studies have attempted to demonstrate hue discrimination in infants (e.g., Chase, 1937; Fagan, 1975; Spears, 1964). Unfortunately, each of these studies failed to eliminate the possibility that infants were basing their discriminations on brightness cues. This is a serious problem because infants' sensitivity to small intensity differences is quite high (Peeples and Teller, 1975; Wooten, 1975).

Recently, however, demonstrations of hue discrimination not confounded by potential brightness cues have appeared (Bornstein, 1976; Oster, 1975; Peeples and Teller, 1975; Schaller, 1975). Peeples and Teller presented a large white field to two-month-olds; one or the other side of the field contained a single red bar of variable luminance. The infants preferentially fixated the side with the red bar for all luminance levels, presumably including the luminance level that matched the white background in brightness. Oster (1975) used a somewhat similar procedure. She adopted von Frisch's (1964) technique of presenting a chromatic stimulus along with a number of achromatic stimuli of various luminances. She found that two and one-half-month-olds reliably fixated the chromatic stimulus despite the fact that its brightness relative to the other stimuli varied from trial to trial. Schaller (1975) employed an operant conditioning paradigm to test hue discrimination in three-month-olds. Infants were able to successfully learn a discriminative response to either red or green patches of light, even though brightness was again varied from trial to trial. These three studies provided persuasive evidence that young infants can discriminate visual stimuli solely on the basis of differences in hue. This in turn implies that some form of chromatic vision is present at this early age.

Bornstein (1976) has noted that none of these studies provide information about the type of chromatic vision present in young infants. Adult dichromats (who are referred to as color-deficient) and normal adult trichromats (who are referred to as color-normal) would exhibit similar discrimination behavior if they served as subjects in the foregoing experiments. Only monochromats (who are totally color-deficient) would be unable to discriminate the stimuli used. One way by which dichromacy and trichromacy can be differentiated is by the neutral-point test. Color-normal trichromats (who possess all three types of cones) see each wavelength in the visual spectrum as possessing hue, and therefore as different from white. On the other hand, color-deficient dichromats (who possess only two cone types) do not see all wavelengths as hued; there is at least one point or zone in the spectrum that is seen as achromatic and indistinguishable from white (Hsia and Graham, 1965). Indeed, the various subclasses of dichromacy can be diagnosed by the point in the spectrum that is perceived as achromatic. This neutral point lies between 489 and 497 nm (protonopia) or 495 and 500 nm (deuteranopia) for the two most common forms of dichromacy.

Bornstein (1976) devised an experimental procedure based on the neutral-point test to investigate whether young infants possess trichromatic or dichromatic color vision. He familiarized three-month-old infants to varying stimulus wavelengths in the 490–500 nm range, the range in which adult dichromats are unable to discriminate chromatic from achromatic stimuli. During familiarization, the luminance of the light was also randomly varied over a fairly broad range. Following habituation, infants showed recovery of looking (dishabituation) to a white light whose luminance was equal to the mean luminance of the monochromatic familiarization stimuli. Bornstein concluded from this that three-month-olds probably possess trichromatic color vision, because no neutral point was observed in the most likely of spectral regions. Although the results of this study are compelling, there are two methodological considerations that make interpretation somewhat difficult. First, Bornstein did not include sufficient control groups to ensure that his infants' recovery of attention was based on a visual discrimination. A within-subject control was used to ensure that response recovery was contingent on stimulus change. Unfortunately, given the cyclic nature of infant attention in habituation experiments, this is not an entirely appropriate control. Specifically, infant habituation studies should in general include a control group that receives the same familiarization sequence as the experimental group, but unlike the experimental group, continues to receive the same stimulus during the test sequence as well. One then statistically compares this "no-shift" group to the "shift" group to ascertain whether recovery of attention is based on the change in stimulus (Cohen and Gelber, 1975). The second methodological problem concerns Bornstein's choice of wavelengths. His experiment was designed to test for neutral points in the spectral range that encompass the neutral points of most adult dichromats. However, one cannot assume trichromacy in infants upon failing to find neutral points in that particular range. It may be that infants are in fact dichromats with neutral points in different spectral regions.

Peeples and Teller (Peeples, 1976; Teller, Peeples, and Sekel, 1978) have also used an adaptation of the neutral-point test to ascertain whether infants are dichromats or trichromats. Their methodology is different from Bornstein's in that a number of spectral regions were sampled. They showed that two-month-olds choose to look at blue, blue-green, yellow, orange, or red bars (generated using wideband filters) on a white background in preference to a uniform white field matched in luminance. The luminance of the chromatic bars was varied, in relatively small steps, over a broad range of luminances, so that presumably the bars and background were also matched in luminance at some point in the experiment. Figure 11 illustrates these results. Interestingly, some infants did not preferentially fixate green, yellow-green, or purple bars for all luminance values. This particular finding led Peeples and Teller to suggest two alternatives. First, two-month-olds may be dichromats with a neutral zone in the green or yellow-green region of the spectrum. None of the classical dichromatic types are characterized by neutral points in this spectral region (Hsia and Graham, 1965), but irregular neutral points have been observed in other sorts of adult color deficiencies. Second, two-month-olds may be trichromats and the neutral zones they exhibit caused by insensitivity to differences in saturation. Bornstein (in press) argues that their data might imply that two-month-olds are "color-weak," deuteranomalous trichromats because deuteranomalous adults perceive midspectral hues as relatively unsaturated and, consequently, not too distinct from white. It is possible that the infants' lack of response to green and yellow-green stripes is not based on an inability to discriminate them from the white background, but rather on a simple lack of preference for those hues (Bornstein, Kessen, and Weiskopf, 1976).

Whatever the true nature of infant chromatic vision, there is recent evidence that some classical types of inherited color deficiencies can be diagnosed in early infancy. Peeples (1976), using the Peeples and Teller (1975) paradigm, found that three of five two-month-old boys with dichromatic maternal grandfathers did not

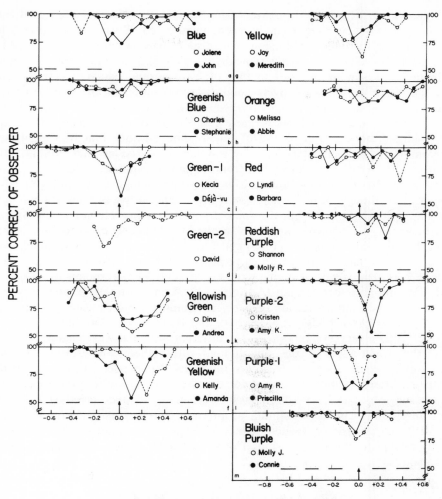

LOG RELATIVE LUMINANCE OF CHROMATIC BAR

Figure 11.   Chromatic discrimination functions for 25 individual infants on 13 chromatic stimuli. Zero on the horizontal axis indicates the adult heterochromatic brightness match. For some chromatic stimuli (blue, blue-green, orange, red, reddish-purple, and bluish-purple), the infants perform above chance for all luminances, indicating the presence of some form of chromatic vision. For yellow-green and mid-purple stimuli, the infants' performance dips to chance, suggesting failures of chromatic discrimination. Other stimuli, particularly greens and yellow, exhibit a minimal dip toward chance. From Teller, Peeples, and Sekel, 1978.

discriminate 496 nm from white. Clearly, a methodology for assessing infant chromatic vision is imminent. As Bornstein (in press) suggests, this venture is not only important for theoretical reasons, but diagnosed deficiencies in color vision can also be used as markers for other hereditary difficulties (McKusick, 1962; Mendlewicz, Fleiss, and Fieve, 1972).

Other facets of infant chromatic vision besides the determination of dichromacy or trichromacy have recently been investigated. Bornstein (in press) has reported that a five-month-old infant can discriminate stimuli differing in wavelength much like adult trichromats typically do. That is, the infant's wavelength discrimination was similar in form to that of color-normal adults: spectral regions where the infant exhibited relatively good discriminability are the same regions in which adult discrimination is high. Bornstein and his colleagues have also investigated the extent to which infants perceive color "categorically." Using an habituation paradigm, Bornstein et al. (1976) found some evidence that four-month-olds showed more recovery of attention if the wavelengths of the test and familiarization stimuli were from different rather than from the same adult color category.

There is also a growing literature on electrophysiological correlates of infant color vision. Although electrophysiological data cannot prove that infants can make dichromatic or trichromatic hue discriminations, it may provide important evidence concerning the mechanisms involved in the development of chromatic vision. Barnet, Lodge, and Armington (1965) and Lodge, Armington, Barnet, Shanks, and Newcomb (1969) have recorded an early positive x-wave in newborn electroretinograms (ERG). The x-wave is a characteristic of adult ERG response to long-wavelength, foveally-presented stimuli (Adrian, 1945, Armington, 1974), and, therefore, is assumed to be a manifestation of cone functioning, a prerequisite for chromatic vision. Fischel (1969), Lodge et al., (1969), and Polikanina (1968) have shown that newborns' VEPs vary systematically for different stimulus wavelengths. Unfortunately, the brightnesses of the stimuli used within these studies have not been equated using infant spectral sensitivity functions. Nonetheless, to the extent that brightness differences do not account for the observed variation in the VEPs, these findings suggest that the newborn visual system up to and including the visual cortex differentially processes stimuli of different wavelengths. It seems likely that such VEP color correlates would reflect a neural representation of color that is causally related to chromatic vision. This relationship, however, remains unproven even in adults (Regan, 1972).

Visual Acuity

Perceiving forms and patterns is the primary function of the visual system. Of course, this function depends on the ability to perceive differences in intensity or wavelength composition (brightness and hue discrimination), because such differences define the contours of forms and patterns in the first place. However, this is not enough. Form and pattern perception further depends on the visual system's ability to encode the spatial distribution of such intensity and wavelength differences. An important experimental question is how accurate is this encoding of spatial distribution. The study of visual acuity is addressed to this question, but in particular to the question of how finely the visual system can partition spatial distributions of intensity and wavelength. Thus, visual acuity refers to the threshold or maximum spatial resolving capability of the visual system.

Measurements of visual acuity generally involve high-contrast, black and white test patterns. A subject's visual performance is assessed as a function of the distance or separation between two reference points within the pattern. The distance for which the subject is just able to detect or resolve the pattern serves as the measure of visual acuity and is generally expressed in degrees of visual angle. This distance, of course, varies depending on the type of pattern used. When the pattern is a single black line on a white background, adults can detect the presence of the line when it is only 0.5 sec wide (Hecht and Mintz, 1939). Acuity measurements such as this, that involve detection of a single line, are termed "minimum visible acuity measurements." Unfortunately, such measurements cannot logically be separated from the intensity discrimination capacity of the eye (Riggs, 1965), and perhaps should not be regarded as measures of acuity, because the spatial distribution of the line need not be encoded for the subject to detect its presence. Acuity is more commonly measured using tasks in which the subject must respond to a separation between elements of the pattern. These are "minimum separable acuity measurements." Minimum separable patterns range from two points or lines separated by a gap, to a series of alternating black and white stripes of equal widths. The second pattern, a so-called squarewave grating, has been the pattern of choice with infants. The width of a single stripe is often taken as the measure of acuity. Threshold stripe widths in adults are as low as $\frac{1}{2}$ minutes of arc (Riggs, 1965; Westheimer, 1972). Two other ways of expressing threshold values numerically have appeared in the literature: 1) spatial frequency (which refers to the number of black stripes per degree of visual angle), and 2) Snellen equivalents. Figure 17 relates these three scales, and shows that a threshold stripe width of $\frac{1}{2}$ min corresponds to a spatial frequency of 60 cycles per degree, or to a Snellen equivalent of 20/10.

There is an extensive literature on infant visual acuity. The consensus is that significant changes in acuity occur during early infancy. These changes presumably have a profound influence on the development of infant visual behavior. Because much is known about the anatomical and physiological bases of adult acuity, the study of acuity growth may also provide some insight into anatomical and physiological development in the infant visual system.

The concept of visual acuity is certainly important to understanding the development of form and pattern perception, but one should keep in mind that acuity concerns only the limiting case in the encoding of spatial distributions of contours. Thus, the understanding of acuity development is an essential, but not sufficient, condition for understanding the development of form vision.

It is somewhat difficult to provide general summary statements concerning the infant acuity literature, because not only have the types of stimuli varied from study to study, but the response measures used have varied as well. Three response measures, optokinetic nystagmus (OKN), visually-evoked cortical potentials (VEP), and preferential looking have been used to measure infant acuity. (For a review of these techniques see Dobson and Teller, in press; Maurer, 1975.) The three techniques use different stimuli to elicit responses from infants and may involve different neural centers in the visual system (Dobson and Teller, in press; Fantz et al., 1962; Maurer, 1975; Regan, 1972).

The OKN procedure typically uses a moving squarewave grating that covers most of the infant's visual field. Pursuit and saccadic refixation eye movements are elicited. The narrowest stripe width for which OKN is observed serves as the estimate of acuity. Figure 12 summarizes the OKN acuity estimates reported by several investigators. Dobson and Teller (in press) describe the various ways these studies have calculated age group averages. There is reasonable agreement among these studies; the narrowest detectable stripe width varies from about 20 min in the newborn to 5 min by six months of age.

The VEP technique involves measurement of the infants' EEG correlated with a change in the visual stimulus. The gratings or checkerboards typically used to elicit the VEP must be periodically flashed (Harter and Suitt, 1970; Harter, Deaton, and Odom, 1977), the stripes or checks within them periodically phase-alternated (Harris, Atkinson, and Braddick, 1976; Sokol and Dobson, 1976), or the striped or checked pattern periodically replaced with a uniform field of equal average luminance (Marg, Freeman, Peltzman, and Goldstein, 1976). Figure 13 shows the acuity estimates of a number of VEP studies. In general, the studies are again in reasonable agreement; threshold stripe width changes from about 15 min at one month to 1–1.5 min at six months. Dobson and Teller (in press) describe the scoring procedures each study used to obtain an acuity estimate.

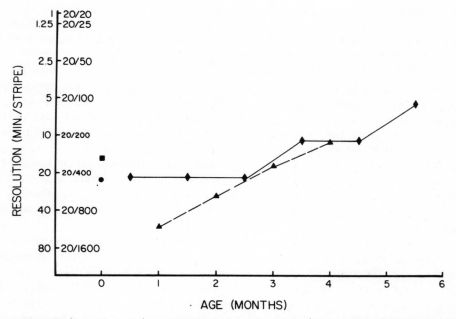

Figure 12. Visual acuity in infants from birth through six months, as estimated with optokinetic nystagmus (OKN) by various investigators. Estimated acuity is plotted in minutes of visual angle at left, and in approximate Snellen equivalent at right. Data points plotted for Dayton, Jones, Aiu, Rawson, Steele, and Rose (1964) and Gorman, Cogan, and Gellis (1957, 1959) are stripe widths at which at least 75% of responsive infants showed OKN. ●—Gorman et al. (1957, 1959); ◆—Fantz et al. (1962); ■—Dayton et al. (1964b); ▲—Enoch and Rabinowicz (1976). From Dobson and Teller, in press.

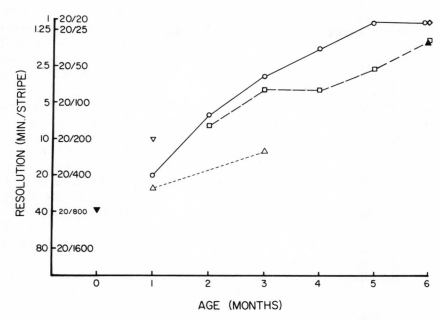

Figure 13. Visual acuity in infants from birth through six months of age as estimated with the VEP. △—Harter and Suitt (1970); ▲—Harris et al. (1976); ○—Marg et al. (1976); ◇—Sokol and Dobson (1976); ▽—Harter et al. (1977, P4 component); □—Sokol (in press); ▼—Atkinson, Braddick, and French (cited in Dobson and Teller, in press). From Dobson and Teller, in press.

The preferential looking technique has been extensively used to study many infant visual capabilities, including visual acuity. The infant is shown two stimuli simultaneously: a grating or checkerboard and a uniform field of equal average luminance. If the infant consistently fixates one stimulus more often than the other, it is inferred that the two stimuli are discriminable. The stripe width of the grating (or check size of the checkerboard) is varied to determine the finest width the infant can reliably respond to. Figures 14 and 15 display the acuity estimates of a number of preferential looking studies. Again there is reasonable agreement among the studies. Acuity increases from about 20 min at one month to 5 min at six months. Dobson and Teller (in press) provide a clear description of the differences in procedure, stimuli, and scoring technique among these studies.

Figures 12 through 15 show that there is reasonable within-technique correspondence. All three techniques indicate a relatively linear increase in acuity with age (Banks 1977b). However, comparison of the figures indicates that the VEP studies generally obtained higher acuity estimates than either the OKN or preferential looking studies. This is most apparent at six months, where VEP estimates are between 2 and 1 min, whereas OKN and preferential looking estimates are about 5 min. Dobson and Teller (in press) argue that this dissimilarity may be attributable to differences in the criteria for what constitutes threshold behavior. In VEP acuity studies, the criteria have generally been rather low. In OKN

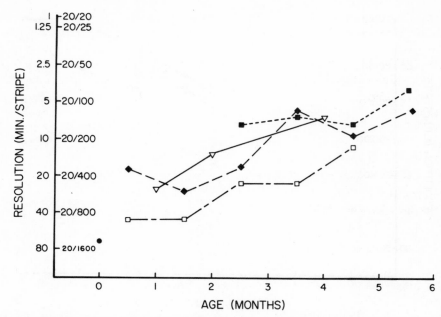

Figure 14. Visual acuity in infants from birth through six months as estimated by Fantz and his co-workers with the preferential looking technique. Data plotted as in Figure 12. Data points shown are stripe widths that, by interpolation within the original data, produce preferential fixation in 75% of infants tested. □—Fantz et al. (1962), Expt. I, 0.8 log cd/m²; ◆— Fantz et al. (1962), Expt. II, approx. 0.8 log cd/m²; ■—Fantz et al. (1962), Expt. III, 1.2 log cd/m²; ●—Miranda (1970), 0.8 log cd/m²; ▽— Fantz (cited in Dobson and Teller, in press). From Dobson and Teller, in press.

and preferential looking studies, the criteria have generally been higher (for example, 75% correct responding or 75% of infants showing OKN or preferential fixation). If lower criteria are adopted, acuity estimates are correspondingly higher. Therefore, the finding of consistently lower acuity values in OKN and preferential looking studies is in large part because of the use of stricter scoring criteria. The fact that the three techniques can yield similar acuity estimates increases our confidence that visual acuity can be measured in infants with reasonable reliability and accuracy. An important consideration for pediatricians and ophthalmologists is the relative ease with which these techniques can be implemented in a clinical setting. Dobson (1976b) has discussed this.

Several stimulus parameters such as luminance, contrast, and field size are known to affect measurements of adult acuity (Riggs, 1965; Westheimer, 1972). Unfortunately, no infant acuity studies to date have systematically varied luminance and field size. The effect of contrast has been investigated (Atkinson, Braddick, and Braddick, 1974; Banks and Salapatek, 1976) and is discussed later in this chapter.

In summary, newborn acuity is very poor in comparison to adults', but improves dramatically during the first six months of life. These observations motivate a two-pronged question: why is infant acuity so poor, and how does it improve so rapidly over the first months of life?

There are several mechanisms that can be proposed to answer this question. Perhaps the simplest is to suppose that the optics of the young infant's eye is the limiting factor in acuity and that as the lens, cornea, and other optic media mature and image quality improves, acuity improves as well. It has been shown in adults that a close correlation exists between image sharpness on the retina (which solely depends on optical factors) and acuity (Campbell and Gubisch, 1966; Green and Campbell, 1965; Westheimer and Campbell, 1962). Several sorts of optical factors affect adult visual acuity: spherical and chromatic aberration (Campbell and Gubisch, 1967), blurring because of diffraction with small pupil sizes (Westheimer, 1963), clarity of the optic media (Bonds and Freeman, 1976; Gstalder and Green, 1971), and accommodative error (Green and Campbell, 1965).

The effect of chromatic aberration on visual performance is limited to relatively narrow grating stripe widths or high spatial frequencies. The effect of spherical aberration is also limited to high frequencies, unless the aberration is extreme (Campbell and Gubisch, 1967). Likewise, blurring because of small pupil size is also a small effect involving relatively high spatial frequencies (Westheimer, 1963). Thus, none of

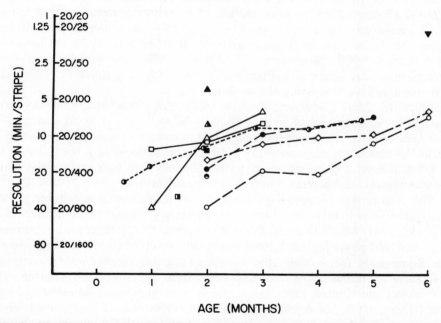

Figure 15. Visual acuity in infants from birth through six months, as estimated using various modified versions of the preferential looking technique. ▲—Atkinson et al. (1974), flashing sinewave gratings, 0.3 log cd/m²; △—Atkinson et al. (1974), drifting sinewave gratings, 0.3 log cd/m²; ○—Teller et al. (1974), squarewave gratings, 0.0 log cd/m²; ●—Teller et al. (1974), squarewave gratings, 1.2 log cd/m²; ■—Banks and Salapatek (1976), sinewave gratings, 1.7 log cd/m²; ▼—Harris et al. (1976), sinewave gratings, 2.5 log cd/m²; ◨—Salapatek et al. (1976), squarewave gratings, 2.1 log cd/m²; △—Atkinson et al. (1977b), sinewave gratings, 1.5 log cd/m²; ◓—Dobson, Teller, and Belgum (in press), 0.8 log cd/m²; □—Banks (1977a), Banks and Salapatek (in preparation), sinewave gratings, 1.7 log cd/m²; ◆—Held et al. (cited in Dobson and Teller, in press), squarewave gratings, 1.5 log cd/m²; ◑—Allen (cited in Dobson and Teller, in press), squarewave gratings, 1.2 log cd/m². From Dobson and Teller, in press.

these seem viable candidates to account for the poor acuity of the infant, because infant acuity (in terms of the highest resolvable spatial frequency) does not approach the spatial frequencies at which these effects are significant.

Blurring of the retinal image because of opacities or cloudiness of the optic media also does not seem to be a significant limitation to acuity in infants; ophthalmoscopic examination of the young infant's eye indicates that the media are relatively free of opacities or cloudiness at birth (Cook and Glasscock, 1951; Hosaka, 1963).

Accommodative error, on the other hand, might be considered a more viable candidate. Haynes et al. (1965) and Banks (1978) have reported that accommodation between two and eight weeks is not as flexible or accurate as it is at later ages. If such accommodative errors are primary limiting factors in infant acuity, then acuity should vary as a function of stimulus distance. Such a correlation between acuity and target distance is not observed in one- or two-month-olds (Fantz et al., 1962; Salapatek et al., 1976). Accommodative error, therefore, does not seem to be a primary limitation to infant acuity either.

One optical factor that would presumably affect visual acuity is the axial length of the eye (distance from anterior surface of cornea to posterior pole of the eye). Retinal image size for a given stimulus is roughly proportional to axial length (Emsley, 1953). Because axial length increases from birth to adulthood by a factor of 1.4 (Larsen, 1971; Scammon and Wilmer, 1950), one would expect similar increases in retinal image size. Presumably, any such magnification of the retinal image would aid the processing of fine visual pattern.

From the above discussion, it seems likely that retinal image quality exceeds behaviorally-measured infant acuity. It must be that physiological and/or attentional factors place the upper limit on infant visual resolution during the first few months. Attentional factors cannot be ruled out at this stage, but the fact that VEP and OKN measures of infant acuity agree relatively well with preferential looking measures suggests that attention may be minimally involved.

The relationship between visual acuity and physiological structures has been investigated extensively in adults and animals (Green, 1970; Kelly, 1975b; Mansfield, 1974; Mitchell et al., 1973; Westheimer, 1972). There are a number of anatomical and physiological factors potentially involved in infant acuity development. Some of the factors that may be involved are: migration of nonrecipient structures, such as retinal ganglion cells away from the foveal pit (Barber, 1955; Hendrickson and Kupfer, 1976; Mann, 1964); average angular separation of foveal cones (Green, 1970; Hendrickson and Kupfer, 1976; Mann, 1964); receptive-field structure of retinal ganglion cells (Rusoff and Dubin, 1977); spatial resolution of geniculate or cortical neurons (Haith, in press; Karmel and Maisel, 1975; Pettigrew, 1974); and delayed maturation of the "primary visual system" (Bronson, 1974; Salapatek, 1975) or of "sustained" or X-type neurons (Ikeda and Wright, 1975). It does seem, however, that the primary resolution limitation lies not in the quality of the retinal image but in the infant's ability to process that image (see also Banks, 1977a; Dobson and Teller, in press; Salapatek et al., 1976).

In the last 10 years we have seen a number of demonstrations that early visual experience can play an important role in visual development. Neurophysiological studies of cats and monkeys have shown that several properties of neurons in the visual cortex are affected by abnormal experience during a specific period of development (Blakemore, 1975; Hirsch and Spinelli, 1970; Wiesel and Hubel, 1963b). Behavioral measures of visual function in these animals also indicate susceptibility to abnormal early experience during this sensitive or critical period (Dews and Wiesel, 1970; Muir and Mitchell, 1973; von Noorden, Dowling, and Ferguson, 1970).

There is now some evidence that abnormal visual experience during infancy and early childhood can result in relatively permanent deficits in human visual acuity. In particular, adults with a history of early astigmatism (Freeman, Mitchell, and Millodot, 1972; Mitchell et al., 1973) or myopia (Fiorentini and Maffei, 1976) exhibit lower visual acuity than normal adults, even if the astigmatic or myopic refractive error was corrected during childhood or adulthood. The presence of cataracts early in life has even more severe effects (Gstalder and Green, 1971; von Senden, 1960).

The importance of establishing developmental acuity norms is indicated by such findings. With such norms, the early detection of visual abnormality would be facilitated. Furthermore, relatively rapid techniques for assessing infant acuity in clinical settings are needed for early visual screening. Dobson and Teller (in press) discuss the advantages and disadvantages of various measurement techniques in this regard.

Enoch and Rabinowicz (1976) have recently published a case history of considerable interest. The history concerns a full-term, healthy infant born with a dense unilateral cataract. The infant was operated upon at four days of age and visual correction was promptly initiated. Visual acuity was then assessed over a period of four and one-half months. The acuity of the good eye steadily improved over this period. The acuity of the aphakic eye, however, did not increase until an adequate visual correction was provided at 25 days. From that age on, acuity improved at similar rates in both eyes such that the aphakic eye exhibited a constant deficit relative to the good eye. It will be of great interest to see if this child's aphakic eye ever develops adult-like acuity. This case history is an important development in the management of congenital cataracts in particular and of problems associated with abnormal sensory experience in general.

Contrast Sensitivity Function

Visual acuity, although an important aspect of form and pattern vision, represents just the limiting case of the finest spatial partitioning of which the visual system is capable. It provides little information about the processing of forms or pattern elements larger than the limit of resolution.

In principle, the contrast sensitivity function (CSF), which has recently been in vogue among students of adult form vision, provides a general index of the visual system's ability to process an infinite variety of forms and patterns (Cornsweet,

1970; Ratliff, 1965). Therefore, measurement of the infant CSF may provide considerable information concerning the development of form and pattern perception.

The CSF is determined by measuring an observer's contrast sensitivity to sinewave gratings of different spatial frequencies. Two examples of sinewave gratings are shown in Figure 16. Sinewave gratings are specified by three parameters: 1) spatial frequency, the number of dark bars per degree of visual angle (spatial frequency is higher in the grating on the right in Figure 16), 2) orientation, the directional disposition of a grating (the ones in Figure 16 are vertically-oriented), and 3) contrast, which is related to the difference between the peak and trough intensities of the grating. (Contrast is actually defined by the equation: $C = I_{max} - I_{min}/I_{max} + I_{min}$ where I_{max} is the intensity of the most intense part of the light stripes, and I_{min} is the intensity of the least intense part of the dark stripes.) Contrast sensitivity is the reciprocal of the grating's contrast at threshold. An example of a typical adult CSF is shown in Figure 17. Note that sensitivity is greatest to intermediate spatial frequencies (2 to 6 cy/deg).

The potential utility of the CSF is derived from Fourier's theorem and linear systems analysis. Fourier's theorem states that any two-dimensional, time-invariant stimulus can be exactly described by the combination of a set of sinewave gratings of various spatial frequencies, orientations, and contrast levels. Thus, even a complex, two-dimensional visual stimulus such as the picture of a face can be exactly reproduced by the combination of various sinewave gratings. In principle, linear systems analysis allows one to predict the visibility of any form or pattern if one knows the observer's CSF. It must be emphasized, however, that rigorous application of linear systems analysis to any system requires that the system have certain strictly defined properties. The visual system does not exactly meet these requirements, so the set of visual stimuli to which the CSF and linear systems analysis can

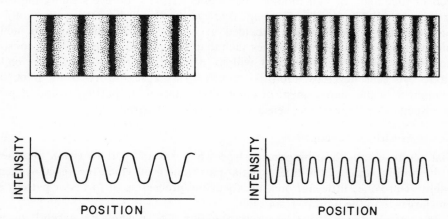

Figure 16.   Two sinewave gratings and intensity distributions. In the upper part of the figure, two sinewave gratings are shown; the grating on the right has a higher spatial frequency. Directly below them are shown the intensity distributions corresponding to the gratings. Intensity is plotted as a function of position.

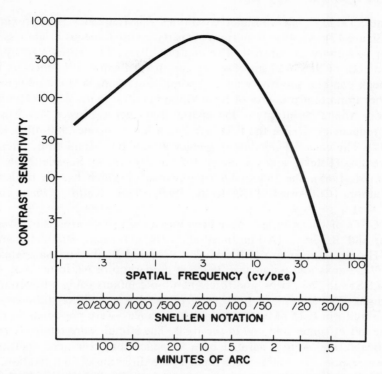

Figure 17. Typical adult contrast sensitivity function (CSF). Contrast sensitivity, the reciprocal of contrast at threshold, is plotted as a function of spatial frequency. Also shown for comparison are scales relating spatial frequency to Snellen equivalents and minutes of arc.

be successfully applied is restricted. Nonetheless, there are numerous examples in the adult literature where the perceived quality of a particular stimulus has been successfully predicted (Campbell, Carpenter, and Levinson, 1969; Davidson and Whiteside, 1971; Lowry and DePalma, 1961). (It is beyond the scope of this chapter to describe the properties required and how systems analysis and the CSF are used to predict input-output relationships, but the interested reader will find informative discussions in Cornsweet, 1970; Goodman, 1968; and Linfoot, 1964.)

There is a second level at which the CSF can be more reasonably applied to the study of form vision. At this level, the CSF is regarded as a describing function rather than a characterizing function from which input-output relationships can be calculated (Cornsweet, 1970). The term describing function is meant to communicate that the CSF provides an approximate description of the form information available to a perceiver and that it can be used to elucidate some basic mechanisms of form vision. This is the level at which the CSF is regarded in the remainder of this section.

Several basic properties of form vision are reflected in the CSF. One of them is visual acuity. The highest spatial frequency an observer can detect is one definition of the observer's limit of resolution or visual acuity (Campbell and Green, 1965;

Westheimer, 1972). Under optimal conditions this frequency is approximately 50 cy/deg (Figure 17). Another important property is simultaneous brightness discrimination, or sensitivity to contrast. The contrast thresholds represented by the CSF provide indices of how well an observer can discern small differences in intensity. Adults' peak contrast sensitivity under optimal conditions is about 500 (Figure 17). Yet another important property of form vision manifest in the CSF is low-frequency attenuation. Adults' sensitivity to low spatial frequencies is lower than it is to intermediate frequencies. Hence the CSF exhibits a low-frequency fall-off in sensitivity (Figure 17). The cause of this low-frequency attenuation seems to be lateral inhibitory processing (Estevez and Cavonius, 1976; Kelly, 1975b; Schade, 1956; Van Nes and Bouman, 1965), the functional significance of which has been discussed by several authors (Cornsweet, 1970; Kelly, 1969, 1975b; Ratliff, 1965; von Bekesy, 1967).

The CSFs of young infants have been measured by two groups of investigators: Atkinson, and Braddick (Atkinson et al., 1974; Atkinson, Braddick, and Moar, 1977a,b; Harris, Atkinson, and Braddick, 1976) and Banks and Salapatek (Banks, 1976, 1977a; Banks and Salapatek, 1976, in preparation). Atkinson et al. (1977a,b) measured CSFs in one-, two-, and three-month-old infants using a preferential looking paradigm. Two stimuli—a sinewave grating (that was either stationary or drifting) and a uniform field of equal average luminance—were presented on each trial, one to the left of center and one to the right. The stimuli were relatively small (15° circular fields), and were separated by a 9° space that contained central fixation lights. Two response measures were used: 1) the direction of first fixation, and 2) a "blind" adult observer's best guess based on the infant's behavior of the side the grating had been on. Generally, three or four spatial frequencies were presented to each infant; contrast threshold for each frequency was estimated as that contrast value that would produce 70% correct responding. The results of the study are discussed in conjunction with Banks and Salapatek's results.

Banks and Salapatek (Banks, 1977a; Banks and Salapatek, in preparation) also measured the CSFs of one-, two-, and three-month-olds. The preferential looking procedure was used, with direction of first fixation serving as the response measure. There were important differences from the Atkinson and Braddick studies, however. The grating and uniform fields were much larger, subtending 48° × 40° each. Furthermore, there was no separation between the two fields. Each infant's contrast threshold for each of five spatial frequencies was estimated as the contrast level that would produce 75% correct responding.

The results of this study are shown in Figure 18. These CSFs are the averages of individual functions from six one-month-olds, six two-month-olds, and eight three-month-olds. The two and three-month CSFs obtained by Atkinson and Braddick are similar to the corresponding functions of Figure 18. Their one-month data are dissimilar, however, because the contrast sensitivity values are considerably lower than Banks and Salapatek's.

As mentioned earlier, the CSF can be used to provide a useful estimate of visual acuity. Acuity estimates are commonly derived from adult CSFs plotted with contrast sensitivity on a logarithmic scale and spatial frequency on a linear scale

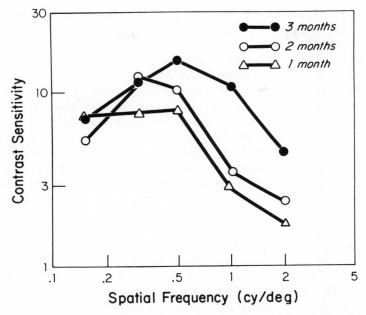

Figure 18.   Contrast sensitivity functions (CSFs) for one-, two-, and three-month-old infants as reported by Banks (1977a) and Banks and Salapatek (in preparation). Contrast sensitivity is plotted as a function of spatial frequency. The functions shown represent the averages of individual CSFs for six one-month-olds, six two-month-olds, and eight three-month-olds.

(spatial frequency is plotted on a logarithmic scale in Figure 18). The high-frequency slope of these functions is extrapolated to find the spatial frequency associated with a contrast sensitivity of 1. This "cut-off" spatial frequency is an estimate of the finest resolvable high-contrast grating. In the Banks and Salapatek study, the "cut-off" frequencies determined in this manner was 2.4 cy/deg for one-month-olds, 2.8 cy/deg for two-month-olds, and 4.0 cy/deg for three-month-olds. These values agree favorably with the acuity estimates of other studies. Atkinson et al. (1977b) used a different procedure to find "cut-off" frequencies, but their stationary grating estimates are similar to Banks and Salapatek's for two of the age groups: 3.1 cy/deg for two-month-olds and 4.2 cy/deg for three-month-olds. Their estimate for one-month-olds, 0.6 cy/deg, is notably lower than Banks and Salapatek's. This difference in the two studies' estimates of one-month acuity may be related to stimulus field size.

One might ask whether the acuity estimates yielded by the CSF are in any sense more reliable or useful than other measures of acuity. An affirmative answer to this question is justified, because one can use the CSF to accurately predict the visibility of different types of acuity targets. Campbell et al. (1969) have shown that adults' single-line acuity (minimum visible) can be predicted by applying the CSF and linear systems analysis. Similarly, Kelly and Magnuski (1975) were able to predict the visibility of fine, circularly-concentric patterns.

Banks and Salapatek (in preparation) have demonstrated that similar predictions can be drawn from infant CSFs. They have reanalyzed two experiments,

Dayton et al. (1964b) and Fantz et al. (1975), which reported acuity estimates out of accord with other reported values. In both cases, application of linear systems analysis and the CSF revealed that the results were actually predictable, and hence consistent with other investigators' estimates.

The CSF also yields information relevant to simultaneous brightness discrimination. Each point on the function represents the contrast (or intensity difference) necessary for an observer to detect the presence of nonuniformity. One of these points, the peak contrast sensitivity value, represents the maximum discrimination capability for sinewave gratings. The average peak values reported by Banks and Salapatek are 9, 12.5, and 15.0 for one-, two-, and three-month-olds respectively. Atkinson et al. (1977b) obtained somewhat lower values of 2.4, 5.5, and 10.4. Peeples and Teller's (1975) measurement of brightness discrimination in two-month-olds has been mentioned. They found that two-month infants could discriminate stripes (squarewave gratings) whose intensity differed by only 10% from background intensity. This corresponds to a contrast sensitivity of about 19 that, despite differences in procedure, agrees fairly well with the Banks and Salapatek result.

Clearly, to describe the contrast sensitivity or brightness discrimination ability of the infant visual system with a single value is inappropriate, because contrast sensitivity highly depends on stimulus size and shape (and other factors such as luminance and adaptation level). Indeed, this interaction between contrast sensitivity and the spatial parameters of stimulation is a crucial aspect of form vision. Adult and infant visual systems are maximally sensitive to certain aspects of form information and relatively insensitive to others. One can see by comparing Figures 17 and 18 that adults exhibit generally higher sensitivity, but also that the frequency region of maximum sensitivity is much higher in adults than in infants. This suggests that adult and infant visual systems are best-tuned to different bands of form information.

As mentioned before, one aspect of form information to which the adult visual system is not very sensitive is low spatial frequencies. The low-frequency insensitivity, or fall-off, observed in adult CSFs is often assumed to be the result of lateral inhibitory processing (Estevez and Cavonius, 1976; Kelly, 1975a,b; Ratliff, 1965; Schade, 1956; Tulunay-Keesey and Jones, 1976). The CSFs of Figure 18 indicate the presence of a low-frequency fall-off for two- and three-month-olds, but not for one-month-olds. Atkinson et al. (1977b) observed the same developmental trend. To the extent that low-frequency fall-offs in CSFs reflect lateral inhibitory processing (a hypothesis that is still somewhat controversial; see Arend, 1976; Estevez and Cavonius, 1976; Kelly, 1975a,b; Savoy and McCann, 1975; Tulunay-Keesey and Jones, 1976), Banks and Salapatek's and Atkinson and Braddick's data suggest that one-month-olds generally do not manifest lateral inhibitory processing, but that two- and three-month-olds do. This hypothesis is supported by the finding that when overall luminance is lowered, the fall-off in the two-month CSF changes in the manner predicted by a lateral inhibition interpretation (Banks, 1976).

The functional significance of lateral inhibition lies in the fact that lateral inhibitory networks, such as those observed in primate retinas, tend to exaggerate or emphasize regions of transition in the retinal image (such as sharp intensity gradients or contours) by attenuating or deemphasizing gradual intensity gradients (such as diffuse shadows). Because areas of intensity transition are the primary defining characteristic of visual forms, the process of contour enhancement is an important facet of form perception.

Each of the properties reflected in the CSF—visual acuity, contrast sensitivity, and low-frequency attenuation—become more adult-like during the first three months of life. There are no published data yet that indicate when the infant and adult CSFs first coincide. It is clear, however, that early visual experience plays a significant role in the development of these properties. Freeman and Thibos (1975) and Mitchell and Wilkinson (1974) have measured the CSFs of persons with histories of early astigmatism, using vertically- and horizontally-oriented gratings. They found the "cut-off" frequencies to be significantly lower when the gratings' orientation coincided with the meridian of the subjects' astigmatic error, despite the fact that this error was carefully corrected during the experiment. In fact, contrast sensitivity was generally lower for a wide range of spatial frequencies in that orientation. The quantitative differences between the CSFs for vertical and horizontal gratings could not be the results of errors of focus in one meridian, so these authors concluded that orientation-specific neural deficits must account for the difference. Such neural deficits are presumed to result from orientational biases in the early visual experience of these subjects. Fiorentini and Maffei (1976) have studied the CSFs of persons with marked myopia, and have found contrast sensitivity to be lower for all spatial frequencies. Again, the authors argued that the reduction in sensitivity results from neural deficits in the processing of form information.

A recent paper has shown that CSFs may provide critical information in visual assessments of amblyopia (reduced acuity that cannot be optically corrected and is not attributable to obvious structural anomalies) that typical measures of visual acuity would miss. Hess and Howell (1977) measured the CSFs of 10 strabismic amblyopes. They found "cut-off" frequency and contrast sensitivity to intermediate spatial frequencies were consistently lower in the amblyopic compared to the non-amblyopic eye. Of most interest, however, is the contrast sensitivity of these patients' amblyopic eyes to low spatial frequencies ($\frac{1}{2}$ to 3 cy/deg): half of the patients showed normal sensitivity, and half showed notably depressed sensitivity. Hess and Howell concluded that there are two classes of strabismic amblyopia; one in which contrast sensitivity is depressed for all spatial frequencies, and one in which it is depressed for only intermediate and high frequencies. It is too early to know how fundamental this classification might be to the understanding and treatment of amblyopia, but Hess and Howell's data effectively argue for the potential utility of CSFs in visual assessment.

Measurement of visual acuity is by far the most common means of clinically evaluating a patient's form vision. The above discussion has shown, however, that some important aspects of form vision are not tapped by measures of visual acuity (see also Bodis-Wollner, 1972). The CSF, on the other hand, provides information concerning contrast sensitivity and low-frequency attenuation in addition to visual acuity. Because these aspects develop relatively rapidly during infancy and are adversely affected by the early presence of ocular abnormality, the CSF might prove to be a useful clinical index of infant visual function.

Binocular Vision

Adults perceive the visual world as three-dimensional even though the retinal image itself is flat. The study of the process by which a two-dimensional image is translated into a three-dimensional percept is one of the classic problems of perceptual psychology. An understanding of the translation process requires consideration of the different kinds of depth information that the visual system can use. Two general classes of information can be distinguished: monocular cues for depth and binocular cues for depth (Gibson, 1966; Kaufman, 1974; Richards, 1975).

There is a lengthy literature on the development of depth perception in infancy. For reviews see Haith and Campos (1977), Pick and Pick (1970), and Yonas and Pick (1975). The majority of infant studies have focused on the global question: when does depth perception first develop? They have not in general attempted to isolate individual depth cues to determine the young infant's ability to utilize such cues. In this section, however, those few studies that are relevant to the development of the primary binocular depth cue—binocular disparity—are discussed.

While one looks at a fairly near object, each eye receives a slightly different view of it. This slight discrepancy between the two retinal images is referred to as binocular parallax. The visual system can use this information to determine the solidity or three-dimensionality of objects. A special case of binocular parallax can be generated with two-dimensional patterns presented separately to the two eyes. The physical difference between the two patterns is called binocular disparity, and the resultant perception of depth is called stereopsis. By varying the amount of binocular disparity, one can create the experience of depth that would result if the retinal images had come from a real object located at different distances from the observer. One can measure the least amount of disparity necessary for an observer to reliably detect the presence of disparity. This threshold is termed stereoacuity. Adults with normal stereopsis can detect disparities as small as 15 sec of arc (Ogle, 1962).

An important aspect of binocular vision is the vergence eye movement system. The visual axes of the two eyes are generally directed toward approximately the same part of an object being fixated. Otherwise, diplopia (perceived double images) or suppression of the input into one eye results. Diplopia or suppression is associated with markedly deficient stereopsis, as witnessed by the fact that persons who cannot appropriately converge show either poor or no stereopsis (Mitchell and Ware, 1974). Because some appropriate vergence movements are observed shortly after birth (Aslin, 1977; Slater and Findlay, 1975), one might expect very young infants to be capable of processing binocular disparity.

Appel and Campos (1977) used a habituation-dishabituation paradigm to investigate two-month-olds' ability to detect binocular disparity. The stimuli presented were stereoscopic photographs (stereograms) of a single object. They found that infants who were first habituated to a stereogram with no binocular disparity would dishabituate when disparity was subsequently introduced into the stimulus. Because the only stimulus difference between the habituation and dishabituation sequences was the amount of disparity, this result indicates some ability to process and respond to binocular disparity by this young age. Unfortunately, significant dishabituation was not observed when the stereogram with disparity was used as the habituation stimulus and the stereogram without disparity as the dishabituation stimulus. Thus, the results are not entirely conclusive.

Atkinson and Braddick (1976) used both a preferential looking and a habituation paradigm to investigate two-month-olds' ability to detect binocular disparity in random-dot stereograms (Julesz, 1971). Both paradigms yielded somewhat ambiguous results. The preferential looking study obtained a few significant preferences for stereograms with disparity over those without disparity. The habituation study obtained similar results: two of four infants exhibited consistent dishabituation to changes in the disparity of the stimulus.

Pipp and Haith (1977) have examined infants' patterns of visual fixation to flat and three-dimensional bar stimuli. They found that two-month-olds scan raised (or recessed) bars differently than they scan flat but otherwise identical bars. Although Pipp and Haith's results indicate that infants are able to discriminate simple three-dimensional and two-dimensional patterns, it is not clear which of many potential depth cues, including binocular disparity, were being used by the infants to distinguish the patterns.

These three studies suggest in conjunction that infants can differentially respond to stimuli differing in disparity by two months of age. Such a finding, however, does not imply that such young infants interpret the presence of binocular disparity as signalling three-dimensionality. Several investigators (e.g., Yonas and Pick, 1975) have recognized that responses appropriate to perceived distance must be recorded to demonstrate this conclusively. With this in mind, Bower, Broughton, and Moore (1970) presented stereograms to neonates and recorded any reaches they made toward the stimulus. Considerable disparity was present in the stimulus so that to adult observers it seemed very close and "reachable." Bower et al. reported that all infants cried after initiating reaches toward the "virtual object." They argue that the emotional outbreaks were evidence for intent to reach and grasp based on the processing of disparity information specifying a reachable (nearby) object. This finding, however, must be questioned, given a recent failure to find visually guided reaching to even real objects (Dodwell, Muir, and DiFranco, 1976). It does seem, however, that infants' reaches to "virtual objects" specified by binocular disparity are distance-appropriate by five months of age (Gordon and Yonas, 1976).

From the above discussion, it is clear that the literature on the development of binocular vision in infancy is as yet somewhat sparse. The age at which binocular disparity can first be used to discriminate stimuli has not been established. No estimates of stereoacuity as a function of age have appeared even though such data would allow one to establish important developmental norms. Amigo (1973) provides estimates for three- to five and one-half year-olds. Although visual acuity and stereoacuity are known to be highly correlated in adults (Frey, 1953), this potentially important developmental relationship has not been studied in infants. Another important but unstudied relationship is that between the development of the vergence eye movement system and binocular disparity detection. This lack of knowledge concerning many aspects of infant binocular vision is primarily attributable to the fact that no effective paradigm for measuring infant stereoacuity has been established to date. Atkinson and Braddick (1976) provide some discussion of the use of different response measures.

There is now considerable evidence that early visual experience significantly influences the development of human binocular vision. Persons with a history of convergent strabismus (crossed eyes), a condition known to deleteriously affect binocular development in cats (Hubel and Wiesel, 1965), do not develop normal binocular vision as indexed by stereoacuity (Burian and von Noorden, 1974; Mitchell and Ware, 1974; Movshon, Chambers, and Blakemore, 1972). This failure to develop normal stereoacuity is presumably because of the absence of corresponding binocular input early in these persons' lives. Recently, two groups of investigators verified this. Banks et al. (1975) and Hohmann and Creutzfeldt (1975) demonstrated that the effects of abnormal visual experience because of strabismus are most severe when the strabismus existed during a specific critical or sensitive developmental period. Both groups measured the quality of binocular vision in persons who had had convergent strabismus some time during their lives and subsequently had had the condition surgically corrected. The response measure used was interocular transfer of the tilt-aftereffect, a measure that is highly correlated with stereoacuity and fusional abilities (Mitchell and Ware, 1974; Movshon et al., 1972). Low interocular transfer values, indicating poor binocular vision, were observed in persons whose period of abnormal experience because of strabismus included the period from six months to four years of age. Higher values were observed in those with late or very early strabismus. Aslin and Banks (in press) have used the data of Banks et al. and Hohmann and Creutzfeldt to calculate the relative importance of normal visual experience at different ages to the eventual development of binocular vision. Figure 19 shows the three functions they calculated. Two of the functions were determined from the two subject populations studied by Banks et al.; one representing subjects who had strabismus from birth (congenital esotropes) and the other representing subjects whose strabismus developed some time after birth (late-onset esotropes). The other function was calculated from Hohmann and Creutzfeldt's data. These functions indicate that the presence of convergent strabismus early in life does indeed adversely affect the development of binocular vision. The critical or sensitive period during which the presence of strabismus is most detrimental seems to begin several months after birth, to reach a maximum during the second year of life, and to decline by six to eight years of age. Other measures of binocular vision besides interocular transfer of the tilt-aftereffect should be studied to determine if sensitive period estimates are the same for the development of other binocular abilities. Nonetheless, the clinical importance of these findings is obvious. For children born with convergent strabismus, surgical intervention is indicated before age two (Taylor, 1972). Early surgery, if successful in realigning the two eyes, can result in minimal functional deficits, at least in terms

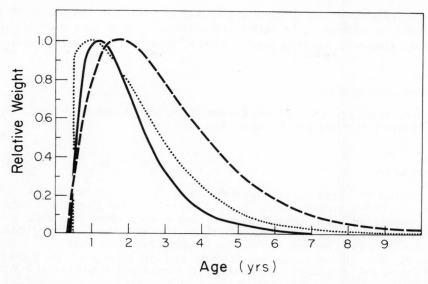

Figure 19.   Functions representing the relative importance of abnormal binocular experience from birth to age 10. The functions shown yielded the highest correlations between observed and predicted interocular transfer for three groups of subjects (see Banks et al., 1975, for further explanation). The dashed curve represents the best-fitting function for the congenital esotropes studied by Banks et al. The dotted curve represents the best-fitting function for the late-onset esotropes studied by Banks et al. The solid curve is the best-fitting function obtained for the late-onset esotropes studied by Hohmann and Creutzfeldt (1975). From Aslin and Banks, in press.

of the interocular transfer measure of binocular vision. For children who develop strabismus some time after birth, the immediacy of surgery does not seem to be as great if the age of onset was later than five or six years of age.

CONCLUDING REMARKS

This chapter summarizes our current knowledge of infant visual capabilities. It is not intended to provide a complete compendium of these abilities, but rather to present a guide to the existing literature. The reader has undoubtedly noticed that the majority of research papers cited have been published in the last decade. This recent surge in infant visual research is attributable in part to the increase in sophistication and effectiveness of measurement techniques. A wide variety of techniques have been discussed in the various sections of the chapter. Some have already been adapted for clinical settings, but others have not. Thus, it is somewhat premature to critically evaluate the advantages and disadvantages of each technique for infant visual assessment. However, it is clear that new adaptations of some of these techniques will eventually result in more accurate and reliable assessment.

Many of the recent studies of infant visual capabilities have used small numbers of highly selected infant subjects. We have yet to verify these findings with large enough samples of normal and abnormal infants to ascertain what constitutes noteworthy deviation from developmental norms. Furthermore, we do not yet fully understand the relationship between visual abnormality in infancy and adult visual capability. However, promising beginnings along these lines are clearly evident.

ACKNOWLEDGMENTS

The authors thank Kay Adams, Karol Kumpfer, Steve Murray, Joanne Bergman, and Loa Magnusson for help in preparing this manuscript.

REFERENCES

Adrian, E. D. 1945. The electric response of the human eye. J. Physiol. 104: 84–104.

Alpern, M. 1969a. Accommodation. In H. Davson (ed.), The Eye. Vol. 3. Muscular Mechanisms. Part 2. Accommodation and the pupil. Academic Press, New York.

Alpern, M. 1969b. Types of movement. In H. Davson (ed.), The Eye. Vol. 3. Muscular Mechanisms. Part 1: Movements of the eyes. Academic Press, New York.

Alpern, M. 1971. Effector mechanisms in vision. In J. W. Kling and L. A. Riggs (eds.), Woodworth and Schlosberg's Experimental Psychology. 3rd ed. Holt Rinehart & Winston, New York.

Amigo, G. 1973. Pre-school vision study. Br. J. Ophthalmol. 57: 125–132.

Appel, M. A., and Campos, J. J. 1977. Binocular disparity as a discriminable stimulus parameter for young infants. J. Exp. Child Psychol. 23: 47–56.

Arend, L. E. 1976. Temporal determinants of the form of the spatial contrast threshold MTF. Vis. Res. 16: 1035–1042.

Armington, J. 1974. The Electroretinogram. Academic Press, New York.

Aslin, R. N. 1975. The development of binocular fixation in human infants. Unpublished doctoral dissertation, University of Minnesota, Minneapolis.

Aslin, R. N. 1977. Development of binocular fixation in human infants. J. Exp. Child Psychol. 23: 133–150.

Aslin, R. N., and Banks, M. S. Early visual experience in humans: Evidence for a critical period in the development of binocular vision. In H. L. Pick, Jr., H. W. Leibowitz, J. E. Singer, A. Steinschneider, and H. W. Stevenson (eds.), Psychology: From Research to Practice. Plenum Press, New York. In press.

Aslin, R. N., and Salapatek, P. 1975. Saccadic localization of peripheral targets by the very young human infant. Percept. Psychophys. 17: 293–302.

Atkinson, J., and Braddick, O. 1976. Stereoscopic discrimination in infants. Perception 5: 29–38.

Atkinson, J., Braddick, O., and Braddick, F. 1974. Acuity and contrast sensitivity of infant vision. Nature 247: 403–404.

Atkinson, J., Braddick, O., and Moar, K. 1977a. Contrast sensitivity of the human infant for moving and static patterns. Vis. Res. 17: 1045–1047.

Atkinson, J., Braddick, O., and Moar, K. 1977b. Development of contrast sensitivity over the first 3 months of life in the human infant. Vis. Res. 17: 1037–1044.

Awaya, S., Miyake, Y., Amaizumi, Y., Shiose, Y., Kanda, T., and Komuro, K. 1973. Amblyopia in man suggestive of stimulus deprivation amblyopia. Jpn. J. Ophthalmol. 17: 69–82.

Banks, M. S. 1976. Lateral inhibition in the infant visual system? Paper presented at Association for Research in Vision and Ophthalmology, April 26–May 1, Sarasota, Florida.

Banks, M. S. 1977a. Infant form vision: The modulation transfer function. Unpublished doctoral dissertation, University of Minnesota, Minneapolis.

Banks, M. S. 1977b. Visual acuity development in human infants: A re-evaluation. Invest. Ophthalmol. Vis. Sci. 16: 191–192.

Banks, M. S. Infant visual accommodation. Paper presented at International Conference on Infant Studies, March 10–12, Providence, Rhode Island.

Banks, M. S., Aslin, R. N., and Letson, R. D. 1975. Sensitive period for the development of human binocular vision. Science 190: 675–677.

Banks, M. S., and Salapatek, P. 1976. Contrast sensitivity function of the infant visual system. Vis. Res. 16: 867–869.

Banks, M. S., and Salapatek, P. Infant Form Perception: A New Approach to an Old Problem. Manuscript in preparation.

Barber, A. 1955. Embryology of the Human Eye. C. V. Mosby Co., St. Louis.

Barnet, A. B., Lodge, A., and Armington, J. C. 1965. Electroretinogram in newborn human infants. Science 148: 651–654.

Beasley, W. C. 1933a. An investigation of related problems in the vision of newborn infants. Psychol. Bull. 30: 626.

Beasley, W. C. 1933b. Visual pursuit in 109 white and 142 Negro newborn infants. Child Dev. 4: 106–120.

Blakemore, C. 1975. Developmental factors in the formation of feature extracting neurons. In F. O. Schmitt and F. G. Worden (eds.), The Neurosciences: Third Study Program. M.I.T. Press, Cambridge.

Bodis-Wollner, I. 1972. Visual acuity and contrast sensitivity in patients with cerebral lesions. Science 178: 769–771.

Bond, E. 1972. Perception of form by the human infant. Psychol. Bull. 77: 225–245.

Bonds, A. B., and Freeman, R. D. 1976. Development of optical quality in the kitten eye. Paper presented at the Association for Research in Vision and Ophthalmology, April 26–May 1, Sarasota, Florida.

Bornstein, M. H. 1976. Infants are trichromats. J. Exp. Child Psychol. 21:425–445.

Bornstein, M. H. Chromatic vision in infancy. In H. W. Reese and L. P. Lipsitt (eds.), Advances in Child Development and Behavior. Vol. 12. Academic Press, New York. In press.

Bornstein, M. H., Kessen, W., and Weiskopf, S. 1976. Color vision and hue categorization in young human infants. J. Exp. Psychol. Hum. Percept. Perf. 2: 115–129.

Bower, T. G. R., Broughton, J. M., and Moore, M. K. 1970. Demonstration of intention in the reaching behaviour of neonate humans. Nature 228: 679–681.

Brazelton, T. B., Scholl, M. L., and Robey, J. S. 1966. Visual responses in the newborn. Pediatrics 37: 284–290.

Bronson, G. W. 1974. The postnatal growth of visual capacity. Child Dev. 45: 873–890.

Burian, H. M., and von Noorden, G. K. 1974. Binocular Vision and Ocular Motility: Theory and Management of Strabismus. C. V. Mosby Co., St. Louis.

Campbell, F. W. 1954. The minimum quantity of light required to elicit the accommodation reflex in man. J. Physiol. 123: 357–366.

Campbell, F. W., Carpenter, R. H. S., and Levinson, J. Z. 1969. Visibility of aperiodic patterns compared with that of sinusoidal gratings. J. Physiol. 204: 283–298.

Campbell, F. W., and Green, D. G. 1965. Optical and retinal factors affecting visual resolution. J. Physiol. 181: 576–593.

Campbell, F. W., and Gubisch, R. W. 1966. Optical quality of the human eye. J. Physiol. 186: 558–578.

Campbell, F. W., and Gubisch, R. W. 1967. The effect of chromatic aberration on visual acuity. J. Physiol. 192: 345–358.

Campbell, F. W., and Robson, J. G. 1968. Application of Fourier analysis to the visibility of gratings. J. Physiol. (London) 197: 551–556.

Charman, W. N., and Tucker, J. 1977. Dependence of accommodation response on the spatial frequency spectrum of the observed object. Vis. Res. 17: 129–139.

Chase, W. P. 1937. Color vision in infants. J. Exp. Psychol. 20: 203–222.

Cohen, L. B., and Gelber, E. R. 1975. Infant visual memory. In L. B. Cohen and P. Salapatek (eds.), Infant Perception: From Sensation to Cognition. Vol. 1: Basic Visual Processes. Academic Press, New York.

Conel, J. L. 1939. The Postnatal Development of the Human Cerebral Cortex. Vol. 1: The Cortex of the Newborn. Harvard University Press, Cambridge, Massachusetts.

Conel, J. L. 1941. The Postnatal Development of the Human Cerebral Cortex. Vol. 2: The Cortex of the One-Month Infant. Harvard University Press, Cambridge, Massachusetts.

Conel, J. L. 1947. The Postnatal Development of the Human Cerebral Cortex. Vol. 3: The Cortex of the Three-Month Infant. Harvard University Press, Cambridge, Massachusetts.

Conel, J. L. 1951. The Postnatal Development of the Human Cerebral Cortex. Vol. 4: The Cortex of the Sixth-Month Infant. Harvard University Press, Cambridge, Massachusetts.

Conel, J. L. 1955. The Postnatal Development of the Human Cerebral Cortex. Vol. 5: The Cortex of the Fifteen-Month Infant. Harvard University Press, Cambridge, Massachusetts.

Conel, J. L. 1959. The Postnatal Development of the Human Cerebral Cortex. Vol. 6: The Cortex of the Twenty-Four-Month Infant. Harvard University Press, Cambridge, Massachusetts.

Conel, J. L. 1963. The Postnatal Development of the Human Cerebral Cortex. Vol. 7: The Cortex of the Four-Year Child. Harvard University Press, Cambridge, Massachusetts.

Cook, R. C., and Glasscock, R. E. 1951. Refractive and ocular findings in the newborn. Am. J. Ophthalmol. 34: 1407–1413.

Cornsweet, T. N. 1970. Visual Perception. Academic Press, New York.

Davidson, M., and Whiteside, J. A. 1971. Human brightness perception near sharp contours. J. Optic. Soc. Am. 61: 530–536.

Dayton, G. O., Jr., and Jones, M. H. 1964. Analysis of characteristics of fixation reflexes in infants by use of direct current electrooculography. Neurology 14: 1152–1156.

Dayton, G. O., Jr., Jones, M. H., Steele, B., and Rose, M. 1964a. Developmental study of coordinated eye movements in the human infant II: An electrooculographic study of the fixation reflex in the newborn. Arch. Ophthalmol. 71: 871–875.

Dayton, G. O., Jr., Jones, M. H., Aiu, P., Rawson, R. A., Steele, B., and Rose, M. 1964b. Developmental study of coordinated eye movements in the human infant I: Visual acuity in the newborn human: A study based on induced optokinetic nystagmus recorded by electrooculography. Arch. Ophthalmol. 71: 865–870.

Dews, P. B., and Wiesel, T. N. 1970. Consequences of monocular deprivation on visual behavior in kittens. J. Physiol. 206: 437–455.

Dobson, V. 1976a. Spectral sensitivity of the two-month infant as measured by the visually evoked cortical potential. Vis. Res. 16: 367–374.

Dobson, V. 1976b. VEP and behavioral measures of visual acuity in infants. Paper delivered at annual meeting of the American Academy of Optometry, December 11–14, Portland, Oregon.

Dobson, V., and Teller, D. Y. Assessment of visual acuity in human infants. In J. Armington, J. Krauskopf and B. Wooten (eds.), Visual Psychophysics: Its Physiological Basis. Academic Press, New York. In press.

Dobson, V., and Teller, D. Y. Visual acuity in human infants: A review and comparison of behavioral and electrophysiological studies. Vis. Res. In press.

Dobson, V., Teller, D. Y., and Belgum, J. Visual acuity in human infants assessed with stationary stripes and phase-alternated checkerboards. Vis. Res. In press.

Dodwell, P. C., Muir, D., and DiFranco, D. 1976. Responses of infants to visually presented objects. Science 194: 209–211.

Doris, J., Casper, M., and Poresky, R. 1967. Differential brightness thresholds in infancy. J. Exp. Child Psychol. 5: 522–535.

Doris, J., and Cooper, L. 1966. Brightness discrimination in infancy. J. Exp. Child Psychol. 3: 31–39.

Duke-Elder, S., and Abrams, D. 1970. System of Ophthalmology. Vol. 5. Henry Kimpton, London.

Emsley, H. H. 1953. Visual Optics. Vol. I.: Optics of Vision. Butterworths, London.

Enoch, J. M., and Rabinowicz, I. M. 1976. Early surgery and visual correction of an infant born with unilateral eye lens opacity. Doc. Ophthalmol. 41: 371–382.

Estevez, O., and Cavonius, C. R. 1976. Low-frequency attenuation in the detection of gratings: Sorting out the artifacts. Vis. Res. 16: 497–500.

Fagan, J. F. 1974. Infant color perception. Science 183: 973–975.

Fagan, J. F. 1975. Infant hue discrimination? Science 187: 227.

Fantz, R. L. 1958. Pattern vision in young infants. Psychol. Rec. 8: 43–47.

Fantz, R. L., Fagan, J. F., III, and Miranda, S. B. 1975. Early visual selectivity as a function of pattern variables, previous exposure, age from birth and conception, and expected cognitive deficit. In L. B. Cohen and P. Salapatek (eds.), Infant Perception: From Sensation to Cognition. Vol. 1.: Basic Visual Processes. Academic Press, New York.

Fantz, R. L., Ordy, J. M., and Udelf, M. S. 1962. Maturation of pattern vision in infants during the first six months. J. Comp. Physiol. Psychol. 55: 907–917.

Fiorentini, A., and Maffei, L. 1976. Spatial contrast sensitivity of myopic subjects. Vis. Res. 16: 437–438.

Fischel, H. 1969. Visual evoked potentials in prematures, newborns, infants, and children by stimulation with colored light. Electroencephalogr. Clin. Neurophysiol. 27 (abstr.): 660.

Fitzgerald, H. E. 1968. Autonomic pupillary reflex activity during early infancy and its relation to social and nonsocial visual stimuli. J. Exp. Child Psychol. 6: 470–482.

Freeman, R. D., Mitchell, D. E., and Millodot, M. A. 1972. Neural effect of partial visual deprivation in humans. Science 175: 1384–1386.

Freeman, R. D., and Thibos, L. N. 1975. Contrast sensitivity in humans with abnormal visual experience. J. Physiol. 247: 687–710.

Frey, R. G. 1953. Die Beziehung zwischen sehschaerfe und Tiefensehschaerfe. Wien. Med. Wochenschr. 103: 436–438.

Gibson, E. J. 1969. Principles of Perceptual Learning and Development. Appleton-Century-Crofts, New York.

Gibson, J. J. 1966. The Senses Considered as Perceptual Systems. Houghton-Mifflin, Boston.

Glickstein, M., and Millodot, M. 1970. Retinoscopy and eye size. Science 168: 605–606.

Goodman, J. W. 1968. Introduction to Fourier Optics. McGraw-Hill, New York.

Gordon, F. R., and Yonas, A. 1976. Sensitivity to binocular depth information in infants. J. Exp. Child Psychol. 22: 413–422.

Gorman, J. J., Cogan, D. G., and Gellis, S. S. 1957. An apparatus for grading the visual acuity of infants on the basis of opticokinetic nystagmus. Pediatrics 19: 1088–1092.

Gorman, J. J., Cogan, D. G., and Gellis, S. S. 1959. A device for testing visual acuity in infants. Sight Sav. Rev. 29: 80–84.

Graham, C. H. 1965. Color: Data and theories. In C. H. Graham (ed.), Vision and Visual Perception. John Wiley and Sons, New York.

Green, D. G. 1970. Regional variations in the visual acuity for interference fringes on the retina. J. Physiol. 207: 351–356.

Green, D. G., and Campbell, F. W. 1965. Effect of focus on the visual response to a sinusoidally modulated spatial stimulus. J. Optic. Soc. Am. 55: 1154–1157.

Gresty, M. A. 1974. Coordination of head and eye movements to fixate continuous and intermittent targets. Vis. Res. 14: 395–403.

Gstalder, R. J., and Green, D. G. 1971. Laser interferometric acuity in amblyopia. J. Pediatr. Ophthalmol. 8: 251–256.

Guernsey, M. 1929. A quantitative study of the eye reflexes in infants. Psychol. Bull. 26: 160–161.

Haith, M. M. Visual competence in early infancy. In R. Held, H. W. Leibowitz, and H. L. Teuber (eds.), Handbook of Sensory Physiology. Vol. 8. Springer-Verlag, New York. In press.

Haith, M. M., and Campos, J. J. 1977. Human infancy. Annu. Rev. Psychol. 28: 251–293.

Harris, L., Atkinson, J., and Braddick, O. 1976. Visual contrast sensitivity of a 6-month-old infant measured by the evoked potential. Nature 264: 570–571.

Harris, P., and Macfarlane, A. The growth of the effective visual field from birth to seven weeks. J. Exp. Child Psychol. 18: 340–348.

Harter, M. R., Deaton, F. K., and Odom, J. V. 1976. Pattern visual evoked potentials in infants. In J. E. Desmedt (ed.), Visual Evoked Potentials in Man: New Developments. Clarendon Press, Oxford.

Harter, M. R., Deaton, F. K., and Odom, J. V. 1977. Maturation of evoked potentials and visual preference in 6 45-day-old-infants: Effects of check size, visual acuity, and refractive error. Electroencephalogr. Clin. Neurophysiol. 42: 595–607.

Harter, M. R., and Suitt, C. D. 1970. Visually-evoked cortical responses and pattern vision in the infant: A longitudinal study. Psychonom. Sci. 18: 235–237.

Haynes, H., White, B. L., and Held, R. 1965. Visual accommodation in human infants. Science 148: 528–530.

Hecht, S., and Mintz, E. U. 1939. The visibility of single lines at various illuminations and the basis of visual resolution. J. Gen. Physiol. 22: 593–612.

Hendrickson, A., and Kupfer, C. 1976. The histogenesis of the fovea in the macaque monkey. Invest. Ophthalmol. 15: 746–756.

Hershenson, M. 1964. Visual discrimination in the human newborn. J. Comp. Physiol. Psychol. 58: 270–276.

Hershenson, M. 1967. Development of the perception of form. Psychol. Bull. 67: 326–336.

Hershenson, M. 1970. The development of visual perceptual systems. In H. Moltz (ed.), The Ontogeny of Vertebrate Behavior. Academic Press, New York.

Hess, R. F., and Howell, E. R. 1977. The threshold contrast sensitivity function in strabismic amblyopia: Evidence for a two type classification. Vis. Res. 17: 1049–1055.

Hickey, T. L. 1977. Human lateral geniculate nucleus: Laminar patterns and postnatal development. Paper delivered at a dedicatory symposium for the College of Optometry, University of Houston, March 28–31, Houston, Texas.

Hirsch, H. V. B., and Spinelli, D. N. 1970. Visual experience modifies distribution of horizontally and vertically oriented receptive fields in cats. Science 168: 869–871.

Hohmann, A., and Creutzfeldt, O. D. 1975. Squint and the development of binocularity in humans. Nature 254: 613–614.

Hollenberg, M. J., and Spira, A. W. 1973. Human retinal development: Ultrastructure of the outer retina. Am. J. Anat. 137: 357–377.

Hosaka, A. 1963. The ocular findings in the premature infants, especially on the premature signs. Jpn. J. Ophthalmol. 7: 77–81.

Hsia, Y., and Graham, C. H. 1965. Color blindness. In C. H. Graham (ed.), Vision and Visual Perception. John Wiley and Sons, New York.

Hubel, D. H., and Wiesel, T. N. 1965. Binocular interaction in striate cortex of kittens reared with artificial squint. J. Neurophysiol. 28: 1041–1059.

Hubel, D. H., Wiesel, T. N., and LeVay, F. 1976. Functional architecture of area 17 in normal and monocularly deprived macaque monkeys. Cold Spring Harbor Symp. Quant. Biol. 40: 581–589.

Ikeda, H., and Wright, M. J. 1975. Spatial and temporal properties of "sustained" and "transient" neurones in area 17 of the cat's visual cortex. Exp. Brain Res. 22: 363–383.

Jones, M. C. 1926. The development of early behavior patterns in young children. Pedagog. Sem. 33: 537–585.

Julesz, B. 1971. Foundations of cyclopean perception. University of Chicago Press, Chicago.

Karmel, B. Z., and Maisel, E. B. 1975. A neuronal activity model for infant visual attention. In L. B. Cohen and P. Salapatek (eds.), Infant perception: From sensation to cognition. Vol. 1: Basic Visual Processes. Academic Press, New York.

Kaufman, L. 1974. Sight and mind. Oxford University Press, New York.

Kelly, D. H. 1969. Flickering patterns and lateral inhibition. J. Optic. Soc. Am. 59: 1361–1370.

Kelly, D. H. 1975a. How many bars make a grating? Vis. Res. 15: 625–626.

Kelly, D. H. 1975b. Spatial frequency selectivity in the retina. Vis. Res. 15: 665–672.

Kelly, D. H., and Magnuski, H. S. 1975. Pattern detection and the two-dimensional Fourier transform: Circular targets. Vis. Res. 15: 911–915.

Kessen, W., Haith, M. M., and Salapatek, P. H. 1970. Human infancy: A bibliography and guide. In P. H. Mussen (ed.), Carmichael's Manual of Child Psychology. Vol. 1 3rd ed. Wiley, New York.

Kiff, R. D., and Lepard, C. 1966. Visual responses of premature infants. Arch. Ophthalmol. 75: 631–633.

Larroche, J. 1966. Development of the nervous system in early life. Part 2: The development of the central nervous system during intrauterine life. In F. Falkner (ed.), Human Development. Saunders, Philadelphia.

Larsen, J. F. 1971. The saggital growth of the eye. IV. Ultrasonic measurement of the axial length of the eye from birth to puberty. Acta Ophthalmol. 49: 873–886.

Linfoot, E. H. 1964. Fourier Methods for Optical Image Evaluation. The Focal Press, London and New York.

Ling, B. C. 1942. A genetic study of sustained visual fixation and associated behavior in the human infant from birth to six months. Pedagog. Sem. J. Genet. Psychol. 61: 227–277.

Lodge, A., Armington, J. C., Barnet, A. B., Shanks, B. L., and Newcomb, C. N. 1969. Newborn infants' electroretinograms and evoked electroencephalographic responses to orange and white light. Child Dev. 40: 267–293.

Lowenstein, O., and Loewenfeld, I. E. 1969. The pupil. In H. Davson (ed.), The Eye. Vol. 3: Muscular Mechanisms. Academic Press, New York.

Lowry, E. M., and DePalma, J. J. 1961. Sine-wave responses of the visual system. I. The Mach phenomenon. J. Optic. Soc. Am. 51: 740–746.

Macfarlane, A., Harris, P., and Barnes, I. 1976. Central and peripheral vision in early infancy. J. Exp. Child Psychol. 21: 532–538.

McGinnis, J. M. 1930. Eye movements and optic nystagmus in early infancy. Genet. Psychol. Monogr. 8: 321–430.

McKusick, V. A. 1962. On the x chromosome of man. Quart. Rev. Biol. 37: 69–175.

Mann, I. C. 1964. The Development of the Human Eye. British Medical Association, London.

Mansfield, R. S. 1974. Neural basis of orientation perception in primate vision. Science 186: 1133–1135.

Marg, E., Freeman, D. N., Peltzman, P., and Goldstein, P. J. 1976. Visual acuity development in human infants: Evoked potential measurements. Invest. Ophthalmol. 15: 150–153.

Maurer, D. 1974. The development of binocular convergence in infants. Unpublished doctoral dissertation, University of Minnesota. Minneapolis.

Maurer, D. 1975. Infant visual perception: Methods of study. In L. B. Cohen and P. Salapatek (eds.), Infant Perception: From Sensation to Cognition. Vol. 1: Basic Visual Processes. Academic Press, New York.

Mendlewicz, J., Fleiss, J. L., and Fieve, R. R. 1972. Evidence for X linkage in the transmission of manic-depressive illness. J. Am. Med. Assoc. 222: 1624–1627.

Millodot, M. 1972. Retinoscopy and the refraction of infants. Ophthalmic Optic. Nov. 11: 1130–1132.

Miranda, S. 1970. Visual abilities and pattern preferences of premature infants and full-term neonates. J. Exp. Child Psychol. 10: 189–205.

Mitchell, D. E., Freeman, R. D., Millodot, M., and Haegerstrom, G. 1973. Meridional amblyopia: Evidence for modification of the human visual system by early visual experience. Vis. Res. 13: 535–558.

Mitchell, D. E., and Ware, C. 1974. Interocular transfer of a visual after-effect in normal and stereoblind humans. J. Physiol. 236: 707–721.

Mitchell, D. E., and Wilkinson, F. 1974. The effect of early astigmatism on the visual resolution of gratings. J. Physiol. 243: 739–756.

Morgan, J. B., and Morgan, S. S. 1944. Infant learning as a developmental index. J. Genet. Psychol. 65: 281–289.

Movshon, J. A., Chambers, B. E. I., and Blakemore, C. 1972. Interocular transfer in normal humans, and those who lack stereopsis. Perception 1: 483–490.

Muir, D. W., and Mitchell, D. E. 1973. Visual resolution and experience: Acuity deficits in cats following early selective visual deprivation. Science 180: 420–422.

Munn, N. L. 1955. The Evolution and Growth of Human Behavior. Houghton Mifflin Co., Boston.

Munsinger, H., and Banks, M. S. 1974. Pupillometry as a measure of visual sensitivity among infants, young children, and adults. Dev. Psychol. 10: 677–682.

Ogle, K. N. 1962. Spatial localization through binocular vision. In H. Davson (ed.), The Eye. Vol. 4: Visual Optics and the Optical Space Sense. Part 2: The optical space sense. Academic Press, New York.

Oster, H. 1975. Color perception in ten-week-old infants. Paper presented at the biennial meeting of the Society for Research in Child Development, April, Denver, Colorado.

Parks, M. M. 1966. Growth of the eye and development of vision. In S. D. Liebman and S. S. Gellis (eds.), The Pediatrician's Ophthalmology. C. V. Mosby, St. Louis.

Patel, A. R., Natarajan, T. S., and Abreu, R. 1970. Refractive errors in full-term newborn babies. J. All-India Ophthalmol. Soc. 18: 59–63.

Peeples, D. R. 1976. Hereditary color deficiencies: Are they congenital? Paper presented at the Spring meeting, Association for Research in Vision and Ophthalmology, April, Sarasota, Florida.

Peeples, D. R., and Teller, D. Y. 1975. Color vision and brightness discrimination in two-month-old human infants. Science 189: 1102–1103.

Peeples, D. R., and Teller, D. Y. 1978. White-adapted photopic spectral sensitivity in human infants. Vis. Res. 18: 49–59.

Peiper, A. 1927. Über die Helligkeits—Und Farbenempfindungen der Frühge burten. Archiv für Kinderheilk. 80: 1–20.

Peiper, A. 1963. Cerebral Function in Infancy and Childhood. Consultants Bureau, New York.

Pettigrew, J. D. 1974. The effect of visual experience on the development of stimulus specificity by kitten cortical neurones. J. Physiol. 237: 49–74.

Pick, H. L. and Pick, A. D. 1970. Sensory and perceptual development. In P. H. Mussen (ed.), Carmichael's Manual of Child Psychology. Vol. 1. 3rd ed. John Wiley and Sons, New York.

Pipp, S. L., and Haith, M. M. 1977. Infant visual scanning of two- and three-dimensional forms. Child. Dev. 48: 1640–1644.

Polikanina, R. I. 1968. Development of color vision in newborn infants. Zh. Vyssh. Nerv. Deiat. 18: 1050–1059.

Pratt, K. L., Nelson, A. K., and Sun, K. H. 1930. The behavior of the newborn infant. Ohio State Univ. Stud. 10: 44–78.

Rabinowicz, T. 1964. The cerebral cortex of the premature infant of the 8th month. Prog. Brain Res. 4: 39–86.

Rabinowicz, T. 1967. Techniques for the establishment of an atlas of the cerebral cortex of the premature. In A. Minkowski (ed.), Regional Development of the Brain in Early Life. Blackwell Scientific Publications, Oxford.

Ratliff, F. 1965. Mach Bands: Quantitative Studies on Neural Networks in the Retina. Holden-Day, San Francisco.

Regan, D. 1972. Evoked Potentials in Psychology, Sensory Physiology and Clinical Medicine. Chapman and Hall, London.

Richards, W. 1975. Visual space perception. In E. C. Carterette and M. P. Friedman (eds.), Handbook of Perception. Vol. 5: Seeing. Academic Press, New York.

Rieser, J., Yonas, A. and Wikner, K. 1976. Radial localization of odors by human newborns. Child Dev. 47: 856–859.

Riggs, L. A. 1965. Visual acuity. In C. H. Graham (ed.), Vision and Visual Perception. Wiley, New York.

Robinson, D. A. 1968. Eye movement control in primates. Science 161: 1219–1224.

Rusoff, A. C., and Dubin, M. W. 1977. Development of receptive-field properties of retinal ganglion cells in kittens. J. Neurophysiol. 40: 1188–1198.

Salapatek, P. 1975. Pattern perception in early infancy. In L. B. Cohen and P. Salapatek (eds.), Infant Perception: From Sensation to Cognition. Vol. 1: Basic Visual Processes. Academic Press, New York.

Salapatek, P., Bechtold, A. G., and Bergman, J. 1977. Pupillary response in 1- and 2-month-old infants. Paper delivered at meetings of the Psychonomic Society, November, Washington, D.C.

Salapatek, P., Bechtold, A. G., and Bushnell, E. W. 1976. Infant visual acuity as a function of viewing distance. Child Dev. 47: 860–863.

Salapatek, P., Haith, M., Maurer, D., and Kessen, W. 1972. Error in the corneal reflection technique: A note on Slater & Findlay. J. Exp. Child Psychol. 14: 493–497.

Savoy, R. L., and McCann, J. J. 1975. Visibility of low spatial frequency sinewave targets: Dependence on number of cycles. J. Optic. Soc. Am. 65: 343–350.

Scammon, R. E., and Wilmer, H. A. 1950. Growth of the components of the human eyeball. II. Comparison of the calculated volumes of the eyes of the newborn and of adults, and their components. Arch. Ophthalmol. 43: 620–636.

Schade, J. P., Meeter, K., and van Groeningen, W. B. 1962. Maturational aspects of the dendrites of the human cerebral cortex. Acta Morphol. Neerl. Scand. 5: 37–48.

Schade, O. H. 1956. Optical and photoelectric analog of the eye. J. Optic. Soc. Am. 46: 721–739.

Schaller, M. J. 1975. Chromatic vision in human infants: Conditioned operant fixation to 'hues' of varying intensity. Bull. Psychonom. Soc. 6: 39–42.

Schulman, C. A. 1973. Eye movements in infants using DC recording. Neuro-pädiatrie 4: 76–87.

Slater, A. M., and Findlay, J. M. 1972a. The corneal-reflection technique: A reply to Salapatek, Haith, Maurer, and Kessen. J. Exp. Child. Psychol. 14: 497–499.

Slater, A. M., and Findlay, J. M. 1972b. The measurement of fixation position in the newborn baby. J. Exp. Child Psychol. 14: 349–364.

Slater, A. M., and Findlay, J. M. 1975. Binocular fixation in the newborn baby. J. Exp. Child Psychol. 20: 248–273.

Smith, J. M. 1936. The relative brightness values of three hues for newborn infants. Univ. Iowa Stud. Child Welfare 12: 91–140.

Sokol, S. 1976. Visually evoked potentials: Theory, techniques and clinical applications. Surv. Ophthalmol. 21: 18–44.

Sokol, S. Measurement of infant visual acuity from pattern reversal evoked potentials. Vis. Res. In press.

Sokol, S., and Dobson, V. 1976. Pattern reversal visually evoked potentials in infants. Invest. Ophthalmol. 15: 58–62.

Spears, W. C. 1964. Assessment of visual preference and discrimination in the four-month-old infant. J. Comp. Physiol. Psychol. 57: 381–386.

Spears, W., and Hohle, R. 1967. Sensory and perceptual processes in infants. In Y. Brackbill (ed.), Infancy and Early Childhood. The Free Press, New York.

Taylor, D. M. 1972. Is congenital esotropia functionally curable? Trans. Am. Ophthalmol. Soc. 70: 529–576.

Teller, D. Y., Morse, R., Borton, R., and Regal, D. 1974. Visual acuity for vertical and diagonal gratings in human infants. Vis. Res. 14: 1433–1439.

Teller, D. Y., Peeples, D. R., and Sekel, M. 1978. Discrimination of chromatic from white light by two-month-old human infants. Vis. Res. 18: 41–48.

Thomas, H. 1973. Unfolding the baby's mind: The infant's selection of visual stimuli. Psychol. Rev. 80: 468–488.

Toates, F. M. 1972. Accommodation function of the human eye. Physiol. Rev. 52: 828–863.

Trincker, D., and Trincker, I. 1955. Die ontogenetische Entwicklung des Helligkeitsund Farbensehens beim Menschen. I. Die Entwicklung des Helligkeitssehens. [The ontogenetic development of brightness and color vision in man. I. The development of brightness.] Graefes Archiv Ophthalmol. 156: 519–534. (Translated and reprinted in Y. Brackbill and G. G. Thompson (eds.). 1967. Behavior in Infancy and Early Childhood. The Free Press, New York.

Tronick, E. 1972. Stimulus control and the growth of the infant's effective visual field. Percept. Psychophys. 11: 373–375.

Tronick, E., and Clanton, C. 1971. Infant looking patterns. Vis. Res. 11: 1479–1486.

Tulunay-Keesey, U., and Jones, R. M. The effect of micromovements of the eye and exposure duration on contrast sensitivity. Vis. Res. 16: 481–488.

van Meeteren, A., and Vos, J. J. 1968. Applicability of Fourier transformation upon contrast sensitivity functions. Institute for Perception RVO-TNO, Report No. IZF, 1968-20.

Van Nes, F. L., and Bouman, M. A. 1965. The effects of wavelength and luminance on visual modulation transfer. Excerpta, Medica, International Congress, Serial no. 125.

von Bekesy, G. 1967. Sensory Inhibition. Princeton University Press, Princeton, N.J.

von Frisch, K. 1964. Bees: Their Vision, Chemical Senses, and Language. Cornell University Press, Ithaca, N.Y.

von Noorden, G. K. 1973. Histological studies of the visual system in monkeys with experimental amblyopia. Invest. Ophthalmol. 12: 727–738.

von Noorden, G. K., Dowling, J. E., and Ferguson, D. C. 1970. Experimental amblyopia in monkeys. I. Behavioral studies of stimulus deprivation amblyopia. Arch. Ophthalmol. 84: 206–214.

von Senden, M. 1960. Space and Sight. Translated by P. Heath. Methuen, New York.

Wald, G. 1945. Human vision and the spectrum. Science 101: 653–658.

Westheimer, G. 1963. Optical and neural factors in the formation of the retinal image. J. Optic. Soc. Am. 53: 86–93.

Westheimer, G. 1972. Visual acuity and spatial modulation thresholds. In H. Autrum, R. Jung, W. R. Lowenstein, D. M. McKay, and H. L. Teuber (eds.), Handbook of sensory physiology. Vol. 7, part 4. Springer-Verlag, New York.

Westheimer, G., and Campbell, F. W. 1962. Light distribution in the image formed by the living human eye. J. Optic. Soc. Am. 52: 1040–1045.

White, B. L. 1971. Human Infants: Experience and Psychological Development. Prentice-Hall, Inc., Englewood Cliffs, N.J.

Wickelgren, L. W. 1967. Convergence in the human newborn. J. Exp. Child Psychol. 5: 74–85.

Wiesel, T. N., and Hubel, D. H. 1963a. Effects of visual deprivation on morphology and physiology of cells in the cat's lateral geniculate body. J. Neurophysiol. 26: 978–993.

Wiesel, T. N., and Hubel, D. H. 1963b. Single-cell responses in striate cortex of kittens deprived of vision in one eye. J. Neurophysiol. 28: 1060–1072.

Wiesel, T. N., and Raviola, E. 1977. Myopia and eye enlargement after neonatal lid fusion in monkeys. Nature 266: 66–68.

Wilson, J. R., and Sherman, S. M. 1977. Differential effects of early monocular deprivation on binocular and monocular segments of cat striate cortex. J. Neurophysiol. 40: 891–903.

Wolff, P. H. 1959. Observations on newborn infants. Psychosom. Med. 21: 110–118.

Wood, I. C. J., and Tomlinson, A. 1975. The accommodative response in amblyopia. Am. J. Optom. Physiol. Opt. 52: 243–247.

Wooten, B. R. 1975. Infant hue discrimination? Science 187: 275–277.

Yakovlev, P. I., and Le Cours, A. 1967. The myelogenetic cycles of regional maturation of the brain. In A. Minkowski (ed.), Regional Development of the Brain in Early Life. F. A. Davis Co., Philadelphia.

Yonas, A., and Pick, H. L. 1975. An approach to the study of infant space perception. In L. B. Cohen and P. Salapatek (eds.), Infant Perception: From Sensation to Cognition. Vol. 2: Perception of Space, Speech, and Sound. Academic Press, New York.

Discussion Summary: Early Assessment

Anne D. Pick

The theme of this conference is optimistic, but achieving its implied goal may be extraordinarily difficult. That goal is to assess in infancy and early childhood the communicative and cognitive functioning of children who subsequently will be, in some way, developmentally disabled. The purpose of such assessment, of course, is to intervene in the children's development so as to design remediation and, eventually, to prevent subsequent problems. The task set by this goal is rather like trying to assess the functioning of caterpillars in order to identify those butterflies that will subsequently be disabled. The human case is even more difficult, however, because we may be deceived by the fact that babies at least look like miniature adults. This resemblance—especially if it is superficial—may mask the fact that the metamorphosis from infancy to adulthood is probably at least as profound as that of the caterpillar to the butterfly. We assume and believe that there is continuity of development, but, as both Horowitz and Scott document, our present measures provide meager evidence for our assumption. Nevertheless, a belief in continuity is the basis for attempting to carry out early assessment for problem remediation and prevention in the first place.

RESEARCH STRATEGIES AND ETHICS IN EARLY ASSESSMENT

Assessment for intervention implies, and requires, an understanding of relations between many aspects of early communicative and cognitive functioning and later development. As the authors of all four papers on early assessment have noted, there are critical gaps in our knowledge of these relations among those complex cognitive processes that are most likely the very processes we must understand in order to remediate the problems that prevent many children from making normal or even adequate progress in school.

Preparation of this paper was supported by a program project grant from The National Institute of Child Health and Human Development to the Institute of Child Development, University of Minnesota (HD05027).

Generally, there are two strategies available for learning how early sensory functioning is related to later learning problems. One is to identify and describe the learning problems, and then to seek their precursors earlier in development. Such a strategy is like working backward from the butterfly to the caterpillar. A second strategy is to seek thorough understanding of the young in order to discover relations between early functioning and subsequent development. By this strategy we would seek knowledge of the caterpillar in hopes of discovering continuities between it and the adult form of the species. Both strategies are reflected in the work on early sensory functioning discussed by Salapatek and by Wilson, although the second strategy clearly dominates studies of infants' vision reviewed by Salapatek, as well as studies of intersensory functioning.

Horowitz and Scott both assert that basic research directed toward understanding of development is essential for successful assessment for prevention and knowledgeable intervention. Also, both suggest that successful assessment and intervention are inseparable conceptually, and that both are also inseparable from research connected with how development occurs. The kind of research that is generated from this position requires consideration of some ethical issues in the conduct of research with infants, young children, and their families.

Researchers necessarily intrude into family privacy when they make direct observations of infants' behavior in the setting in which that behavior normally occurs, instead of in the laboratory. The degree of intrusion that is justified may depend, in part at least, on the usefulness of the knowledge obtained for intervention design and problem prevention.

Although researchers' intrusions into the privacy of families are unavoidable, evaluative judgments about those families and the upbringing they provide their children can be appropriately eschewed. Our present state of knowledge about the developmental outcomes of growing up in one or another family setting does not support precise predictions and appraisals for individual children and particular families. Obviously, researchers ought to intervene when they identify an infant or child who has a problem. That is quite different, however, from a judgmental evaluation of that child's family. What is honestly justified by our current knowledge is that researchers seek the cooperation of families in an enterprise that has as its goal the understanding of how development occurs.

There are ethical issues inherent in the concepts of risk and risk registries discussed by Scott. He has pointed out that many children who eventually will have school problems will not be identified early by the use of such registries. In addition, because prediction of most developmental problems is far from perfect, except in extreme and severe cases, many children may be identified as potentially disabled whose course of development would, in fact, be perfectly normal. Identifying children as at risk for developing problems that, among other things, will interfere with their progress in school may have profound effects on their parents' behavior toward them and expectations for them, as well as on the children's own view of themselves and their capabilities. These effects may impede the children's development and create needless problems for them. On the other hand, where precise prediction is possible, as in the case of some hearing disorders, early identification can allow appropriate intervention with remediation to minimize the effects of the disorder—both on the children's functioning and on their self-evaluations.

A general ethical issue that emerges from research on assessment and intervention is the role of the researcher in social planning and decision making. On the one hand, there are scientists who hold to the view that they should have no role in the formation of social policy except to make available their research findings. According to this view, we should focus, for the present, on acquiring knowledge about the processes of development, and even suspend assessment and intervention until those processes are more thoroughly understood. On the other hand, there are scientists who believe they do properly have a role in formulating social policy, and that they cannot avoid one even if they wished. They believe that their first responsibility is to disseminate and interpret research findings and to urge their use appropriately in social planning. However, they also believe that scientists must be involved in setting research priorities, and in educating the public about the nature of behavioral research, the rules of inference making, and in social policy decision making itself.

THE VALIDITY OF EARLY ASSESSMENT: WHAT TO ASSESS? AND WHY?

Both Horowitz and Scott emphasize that the most widely used assessment measures, those constructed in the psychometric tradition, are not the most appropriate for early identification of developmental problems. Although these are standardized and are probably the most reliable measures, they do not provide information about behavior processes, i.e., how infants or young children solve the problems or accomplish the tasks required by the tests. In order to predict outcomes in terms of disability and to design appropriate intervention strategies, it will be necessary to assess not just *what* infants can and cannot do at a given chronological age, but *how* they do what they do. We need to understand the processes of behavior and its development, i.e., *how* it happens rather than the present *outcome* of development, because only the former will allow the design of appropriate and effective intervention. Furthermore, because of individual variation in rates of development, and the fact that the timing of transitions in development vary for different children, it is difficult to acquire information allowing for prediction of developmental outcome from a cross-sectional comparison.

The inadequacy of the psychometric model for early assessment and intervention reflects the fact that standardized tests have been misused by being used for too many purposes. For example, they are used to indicate the developmental status of individual children in the terms of chronological age norms, to identify and describe children whose development is abnormal, and to evaluate the effects of intervention programs. The same instrument cannot be adequate for all these purposes. Instruments for different purposes have to be differently constructed, and infant tests have not been constructed with a view toward developing intervention strategies.

Unfortunately, it is not as easy to describe and construct an appropriate instrument for identifying babies whose development may not be normal as it is to specify why the most-used existing instruments are inadequate for the task. The difficult problem to solve is what to measure, because as Scott and others have noted, the meaning of specific isolated behaviors changes with development. Behaviors such as looking or head-turning, that are *elicited* as responses to specific isolated events in early infancy, subsequently reflect the baby's ability to initiate search and exploration of the environment. Horowitz has noted that infants have a much more extensive behavior repertoire that can be used for assessment than has been assumed previously. She has also pointed out that, with more sensitive measures, we can observe individual differences, even in very young babies. This may make assessing the course of infant development even more difficult as the wide range of normal individual differences becomes more apparent. As we develop increasingly sensitive assessment devices for descriptive observations of early behavior, the identification of deviant behavior may be accomplished with greater accuracy, but also with greater difficulty.

Awareness of consistent individual differences, even in infancy, implies the need to assess directly behavior variability across infants. Horowitz has elaborated on the need to consider the match between infant characteristics and the environment in which that infant functions and develops. The infant's setting itself affects the baby's behavior in that setting, and may be an important determinant of the observed early individual differences. An analysis of behavior settings in terms of those that seem to encourage or discourage certain kinds of behaviors should be extremely useful once there are behaviors identified that are precursors of aspects of later development. Furthermore, important information may also be gained by observing the variability across settings of individual infants' behavior. Are there consistent individual differences in *variability* of behavior in different settings? If so, does high variability imply vulnerability to environmental impact? Or instead, does it reflect flexibility and adaptability? Information about such individual differences might prove useful or even crucial for identifying babies whose development may not be normal.

As Horowitz discussed, one of the problems that has plagued those engaged in early infant assessment for prediction is the absence of any clear relations between behavior in infancy and later. Obviously, this problem of the validity of early assessment is of critical relevance to the goals of this conference. One implication, of course, is that earlier assumptions about what is developing during infancy were too simplistic.

The validity of infant assessment must be clearly established if it is to be used to detect babies who will have problems and design intervention for them. It would be worthwhile to determine whether infants' sensitivity to relatively complex, naturally occurring stimuli and events in meaningful settings might be more predictive of the course of their subsequent development than is their sensitivity to some of the items currently used for assessment and diagnosis. There already is some information available about infant's responsiveness to a visual cliff, to looming or apparent impending collision, to animate versus inanimate motion, to human voices, and to human speech. Horowitz (1975) has used an intermodal procedure to assess infants' attention to auditory events on the ground that intermodal functioning reflects important aspects of an infant's natural learning environment. She observed that the babies recovered attention to a visual stimulus after she introduced a meaningful auditory stimulus—the sound of their mothers' voice—and the babies thereby demonstrated sensitivity to aspects of human voices. It is possible that sensitivity to social stimuli—to such things as faces and voices—are implicated in normal social development, and that profoundly atypical development might be accompanied by relatively greater sensitivity to non-social stimuli. The several reports made by now of imitation by extremely young infants suggest that there may ordinarily develop very early a synchrony to many parent-infant interactions.

SENSITIVITY AND SENSORY DEFICITS

A child's sensitivity to pure tones and to meaningless, although complex, noise does not predict as well as would be desired whether the child can extract information from speech, vision, or if he can, how he does so. With regard to vision it is simply not known in any detail how the assessment of various kinds of simple acuity are related to functional vision and visual perception. For assessing children's hearing, it may still turn out that even though pure tones and complex noise do not provide information about language and communication, they do provide information about the auditory system. Children with hearing impairments might respond like nonimpaired children to meaningful speech and other sounds, and it may be only their differential sensitivity to the simple pure tone sounds that allows for their identification and remediation of the impairment. Still, the notable lack of relation, in many areas of functioning, between predictions from early assessment and subsequent development makes consideration of the importance for prediction of naturally occurring behaviors and settings at least reasonable.

It has been suggested that there is a potential disadvantage in removing the stimulus dimension for which sensitivity is being assessed from the setting in which it normally occurs. For example, the adequacy of amplification for remediating a hearing impairment is usually evaluated in a setting without reverberation. However, the condition in which an amplifier nearly always is used is a reverberating one. One influence of laboratory research on assessment—in addition to providing new knowledge about how children function—is to develop technology and methodology that gets transferred from the laboratory to the clinic. However, the quest for precision in measurement of sensory functioning might preclude proper evaluation of the tacit assumption that the isolatable, separable stimulus parameters are the ones most appropriately assessed, even for making inferences and predictions about complex tasks like speech or communication.

It is obviously not easy to decide what the most appropriate indices of sensitivity are and in what setting they should be obtained. Requiring that a specific response be made in the presence of a stimulus event may mask sensitivity that could be demonstrated by requiring only a simple discrimination between that event and another. Humans whose sight is restored after they have been deprived of vision for long periods of time often recognize many visible objects that previously they only handled. On the other hand, sensitivity assessed passively may not be most relevant for evaluating how an individual can function in complex tasks and settings that require *using* the modality in question. Thus, humans with restored sight after many years of blindness find it difficult or impossible to perform many tasks requiring visually guided behavior. The facts of their visual pattern recognition are not informative about their active functional visual perception. In assessing sensitivity to various stimulus dimensions and events, it therefore may be necessary to ask, "Sensitivity for what?" The answer to that question may then determine what is the *appropriate* index of that sensitivity. The appropriate index may often be the behavior that is based on the stimulus event or the action that is guided by it. In other words, one wants to know what the *meaning* of the event is in terms of actions or behaviors.

Early sensory deficits can logically have a variety of different influences on subsequent cognitive development, and in order to design appropriate intervention programs it will be necessary to understand better what these different effects are. Many profound sensory problems are technically easy to identify in contrast to more subtle problems that are also more difficult to detect. However, the specific effects of even the profound problems are not clearly identifiable. It is obvious that blind babies will show no visual response to light. The cognitive outcome is not so obvious. For example, a sensory deficit may be a concomitant of a more general one, e.g., some type of brain damage. In such a case, the effects on cognitive development may differ from those in which the sensory deficit is not also accompanied by a central deficit. On the other hand, the sensory deficit may by itself be responsible for lack of input or activity that is necessary for normal development. For example, the cognitive development of babies blind from birth may not be generally slowed, but it may be that their spatial abilities, their knowledge about the representation of space, are adversely affected by their lack of vision. Another example may be found in the case of deaf children, who typically do not acquire language as early as normally hearing children do. Their retarded language development may, in turn, profoundly affect their cognitive development and functioning. In order to design appropriate interventions, we need much more precise information about what types of cognitive problems are the result of what types of peripheral sensory deficits. Wilson made the point that assessment and intervention cannot wait until the basic processes of sensory development are well understood. However, the case of hearing, about which he made the point, may be special because we currently have *sufficient* knowledge to identify appropriate interventions. Salapatek has also made the point that deficiencies in the visual system have important effects on the quality of visual perception, but in order to design appropriate interventions, we need much more knowledge about exactly what those effects are and how they occur, i.e., the processes by which they develop.

INTERMODAL FUNCTIONING

Because much ordinary perceptual and cognitive functioning is intermodal, it is important to ask how intermodal relations develop. Also, because the infant's everyday environment includes stimulation for several modalities, we need to understand how that stimulation is organized, in order to understand the infant's effective environment. Is intermodal functioning possible from an early age, or must mechanisms of contiguity and association come into play in order for modalities to function in an integrated way?

Knowledge about how sensory systems function together is important to attain in order to remediate problems for children whose functioning in one or more modalities is impaired. On the one hand, there is the view espoused by Turkewitz (1976), among others, that information or input to different senses from the same source becomes associated via contiguity. By such a process, a variety of relations among modalities are established: e.g., dominance, compensatory, equivalence. Likewise, disabilities in one sensory system have a variety of possible consequences for functioning in other modalities. For example, the fact of a disability in one system may simply be irrelevant for other systems, or one system may be able to compensate for a disability in another system. Turkewitz has found that kittens whose whiskers were shaved off at birth, and who thus were deprived of some tactile input about surfaces and objects, discriminated depth visually at an earlier age than kittens not so deprived. Still another outcome of a disability in one system is difficulty in using others as well. There may be instances in which the development of competence in one system requires prior proficiency in another. Therefore, multisensory deficits may have either common or sequential etiology.

The most controversial aspect of Turkewitz's position is probably the assertion that intersensory relations are established according to a process of association-by-contiguity, and that such relations form before subsequent cognitive development, and are the basis for such development. One logical difficulty for such a position is to account for how input into two modalities from the same source becomes associated, if the association is not already present. For example, one might look at and hold an object while simultaneously touching or hearing something else. How is it known which inputs emanate from a common source and which do not, unless the systems already can identify equivalent inputs? One suggestion is that the basis for establishing appropriate associations is repetition and regularity in the pattern of stimulation to the sensory systems. For example, we learn about people and their identities because they have an auditory referent, a visual referent, etc., and these become associated because they occur regularly together. Still, it is not obvious whether this account solves the problem of how input to two sensory systems can be identified as being from the same event if those systems are not already coordinated.

An alternative to the idea that intermodal coordination occurs before, and is basic to, cognitive development is the idea that intermodal integration is a concomitant of cognitive development. Several observations lend plausibility to such an idea. First, in much of the work on habituation in infancy, intermodal procedures are used, implying that intermodal functioning does indeed characterize the infant's ordinary learning environment. If intermodal procedures are used successfully to induce learning in the laboratory, then that success implies also that the infants *can* function intermodally in other settings as well. There is other recent work that suggests that this is so. For example, Spelke (1976) has found that four-month-old infants, when presented with two movies and a sound track appropriate to one, will look more at the movie specified by the sound track than at the other movie. This behavior implies integration of complex visible and audible information emanating from the same event. Similar capability is implied by Horowitz's (1975) observation of infants' recovery of attention to a visual stimulus by the introduction of a meaningful auditory stimulus. Likewise, Wilson exploited the effectiveness of intermodal information by using a complex, presumably interesting visible object to reinforce infants' localizing the direction of the source of a sound. Finally, the idea that intersensory coordination is a concomitant of cognitive development instead of a precursor to it is supported by the fact that even people with disabilities in more than one sensory system achieve sophisticated levels of complex cognitive and linguistic functioning.

However it is achieved, intersensory functioning implies precise coordination among and within modalities. Disruptions in that coordination may also initiate developmental disabilities. For example, if the two eyes are not synchronized, strabismus develops, and eventually vision in at least one eye is often affected adversely. Strabismus may be adaptive however, because if one experienced instead constant rivalry or double imaging, directional information for spatial localization would either be absent or at least imprecise. There are also children with middle ear problems who may experience prolonged distorted or discontinuous input. For the development of some skills, such as speech, synchrony between modalities may be crucial. If audition is slow, and out of synchrony with vision and proprioception, speech acquisition may be more difficult than if there is no auditory input at all. At least one theory of stuttering is that it is based on asynchrony between audition and other modalities. In short, asynchronous or distorted processing may in some cases be more disabling than simple deficits.

An observation made in conclusion is that sensory deficits and distortions probably can occur at many points during the course of information transmission, and it is possible that the sensory systems can make some accommodations. In any case, the nature and varieties of intersensory functioning are poorly understood at present, and understanding is vital for remediating many complex and disabling developmental problems.

REFERENCES

Horowitz, F. D. (ed.). 1975. Visual attention, auditory stimulation, and language discrimination in young infants. Monogr. Soc. Res. Child Dev. Vol. 39, no. 158.

Spelke, E. 1976. Infants' intermodal perception of events. Cog. Psychol. 8: 553–560.

Turkewitz, G. 1976. Intersensory relationships during infancy. Paper presented at the Conference on Early Behavioral Assessment of the Communicative and Cognitive Abilities of the Developmentally Disabled, May 2–6, Orcas Island, Washington.

MEMORY, SENSORIMOTOR, AND COGNITIVE DEVELOPMENT

Infant Recognition Memory and Early Cognitive Ability: Empirical, Theoretical, and Remedial Considerations

Joseph F. Fagan, III

The goal of the present chapter is to point out the potential clinical value of infant visual recognition as an instance of early cognitive ability. In the experimental psychology of mental retardation, any task involving cognitive functioning attracts the attention of researchers when three criteria are met. First, the task must be empirically sensitive to variations in age and intelligence. In other words, the older and more intelligent the subject, the better the performance. Second, the processes underlying the task must be amenable to theoretical interpretation. Third, some remediation is possible, as shown by improved performance because of alterations in task conditions, alterations suggested by theory. The study of short-term verbal recall in normal and retarded children is one example of how these empirical, theoretical, and remedial criteria may be fulfilled for a particular cognitive task. In the 1960s, a number of studies with children demonstrated advantages in short-term verbal recall as a function of increased age or higher intelligence (e.g., Belmont and Butterfield, 1969). Ellis (1970) interpreted these data in the light of a popular model of adult verbal recall originally developed by Atkinson and Shiffrin (1969), that focused on transfer of information among memory stores, accomplished by control processes such as rehearsal. Remedial implications of Ellis's formulations were pursued in studies of improved recall as a function of particular rehearsal strategies (e.g., Butterfield, Wambold, and Belmont, 1973).

Following a brief discussion of operational definitions of infant visual recognition, evidence that suggests that all three criteria may be met in tests of infant recognition is reviewed. Empirically, evidence of superior recognition performance with age and on the part of infants expected to be more intelligent than other infants later in life is considered. Theoretically, it is demonstrated that the infant's recogni-

The preparation of this paper was supported by a Career Development Grant (1 KO4 HD-70144) to the author from the National Institute of Child and Health and Human Development.

117

tion performance can be conceptualized both qualitatively and quantitatively by variants of attention theories of discrimination learning. Both descriptive and predictive functions of such theorizing are illustrated. With regard to remediation, it is noted that recognition can be facilitated by changes in stimulus conditions, changes suggested by the attention model of infant recognition.

OPERATIONAL DEFINITIONS

Fantz (1956) developed "visual interest" as a test of infant perception. The response that he chose to measure discriminative ability was the activity of the eyes themselves, the assumption being that if infants consistently gaze at some stimuli more often than at others, they must be able to perceive and differentiate among them. Differential visual fixation, then, constitutes an operational definition of discrimination and is obtained when, for example, one of a pair of targets elicits significantly more than 50% of an infant's fixation. If the two targets to be discriminated differ in that one has been seen before and one has not, it is assumed that an unequal distribution of fixation between the novel and the previously exposed target indicates recognition memory. Various procedures have been developed to test infant recognition memory. The studies reviewed here were based on the paired-comparison approach. The specific procedure is to expose the infant to a target for a certain study period, usually 30–60 sec, and then to present him with the recently exposed and novel target simultaneously. When tested in this manner, infants typically devote the greater part of their visual fixation to the novel target. This differential fixation to a novel over a previously exposed stimulus demonstrates that the infant finds the two targets discriminable, and indicates that he recognizes one as having been seen before. Furthermore, by controlling the manner in which the novel and the familiar target differ and by varying the amount of study time allowed before the pairing of stimuli, some inference can be made as to which stimulus characteristics served as the basis of the infant's recognition, and when they did so.

EMPIRICAL CONSIDERATIONS

Stimuli, Age, and Study Time

The age at which an infant demonstrates recognition depends on the nature of the previously exposed and novel targets with which he is faced. Generally, targets differing along a variety of dimensions are differentiated at an earlier age than are pairs of stimuli with fewer between-target differences. Examples of both kinds of discrimination tasks are contained in Figure 1. The top row of Figure 1 contains three abstract black and white targets that differ from one another along a number of dimensions (e.g., size, number, and form of elements). Such patterns were employed in a study by Fagan, Fantz, and Miranda (1971) to estimate age trends in recognition on the part of selected samples of infants born at various lengths of gestation, and tested at postnatal ages from 5 to 20 weeks. Fagan et al. found that infants demonstrated more interest in novel than in previously exposed targets by at

Figure 1.   Stimulus targets.

least the third month of age (about 10 weeks), with total maturational level, rather than simply age from birth, playing the more important role in determining when preferences for novelty appeared. The stimuli in the bottom row of Figure 1 vary along more restricted dimensions defining patterning, each being composed of the same number and size of linear elements, and differing only in how the linear elements are arranged to form an overall pattern. Unlike discrimination tasks composed of targets varying along many dimensions, stimuli differing only in pattern arrangement are not recognized until approximately 16 weeks of age (Fagan, 1970, Experiment I; see Fantz, Fagan, and Miranda, 1975, pp. 274–276). In effect, then, varying the type of stimuli to be discriminated reveals age differences in recognition memory in the early months of life.

In the research just noted, the amount of study time allowed the infant before recognition testing ranged from 1 to 2 min. A further experiment (Fagan, 1974) asked whether brief amounts of study are effective in allowing recognition memory. A related question was whether longer study time was necessary for more difficult discriminations. Among the tasks included in the Fagan (1974) study were discriminations among stimuli varying along a number of dimensions and among targets varying in pattern arrangement. Examples of each task have already been noted in Figure 1. The general procedure, employing separate groups of subjects, was to allow infants a set study time, ranging from 5 to 30 sec over these particular discrimination tasks, before recognition testing. The amount of study time necessary to elicit a novelty preference on recognition testing varied from task to task. As little as 3 to 4 sec of study time were needed to differentiate a novel from a previously exposed target when the targets varied widely, while a similar level of novelty preference was not reached for the pairs of targets differing solely in patterning until 17 sec of study time had passed. In other words, brief periods of familiarization led to recognition, and the order in which discriminations are solved over age was recaptured at a single age by varying study time.

In summary, the infant's age, the nature of the stimuli, and the amount of study time devoted to a target all affect the infant's tendency to devote more fixation to a novel than to a previously exposed target. In general, discriminations between stimuli varying along a number of dimensions following long study are possible at 10 weeks of age for infants born at term. Given equivalently long study times, more subtle discriminations are not evidenced until 16 or more weeks of age. By five to six months, recognition follows upon relatively brief amounts of study time, although more time is needed for more difficult discriminations. In addition, the order in which stimuli are differentiated over age may be reconstructed within an age by varying study time, i. e., stimuli differentiated on a recognition test at an early age also require less study time at a later age.

Comparisons of Normal and Down's Syndrome Infants

As we have seen, the infant's recognition ability grows from the second through the sixth month. Recognition tests also discriminate "normal" from "retarded" infants. The common approach of the studies reviewed here was to compare groups of infants on recognition tests when there was some reason to expect that one sample would be more intelligent than the other later in life. Specifically, the comparisons were between normal and Down's Syndrome infants, because Down's Syndrome is diagnosable at birth and virtually certain to result in retarded intelligence. Initial studies conducted in our laboratory by Miranda (1970) and Fagan (as reported in Fantz et al., 1975, p. 393) demonstrated reliable novelty preferences on the part of Down's Syndrome infants from 22 to 34 weeks of age when recognition was tested with pairs of abstract black and white patterns varying along a number of dimensions. In fact, Down's Syndrome infants functioned equally well as normal infants. We took these results to mean that recognizing which of two widely varying stimuli was seen before was a relatively simple feat. If the tasks were, indeed, too easy, it seemed likely that the use of more difficult discriminations to test recognition would reveal normal-Down's Syndrome differences. These expectations were met in a study of Miranda and Fantz (1974), in which samples of Down's Syndrome infants, matched with normal controls for sex and length of gestation, were tested at 13, 24, and 36 weeks. One of the three tasks administered at each age employed widely different abstract patterns, another was based on targets differing in arrangement of pattern elements (as in the bottom row of Figure 1), and the third involved a dis-

crimination of photos of faces. The results from each task indicated a clear supe-
riority on the part of the normal infants. Novel targets from easily discriminable
pairs of stimuli were preferred by normals at 13 weeks, but Down's Syndrome
infants did not evidence such preferences until 24 weeks. Distinctions among photos
and between targets varying in arrangement of pattern elements were accomplished
on recognition tests by 24 weeks for normals. Down's Syndrome infants preferred a
novel face photo at 36 weeks, but showed no recognition at any age when abstract
targets varying in pattern were to be differentiated.

Preliminary testing by Miranda and Fantz ruled out the possibility that the
Down's Syndrome infants' lack of recognition was attributable to an inability to
resolve pattern, because the pattern detail in all the stimuli used by Miranda and
Fantz were shown to be well within the acuity range of the Down's Syndrome
infants. There is also the possibility that two particular patterns, although resolvable, simply cannot be discriminated by a Down's Syndrome infant. Hence, an
apparent failure to recognize is really a failure in discrimination. In a later study,
Miranda (Miranda, 1976) tested normal and Down's Syndrome infants with abstract patterns known to be discriminable. Specifically, Down's Syndrome infants
had shown a natural preference for one pattern over the other (i.e., when both were
"novel") as early as five weeks of age. When these two patterns were employed for
recognition testing, however, Down's Syndrome infants failed to show a novelty
preference until 17 weeks of age, a preference evidenced at nine weeks on the part of
normals. In short, these studies, taken together, imply a deficit in visual recognition
memory on the part of Down's Syndrome infants, a deficit quite apart from any difficulties in simple visual functioning.

AN ATTENTION MODEL OF INFANT RECOGNITION

Overview

As noted earlier, one feature of a paradigm that attracts experimental psychologists
interested in mental retardation is the possibility that the processes underlying the
task are amenable to theoretical analysis. The present aim is to illustrate how
variants of attention theories of discrimination learning can provide one basis for a
theoretical interpretations of infant visual recognition. The material given here is
adapted from a more detailed report by Fagan (1977). In the current presentation, a
model of infants' visual recognition is first considered. In brief, the model assumes
that one "look" consisting of a chain of two covert responses is made when the
infant is faced with a novel and a previously exposed target. An attentional, observing response is made to a dimension followed by a fixation response to a cue. Each
response has some probability of occurrence. From the model, equations can be
derived to estimate the probability of infants observing the dimension(s) providing a
novel and a familiar cue in a given situation. We then focus on the desciptive use of
the model by estimating probabilities of observing particular dimensions as sources
of recognition. To do this, data are obtained from studies designed to separate attention to compound and component dimensions. Finally, we see how these estimates

are used to predict novelty preferences under different conditions, with the observed and predicted preferences closely agreeing in each case.

The Model

The basic question that motivated development of the model is: What information does the infant encode during study to serve as a basis for later recognition? The supposition was that attention theories of discrimination learning may aid in answering this question. The basic attitudes and terms of one such theory, initially presented by the Zeamans (House and Zeaman, 1963; Zeaman and House, 1963) provided a starting point. The Zeamans proposed that in order to solve a discrimination problem, a child must first make a cognitive attentional or observing response to a dimension (e.g., form), and then an instrumental response to a cue from that dimension (e.g., square). Furthermore, each dimension has some probability of being observed, although some dimensions may be more readily attended to than others. The Zeamans stress the role of the attentional response in the solution of a discrimination task. The quantitative model of infant recognition presented here shares many of the features and some of the language of the Zeaman and House (1963) model of discrimination learning. For example, a chain of two responses is inferred, and terms like "observing response," "probability of attending," etc. are used. No precise analogy, however, is either intended or drawn between 1) a discrimination learning task in which a child must discover which of two stimuli is, over trials, consistently associated with a reward, and 2) a recognition task in which the infant, by his looking time to paired novel and familiar targets, demonstrates that certain dimensions have or have not served as a basis for recognition.

The model is addressed to the infant's behavior on recognition testing. In other words, its domain is the situation in which the infant, after having been exposed to a target, is now confronted with two targets that contain a novel and a familiar cue along some dimension(s). The behavior to be predicted is the probability (P) of viewing the target designated by the experimenter as novel. Operationally, P is approximated by the percentage of total viewing time elicited by the novel target (%N). The model is diagrammed on the left in Figure 2. Faced with two targets, the infant is assumed to take one "look" that consists of a chain of two responses, an attentional or observing response, O, to a dimension and a fixation response, R, to a cue. The only observable behavior is the actual amount of time spent viewing the two targets, because both the attentional and fixation responses are covert. Two observing responses are listed in Figure 2. The first, $O_{(fn)}$, is an attentional response to the dimension containing, for the infant, a familiar and a novel cue. The second, $O_{(\overline{fn})}$, is a response to a dimension that does not, for the infant, contain a novel and a familiar cue. In making the attentional response, $O_{(fn)}$, the infant has, by definition, achieved recognition. In making the response $O_{(\overline{fn})}$, the infant is not evidencing recognition. If $O_{(fn)}$ is made, the infant is faced with the novel stimulus, S_n, and the familiar stimulus, S_f. If the attentional response is $O_{(\overline{fn})}$, then targets coincident with the novel and familiar cues, S_1 and S_2, respectively, constitute the array of cues for further response. Two fixation, R, responses are open to the infant. The infant

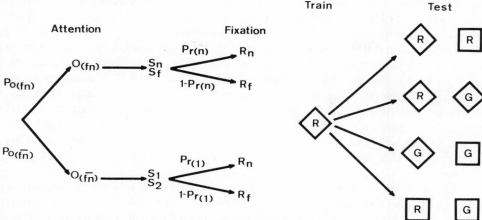

Figure 2.   Summary of the model and of the experimental design.

may make the response R_n to the cue the experimenter has designated as novel, or he may make the response R_f to the cue designated as familiar.

As illustrated in the diagram, the cue designated as novel may be viewed by following either one of two paths. The infant may make the attentional response $O_{(fn)}$ with probability $Po_{(fn)}$, and then make the fixation response R_n with probability $Pr_{(n)}$. Taking the second path, the $O_{(\overline{fn})}$ response may be made with probability $Pr_{(\overline{fn})}$ followed by the R fixation response with probability $Pr_{(1)}$. Thus, P, which is the probability of viewing the cue specified by the experimenter as novel, is given by the formula in Equation 1:

$$P = Po_{(fn)} \cdot Pr_{(n)} + Po_{(\overline{fn})} \cdot Pr_{(1)}$$

In order to simplify Equation 1, two assumptions are made. The first assumption is that $Po_{(fn)}$ and $Po_{(\overline{fn})}$ sum to one. The second is that $Pr_{(fn)}$ is equal to one. Hence, the basic formula may be reduced to Equation 2:

$$P = Po_{(fn)} + (1 - Po_{(fn)}) \cdot Pr_{(1)}$$

Finally, the value of $Pr_{(1)}$ may be set at $\frac{1}{2}$ by ensuring that the targets employed on recognition testing serve equally often, over subjects, as novel or familiar, and Equation 2 may be solved for $Po_{(fn)}$ as follows in Equation 3:

$$Po_{(fn)} = 2P - 1$$

Description

With this model, if test conditions can be arranged to obtain novelty preferences (i.e., estimates of P) given particular dimensions as bases for recognition, Equation 3 may then be used descriptively to assign $Po_{(fn)}$ values to various outcomes. A means of empirically specifying which dimensions the infant has relied on as a basis for recognition was derived from a consideration of the issue of attention to compound and component dimensions—an issue germane to attention theories of discrimination learning. As House and Zeaman (1963) point out, the child faced with a choice between two stimuli that vary along one dimension, but that are constant along another dimension, may base his solution of the discrimination task on the relevant component dimension or on the compound dimension. The problem of distinguishing between component and compound solutions is also present in studies of infant recognition whenever the stimulus used during familiarization also appears on test. If, for example, the infant devotes more fixation to a red square than to a green square on recognition testing after having studied a green square, we might infer either that he had been attending to the component dimension of color (red versus green) or to the compound dimension of form-color (red square versus green square).

The problem is to control conditions so that attention to a compound dimension can be separated from attention to component dimensions. Investigators of discrimination learning solve the problem by preserving or destroying stimulus compounds from trial to trial in a discrimination task, and by testing for gain or loss in performance. Similarly, a test of attention to component dimensions, undertaken in an experiment that we now consider and that was reported more fully in Fagan (1977), was to familiarize the infant to a form-color compound, and then to present a pair of targets with a familiar and a novel cue along one dimension and the same two novel cues along the other. To test whether the component dimensions of color served as a basis for recognition, for example, the infant might be shown a red diamond during familiarization, and then tested on the pairing red square versus green square. Because the only simultaneous pairing of a novel and a previously exposed cue is the pairing red versus green, a reliable preference for the novel color cue (green in this example) would indicate that color had provided a component solution. Evidence for a compound dimension as a basis for recognition would be provided if other infants, given the familiar compound on test (e.g., shown a red diamond for study and presented later with a red diamond versus a green diamond), showed higher preferences for novelty than infants allowed only a component solution. In other words, both the component (red versus green) and the compound dimension (red square versus green square) provide a choice between a novel and a previously exposed cue for infants in our example, given the familiar compound on test.

In the experiment, which employed infants five to seven months of age, differences in form were achieved by the use of patterns that were composed of the same size and number of elements, and that differed only in how the elements were arranged to form a particular pattern (the overall square and diamond patterns in the second row of Figure 1). Variations in color were accomplished by constructing patterns from Munsell papers of either red or green hue. The general procedure was to expose the infant to a pair of identical targets for a set study period (e.g., red diamond - red diamond for 40 sec), and then to give a recognition test by pairing two targets for two 5-sec periods, reversing left-right positions from one period to the next (e.g., red diamond-red square, red square - red diamond). Study periods varied from 30 to 90 sec to produce groups of subjects with more or less study time. Examples of the four types of pairings that an infant could receive on recognition testing, depending on which test condition he was in, are illustrated in the design pictured to the right in Figure 2. The top two test conditions in the design are distinguished by the presence of the previously exposed form-color stimulus on test. Hence, attention to the compound dimension could serve to mediate recognition. The first condition contained form as a component dimension; the second, color. In the next two conditions the previously exposed form-color compound was absent on recognition testing. The infants in the third condition had to rely on attention to form as a component dimension to notice novelty. Attention to color as a component dimension was required for infants in the fourth condition.

The percentages of fixation paid to the novel target are listed in Table 1. The data in Table 1 are given for the four conditions illustrated in the design to the right in Figure 2. The four conditions are defined as to whether the familiar form-color stimulus was present or absent on test, and whether form or color served as the relevant component dimension. The results presented in Table 1 are, however, divided into two groupings based on length of fixation during the study period. The left column of figures in Table 1 presents results from infants allowed "low" study time, averaging about 17.0 sec of fixation during study. The second grouping (right column of figures in Table 1) includes infants allowed "high" study time, with a mean of about 30.0 sec of fixation during familiarization. As can be seen from the means in Table 1, more preference for novelty was found for all test conditions when the previously exposed compound was present on test than for conditions in which the familiar compound was absent. In other words, recognition based on the compound plus the component solution led to reliably greater novelty preferences relative to conditions in which infants had to rely solely on attention to a component dimension. Infants also demonstrated the ability to respond to component dimensions. This is most clearly seen in Table 1, for 1) infants with high study times, where reliable preferences for novelty were evident when the familiar compound was absent and either form or color was the component dimension underlying recogni-

Table 1.   Percent fixation to novel targets for groups with Low or High study time under conditions where the familiar form-color compound was present or absent on test and either form or color served as the component dimension

Familiar compound	Component dimension	Measure	Study time	
			Low	High
Present	Form	M	56.3[a]	61.9[a]
		N	72	72
	Color	M	61.3[a]	60.9[a]
		N	72	72
Absent	Form	M	51.5	59.2[a]
		N	48	72
	Color	M	55.6[a]	55.4[a]
		N	56	72

[a] $p < .01$.

tion, and for 2) low study time infants who responded to the component dimension of color.

In short, conditions may be arranged to discover if particular dimensions serve as a basis for infant visual recognition. In the experiment given as an illustration of such procedures, we found that infants five to seven months of age were capable of distinguishing novel from familiar cues along the component dimensions of either form or color. In addition, evidence was presented to show that a compound dimension as well as specific components may serve as a basis for recognition. Finally, given the stimuli employed, less study time was required before recognition when one dimension (color) served as the component dimension underlying recognition than when attention to another dimension (form) was required as a source of recognition.

To return to our illustration of the descriptive use of the attention model of infant recognition, let us consider, for example, how $Po_{(fn)}$ values may be derived from the data provided by these five- to seven-month infants. The reader may find it helpful to refer to Table 1 for the percentages to novelty obtained in the experiment as we proceed through this example. Low study time subjects allowed the component dimension of color as the sole basis for recognition obtained a %N score of 55.6%. According to the Equation 3, the $Po_{(fn)}$ under such conditions is 11.2%. The %N of 51.5 for low study time infants tested with form as the component dimension did not differ reliably from a chance preference of 50%, indicating that the probability of observing form as the dimension containing the familiar and novel cues was, in effect, zero.

Infants who had the previously exposed target present on test had the compound dimension available as a basis for recognition along with a component dimension. The presence of the familiar compound on test facilitated recognition for low and high study time subjects. Hence, values of $Po_{(fn)}$ may be calculated for the compound dimension for each study time sample. An interesting feature of the data was that low study time infants varied in responsiveness to novelty depending on which component dimension was provided along with the compound solution. Thus, we may obtain, and note the agreement between, two estimates of $Po_{(fn)}$ for the compound dimension under low study time conditions, one estimate under the condition in which color was the component dimension, and another for form. When the color component was also present, infants given low study time responded with 61.3% to the novel target, indicating a $Po_{(fn)}$ value of 22.6%. This score, however, results from two $Po_{(fn)}$ values—a $Po_{(fn)}$ for the color component that we previously estimated as 11.2%, and a value of 11.4% for the compound obtained by subtracting 11.2% from 22.6%. When form was present on test along with the compound, a value of 56.3% to the novel target was obtained and the $Po_{(fn)}$ value, under such conditions, is 12.6%. Because $Po_{(fn)}$ was estimated at zero for the form component, this entire $Po_{(fn)}$ of 12.6% may be attributed to the compound dimension. The two estimates of $Po_{(fn)}$ for the compound dimension under low study time, 11.4% and 12.6%, are not identical, but are so close that the disparity between them is of little concern. For our present purpose, the mean of these values, 12.0%, may be taken as the estimate of $Po_{(fn)}$ for the compound dimension.

Computations of $Po_{(fn)}$ are somewhat simplified under the high study time condition, because there were no differences in how responsive infants were to novelty when either form or color served as the component dimension. The mean percent to novelty score was derived for all subjects given high study time and serving under conditions where the familiar compound was absent on test, to obtain the best estimate of $Po_{(fn)}$ when a component dimension (either form or color) served as the sole basis for recognition. Similarly, the best estimate of $Po_{(fn)}$ for the compound dimension was calculated by taking the mean percent to novelty value for the two conditions where the familiar compound was present on test. As a brief summary, the $Po_{(fn)}$ values estimated for color or for form as component dimensions or for the compound dimensions are listed in the first column of figures in Table 2 for low and high study time samples.

As a final example of the descriptive use of the model, let us note an experiment by Cornell (1975), in which 18-week infants evidenced reliable and approximately equal responsiveness to novelty on the basis of the component dimensions of pattern arrangement and orientation (called PaOr in Table 2). Using the data reported by Cornell (1975 Table 1, p. 232) to obtain mean novelty preferences for conditions in which the familiar compound was either present or absent on test, yields $Po_{(fn)}$ values of 15.7% for pattern arrangement or for orientation as component dimensions, and a $Po_{(fn)}$ of 5.7% for the compound dimension.

Prediction

Let us now see how the model may be used to predict infants' visual recognition. According to Equation 2, if $Po_{(fn)}$ and $Pr_{(1)}$ are known, then P (or %N) may be predicted. A second experiment (also reported in Fagan, 1977), that we now consider, was designed to test three such predictions of novelty preference. Two predictions were based on data provided by the five- to seven-month infants in the experiment just discussed, and a third prediction was made on the basis of the results obtained independently by Cornell (1975). With regard to the first two pre-

Table 2.   Values of $Po_{(fn)}$ and $Pr_{(1)}$ and predicted and observed percent fixation to novelty (%N) for groups of infants presented with form and color stimuli and allowed Low study time (FC, Low) or High study time (FC, High) and for infants exposed to targets varying in pattern arrangement and orientation (PaOr)

Group	Dimension	$Po_{(fn)}$	$\Sigma Po_{(fn)}$	$Pr_{(1)}$	Predicted	Observed
FC, Low	Form	0.0				
	Color	11.2	23.2	50.0	61.6	61.4
	Compound	12.0				(N = 48)
FC, High	Form	14.6				
	Color	14.6	37.4	50.0	68.7	66.8
	Compound	8.2				(N = 32)
PaOr	Pattern	15.7				
	Orientation	15.7	37.1	57.4	73.2	73.9
	Compound	5.7				(N = 14)

dictions, five- to seven-months infants were placed in a situation in which both form and color as component dimensions were present, along with the compound dimension, as bases for solution. For example, a typical subject would be shown a red diamond for study and then, on test, would be faced with a red diamond and a green square. Furthermore, conditions were arranged so that some infants averaged 17 sec of fixation during the study period, a low study time sample, while others averaged 30 sec to constitute a high study time group. Given such stimulus conditions, predictions of %N were made for each study time sample based on the estimates of $Po_{(fn)}$ derived above from the data provided by infants in the initial experiment. In the case of infants allowed approximately 17 sec of study fixation, $Po_{(fn)}$ values of 11.2%, zero percent, and 12.0% were estimated for the component dimensions of color, form, and the compound dimension, respectively. Summing these values yields a $Po_{(fn)}$ of 23.2%, as listed in the second column of figures in Table 2. Employing this estimate of $Po_{(fn)}$ and setting $Pr_{(1)}$ at 50.0% (third column in Table 2) by ensuring that all stimuli served equally often over subjects as novel or familiar, Equation 2 yielded a value of 61.6% (fourth column in Table 2) for %N under Low study time conditions, where the components form and color and the compound dimension each provided a basis for recognition. In the same vein, infants allowed High study time would be expected to devote about 68.7% to the novel target on test. This value of 68.7% follows from a $Po_{(fn)}$ of 37.4% and a $Pr_{(1)}$ of 50.0%. As a final prediction, based on the Cornell (1975) study, four-and-one-half-month infants were tested in the second experiment for recognition when pattern arrangement and orientation as component dimensions and the resulting compound dimension were each available as sources of recognition (summary data in row labeled PaOr, Table 2). Stimuli patterned after those employed by Cornell were shown, and $Po_{(fn)}$ was estimated at 37.1%. For this last prediction of %N, however, a value of 57.4% was used for $Pr_{(1)}$, because the pattern arrangement that served as the novel stimulus for all the four-and-one-half-month subjects had been shown in earlier work (Fantz et al., 1975) to elicit an initial preference of 57.4% when paired with the pattern always employed in this second experiment as familiar. Hence, the predicted %N for the sample based on Cornell's study was derived from a $Po_{(fn)}$ of 37.1% and a $Pr_{(1)}$ of 57.4% to yield a value of 73.2%.

Obtained means for responsiveness to novelty on recognition testing are listed in the fifth column of figures in Table 2, next to the predicted novelty preferences for each of three samples of infants. Inspection of the last two columns in Table 2 shows that observed preferences for novelty were comfortably close to the predicted values generated by the model. The mean novelty preference on the part of infants allowed low study time and tested with form-color stimuli was within 0.2% of the predicted score of 61.6%. In effect, the results confirmed the expectation that providing the form component as an additional basis of recognition for low study time subjects would add nothing to ease of recognition above and beyond that already provided by the color component and the compound dimension. Higher novelty preferences than had been found in the first experiment and in the Cornell (1975) study were expected for the subjects allowed high study time and provided with form and color components and the compound dimension as bases for solution, and for the four-and-one-half-month infants given pattern arrangement and orientation as component bases along with the compound. On an absolute and a comparative basis, the obtained scores for these two groups were also satisfactory, differing from predicted values by only 1.9% (68.7% versus 66.8%) or by as little as 0.7% (73.2% versus 73.9%).

FACILITATING RECOGNITION

Thus far we have seen that infants' visual recognition performance varies with age and with assumed level of later intelligent functioning. The processes underlying infants' recognition have also been demonstrated to be amenable to theoretical analysis. In the present section, we note that recognition can be improved by alterations in task conditions, alterations suggested by the attention model. Our concern is with initial findings from an ongoing series in which naturally occurring stimulus preferences were used to direct the infant's attention during study to a particular dimension. Tests for recognition were then made with either the directed dimension or some other component dimension as the basis for recognition. Directing attention to a particular dimension during study seems to facilitate later recognition based on that dimension.

As noted earlier, manipulating amount of study time and controlling the manner in which novel and previously exposed targets vary allows us some estimate of which stimulus dimension(s) served as a basis for recognition, and in what order they were processed. For example, given the particular stimulus and temporal conditions of the experiment discussed earlier (data in Table 1), infants seemed not to rely on the component dimension of form as a basis for recognition after having viewed a target for about 17 sec during the study period. To elucidate such a finding, we asked what circumstances the attention model would suggest for facilitating infants' recognition of form given limited study time. The model emphasizes the distribution of attention to various dimensions at the time of recognition testing as the key determinant of performance. Obviously, the distribution of attention to dimensions present at time of test depends on the infant's experience during the study period. If infants must limit their attention during a brief study period to some dimensions while excluding others, we would expect only those dimensions that have received attention to serve as bases of later recognition. Furthermore, it would seem reasonable to suppose that directing the infant's attention to a particular dimension during the study period would increase the probability of that dimension serving effectively as a basis for recognition.

One procedure by which we might reasonably infer that the infant's attention had been directed to a particular dimension during study is to present two stimuli and to assume from the natural visual preference infants display for one stimulus over the other than attention had been paid to the dimension along which those stimuli vary. One of the best documented preferences among forms, for example, is the infant's tendency to devote more fixation to curved than to straight contours (Fantz et al., 1975, pp. 260–269). Specifically, in the present experiment, a pilot study with five- to seven-month infants revealed that the overall circular arrangement of small linear elements pictured to the left in the bottom row of Figure 1 elicited about 70% of total fixation when paired with either overall square or diamond arrangements also pictured.

Hence, in the experiment we now consider, a sample of 138 five- to seven-month infants were allowed to study two forms of the same color. One form was always the circular arrangement and the other was the linear arrangements (e.g., red circle paired with red square). Exposure duration for study was manipulated so that actual viewing time for the linear arrangement was limited, on the average, to less than 17 sec. Following study, the infant was tested with a pairing of the previously exposed linear arrangement and a novel linear arrangement of the same color, a color not seen during study (i.e., in this example the test would be green square versus green diamond). Note that the circular pattern only appeared during study, never on recognition testing. In effect, the design was identical to that used in the initial experiment (data in Table 1) for the condition in which form, following low study time, served as the sole basis for recognition. The only difference is that in the present experiment, the "familiar" form cue was always paired during study with the circle rather than with a duplicate of itself, as had been the case in the initial experiment. To test the durability of any facilitation in recognizing form that might result from directing attention to form during study, 86 of the infants were tested for recognition immediately following study, and 52 were tested 60 sec after the end of the study period.

During study, the 86 infants tested for immediate recognition averaged 32.4 sec of fixation to both targets (SD 13.2), with 66.7% (SD 14.0) of that total paid to the circular pattern, a percentage reliably greater than a chance value of 50%, $t = 11.1$, df 85, $p < .001$. Hence, attention had been paid to the form dimension, and an average viewing time of less than 17 sec (actual mean 10.7 sec, SD 6.4) was accorded the square or diamond arrangement during study. On immediate recognition testing, these infants averaged 56.8% (SD 17.2) of their total test fixation of 7.1 sec to the novel form cue, a reliable preference, $t = 3.4$, df 85, $p < .001$. In other words, despite "low" study time for the previously exposed cue, recognition on the basis of form was demonstrated following directed attention to the form dimension during study. To insure against the unlikely possibility that a viewing time of 10 sec or less to the linear arrangement during study would have resulted in reliable recognition whether or not the circular form was present, a sample of 10 infants were tested in the same manner as the experimental subjects, except that one of the linear patterns was paired with itself during a study period of 10 sec. These control subjects averaged 6.2 sec of viewing time during study with a range from 4.2 to 8.9 sec. On immediate recognition testing, their differential fixation did not differ from chance with 50.3% (SD 18.4) paid to the novel form cue. In contrast, experimental subjects whose viewing times to the linear arrangement during study ranged from 4.2 to 8.9 sec, demonstrated reliable immediate recognition with 59.1% (SD 17.4) of total fixation to the novel target; $t = 3.9$, df 55, $p < .001$.

The behavior of the infants whose attention was directed to the form dimension during study, but whose recognition was tested following a 60-sec delay, was comparable, in all respects, to that of the other experimental sample who had been tested for immediate recognition. During study, the sample given delayed testing averaged 29.4 sec to both form cues with 71.4% (*SD* 13.3) of that time to the circular form, a reliable preference, $t = 11.6$, df 51, $p < .001$. A mean viewing time of 8.5 sec (*SD* 4.4) was accorded the square or diamond during study. On delayed recognition testing, infants averaged 56.6% (*SD* 14.5) of total fixation to the novel target, a preference greater than chance, $t = 3.3$, df 51, $p < .001$, and virtually identical to 56.8% preference obtained for the group tested immediately.

In short, working from theory to alter task conditions, a naturally occurring stimulus preference was used to guide infant's attention to the form dimension during study. Following this direction of attention, form served as a reliable basis of recognition, as demonstrated by novelty preferences—preferences not shown in an initial experiment that had not included the direction of attention to form during study. In addition, the facilitation of recognition occasioned by altering task conditions during study was shown to be lasting, with reliable preferences for a novel form cue shown on delayed as well as on immediate recognition tests.

SUMMARY AND DISCUSSION

Empirically, the infant's ability to recognize a visual stimulus, as indexed by responsiveness to novelty, develops over the early months of life. In addition, groups of infants who are certain to differ in measured intelligence some years later also differ in their ability to recognize familiar targets when tested during the first year. Theoretically, the present report discussed a model of infants' responsiveness to novelty, a model derived from an attention theory of discrimination learning. The model assumes that an attentional response to a dimension and then a fixation response to a cue is made during recognition testing. Attached to each response is some probability of occurrence. Equations were derived to estimate the probability of infants' observing the dimension(s), providing a basis for recognition in a given situation. Such estimates were obtained and were then used to predict the novelty preferences of infants under other conditions. The fact that observed and predicted novelty preferences were in close agreement does not mean that this particular model has proved valid to the exclusion of other conceptualizations of infant recognition. The emphasis, rather, is that adapted versions of sophisticated attention theories and quantitative models of discrimination learning can be profitable both for describing and predicting infants' visual recognition. Finally, a demonstration of how stimulus conditions may be altered to improve recognition was provided. Most importantly, the manner in which this instance of remediation was effected was derived from the assumptions underlying the attention model of recognition.

Further determination of which stimulus dimensions at what time serve as bases for recognition for normal infants and for infants likely to be retarded later in life would be useful for three reasons. The first would be for test construction, i.e., to provide specific items to be included in the measurement of individual differences in early perceptual-cognitive functioning. Because the attention model of infant recognition should be viewed as an initial statement subject to modificiation, the second use of further studies would be to provide data for a more refined theoretical account of infant recognition. Some of the areas within the model particularly subject to modification are given in Fagan (1977). For our present purposes, however, the two main refinements would be a specification of the processes relating to individual differences and an elaboration of the conditions necessary for facilitating recognition. Finally, because we know from the studies cited earlier that, for example, Down's Syndrome infants are indeed capable of recognizing what they have seen before, a third use of the data would be to describe the kind of visual environment in which a retarded infant can profit. It might be possible, in other words, to provide baselines for future remedial programs in terms of the kind of visual dimensions known to serve as bases for recognition for retarded infants, and in terms of the alterations in study and test conditions that improve recognition, and to which a retarded infant would respond.

REFERENCES

Atkinson, E. C., and Shiffrin, R. M. 1969. Human memory: A proposed system and its control processes. In K. W. Spence and J. T. Spence (eds.), The Psychology of Learning and Motivation: Advances in Research and Theory. Vol. 2. Academic Press, New York.

Belmont, J. M., and Butterfield, E. C. 1969. The relations of short-term memory to development and intelligence. In L. C. Lipsitt and H. W. Reese (eds.), Advances in Child Development and Behavior. Vol. 4. Academic Press, New York.

Butterfield, E. C., Wambold, C., and Belmont, J. M. 1973. On the theory and practice of improving short-term memory. Am. J. Ment. Def. 77: 654–669.

Cornell, E. H. 1975. Infants' visual attention to pattern arrangement and orientation. Child. Dev. 46: 229–232.

Ellis, N. R. 1970. Memory processes in retardates and normals. In N. R. Ellis (ed.), International Review of Research in Mental Retardation. Vol. 4. Academic Press, New York.

Fagan, J. F. 1970. Memory in the infant. J. Exp. Child Psychol. 9: 217–226.

Fagan, J. F. 1974. Infant recognition memory: The effects of length of familiarization and type of discrimination task. Child Dev. 45: 351–356.

Fagan, J. F. 1977. An attention model of infant recognition. Child Dev. 48: 345–359.

Fagan, J. F., Fantz, R. L., and Miranda, S. B. 1971. Infants' attention to novel stimuli as a function of postnatal and conceptional age. Paper presented at Society for Research in Child Development Meeting, April 4.

Fantz, R. L. 1956. A method for studying early visual development. Percept. Mot. Skills 6: 13–15.

Fantz, R. L., Fagan, J. F., and Miranda, S. B. 1975. Early perceptual development as shown by visual discrimination, selectivity, and memory with varying stimulus and population parameters. In L. Cohen and P. Salapatek (eds.), Infant Perception: From Sensation to Cognition: Basic Visual Processes. Vol. 1. Academic Press, New York.

House, B. J., and Zeaman, D. 1963. Miniature experiments in retardate discrimination learning. In L. P. Lipsitt and C. C. Spiker (eds.), Advances in Child Development and Behavior. Vol. 1. Academic Press, New York.

Miranda, S. B. 1970. Response to novel visual stimuli by Down's Syndrome and normal infants. Proceed. 78th Ann. Conv. APA 275–276.

Miranda, S. B. 1976. Visual attention in defective and high-risk infants. Merrill-Palmer Quart. 22: 201–228.

Miranda, S. B., and Fantz, R. L. 1974. Recognition memory in Down's Syndrome and normal infants. Child Dev. 45: 651–660.

Zeaman, D. and House, B. J. 1963. The role of attention in retardate discrimination learning. In N. R. Ellis (ed.), Handbook of Mental Deficiency. McGraw-Hill, New York.

Sensorimotor and Cognitive Development

Ronald S. Wilson

The course of early mental development is one in which the primitive sensorimotor functions of the neonate gradually become transformed into the more complex and abstract cognitive processes of the child. The rate of gain is rapid in the early years, although in comparison with other species it may seem agonizingly slow, and the massive registration of experience seems to supply the foundation elements for the gradual elaboration of cognitive functions.

Recent developments in evolutionary theory (Freedman, 1974) would call attention to this process as an example of species programming, in which the unfolding of capabilities is determined by inherent and species-wide developmental processes plus the accumulation of experience. Although the steady input of sensory experience plays an influential role in cognitive development, it seems that a certain degree of patterning and organization is also imposed on this experience by inherent neural processes. Indeed, the progression to more complex cognitive functions is jointly provided for by cumulative experience plus innate neural programming.

Piaget's description of cognitive development (Piaget, 1952; Phillips, 1975), with its emphasis on successive stages unfolding in invariant order and building on the experiences of the preceding stages, may be regarded as the basic itinerary for the species. It touches on the fundamental operations and transformations accomplished by all human infants, and as such it gives expression to the species-wide programming that regulates mental development. Although individual differences are acknowledged, they play a minor role in Piaget's formulations about cognitive development—the principal emphasis is on the main trend.

The main trend is subdivided into six stages, ranging from the primitive reflexes of the neonate to the solution-seeking efforts of the two-year-old. The cognitive operations at each stage gradually construct a mental representation of the external world for the infant, and a repertoire of adaptive action-patterns for dealing with the world. These operations are substantially facilitated by two pervasive features of the infant's behavior, imitation and play, that enable the infant to model the actions of

The research for this paper was supported in part by PHS grants MH 23884 and HD 07200.

others and to perfect these actions through endless repetition. In the Piagetian view, the experiences registered during these stages and the resultant cognitive structures comprise the foundation elements of intelligence.

This orientation, particularly as interpreted by many U.S. investigators, accepts the premise that all infants pass through all stages, and implicitly concludes that any infant reaching a given stage is essentially comparable in cognitive functioning to any other infant at that stage. Individual differences are limited to acceleration or delay in reaching a stage, and such differences are attributed to familial/cultural variations in development-fostering experiences.

The assessment of infant cognitive development from this perspective is perhaps best illustrated by the work of Uzgiris and Hunt (1975), whose scales have recently been published after nearly a decade of informal use. The six scales touch on the major aspects of cognitive development (e.g., the development of visual pursuit and object permanence, the development of causality), and within each scale the eliciting situations are arranged in hierarchical order, from simple to more advanced. The infant's progression through each scale reveals the stage of cognitive functioning he has reached. Because the scales presumably tap semi-independent developmental sequences, each of which may be susceptible to acceleration or lag in accordance with prior cumulative experience, the results are purely idiographic in nature. Each infant is regarded as a unique product of his experiences, interpretable only in reference to himself, and indeed Uzgiris and Hunt disclaim any interest in standardizing the scales to measure the relative differences between infants.

From an assessment standpoint, these assumptions create certain inherent limitations to the scales with respect to scoring and predictive validity. Some reference comparison is essential to determine whether an infant is developmentally delayed or advanced, and whether this deviation at a particular stage of sensorimotor development has a significant bearing on later intellectual status at school age.

BAYLEY AND INFANT TESTING

The other research area that has been concerned with early mental development is in the psychometric tradition, where the assessment of individual differences has been the paramount interest. Continuing from Binet's early interest in identifying children who would not profit from schooling, this area has focused on the measurement of intelligence, and ultimately on detecting the earliest indicators of intelligence during infancy. Primary importance has been attached to whether a child is precocious or slow in relation to his age-peers, and consequently the scales have been constructed to give maximum exposure to individual differences. Although the growth of intelligence as an age-linked process has been recognized as a major parameter of development (Bayley, 1955), the principal efforts at measurement and prediction have been concerned with individual differences—specifically, how early were they apparent, and how reliable were they in predicting later measures of intelligence?

This approach is best illustrated in the work of Bayley, which culminated in the first well-standardized test of infant mental development (Bayley, 1969). Indeed, much of what there is to be said in this area has its roots in Bayley's work, both in infant testing and in the longitudinal study of mental development. She remarked long ago on the poor predictability of infant tests in the first year (Bayley, 1955), a fact that has been rather dramatically rediscovered by certain recent investigators who use it as a pretext for dismissing the validity of infant tests (e.g., Lewis and McGurk, 1972).

However, Bayley also noted a change in the functions measured by the test during the latter half of the second year, turning from primitive sensorimotor functions to more abstract and symbolic processes, and this transition signalled the emergence of intelligence (Bayley, 1965). Bayley further observed that each infant followed his own distinctive path of development—whether slow initially and bright later, or vice versa—and the unfolding of this developmental pattern was largely independent of major environmental events.

The inferences to be drawn from Bayley's work are twofold: 1) there is a qualitative change in the functions measured during infancy, and the transition to the functions connoting intelligence seems to occur around 18 months, and 2) each infant may be subject to developmental spurts and lags that produce temporary phases of advancement or delay in reference to other infants.

The major thrust of the present article concerns the first inference, namely the transition from sensorimotor processes to the more abstract, conceptual modes of thought. It examines the performance of infants on items from the Bayley Scale as a means of detecting the cognitive functions engaged by these items, and the relationship of such cognitive functions to later measures of intelligence. The analysis focuses on emerging individual differences during the transition stage as early indicators of differential capability, and inquires into the cognitive functions that are notably advanced for these precocious infants. Finally, the inferences from this analysis are coordinated with Piaget's description of cognitive functioning during the final stage of the sensorimotor period, 18–24 months.

Background

By way of background, the Bayley Mental Scale is composed of 163 items, beginning with the most rudimentary responses to auditory and visual stimuli and extending through measures of word comprehension and form perception. The items represent a diverse assortment of tasks selected according to the general criteria of apparent relevance to adaptive functions, internal consistency, and increasing percentage of passes with increasing age. The items are arrayed by order of difficulty and cover a prospective age range of 1 to 30 months. An infant is examined over a limited number of items appropriate to his age, and the raw score is based on the total number of items passed. This score is then transformed to a standardized Mental Development Index (MDI) score based on the published norms for that age, with a mean of 100 and SD of 16. The overall score, of course, takes no cognizance of which items were passed, and the question is whether any subset of items is predictive of later measures of intellectual functioning.

Ideally, one would like to coordinate the Bayley data with a measure of school-age intelligence, because individual differences are more securely established. However, the sample for whom we have both Bayley data and school-age data is quite small; the Bayley Scale has been available only since 1969. Therefore, we have used the three-year Binet IQ score as the criterion by which to evaluate the predictive power of the infant tests. Age three is an excellent age for testing, and it is enough of a stable landmark for revealing individual differences that it qualifies as a significant criterion age. The predictive correlation between age three and age six for other children in this sample is $r = 0.72$ (n = 211), so there is reasonable stability in the ordering of individual differences. As subsequent data shows, this correlation between three and six years is higher than many of the correlations in earlier infancy across periods as short as six months.

Results

The data are drawn from a longitudinal study of infant twins in which they were tested at 3, 6, 9, 12, 18, and 24 months of age on the Bayley, and at three years on the Binet Form L-M. Except for occasional missed visits, most of the sample has been carried through the entire testing period, so the continuity in infant mental development can be appraised. Correlations were computed between the scores at each age, and the results are shown in Table 1.

The correlations display the classical simplex pattern—they are higher for adjacent ages than for distal ages, and they also become larger as the infants get older. The correlation between 24 and 36 months ($r=.73$) is substantially larger than the correlation for any three-month interval in the first year, so the ordering of individual differences has begun to stabilize. The pattern of correlations is coherent and orderly, and perhaps the most interesting feature is the substantial gain in predictive power at 18 months. It suggests an emerging dimension of cognitive functioning that becomes more fully operative with age, but that is only modestly related to earlier functions.

Given the increasing predictive power of the global MDI scores, the next question was whether there were specific items at each age that had particular power for predicting three-year IQ, and if so, did they represent some distinctive aspect of cognitive functioning?

This was examined by dividing the sample into quartiles on the basis of the three-year Binet IQ scores. With approximately 55 cases per quartile, the items from the earlier Bayley tests were analyzed for percent passing and then graphed for the Hi-Quartile and Lo-Quartile groups. The results for the six-month Bayley tests are shown in Figure 1.

Table 1.   Intercorrelations between mental development scores at ages 3 to 36 months

	3	6	9	12	18	24	36
3		0.57	0.44	0.44	0.37	0.22	0.20
6			0.58	0.53	0.42	0.25	0.26
9				0.57	0.43	0.30	0.34
12					0.55	0.43	0.38
18						0.61	0.57
24							0.73

N between 177 and 335 for each correlation.

The pass percentages generally decline over successive items and the curves for both groups are similar, especially in the latter half of the test. There are some intermediate items, however, that do display a differential pass percentage of 20% or more, and these items are listed below.

Six-month mental	Pass percentage	
	Hi-Q	Lo-Q
38. Watches ball roll across table	98	78
40. Turns head to follow ring visually	97	73
42. Awareness of strange place	82	63
47. Turns head to sound of bell	93	63
48. Turns head to sound of rattle	87	63
53. Responds to image in mirror	77	56
57. Exploitive paper play	75	56

Although it would be premature to abstract a common theme from these items, they do seem to touch on attentiveness and responsiveness to external stimuli.

Turning to the item analysis for the 12-month Bayley tests, the results were notable for a lack of any consistent differential between the Hi-Quartile and Lo-Quartile groups. Only two items showed a 20% pass differential in favor of the Hi-Quartile group, and this was offset by two other items in which the pass differential was reversed. Evidently there was no distinctive cluster of attributes in the mental functioning of 12-month infants that would furnish a predictive marker for individual differences at three years of age. Indeed, this was the essential thrust of the entire first-year results from the Bayley Mental Scale.

The Motor Scale from the Bayley was also given during the first-year visits, and it is more specifically oriented toward postural adjustments and psychomotor coordination. Fewer cases were available for the item analysis, but those items that seemed to be clearly differentiated for the Hi-Quartile and Lo-Quartile groups are shown below.

Six-month motor	Pass percentage	
	Hi-Q	Lo-Q
22. Pulls to sitting position	70	40
25. Attempts to secure pellet	48	24
26. Rotates wrist freely with toys	56	28
28. Rolls from back to stomach	67	40
Nine-month motor		
30. Scoops pellet	83	50
31. Sits alone, good coordination	89	67
34. Early stepping movements	83	44
37. Raises self to sitting position	67	39
38. Pulls self to standing position	72	39
40. Stepping movements when held by hands	56	28
Twelve-month motor		
43. Sits down intentionally	96	72
46. Walks alone	50	32
47. Stands up from recumbent position	37	12

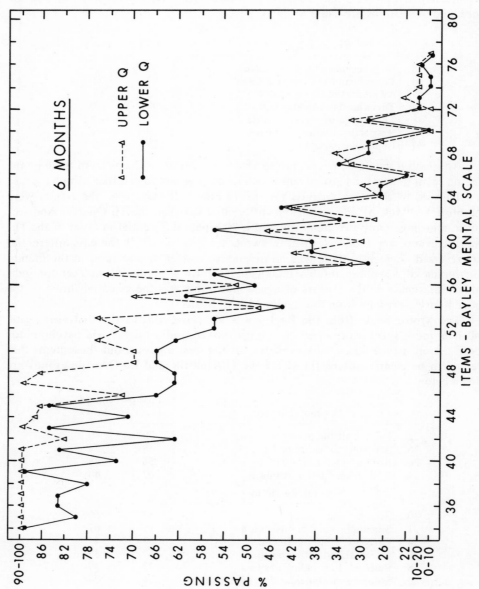

Figure 1.   Percentage of passes on six-month Bayley Mental items for Hi-Quartile and Lo-Quartile three-year infants (see text).

These items of postural control and efforts to improve mobility are far removed from the content of the Binet, yet the Lo-Quartile Binet infants were the ones who were delayed on these postural/mobile adjustments in the first year. It suggests a linkage between the mechanisms of balance plus the impetus to attain upright posture and mobility with the more cognitive mechanisms engaged by the Binet. A discussion of such mechanisms falls outside the limits of this paper, but it is notable that most of the same items differentiated between normal and neurologically suspect eight-month infants (Honzik, Hutchings, and Burnip, 1965). A broader discussion of postural adjustments in sitting and standing, and their relationship to developmental status, may be found in Milani-Comparetti and Gidoni (1967).

Second Year Item Analysis

Returning to the Mental Scale of the Bayley, the results for the item analysis of the 18-month tests are shown in Figure 2.

The two groups have become more clearly differentiated, with the Hi-Quartile group maintaining a consistently higher pass percentage throughout the test. Recalling that the items are arrayed in order of difficulty, it is interesting to note the abrupt fluctuations in pass percentages for the Lo-Quartile group on some adjacent items. Perhaps these items draw on capabilities that are susceptible to lag for the Lo-Quartile infants.

Which items show the largest pass differential between the Hi-Quartile and Lo-Quartile groups?

18-month mental	Pass percentage	
	Hi-Q	Lo-Q
106. Imitates words	86	51
112. Spontaneous scribble with crayon	86	56
113. Says 2 words in imitation	85	29
117. Points to shoes upon request	90	49
118. Pegboard: All pegs in 70 sec	86	41
119. Tower of 3 cubes	49	27
124. Names one object correctly	59	12
126. Follow directions with doll (put in chair, wipe nose, give drink)	68	27
127. Uses words to make wants known	66	15
128. Points to parts of dolly	53	5
130. Names one picture correctly from 4-picture card	36	5
131. Finds correct hidden object	51	15

These items seem to draw on aspects of word knowledge, object recognition, and psychomotor dexterity. An analysis of the underlying cognitive processes engaged by these items is deferred until the 24-month data are presented.

The item pass percentages for the Hi- and Lo-Quartile groups at 24 months are plotted in Figure 3.

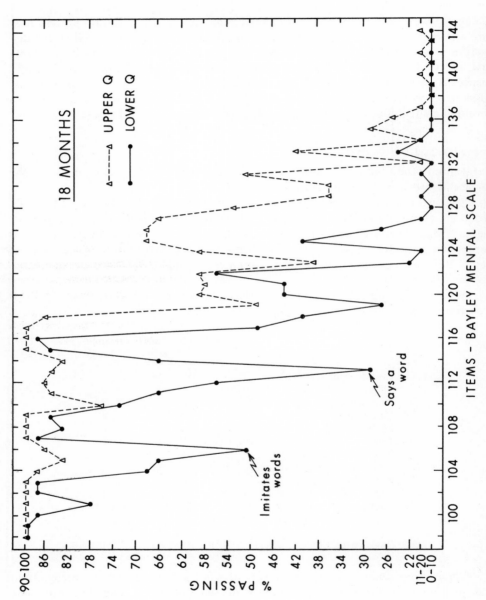

Figure 2.   Percentage of passes on 18-month Bayley Mental items for Hi-Quartile and Lo-Quartile three-year infants (see text).

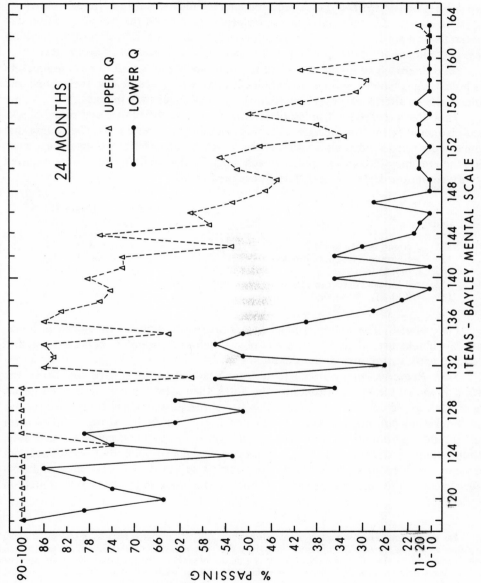

Figure 3.   Percentage of passes on 24-month Bayley Mental items for Hi-Quartile and Lo-Quartile three-year infants (see text).

The differentiation between groups is very sharp at 24 months, and evidently the capabilities assessed by these items are precursors of the capabilities measured on the three-year Binet. What inferences can be drawn about the nature of these capabilities by surveying the task requirements for the high-differentiation items?

For clarity, the items have been grouped according to the use of common test materials or a similarity in task requirements. The task is briefly described, the item pass percentages are shown for 24 months, and also for 18 months, if given then.[1]

Blue Board   The infant is handed a round block and is told to put the block in its hole, then is handed another round block, then two square blocks, then round and square blocks alternately, until the infant fails or all blocks are in place.

Task Requirements   The infant must differentiate the square and round blocks and also identify the appropriate matching hole on the form board. The square and round blocks are handed alternately to the infant, so form differentiation must override the tendency to continue putting each block in any available hole. Also required are psychomotor dexterity, task persistence, and speed.

Item	Credited for	24-month Hi-Q	24-month Lo-Q	18-month Hi-Q	18-month Lo-Q
121.	2 round blocks in place	93	74	58	44
129.	2 round and 2 square blocks in place	91	63	36	15
142.	6 blocks in place	72	35	17	5
155.	All blocks correct in 150 seconds	50	7	—	—
159.	All blocks: 90 seconds	41	5	—	—

Pink Board   The board is placed in front of the infant with blocks in holes, then the blocks are taken out by *E* and placed before *S,* in order round, square, and triangle, with instructions to put them back in.

Task Requirements   A triangular form is added to the square and circle; the infant is shown the blocks fitted into the holes, then after removal instructed to put them back in the correct holes. Once this is completed, the board is reversed so that the blocks are no longer directly in front of holes they fit in. More complex form perception is required, as well as a sensitivity to the fit between block and hole. Additionally, a degree of form constancy is demanded such that the infant can relocate the appropriate hole when the board is reversed. The matching of forms must override the earlier experience of putting the block in the hole immediately in front.

---

[1] The temptation to perform a factor analysis has been resisted, primarily because of serious technical questions about the applicability of factor analysis to this type of developmental data (Cronbach, 1967). The issue is treated more fully elsewhere, but it is a matter of certain inherent properties of any simplex matrix, where adjacent measures correlate more highly than distal measures. When these measures come from successive tests given over ages, as in the Bayley data, or from item correlations where the items are arrayed by order of difficulty, the resulting correlation matrix will generate a known set of factors regardless of the tests or items involved. The interpretation of such factors is necessarily an exercise in futility, and it has the unfortunate consequence of seeming to find meaning and coherence among the measures involved, when in fact the obtained factor structure is built into a simplex matrix and devoid of any such meaning.

Item	Credited for	24-month Hi-Q	24-month Lo-Q	18-month Hi-Q	18-month Lo-Q
120.	Round block placed correctly	90	65	59	44
137.	All 3 blocks placed correctly	83	28	17	2
151.	Board reversed, then all 3 blocks placed correctly (i.e., blocks are no longer in front of hole they fit)	55	12	—	—

Tower of Cubes   *E* places cubes in front of infant and stacks 3 of them, saying, "Let's make a house." Credit for largest number of cubes stacked by infant in three trials.

Peg Board   *E* places pegboard in front of infant with pegs in place, then removes pegs and instructs infant to put them in the holes. When completed, pegs are removed and two more trials are given.

Task Requirements   Aside from the fine motor coordination required to stack the cubes and insert the pegs in the board, perhaps the important attribute here is the infant's matching the model provided by the examiner, and responding to the instructions, "You do it." The infant is making a replica of the examiner's model, and it requires sustained concentration and activity toward that end, rather than drifting into aimless play behavior. It also requires what might be called a constructionist attitude, with the focus on combining the cubes into an organized end product, rather than scattering them in disarray. The latter is a basic tendency (ask any parent) that is superseded only with difficulty by the constructionist attitude, and it remains as a potent undercurrent in the event of frustration or fatigue.

Item	Credited for	24-month Hi-Q	24-month Lo-Q	18-month Hi-Q	18-month Lo-Q
119.	3-cube tower	95	79	49	27
143.	6-cube tower	53	30	—	—
123.	Completes pegs in 42 sec, best trial	98	86	39	22
134.	Completes pegs in 30 sec, best trial	86	56	14	12
156.	Completes pegs in 22 sec, best trial	41	21	—	—

Names Objects   Infant is shown a ball, watch, scissors, pencil, and cup, and is asked, "What is it?" Infant must pronounce name of object for credit.

Task Requirements   The infant must have an appropriate vocal utterance associated with each object, and must also be able to express this utterance selectively when confronted with different objects. The linkage between visual image and appropriate utterance involves perceptual recognition plus both imitation and differential shaping of vocalizations. Because most infants immediately reach for the object when shown, the task requires the infant to insert an intermediary vocal response in the chain before obtaining the object.

Item	Credited for	24-month Hi-Q	24-month Lo-Q	18-month Hi-Q	18-month Lo-Q
124.	1 correct response	91	53	59	12
138.	2 correct responses	76	23	10	0
146.	3 correct responses	60	7	—	—

Names Pictures   E presents four-picture card to infant, points to dog and asks, "What is this?" Remaining pictures are presented with same query, to make it a naming game. E continues with six-picture card. For each picture not named, E says to infant, "Put your finger on the _____."

Task Requirements   The infant must recognize the picture of an object, which is one step more abstract than the object itself, and also must have the appropriate vocal expression linked to the object. For those pictures not named by the infant, the examiner says the name and the infant then points to the appropriate picture. These two memory measures of recall and recognition display the infant's repertory of acquired verbal symbols, and are frequently designated as expressive and receptive language functions. It is an important demonstration of the use of symbols for identification and communication, and of the refinement of primitive babbling into comprehensible words.

Item	Credited for	24-month		18-month	
		Hi-Q	Lo-Q	Hi-Q	Lo-Q
130.	Names 1 picture correctly	90	35	36	5
132.	Points to 3 pictures	86	26	20	2
139.	Points to 5 pictures	74	2	—	—
141.	Names 3 pictures	72	9	—	—
148.	Points to 7 pictures	47	0	—	—
149.	Names 5 pictures	45	0		

Selection of Objects   A cup, blue box, and plate are placed in front of infant, then E requests, "Please give me the cup." Repeated for box and plate.

Task Requirements   Similar to the preceding tasks, except the examiner provides the name and the infant chooses the correct object from three on display. The infant must attend to E's instruction and override any inclination to make his own selection exclusively.

Item	Credited for	24-month		18-month	
		Hi-Q	Lo-Q	Hi-Q	Lo-Q
144.	Credit if infant selects 2 objects correctly (even if he does not hand them over)	76	21	Not given	
152.	Credit if all 3 are correctly selected	48	9	Not given	

Word Usage   The examiner notes whether the infant uses words to make his wants known, and whether he can combine two words denoting two concepts. It represents an early and primitive use of language to convey feelings and describe events.

Item	Credited for	24-month		18-month	
		Hi-Q	Lo-Q	Hi-Q	Lo-Q
127.	Uses words to make wants known (usually one word signifying what the child wants)	91	63	66	15
136.	Sentence of 2 words signifying 2 concepts together; i.e., "shut door, daddy gone"	86	40	25	10

Activity With Doll   The infant is instructed to carry out certain actions with the doll (put in chair, wipe nose, give drink) that are replicas of earlier actions involving the infant.

Task Requirements   Aside from understanding the words, the earlier actions must now be recalled and imitated in a play-type situation with the infant being the active agent rather than the recipient. Infants who are precocious in this regard may be said to assimilate more readily from their past experience certain behaviors that can be imitated, practiced, and ultimately employed in play activities or problem solving.

Item	Credited for	24-month		18-month	
		Hi-Q	Lo-Q	Hi-Q	Lo-Q
126.	Following directions: a) put dolly in chair, b) give dolly drink, c) wipe dolly's nose. Credit if 2 correct.	93	79	68	27

Identifying Parts of Doll   The infant is presented with the complete gestalt of the doll and then is asked to identify certain parts of the body. He must be able to differentiate the component parts and give the correct name.

Item	Credited for	24-month		18-month	
		Hi-Q	Lo-Q	Hi-Q	Lo-Q
128.	Infant is asked to point to dolly's hair, mouth, ears, hands, eyes, feet, nose. Credit if 3 correct.	93	51	53	5

Mending Broken Doll   A small plastic doll with the head separated is placed in front of infant with instructions to fix it.

Task Requirements   This task extends to a further limit than the preceding one; the infant must be able to infer what the object is from an incomplete specimen, and to identify the separated component. It requires a type of object constancy in which the memory representation of the object can compensate for the separated component and enable the infant to relocate the piece correctly. Infants who perform well on this task are precocious in their ability to transcend the immediate stimulus boundaries of an object and to recombine separated components in accordance with the internalized image of the whole.

Item	Credited for	24-month		18-month	
		Hi-Q	Lo-Q	Hi-Q	Lo-Q
133.	Credit if infant makes any attempt at replacement by touching head against neck or shoulders	84	51	42	24
140.	Places head on neck in any position	78	35	14	10
153.	Places head correctly	33	12	—	—

DISCUSSION

It is evident that infants differ appreciably in how they respond to these task demands, and such differences are predictive of later measures of intelligence. The emergent cognitive functions that begin to consolidate after 18 months represent a more advanced mode of central processing than earlier sensorimotor functions, and within this broad category, some infants are more efficient than others.

The focus on task demand and emergent cognitive functions returns attention to Piaget's description of cognitive development. Other investigators (Gottfried and Brody, 1975; Matheny, 1975) have noted a similarity between certain test items from the Bayley and the Piaget-oriented scales, and have suggested that both are measuring the same fundamental aspects of mental development. This author believes this to be the case, and it might be useful to touch briefly on Piaget's formulations about the particular cognitive functions that are prominent during the 18 to 24 month period.

Recall that in the preceding period the infant had begun to show evidence of object permanence and the representation of objects in memory, an awareness of causality and the use of adults to attain desired goals, purposiveness and intentionality in pursuing a particular goal, and the use of imitation in acquiring certain action patterns. All of these functions become refined and more widely employed during the final stage. Furthermore, internalized symbols play an increasingly important role in the child's construction of time and space, bringing to bear the recollection of past events with the anticipation of future ones. Such recollections gradually create a sense of what is constant and what is permanent among the attributes of the physical world. It makes available an internal monitor for appraisal of current perceptions and prediction of likely outcomes.

In the bridge between the sensorimotor and the preoperational periods, the representation of experience by symbols and the manipulation of such symbols are the primary features. The infant of 24 months has signifiers (words or images) that are differentiated from the significates, i.e., the memory of experiences to which the words or images refer. Words become absorbed into the signifier system via imitation and practice, and although they are not essential to representational thought, they do reveal how socially mediated symbols become associated with internalized experiences. The development of this symbol system and its use in communication is a major milestone, because it makes accessible the experience of others in summary form as a guide to adaptive behavior.

Are these cognitive functions as described by Piaget comparable to the functions engaged by the high-differentiation items of the Bayley? It would seem so. The knowledge and use of words, the propensity to imitate the examiner's model, the internal representation of figures and shapes, the linkage between object and verbal symbol—all these attributes are clearly involved in both systems.

Thus, it would seem that precocious performance on the Bayley at 24 months draws heavily on the more advanced cognitive functions available in the final sensorimotor stage. Infants who use these functions most effectively are not only precocious at this age; they also remain precocious at later ages. Therefore, the functions that are singularly enhanced during this stage, particularly the representation of experience by symbols and the manipulation of such symbols, become the rudiments from which intelligence is realized.

If this is the case, we might go one step further and assert that individual differences are as prominent and as biologically based in the Piagetian model as in the psychometric model. Such differences are not to be passed off purely as a consequence of lesser or greater registration of experience, but deserve separate study as inherent dispositions that modulate the effects of experience. The breadth and generality of each schema, the rate of development and degree of organization among structures, the elaboration of metastructures—all are accomplished with varying degrees of efficiency among infants. Such variation must be largely biological in origin, just as the overall trend is rooted in, the species programming. The variation eventually becomes the normal distribution of intelligence, and it reflects those idosyncrasies of spurts and lags and ultimate terminal level that make each child a law unto himself.

The Piagetian model has revolutionized our understanding of the stages of cognitive development in terms of the main trend. Perhaps now is the time for an equivalently detailed study of individual differences in progression through the stages, and in the extensiveness and diversity of cognitive operations at each stage. From an assessment standpoint, such a perspective on individual differences is crucial if the diagnosis and remediation of developmental lags are sought.

ACKNOWLEDGMENT

I am indebted to Dr. Adam Matheny for many helpful comments and suggestions concerning this paper.

REFERENCES

Bayley, N. 1955. On the growth of intelligence. Am. Psychol. 10: 805–818.

Bayley, N. 1965. Comparison of mental and motor test scores for ages 1–15 months by sex, birth order, race, geographical location, and education of parents. Child Dev. 36: 379–411.

Bayley, N. 1969. Bayley Scales of Infant Development. Psychological Corporation, New York.

Cronbach, L. J. 1967. Year-to-year correlations of mental tests: A review of the Hofstaetter analysis. Child Dev. 38: 283–289.

Freedman, D. G. 1974. Human Infancy: An Evolutionary Perspective. Erlbaum, Hillsdale, N.J.

Gottfried, A. W., and Brody, N. 1975. Interrelationships between and correlates of psychometric and Piagetian scales of sensorimotor intelligence. Dev. Psychol. 11: 379–387.

Honzik, M. P., Hutchings, J. J., and Burnip, S. R. 1965. Birth record assessments and test performance at eight months. Am. J. Disord. Child. 109: 416–426.

Lewis, M., and McGurk, H. 1972. The evaluation of infant intelligence. Science 178: 1174–1177.

Matheny, A. P. 1975. Twins: Concordance for Piagetian-equivalent items derived from the Bayley Mental Test. Dev. Psychol. 11: 224–227.

Milani-Comparetti, A., and Gidoni, E. A. 1967. Routine developmental examination in normal and retarded children. Dev. Med. Child Neurol. 9: 631–638.

Phillips, J. L., Jr. 1975. The Origins of Intellect: Piaget's Theory. 2nd ed. Freeman, San Francisco.

Piaget, J. 1952. The Origins of Intelligence in Children. International Universities Press, New York.

Uzgiris, I. C., and Hunt, J. McV. 1975. Assessment in Infancy. University of Illinois Press, Urbana.

Object Permanence, Imitation, and Language Development in Infancy: Toward a Neo-Piagetian Perspective on Communicative and Cognitive Development

M. Keith Moore and Andrew N. Meltzoff

A conceptual revolution is brewing in our understanding of infant cognition, which could potentially reorganize our most fundamental theoretical ideas and established clinical practices. In large measure, it is a revolution of rising expectations engendered by various successes of the Piagetian conception of infancy. However, there have been two almost diametrically opposed responses to these successes. On the one hand, clinicians and educators have been inspired to attempt widespread applications of Piaget's ideas in remedial training programs, special educational endeavors, and the construction of instruments for assessing progress in mental development. On the other hand, developmental psychologists have been inspired to scrutinize more closely Piaget's assumptions and assertions about infant development. The result has been, paradoxically, that the burgeoning practical application of Piaget's ideas has coincided with growing challenges to them.

In general terms, this chapter offers a revision of Piagetian theory within the context of recent infant research and spells out the consequences of this revision both for theory and practice. More specifically, the chapter analyzes the potential significance of development in imitation, object permanence, and language for the growth of communicative and cognitive competence, outlines the impact of recent

This work was supported in part by grants from the National Science Foundation (GS-42926), the Spencer Foundation, the Washington Association of Retarded Citizens, and the Child Development and Mental Retardation Center of the University of Washington (HD 02274).

research on Piaget's theory of infancy, and traces the implications of this new evidence for the construction of assessment instruments.

The organization of the chapter is as follows: first considered is Piaget's theory of sensorimotor functioning, with particular focus on his account of the development of imitative competence and its most direct developmental sequela: mental representation. Next reviewed is recent evidence showing that 12- to 21-day-old infants are able to imitate facial gestures—a feat Piagetian theory claims to be possible only at about 12 months of age. This finding leads to a revision of Piaget's account of imitative development. The implications of this revision for Piagetian-based theories of language development are next explored and a new account of the role of infant cognition in language acquisition is offered. Specifically, it is argued that a major prerequisite determining the onset of meaningful speech is the development of the infant's rules for maintaining the identity of objects through spatial and featural transformations of them. General conclusions are drawn for: 1) theories of infant cognitive and communicative development, 2) the construction of assessment instruments, and 3) priorities for future research.

SENSORIMOTOR INTELLIGENCE AND THE DEVELOPMENT OF IMITATION IN PIAGETIAN THEORY

Piaget (1952, 1954, 1962) has organized the major developments in infancy into six invariantly ordered stages. According to him, developments in such diverse areas as visual-manual coordination, imitation, and object permanence are linked together through the unitary organization of the action structures which underlie them. Piaget terms these action structures, "schemes." By approximately 18 months of age, the development of these action structures is said to have advanced far enough to allow the infant to construct an internal representation or image of absent objects and events. When the infant can act on the basis of such internal representation he has, by definition, passed beyond Piaget's sensorimotor period and would then possess the cognitive competencies needed for acquiring a linguistic system. The Piagetian formulation of infant development thus allows for considerable economy in the assessment of communicative and cognitive development. For example, the determination of an infant's stage of imitative development would, in principle, predict both his level of object permanence development and the extent of his progress toward the onset of meaningful speech. For theoretical, empirical, and practical reasons, therefore, a systematic validation of Piaget's account seems well worthwhile.

Sensorimotor Intelligence

Piaget is extremely sparing in his assumptions about the psychological sophistication of the newborn infant. Indeed, the initial building blocks for psychological development he postulates are action structures such as sucking, the palmar grasp, etc. (Piaget, 1952). Kohlberg (1969) aptly summarizes Piaget's account of the development of these action structures as follows:

The fundamental unit of directed behavior in infancy is a circular reaction, that is, a patterned action which produces feedback stimuli which are the natural elicitors of the act in question. The first and simplest circular reactions are those innately wired to produce such a reaction (sucking which itself produces the tactile pressure on the mouth which naturally elicits sucking, or clenching the fist which produces the pressure on the child's palm naturally eliciting further clenching). These behaviors, then, naturally lead to cycles of repetition, and soon generate integrations in which activities in one modality (waving the hand) lead to sensory feedback in another modality (the spectacle of a moving hand) which leads to repetition of the activity in the first modality, repetitions with functional value (developing eye-hand coordination). This is termed "primary circular reaction," and is in turn followed by a stage of "secondary circular reaction" (the feedback from the act is from its effect in moving an external object), "tertiary circular reaction," etc. (p. 437). (Reprinted from "Stage and Sequence: The Cognitive-Developmental Approach to Socialization," in David A. Goslin (ed.), *Handbook of Socialization Theory and Research,* © 1969 Rand McNally College Publishing Co., by permission.)

In brief, the infant is seen as gradually constructing ever more elaborate and intercoordinated modes of acting on the environment. One central problem for Piaget's theory of psychological development then is to answer the following question: How does an infant who is essentially evolving more complex and adaptive *sensorimotor* patterns for interacting with the here-and-now world ever become able to evoke an object or event that is absent from his perceptual field by means of some sort of "internal representation" of the perceptually absent reality? Herein lies the importance of imitation for Piaget's overall theory of infancy. He maintains that the ability to construct an internal representation of the external world is a direct outgrowth of the stages of imitative development. Moreover, the development of this representational capacity is seen as an essential precursor to subsequent forms of higher order mental activity such as play, dreams, drawing, and perhaps most importantly, language.

Below, Piaget's account of the development of imitation in infancy will be considered in more detail for two reasons. First, it illustrates the manner in which sensorimotor development is claimed to lay the foundation for later representational activity. Second, Piaget's behavioral predictions concerning the stages of imitative development are unusually clear. Therefore, imitation affords an ideal opportunity for an empirical test of the Piagetian position, which the current growth of practical applications suggests is urgently needed.

Imitative Development: Theory and Evidence

The six stages of imitative development and their links to the six levels in the organization of action structures are outlined in abbreviated form in Table 1. Notice that there is a development from the imitation of familiar gestures *one can see oneself perform* (visible imitation), to the imitation of gestures *one cannot see oneself perform* (nonvisible imitation), to imitation that occurs when *one can no longer see the gesture-to-be-imitated* (deferred imitation).

Piaget argues that the stage of visible imitation occurs early in development because when the infant sees an adult performing gestures he has seen himself perform, he fails to distinguish the adult's behavior from his own, and then repeats

Table 1.   Summary of Piaget's stages of imitation in infancy

Stage	Approximate age (months)	Level of organization of sensorimotor intelligence	Developments in imitation
1	0–1	Reflexive	Imitation of crying
2	1–4	Primary circular reactions	Imitation of visible behaviors (e.g., hand clasping) or sounds (e.g., "le")
3	4–8	Secondary circular reactions	Imitation of actions on objects (e.g., hitting or banging an object)
4	8–12	Coordination of secondary circular reactions	Facial imitation
5	12–18	Tertiary circular reactions	Imitation of certain new behaviors never before performed by the infant
6	18–24	Mental recombination and adjustment of schemes	Deferred imitation

the gesture by virtue of his own circular reaction. For example, if an infant who has already constructed the circular reaction of clasping and unclasping his hands sees an adult demonstrating this behavior, the infant incorporates this sensory input into his sensorimotor circular reaction of repetitive hand clasping, and thus performs the motor component. What the observer sees, then, is the infant imitating hand clasping. The infant presumably is unaware that he is imitating anyone; he is merely exercising his circular reaction.

This lack of differentiation between the actions of the self and the actions of another may provide a basis for imitating gestures that the infant can see himself perform (see Parton, 1976, for a review and critique of this point), however, it cannot account for the imitation of gestures that the infant cannot see himself perform—e.g., facial gestures. Thus, Piagetian theory predicts that facial imitation must wait until the infant can establish the correspondence between the visual perceptions of another's facial movements and his own unseen movements. The construction of these correspondences is hypothesized to be accomplished through various intermediaries such as touching one's own face and another's face to establish the correspondence tactually:

> An important new phase begins with the imitation of facial movements (opening and closing the mouth or eyes, etc.). The difficulty is then that the child's own face is known to him only by touch and the face of the other person by sight, except for a few rare tactile explorations of the other person's face. Such explorations are very interesting to note at this level, when the child is forming correspondences between the visual and tactilo-kinesthetic sensations in order to extend imitation to the non-visible parts of the body. Until these correspondences are elaborated [at about 8 to 12 months of age], imitation of facial movements remains impossible or accidental. (From *The Psychology of the Child,* by Jean Piaget and Barbel Inhelder, translated from the French by Helen Weaver, p. 55, © 1969 by Basic Books, Inc., Publishers, New York.)

Although facial imitation marks a developmental milestone in Piagetian theory, it does not indicate to Piaget that the infant has progressed to the level of utilizing any form of internal representation of the external stimulus. In fact, it is only when the infant has reached the last stage of imitative development and can imitate gestures no longer in the perceptual field (deferred imitation) that the question of representation is raised for Piaget. Certainly, deferred imitation requires that the infant's actions be somewhat liberated from the here-and-now perceptual world. It is a way of re-presenting an absent object or event. However, this re-presentation is still carried out in overt action, and according to Piaget, it is only after the infant has developed this capacity that he can then "internalize" his imitation, and thus create a kind of "internal imitation" or mental image of an external object or event (see for example, Piaget and Inhelder, 1969, pp. 55–56). This new capacity for constructing internal representations can now be utilized by the infant in problem-solving situations. For example, when Piaget's (1952, p. 338) daughter was having difficulty trying to open a matchbox while she was still in the sensorimotor period, she was observed to stop acting, look at the box, and open and shut her mouth several times. With this aid in defining the goal she was trying to attain, she succeeded in opening the box. In contrast, after accomplishing the final stage in imitation, she was able to solve such problems without resort to overt modeling in action. Piaget maintains that at this point she is able to represent the goal internally.

The existing empirical research seems to support Piaget's claims about the development of imitation. Several investigators have provided evidence that infants progress through the six stages of imitative development predicated by Piaget (Giblin, 1971; Paraskevopoulous and Hunt, 1971; Uzgiris, 1972; Wachs, Uzgiris, and Hunt, 1971). Indeed, the developmental ordering of the imitative behaviors originally observed by Piaget seems to be so stable that at least one widely used scale of infant psychological development has been constructed on this basis (Uzgiris and Hunt, 1975). Morehead and Morehead (1974) rely on Piaget's sequencing of imitation and his idea that sensorimotor imitation is a key developmental precursor of higher mental functioning to outline a program of training in gestural imitation with the goal of fostering language acquisition and habilitating language-deficient children. Still others have used Piaget's conceptualization of the developmental process as the justification for introducing imitation training as a central part of infant curricula (Winkelstein, 1974).

However, from the point of view of a clinician hoping to use an assessment of imitation to identify an abnormal infant or to ameliorate a case of language-delay through imitation training, these replication studies provide only weak evidence on which to base such critical decisions. This is claimed because Piaget's predictions were made at the level of the infant's *competence* to perform certain imitations, but the tests of them have been at the level of the infant's imitative *performance* under certain restricted conditions. For example, in these studies a particular gesture-to-be-imitated was presented in a more or less uniform manner to infants of various ages, and instances of imitation were recorded. Given this procedure, the invariant order Piaget originally observed was confirmed. However, few attempts were made to accommodate for factors that might interfere with offering the younger infants an equivalent opportunity to display their highest level of imitative capacity—e.g., younger infants may require longer response times for the organization of motor activity, they may be subject to greater memory limitations, etc. Thus, Piaget's crucial theoretical hypotheses about a necessary progression in the development of imitative competence have, by and large, not been rigorously tested.

Some Counterevidence and Implications

Because Piaget's behavioral prediction that infants younger than 8 to 12 months of age (Stage 4) do not have the competence to imitate facial gestures is so clearly stated and so intimately tied to his most fundamental theoretical postulates concerning the stages of sensorimotor development, the authors sought to evaluate this empirical claim in a carefully controlled laboratory setting (Meltzoff and Moore, 1977). The environmental conditions were regulated to maximize the infant's alertness and responsivity—e.g., indirect, subdued lighting was maintained and the experimental room was kept as free from auditory distractions as possible. Some investigators have reported that general anesthesia administered to the mother during childbirth negatively affects the neonates' performance on various behavioral tasks (Aleksandrowicz, 1974; Bower, 1972; Conway and Brackbill, 1970) so only infants whose mothers received no such medication were admitted to the study. Within this context, two studies aimed at assessing the ability of 12- to-21-day-old infants to imitate three facial and one manual gesture were conducted. In one study the infants were shown the following four gestures: tongue protrusion, mouth opening, lip protrusion, and sequential finger movement (an opening and closing of the hand by serially moving the fingers). In a second study, using a different design, the infants were shown the gestures of tongue protrusion and mouth opening. In both studies the experimenter simply demonstrated the gesture to the infant during a stimulus-presentation period, then stopped the demonstration and sat with an unreactive, neutral face during the response period. In short, no training or reinforcing procedure was employed. In both studies the infants were videotaped, and the videotaped segments were examined in random order by scorers who were uninformed as to which gesture had been shown to the infant they were scoring. The results indicate that the infants could successfully imitate all four of the gestures tested when they were examined in this controlled environment. In other words, it seems that two- and three-week-old infants do have the *competence* to imitate facial gestures.

How could such young infants match a gesture they saw another person perform with a gesture of their own which they could not see? It is unlikely that Piaget's Stage 4 mechanism could be utilized. For example, it seems highly improbable that infants this young could have had the experiences necessary to construct the correspondences between their own facial movements and the gestures demonstrated, through intermediaries such as tactual explorations of the mother's and their own face. Similarly, it is unlikely that infants of this age could have learned to associate the visual and proprioceptive components of facial movements by observations of themselves in a mirror. It was therefore hypothesized that this early facial imitation is based on the infant's capacity to represent gestures he visually perceives and gestures he "feels" himself perform in a common form (see Meltzoff and Moore, 1977). The infant is thus envisioned as comparing his own (unseen) facial movements to what might be called a "supramodal representation" of the gestures he sees, and then as actively constructing the match required. Such a representation is termed "supramodal" (after Bower, 1974) inasmuch as it is not particular to one sensory modality. If infants do indeed imitate facial gestures on the basis of such a supramodal representation, then the implications of this finding go beyond a simple demonstration that neonates can perform tasks normally assigned to much older infants. Rather, this phenomenon raises serious questions about the Piagetian, action-based theory of infant sensorimotor development. The capacity for acting on the basis of an internal representation of the external world may not be the culmination of psychological development in infancy as Piaget conceived—but merely its starting point.

If one adopts the hypothesis that the infant begins life with some representational capacities, one is immediately struck by several dilemmas. First, there is the problem of Piaget's stages of imitative development. They seem to be robust enough for several investigators to have replicated them in a wide range of settings. However, these findings of neonatal facial imitation cast doubt on Piaget's interpretation of these stages, especially his idea that they are steps toward the capacity to form internal representations accomplished through a reorganization of the infant's circular reactions. What, then, underlies these apparent stages of imitative development? The authors hypothesize that portions of the Piagetian progression should be reinterpreted as a change in the *function* that imitation serves. Specifically, if the neonatal imitation rests on an innate competence, Piaget's "stage" of facial imitation at one year of age may mark the infant's use of this competence to serve a new, self-representative function. According to this view, the 12-month-old realizes that when he imitates another person, *he looks like the other and the other looks like him.* That is, he can now understand the correspondence in visual terms. Imitation on this basis would be quite different from the imitation of neonates, which is based on the supramodal unity of visually and proprioceptively perceived information. Presumably, this new realization motivates an increase in imitative performance as the infant tries to explore his visual appearance, and this accounts for the apparent increase in imitative performance during Piaget's Stage 4. (This hypothesis is further elaborated later, and is used in explaining how infants might solve certain problems in language acquisiton.)

A second dilemma to be considered is Piaget's argument that the 18-month-old's new capacity to construct internal representations is an important step toward the onset of meaningful speech. If the authors' findings are taken to show that neonates already possess some representational capacity, one must also re-raise the question of what governs the timetable of language acquisition. Whatever determines the onset of meaningful speech, it is not the de novo development of a capacity for representation. In the following section, the implications of this viewpoint for Piagetian-based theories of language development are explored.

Summary

Imitation plays a key role in Piagetian theory because the capacity to construct internal representations is seen as a direct outgrowth of this activity. Although Piaget postulates six invariantly ordered stages in the infant's imitative competence, there is, as yet, very little data evaluating this hypothesized progression. The authors have shown that infants as young as 12- to 21-days-old can already imitate gestures they cannot see themselves perform (facial imitations) and this led to the postulation that neonates can act on the basis of a supramodal representation of visually perceived stimuli. Such a revision raises questions about the meaning of Piaget's stages of imitative development, and it is suggested that at least some of these stages might index a change in the function of imitation. A question that remains to be answered is how these revisions affect our notions of language development, because the growth of the infant's capacity for internal representation and the capacity for using representational (symbolic) systems such as language are intimately linked in the Piagetian view of infancy.

THE ROLE OF COGNITION IN LANGUAGE DEVELOPMENT

This section briefly considers the empirical evidence concerning Piaget's argument that certain sensorimotor attainments are necessary preconditions for the acquisition of language. A reformulation of Piaget's general hypothesis that there are important cognitive precursors to language acquisition is then advanced. Several predictions about the nature of the first words that infants comprehend and produce are derived from this new perspective, and a preliminary empirical test is presented.

Piagetian Approaches to Language and Cognition

Underlying many current theories of language acquisition is the belief that there are necessary cognitive precursors to the onset of meaningful speech. Piaget's stages of sensorimotor development have been a primary resource for developmental psycholinguists speculating about the nature of these precursors (Bates, 1976; Bloom, 1973; Bowerman, 1974; Ingram, in press; Mehrabian and Williams, 1971; Sinclair-de Zwart, 1971, 1974). Although the particular positions advanced differ in significant ways, the general outline of the argument proceeds from certain premises about the requirements that must be met in order for the infant to use words meaningfully. These are as follows:

1. Words and sentences have a symbolic relationship to objects and events in the world. Therefore, the infant must understand the way in which words can stand for (symbolize) objects and events in order to comprehend or to use language. This capacity for symbolic representation is linked to imitative development according to Piaget—therefore, the onset of meaningful speech should be related to imitative development.
2. In order to talk about objects and events not perceptually present, the infant is required to conceive of the continued existence of absent objects. Piaget has postulated that the capacity for understanding that objects continue to exist while they are out of sight—"object permanence," as he calls it—develops through a series of qualitatively different stages over the first two years of life. Presumably, the potential referents of an infant's words should partially depend on his stage of object permanence.

3. Words in sentences may express spatial, causal, and temporal relationships between persons and objects. Again, Piaget has postulated that these concepts are developing over the first two years of life. Thus, the infant's ability to express or understand sentences involving these concepts should be limited by his stage in the development of these concepts.

In principle, then, an infant's cognitive development should greatly influence his language development. However, there are two common observations at odds with Points 1 and 2 above. First, the infant's earliest words begin to appear around 12 months of age—well before Piaget presumes infants to possess the capacity for symbolic representation of objects and events (Piaget, 1952). Second, most of the infant's first communications about objects concern things within the infant's perceptual field; consequently, it is not obvious why object permanence need play a fundamental role in determining the onset of meaningful speech.

One way of interpreting these discrepancies while still preserving the *general* Piagetian hypothesis that there are important cognitive percursors to language development is to suggest that the particular stages of sensorimotor development proposed by Piaget are incorrectly conceived. This would then obscure the genuine relations between representation, object permanence, and language. According to this view, Piaget could still be correct in his delineation of the essential cognitive precursors to language acquisition, and discrepancies from his predictions would be the result of errors in his particular formulations of the stages of cognitive development. This is the view adopted by the authors. Thus, in the following sections, the authors accept Piaget's general hypothesis of a cognition-language relationship, but revise the details of this relationship in the light of new ideas in cognitive development.[1]

A Neo-Piagetian Approach to Language and Cognition

The authors maintain that the acquisition of language is a developmental process in its own right. That is, *the infant must develop a conception of language as a communicative system, and the nature of this conception will be a function of his level of cognitive development.* From this perspective, then, the infant should treat language as an "object of thought" before it becomes an "instrument of thought." Moreover, his understanding of language as "object of thought" should emerge from the interaction between his stage-determined cognitive structures and the linguistic

---

[1] It is worth noting that the parallelisms between language and cognition expressed in Points 1–3 above leave the functional and developmental aspects of the relationship undefined. Nothing is said about how the knowledge acquired through cognitive development is used in language acquisition, or where the notion of language as a communicative system arises. For example, Point 3 implies that a child will not understand or produce the sentence *John hit the ball* before differentiating the concepts of "past" and "present" and the concepts of "agent, action, and object." Although this is true by definition, it offers no suggestions about how these new concepts are translated into the infant's language. Moreover, this parallelism could assume that the infant's general conception of language as a communicative system originates independently of these cognitive developments. The parallelism of points 1–3 alone, therefore, suggests that certain cognitive structures are necessary prerequisites for language acquisition, but they are not sufficient. The approach offered in the next section takes both functional and developmental problems as central to constructing an adequate theory of language acquisition.

behavior he observes. This section, then, presents an overview of the language-cognition relationship, and this serves as a framework for the remainder of the chapter.
The approach is termed "neo-Piagetian," because the authors agree with Piaget that
imitation, object permanence, and internal representation are the appropriate concepts to consider in the search for precursors to language development, but wish to
revise his specific formulations of the stages of sensorimotor development.

　　If we are to understand how the infant comes to conceive of language as a
holistic system based on the information available in his environment, we need a
description of the system he is trying to understand. In the simplest terms, a mature
speaker utters sentences, represented by sequences of sound, with the intention of
conveying a message to a hearer. One major task for the infant is to discover that
these "sentences" have a meaning (the message), and that they are uttered with the
intent to communicate it. This description of the infant's task is generally compatible with recent attempts in semantics to analyze sentences as complex speech acts
containing both a propositional or locutionary component and a performative or
illocutionary component (see Austin, 1962; Fodor, 1977).

　　An attempt to explain how infants initially understand the *performative aspect*
of the language has already been undertaken by Bates and her colleagues (Bates,
1976; Bates, Camaioni, and Volterra, 1975). Bates, Camaioni, and Volterra offer an
account of the way an infant's developing conceptions of causality might be implicated in language development. The basic cognitive-linguistic continuity they
hypothesize stems from the infant's functional use of language as a *tool*—as a means
to an end. They see the infant's initial schemes for tool use (e.g., the action structures that underlie the use of a stick or string to obtain another object) as the
precursors to the infant's use of preverbal gestures as a tool (e.g., pointing to obtain
an object), which in turn serve as precursors to the use of verbal communication as a
tool (e.g., uttering the name of an object with an imperative intonation in order to
obtain it). Thus, they predict that the emergence of both gestural and verbal communication employed as a tool will depend on the infant's attainment of Piaget's
Stage 5 (during which the infant first exhibits tool use with physical objects). This
prediction also follows from an analysis of the infant's cognizance of communication per se, because Piaget (1954) argues that the infant does not attribute independent causality to others until Stage 5. Thus, gestures and vocalizations to others
would not be "communicative" from the infant's viewpoint until Stage 5, when an
indication of the infant's intentions or wishes can be seen as causing the *other* to
carry them out. Bates therefore argues that the Stage 5 action structures (schemes)
underlying tool use and means-end relations are prerequisites to developing a linguistic means for expressing the functional intentions of verbal communication.
That is, these action structures are precursors to the performative (or illocutionary)
component of sentences—that aspect expressing the act intended by the sentence
(e.g., declaring, questioning, commanding, etc.)

　　In sum, Bates, Camaioni, and Volterra argue for a developmental progression
in which some language functions emerge from cognitive precursors. Their data support the following conclusions: a) once infants solve Piaget's Stage 5 means-ends
tasks, they also begin using objects gesturally to get adult attention and using adults
to get objects through gestures, and b) when they subsequently enter Piaget's Stage

6, they begin to use words for the same purposes. Although this work is still preliminary, this general model of earlier cognitive functions being translated into later communicative and linguistic forms seems a more adequate interpretation of the Piagetian claim that language develops from thought than the simple parallelism between language and causal concepts offered in the previous section. In what follows, a revision of the Piagetian claims concerning the role of object permanence and internal representation in language development is offered.

The authors postulate the infant's early (and developing) representational system serves as a functional precursor to the *referential and propositional functions* achieved through sentences. In particular, the relationship an infant constructs between his internal representation of an external object and the thing itself is one of the precursors to the linguistic notion of reference. Moreover, because the infant's cognitive structures serve to interpret the external world, these interpretations are among the precursors to the propositional (as opposed to performative) component of sentences. In short, because the infant's cognitive interpretations of the world can be violated and confirmed (i.e., he has true and false expectations), they prefigure that aspect of sentences that allows one to say that a sentence is true or false. Thus, the function of representing the external world, which is initially performed for the infant through internal cognitive structures, is subsequently performed through language.[2]

If the infant is to learn to use language meaningfully, he must understand how adults use it meaningfully. This implies that *until the infant understands those aspects of a situation to which an adult is referring in much the same way as the adult does, he will not be able to determine any systematic correspondence between adult words and their referents.* According to the authors' approach, then, an explanation of how infants learn to comprehend and subsequently to produce speech depends in part on an account of how an adult and infant might succeed in establishing a common interpretation for some aspect of their worlds.

Bruner (1975) has addressed the issue of how the infant and adult might develop a shared view of the world. Bruner discusses this problem in terms of the development of means by the mother and infant for mutual control of the focus of attention—specifically, the line of visual regard. He goes on to point out the limitations of this procedure:

> Plainly, such devices for assuring a joint focus are insufficient for indicating what feature of a focus of attention is being abstracted—by the mother or by the child. That, of course, is the shortcoming of all ostensive indication. What has been mastered is a

---

[2] It is interesting that this hypothesis about the relationship between internal representations and representation in language has been argued from a purely logical consideration of languages and cognitive psychology by Fodor (1975). In fact, Fodor contends from such considerations that language learning is best conceived as a process of translating the external language-to-be-learned into the terms of an unlearned, but equally rich, inner representational system, which he calls a private language. Given that humans can learn the languages of any culture, he equates this private language with the universal representational system underlying all human cognitive processes. The authors agree with Fodor's arguments for the existence of a rich representational system before language acquisition, but disagree with Fodor on two major points. First, the initial system could be much less powerful than Fodor supposes, because as becomes clear later, this system is itself developing. Second, there are developmental mechanisms for "stage change" (the reorganization of rules governing representations) that are not reducible to the psychological processes of association, maturation, or concept formation.

procedure for homing in on the attentional locus of another: learning where to look in order to be tuned to another's attention. It is a discovery routine and not a naming procedure. It is totally generative within the limited world inhabited by the infant in the sense that it is not limited to looking at oranges or dolls or rattles (p. 269).

Bruner is thus suggesting that the gap between the mother's and infant's view of the relevant part of the world is narrowed by these generative procedures. Yet, as he correctly notes, the fundamental problem of establishing some precisely shared object, or event-to-be-referred-to, has still not been solved. It cannot be solved until one considers how infants interpret these joint foci of attention. Only then could one specify what feature of a focus of attention was being abstracted. What we need, therefore, is some description of how infants understand these aspects of their world, and to do that we must consider how the infant's cognitive capacities are employed in these situations.

Infant cognitive development is primarily involved in language acquisition in two ways. First, it provides the cognitive processes with which the infant understands the *context* of a potentially communicative interaction so that he shares some mutual meaning with a mature speaker of the language. Second, it provides the *cognitive processes* that allow him to learn how the speaker's verbalizations relate to these shared meanings. In this case, "meaning" refers to how the external world is understood by the infant or adult. These premises are based on the assumption that many aspects of the adult's world will not be initially understood by infants and, thus, infants will not be able to learn how adult discourse relates to these aspects until they acquire a similar view of the world. Adult speech in these cases will be meaningless to the infant. The converse case will also occur, where infant conceptions of the world will be incomprehensible to the adult. Thus, although these infant conceptions may underlie some infant babbling and early vocalizations, it will be difficult, if not impossible, for an adult to detect any regularities between the infant's vocalizations and his adult interpretation of the world.

The Infant's Conception of his World

Recent research shows just how different the infant's and adult's interpretations of the world can be. Consider, for example, the reports of infant visual tracking behavior at three months of age (Bower, 1971; Bower, Broughton, and Moore, 1971; Gardner, 1971). Bower and his colleagues initially observed that the infant would visually follow an object to the edge of a screen, then, after the object's occlusion, his eyes would jump to the other edge of the screen in apparent anticipation of the object's reappearance. These authors were impressed with this evidence of early sophistication, until they performed the following control procedure. When the object was started toward the screen, but stopped in sight before occlusion, the infants briefly arrested their gaze on the stopped object and then resumed tracking the path of the moving object. Subsequent experiments showed that this effect could be obtained both without occlusion of the object and on circular as well as linear trajectories of motion (Bower, 1971; Bower and Paterson, 1973). The authors concluded that the infants did not understand that when the object was at rest it was the same object as the one that was in motion. For the three-month-old infants, there were two different objects: a moving object and a stationary one. It seems, therefore, that three-month-old infants use spatial rules to determine object identity—namely, a moving object is identified by its trajectory of motion and a stationary object is identified by its location in space. Moreover, it is not until five months of age that these two rules for identifying objects are coordinated into a single rule, enabling the infant to recognize an object moving from place to place as a unitary one.[3]

It has been proposed that the infant's conception of object identity continues to develop throughout the first 18 months of life (see Moore, 1973, 1975). The authors now wish to postulate that the whole of what is called object permanence development in Piagetian theory is better accounted for as a development of rules for object identity than by a development of the underlying sensorimotor schemes. "Object identity" here refers to the concept by which an infant determines whether an object remains the same with itself throughout a transformation, such as moving from place to place or disappearing and reappearing. The concept of object identity, then, refers to an object's *sameness with itself*, its *unique identity*, not to its featural similarity to another object (as in the usage *two identical objects*).

What, then, is the link between "object identity" thus conceived, and what Piaget has termed the problem of "object permanence?" This question is best answered by considering the infant before he has a concept of object permanence and asking: How can the numerous disappearances and reappearances of objects that he witnesses every day be of any help to him in constructing this concept? If disappearance annihilates the object for the infant (i.e., "out of sight is out of mind"), then when that object reappears there is no reason why it must be viewed by the infant as the *same* object. It could just as well be a *different* object that has now appeared in the same place that the *first* object disappeared. *It would thus seem that before an infant can utilize the disappearances and reappearances of objects as data bearing on their permanence, he must see the pre- and post-disappearance object as the same object.* Otherwise, he merely witnesses two unrelated events. Consequently, rules for object identity would seem to be logical prerequisites for the development of object permanence (see also Moore, Borton, and Darby, 1978).

Given this analysis, two hypotheses can be advanced: First, it is only through development of the concept of object identity that the infant (like the adult) can come to understand that two instances of contact with the same object imply that the object was permanent during an intervening period when it was out of sight. Second, as the infant's concept of object identity develops there will be a concomitant development of what is called object permanence.

The authors postulate three levels in the development of object identity (see Table 2). Level 1 comprises the identity problems associated with the steady-state structure of the visual world: objects in motion continue in motion; objects at rest stay at rest, etc. Thus, an infant can determine that the identity of an object in motion is the same at any point on its path, that an object in the same place is the

---

[3] One reason, then, that infants may not learn to use words pertaining to objects and events before five months of age arises from the problems they have in identifying unique objects. If the movement of a stationary object creates two objects for the infant, then finding a joint adult-infant meaning on which to base a "name" for this event will be difficult, to say the least.

Table 2. Developmental levels postulated by Identity Theory

Level	Age (months)	Description of levels	Examples of transformations for which an object's unique identity is maintained
1	0–4	Identity maintained for steady-state transformations of the visual world	Objects in motion Objects at rest
2	5–8	Identity maintained for transformations of visible objects	Objects in motion stopping Objects at rest starting to move
3	9–18	Identity maintained for transformations producing occluded objects	Objects disappearing in motion Object disappearing at rest

same object each time he looks at it, and so on. Level 2 comprises the identity problems associated with changes from the steady-state structure of the visual world: the visible transformations of visible objects such as an object in motion stopping, a stationary object moving, etc. Level 3 comprises the identity problems associated with changes from the world of visual objects to mental representations of objects: the transformations producing occluded objects such as a stationary object being covered by a moving screen or a moving object going behind a stationary screen. Within this framework the rules for identity employed in solving Level 1 problems are postulated to be developmentally reorganized to solve Level 2 problems, and these are developmentally reorganized to solve those of Level 3.

In brief, according to the authors' "Identity Theory" the infant's conservation of the permanence of objects across transformations of disappearance and reappearance arises from his conservation of the unique identity of objects across spatiotemporal transformations of them. The underlying basis for the stages of object permanence development lies in the gradual elaboration identity rules rather than in the progressive intercoordination of action structures (schemes), as Piaget claims.

The preceding discussion has argued for a revision of Piaget's theory of imitative and object permanence development. Current work on neonatal sensorimotor coordination suggests additional revisions in Piaget's position. According to Piaget, the infant is initially incapable of differentiating himself from the world around him. Thus, for example, the infant is presumed to confuse his own acts with events in the world, to believe that objects exist only as he interacts directly with them, and to confuse changes of object position with changes in object size. More recent research leads one to question this view. For instance, Bower, Broughton, and Moore (1970a) and Ball and Tronick (1971) have shown that neonates will interpose their arms between an approaching object and their face, as though defending against being hit. The infants apparently did not see the looming object as merely growing larger while remaining stationary, as would be expected according to the Piagetian perspective. In addition, Bower, Broughton, and Moore (1970b) found that neonates will reach to an object they see, thereby supporting the idea that they innately possess a sophisticated sensorimotor coordination. Bruner and Koslowski (1972) report similar behavior by slightly older infants. Piaget does not expect reaching behavior until about four months of age. According to his theory, it is only at that age that infants begin to coordinate their visual and tactual perception of objects, thereby leading to accurate, visually guided attempts to grasp. (It must be noted that the studies cited here are controversial, and more rigorous empirical work is needed before firm conclusions are justified; see also Bower, 1972, 1974, 1977; Dodwell, Muir, and Di Franco, 1976; Field, 1977; Ruff and Haltan, 1977; von Hofsten, 1977; Yonas et al., 1977.)

In brief, evidence from several lines of work in early infancy—sensorimotor coordination, imitation, and object permanence—suggests that a fundamental reorganization of Piaget's conception of the infant is required. At the risk of oversimplifying these complex issues, the points included in this revised concept as they emerge from this work are:

1. The infant possesses at birth a well-organized perceptual world, differentiated from himself, in which objects are seen as stable wholes located within an external, three-dimensional space.
2. The infant possesses at birth some ability to act upon a supramodal representation of this perceptual world.
3. Through development, the infant reorganizes his innate representational capacities to conserve the identity and permanence of objects across increasingly complex transformations of his perceptual world. That is, he constructs rules that maintain invariants over perceptual change (e.g., rules for object identity and object permanence).

Points 1 and 2 deal with what has usually been called perception—i.e., cases where the relevant behaviors are determined by parameters of the stimulus. Point 3 deals with what has usually been called cognition—i.e., cases where behavior is not under stimulus control, but depends on the organism's interpretation of the stimulus. The difference between cognition and perception can be illustrated by returning to the three-month-old in the tracking situation. As the object moves along its path, the infant follows it visually; when it stops, his eyes stop with it. Then he resumes tracking along the original path. However, there is no external stimulus to start his eyes tracking again. In this case, the effective stimulus is his *interpretation* that the stopped object is not the one he was originally tracking, and his continued tracking is an attempt to maintain the steady-state structure of the visual world. A primary function of cognition, then, is to extend the infant's capacity to cope with changes in his perceptual world by discovering the stability that underlies the variations in surface appearances. This function is the reason why identity maintenance plays so central a role in infant development, because both an understanding of stability and of predictable change depend on a means of determining what has stayed the same in the face of apparent flux.

The infant's identity rules determine the meaning that a particular event will have for the infant. For example, the three-month-old is postulated to identify a moving object as the *same* object at different points along its path of motion by means of a "trajectory" rule for object identity (see Table 2). For the case of a moving object, the infant interprets that it is the *same* object that has moved from one point A at time t_1 to point B at t_2 by comparing his stored representation of the object and its trajectory at A with his perception of the object and its trajectory at B. If the trajectories are the same, the objects are the same, according to his identity rule. If the trajectories are different, the infant thinks the objects are also different. With development, these rules are reorganized to encompass increasingly complex events, and the infant's interpretations of events become both more comprehensive and more similar to those of an adult.

What is the relevance of these developing cognitive rules for language development? The infant's interpretations of transformational events are among the first "meanings" the infant could express in his own utterances. They are also the first "meanings" he could potentially share with an adult and in terms of which he could comprehend an adult's utterances.

The Infant's Conception of Adult Language

The previous section emphasized the central role transformational events play in the infant's world. One might suspect, then, that one reason people are so interesting to infants is because they are self-transforming objects. Furthermore, it has been claimed that transformational events the infant can control or create himself maximally capture his attention (Piaget, 1952; Watson, 1972). It is possibly for this reason, then, that repetitive and predictable sequences of social interaction (i.e., games and rituals) are so fascinating to infants (Watson, 1972). Moreover, Bruner (1975) suggests that it is within the context of such social interaction that infants develop their skills in turn-taking in terms of sequencing both actions and speech (dialogue). In this section the authors propose that within such contexts of mutual interaction, it is the infant's cognitive structures (e.g., the object identity rules described above) that enable him to detect the correspondences between adult speech and the concurrent transformational events. Through the detection of these correspondences, he comes to comprehend the referential and propositional components of speech about these events.

With regard to the infant's *production* of utterances, however, we must resort to additional mechanisms: imitation and feedback from the effects of infant utterances. The authors most emphatically are not proposing that these imitative and feedback processes are involved in the comprehension of adult speech about transformational events. Others (e.g., Sherman, 1971; Skinner, 1957) have proposed such programs, which seem to be inadequate, and the proposals herein should not be confused with them. Rather, imitation will motivate the infant to produce the vocal-event correspondences of adults *as the infant construes or understands them.* As his understanding of the correspondence develops, so will his productions. Two kinds of feedback from the effects of his utterances will be important. With regard to the acquisition of phonetically correct forms, one would expect the efficacy of the infant's verbalizations in gaining adult attention and response to be the most important. This

Table 3.   Four initial phases in the infant's imitation of adult speech about transformational
events

Phase	Imitative behavior
1	Imitation of adult behavior toward objects *or* imitation of adult vocalizations regardless of the event
2	Imitation of the temporal relationship between adult vocalizations and transformational events: Infant vocalizations occur when watching or performing transformational events
3	Imitation of the consistency relationship between adult vocalizations and transformational events: Particular but idiosyncratic infant vocalizations consistently occur in conjunction with particular transformational events
4	Imitation of the specific relationship between particular adult utterances and particular transformations or objects transformed: Infants produce the particular adult utterance pertaining to the transformation observed or the object transformed

kind of feedback enables the infant to discover that verbalizations can be used to control others. Once adult attention and response have been attained, it is feedback about the *truth* of his utterance that matters (i.e., did what he say correctly correspond to the transformational event). This kind of feedback enables the infant to discover that verbalizations can be used to communicate states of affairs in the external world. Initially, then, one would not expect adult corrections, restatements, expansions, simplifications, and so on to provide the main form of feedback.

The authors postulate four initial phases in an infant's understanding of adult linguistic behavior with corresponding attempts by the infant to imitate the adult (see Table 3):

1. The infant's first vocalizations in relation to transformational events are primarily expressions of the affective state induced by the infant's understanding of transformation. When the infant understands it correctly, that is when his expectations are confirmed, he initially smiles, gurgles, and coos. When he does not understand the event, he responds either with surprise (when his expectations are disconfirmed) or with avoidance and fretting (when he has two contradictory expectations). From the infant's point of view, adult behavior has no systematic relation to these transformational events, because the infant focuses either on the adult behavior *or* on the transformational event alone. Thus, two behavior patterns occur. If the infant focuses on the transformational event, he responds with vocalizations determined by the degree of his understanding of the event. If he focuses on the adult, he may attempt to imitate the adult's behavior or vocalizations without regard to their relation to the transformational event.

2. Once the infant's understanding of transformations begins to overlap those of the adults around him, the infant notices that there is a *systematic temporal relationship* between adult vocalizations and these transformations. In this

phase, the infant can be imagined as seeing adults "babbling" when they watch or perform transformations. Infants will attempt to imitate this purely temporal relationship between vocalizations and transformational events. Such imitation would consist simply of making sound when acting on objects or watching them transformed. In this phase the infant realizes only that vocalizations are temporally linked to transformational events (at least to the ones he can understand). Therefore, his imitation arbitrarily links a variety of sound sequences to any transformational event. Adults typically see this as the infant babbling happily while playing with toys.

3. The imitative relationship becomes more specific as the infant notices repetitions of the particular sound sequences that adults employ with particular kinds of transformational events. The infant now recognizes that adults use sound sequences consistently, yet he attaches no significance to *which* sound sequences are used. In this phase, then, the infant's imitation of the relationship between adult utterances and external events takes the form of the infant vocalizing in his own idiosyncratic fashion, but employing these vocalizations *consistently* with particular transformational events.

4. Finally, the infant notices that particular adult sound sequences co-vary in regular fashion with particular transformations and particular objects. (From now on, "transformation" is used in a technical sense, referring only to the spatiotemporal change specified by the infant's identity rules. An event, therefore, can be decomposed into the transformation and the object undergoing transformation.) Thus, some adult utterances remain invariant as long as the *same transformation* is involved, regardless of the objects transformed   (e.g., adult words for transformations, such as *bye-bye* or *more*). Conversely, some adult utterances are invariant as long as the *same object* is involved regardless of the transformations employed (e.g., words naming particular objects, such as *Mommy* or *Teddy*). These differential situations provide the basis for the infant's segregating which adult words pertain to transformations and which pertain to the objects transformed. In this phase, specific relationships are imitated by the infant, yielding correspondences between infant utterances and particular transformations or objects that correspond to adult usage.

It is vital to note that the hypothesized process of extracting a relationship between adult words and events requires that the relationship between the sound sequence and some aspect of the transformational event remains invariant, but that the event as a whole varies. Simple repetitions will not be effective. This can be illustrated by considering the regularities that occur in the adult's use of words standing for transformations (see the description of *bye-bye* in 4 above). In this case, the *type of transformation* applied to objects remains invariant even though many different objects are transformed. Similarly, the *words* standing for these transformations will remain invariant, but the words standing for the different objects will vary. This circumstance, then, effectively isolates an invariant relationship between occurrences of the word for the transformation and instance of the particular transformation. The converse occurs in the infant's isolation of the word for a particular object. In this case, only the word corresponding to that object will remain invariant as that object is transformed in different ways. Again, an invariant relationship can be extracted between the occurrences of the word for that particular object and instances of that object being transformed.

The infant is seen as applying the same basic cognitive process first to transformations of the physical world to extract *invariant objects* (see discussion of "object indentity" in previous section) and then to the communicative encounter to extract *invariant relationships between adult words and these transformational events*. In short, the authors' viewpoint, which might be called a "transformational approach" to the specification of joint reference, helps to solve the problem of ostensive definition that has plagued previous accounts of language acquisition.

Below hypotheses about the necessary structural relationships that hold between infant cognitive development and language acquisition are more specifically summarized (see also Table 2):

1. Until approximately five months of age, the infant's cognitive system limits the range of potentially shareable meaning so severely that there is virtually no basis for the infant to learn that adult words relate systematically to aspects of the world that the infant understands. That is, from the infant's point of view, there simply *is* no systematic relationship between the words he hears used and the way he understands events.
2. Among the first meanings that infants could potentially share with an adult are those interpretations of transformational events that the infant bases on his developing cognitive rules for maintaining an invariant over transformation— e.g., the identity of an object undergoing a particular visible change.
3. The development of rules for object identity allows the infant to conceive of objects as invariant across some transformations of the steady-state structure of the world, so that at about five months of age, the infant sees an object as maintaining its unique identity even when it visibly starts or stops moving. This is the first opportunity for shared meaning with an adult regarding objects. Further development of object identity and object permanence provides a major basis for an increasingly similar adult-infant view of the contexts in which communication could occur.
4. The infant can learn to relate adult words correctly to those aspects of a situation that he understands as invariant over different transformations (e.g., objects), because it is only those adult words referring to that aspect of the situation that will remain the same over different transformations. Similarly, infants can correctly learn to relate adult words to the transformations because those words will remain the same, regardless of the objects transformed.

It may seem that the authors have labored to account partially for a very small accomplishment: the infant's acquisition of the simplest declarative speech. Certainly, all of the power of the infant's initial cognitive structures have not been explored, nor have even modestly sophisticated declaratives been treated. However, we contend that this accomplishment, coupled with the acquisition of some performatives (Bates, 1976) is significant because it gives the infant a conception of language as a symbolic system capable of representing affairs in the world (the propositional component) and capable of serving a communicative purpose (the functional component). This initial conception captures the fact that sentences can be used to declare, to command, to question, etc. that they can be true or false as descriptors of the world, and that others respond to these truth values.

The neo-Piagetian perspectives afforded by recent research in early infancy suggest a plausible means through which the infant and adult might establish shared meanings which could then be utilized in both infant and adult verbalizations. Moreover, although this account differs substantially from Piaget's in the way in which cognitive development plays a role in language development, it does agree that certain prelinguistic attainments constititue important cognitive precursors to language acquisition.

Some Empirical Predictions   It has been argued that the relationships between adult utterances and shared adult-infant meanings provide a basis for the infant's comprehension of adult speech and his own meaningful use of speech. Although predictions from this line of argument are made most directly for comprehension, it is assumed that they will be mirrored subsequently in the first words that infants produce. The first words to appear will be words pertaining to visible transformations and words referring to objects that the infant can observe transformed. Below, the authors develop more detailed predictions, first for words pertaining to transformations, and then for words referring to objects.

The infant's first words for transformations will be determined by his understanding of transformations preserving object identity. Infants at Level 1 (i.e., infants capable of maintaining identity only for the steady-state structure of the visual world), will not be able to employ the process of isolating transformations by variation in the objects transformed. This will be true because to them, objects are not transformed at all—rather, the visual world is transformed. Thus, Level 1 infants will not extract any invariant relationship between adult speech and events, and so will not produce any socialized speech. An infant at Level 2 (i.e., an infant capable of preserving identity over an object's visible transformations) will produce words for visible transformations of objects. They will use words such as *up* and *down*, words for exchanging objects with others like *give* and *thanks* (where the object is moved but not hidden), and words for recognizing the same object again after transformation, such as *see* and *look*. A Level 3 infant (i.e., an infant capable of understanding transformations that cause an object to disappear) will produce words for disappearances and reappearances, such as *where, more, all gone*. (It is the meaning that the word has for the child that is being predicted, not the word the child uses per se. For example, an infant could use *bye-bye* in association with an object's or person's disappearance, which would suggest that Level 3 object permanence was involved. He could also use it only in association with the object's moving away from him, which would suggest a Level 2 visible transformation.)

Hypotheses with regard to object words are also intimately tied to the development of object identity and permanence. Consider the six-month-old. He can maintain the unique identity of an object that starts and stops moving in full view, and thus can notice an adult's systematic use of a sound sequence in relation to these visible transformations of that object. He would think that the word *cup*, for instance, was the *proper* name for the specific object he saw transformed, rather than the "common" name for all objects with cup-like functions and features. Because the six-month-old lacks object permanence, he has no way of recognizing that particular cup as the same object, should he encounter it again in a different situation. Consequently, he would think that it was a different object, and would be confused by an adult's use of what he thinks is the proper name for the original object in this second encounter. Given this falsification of his hypothesized relationship between the object and the adult utterances, he would not continue to think that *cup* was a name for the object.

Only around 11 months of age, when the infant has acquired permanence for some transformations of an object, its features, and its functions (Moore and Clark, 1975) will the infant, through these properties, have a means of identifying the object on a subsequent encounter. At this point then, he could learn proper names for objects from adult discourse. However, comprehending most adult names for objects must wait until the infant realizes that an adult's utterances refer generically to the class of objects defined by the features and functions of the object currently being named: e.g., *cup* refers to all cup-like objects. Before this realization, the infant will misinterpret generic object names as proper names. If the infant produces these names himself, they will be unstable productions, because he will soon discover that adults do not use them in this way. After he realizes that these are generic names, however, one might expect an idiosyncratic under- and overgeneralized use of words based on the infant's choice of the features and functions defining the generic class. This realization that objects are usually named generically could well account for the often found vocabulary "explosion" after the first 50 words or so are acquired.

The prediction that infants will first comprehend object words as proper names before they comprehend them as generic names needs two qualifications before translation into a prediction about infant verbal productions. First, for some infants, the misinterpretation of generic names may only appear in comprehension, because this problem is resolved there before any generic names are produced. Second, for other infants, only a few generic names may be produced as though they were proper names, because the discrepancies associated with these words will be sufficient for them to realize how adults name objects. Then, subsequent names will be treated as generic ones.

It should also be noted that all of these predictions regarding the infant's first words are made for English. The nature of English, like most languages, creates some interesting problems for infants in learning the meaning of words either for transformations or for objects. The problem with object names has already been examined—the infant has to learn that most adult object words are generic names for the superordinate class of which the object is a member, rather than the proper names for the specific objects as he initially interprets them. For transformation words the problem is the opposite, because most visible transformations in English have been mapped onto a topological or Cartesian spatial reference system—up, down, left, right, in front of, behind, etc. The infant has to learn that most adult words for spatial transformations pertain only to a subclass of the transformational categories with which he is initially concerned. (It may be that there are languages whose categories for objects and transformations would correspond more closely to the infant's. If so, more rapid acquisition for these cases is likely.)

Very little data directly relevant to these hypotheses exist. However, some support for them can be found in the literature. For instance, Hilke and Clark (1978) have found that infants being tested for object permanence will vocalize more when presented with transformations they partially understand than for those they completely understand (correct search) or completely do not understand. This result is consistent with the prediction for Phase 1 (Table 3), where the infant's initial vocal reactions to transformational events are solely a function of his understanding of the event. Moreover, Dore, Franklin, Miller, and Ramer (1976) have found evidence that infants will consistently produce the same phonetic form over repeated encounters with the same events in the transition period between prelinguistic vocalizations and one-word speech. This finding is compatible with our idea that there is a time (in Table 3 it is called Phase 3) when infants use their own idiosyncratic utterances to imitate the consistency relationship between adult vocalizations and transformational events from their point of view. The de Villiers (this volume) report that:

> Greenfield and Smith (1976) and Veneziano (cited in Bates, 1976) claim that children in the one-word stage of development almost always encode that element undergoing greatest change or emphasis. For example, if the child is placing toys in a bucket, he tends to name them individually rather than saying *put* or *bucket*, which remain constant in the situation.

Similarly, Nelson (1973) summarizes her study of infants' first 50 words as follows:

> The common attribute of all of the most frequent early referents is that they have salient properties of change—that is, they do things (roll, run, bark, meow, go r-r-r and drive away). In this connection, sound is as relevant as movement; both exhibit temporal change. The omissions are in general of things that—however obvious and important— just sit there: sofas, tables, chests, windows, plates, overalls, trees, grass. The words that are learned are not only the ones the child acts upon in some way (shoes, bottle, ball) but also ones that do something themselves that the child only observes—trucks, clocks, buses, and all the animals. This general conclusion is of course in accord with cognitive theories (e.g., Piaget's emphasizing the importance of the child's action to his definition of the world, but it implicates equally the importance of actions external to the child).

These two reports are consistent with the overall prediction that objects the infant sees and hears transformed (and not only those which the infant can manipulate, as Piagetian theory might predict) are the ones that infants name first.

The Role of Imitation in Acquiring Words Referring to the Self and to Subjective States The difficulty that infants face in establishing exactly which aspect of a situation is being referred to by the usage of a specific word has already been underscored. In this section we explore the special difficulty that infants face in learning the meaning of words that refer to the self (such as the pronoun *I*) and words that refer to subjective states of feeling and emotion. These words pose an additional problem because the infant and adult cannot orient in the same way to the referents as they can in regard to objects and events external to themselves. The transformational mechanism proposed above will therefore be less effective in these cases. For these problems, the development of imitative functions may play a uniquely valuable role.

Consider first the problem of learning the meanings of *I* and *you:*

> We shall call attention to a fundamental and moreover obvious property of *I* and *you* in the referential organization of linguistic signs. Each instance of use of a noun is referred to a fixed and "objective" notion, capable of remaining potential or of being actualized in a particular object and always identical with the mental image it awakens. But the instances of the use of *I* do not constitute a class of reference since there is no "object" definable as *I* to which these instances can refer in identical fashion. Each *I* has its own reference and corresponds each time to a unique being who is set up as such.
>
> What then is the reality to which *I* or *you* refers? It is solely a "reality of discourse," and this is a very strange thing. *I* cannot be defined except in terms of "location," not in terms of objects as a nominal sign is. *I* signifies "the person who is uttering the present instance of the discourse containing *I*." Consequently, by introducing the situation of "address," we obtain a symmetrical definition for *you* as the "individual spoken to in the present instance of discourse containing the linguistic instance *you*." These definitions refer to *I* and *you* as a category of language and are related to their position in language (Benveniste, 1971, pp. 217–218).

In attempting to account for how self-reference pronouns might be acquired, it is useful to link the neonatal facial imitation reported earlier both to Piaget's presumed stage of nonvisible imitation (that emerges between 8 to 12 months of age) and to the stable appearance in speech of the personal pronoun *I* between two and one-half to three years of age. In making these linkages, the authors hypothesize that the putative burst of facial imitation marking Piaget's stage of nonvisible imitation occurs because facial imitation serves a new function for the infant—namely that of self-representation. At 8 to 12 months, infants come to realize that when they make the same facial movements as another, they also look like the other and the other looks like them. Thus, their facial imitation at this age could be seen as a step forward in their representation of themselves. The presumed burst of facial imitation then, is interpreted as a change in their motivation to imitate and an interest in exploring what they look like, which results from this new development.

One piece of evidence supporting this hypothesis comes from Lewis and Brooks' study (1975) of infants looking at themselves in mirrors. They found a low probability that nine-month-old infants with rouge on their noses would touch their noses when looking into a mirror. From nine months on, however, the probability of touching their noses increased. It is tempting to argue that the onset of this phenomenon is tied to the onset of Piaget's stage of nonvisible imitation, because until the infant begins to represent himself as others see him, he has no basis on which to relate the appearance of the mirror image to his own appearance.

Fraiberg and Adelson (1975) have conducted a provocative study of self-representation in blind children that can be interpreted along these same lines. They argue that the stable use of the personal pronoun *I* between two and one-half and three years of age is related to the symbolic representation of the self in imaginative play. They base this conclusion on a study in which three blind children with otherwise normal language development up to two years of age showed striking delays in two areas: the productive, rule-governed use of the personal pronouns *I/me* and the children's self-representation in play. The delay in the development of self-representation was restricted to play in which the children imitated the roles that others take toward them. Notice that in this form of play, the children have to represent symbolically both themselves (e.g., through dolls) *and* the relationship they are engaged in (e.g., giving dolly a bottle). When such imaginative role-reversal did begin to emerge for these blind children, between four and five years of age, so did the self-reference pronouns. Thus, the representation of self, which develops through nonvisible imitation of others in the first half of the second year, seems to incorporate the roles that the self engages in through imitative role-play later in development. This developing representation of the self in relationship to others may be a prerequisite for the development of self-reference in speech. This would follow because the representational requirement for using *I/you* is similar to that required in imaginative role-reversal, given that correct usage of such pronouns depends on referring to the role that the self plays in the dialogue.

The above ideas resemble those of James Mark Baldwin (1906) regarding the centrality of imitation in the development of a concept of self. In fact, they suggest an extension of Baldwin's argument to include the affective dimension of social interactions in a way that might assist the child in acquiring the meaning of words referring to feelings and emotions. Kohlberg (1969) summarizes Baldwin's position as follows:

> According to Baldwin, then, there are two intertwined mechanisms of society, of sharing. The first is imitation of the other, the second is "ejection," i.e., empathy or "projection" of one's own subjective feelings into the other. Imitation of the other not only leads to a changed self-concept (e.g., a self who rides the bicycle), but also leads to a changed concept of the other because the activity (bicycle-riding) has a new meaning after it is done by the self, and this meaning is read back as part of the other (pp. 415–416).

Building from this idea, the authors postulate that imitation may provide an initial means by which the equivalence of subjective feelings can be established in two different individuals. Therefore, the imitative situation would seem to be an ideal context for the child to establish the referents for words describing subjective states of feeling and emotion. We were particularly struck by the aptness of this possibility when a three-year-old of our acquaintance was asked: "How's Mommy?" She replied, "Mommy made a [cry] face." Although she had no words to describe her mother's feelings, she attempted to convey her mother's state by imitating the facial expression. She also sought to comfort her mother when her mother made these faces, presumably because she could understand the feelings they indicated, if not the word. Subsequently, she began to use the words *sad* and *upset* to describe her mother when her mother made the cry face.

In sum, although the arguments presented in this section have been speculative, they do suggest that the developing functions that imitation serves may prove a fruitful area in which to seek the cognitive precursors for the acquisition of words referring to the self and to subjective states.

An Empirical Test of the Neo-Piagetian View of the Relation Between Cognitive Development and Language

In the foregoing sections, an argument has been developed regarding the role that cognition—most fundamentally the infant's notion of object identity and object permanence—plays in early language development. These cognitive developments have been distinguished from the infant's capability for representing the perceptual world per se, which the work on early imitation suggests is already present in the neonate. One preliminary test of the neo-Piagetian account would be to show that the development of object identity and permanence—at least as conceived of in this chapter—is indeed the crucial cognitive precursor to language acquisition. There are three methods that could be used. First, correlational studies of language and object permanence development could be undertaken. Second, one could attempt to accelerate object permanence development selectively and ascertain whether language development is also accelerated. A third alternative is what might be called a natural deceleration study. That is, by investigating the relationship between the variables of interest in a developmentally delayed population, one could determine which facets of cognitive development are delayed along with language development.

Previous studies have searched for a relationship between object permanence and language development in normal infants with mixed success (Bates, 1976; Ingram, 1974, in press; see also Bowerman, this volume). Unfortunately, the object permanence measures used were not based on a transformational model of cognitive development such as the one described in this chapter, and only rarely were both language and cognitive variables actually measured (instead one variable was often inferred from age norms).

Corrigan (1975) improved on these studies by separately assessing the development of three normal children in terms of mean length of utterance as defined by Brown (1973) and Piagetian object permanence as measured by the Uzgiris and Hunt Scale (1975). If object permanence were a cognitive precursor to language development, then a strong, positive correlation should exist between her two measures. In fact, she found rank-order correlations (Tau) of 0.75, 0.78, and 0.89 between them. However, because both measures have strong relationships to chronological age, she noted the possibility that these findings may reflect a parallel, but causally independent, course of development. Indeed when age was partialled out of the relationship to test this possibility, the correlations dropped to 0.00, 0.46, and 0.89. Given this drop, Corrigan concluded that the original correlations did not reflect any causal relationship. Again, however, the object permanence measure was based on a Piagetian scale.

Moore, Clark, Mael, Myers, Rajotte, and Stoel-Gammon (1977) conducted a study that takes advantage of the deceleration method. They employed the model of object permanence development described in this chapter. Table 4 provides a general outline of the object permanence tasks used in this scale (see Moore, 1973, 1975, for a more complete description). The sample consisted of eleven Down's infants and children ranging in age from 3:8 to 5:3. With one exception, all of the children had begun to talk. Of the 10 who were talking, nine had a mean length of utterance (MLU) under 1.8, and one had an MLU of 2.8 morphemes. In order to control for the effects of the experimenter's expectations, the language assessors were not informed of the children's performance on the cognitive measures, and the cognitive assessors were not informed of their level of language development. One-hour speech samples taken on visits to the infants' homes were used to assess the mean length of utterance (Brown, 1973) and the mean length of the five longest utterances. The order of difficulty for the object permanence tasks was found to be identical to that for normal infants; however, the age at which the Down's children solved these tasks was much later than for normals. In fact, some of these Down's children could only

Table 4.   Stages within Level 3 object identity[a]: Invariant developmental sequence in the solution of search tasks for stationary objects

Stage	Description of task[b]
3.1	Recovery of an object hidden partially by the movement of a screen
3.2	Recovery of an object placed within reach, and hidden completely by the movement of a screen A. in one location B. in one of two locations
3.3	Recovery of an object, initially placed out of reach and hidden completely by movement of a screen; the screen is then pushed within reach with the object remaining under the screen A. in one location B. in one of two locations
3.4	Recovery of an object hidden under/behind a stationary screen by visible movement of the object on a carrier A. in one location B. in one of two locations
3.5	Recovery of an object hidden successively under/behind two stationary screens and left behind one of them by visible movement of the object on a carrier
3.6	Recovery of an object hidden completely by movement of a screen and then moved invisibly by means of the screen to a location behind a second stationary screen A. in one location B. in one of two locations
3.7	Recovery of an object hidden completely by movement of a screen and then moved invisibly by means of the screen to successive locations behind additional stationary screens

[a] In Level 3 the infant can maintain identity for transformations from visible to invisible objects. There are 7 stages within Level 3—the first of which is termed 3.1, the second 3.2, and so on. There are two levels of object identity that occur developmentally earlier than Level 3 (see Table 2).

[b] These descriptions are not procedures for task administration and do not include criteria for successful recovery, such as the requirement that the infant not be in the act of reaching for the object while the task is being presented, etc.

Table 5.   Correlations between chronological age, object permanence, and language measures[a]

N = 11

	MLU	X̄	OP
Chronological age	.28	.38	.40[d]
Object permanence (OP)	.75[c]	.81[c]	
Object permanence with age removed[b]	.73	.78	

[a] MLU represents mean length of utterance as defined by Brown (1973). X̄ represents the mean of the five longest utterances. Correlations are Kendall Tau. Subjects are Down's children.

[b] No significance can be estimated for partial correlations.

[c] $p < .001$

[d] $p < .05$

solve object permanence tasks typically solved by normal 12-month-old infants at five years of age.

Table 5 shows the intercorrelations obtained between the object permanence and language measures. There is a significant positive correlation, and this correlation is not appreciably reduced when age is partialled out of the relationship. One might still object that partialling out chronological age is not an adequate control. If the Down's children's rate of development is equally retarded in both the linguistic and cognitive domains, the resulting correlations would not be expected to decrease after partialling out age, even if the two measures were actually independent. To assess this hypothesis, the authors examined data gathered with the Bayley Scale of Infant Development (BSID) on five of the children in the study. The Bayley Scale provides a standardized measure of general rate of intellectual development. As can be seen in Table 6, mental age as indexed by the BSID does not correlate significantly with the language measures, and more importantly, partialling it out of our language-cognition correlation does not reduce that relationship. We are left with

Table 6.   Correlations between chronological age, cognitive development, and language measures

N = 5

	MLU	X̄	OP	MA
Chronological age	.40	.40	.20	.60
Mental age (MA)[a]	.40	.40	.20	
Object permanence (OP)	.80[b]	.80[b]		
Object permanence with MA removed	.80	.80		

[a] Mental age determined by the Bayley Scale of Infant Development

[b] $p < .05$

reasonably strong evidence that object permanence development—at least as measured by tasks derived from the identity-based theory presented earlier—is associated with language development independent of chronological age or overall mental age.

Summary

This section has explored the implications of some recent research in perceptual and cognitive development for our conceptions of early communicative development. Their major impact has been to demonstrate that the developmental unity that Piaget ascribed to object permanence, imitation, and mental representation is not evident. For this reason, Piaget's theory about the relation between cognitive development and language has been substantially revised, and a neo-Piagetian position has been advanced. According to this view, mental representation is a necessary, although not sufficient, condition for the acquisition of language; moreover, some representational capacities are present at birth. The developmental precursors that determine the onset of speech build on this early representational system. The development of object identity and object permanence are crucial to the acquisition of language for two reasons. First, their development sets limits on the degree to which the infant and adult can share a common interpretation of their worlds. Second, the cognitive processes underlying object identity and permanence provide a means for the infant to determine the correspondence between transformational events and the adult's utterances about them. These constructed relationships between adult utterances and shared adult-infant interpretations are seen as giving a structural basis to the infant's comprehension of adult speech and to his own meaningful use of speech. Predictions derived from this position were in accord with previous studies of infants' first words and were supported by a test of the relationship between this identity-based model of object permanence development and the onset of speech in Down's children.

The neo-Piagetian view also suggested new roles for imitation in language acquisition. First, several developmental steps in the infant's production of vocalizations were hypothesized. These were derived from steps in the infant's interpretation and subsequent imitation of the relationship between adult utterances and transformational events. Second, Piaget's stages of imitative development were reinterpreted as reflecting in part the development of self-representation, and were then implicated in the acquisition of the meaning of words referring to the self and of words referring to subjective states.

CONCLUSIONS

The research on infant imitation conducted by the authors suggests that the capacity to construct internal representations should be considered a basic building block from which infant cognitive development proceeds, rather than its endpoint as Piaget assumes. Recent research on early infant perceptual-motor development and longitudinal studies of cognitive development (e.g., object identity) also suggest that a fundamental revision of Piaget's theory of infant development is needed. Considered as a whole, this research suggests that both the infant's perceptual world and his sensorimotor coordination are far more sophisticated and well-organized than Piaget claimed. However, this research also reveals that the infant has difficulty with *transformations* of his perceptual world. In understanding transformations of the perceptual world, the infant seems to progress through a series of developmental stages that are perhaps Piagetian in spirit, if not in precise detail.

These findings, hypotheses, and their implications led to the broad outline of a neo-Piagetian approach to cognitive functioning in infancy. This approach assumes that infants possess some representational capacity at birth, and cognitive development is interpreted as the progressive resolution of problems in the management and reorganization of these internal representations (e.g., the development object identity). A major consequence of such a reconceptualization is an abandonment of the Piagetian hypothesis that development in the organization of *action* provides the basis for the invariant ordering of stages of infant cognition. This revision raises two theoretical questions: 1) are there actually stages of cognitive development (in the sense of a series of wholistic organizations of cognitive processes) that encompass a variety of apparently diverse phenomena and 2) if there are such stages, what is their underlying organizational principle, given that the Piagetian action-basis has been rejected? The authors maintain that unified stages do exist, at least with regard to the infant's conception of objects, space, causality, and time. Because these phenomena all concern the transformations of objects, the authors furthur propose that the infant's developing rules for maintaining object identity (see Table 2) provide the necessary organizing principle.

It is worth highlighting the kinds of implications which this neo-Piagetian view suggests with respect to developmentally disabled populations. On the other hand, it implies that we should be circumspect in our justification of intervention strategies for the disabled by appeal to the Piagetian linkage between action and cognition— (e.g., attempts to accelerate cognitive development by exercising circular reactions or teaching infants to imitate as a means of fostering language (Morehead and Morehead, 1974)). On the other hand, even in areas where both Piagetian and neo-Piagetian approaches postulate similar developmental relationships (e.g., object permanence and language development), the respective intervention strategies are likely to differ significantly, because the presumed mechanisms of development are so different. Inescapably, the appropriate basis for an intervention program is not merely an academic question—it might well determine the number of years that some disabled individuals spend with only the most rudimentary understanding of their world or without the benefits of language.

The neo-Piagetian perspective affords new suggestions concerning two categories of research that seem especially fruitful to explore: (1) research on imitative development, and (2) research on the cognitive precursors to language development.

Research on Imitative Development

Further research on infant imitation is needed before the development of assessment instruments is undertaken, or a large-scale screening of infant populations on the basis of available instruments is warranted. There are, therefore, two areas of particularly high priority for research in infant imitative development:

1. Piaget's original aim was to chart the development of imitative competence in infancy. That task remains to be done, and the potential theoretical and practical significance of such research seems to justify this endeavor. Some possible examples of the developmental progression of imitative competence might be: actions of self, actions on self, actions on objects, actions relating objects, roles, etc.

2. Piaget's behavioral observations create another task that ought to be undertaken—that of determining the meaning of the developmental progression he did discover. The evidence of neonatal facial imitation suggests that the Piagetian stages do not describe the first attainment of new imitative abilities, although they may reflect new imitative preferences, the effects of performance limitations, or the use of available competencies in the service of new functions. One example of a functional approach to a reinterpretation of Piaget's stages in terms of the development of self-representation and an empathetic understanding of others was offered in this chapter. At the very least, such research would enable us to understand better what Piagetian-based instruments such as the Uzgiris and Hunt Scales (1975) are actually measuring.

Research on the Cognitive Precursors to Language Development

In trying to determine the relation between cognitive development and language acquisition, a primary problem is to find a method that could sort among the many potential cognitive precursors of language development and to isolate the genuine contributors. The problem is difficult both at the theoretical and empirical levels, especially when the host of potential masking factors is taken into account, for example: the lag between the appearance of a cognitive attainment and linguistic utilization of that attainment, the lag between comprehension of a linguistic form and the production of it, etc. The neo-Piagetian approach suggests some ways that future research might deal with these problems:

1. Developmentally delayed populations could be studied to identify the particular cognitive attainments that are related to a particular linguistic one. Because delayed infants spend a longer time in each cognitive stage than normal infants do, their first expression of a potentially related linguistic form should also be delayed, if there is indeed any cognition-language relationship. In order to determine the specific relationships, one could study several delayed populations and thereby isolate any cognition-language relationships that remain invariant over these populations. The use of a variety of delayed populations also could be utilized to help estimate the minimum cognitive attainment necessary for a given linguistic achievement, because unnecessarily powerful cognitive prerequisites might be revealed.

2. In order to confirm any relationships discovered by the above method, acceleration experiments could be undertaken. The most powerful evidence in favor of a

causal relationship would be obtained if selective acceleration of a cognitive attainment results in accelerating the appearance of a linguistic form. Such studies would have profound implications for language programs for the disabled, because they would suggest where intervention directed toward the cognitive precursors might fruitfully precede attempts to assist linguistic development through verbal means.

3. Future efforts could profitably be expended in discovering the mechanisms fostering transitions between developmental stages, because such descriptions of developmental mechanisms would provide a basis for the conduct of an acceleration study. When applied to language development, for example, the neo-Piagetian perspective suggests different domains of investigation (e.g., object identity versus imitation), and different potential mechanisms (e.g., transformational rules instead of action structures) from Piagetian theory.

Summary

In summary, there has been proposed a reorganization of Piaget's account of the interrelation between imitation, object permanence, and language development in infancy. The charge to the authors was to focus on early behavioral assessment and its special application to the developmentally disabled. Our appraisal of the current ferment in infant cognition led us to focus primarily on theoretical conceptions of the infant and his development. These conceptions promise not only to further our abilities to assess cognitive development in the disabled, but also to enrich our hypotheses about the nature of cognitive impairments and our strategies for their amelioration.

ACKNOWLEDGMENTS

The authors gratefully acknowledge the assistance of Jerald Dirks, Mary Durkanjores, Olga Maratos, and Carol Swartz in the development of the imitation research and the collaboration of the Child Language Acquisition Study at the University of Washington in facilitating the language research. We thank John Churcher, Dedre Gentner, Alison Gopnik, Geraldine Myers, Paul Potter, Peggy Rajotte and Carol Steol-Gammon for helpful critiques.

REFERENCES

Aleksandrowicz, M. 1974. The effect of pain relieving drugs administered during labor and delivery on the behavior of the newborn: A review. Merrill-Palmer Quart. 20: 121–141.

Austin, J. 1962. How To Do Things with Words. Oxford University Press, Cambridge.

Baldwin, J. M. 1906. Social and Ethical Interpretations in Mental Development. Macmillian, New York.

Ball, W., and Tronick, E. 1971. Infant responses to impending collision: Optical and real., Science 171: 818–820.

Bates, E. 1976. Language and context: The Acquisition of Pragmatics. Academic Press, New York.

Bates, E., Camaioni, L., and Volterra, V. 1975. The acquisition of performatives prior to speech. Merrill-Palmer Quart. 21: 205–266.

Benveniste, E. 1971. Problems in General Linguistics. Translated by M. E. Meek. University of Miami Press, Coral Gables, Florida.

Bloom, L. 1973. One Word at a Time: The Use of Single-Word Utterances Before Syntax. Mouton, The Hague.

Bower, T. G. R. 1971. The object in the world of the infant. Sci. Am. 225: 30–38.

Bower, T. G. R. 1972. Object perception in infants. Perception 1: 15–30.

Bower, T. G. R. 1974. Development in Infancy. W. H. Freeman, San Francisco.

Bower, T. G. R., Broughton, J. M., and Moore, M. K. 1970a. Infant responses to approaching objects: An indicator of response to distal variables. Percept. Psychophy. 9: 193–196.

Bower, T. G. R., Broughton, J. M., and Moore, M. K. 1970b. Demonstration of intention in the reaching behavior of neonate humans. Nature 228: 679–680.

Bower, T. G. R. 1977. Comments on Yonas et. al. "Development of sensitivity to information for impending collision." Percept. Psychophys. 21: 281–282.

Bower, T. G. R., Broughton, J. M., and Moore, M. K. 1971. Development of the object concept as manifested by the changes in the tracking behavior of infants between 7 and 20 weeks of age. J. Exp. Child Psychol. 11: 182–193.

Bower, T. G. R., and Paterson, J. G. 1973. The separation of place, movement, and object in the world of the infant. J. Exp. Child Psychol. 15: 161–168.

Bowerman, M. 1974. Discussion summary—Development of concepts underlying language. In R. Schiefelbusch and L. Lloyd (eds.), Language Perspectives—Acquisition, Retardation, and Intervention. University Park Press, Baltimore.

Brown, R. 1973. A First Language: The Early Stages. Harvard Press, Cambridge.

Bruner, J. S., and Koslowski, B. 1972. Visually preadapted constituents of manipulatory action. Perception 1: 3–14.

Bruner, J. S. 1975. From communication to language—A psychological perspective. Cognition 3: 255– 287.

Conway, E., and Brackbill, Y. 1970. Delivery medication and infant outcome: An empirical study. Monogr. Soc. Res. Child Dev. 35: 24–34.

Corrigan, R. 1975. Relationship between object permanence and language development: How much and how strong? Paper presented at the Eighth Annual Stanford Child Language Forum, April, Stanford, California.

Dodwell, P., Muir, D., Di Franco, D. 1976. Response of infants to visually presented objects. Science 194: 209–211.

Dore, J., Franklin, M., Miller, R., and Ramer, A. 1976. Transitional phenomena in early language acquisition. J. Child. Lang. 3(1): 13–28.

Field, J. 1977. Coordination of vision and prehension in young infants. Child Dev. 48: 97–103.

Fodor, J. A. 1975. The Language of Thought. Crowell, New York.

Fodor, J. D. 1977. Semantics. Crowell, New York.

Fraiberg, S., and Adelson, E. 1975. Self-representation in language and play: Observations of blind children. In E. H. Lenneberg and E. Lenneberg (eds.), Foundations of Language Development: A Multi-disciplinary Approach. Vol. 1. Academic Press, New York.

Gardner, T. K. 1971. The development of object identity in the first six months of human infancy. Paper presented at the meeting of the Society for Research in Child Development, April, Minneapolis, Minnesota.

Giblin, P. 1971. Development of imitation in Piaget's sensory-motor period of infant development (Stages III–VI). Proceed. 79th Ann. Conv. Am. Psychol. Assoc. 6: 141–142.

Greenfield, P., and Smith, J. H. 1976. Language Beyond Syntax: the Development of Semantic Structure. Academic Press, New York.

Hilke, D. D., and Clark, D. E. 1978. The cognitive context of infant vocalizations: A case study. Paper presented at the meetings of the Eastern Psychological Association, March, Washington, D. C.

Ingram, D. Sensorimotor intelligence and language development. In A. Lock (ed.), Action, Gesture and Symbol: The Emergence of Language. Academic Press, New York. In press.

Kohlberg, L. 1969. Stage and sequence: The cognitive-developmental approach to socialization. In D. A. Goslin (ed.), Handbook of Socialization Theory and Research. Rand McNally and Company, New York.

Lewis, M., and Brooks, J. 1975. Infant's social perception: A constructivist view. In L. B. Cohen and P. Salapatek (eds.), Infant Perception: From Sensation to Cognition. Vol. 1. Academic Press, New York.

Mehrabian, A., and Williams, M. 1971. Piagetian measures of cognitive development up to age two. J. Psycholinguist. Res. 1: 113–126.

Meltzoff, A., and Moore, K. 1977. Imitation of facial and manual gestures by human neonates. Science 198: 75–78.

Moore, M. K. 1973. The Genesis of Object Permanence. Paper presented at the Society for Research in Child Development meetings, March, Philadelphia, Pennsylvania.

Moore, M. K. 1975. Object permanence and object identity: A stage-developmental model. Paper presented at the meeting of the Society for Research in Child Development, Denver, Colorado.

Moore, M. K., Borton, R., and Darby, B. 1978. Visual tracking in young infants: Evidence for object identity or object permance? J. Exp. Child Psychol. 25: 183–197.

Moore, M. K., and Clark, D. 1975. Piaget's Stage IV Error: An Identity Theory interpretation. Paper presented at the Society for Research in Child Development meetings, April, Denver, Colorado.

Moore, M. K., Clark, D., Mael, M., Rajotte, P., and Stoel-Gammon, C. 1977. The relationship between language and object permanence development: A study of Down's infants and children. Paper presented at the meeting of the Society for Research in Child Development, March, New Orleans, Louisanna.

Morehead, D. M., and Morehead, A. 1974. From signal to sign: A Piagetian view of thought and language during the first two years. In R. L. Schiefelbusch and L. L. Lloyd (eds.), Language Perspectives—Acquisition, Retardation, and Intervention. University Park Press, Baltimore.

Nelson, K. 1973. Structure and strategy in learning to talk. Monogr. Soc. Res. Child Dev. 149(38): 1–2.

Paraskevopoulos, J. and Hunt, J. McV. 1971. Object construction and imitation under differing conditions of rearing. J. Genet. Psychol. 119: 301–321.

Parton, D. 1976. Learning to imitate in infancy. Child. Dev. 47: 14–31.

Piaget, J. 1952. The Origins of Intelligence in Children. W. W. Norton and Co., New York.

Piaget, J. 1954. The Construction of Reality in the Child. Basic Books, New York.

Piaget, J. 1962. Play, Dreams and Imitation in Childhood. W. W. Norton and Co., New York.

Piaget, J., and Inhelder, B. 1969. The Psychology of the Child. Norton, New York.

Ruff, H., and Halton, A. 1977. Is there directed reaching in the human neonate. Paper presented at the meeting of the Society for Research in Child Development, March, New Orleans, Louisiana.

Sherman, J. A. 1971. Imitation and Language Development. In H. W. Reese (ed.), Advances in Child Development and Behavior, Vol. 6, pp. 239–272. Academic Press, New York.

Skinner, B. F. 1957. Verbal Behavior. Appleton-Century-Croft, New York.

Sinclair-de Zwart, H. 1971. Sensori-motor action patterns as a condition for the acquisition of syntax. In R. Huxley and E. Ingram (eds.), Langue Acquisition: Models and Methods. Academic Press, New York.

Sinclair-de Zwart, H. 1974. On pre-speech. In E. V. Clark (ed.), Papers and Reports on Child Language Development. Stanford University, Stanford.

Uzgiris, I. 1972. Patterns of vocal and gestural imitation. In F. Monks (ed.), Determinants of Behavioral Development. Academic Press, New York.

Uzgiris, I., and Hunt, J. 1975. Assessment in infancy. University of Illinois Press, Chicago.

von Hofsten, Claes. 1977. Binocular convergence as a determinant of reaching behavior in infancy. Perception 6: 139–144.

Yonas, A., Brechtold, G., Frankel, D., Gordon, F., McRoberts, G., Norcia, A., Sternfels, S.

1977. Development of sensitivity to information for impending collision. Percept. Psychophys. 21: 97–104.

Wachs, T., Uzgiris, I., and Hunt, J. McV. 1971. Cognitive development in infants of different age levels and from different environmental backgrounds: An exploratory investigation. Merrill-Palmer Quart. 17: 283–317.

Watson, J. S. 1972. Smiling, cooing and the "game." Merrill-Palmer Quart. 18: 323.

Winkelstein, E. 1974. The development of a systematic method by which day care staff can select gestural imitation curriculum procedures for individual infants. Child Stud. J. 4: 169–178.

Discussion Summary: Memory, Sensorimotor, and Cognitive Development

Philip S. Dale

The three papers included in this section are concerned with the issue of continuity and discontinuity in development. How are the many behaviors observed at a particular age related to each other? Which lead to important later developments? The papers illustrate the three major approaches to the study of cognitive development: Fagan's paper illustrates the information-processing approach (see also Hamilton and Vernon, 1977); Wilson's paper, the psychometric tradition (see also Lewis, 1976), and Moore and Meltzoff's paper, the Piagetian (or neo-Piagetian, as many investigators who share Piaget's paradigm, but not theory, prefer).

Scott, in the previous section, proposed a set of minimal criteria for deciding if a program of basic research might have any clinical utility. The procedure for data collection must be adequately described to make a judgment about feasibility and cost effectiveness. In particular, assessments of reliability are even more important than they are for basic research purposes. A compelling theoretical case, not just an intuitive appeal, must then be made for the clinical importance of what is being assessed. This is most often done (because it is easiest) at the level of group differences. Fagan's recognition memory paradigm, for example, differentiates Down's Syndrome and normal infants. The critical question, however, is whether variability within groups is predictive of later performance in the same domain, or in others. The most important criterion is the demonstration that the processes studied are subject to environmental modification. Individual differences that cannot be affected are of little interest for remediation efforts. Modification is most often (again, because it is easiest) demonstrated in short-term performance. The problem of the relationship between short-term changes within a restricted behavioral domain and longer-term, broader changes is pervasive in developmental psychology, as a literature of literally hundreds of conservation training experiments demonstrates (see Flavell, 1977, for a discussion of the theoretical questions).

MEMORY DEVELOPMENT

Fagan's research program is an attempt to decompose performance on cognitive tasks into underlying processes, processes that are amenable to either short- or long-term modification by the experimenter or other designer of the environment. In particular, an analysis of recognition memory in terms of attention theory is proposed as a first attempt. It describes performance in a number of experimental conditions and makes predictions within this limited range of conditions. The discussion of the paper centered around three issues: the nature of the procedures and the subjects tested, implications for understanding abnormal development, and the possible clinical utility of the procedure.

In the discussion, Fagan pointed out that the experimental procedure, which typically requires 10–15 minutes, is generally conducted in the infant's home with the infant seated on the mother's lap, without restraint. Because the mother is asked to specify a time when the infant is awake and attentive, at least 75% of the infants whose parents agree to participate complete the experiment. In fact, according to Fagan, the test actually calms some upset infants by giving them an interesting activity.

It was pointed out at the conference that the recognition memory paradigm demonstrates retention of at least a few minutes, which is longer than would be shown by the habituation paradigm. The question of false alarms was also raised: infants look at the new pattern about 60% of the time, which seems significant, but might they look 60% of the time at one of a pair of identical, old patterns, perhaps on the basis of position preferences? For the purpose of group comparisons such as Fagan has made, such preferences would "wash out," but their incidence would be important for understanding individual differences.

Another question concerned the relevance of recognizing a change in form or color. Faces are ecologically more significant. Fagan has also conducted research on recognition memory for faces, but it was not included in the present paper because it is not as developed theoretically. He argued that colors and forms are as basic as features discriminating faces: "Ultimately all you can answer to questions like that is that it seems like a good idea at the time."

Like research with older children, Fagan's work suggests that the difference between Down's Syndrome and normal children is not so much a global deficit as a set of specific task component deficits. The methodology here is significant. Comparisons of Down's Syndrome, or any handicapped group, with normals are not very informative in themselves, for the same reasons that cross-cultural comparisons, or even cross-sectional comparisons of normal four-year-olds with normal six-year-olds, are not very informative: they are simply too ambiguous, too susceptible to multiple interpretations. Where we really gain information is from task comparisons *within* groups or age levels or cultures, as Fagan's work demonstrates for Down's Syndrome children, and as the work of Cole, Gay, Glick, and Sharp (1971) demonstrates for cross-cultural research on memory.

In the recognition memory paradigm, as in most procedures for infant research, negative results are highly ambiguous. A failure to observe a preference for the new patterns does not establish that memory did not persist. This ambiguity limits to some extent our ability to compare performance with various patterns. Still, if a group of infants does better under one condition than another group of infants does under another condition, there is *some* difference between the conditions. The latter condition is in some sense (perhaps memorial, perhaps not) harder. The relationship of preference to memory is only partially understood. We know that it is not a simple one. Wetherford and Cohen (1973) demonstrated that six- and eight-week-old infants remember a pattern, but prefer to look at the familiar, whereas ten- and twelve-week-old infants prefer to look at the novel. The shift between eight and twelve weeks is not one of memory development, but of a change in the relationship between memory and preference. One interpretation of Wetherford and Cohen's results is that for the infant of six weeks, who is just developing internal representations of events and patterns, the memory is sufficiently imprecise that exact repetitions are not recognized as such. Repetitions are recognized as similar but not identical, and therefore do not build up inhibitory force. A few weeks later, memory processes may have improved enough to detect exact repetitions, which may lead to a preference for novelty. If this proposal is along the right track, dichotomizing patterns as familiar/novel is much too simple, and we should expect a more complex relationship between degrees of familiarity and attention. (Kagan, 1972, has proposed one hypothesis, the "moderate discrepancy hypothesis," but the evidence thus far is inconclusive.)

There was considerable agreement among the discussants that the issue of clinical usefulness of infant recognition memory research cannot be decided until more is known about individual differences in response. In the experiments reported in the paper, the proportion of time spent looking at the new pattern is seldom much over 60%, and the standard deviations are sizable. Furthermore, some infants spend more time looking overall than others. It has not yet been established whether "short lookers" are really short lookers across a series of conditions, or whether infants who show a large preference for the novel pattern in one condition will do so in other conditions.

Fagan pointed out that one particularly encouraging aspect of his findings is that it is possible to reproduce what happens with age by varying study time; that is, the same factors determine difficulty at one developmental point that determine the course of development. A promising tack for assessing individual differences would be to compute indices based on differences between tasks for individual infants.

SENSORIMOTOR AND COGNITIVE DEVELOPMENT

Wilson's paper illustrates well a point made early in the conference discussions: there is a great deal of data already available that could properly be mined for information on some important theoretical questions. Longitudinal records of the Bayley test are used to address the question of continuity in development. Items that successfully predict later performance have been grouped, and the demands of particular tasks have been identified.

The Bayley is a diverse collection of test items. They have been chosen primarily on two grounds: first, that they engage the interest of the child; and second, that they discriminate children at different ages. Although the former criterion is also relevant for Piaget-based tests, such as the Uzgiris-Hunt scales, the items for those tests are selected primarily on the basis of theory. Another major difference between the two types of scales stems from Piaget's concern with universals of human development. Tests inspired by his theories are developed by selecting a set of items that form a good scale, in the Guttman sense of an invariant ordering. In contrast, in the construction of tests such as the Stanford-Binet or the Bayley, items are selected largely on the basis of their ability to show variation. Thus, it is not surprising that psychometric tests such as the Stanford-Binet show differences, and Piaget-inspired tests reveal universal patterns of development. Given these fundamental differences in approach, attempts such as Wilson's to bridge the gap are of great interest. Particularly interesting are the suggestions concerning the role of postural development and attention.

One conference participant inquired about the 50% of sample that is missing in Wilson's Hi-Quartile/Lo-Quartile comparison method. She also questioned the interpretation of differences such as 41%/5%, because 59% of the subjects in the Hi-Quartile would have failed to pass the item. Wilson reported that the intermediate quartiles generally showed the same trend as the extreme quartiles. Furthermore, the actual items on the test might be thought of as selected points on one or more continua of development, so that infants in the Hi-Quartile group might be thought of as farther along, even though not sufficiently so to pass the hypothetical example above.

A major focus of the discussion was the extent to which development can in fact be adequately represented by one or more invariant sequences. This was perceived to be a primary tenet of Piaget's account. Although infants may differ in rate, all acquire the same cognitive capacities in the same order. Tests, however, measure only a small sample of behavior, and given the way in which Piaget-inspired tests, in particular, are constructed, undoubtedly far larger variations exist among children than are generally recognized. Much interest was expressed in Guttman scaling and similar procedures for tests such as the Bayley. Dale reported a scaling analysis performed on Bayley scores for 25 Down's Syndrome children that determined that a scale did not in fact exist, a conclusion consistent with the common observation that the performance of such children is unpredictable from item to item. However, little is known about the scalability of the Bayley test for normal infants.

Wilson argued in his paper that although virtually all humans complete sensorimotor development in some sense, the strength and breadth of the cognitive operations vary. For example, the generalization of operations to other objects, to remembered information, and to a variety of persons may vary substantially. A diversified set of items may be needed to assess the variation among children. Although Piaget himself distinguished between horizontal and vertical development—vertical referring to the primary line of development, and horizontal to generality—the relationship between the two is far from understood. Are the two correlated, so that experiences faciliting each are mutually supportive? Are they opposed, as Piaget suggests in his criticism of acceleration experiments? Or are they simply independent dimensions of development?

There was a lively discussion at the conference concerning the possibility of relating the psychology of sensorimotor and cognitive development to physiological and neuropsychological processes. The question of whether we can "open up the black box of the central nervous system in relation to human development of sensorimotor cognitive functions" was raised. There seemed to be agreement that we need a better understanding of both biological development and behavioral development, but that it would be a mistake to expect either to explain the other. Like all correlations, any relationship between biological development and behavioral development has at least three interpretations; in fact, examples can be, and were, cited of effects in each direction.

IMITATION AND LANGUAGE DEVELOPMENT

The paper presented by Moore and Meltzoff at the conference was primarily a report of their research on imitation in early infancy, then not widely known. The results are stunning, with potential implications for many aspects of infant cognitive development, including perception, intersensory integration, object permanence, and communicative development. The conference discussion consisted in large part of a careful examination of the procedures used, with the participants eventually convinced of the results and their theoretical importance. Since the conference, the research has been reported in Meltzoff and Moore (1977). For the present volume, Moore and Meltzoff have prepared an extended theoretical treatment of the role of imitation and mental representation in development. This paper, together with Bowerman's review of empirical research on language and cognitive development in infancy (this volume), provides an excellent overview of current theorizing and research on this difficult question. Because much of the material in the Moore and Meltzoff paper was not presented at the conference, the following remarks, which are primarily the responsibility of the author of this summary, are presented here as supplementary commentary.

The most radical change in Piaget's theory offered in this paper is the downgrading in both a developmental and a theoretical sense of the role of mental representation. In Piaget's account, this is the endpoint of sensorimotor development and the foundation of the symbolic use of language. In Moore and Meltzoff's account, it is in some sense the *beginning* of sensorimotor development, and at best, one necessary process for language. What changes during the first year or so of life is *how* mental representations (exemplified in imitation) are used. This proposal is, however, in spirit with a number of other theoretical revisions to Piaget's theory. In many areas—object permanence, number concepts, formal operations, etc.— Piaget's emphasis on the development of structures that are generally operative seems excessive. Cognitive advances more often appear first in restricted domains, and generalization is a time-consuming process that varies from child to child, a process that is at least as interesting as the first appearance of the advance. (Much of the discussion of Wilson's paper was relevant to this issue; see also Flavell, 1977.)

Moore and Meltzoff make a number of predictions; for most of them we simply do not yet have relevant evidence. Nevertheless, the fact that at least some of the predictions are both specific and somewhat counterintuitive suggests that their theory has substantial content, unlike some other Piaget-inspired accounts of language. One striking prediction is that object names should first be interpreted as proper nouns, and only later as common nouns. Most students of child language have observed that even very young children generally use object names as category labels, superficially disconfirming Moore and Meltzoff's prediction. However, it is also generally agreed that it is possible that particular words might be first, and very briefly, underextended (used as proper nouns) before being overextended (Anglin, 1977; Dale, 1976). Much more temporally fine-grained evidence on the meanings of early words will be necessary to settle this question. Curiously, the evidence would seem to be more in Moore and Meltzoff's favor in the case of transformation words—up, down, etc. Many of the examples of underextension cited in Bowerman's paper (this volume) are drawn from this set of words.

Some of Moore and Meltzoff's predictions seem to be tied too closely to the actual words first acquired by children (vocabulary) and by implication to their meaning for adults, whereas the predictions would most reasonably be related to the meanings for the children (semantics) and to how the words are used (pragmatics). For example, the distinction between Level 2 and Level 3 amounts to a prediction that words should be used to refer to object exchanges and to object recognition before they are used to refer to disappearance and reappearance. The actual words used for these purposes might vary considerably from child to child. It is even possible that the same word might be used for several purposes, in which case the crucial evidence would be to determine the pragmatic functions for that word at two or more developmental points.

In the absence of research on individual differences, it is somewhat premature to speculate on possible clinical applications of this imitation research, either for diagnosis or for remediation. However, as the example of the blind children studied by Fraiberg and Adelson (cited in Moore and Meltzoff, this volume) suggests, self-representation is a central process of cognitive development, and its disruption can have far-reaching effects. It would be equally interesting to look at the development of autistic children in this light (Lovass, 1977). It is important to note that if Moore and Meltzoff's views are correct, it is not facial imitation per se that needs to be developed, but a particular way of using that process.

CONCLUSION

Together, the three papers of this section argue for a multidimensional view of cognitive development in the first two years. No single dimension, however theoretically sophisticated, can account for the many changes that occur. The most important implication of this conclusion for clinical purposes is that both assessment and remediation are likely to be even more difficult than might have been thought. Assessment rests on an identification of a small number of behaviors that predict a wider range; remediation depends on the identification of a small number of behaviors that, when modified environmentally, will have wide ranging effects. On a more optimistic note, the papers of this section also demonstrate that it is possible to devise relatively brief procedures for eliciting extremely sophisticated cognitive behaviors from infants, proving that our goal of assessment and remediation is attainable.

REFERENCES

Anglin, J. M. 1977. Word, Object, and Conceptual Development. Norton, New York.

Cole, M., Gay, J., Glick, J., and Sharp, D. W. 1971. The Cultural Context of Learning and Thinking. Basic Books, New York.

Dale, P. S. 1976. Language Development: Structure and Function. 2nd ed. Holt, Rinehart and Winston, New York.

Flavell, J. S. 1977. Cognitive Development. Prentice-Hall, Englewood Cliffs, N.J.

Hamilton, V., and Vernon, M. D. 1977. The Development of Cognitive Processes. Academic Press, New York.

Kagan, J. 1972. Do infants think? Sci. Am. 226: 74–82.

Lewis, M. (ed.). 1976. The Origins of Intelligence. Plenum, New York.

Lovass, O. I. 1977. The Autistic Child. Irvington Publishers, New York.

Meltzoff, A. N., and Moore, K. M. 1977. Imitation of facial and manual gestures by human neonates. Science 198: 75–78.

Wetherford, M. J., and Cohen, L. B. 1973. Developmental changes in infant visual preferences for novelty and familiarity. Child Dev. 44: 416–424.

DEVELOPMENT OF PHONOLOGY

Infant Speech Perception: Origins, Processes, and *Alpha Centauri*

Philip A. Morse

According to Plato, the human mind was thought to differ radically from that possessed by animals. Although Darwin's proclamation of kinship between *Homo sapiens* and other species forced us to reexamine aspects of our human physiological heritage, it was not until the chimpanzee, Washoe, began to learn sign language in 1966 that the sanctity and uniqueness of the human mind was seriously threatened (Gardner and Gardner, 1969; Linden, 1976). Specifically, one of *Homo sapiens'* primary unique mental abilities, "language," no longer seemed quite so special.

Although research with Washoe, and more recently with other chimpanzees and human children, has suggested that at least the *early* stages of syntax acquisition may depend on the development of certain cognitive/semantic abilities shared by both the chimp and human child (e.g., Brown, 1973), the speech mode of human language and its acquisition are unique to *Homo sapiens*. Efforts to teach nonhuman primates the articulation of human speech sounds (e.g., Hayes, 1951) combined with studies of the vocal tracts of fossil hominids and living nonhuman primates (Lieberman, 1975) indicates that the *production* of human speech is definitely restricted to our species. Given what we know about the auditory/vocal communication systems of other species (e.g., Frischkopf, Capranica, and Goldstein, 1968; Wollberg and Newman, 1972), we might expect that *Homo sapiens* have also evolved correspondingly unique capacities for the *perception* of speech. Thus, studies of speech perception and its ontogenetic and phylogenetic development in the human infant and nonhuman primate, respectively, may contribute important information about the uniqueness of our human linguistic abilities. As part of this quest, the present chapter examines the major research findings in infant speech perception with special focus on the *origins* of these ontogenetic and phylogenetic abilities, on the physiological and psychological *processes* that underlie these abilities, and on those bright, exciting, unexplored worlds that lie beyond our present scope of inquiry (*Alpha Centauri*).

The preparation of this chapter was supported in part by NICHD grants HD-08240 and HD-03352.

Studies of infant speech perception have relied primarily on two paradigms in probing the infant's discriminative abilities: an operant nonnutritive sucking method and a heart-rate orienting response procedure. In the nonnutritive sucking paradigm, a speech sound (syllable) is presented to the infant contingent upon the infant's rate of hard (high-amplitude) sucking. As the infant discovers this contingent relationship, the rate (per minute) of high-amplitude sucking (HAS) increases (acquisition). Eventually, the infant begins to satiate or habituate the HAS response and the rate decreases. If the rate decreases in accordance with a predetermined criterion, then the sound is changed and a subsequent increase in responding relative to a no-change control condition is interpreted as discrimination of the two sounds. In the heart rate (HR) paradigm a series of one sound is also presented to the infant (but not contingent upon the infant's response) and discrimination of a second sound is indexed by a deceleration in heart rate (an orienting response) to the stimulus change. Later in this chapter we shall have an opportunity to examine more closely the developmental implications of these two paradigms (also see Morse, 1974), but this brief methodological overview will permit us to appreciate how the basic data in infant speech discrimination were gathered.

THE FOUNDATIONS OF INFANTS SPEECH DISCRIMINATION

Because several extensive reviews of the research in infant speech perception before 1973 have appeared elsewhere (Butterfield and Cairns, 1974; Eimas, 1974b, 1975b; Morse, 1974), in this section the earlier studies are briefly summarized, and attention is concentrated instead on more recent findings. One way of organizing the data in infant speech discrimination is to distinguish between studies that provide evidence of *auditory* versus *phonetic* discriminative abilities. For example, if infants demonstrated discrimination (using either the HAS or HR paradigm) of the sound of the garbage truck versus that of a fire engine, we might hesitate to infer that they knew anything about the sound categories of these two vehicles. Instead, a more conservative conclusion might be that some auditory difference between the two sounds was discriminated. Similarly, if infants discriminated [ba] versus [ga], it might be premature to conclude that this differential responding was based on the phonetic consonant categories [b] and [g]. Thus, although Moffitt (1971) and Morse (1972) have both shown that four- to five-month and six-week infants, respectively, can discriminate the syllables [ba] and [ga], we cannot conclude from these studies that infants can discriminate the phonetic consonant categories [b] and [g].

Some Basics of Speech Production and Perception

In contrast, the phenomenon of *categorical perception* does provide one way of assessing the infant's appreciation of phonetic categories. However, in order to understand the contribution of categorical perception, a few of the basics of speech production and perception must first be reviewed. In speech production a sound *source,* usually produced by the vocal cords in the larynx, is *filtered* by the chamber or vocal tract above the larynx. This filtering process, much like what occurs when we hum into a milk bottle, produces concentrations of resonating frequencies that are a function of the size and shape of the supralaryngeal vocal tract (compare humming into a milk bottle to humming into a soda pop bottle). These concentrated resonating frequency bands are referred to as *formants*. When the frequencies of these formants are displayed over time with the aid of a machine called a sound spectrograph, they appear as in Figure 1 for the natural speech sound [bɛ] (upper portion) and its synthetic counterpart (lower portion). According to convention, the formant patterns are labeled in an ascending frequency order: first formant, second, third, etc. Extensive research with synthetic speech on the acoustic cues of adult speech perception has revealed that changes in the initial transition of the second formant (F2) are sufficient to cue the distinction between [b], [d], and [g] (e.g., Mattingly, Liberman, Syrdal, and Halwes, 1971). Thus, holding all other cues constant we may vary along a continuum the starting frequency of the F2 transition to create a set of syllables, illustrated in Figure 2, that move from [ba] (low F2 starting frequency, rising transition) to [da] (medium F2 starting frequency, slightly falling transition) to [ga] (high F2 starting frequency, greatly falling transition). If pairs of stimuli along this synthetic F2 transition continuum are presented to adult listeners for discrimination, they will be able to discriminate between stimuli in a pair quite well if the stimuli are selected from different phonetic categories (e.g., [da] versus [ga]). However, if a stimulus pair is selected that contains the same acoustic difference in initial F2 starting frequency, but both stimuli are from the same category, then adult listeners typically do not discriminate this within-category contrast much better than chance. This phenomenon, in which listeners' discrimination of two stimuli is limited to those stimuli that they can label or identify differentially, is referred to as *categorical perception*.

Infant Auditory versus Phonetic Abilities

By adapting the phenomenon of categorical perception for studies of infant speech perception, we can ask if the infant's discrimination of speech contrasts reflects any knowledge of the adult phonetic categories and is not merely indicative of simple auditory discriminative abilities. Accordingly, Eimas (1974a) presented two- to three-month-old infants, using the HAS paradigm, with either a *between-category* discrimination (e.g., [dae] versus [gae]), a *within-category* discrimination (e.g., within-[dae] or within-[gae]), or a no-shift *control* condition. Infants demonstrated adult-like (phonetic) discrimination of these contrasts in that *only* in the between-category change did infants show a recovery of their HAS response or differ reliably from the control condition. Because this finding of categorical discrimination has been replicated by Eimas (1974a) with a second set of stimuli differing along the [dae-gae] continuum and in studies using a HR paradigm by Miller and Morse (1976) and by Till (1976), we may conclude that infants do indeed discriminate differences in place of articulation ([d] versus [g]) not only auditorily, but also phonetically.

In addition to the phonetic discrimination for place of articulation, infants as young as one month of age exhibit phonetic discrimination of voicing cues (voice-onset-time) in the contrast [ba] versus [pa] (Eimas, Siqueland, Juszyck, and Vigorito, 1971). More recently, Eimas (1975a) has also found that infants discriminate the liquid contrast [ra] versus [la] categorically. Additional infant studies investigating the auditory discrimination of consonant contrasts have observed dis-

[bɛ]

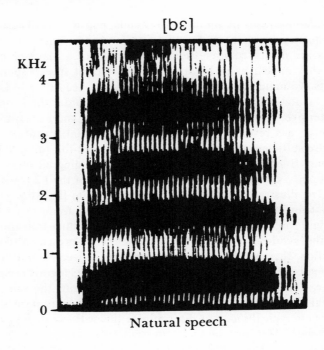

Natural speech

Synthetic speech

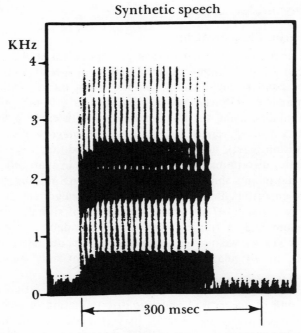

Figure 1.   Spectrograms of natural and synthetic [bɛ] stimuli. (From Mattingly, I. 1972.) Speech cues and sign stimuli, *Am. Sci. 60:* 327–337. Reprinted by permission.

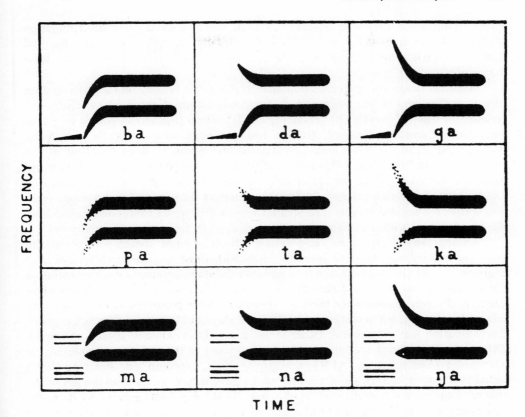

Figure 2. Hand-painted spectrograms of some of the major consonant contrasts. Columns differ in their place of articulation, rows in their voiced, voiceless, and nasal qualities. (From Liberman, A., Delattre, P., Gerstman, L., and Cooper, F., 1956). Tempo of frequency change as a cue for distinguishing classes of speech sounds, *Journal of Experimental Psychology,* 1956, *52,* 127–137. Reprinted by permission.

crimination of initial burst cues (8–32 msec in duration) for the consonants [bu] and [gu] (Miller, Morse, and Dorman, 1977) and fricative cue discrimination with the pairs [sa] versus [va], [sa] versus [ʃa], but not [sa] versus [za] (Eilers and Minifie, 1975).[1] Except for the absence of discrimination with [sa] versus [za], all of these

---

[1] Eilers and Minifie have suggested that their failure to find voicing discrimination for the contrast [sa]-[za] is inconsistent with the Eimas et al. (1971) voicing findings with stop consonants. However, inspection of the Eilers and Minifie natural speech [sa] and [za] stimuli reveals that at least they differed both in initial fundamental frequency and in VOT. Furthermore, although the voice-onset-time difference between [za] (0 VOT) and [sa] (at least +100 VOT) was large, it occurred primarily during the period of friction noise. If for these infants the higher frequency friction masked the lower frequency F1 differences and the fundamental frequency cue was insufficient for discrimination, then the absence of [sa]-[za] discrimination in Eilers and Minifie's three-month-olds need not be in conflict with the Eimas et al. evidence of voicing discrimination. More recently, Eilers, Wilson, and Moore (1977) have shown that six- to eight-month-olds can discriminate [sa]-[za] using a different paradigm. Until synthetic stimuli are employed that permit the separate manipulation of these voice-onset-time and fundamental frequency cues (e.g., Massaro and Cohen, 1977), it remains unclear whether these developmental differences reflect a maturational change in infants' processing of these two cues, or a paradigm difference.

infant findings parallel those observed in adult listeners using other discrimination methods. In summary, infants and adults both discriminate place, voicing, and liquid contrasts phonetically, and several other consonant contrasts at least auditorily.

Needless to say, the perception of speech also relies heavily on the participation of vowels. Trehub (1973b) has reported that young infants discriminate auditory differences in isolated vowels ([i] versus [a] and [i] versus [u]) and in vowels in a consonant-vowel context ([pa/pi], [ta/ti], and [pa/pu]). More recently, Swoboda, Morse, and Leavitt (1976) have investigated the phonetic discrimination of the vowels [i] (as in "beet") and [I] (as in "bit"). In contrast to the categorical discrimination evidenced by adults for consonants, vowels tend to be perceived continuously, i.e., both good between-category *and* within-category discrimination. Swoboda et al. found that 8-week-old infants also treated vowels differently than consonants: both the between- and within-category vowel contrasts were discriminated equally well.

Another way of examining the phonetic aspects of infant speech perception is to compare infants' responses to speech stimuli with those to nonspeech sounds. For example, Eimas (1974a) observed that infants exhibited *continuous* discrimination of the F2 transitions that cued the [d]-[g] contrasts (i.e., good between- *and* within-category discrimination) when these F2 transitions were presented in isolation to the infant. In contrast, when these transitions were played to infants in a speech context, discrimination was categorical. Other investigators have explored speech-nonspeech differences by studying the lateralization of response to these signals. Employing an averaged evoked response (AER) measure, Molfese, Freeman, and Palermo (1975) found that young infants, children, and adults gave larger AERs over the left hemisphere to the speech stimuli: [ba], [dae], "boy," and "dog," and greater AERs to the nonspeech sounds: C major chord and 250 Hz-4KHz noise burst, when recorded over the right hemisphere. Finally, Entus (1975, 1977) has recently demonstrated that infants show greater recovery of the HAS response to a change in dichotically presented sounds that occurs in the right ear if the sounds are speech ([ba], [da], [ga], [ma]), but in the left ear if musical stimuli are employed (a 440 Hz A played on a piano, viola, bassoon, or cello).[2] Because all of these patterns of speech/nonspeech responding are similar to those obtained in adult listeners, one may conclude (at least for the small sample of stimuli employed to date) that young infants also seem to treat speech/nonspeech contrasts in an adult-like manner.

FRONTIERS AND ISSUES IN INFANT SPEECH PERCEPTION

According to this brief overview of the basic findings in infant speech perception, infants as early as one to three months of age respond in a manner similar to adult listeners in their differential treatment of certain speech and nonspeech signals and in their pattern of auditory and phonetic discrimination of consonants and vowels.

---

[2] Recently Khadem and Corballis (1977) have presented data that fail to replicate Entus's HAS results, although Glanville, Best, and Levenson (1977) have demonstrated infant laterality effects using a heart-rate paradigm.

Furthermore, because the evidence of infant phonetic discrimination in consonants has been replicated for voicing (Eimas, 1975b; Miller, 1974) and place of articulation (Eimas, 1974a; Miller and Morse, 1976; Till, 1976), we may regard categorical discrimination in young infants as a well-established finding. Although additional studies certainly need to investigate other auditory/phonetic discriminative abilities in infancy, the most exciting frontiers and issues in the field of infant speech perception are to be currently found in: 1) the *origins* of these categorical abilities, 2) the perceptual, learning, and memory *processes* involved in the *paradigms* employed in assessing these categorical abilities, and 3) the *organization* and *elaboration* of phonetic perception beyond the scope of previous research questions (*Alpha Centauri*).

Origins: Ontogeny, Phylogeny, and Physiologic Aspects of Phonetic Categories

Some early accounts of speech sound acquisition (e.g., Allport, 1924) presumed that infants learned the sound categories of speech from the auditory feedback of their own babbling, coupled with some degree of external reinforcement from the babbled-at community. Unfortunately, this cannot explain the development of the phonetic categories that underlie infant categorical discrimination. According to studies of infant speech production, infants are not yet producing in any consistent manner the sound contrasts that they can discriminate perceptually (e.g., Kewley-Port and Preston, 1974; Pierce, 1974). If infants do not generate these sound categories themselves, the possibility remains that their experience in listening to other speakers produce these categories during the first few months after birth may play a major role in the acquisition of these phonetic capabilities. Although no data are as yet available that describe the early phonetic input to the infant, several studies have explored infants' discriminations of cross-language contrasts using speech categories not heard in the languages of their parents or immediate linguistic community.

Cross-Language Studies   The majority of the studies of infant cross-language discrimination has examined the voicing distinction, as cued by voice-onset-time (VOT). The dimension of voice-onset-time consists of a complex of acoustic cues, the primary of which is the relative lag or lead in onset of the first and second formants. Figure 3 illustrates these voice-onset-time differences for the three major voicing categories. In English, voiceless consonants (e.g., [p, t, k]) are produced by a delay in voicing (at the larynx) after the mouth has released the sound. For example, in the English pair [ba-pa], the onset of F1 in [pa] *lags* in time behind that of F2 by at least 30 msec (+30 VOT). If the onset of F1 lags behind F2 less than 30 msec or leads the onset of F2, then the syllable is generally categorized in English as a voiced sound ([ba]).

Using contrasts along this VOT continuum, Eimas et al. (1971) observed that infants discriminated the VOT values +20/+40 ([ba] versus [pa]), but not a within-[ba] (−20/0) or within-[pa] (+60/+80) contrast. In a replication of these categorical findings with [da] and [ta], Eimas (1975b) also reported that infants discriminated +10/+60 ([da] versus [ta]), but not within-[da] (−30/+20) or within-[ta] (+50/+100). In contrast to English, other languages (e.g., Lebanese Arabic, Spanish) may distinguish between a *pre-voiced* category (long F1 lead) and a voiced

Three Conditions of Voice Onset Time
Synthetic Labial Stops

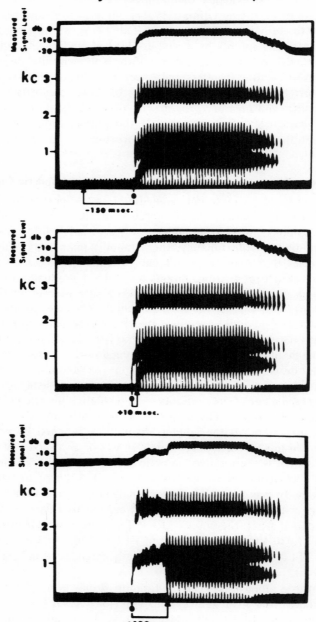

Figure 3.   Spectrograms of the types of voicing. From top to bottom: "prevoiced" or voicing lead (−150 VOT), "voiced" or slight lag (+10 VOT), and "voiceless" or long lag (+100 msec). (From Abramson, A., and Lisker, L., 1973.) Voice-timing perception in Spanish word-initial stops, *Journal of Phonetics,* 1973, *1,* 1–8. Copyright by Academic Press Inc. (London) Ltd. Reprinted by permission.

category (corresponding to our English voiced [b, d, g] category (Lisker and Abramson, 1964). Finally, some languages such as Thai employ all three categories: pre-voiced, voiced, and voiceless.

Thus, by presenting infants in an English-speaking community with the prevoiced/voiced distinction or infants living in a community where only the prevoiced/voiced contrast is employed with a voiced/voiceless comparison, one can determine if discrimination of voicing categories requires any previous language experience or whether infants may possess these discriminative abilities independent of such experience (innately). To this purpose, Streeter (1976) used the HAS paradigm to test two-month-old infants in Kenya whose parents spoke only Kikuyu, a Bantu language. Kikuyu does not have the English voiced/voiceless contrast, but uses instead the prevoiced/voiced distinction. Similarly, Lasky, Syrdal-Lasky, and Klein (1975), using an HR procedure, studied voicing discrimination in four- to six and one-half-month-old Guatemalan (Spanish) infants. In both studies, infants discriminated the "foreign" English [ba/pa] contrast (Streeter: +10/+40; Lasky et al.: +20/+60). In addition, for the Kikuyu infants, discrimination of the contrast appropriate for their native language was equally well discriminated (−30/0).[3] Finally, in an attempt to investigate the prevoiced/voiced boundary in American infants, Eimas (1975b) presented infants with the following apical ([da]) VOT contrasts: Expt. I: −100/−40, −40/+20; Expt. II: −150/−70, −70/+10. No significant differences in recovery were obtained in Expt. I, although the −100/−40 condition exhibited slightly more recovery. In Expt. II, only the −70/+10 pair yielded reliable recovery, but the difference between the −70/+10 and −150/−70 pairs did not reach significance. Thus, American infants can discriminate a change across the prevoiced/voiced boundary (similar to the Kikuyu infants: −30/0), but not categorically, as they do the English [ba/pa] contrast. Inspection of Streeter's Kikuyu data reveals an analogous pattern of responding. Although her infants discriminated a change across their own boundary (−30/0) and the English boundary (+10/+40), their discrimination within-[pa] (+50/+80) failed to differ significantly from the +10/+40 pair, even though it was not statistically different from a no-shift control condition. Thus, as in the Eimas study, Streeter's infants also failed to exhibit significant *categorical* discrimination for a category that is not in the native language of their parents. In contrast, discrimination of voicing categories that do

---

[3] The exact location of the Spanish labial boundary is not yet clear (e.g., Abramson and Lisker, 1973; Williams, 1974). Williams's recent study of monolingual Puerto Rican speakers suggests a discrimination peak at −20/0 VOT. Within this context, the failure of the Lasky et al. infants to discriminate the contrast −20/+20 (coupled with their reliable discrimination of the −60/−20 contrast) remains something of an anomaly. It is possible that these experimental outcomes may have been attributable to the data collection methods employed by Lasky et al. In their study, heart-rate data were collected from the polygraph output of the cardiotachometer. Because the paper speed of the polygraph was not reported in their study, it is possible that the differences in mean heart-rate values may have fallen within the error of measurement of such a procedure. Furthermore, because there is no indication that these records were interpreted blindly for each infant (re: assignment to condition), the possibility of bias cannot be ruled out. Finally, however, in the defense of the Lasky et al. findings, it should be noted that the reliable effects that they report for the −60/−20 and +20/+60 conditions differ markedly from the results in the −20/+20 condition. Clearly, additional studies with Spanish-speaking infants using other paradigms would greatly aid in resolving these puzzling findings by Lasky et al.

occur in the infant's native language seems to be categorical for the English contrast, i.e., no within-category discrimination (Eimas et al., 1971: $+60/+80$, $-20/0$).[3]

In sum, these cross-language VOT studies suggest that young infants can detect auditorily specific category boundaries not available in the languages of their communities, but that the categorical nature of discrimination, although approaching, does not attain statistical significance. Therefore, the role of experience with a specific language may be posited to be at least two-fold: 1) it is unnecessary for the emergence of the infant's ability to discriminate the major VOT boundaries between prevoiced and voiced stop consonants (approx $-30/0$ VOT)[3] and between voiced and voiceless stop consonants (approx $+20/+40$), and 2) it may result in a particular VOT category, that is employed in that language, becoming *more* categorical (this is also reminiscent of the *suggestion* of the disappearance by four months of the slightly better within-category discrimination of the one-month-olds in the Eimas et al., 1971 study). Indirect support for this suggestion also derives from a developmental study by Zlatin and Koenigsknecht (1975), who observed that the voiced-voiceless category boundary in identification tasks becomes sharper (narrower) for English-speaking children as they progress from two years to six years to adulthood. Finally, the studies of adult listeners have revealed that the prevoiced/voiced boundary is generally not discriminated by English-speaking adults (Abramson and Lisker, 1970), thus suggesting that these category boundaries may disappear developmentally in the absence of the appropriate experience (i.e., through disuse). A similar point has been made by Trehub (1976) in explaining her finding of infant discrimination of the Czech contrast [ža/řa] in the face of non-Czech adult listeners' difficulties in discriminating this contrast (although their performance did exceed chance levels). Whereas this developmental "disappearance" proposal may be true for the non-English boundary, the case is far less clear for the English boundary and Kikuyu adults. Streeter (1974) found that monolingual Kikuyu adults, like their infants, discriminated across the English VOT boundary, suggesting that there may be something special acoustically about this particular VOT boundary. Whether or not this special status of the English boundary primarily involves a difference in the presence versus absence of an F1 transition is currently a topic of considerable interest in the adult literature (Lisker, 1975a,b; Stevens and Klatt, 1974; Summerfield and Haggard, 1975), but has not yet been directly studied in infants (i.e., can infants of English-speaking parents discriminate a voiced/voiceless distinction in which changes in the F1 transition do not covary with a change in the lag and lead relations of F1 and F2?

Phylogenetic Origins? If the young infant's special ability to discriminate changes at specific phonetic category boundaries does not depend on his own experience in producing these categories or in listening to them in the speech of other speakers, how is it acquired? Because the articulatory apparatus necessary for the production of the categories of human speech is unique to our species (Lieberman, 1975), one possible explanation is that these perceptual categories may have developed phylogenetically to match our phonetic production abilities. In other words, these perceptual capabilities may have evolved as part of the basic organization of the human auditory system, and may be functional in the very young infant as soon as his auditory system is sufficiently developed.

One indirect way of investigating this phylogenetic account is to examine the categorical discrimination of nonhuman primates who do not possess the ability to produce the full range of human speech categories. Presumably, according to the above argument, categories should be absent in their perception. In order to test this hypothesis, Morse and Snowdon (1975) presented rhesus monkeys with a [bae/dae] categorical discrimination task in which each monkey received a between-category, a within-category, a no-shift control, and a two-category ([bae/gae]) change. Analyses of the monkeys' heart-rate responses revealed a reliable orienting response to the within-category change (compared to the control trial), but also significantly larger orienting responses to the between-category and the two-category changes than to the within-category shift. Comparing these results to those obtained with three-month-old human infants and the identical HR paradigm (Miller and Morse, 1976), using the [dae/gae] portion of the same stimulus continuum, shows that rhesus monkeys, relative to human infants, are less limited in their ability to discriminate *within* a phonetic category (Morse, 1976). However, both types of subjects *do* exhibit better between- than within-category discrimination. Sinnott, Beecker, Moody, and Stebbins (1976), employing an appetitive discrimination task, also tested rhesus monkeys on a [ba/da] continuum. According to their latency data, the nonhuman primate subjects (unlike human adults tested with the same procedure) discriminated differences within a phonetic category.

Finally, two recent identification training studies have provided data on VOT category responding in the rhesus monkey (Waters and Wilson, 1976) and the chinchilla (Kuhl and Miller, 1975). Waters and Wilson trained rhesus monkeys using an avoidance task to differentiate a −140 [ba] from a +140 [pa] and tested their generalizations to VOTs of −70, 0, and +70. In general, all animals demonstrated a boundary in their generalizations between +20 and +40, although the boundary shifted to +66 when the endpoint stimuli were 0 and +140 and the test stimuli were +35, +70, and +100. Using a slightly different avoidance paradigm, Kuhl and Miller trained chinchillas on [da] (0) and [ta] (+80) and tested them with stimuli ranging between these two points in 10 msec VOT increments. The chinchillas yielded a [da/ta] boundary of +33.5, very similar to that obtained for the human adults tested in their study (+35.2). In general, these training studies demonstrate that other species can learn to generalize along the VOT continuum, to divide it approximately at the voiced/voiceless boundary employed by speakers of English, and even to generalize their boundaries to other voicing contrasts differing in place of articulation, speaker, and vowel environment (Kuhl and Miller, 1975). However, one important factor distinguishes these studies from the human infant and monkey research described earlier. These identification training studies do *not* provide a measure of the subject's ability to discriminate VOT differences independent of trained reference points in the study. The boundary movement observed in the Waters and Wilson study as a function of endpoint training conditions and the fact that the boundary observed by Kuhl and Miller almost bisects the range of the VOT continuum employed with the chinchillas, suggests that these estimates of a voiced/

voiceless VOT boundary may not prove to be as stable as they have been observed to be in one human study (Sawusch, Pisoni, and Cutting, 1975).[4] Nevertheless, the fact that in both of these training studies the boundary hovered approximately between +10 and +30 raises the possibility that the mammalian auditory system may be psychophysically sensitive to differences in VOT in this particular region. Some support for this suggestion derives from recent studies with human adults using lag/lead comparisons in nonspeech stimuli (Miller, Weir, Pastore, Kelly, and Dooling, 1976; Pisoni, 1977).

In summary, these speech perception findings with nonhuman primates and the chinchilla indicated that these animals seem capable, under some training conditions, of categorizing VOT stimuli into the human voiced and voiceless categories. However, additional research is necessary to determine whether these VOT categories will withstand considerable variation in the training stimuli or exhibit categorical discrimination in tasks without endpoint training stimuli.[4] In contrast, the rhesus monkey's discrimination of the [b] and [d] categories of place of articulation is somewhat categorical in the sense that between-category discrimination exceeds that within a category. In this respect, the rhesus monkey seems to discriminate place boundaries phonetically, as does the human infant tested with the same paradigm (Morse, 1976). However, unlike the human infant and adult who do not easily exhibit discrimination within place categories, the rhesus monkey does respond differentially to within-category contrasts.

If aspects of "phonetic" perception continue to be demonstrated in organisms incapable of human speech,[5] then a more sophisticated approach to the origins (ontogenetic and phylogenetic) of human speech perception will be required. First, a better understanding will be necessary of the acoustics of stimuli that do or do not yield categorical discrimination in these development subjects, and second, we shall need to learn more about the neurophysiological bases responsible for these phonetic abilities.

Feature Detectors for Speech?   Recent findings implicating the adaptation of feature analyzers in adult speech perception have provided one very promising avenue for approaching the possible neurophysiological bases involved in the categorical discrimination of human infants and nonhuman primates. In 1973, Eimas and Corbit reported the results of a speech adaptation paradigm that they felt suggested the importance of auditory feature analyzers or detectors in the human's coding of phonetic categories. These auditory feature analyzers were presumed to be analogous to those investigated in the human visual system (Blakemore and Campbell, 1969; McCollough, 1965) and those that have been studied by

---

[4] Since this paper was initially written, Kuhl (1976) has reported evidence of categorical discrimination of VOT differences in chinchillas.

[5] Lieberman's original formulation of the articulatory abilities of the rhesus monkey (Lieberman, Klatt, and Wilson, 1969) related primarily to deficiencies in its production of the vowel triangle ([i, a, u]), which are presumed to preclude the perceptual decoding of consonant cues in the varying vowel environments of human speech. More recently Lieberman (1976) has raised the possibility that some consonant contrasts may be possible for the *chimpanzee* (although they are not used), and thus additional studies of categorical discrimination in rhesus monkeys using other categories than [bae] and [dae] would help establish the generality of the Morse and Snowdon results.

neurophysiologists in the auditory systems of other species (e.g., Nelson, Erulkar, and Bryan, 1966; Whitfield and Evans, 1965). Finally, based on the feature adaptation results in human adults, Eimas (1974b, 1975b) has posited that the human infant's phonetic discrimination abilities may reflect the functioning of underlying feature detector mechanisms that may be temporarily adapted within the infant discrimination paradigms.

Because several excellent reviews are available elsewhere of the speech adaptation literature (Cooper, 1975; Cutting and Eimas, in press; Eimas, 1974a, 1975b), only a brief overview of the basic paradigm and its results is included here. In a typical speech adaptation study, subjects are presented with a specific stimulus (e.g., a −10 VOT [ba]) that is repeated very quickly in one-minute blocks over the course of approximately one hour. Interspersed between these adaptation strings are tokens of different stimuli varying along a test continuum (e.g., VOT) that the listener is asked to identify. When the subject's adapted identifications are subsequently compared with the identification responses elicited *before* adaptation, differences are usually found in the category boundaries. For example, adaptation with −10 [ba] results in the shifting of the [ba/pa] boundary toward the [ba] category and adaptation on +80 [pa] in a shift toward the [pa] end of the continuum. To explain this outcome, Eimas and his colleagues hypothesized that there are separate feature analyzers in the auditory system that respond to the voiced feature of [ba] and the voiceless feature of [pa], and that the phonetic boundary between [ba] and [pa] represents that point along the VOT continuum that activates both feature analyzers equally. Thus, adaptation with a token from one end of the continuum (e.g., [ba]) might be expected to fatigue the feature analyzer for that part of the continuum, thereby shifting the point of equilibrium between the two detectors *toward* the adapting stimulus.

Since this initial Eimas and Corbitt (1973) experiment, several studies of speech adaptation have been conducted to explore the basis for this adaptation phenomenon. Eimas, Cooper, and Corbit (1973) demonstrated that the adaptation effect is a central and not peripheral auditory effect. Eimas and Corbit (1973) showed in a second experiment that it was not specific to the adapting stimuli. For example, if [da] and [ta] are the adapting stimuli, reliable shifts in the appropriate direction are obtained along the [ba/pa] test continuum, and vice versa. Eimas and Corbit interpreted these results as suggesting that abstract *phonetic* features (voiced, voiceless) were being selectively adapted in this procedure, and not just *auditory* feature analyzers (which would require acoustically similar patterns in the adapting and test stimuli). Cooper and Blumstein (1974) demonstrated similar adaptation results for stimuli varying in place of articulation, i.e., [bae], [bi], [mae], and [vae] all separately shift the [bae/dae] but not the [dae/gae] boundary toward [bae].

More recently, investigators have begun to scrutinize the phonetic nature of these adaptation effects (e.g., Cooper, 1975; Diehl, 1975). For example, Ades (1974) observed that when the stimuli [bae-dae-gae] were employed as adapting stimuli and the test continuum consisted of the same stimuli, but with the vowel-consonant order reversed in each syllable, no reliable adaptation effects were obtained, despite the similarities in phonetic features. In addition, other studies have demonstrated reliable adaptation effects using the critical acoustic cues of speech stimuli in isolation as adapting stimuli. However, these effects are generally of a lesser magnitude than those observed for the entire syllable (e.g., Ades, 1973; Tartter and Eimas, 1975). Although Cooper (1974b) and Diehl (1975) have recently provided slightly more convincing evidence of phonetic feature adaptation for voicing and place features, respectively, the picture that is beginning to emerge from these feature adaptation studies is that many of the previously published "phonetic" adaptation studies may have reflected, instead, the adaptation of *auditory* feature analyzers.

Feature Analyzers and Infant Speech Discrimination   Although the status of phonetic feature analyzers in adult adaptation studies is currently unclear, this should not detract from the relevance of these adaptation studies to the origins of infants' categorical abilities. Adult adaptation studies have demonstrated reliable adaptation effects for stimuli along acoustic continua for voicing (Eimas and Corbit, 1973), place of articulation (Cooper, 1974a), and vowels (Morse, Kass, and Turkienicz, 1976). The importance of these studies for infant speech perception is that they provide indirect evidence of the functioning of *some* types of feature analyzers that may be responsible for the perception of category boundaries in infant categorical discrimination. In the adult adaptation literature, a "phonetic" level of feature adaptation is *supported* if the relevant acoustic cues in isolation do *not* yield the same adaptation effects, or if adaptation effects *are* produced either with the same acoustic cues rearranged in time, or with completely different acoustic cues.

Although this is one way of defining the level of "phonetic" perception, it assumes much more abstract phonetic categories than have generally been ascribed to the infant categorical discrimination findings. In the infant studies described above, "phonetic" discrimination has been confined to the demonstration of a category boundary in the context of a constant vowel environment (e.g., [ba], [da], [ga]). It is entirely possible and reasonable that this categorical discrimination might involve some relatively "low-level" phonetic feature detectors, rather than the more abstract phonetic feature analyzers sought after in adult adaptation studies.

Although Eimas' (1974a) demonstration of continuous discrimination in infants for nonspeech, isolated F2 transitions suggests that the infant's categorical discrimination of consonants is not because of a simple auditory feature analyzer, it does not reveal what complex acoustic events are sufficient for the infant to perceive a discontinuity in the place continuum. In a related vein, the categorical sensitivity observed for place contrasts in rhesus monkeys (Morse and Snowdon, 1975), as well as the VOT identification behavior in the Kuhl and Miller (1975) and Waters and Wilson (1976) studies, may reflect the operation of either auditory feature analyzers responsive to certain of the complex acoustic characteristics of these continua or "low-level" phonetic feature analyzers. Until a variety of other speech and nonspeech comparisons are presented to these nonhuman species, we will not be able to determine the level(s) of feature analysis involved in these animal studies. In summary, a determination of the specific feature analysis systems that may underlie categorical discrimination in human infants and other mammalian species must await future studies of speech, and especially nonspeech, discrimination in both types of populations, coupled with a continued exploration of adaptation effects in human adults.

The link between the adult adaptation studies, feature analyzers, and the basis for infant categorical discrimination relies on several assumptions recently articulated by Eimas (1975b). First, these feature analyzers are presumed to be functional in the infant soon after birth. Second, within the infant testing paradigms, the presentation of a particular speech sound is assumed to excite the appropriate feature analyzers. Furthermore, if a second stimulus is presented that excites the same detectors (within-category shift), then no difference is noted by the infant. In contrast, if a stimulus change occurs that excites different feature analyzers (between-category shift), then the infant will discriminate the two stimuli.

Although these assumptions alone are sufficient to account for the infant's categorical discrimination, Eimas (1975b, p. 223) also suggests that adaptation of these feature detectors may play a role in the infant HAS paradigm. First, he suggests that the repeated stimulus presentation format will result in adaptation of the appropriate detector, and second, that this adaptation may be directly or indirectly responsible for the satiation observed to the familiar stimulus in the HAS procedure. In order to explore the possibility that adaptation may be an underlying process in the first phase of infant discrimination paradigms, one must first determine whether adaptation could take place within the very brief durations of the preshift period employed in most infant studies. In the majority of adult adaptation studies, listeners receive over the course of an hour several thousand presentations of the adapting stimulus (e.g., Cooper, 1974b = 1960; Cooper and Blumstein, 1974 = 3300; Eimas and Corbit, 1973, Expt. I = 5400; Eimas, Cooper, and Corbit, 1973, Expt. I = 2775). In contrast, nonnutritive sucking studies typically provide the infant with 5–10 minutes of somewhat aperiodic exposure to the "adapting stimulus." One estimate of the average number of adapting stimulus presentations in a typical infant HAS discrimination study (Swoboda et al., 1976) indicates that 161 "adapting stimuli" (range: 81–271) were heard before a between-category change, which occurred after 9 minutes (range: 5–12). Furthermore, investigators using a heart-rate paradigm have obtained similar infant discrimination findings with only 20 presentations of the preshift stimulus (Miller and Morse, 1976; Till, 1976). Thus, if the process of adaptation is involved in either the HAS satiation effects or the HR habituation effects, then it is occurring with considerably fewer stimulus presentations than are generally used to elicit adaptation effects in adults. Some encouragement may be derived from recent studies by Hillenbrand (1975), in which reliable adaptation effects were observed for as few as 280 and 700 adapting presentations, and by Bryant (1977), in which adaptation effects were obtained after only 60 adapting stimuli. A more direct test of the possible role of the adaptation process in the satiation/habituation portion of the infant paradigms was recently carried out in the author's laboratory. Miller and Morse (1978) presented adult listeners with adapting stimuli that conformed in number and format to the sequencing of the "familiar" stimulus in the infant HR (20/20) and HAS paradigms. Despite the small numbers of adaptive stimuli, reliable adaptation effects for place of articulation obtained in *both* the HR and HAS paradigms. Thus, these results provide indirect support for Eimas's suggestion about the role of adaptation in infant speech perception studies. In sum, continued research on the role of feature detectors, such as that conducted by Eimas and his colleagues, coupled with additional investigations of the role of adaptation, promise to tell us much about the underlying processes and mechanisms to these infant studies.

Structural and Functional Development Aspects of the Auditory System
Although the feature adaptation explanation may provide a viable hypothesis for the ontogenetic bases of the infant's phonetic perception, its ultimate usefulness and verification depend on our understanding of the structural and functional development of the auditory system as they relate to these speech perception abilities. According to a recent review of the structural development of the auditory system (Hecot, 1975), the development of the peripheral auditory apparatus is nearly complete at birth. The exceptions to this are that the external auditory canal, the tympanic membrane, and the middle ear cavity do not attain their adult dimensions until the age of one year, and the outermost row of hair cells and the basalward portion of the cochlea may be immature at birth. As a consequence of these later developments, the infant experiences: 1) some developmental change in the resonance properties of the external and middle ear cavities and thus in the frequency dependency of the middle ear transfer function, 2) some improvement in the impedance matching properties of the middle ear and thus a slight reduction in hearing threshold, and 3) possibly an improvement (above 2 KHz) in high-frequency sensitivity. Farther upstream in the auditory system, the auditory nerve seems to be completely myelinated at birth, as are the structures of the lower brain stem (e.g., cochlear nucleus, superior olive). In contrast, myelinization at the inferior colliculus and medial geniculate is not complete at birth. Finally, the auditory cortex undergoes myelinization and changes in axonal and dendritic length and diameter from about two to three months postnatally until four years of age, although some anatomical differences in the left (speech) versus right temporal cortex are evident at or before birth (Wada, Clarke, and Hamm, 1975; Witelson and Pallie, 1973).

Unfortunately, what we know about the functional aspects of these developing structures is considerably less (e.g., is it critical that the auditory cortex is not myelinated by the earliest age at which infants exhibit categorical discrimination?). However, recent electrophysiological studies using auditory evoked responses have begun to shed some light on the functional activity of the developing auditory system. For example, according to Hecot (1975), infant eighth nerve action potentials, brain stem, and cortical evoked responses all exhibit prolonged latencies, diminished amplitudes, and elevated thresholds, with the order of maturation in these responses proceeding from caudal to rostral structures. Other investigators have begun to report developmental changes in cortical responsiveness to speech and nonspeech signals (Barnet, Ohlrich, Weiss, and Shanks, 1975; Molfese, Nunez, Seibert, and Ramanaiah, 1976; Ohlrich, Barnet, and Weiss, 1975). In addition, recent research with the evoked eyeblink startle reflex (Graham, 1975; Strock, 1976) and the heart-rate orienting response (Leavitt, Brown, Morse and Graham, 1976; Till, 1976) has suggested that other psychophysiological measures may also aid in tracing developmental changes in auditory function from brain stem to cortex. Although these developments in human physiology and psychophysiology are promising, it is still a large jump from these findings to the specific neuronal transformations that occur in the auditory system as the complex features of speech and other acoustic events are analyzed. The neurophysiologist's recordings of the different levels of auditory processing in nonhuman species could help us bridge this gap and bring us closer to a physiological understanding of the infant's speech perceptual abilities.

More on Acoustic Parameters and Infant Perception In addition to the developmental value of adaptation and neurophysiological studies, it is important to bear in mind that *behavioral* indices of the infant's developing responsiveness to the acoustic parameters of simple and complex sounds continue to provide a source of interesting speech perception questions that we may pose for the comparative neurophysiologist and students of human adaptation effects. Although a vast body of research has demonstrated that the young infant is sensitive to and discriminates differences in the basic auditory dimensions of frequency, intensity, and duration (see Eisenberg, 1976; Morse, 1974 for reviews of this literature), a very different picture emerges when we turn to studies of the infant's perception of speech or speech-like sounds. Either natural speech stimuli have been employed, and thus many of the exact acoustic parameters of the stimuli are unknown (e.g., Eilers and Minifie, 1975[1]; Trehub, 1973a) or synthetic stimuli were generated (as in studies of categorical discrimination) and the critical parameters (such as VOT, F2 transition frequencies, etc.) are provided, but other potentially interesting acoustic information is usually omitted. For obvious reasons, none of the investigators employing synthetic speech stimuli with infants has described *all* of the detailed changes in the parameters used in synthesizing the stimuli. In addition, few have subsequently analyzed their synthetic continuum for frequency or intensity related discontinuities that may have unknowingly been introduced by synthesis (see Popper, 1972 for a good model in the adult literature). For example, some synthesizers permit the assignment of amplitude and frequency values for each of the formants, but only the formant frequency information is generally reported by the investigator. Yet in determining how the auditory system may respond to this complex of formants, relative formant intensities within the stimulus may be of considerable import, especially as the speech stimulus is "pulled-apart" and dissected in studies of nonspeech stimuli. One particularly good nonspeech example that underscores the importance of a systematic pursuit of the role of various acoustic parameters in infant auditory perception is a recent study by Juszcyk, Rosner, Cutting, Foard, and Smith (1977). Juszcyk et al. found that two-month-old infants exhibited categorical discrimination for a pluck/bow continuum consisting of saw-tooth wave stimuli varying in rise time from rapid (less than 35 msec = pluck) to gradual (greater than 35 msec = bow). Although these infant categorical findings are similar to those obtained with adult listeners, this study reminds us that our understanding of the acoustics responsible for infant categorical discrimination and of the relationship between categorical discrimination and "phonetic" abilities in infants is still very much in its "infancy."

In summary, now that the categorical discrimination of some speech sounds (and even an occasional nonspeech sound) has been demonstrated satisfactorily in the human infant and we have begun to progress in our pursuit of some of the potential origins of these abilities, we need to advance our understanding of structure and function within the developing auditory system, to examine the stimulus parameters of those sounds that do and do not yield categorical discrimination, and to explore both of these avenues within the laboratory of the neurophysiologist and the behavioral paradigms of adaptation and developmental psychophysiology.

Infant Paradigms and Processes

As research in early language development has progressed over the past decade, investigators have had occasion to learn and relearn the usefulness of the distinction between the child's competence (knowledge of the world) and performance (behavior observed). This is nicely illustrated by the historical changes in the syntax acquisition literature, in which inferences about child syntax (competence), initially based on tape-recorded utterances (performance), gradually became transformed into inferences about a more restricted set of semantic and cognitive rules, as investigators began to explore other aspects of the child's performance—namely the context of the communicative act and the child's cognitive skills. Similarly, in the area of infant speech perception, our understanding of the infant's perceptual competence has gradually been undergoing some exciting changes as we have begun to consider the constraints of the testing situation and to examine the processes (including adaptation) that may underlie the infant's discriminative abilities.

Initially, interest in aspects of the infant testing situation focused on the importance of natural versus synthetic speech stimuli (Butterfield and Cairns, 1974; Doty, 1974), the importance of infant state factors (Doty, 1974; Trehub, 1975), and the possible advantages and disadvantages of the HAS and HR paradigms (Butterfield and Cairns, 1974; Doty, 1972; Morse, 1974). Although agreement is currently far from unanimous on the stimulus issue, the general consensus seems to be that at least both natural and synthetic speech have a place in studies of infant speech perception. Which is employed in a particular study is best determined by the importance of controlling parameters that are inaccessible in the wave-form of the stimulus. Thus, control over the second formant transition frequencies requires synthetic speech (Eimas, 1974a), whereas control of overall intensity duration, or even some consonant burst cues (e.g., Miller et al., 1977) may be accomplished using an oscilloscope and natural speech tokens. The controversy over state factors concerns the basis for and importance of eliminating infants who change state (e.g., become sleepy, fussy, etc.) during the experimental session. In heart-rate studies, changes in state have been shown to affect dramatically the infant's responsiveness to auditory stimuli (Berg, Berg, and Graham, 1971; Eisenberg, 1976; Rewey, 1973) and consequently, investigators attempting to assess the infant's auditory competence have been careful to select only those infants who remain calm and alert *throughout* the session (e.g., Berg, 1974; Brown, 1972; Leavitt et al., 1976). The sensitivity of the nonnutritive sucking paradigm has been more controversial. In the only published comparison of infants who did not complete the full 4-min postshift period because of major state changes, Swoboda et al. (1976) found that these infants' shift data collected *before* state changes did not exhibit the same discrimination as evidenced by infants who completed the experiment without a change in state. Similar effects have also been reported for heart rate in six-week-olds (Leavitt et al., 1976). Unfortunately, the selection of infants on the basis of acceptable state criteria often results in a high attrition rate. Although there is no published evidence that infants who are thus rejected differ in their discrimination from infants who complete the session, periodic attempts in our laboratory to retest infants rejected for state on a previous visit indicate that their discriminative responding is similar to that of infants successfully tested on their first visit. Thus, in an effort to assess the infant's speech perceptual *competence,* it seems wise to continue to select only those infants who remain in a state optimal for the processing of and responding to speech information.

More recently, investigators have become more concerned with the infant testing situation as it relates to other aspects of the infant's speech discrimination. This concern includes an interest in the experimental factors that govern the response to the preshift stimulus, the infant's memory for the preshift stimulus, the discrimination of a change (categorical or otherwise), and individual differences that may exist among infants of normal medical histories versus those "at risk" for later developmental problems. In the discussion of these factors that follows, we first consider the HAS and HR procedures separately, then proceed to a more general discussion of memory factors and individual differences in studies of infant speech discrimination.

HAS Paradigm: Acquisition and Discrimination   The nonnutritive sucking paradigm provided the earliest evidence of infant categorical discrimination (Eimas et al., 1971), and it was only natural that along with the VOT stimuli of that first study (Stevens and Klatt, 1974), it should also be subjected to intense examination (Butterfield and Cairns, 1974). In their review of the HAS literature, Butterfield and Cairns wrote that "the HAS shift effect cannot be clearly interpreted" on several counts. First, they argued that no data demonstrating that the contingent auditory stimulation accounted for an increase in HAS rate were available. Two recent studies have since directly examined this aspect of the infant's preshift performance. Swoboda, Morse, and Leavitt (1976) divided into fifths the period between baseline and the stimulus shift for each infant in their HAS study of vowel discrimination, and observed an orderly increase in sucking rate between sections 2 and 3, 3 and 4, and 4 and 5. Trehub and Chang (1977) have more recently explored the infant's appreciation of the contingency between sound and HAS by testing infants with [ba] or [pa] stimuli in one of three presentation conditions: a) contingent upon their HAS, b) in a contingency-withdrawal condition (HAS terminated stimulus presentation), or c) in a noncontingent condition yoked to the stimulus sequence of the two contingency groups. In addition, d) a no-sound condition was also tested. The infants in the contingency-presentation condition exhibited an orderly increase in rate of HAS over the six minutes of the "conditioning period;" in contrast, no other group demonstrated any reliable change from baseline during this period. Thus, the results of both of these studies provide evidence that during the preshift period infants do exhibit a learning of the contingency between HAS and the presentation of speech sounds.

A second problem that Butterfield and Cairns observed in the infant HAS studies was that the no-change control condition was inadequate. They argued that a shift to no stimulus (following habituation) was necessary to rule out the possibility that infants were responding to the *removal* of the initial stimulus, rather than the discrimination of the postshift sound from the preshift stimulus. Such a no-stimulus control would be of interest for a number of reasons, e.g., it is often used to examine offset orienting responses with heart rate. However, in a typical HAS experimental condition, "removal" of the preshift stimulus is signalled by the introduction of a different (postshift) stimulus. Thus, the critical question is whether this stimulus difference is a sufficient cue for infant discrimination, and for this purpose the *no-change* control condition traditionally employed in this paradigm would seem to be adequate.

Finally, Trehub (1973a) and Butterfield and Cairns (1974) have both criticized the interpretation of HAS studies of categorical discrimination, because the *failure* of an increase in a *voluntary* response (HAS) following a within-category shift does not necessarily demonstrate that the infant *cannot* discriminate such a change. In general, they are absolutely correct. However, one should not lose sight of the fact that, like adults in a variety of discrimination paradigms, infants in HAS studies consistently *do not* discriminate within-category changes (as compared to between-category shifts). Furthermore, the recent replication of the HAS evidence of categorical discrimination using a relatively involuntary response, the heart-rate orienting response (Miller and Morse, 1976; Till, 1976), suggests that young infants do treat within- and between-category contrasts differently. Nevertheless, one cannot ignore the possibility that, under some very special testing conditions, sensitivity to within-category differences in consonants may also be within the infant's auditory/linguistic competence (as is the case for adult listeners) (Lazarus and Pisoni, 1972; Pisoni and Tash, 1974). This is indeed an intriguing possibility, and it is treated in more detail when the role of memory factors in categorical discrimination is considered.

In summary, both the acquisition aspects and the categorical discrimination results of the HAS paradigm seem to be fairly well-established. This does not mean, however, that all of the processes involved in this procedure are completely understood. Specifically, the possible role of the adaptation of feature analyzers and conditions that would facilitate demonstrations of within-category discrimination are two areas of research that will greatly deepen understanding of the HAS paradigm.

HR Paradigms: Discrimination and Orienting   Although the landmark study in infant speech discrimination (Moffitt, 1971) employed a heart-rate measure, few systematic investigations have been conducted of heart-rate indices of infant speech discrimination until recently. Moffitt (1971), Berg (1974), and most recently Lasky et al. (1975) have demonstrated that infants older than four months of age evidence auditory discrimination when habituation/dishabituation HR paradigm is employed. In this particular HR paradigm, the infant receives several trials (usually six to eight) of one stimulus (each perhaps consisting of 5–10 sec of stimulation), followed by a couple of trials (usually two) of a change stimulus; an intertrial interval ITI of 20–30 sec is generally employed. Over the course of the six or eight trials of the preshift stimulus, the initial orienting response (OR) to trial onset exhibits progressive habituation. If the trials of the change-stimulus re-elicit an OR (i.e., result in dishabituation), then discrimination of the stimulus contrast is inferred.

Although the habituation/dishabituation procedure provides a reliable measure of auditory discrimination in infants four months of age and older, as well as in adult listeners (Morse, Leavitt, Miller, and Romero, 1977), it has consistently failed to demonstrate auditory discrimination in younger infants (Berg, 1974; Brown, 1972; Leavitt et al., 1976; Miller et al., 1977). For example, Leavitt et al. presented six-week-olds with a [ba]/[ga] discrimination using a 6/2 (6 habituation/2 dishabituation trials) HR paradigm, and Miller et al. played [bu] versus [gu] to three-month-olds in an 8/2 paradigm. Although infants in both studies responded to the initial trials with a large orienting response that subsequently habituated over trials, no evidence was even suggestive in either study of a recovery of the OR to the stimulus change. In contrast, when Leavitt et al. presented the same stimuli in a paradigm in which the long ITIs of the 6/2 paradigm were eliminated, reliable discrimination of the stimulus change was observed. In this no-ITI paradigm, several tokens (e.g., 20 or 30) of one stimulus are typically followed immediately by several tokens (e.g., 20 or 30) of a second sound, with the interstimulus interval (e.g., 500 msec or 1 sec) held constant throughout the entire train of stimuli. Variations of this no-ITI HR paradigm have been used successfully in studying auditory discrimination not only in six-week-olds, but also in three-month-olds (Miller et al., 1977), and categorical discrimination in three-month-olds (Miller and Morse, 1976), four-month-olds (Till, 1976), and rhesus monkeys (Morse and Snowdon, 1975). Thus, this particular version of the HR paradigm would seem to be an excellent candidate for developmental comparisons across a wide and early age range, including nonhuman primates. However, before developmental enthusiasm for this procedure becomes unbounded, it should be noted that unless the task demands are reasonably complex, such as in a dichotic listening study (Cowan and Morse, 1975), human adults are easily bored with such a presentation procedure and, consequently, either instructions to pay attention (Brown, Morse, Leavitt, and Graham, 1976) or incentives may be necessary to induce their cooperation.[6]

Although it is exciting that the no-ITI paradigm provides us with a method for assessing early infant auditory discrimination, it is unclear at present which of the parameters and processes that differentiate the no-ITI and habituation/dishabituation paradigms are responsible for these consistent discrimination differences in early infancy. Both Leavitt et al. and Miller et al. failed to find evidence of speech discrimination with a habituation/dishabituation paradigm, but they did obtain reliable discrimination of the same speech contrasts when a no-ITI procedure was utilized. In both studies, the actual number of preshift stimulus presentations was either equal to or less than that employed in the habituation/dishabituation conditions. Therefore, differences in the number of presentations could not account for the advantage observed with the no-ITI paradigm. Second, because both studies found reliable habituation of the OR over trials, infants were obviously remembering something of the stimuli as the experimental session progressed. One hypothesis is that over the course of the long ITIs of the habituation/dishabituation paradigm,

---

[6] However, in a recent series of studies in this author's laboratory, this version of the heart-rate paradigm was applied to VOT discrimination without such success (Miller and Ruzicka, 1978; Roth and Morse, 1975). The basis for these discrepancies in the VOT and place of articulations findings is currently under investigation, but the Miller and Ruzicka analyses of full-session heart-rate data suggest that investigators should pay particular attention to cyclical heart-rate activity, and differences in prechange baseline levels.

the young infant's memory of the critical stimulus features employed in these two studies may begin to decay and become relatively undifferentiated. However, if this is the only factor operating, one might expect that a change stimulus would nevertheless be discriminated from this undifferentiated memory of the preshift sound (if one accepts Sokolov's account of habituation). Alternatively, perhaps the brief number of stimuli presented on each trial (i.e., the distribution of stimuli during the habituation phase) contributes to a relative difference in the encoding of the critical stimulus cues. With the longer strings of the no-ITI paradigm, this stimulus representation may become relatively more consolidated. Although these two accounts are by no means mutually exclusive, it remains for future parametric investigations to elucidate the relative importance of memory decay and encoding factors. Finally, the observation that adaptation effects may be observed in adult listeners with as few as 20 presentations of the same stimulus (Miller and Morse, 1978) suggests that the adaptation of feature analyzers also needs to be explored among the processes involved in HR measures of infant discrimination. In sum, what is of particular interest in these HR paradigm differences is the suggestion that young infants may be developmentally deficient *not* in their discrimination of particular speech contrasts, but in the processes that are involved in their ability to code, remember, or compare acoustic events. Older infants studied with the habituation/dishabituation procedure, and even younger infants examined with the HAS paradigm, *do* exhibit reliable speech discrimination (e.g., Eimas et al., 1971; Moffitt, 1971; Morse, 1972).

In addition to providing an important method for assessing infant auditory discrimination, the cardiac orienting response also permits an examination of how different acoustic events are processed by the developing infant. For example, a stimulus with a high intensity and/or rapid rise time is more likely to elicit an accelerative rather than a decelerative response, and both of these parameters need to be considered in studies with young infants (Berg et al., 1971; Graham and Jackson, 1970). Furthermore, it is extremely difficult to elicit orienting responses in newborns to auditory stimuli, even when intensity and rise-time are optimized (Kearsley, 1973), although it becomes progressively easier to elicit an OR as the infant matures (Graham, Berg, Berg, Jackson, Hatton, and Kantowitz, 1970). Another factor that seems to affect the OR in six-week-olds is the pulsed (containing an interstimulus interval) versus non-pulsed (continuous with no interstimulus interval) nature of the acoustic stimulus (Berg, 1974; Brown, 1972; Leavitt et al. 1976). For example, a pulsed speech stimulus (such as the syllables, [ba] . . . [ba]) elicits a large OR in six-week-olds, as does a pulsed sine wave (Leavitt et al., 1976); but when a nonpulsed complex triangular wave is employed, it fails to elicit an OR at six weeks, but does elicit an OR at nine weeks of age (Brown, 1972). In contrast, if the interstimulus intervals are removed from the speech stimuli (e.g., [bababa . . .]), an orienting response is still evidenced in six-week-olds (Morse, Leavitt, Brown, and Graham, in preparation). Although these findings are necessarily limited by the particular speech and nonspeech stimuli employed, as well as by the eternal problem of developing an appropriate "nonspeech control" stimulus, they do suggest that young infants attend differently to pulsed and nonpulsed, speech and nonspeech events.

Some additional evidence that six-week-old infants may attend to speech and nonspeech signals differently may be found in the acceleratory response observed to a [ba/ga] speech *change* versus a deceleratory response to a sine wave change in the same frequency range (Leavitt et al., 1976). Similarly, Till (1976) observed that four-month-olds responded to a [ba]-[da] change in a no-ITI paradigm with heart rate *deceleration*. However, when nonspeech control stimuli were synthesized (using the [ba]-[da] second formant transition differences, but with the first formant transition inverted), infants responded to the change with heart-rate *acceleration*. In both the Leavitt et al. and Till studies, infants responded to the *initial* presentation of these stimuli with an orienting response. These findings suggest that in a discrimination situation (in the context of other auditory events), infants may experience some relative difficulty encoding rapidly changing (40–45 msec) formant transition cues. It is tempting to speculate that for young infants (six-week-olds), even if the change stimulus is speech, this will be the case; the older infant (four-month-old), however, who has had more experience with human speech, more readily encodes the speech change, but does not encode as easily a very similar but unfamiliar nonspeech change. Alternatively, these acceleratory/deceleratory response differences may reflect the development of different levels of processing in the auditory system, similar to the "short-time constant" (cortical) and "long-time constant" (subcortical) processing systems of Gersuni (1971). The further pursuit of these effects promises to be an exciting frontier of developmental research for the HR orienting response and other psychophysiological methods.

Taken together, these recent heart-rate findings reflect a growing interest in exploring the *microgenetic* aspects of infant speech perception (Morse, 1974), i.e., the encoding and memory processes that underlie the infant's perception of human speech. These include the study of general orienting and habituation to different acoustic stimuli, as well as the contrasting results obtained for younger infants with the habituation/dishabituation and no-ITI procedures. Although our earlier discussion of HAS research primarily focused on the underlying processes of the method, an interest in how encoding or memory processes might be studied with the HAS paradigm is just beginning to be awakened. For example, Swoboda et al. (1976) observed, in response to the onset of sound, a consistent drop in HAS following the silent baseline minute. It is possible that this onset response will prove useful in assessing an infant's differential attention to various speech and nonspeech stimuli.

Memory and the HAS Paradigm   The investigation of the role of memory processes in HAS measures of speech discrimination has been recently stimulated by some of the adult research on the categorical/continuous perception of vowels. Pisoni (1973, 1975) and Fujisaki and Kawashima (1970) have both suggested that an auditory short-term memory (STM) and a phonetic STM component play an important role in adult speech discrimination. In general, the auditory STM is presumed to retain a reasonably faithful auditory copy of the original stimulus, whereas phonetic STM only retains information about the phonetic category assignment of the stimulus. Accordingly, if testing conditions permit the listener access to an auditory STM of the stimuli, then within-category discrimination might be expected to be continuous, or relatively good. In studies of adult vowel discrimination, this is accomplished by using relatively long vowels or short interstimulus intervals between the stimuli to be compared. In contrast, if conditions force the listener to rely primarily on a phonetic STM of the stimuli, then within-category discrimination would be expected to be poor, and thus overall discrimination more categorical. This latter outcome occurs for adult listeners if relatively brief vowels or long interstimulus intervals are employed (Pisoni, 1973, 1975).

If this analysis of adult vowel discrimination is applied to the infant's phonetic responding, the phenomenon of categorical discrimination begins to assume another dimension: it can be seen as a "state of mind," subject to the memory constraints of the paradigm and stimuli. To explore this "state of mind" hypothesis in infant vowel discrimination, Swoboda, Kass, Morse, and Leavitt (1978), using the HAS paradigm, presented eight-week-old infants with the [i] and [I] vowel changes of the Swoboda et al. (1976) study, except that the stimulus duration was 60 msec rather than the 240 msec of the Swoboda et al. (1976) study. Two interesting results emerged from this investigation. First, although discrimination differences between the two vowels were observed, overall the between-category shift exhibited discrimination, whereas the within-category shift did not. However, the difference between the two conditions did not reach significance. This latter finding is not entirely unexpected, in view of the incomplete categorical discrimination observed by Pisoni (1973) for the same short vowels. A second interesting finding in the Swoboda et al. short vowel study was that between-category discrimination (amount of HAS recovery in the first postshift minute) was significantly inversely correlated with the number of seconds intervening between the last preshift stimulus and the first change stimulus heard by the infant. In other words, the longer the silent delay, the worse the between-category discrimination. Interestingly, Pisoni (1973) observed a similar progressive reduction in adult within-category discrimination for short vowels as the delay interval in a same/different task was lengthened. However, because Pisoni's adults did not yield such a reduction in between-category discrimination, the infant short vowel findings suggest that infants' phonetic STM for vowels may not be as robust as that evidenced by adults. In summary, the extent to which vowel discrimination is categorical or continuous seems to depend on memory factors for the infant as well as for the adult. Both the manipulation of stimulus duration and correlations of the preshift-postshift silent interval with shift recovery provide ways of assessing these memory effects in the HAS paradigm. If categorical discrimination for the infant is considered a "state of mind," then the issue raised earlier by Trehub (1973a) and Butterfield and Cairns (1974) regarding the lack of recovery to within-category consonant discrimination in the HAS paradigm takes on a very different significance. Within this framework, it may only be a matter of time before a clever paradigm is developed that reveals continuous discrimination of consonants in infants.

Individual Differences   These recent advances in the development of the HR and HAS paradigms have made it possible to begin to explore individual differences in infants' responses to speech and other acoustic stimuli. First, these procedures can be used to assess differences in consonant versus vowel and categorical versus continuous discrimination. In addition, the HR paradigm permits an assessment of individual differences in initial orienting and the rate of habituation to different acoustic events. Similarly, the HAS paradigm also permits the examination of individual differences in rate of acquisition. Finally, both the HR and HAS paradigms enable us to study the role of encoding and memory factors in affecting individual differences in infant speech discrimination. It may well be these latter manipulations of the perceptual problem presented to the infant that result in the most sensitive measures of individual differences.

At present, data on individual differences in infant speech perception are almost nonexistant. Only one published study has directly compared infants who have normal medical histories with infants (primarily premature) whose medical records placed them "at risk" for later developmental problems. Swoboda et al. (1976), in their study of continuous vowel discrimination in eight-week-olds, observed a *tendency* for at risk infants not to exhibit the gradual acquisition function of "normal" infants, and for infants judged at "high risk" to show a different pattern of within-category discrimination. More recently, in the short vowel study of Swoboda et al. (1978), at risk infants, in contrast to "normal" infants, were found not to exhibit the negative correlation between the magnitude of HAS recovery to a between-category shift and the interval separating the last preshift and first postshift stimulus. Although these findings can only be considered suggestive at present, they nevertheless do indicate that continued exploration of individual differences in infant speech discrimination may eventually prove useful in the early identification of later language problems. Finally, in addition to the use of the HR and HAS paradigms with very young infants, the assessment of speech discrimination in older infants and children may also benefit from the use of Friedlander's Playtest apparatus (e.g., Friedlander, McCarthy, and Soforenko, 1967) or from a recent and innovative audiometric-based head-turning paradigm developed by Eilers, Wilson, and Moore (1977).

Beyond Categorical Discrimination?: *Alpha Centauri*

In the previous sections, it has been established that infants do indeed discriminate consonants categorically, questions about the origins of these abilities have been pursued, and the processes that underlie the paradigms employed in assessing these abilities that may affect the presence of discrimination or the "state of mind" observed have been explored. Clearly, many exciting answers to these latter problem areas remain before us in the future, but they should not be considered the limits of research in infant speech perception. Although the domain of categorical discrimination and the related paradigm/process frontiers discussed above clearly constitute an important aspect of infant speech perception, the infant's phonetic abilities must eventually extend far beyond his categorizing of consonants along a continuum in which the vowel environment is held constant (e.g., [bae/dae/gae]). To begin with, as we know from adult speech perception studies, the particular acoustic cues that signal a given consonant differ radically as a function of vowel context, position in the syllable, sex of the speaker, etc. For example, in the familiar example of [di] and [du] shown in Figure 4 (Liberman, 1970) the [d] consonant may be cued by a rising F2 transition in [di] and a falling F2 transition in [du], yet we consistently identify

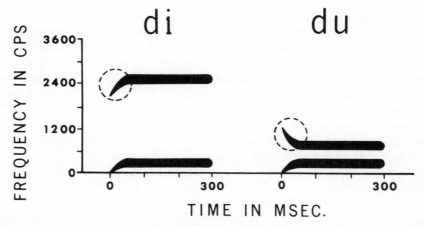

Figure 4.   Hand-painted spectrograms illustrating the second formant frequency transition differences for the consonant [d] in the context of the vowels [i] versus [u]. (From Liberman, A., 1970). The grammars of speech and language, *Cognitive Psychology,* 1970, *1*, 201–323. Reprinted by permission.

the initial consonant in both syllables as the same. To test this phonetic ability in young infants requires a paradigm that is not merely capable of measuring discrimination, but one that can also assess the infant's identification or generalization responses. As presently conceived, neither the HAS nor HR paradigms is adequate for this purpose. In contrast, two alternative training procedures, analogous to those employed in testing nonhuman species, do permit the assessment of identification responses.

In the only published attempt to address these problems of abstract phonetic invariance, Fodor, Garrett, and Brill (1975) presented infants in a conditioned head-turning paradigm with the natural speech stimuli [pi, pa, pu, ki, ka, ku]. For a given set of three syllables (e.g., [pi, ka, pu]), infants were either conditioned to turn their heads only for the syllables that contained the *same* initial consonant (e.g., [pi] and [pa]) or to turn their heads for a pair in which the initial consonant was different (e.g., [pi] and [ka]). Fodor et al. observed that infants 14 to 18 weeks of age gave more conditioned head-turns to the pair that contained the same initial consonant than to the pair that contained different ones. Unfortunately, because Fodor et al. employed natural speech sounds, this "phonetic" effect may have been attributable to acoustic cues that were similar in the "same" condition, such as amount of voicing or the consonantal release burst. Nevertheless, this study represents an important beginning in the investigation of the more complex phonetic decisions that the infant must eventually make.

Another aspect of the abstract phonetic domain that the infant must also master, the discrimination of speech contrasts in different positions within an utterance, was explored by Trehub (1973a). Using the HAS paradigm, she observed that infants 4 to 17 weeks of age could discriminate the contrast [aba] - [apa], but not [atapa] - [ataba] or [mapa] - [pama]. However, because natural speech stimuli were also employed in this study, it is not certain whether these failures of discrimination were attributable to the acoustic cues specific to the [p] and [b] consonants in these contexts or to the greater complexity of the utterances. In addition, inspection of her data for the two conditions that did not result in discrimination suggests that an assessment of the change in responses *immediately* after the stimulus shift might have evidenced reliable discrimination. In any event, Trehub's study also constitutes an important beginning in the investigation of other aspects of phonetic perception that the developing infant must confront.

However, the magnitude of the phonetic categorization task that the infant must eventually solve is not limited to problems such as [di] and [du] or the coding of consonants in different positions in an utterance. The infant must also be able to correctly categorize consonants articulated by different speakers who have radically different vocal tracts (Rand, 1971) and consonants that occur in various combinations or clusters. This general problem of acoustic invariance in consonants is illustrated in the following examples. In English, the [p] sound may be cued in the contrast [bit] - [pit] by VOT, in [sib] - [sip] by vowel duration, and in [slit] - [split] by a brief interval of silence. Thus, eventually the infant must arrive at a phonetic category for [p] that permits all of these versions: a much more abstract phonetic problem than that posed for categorical discrimination. A similar problem of invariance also exists for vowel perception (Shankweiler, Strange, and Verbrugge, in press). In running speech, the consonant cues that surround a vowel are critical for its identification, and listeners cannot just rely on a portion of the vowel's steady state in categorizing it. Thus, in the case of both consonant and vowel classes, the infant must come to appreciate that phonetic categories are much more than the decisions involved in categorical discrimination. Instead, they require the assignment of speech sounds with widely differing acoustic patterns in a variety of contexts to the same abstract phonetic category. Finally, as the developing child begins to treat these phonetic categories as important in distinguishing differences in the meaning of words in a particular language (i.e., phonemes), further reorganization and refinement of categories will also be necessary. For example, the category boundaries along consonant continua may become progressively sharper with development (Streeter and Landauer, 1976; Zlatin and Koenigsknecht, 1975).

Unfortunately, the challenges in speech perception for the developing infant will not be put to rest by the formulation of abstract phonetic and phonemic categories. The infant must also come to appreciate the complexities of entire utterances. This includes the perception of differences in intonation, stress, and speaking-rate patterns, as well as the segmentation of utterances into syllables and words (e.g., *ice cream* versus *I scream*). Although some available data suggest that infants as young as six weeks can discriminate changes in rising versus falling intonation contours (Morse, 1972), these findings are limited to a single syllable and need to be extended to more complex intonation contours and utterances (e.g., Hadding-Koch and Studdert-Kennedy, 1964). Finally, perhaps one of the most interesting challenges that lies in store for the infant (and investigators) is the adult's appreciation of *silence* in continuous speech perception (Dorman, Raphael, Liberman, and Repp, 1975). For example, Dorman et al. found that if the silent interval is varied between the friction noise of [ʃ] and the syllable [pɛ], the listener will hear either [ʃɛ] (short interval) or [ʃpɛ] (long interval). Similarly, if the silent interval between [bɛb] and [dɛ] is varied, adults hear either [bɛdɛ] (short interval) or [bɛbdɛ] (long interval). In a series of very clever experiments, Dorman et al. demonstrated that these effects could not be attributed to simple forward and backward masking, but instead might be attributable to the listeners' understanding of the time that is necessary to articulate a particular sequence (e.g., it takes time to move the articulations from the final [b] in [bɛb] to the [d] in [dɛ]). The development of this sophisticated perceptual ability will also certainly be of interest (Liberman, 1976).

In summary, we have seen in this review that the study of infant speech perception involves much more than the demonstration of categorical discrimination in small humans. The auditory and phonetic bases of infant categorical discrimination are beginning to be explored in terms of phylogenetic origins, memory factors, specific acoustic cues, and the adaptation of feature analyzers. Furthermore, as some of these human infant and adult and animal studies indicate, we may need to reconsider the usefulness of the simple distinction between "auditory" and "phonetic" levels of processing and begin to explore the organization of the continuum of auditory-phonetic events.[7]

Thus, the phenomenon of infant categorical discrimination, when viewed as a "state of mind" that depends on these various factors, begins to assume a very exciting and different importance in research on infant speech perception. Furthermore, when we consider the phonetic and other speech perceptual tasks that confront the developing infant in addition to the research questions related to categorical discrimination, we begin to realize that this area of research contains some of the most interesting prospects for discovering those aspects of speech perception and language in general that *do develop* later in infancy and *are* unique to the human species. Finally, these new research frontiers in infant speech perception promise to provide a host of more sensitive assessment tools for probing individual differences in infants considered at risk for later developmental problems.

ACKNOWLEDGMENTS

The author would like to express his gratitude to Professor Jerzy Rose for his Principle of Alpha Centauri: the comparative neurophysiologist's conception of research on speech perception.

REFERENCES

Abramson, A., and Lisker, L. 1970. Discriminability along the voicing continuum: Cross-language tests. Proceedings of the Sixth International Congress of Phonetic Sciences, Prague, 1967, pp. 569–573. Academic, Prague.

Abramson, A., and Lisker, L. 1973. Voice-timing perception in Spanish word-initial stops. J. Phonet. 1: 1–8.

---

[7] The need to redefine what is meant by "phonetic" in infant speech perception is also voiced by Kuhl in her paper at this conference. Although she assumes a somewhat more extreme position on this issue, she basically agrees regarding the limited "phonetic" meaning of infant categorical discrimination.

Ades, A. 1973. Some effects of adaptation on speech perception. MIT Res. Lab. Electron. Quart. Progr. Rep. 111: 121–129.

Ades, A. 1974. How phonetic is selective adaptation? Experiments on syllable position and vowel environment. Percept. Psychophys. 16: 61–66.

Allport, F. 1924. Social Psychology. Houghton Mifflin, Boston.

Barnet, A., Ohlrich, E., Weiss, I., and Shanks, B. 1975. Auditory evoked potentials during sleep in normal children from ten days to three years of age. Electroenceph. Clin. Neurophysiol. 39: 29–41.

Berg, W. 1974. Cardiac orienting responses of 6- and 16-week-old infants. J. Exp. Child Psychol. 17: 303–312.

Berg, K., Berg, W., and Graham, F. 1971. Infant heart rate response as a function of stimulus and state. Psychophysiology 8: 30–44.

Blakemore, C., and Campbell, F. 1969. On the existence of neurons in the human visual system selectively sensitive to the orientation and size of retinal images. J. Physiol. 203: 237–260.

Brown, J. 1972. Orienting responses to repeated auditory stimuli in alert six- and nine-week-old infants. Unpublished master's thesis, University of Wisconsin, Madison.

Brown, R. 1973. A First Language: The Early Stages. Harvard University Press, Cambridge.

Brown, J., Morse, P., Leavitt, L., and Graham, F. 1976. Specific attentional effects reflected in the cardiac orienting response. Bull. Psychonom. Soc. 7: 1–4.

Bryant, J. 1977. The effects of numbers of presentations and processing time on the selective adaptation of speech. Unpublished master's thesis, University of Wisconsin-Madison.

Butterfield, W., Cairns, G. 1974. Discussion summary—Infant reception research. In R. Schiefelbusch and L. Lloyd (eds.), Language Perspectives—Acquisition, Retardation, and Intervention, pp. 75–102. University Park Press, Baltimore.

Cooper, W. 1974a. Adaptation of phonetic feature analyzers for place of articulation. J. Acoustic. Soc. Am. 56: 617–627.

Cooper, W. 1974b. Selective adaptation for acoustic cues of voicing in initial stops. J. Phonet. 2: 303–313.

Cooper, W. 1975. Selective adaptation to speech. In F. Restle, R. Shiffrin, N. Castellan, H. Lindman, and D. Pisoni (eds.), Cognitive Theory: Vol. 1, pp. 23–54. Wiley and Sons, New York.

Cooper, W. and Blumstein, S. 1974. A "labial" feature analyzer in speech perception. Percept. Psychophys. 15: 591–600.

Cowan, N., and Morse, P. 1975. Detection and report processes in dichotic listening. Infant Development Laboratory Research Status Report, II. Univ. of Wisconsin, Madison.

Cutting, J., and Eimas, P. Phonetic feature analyzers and the processing of speech in infants. In J. Kavanaugh and J. Cutting (eds.), The Role of Speech in Language. MIT Press, Cambridge. In press.

Diehl, R. 1975. The effect of selective adaptation on the identification of speech sounds. Percept. Psychophys. 17: 48–52.

Dorman, M., Raphael, L., Liberman, A., and Repp, B. 1975. Some masking like phenomena in speech perception. Haskins Laboratories Status Report on Speech Research, SR-42/43, pp. 265–276.

Doty, D. 1974. Infant speech perception: Report of a conference held at the Univ. of Minnesota, June 20–22, 1972. Hum. Dev. 17: 74–80.

Eilers, R. 1975. Infant speech perception: Context sensitivity. Paper presented at Asha, November, Washington, D.C.

Eilers, R., and Minifie, F. 1975. Fricative discrimination in early infancy. J. Speech Hear. Res. 18: 158–167.

Eilers, R., Wilson, W., and Moore, J. 1977. Developmental changes in speech discrimination in infants. J. Speech Hear. Res. 20: 766–780.

Eimas, P. 1974a. Auditory and linguistic processing of cues for place of articulation by infants. Percept. Psychophys. 16: 513–521.

Eimas, P. 1974b. Linguistic processing of speech by young infants. In R. Schiefelbusch and L. Lloyd (eds.), Language Perspectives—Acquisition, Retardation, and Intervention, pp. 55–73. University Park Press, Baltimore.

Eimas, P. 1975a. Auditory and phonetic coding of the cues for speech: Discrimination of the [r-1] distinction by young infants. Percept. Psychophys. 18: 341–347.

Eimas, P. 1975b. Speech perception in early infancy. In L. Cohen and P. Salapatek (eds.), Infant perception: From Sensation to Cognition, Vol. II, pp. 193–231. Academic Press, New York.

Eimas, P., Cooper, W., and Corbit, J. 1973. Some properties of linguistic features detectors. Percept. Psychophys. 13: 247–252.

Eimas, P., and Corbit, J. 1973. Selective adaptation of linguistic feature detectors. Cog. Psychol. 4: 99–109.

Eimas, P., Siqueland, E., Juszyck, P., and Vigorito, J. 1971. Speech perception in infants. Science 171: 303–306.

Eisenberg, R. 1976. Auditory Competence in Early Life: The Roots of Communicative Behavior. University Park Press, Baltimore.

Entus, A. 1975. Hemispheric asymmetry in processing of dichotically presented speech and nonspeech stimuli by infants. Paper presented at Society for Research in Child Development, April, Denver, Colorado.

Entus, A. 1977. Hemispheric asymmetry in processing dichotically presented speech and nonspeech stimuli by infants. In J. Segalowitz and F. Gruber (eds.), Language Development and Neurological Theory, pp. 64–73. Academic Press, New York.

Fodor, J., Garrett, M., and Brill, S. 1975. Pi ka pu: The perception of speech sounds by prelinguistic infants. Percept. Psychophys. 18: 74–78.

Friedlander, B., McCarthy, J., and Soforenko, A. 1967. Automated psychological evaluation with severely retarded institutionalized infants. Am. J. Ment. Def. 71: 909–919.

Frischkopf, L., Capranica, R., and Goldstein, M. 1968. Neural coding in the bullfrog's auditory system: A teleological approach. Proceed. IEEE 56: 969–988.

Fujisaki, H., and Kawashima, T. 1970. Some experiments on speech perception and a model for the perceptual mechanisms. Faculty of Engineering, University of Tokyo, Japan. Eng. Res. Inst. 29: 207–214.

Gardner, R., and Gardner, B. 1969. Teaching sign language to a chimpanzee. Science 165: 664–672.

Gersuni, G. 1971. Temporal organization of the auditory function. In G. V. Gersuni (ed.), Sensory Processes at the Neuronal and Behavioral Levels, pp. 85–114. Academic Press, New York.

Glanville, B., Best, C., and Levenson, R. 1977. A cardiac measure of cerebral asymmetries in infant auditory perception. Dev. Psychol. 13: 54–59.

Graham, F., and Jackson, J. 1970. Arousal systems and infant heart rate responses. In L. Lipsitt and H. Reese (eds.), Advances in Child Development and Behavior, Vol. 5, pp. 54–117. Academic Press, New York.

Graham, F. 1975. The more or less startling effects of weak prestimulation. Psychophysiology 12: 238–248.

Graham, F., Berg, K., Berg, W., Jackson, J., Hatton, H., and Kantowitz, S. 1970. Cardiac orienting responses as a function of age. Psychon. Sci. 19: 363–365.

Hadding-Koch, K., and Studdert-Kennedy, M. 1964. An experimental study of some intonation contours. Phonetics 11: 175–185.

Hayes, C. 1951. The Ape in Our House. Harper and Row, New York.

Hecot, K. 1975. Electrophysiological correlates of human auditory development. In L. Cohen and P. Salapatek (eds.) Infant Perception: From Sensation to Cognition, Vol. II, pp. 151–191. Academic Press, New York.

Hillenbrand, J. 1975. Intensity and repetition effects on selective adaptation to speech. In D. Pisoni (ed.), Research on Speech Perception—Progress Report No. 2, pp. 59–137. Department of Psychology, Indiana University, Bloomington, Indiana.

Jusczyk, P., Rosner, B., Cutting, J., Foard, C., and Smith, L. 1977. Categorical perception of nonspeech sounds by 2-month-old infants. Percept. Psychophys. 25: 50–54.

Kearsley, R. 1973. The newborn's responses to auditory stimulation: A demonstration of orienting and defensive behavior. Child Dev. 44: 582–590.

Kewley-Port, D., and Preston, M. 1974. Early apical stop production: A voice onset time analysis. J. Phonet. 2: 195–210.

Khadem, F., and Corballis, M. 1977. Cerebral asymmetry in infants. Paper presented at biennial meetings of Society for Research in Child Development, New Orleans.

Kuhl, P. 1976. Speech perception by the chinchilla: Categorical perception of synthetic alveolar plosive consonants. J. Acoustic. Soc. Am. 60(suppl. 1): S81(A).

Kuhl, P., and Miller, J. 1975. Speech perception by the chinchilla: Voiced-voiceless distinction in alveolar plosive consonants. Science 190: 69–72.

Lasky, R., Syrdal-Lasky, A., and Klein, D. 1975. VOT discrimination by four- to six-month-old infants from Spanish environments. J. Exp. Child Psychol. 20: 215–225.

Lazarus, J., and Pisoni, D. 1972. Categorical and non-categorical modes of speech perception along the voice-onset-time continuum. Paper presented at 84th meeting of the Acoustical Society of America, December, Miami, Florida.

Leavitt, L., Brown, J., Morse, P., and Graham, F. 1976. Cardiac orienting and auditory discrimination in 6-week infants. Dev. Psychol. 12: 514–523.

Liberman, A. 1970. The grammars of speech and language. Cog. Psychol. 1: 301–323.

Liberman, A. 1976. Comments on the session: Perception and production of speech II; Conference on origins and evaluation of language and speech. Ann. N.Y. Acad. Sci. 280: 718–724.

Liberman, A., Delattre, P., Gerstman, L., and Cooper, F. 1956. Tempo of frequency changes as a cue for distinguishing classes of speech sounds. J. Exp. Psychol. 52: 127–137.

Lieberman, P. 1975. On the Origins of Language; An Introduction to the Evolution of Human Speech. Macmillan, New York.

Lieberman, P., Klatt, D., and Wilson, W. 1969. Vocal tract limitations on the vowel repertoires of rhesus monkeys and other nonhuman primates. Science 164: 1185–1187.

Linden, E. 1976. Apes, Men, and Language. Penguin, New York.

Lisker, L. 1975a. Is it VOT or a first-formant transition detector? J. Acoustic. Soc. Am. 57: 1547–1551.

Lisker, L. 1975b. Stop voicing production: Natural outputs and synthesized inputs. Paper presented at 90th meeting of Acoustical Society of America, November, San Francisco.

Lisker, L., and Abramson, A. 1964. A cross-language study of voicing in initial stops: Acoustical measurements. Word 20: 384–422.

Massaro, D., and Cohen, M. 1977. Voice onset time and fundamental frequency as cues to the /zi/-/si/ distinction. Percept. Psychophys. 22: 373–382.

Mattingly, I. 1972. Speech cues and sign stimuli. Am. Sci. 60: 327–337.

Mattingly, J., Liberman, A., Syrdal, A., Halwes, T. 1971. Discrimination in speech and nonspeech modes. Cog. Psychol. 2: 131–157.

McCollough, C. 1965. Color adaptation of edge-detectors in the human visual system. Science 149: 1115–1116.

McNabb, S. 1975. Must the output of the phonetic feature detector be binary? In D. Pisoni (ed.), Research on Speech Perception—Progress Report No. 2. Department of Psychology, University of Indiana, Bloomington, Indiana.

Miller, C., and Morse, P. 1976. The 'heart' of categorical speech discrimination in young infants. J. Speech Hear. Res. 19: 578–589.

Miller, C., and Morse, P. 1978. Selective adaptation effects in infant speech perception paradigms. Research Status Report II. Infant Development Laboratory, University of Wisconsin, Madison. In press.

Miller, C., Morse, P., and Dorman, M. 1977. Cardiac indices of infant speech perception: Orienting and burst discrimination. Quart. J. Exp. Psychol. 29: 533–545.

Miller, C., and Ruzicka, E. 1978. A parametric investigation of the cardiac no-delay discrimination paradigm and voice-onset-time discriminations in infants. Research Status Report II. Infant Development Laboratory, University of Wisconsin, Madison. In press.

Miller, J. 1974. Phonetic determination of infant speech perception. Unpublished doctoral dissertation, University of Minnesota, Minneapolis.

Miller, J., Weir, C., Pastore, R., Kelly, W., and Dooling, R. 1976. Discrimination and labeling of noise-buzz sequences with varying noise-lead times: An example of categorical perception. J. Acoust. Soc. Am. 60: 410–417.

Moffitt, A. 1971. Consonant cue perception by twenty- to twenty-four-week old infants. Child Dev. 42: 717–731.

Molfese, D., Freeman, R., and Palermo, D. 1975. The ontogeny of brain lateralization for speech and nonspeech stimuli. Brain Lang. 2: 356–368.

Molfese, D., Nunez, V., Seibert, S., and Ramanaiah, N. 1976. Cerebral asymmetry: Changes in factors affecting its development. Ann. N.Y. Acad. Sci. 280: 821–833.

Morse, P. 1972. The discrimination of speech and nonspeech stimuli in early infancy. J. Exp. Child Psychol. 14: 477–492.

Morse, P. 1974. Infant speech perception: A preliminary model and review of the literature. In R. Schiefelbusch and L. Lloyd (eds.), Language Perspectives—Acquisition, Retardation, and Intervention, pp. 19–53. University Park Press, Baltimore.

Morse, P. 1976. Speech perception in the human infant and rhesus monkey. Ann. N.Y. Acad. Sci. 280: 694–707.

Morse, P., Kass, J., and Turkienicz, R. 1976. Selective adaptation of vowels. Percept. Psychophys. 19: 137–143.

Morse, P., and Snowdon, C. 1975. An investigation of categorical speech discrimination by rhesus monkeys. Percept. Psychophys. 17: 9–16.

Morse, P., Leavitt, L., Miller, C., and Romero, R. 1977. Overt and covert aspects of adult speech perception. J. Speech Hear. Res. 20: 40–54.

Morse, P., Leavitt, L., Brown, J., and Graham, F. Cardiac orienting to "familiar" sounds in 6-week-olds. In preparation.

Nelson, P., Erulkar, S., and Bryan, S. 1966. Responses of units of the inferior-colliculus to time-barying acoustic stimuli. J. Neurophysiol. 29: 834–860.

Ohlrich, E., Barnet, A., and Weiss, I. 1975. Longitudinal study of averaged auditory evoked potentials in normal children from birth to three years of age. Paper presented at Society of Research in Child Development, April, Denver, Colorado.

Pierce, J. 1974. A study of 750 Portland, Oregon children during the first year. Stanford Univ. Pap. Rep. Child Lang. Dev. 8: 19–25.

Pisoni, D. 1973. Auditory and phonetic memory codes in the discrimination of consonants and vowels. Percept. Psychophys. 13: 253–260.

Pisoni, D. 1975. Auditory short-term memory and vowel perception. Mem. Cog. 3: 7–18.

Pisoni, D. 1977. Identification and discrimination of the relative onset time of two component tones: Implications for voicing perception in stops. J. Acoustic Soc. Am. 61: 1352–1361.

Pisoni, D., and Tash, J. 1974. Reaction times to comparisons within and across phonetic categories. Percept. Psychophys. 15: 285–290.

Popper, R. 1972. Pair discrimination for a continuum of synthetic voiced stops with and without first and third formants. J. Psycholing. Res. 1: 205–219.

Rand, T. 1971. Vocal tract size normalization in the perception of stop consonants. Haskins Lab. Stat. Rep. Speech Res. SR-25/26: 141–146.

Rewey, H. 1973. Developmental change in infant heart rate response during sleeping and waking states. Dev. Psychol. 8: 35–41.

Roth, P., and Morse, P. 1975. An investigation of infant VOT discrimination using the cardiac OR. Research Status Report I, pp. 207–218. Infant Development Laboratory, University of Wisconsin, Madison.

Sawusch, J., Pisoni, D., and Cutting, J. 1975. Category boundaries for linguistic and nonlinguistic dimensions of the same stimuli. In D. Pisoni (ed.), Research on Speech Research—

Progress Report No. 2, pp. 162–173. Department of Psychology, University of Indiana, Bloomington, Indiana.

Shankweiler, D., Strange, W., and Verbrugge, R. Speech and the problem of perceptual constancy. In R. Shaw and J. Bransford (eds.), Perceiving, Acting, and Comprehending: Toward an Ecological Psychology. Lawrence Erlbaum Assoc., Hillsdale, N. J. In press.

Sinnott, J., Beecker, M., Moody, D., and Stebbins, W. 1976. Speech sound discrimination by humans and monkeys. J. Acoust. Soc. Am. 60: 687–695.

Stevens, K., and Klatt, D. 1974. Role of formant transitions in the voiced-voiceless distinction for stops. J. Acoust. Soc. Am. 55: 653–659.

Streeter, L. 1974. The effects of linguisitic experience of phonetic perception. Unpublished doctoral dissertation, Columbia University, New York.

Streeter, L. 1976. Language perception of 2-month-old infants shows effects of both innate mechanisms and experience. Nature 259: 39–41.

Streeter, L., and Landauer, T. 1976. Effects of learning English as a second language on the acquisition of a new phonemic contrast. J. Acoust. Soc. Am. 59: 448–451.

Strock, B. 1976. Inhibition of acoustic startle response in six and nine week infants. Unpublished master's thesis, University of Wisconsin, Madison.

Summerfield, Q., and Haggard, M. 1975. First formant onset frequency as a cue to the voicing distinction in pre-stressed, syllable-initial stop-consonants. Paper presented at 90th meeting of Acoustical Society of America, November, San Francisco, California.

Swoboda, P., Kass, J., Morse, P., and Leavitt, L. 1978. Memory factors in vowel discrimination of normal and at-risk infants. Child Dev.

Swoboda, P., Morse, P., and Leavitt, L. 1976. Continuous vowel discrimination in normal and at risk infants. Child Dev. 47: 459–465.

Tartter, V., and Eimas, P. 1975. The role of auditory feature detectors in the perception of speech. Percept. Psychophys. 18:293–298.

Till, J. 1976. Infants' discrimination of speech and nonspeech stimuli. Unpublished doctoral dissertation, University of Iowa, Iowa City.

Trehub, S. 1973a. Auditory-linguistic sensitivity in infants. Unpublished doctoral dissertation, McGill University, Montreal, Quebec, Canada.

Trehub, S. 1973b. Infants' sensitivity to vowel and tonal contrasts. Dev. Psychol. 9: 81–96.

Trehub, S. 1975. The problem of state in infant speech discrimination studies. Dev. Psychol. 11: 116.

Trehub, S. 1976. The discrimination of foreign speech contrasts by infants and adults. Child Dev. 44: 466–472.

Trehub, S., and Chang, H. W. 1977. Speech as reinforcing stimulation for infants. Dev. Psychol. 13: 170–171.

Wada, J., Clarke, R., and Hamm, A. 1975. Cerebral asymmetry in humans. Arch. Neurol. 32: 239–246.

Waters, R., and Wilson W. 1976. Speech perception by rhesus monkeys: The voicing distinction in synthesized labial and velar stop consonants. Percept. Psychophys. 19: 285–289.

Whitfield, I., and Evans, E. 1965. Responses of auditory cortical neurons to stimuli of changing frequency. J. Neurophysiol. 28: 655–672.

Williams, L. 1974. Speech perception and production as a function of exposure to a second language. Unpublished doctoral dissertation, Harvard University, Cambridge.

Witelson, S., and Pallie, W. 1973. Left hemisphere specialization for language in the newborn: Neuroanatomical evidence of asymmetry. Brain 96: 641–646.

Wollberg, Z., and Newman, J. 1972. Auditory contex of squirrel monkey: Response patterns of single cells to species-specific vocalizations. Science 175: 212–214.

Zlatin, M., and Koenigsknecht, R. 1975. Development of the voicing contrast: Perception of stop consonants. J. Speech Hear. Res. 18: 541–553.

Predispositions for the Perception of Speech-Sound Categories: A Species-Specific Phenomenon?

Patricia K. Kuhl

Language has traditionally been considered an exclusively human endeavor, an example of true "emergence" in the evolutionary sense of the term (Lenneberg, 1967). Had we asked, then, twenty years ago, whether nonhuman animals were capable of any of the behaviors we call linguistic, the answer would have been a resounding "No." The answer now is equivocal. The once-considered quantal gap between present-day apes and man seems to be narrowing as we discover what may be the underpinnings of the cognitive, physiologic, and perceptual substrates of our language competencies and behaviors evidenced in nonhuman primates.

Take hemispheric asymmetry as an example. Man's asymmetrical brain has long been associated with his linguistic prowess (Jackson, 1884), but Dewson, Burlingame, Kizer, Dewson, Kenny, and Pribram (1975) have recently demonstrated functional hemispheric asymmetry in Old World monkeys using an auditory-visual association task in a delayed-response recall paradigm. The stimuli were simple tones and noises. In essence, they demonstrated that a rhesus monkey could "remember" an auditory-visual code for about 15–20 sec, but after ablation of the left-temporal cortex (Wernicke's Area in man) performance was at chance. No impairment occurred for animals whose right-temporal cortex had been destroyed. Nottebohm, Stokes, and Leonard (1976) demonstrated functional hemispheric asymmetry for the production of biologically relevant sound in song birds. Ablation of the highest motor areas in the left hemisphere of the canary brain resulted in

During the preparation of this manuscript, the author was supported by the U.S. Public Health Service, Department of Health, Education and Welfare research grant NS03856 from the National Institute of Neurological and Communicative Disorders and Stroke awarded to Central Institute for the Deaf.

229

almost complete absence of meaningful units ("syllables") in the bird's song repertoire; ablation of the corresponding areas of the right hemisphere had no effect. To make the parallel even more compelling, if ablation of the left motor area preceded song "crystalization," that is, occurred before the bird had passed the critical period for vocal learning (Marler, 1973), the bird's song developed normally using the subordinate right motor area. Molfese, Freeman, and Jones-Molfese (cited in Molfese, Nunez, Siebert, and Ramanajah, 1976) found hemispheric differences in the auditory evoked responses of the cat in response to stimuli that differed in bandwidth, in the presence or absence of frequency transitions, and in the number of formants. In other words, functional asymmetries are not unique to man, and in some instances (the canary) it is tempting to argue that the functional asymmetries in animals are somehow related to the production and/or perception of biologically relevant signals, and therefore parallel man's use of the left hemisphere for linguistic functions.

At a more linguistic level, Premack (1971), Gardner and Gardner (1969), and Rumbaugh (1976) have demonstrated that a Great Ape species (chimpanzee) can create simple sentences using sign language, plastic chips, and computer keys to string words together. Some of their constructions are novel. The chimpanzee Washoe saw a duck and signed "water bird," and called watermelon "candy water." The chimpanzee Lana, using computer keys, asked for coffee in 23 different ways. None of these nonhuman primates are capable of producing "speech," however (Hayes, 1951; Kellogg and Kellogg, 1933), perhaps because they lack man's supralaryngeal vocal tract and, thus, cannot create the cross-sectional area required to produce the full complement of speech sounds produced by the adult human (Lieberman, Crelin, and Klatt, 1972).

The tacit assumption in the field of speech perception is that there is a corresponding lack of the special mechanisms involved in the perception of speech sounds in animals that would enable them to perceive speech-sound categories (Liberman, 1970; Liberman, Cooper, Shankweiler, and Studdert-Kennedy, 1967; Liberman, Mattingly, and Turvey, 1972). These special mechanisms are presumed to be species specific and perhaps innate. The data on the perception of speech by human infants are not inconsistent with this view because the perceptual proclivities of infants when listening to speech are amazingly "adult-like." In fact, the data gathered on young infants have been interpreted to mean that infants process speech in a "linguistic mode" (Eimas, 1974b; Morse, 1974). However, the species-specificity hypothesis has only recently been tested, and this review compares the speech-perception capabilities and proclivities of the human newborn with those of nonhuman mammals. The human newborn brings to the task all of the predispositions that allow him to acquire language in a natural setting—that is, the cognitive, physiologic, and perceptual substrates of linguistic capability. The animal brings to the task the predispositions that are part of the general perceptual capabilities of mammals, but these are not destined to provide him with language. By examining the set of behaviors evidenced by both groups and discovering to what extent they overlap, we might make inferences about the origins of the infants' predispositions, and what, if anything, makes them unique, as well as contributing to the more general question of the evolution of language.

THE PERCEPTION OF SPEECH-SOUND CATEGORIES

Two kinds of perceptual behavior have been considered to be behavioral manifestations of "linguistic" processing at the phonological level, and they will be used to compare infants and animals. Both have to do with a listener's perception of speech-sound categories. One is a highly restricted and narrowly defined set of conditions called "categorical perception," in which a listener's ability to discriminate stimuli that form an acoustic continuum is predicted by his ability to label the two stimuli differently. To test this phenomenon, a critical acoustic cue differentiating two speech sounds is manipulated in computer-synthesized syllables while all other noncritical dimensions, such as fundamental frequency and intensity, are held constant. The other perceptual behavior is phenomenological, and therefore does not require experimental test for adult listeners. For example, adult listeners perceive the steady-state vowel /a/, produced by a male talker, a female talker, and a child talker, as being somehow similar, despite the fact that the critical cues (formant frequencies) of these vowels are different (Peterson and Barney, 1952), and that many of the noncritical dimensions, such as fundamental frequency, also vary. This perceptual "constancy" in the face of what seems to be widely diverse acoustic dimensions of sounds characterizes speech-sound perception in general. In fact, the lack of acoustically "invariant" cues for particular phonetic distinctions is the major phenomenon that initially led theorists to the drawing boards, and identifying the invariant or prototypical acoustic dimensions of speech sounds is still the major business of researchers in the field (Fant, 1973; Stevens, 1975; Stevens and Blumstein, 1976).

Both of these behaviors tap a listener's proclivity to form acoustic categories: "categorical perception" concerns a listener's ability, under precisely specified conditions, to perceive small differences in the acoustic variables critical to a particular speech-sound distinction, and has been widely studied; the perception of constancy, on the other hand, takes a broader view of category formation, and asks whether a listener perceives a similarity despite differences in both the critical and noncritical acoustic dimensions. The critical acoustic dimensions are widely divergent because of phonetic context and talker differences, and the noncritical dimensions—those that are not critical to the phonemic distinction—also vary widely. This phenomenon, although germinal from a theoretical standpoint, has only recently been examined in nonhuman animals and infants.

INFANT SPEECH PERCEPTION

This review is directed toward three specific questions (Kuhl, 1976a): 1) Do young infants discriminate single pairs of speech sounds when only the phonetically relevant acoustic dimensions are varied? 2) Does the infant perceive "constancy" when both the phonetically relevant and phonetically irrelevant acoustic dimensions are allowed to vary? and 3) Is perception categorical—is the infant's discrimination characterized by the same constraints shown by adult listeners?

Discrimination of the Phonetically Relevant Dimensions of Speech Sounds

Using the high-amplitude sucking (HAS) paradigm (Eimas, Siqueland, Jusczyk, and Vigorito, 1971) and synthetically generated speech-sound pairs, in which the nonphonetic dimensions such as fundamental frequency, intensity, and duration are identical, it has been demonstrated that normal infants ranging in age from four to seventeen weeks discriminate consonants that differ with respect to voicing (Eimas et al., 1971) and place of articulation (Eimas, 1974a; Morse, 1972), and that they discriminate among fricatives (Eilers and Minifie, 1975) and liquids (Eimas, 1975a). The discrimination of nasals and glides has not been examined. Infants discriminate spectrally dissimilar vowels, /a/ versus /i/ (Kuhl, 1976a; Kuhl and Miller, 1975b), as well as those that are spectrally similar, /i/ versus /I/, (Swoboda, Morse, and Leavitt, 1976). These data generally support the hypothesis that the young infant discriminates all of the contrasts that are phonemically relevant in English. This conclusion, given that it is true, is noteworthy in at least two respects. First, the infant does not seem to have to "learn to hear" the appropriate differences between speech sounds; he does so naturally. Second, contrary to previously suggested hypotheses, we observe no "progressive differentiation" of the phonemic repertoire (Jakobson, 1941) using this particular testing paradigm and stimuli that differ in a single acoustic detail.

The recent reviews of the available data (Eimas, 1974a; Kuhl, 1976a; Morse, 1974) concluded that there was little existing evidence to suggest that speech-sound differentiation was a developmental process. Two factors suggest that this conclusion is premature. First, recent results on the discrimination of fricatives by Eilers and Minifie (1975), Eilers (1977), and Eilers, Wilson, and Moore (1977) suggest that fricatives are considerably more difficult to discriminate. Eilers and Minifie (1975) and Eilers (1977), testing normal one- to four-month-olds in the HAS paradigm, demonstrated that although the voicing feature was discriminable in prevocalic stop consonants, it was considerably more difficult to demonstrate discrimination of voicing in prevocalic fricatives (/sa-za/). Eilers (1977) further demonstrated that in final position (/as-a:z/), when information concerning voicing is carried by additional cues such as the duration of the preceding vowel, discrimination was obtained. However, when the additional durational cues were removed (/a:s-a:z/), infants again failed to discriminate. This did not hold for stops in final position. Both the /at-a:d/ contrast and the /a:t-a:d/ contrast were discriminable. Eilers (1977) makes two points about these data. First, they indicate that the infant's perceptual abilities may demonstrate developmental trends, and second, the fact that results depend on a feature's context detracts from the Eimas (1974a) feature detection model, which assumes a mechanism that recognizes features, regardless of context.

These notions were more fully developed in a report of continued research by Eilers et al (1977). In this report, two more contrasts were added to the list of those tested using the HAS paradigm and young infants (one- to four-month-olds). The two contrasts were /fa-θa/ and /fi-θi/, and again, infants tested in HAS showed no evidence of discrimination. The report also extended these results on very young infants to two older groups of infants, six- to eight-month-olds and 12- to 14-month-olds, using a visually reinforced head-turn technique and the same stimuli. The data were then compared across age. The data demonstrate that by six months of age, the infants are making the /sa-za/ and the /a:s-a:z/ distinction, two that they were not making in the one- to four-month-old age range. The six-month-olds continue to fail to discriminate three contrasts, /a:t-at/, /fa-θa/, and /fi-θi/. Twelve- to 14-month-olds demonstrate further advances in that more subjects in this age range discriminate the contrasts; for example, in the six- to eight-month-old group, one infant discriminated /a:t-a:d/ and /a:t-at/, but in the 12- to 14-month-old group, four infants discriminated /a:t-at/. No improvement in the discrimination of /fa-θa/ occurred, but the eight of the older infants discriminated /fi-θi/. In contrast to the experiments previously cited, the studies on the discrimination of fricatives employed stimuli that were naturally produced. A computer-analysis program was used to plot the fundamental frequency contours, intensity changes, and durational characteristics of these syllables so that tokens could be matched, as closely as possible, on their irrelevant dimensions. These data provide the first suggestion that some speech-sound contrasts are not differentiated by the young infant.

The second factor, which suggests that the conclusion that young infants discriminate all phonemically relevant contrasts at birth is premature, is a more fundamental one. It is a basic question concerning the validity of conclusions regarding the discrimination of a phonetic contrast when only a single exemplar of both categories is employed. As Kuhl (1976a) reviewed, all of the procedures used to date are supposedly aimed at assessing an infant's ability to differentiate a phonemic contrast, but they test the infant's ability using two single tokens to exemplify that contrast. For example, one wishes to examine an infant's perception of the voicing contrast. Our current techniques (High-Amplitude Sucking, Visually Reinforced Head-Turning) involve the presentation of a single voiced (/ba/) syllable and a single voiceless (/pʰa/) syllable, and the results are "stimulus-bound;" that is, they reflect the infant's ability to detect this relatively simple psychophysical change. If the difference between /ba/ and /pʰa/ somehow encapsulated the critical difference between voiced and voiceless tokens in general, then this strategy would be satisfactory. What we know about speech sounds, however, suggests that this is not the case. Both speech analysis and speech synthesis techniques suggest that the critical cues for phonetic differentiation vary with phonetic context, talker, and position in a word. The fact that adult listeners recognize a particular phonetic feature across context, talker, and position in a word, in spite of wide diversity in its acoustic realization ("constancy"), still constitutes the main "problem" in explaining speech perception. Therefore, what we need to know about an infant's perception is whether this "perceptual constancy" for phonetic features is characteristic of the infant's perception, or whether "perceptual constancy" is a learned phenomenon.

Burdick and Miller (1975) and Kuhl and Miller (1975a) were faced with the same problem in attempting to validly assess whether a nonhuman animal was capable of differentiating speech-sound categories. They argued that the use of a single pair of syllables would not tell them much about an animal's ability to differentiate the category as a whole. They solved the problem by requiring the animal to categorize, in a typical identification-task format, a large number of exemplars from two phonetic categories. This multiple-token approach has been successfully applied to the testing of young infants (Kuhl, 1976c), as is described in the following section.

The Perception of Constancy

At least two processes are involved in perceptual constancy for speech-sound categories. First, an infant must discover and focus on acoustic dimensions that are relevant to a particular phonemic contrast. This may be relatively easy when the phonetic context and "talker" are held constant, such as in the experiments just reviewed, but when these aspects are allowed to vary, the prototypical dimensions of a particular phonemic category must be abstracted from a set of cues that are not invariant. What we know about speech sounds tells us that these attributes are abstract and relational (Fant, 1973; Stevens, 1975). One would predict, then, that exposure to a set of exemplars that differ with respect to phonetic context and talker is essential to discovering these prototypical attributes. On the other hand, we know little about complex auditory functions, particularly for signals of this kind. It may be the case that as we become more aware of the nature of the cues for speech and more aware of how the auditory system processes complex signals, we will discover that the two are ideally matched. That is, the mammalian auditory system may function in ways that make these relational abstractions obvious even though the sound spectrograph does not. If this were the case, the learning process might not be so complex.

The second process involved in the perception of constancy is necessitated by the first. When the phonetic context and the talker are varied, acoustically prominent but phonemically irrelevant acoustic dimensions are introduced. If an infant recognizes that /di/ and /du/ are somehow similar, he must ignore the most prominent difference between them, that is, the vowel. Other prominent acoustic dimensions, such as fundamental frequency and timbre differences between male and female voices and pitch contour, are characteristics that do not differentiate phonemic categories, and must also be ignored.

As a preliminary step toward testing perceptual constancy, Kuhl and Miller (1975b) asked whether 4- to 16-week-old infants could detect a change in a target dimension if an irrelevant dimension was randomly varied throughout the experiment, serving as a kind of "distracting" stimulus. The sucking paradigm was employed. A change in the "target" dimension occurred at the "shift-point" while an "irrelevant" dimension was randomly varied throughout both the pre- and postshift periods. In one condition, the target dimension was a phonemic change in the vowel and the irrelevant dimension was the pitch contour of the vowel; in a second condition, the target dimension was the pitch contour of the vowel and the irrelevant dimension was the vowel color. The choice of pitch contour as a "distracting" acoustic dimension is particularly appropriate, because the literature is replete with suggestions that suprasegmental dimensions such as pitch contour, loudness, and stress pattern are more salient than segmental (phonetic) dimensions at this age (Crystal, 1973; Lewis, 1936; Leopold, 1949). The stimuli were two /a/'s and two /i/'s synthesized such that one /a/ and one /i/ had identical monotone pitch contours, and one /a/ and one /i/ had identical rise-fall pitch contours. Discrimination of vowel color and pitch contour "targets" were tested with and without irrelevant variation in the second dimension. The data demonstrated that infants detect a vowel change regardless of the distraction posed by a random change in the pitch contour of the vowel. In contrast, infants detected a change in the pitch contour of a vowel when all other dimensions were held constant, but failed to respond to a pitch contour change when the vowel color was randomly changed. In addition, infants responded for a significantly longer period of time before habituating (preshift) when the vowel color was constantly changing than when the pitch contour was randomly changing. Using these stimuli, then, it would seem that the vowel-color dimension captured the infant's attention more readily than pitch contour both when it was the target and when it served as the distractor. This research demonstrated the infant's ability to tolerate some degree of distraction and still make the discrimination, but it did not demonstrate the infant's ability to recognize the phonetic similarity among vowel tokens whose critical acoustic dimensions varied.

Fodor, Garrett, and Brill (1975) examined the acquisition of a head-turn response for visual reinforcement in 14- to 18-week-old infants under two stimulus conditions. In both conditions, three syllables were randomly presented (/pi/, /ka/, /pu/), but only two of the three were reinforced. In one condition, the stimuli being reinforced were phonetically similar (/pi/ and /pu/); in the other, they were not (/pi/ and /ka/). Although the differences in the proportions of head turns in the two conditions were not striking, they reached statistical significance; the proportion of head turns was greater when phonetically similar sounds were reinforced.

In order to extend these results to a situation in which the infant had to contend with variation in both the critical and noncritical dimensions of the signals, Kuhl (1976c) combined the use of a head-turn technique for visual reinforcement with the multiple-token approach of Kuhl and Miller (1975a). The head-turn technique was developed at the University of Washington in Seattle (see Wilson, this volume). Wilson, Moore, and Thompson (1976) reported that infants as young as five months could be tested on simple audiometric tasks. In these tasks, the infant is held by the mother so that he faces an assistant. A loudspeaker is positioned at a 90° angle relative to the assistant, and, in front of it, an animated toy is housed in a dark plexiglass box, so that it is not visible until the lights inside the box are illuminated. During observation intervals, a tone is presented from the loudspeaker, and if the child turns toward the loudspeaker, the visual reinforcer is activated for a short period of time. Eilers et al. (1977) employed the technique to study speech-sound discrimination in 6- to 8- and 12- to 14-month-old normal infants by presenting a single speech stimulus, like /sa/, over the loudspeaker at 1 sec intervals. During half of the observation intervals, the sound was changed from /sa/ to /za/ and the infant was reinforced for turning toward the loudspeaker. During the other half of the observation intervals, the sound was not changed, but the infant was monitored for a head turn. If a head turn occurred during this period, it was scored as an error.

Kuhl (1976c) modified the procedure to test perceptual constancy for the vowel categories /a/ and /i/. In this modified procedure, the infant is trained just as he would be in the original head-turn technique (Eilers et al., 1977). That is, the infant is trained to turn his head to view an animated toy when the "background" stimulus, the phoneme /a/ presented every 2 sec, is changed to the "comparison" stimulus (/i/). In the initial-training condition, the /a/ and /i/ stimuli are synthesized to simulate a male voice with a rise-fall intonation contour, and are therefore matched on all the irrelevant dimensions. In the next four successive conditions, the number of /a/'s in the "background" category and the number of /i/'s in the "comparison" category are systematically increased until the set includes those synthesized with a male, a female, and a child's voice, each with two pitch contours, rise and rise-fall, for a total of six stimuli in each category. In all stages, the stimuli in the background and comparison categories are randomly presented. At each stage in training, the infant must meet a performance criterion before progressing to the next stage. The criterion is nine out of ten consecutive trials correct; a trial consists of a 6-sec observation interval, during which the child is monitored for a head turn. Half of the trials are "change" trials, in which the signal actually changes from the "background" category to the "comparison" category; the other half of the trials are "control" trials, in which no change occurs. If a head turn occurs during a change trial, the infant is reinforced with the visual stimulus and the trial is scored correct; if a head turn occurs during a control trial, the infant is not reinforced and the trial is scored as incorrect.

As the testing progresses, the infant must learn to recognize the essential differences between the two categories, and to ignore the irrelevant changes that occur when the number of stimuli increase. The results suggest that the six-month-old infant readily perceives the abstract similarity between the vowels of male, female, and child talkers, and therefore demonstrates perceptual constancy for some phonetic categories. This method and approach provide a vehicle for testing perceptual constancy for auditory stimuli in young infants, and the data should prove to be theoretically germane.

Categorical Perception in Early Infancy

The criteria for categorical perception have been well described (Studdert-Kennedy, Liberman, Harris, and Cooper, 1970). Essentially, it is said to occur when a listener's ability to discriminate two stimuli is predicted by his ability to label them differently. To demonstrate categorical perception, then, two tasks must be compared: one in which the subject "labels" each of the stimuli from an acoustic continuum when presented randomly one at a time, and one in which the subject attempts to discriminate pairs of stimuli taken from the continuum. These pairs of stimuli can be said to be drawn from the same phonetic category or from different phonetic categories, according to how the stimuli were labeled. Typically, when speech stimuli from a computer-synthesized continuum are presented in pairs for discrimination, the listener's performance is at chance for stimuli drawn from the same phonetic category—that is, for stimuli that were labeled similarly—and near perfect for stimuli drawn from different phonetic categories—that is, for stimuli that were labeled differently (Liberman, 1957; Liberman et al., 1967; Liberman, Harris, Hoffman, and Griffith, 1957).

Infants, of course, cannot "label" stimuli, but when it was demonstrated that an infant's discrimination was enhanced for stimulus pairs drawn from different rather than the same adult-defined categories—and this has now been demonstrated for a voiced-voiceless (Eimas et al., 1971), a place of articulation (Eimas, 1974a), and a liquid (Eimas, 1975a) continuum—the infant's responses were considered to be behavioral manifestations of perception in a "linguistic mode." In other words, the infant's responses were taken as evidence that the infant was processing these stimuli as linguistic units (Eimas, 1974b).

Whether or not infants respond categorically to all of the phonemic contrasts employed in the languages of the world is not yet known. The English voiceless-unaspirated versus voiceless-aspirated pair (/pa/ versus /pʰa/) is discriminated by two-month-old Kikuyu (Streeter, 1976) and Spanish (Lasky, Syrdal-Lasky, and Klein, 1975) infants, even though this contrast is not used in either language. On the other hand, interpreting the data collected for stimulus pairs in the prevoiced region of the VOT continuum is more difficult. Williams (1977a) identified the phoneme boundary for monolingual adult Spanish listeners at approximately −5 msec VOT. It has yet to be demonstrated that American infants discriminate stimuli that straddle this boundary (Eimas, 1975b), although Kikuyu infants (Streeter, 1977) and Spanish infants (Lasky et al., 1975) have been shown to make this discrimination. Some of the differences obtained across studies may be attributable to the fragility of the acoustic cue used to simulate prevoicing, in that it is very low in frequency (150 Hz) and in amplitude, and is more likely to depend on the specific levels and frequencies of ambient noise, loudspeaker or earphone characteristics, and the recorded signal-to-noise ratio. There is some evidence from manipulation of natural-speech tokens produced by monolingual Spanish speakers that prevoicing is not the only cue responsible for /ba/ judgments by Spanish listeners (Williams, 1977b). In addition, analysis of naturally produced prevoiced tokens (Williams, personal communication) reveals certain other acoustic cues, such as amplitude envelope variations, that may serve to make prevoicing more acoustically prominent. It is important to point out that no one has compared the responses of infants from two diverse linguistic environments in the same laboratory under the exact same listening conditions. Also, no one has examined the perception of prevoiced and voiceless-unaspirated tokens that are naturally produced by monolingual Spanish talkers.

In summary, the data gathered both on categorical perception and on perceptual constancy suggest that the infant's auditory perception may not differ greatly from that of the adult. What does this mean in light of our current theories of speech perception? Is the infant endowed with perceptual capabilities that are part of his unique linguistic potential? More generally, do these specific behaviors reflect the workings of a unique linguistic process? This author has argued that a critical test of the notion that these behaviors are specifically linguistic involves testing nonhuman listeners on these same tasks, and therefore those data are later reviewed. First, however, there is a slight diversion. In order to adequately interpret the categorical perception data gathered on both infant and animal listeners, the phenomenon itself, and what we have recently learned about it, is discussed.

CATEGORICAL PERCEPTION

General Considerations

The apparent inability to discriminate within-category stimuli was hypothesized to be a result of the speech-perception process; that is, it was considered to be a direct result of the phonetic categorization process. As described by Liberman et al. (1972), the listener "has no auditory image of the signal available to him, but only the output of a specialized processor that has stripped the signal of all normal sensory information and represented each phonetic segment (or feature) categorically by a unitary neural event" (p. 320).

Recent data do not allow us to view categorical perception as an automatic definition for processing stimuli in a "linguistic mode." Contrary to the original hypothesis, it is not unique to speech-sound perception, and when the signal is speech, categorical perception is not unique to human listeners.

Nonspeech Data

Miller, Pastore, Wier, Kelly, and Dooling (1976) demonstrated categorical perception for noise-buzz sequences designed to simulate the gross spectral characteristics of stop consonant-vowel syllables without being perceived as speech. The "noise" was band-pass filtered (900–2700 Hz) and the "buzz," a 1-msec square wave with a 100-Hz repetition rate, was band-pass filtered (500–3000 Hz). The noise-buzz continuum was generated by manipulating the degree to which the noise would "lead" or "lag" the buzz, ranging from an 80-msec noise lead to a 10-msec noise lag in 5-msec steps. Listeners labeled the stimuli as "noise" or "no noise," and an oddity discrimination procedure was used to test pairs of stimuli whose noise-lead times varied by 10 msec. The boundary between categories identified in the labeling task was approximately 15-msec noise lag, a value that is in good agreement with the data on the perception of the temporal order of two stimuli. Two stimuli must be separated by 17 msec to obtain 75% correct identification of the order of the two stimuli (Hirsh, 1959). A sharp peak in the discrimination function occurred at the noise-lead boundary; that is, discrimination was excellent for stimulus pairs drawn from different categories, but performance was near chance for stimulus pairs drawn from the same category.

Cutting and Rosner (1974) demonstrated categorical perception for sawtooth-wave stimuli varying in rise time between 10 and 80 msec in 10-msec steps. Listeners labeled the stimuli "pluck" or "bow" because they resembled the sounds produced by stringed instruments when played in these two manners. Discrimination was tested using an ABX format with stimulus pairs whose rise times differed by 10 msec. Again, the data meet all the criteria for categorical perception. The stimuli are perceived as falling into two discrete categories and the listener's tendency to give two stimuli the same label predicts his ability to discriminate those two stimuli almost perfectly. Using the same stimuli and the high-amplitude sucking technique, infants have been shown to discriminate pairs of stimuli that were labeled differently by adults, and to fail to discriminate pairs of stimuli that were labeled similarly by adults (Jusczyk, Rosner, Cutting, Foard, and Smith, 1977).

More recently, Pisoni (1977) varied the onset times of two pure tones (500 Hz and 1500 Hz) in 10-msec steps. The continuum varied in 10-msec steps from a 50-msec low tone lead to a 50-msec low tone lag. In the labeling task, listeners were instructed to listen to the stimuli and to respond by pressing one of two keys. ABX discrimination was tested for stimulus pairs differing in tone-onset-time by 10 msec. The results followed the familiar pattern. The boundary between categories identified by the labeling functions correlated with a peak in the discrimination function. That is, discrimination between stimuli that were given different labels was very good, but discrimination between stimuli that were given the same label was very poor.

In another experiment reported by Pastore (1976), categorical perception was obtained with a simple visual continuum generated by manipulating the frequency with which a light-emitting diode was gated on and off. Subjects labeled the stimuli "flicker" or "fusion" and ABX discrimination was examined for stimuli whose periods (time in msec for one on and off cycle) differed by 6 or 8 msec. Discrimination was excellent for pairs of stimuli that were assigned different labels, but discrimination was near chance for pairs of stimuli that were assigned the same label.

Quite by accident, Wroton and Watson (1974) demonstrated categorical perception for a complex auditory stimulus varying in frequency. The authors were examining the perception of 40-msec tones differing in frequency by 6 Hz when these tones were embedded between a single-frequency "leading" and "trailing" tone. The variable manipulated to create a continuum was the frequency of the 40-msec test tone relative to the leading and trailing "reference" tones. For example, at one end of the continuum, the 40-msec test tone was 16 Hz above the reference tone; at the other end the 40-msec test tone was 16 Hz below the reference tones. Test tones that were adjacent on the continuum differed by 1 Hz. Listeners were instructed to label the stimuli by pressing one of two response keys as they were presented singly; subjects reported hearing a "smooth warble" quality or a "discrete change" quality. Discrimination for stimuli that were labeled similarly was generally poorer than discrimination for stimuli that were labeled differently, but more importantly, Wroton and Watson demonstrated the importance of a stimulus context; that is, discrimination of a 6-Hz difference in 40-msec tones was unaffected by the absolute frequencies of the test tones when they were presented in isolation—without the leading and trailing tones.

These demonstrations of categorical perception for nonspeech signals lead to a number of conclusions. First, and most obvious, categorical perception is not a direct result of phonetic categorization as previously hypothesized. More subtly, it is not a direct result of categorization, whether phonetic or not. Early experiments by Lane (1965) demonstrated that training subjects to "label" stimuli on a continuum in a binary fashion does not produce categorical perception. Steady-state vowels (300-msec durations) ranging from /i/ to /I/ to /ɛ/ on a synthetic continuum have been shown to produce similar identification functions, but discrimination for within-category pairs is significantly above chance (Fry, Abramson, Eimas, and Liberman, 1962).

Another obvious conclusion is that categorical perception does not depend on the use of categories that are meaningful in everyday life. Noise-buzz sequences, temporally offset tones, or "warbled" tones enjoy no special status in our auditory worlds, although "plucked" and "bowed" stimuli might, and speech sounds obviously do; nevertheless, all are perceived categorically.

These diverse examples have a number of things in common, however. In each case, an abrupt change in the percept occurs some place along a continuum. In other words, the acoustic changes are not readily perceived until a kind of "threshold" is passed. Miller et al. (1976) put it succinctly: "We argue that categorical perception may be usefully approached in terms of psychophysical boundaries or thresholds for perceptual effects that are encountered as one component of a stimulus complex is changed relation to the remainder of the complex. In the region of a threshold the effects of the varied component undergo rapid changes in detectability, discriminability, clarity, or perceived magnitude" (p.415).

As these authors note, in the typical speech examples, a change in one variable (VOT, the starting frequency of the F2 transition) occurs against a constant background (the formant frequencies of the vowel, or, in the latter case, the F1 transition) and does not occur when the changing variable is removed from its context. F2 transitions in isolation are not perceived categorically (Mattingly, Liberman, Syrdal, and Halwes, 1971), just as Wroton and Watson's 40-msec tones without "leaders" and "trailers."

One could still argue, however, that the nonspeech examples of categorical perception obtain precisely because they replicate the critical components of speech sounds; that is, one could argue that the noise-buzz sequences are perceived categorically not because they sound like speech, because they do not, but because they replicate one of the critical components of speech sounds. In other words, should we argue that noise-buzz sequences are perceived categorically because they are in some respects like da's and ta's and may "fool" the relevant feature detector, or that da's and ta's as well as noise-buzz sequences are perceived categorically because they both have stimulus configurations that produce sudden different percepts? The data gathered using animal listeners tend to support the latter notion.

Memory Constaints and Stimulus Uncertainty

We are becoming increasingly aware of the role of memory in obtaining categorical-like results (Barclay, 1972; Fujisaki and Kawashima, 1969, 1970; Pisoni and Lazarus, 1974). The clearest demonstrations of categorical perception are obtained when the psychophysical testing procedures used in discrimination testing require the subject to somehow "remember" the stimuli. The often-used ABX procedure requires the listener to remember something about A and B until X occurs so he can decide whether X is more like A or more like B. The oddity procedure is similar. The first and second stimulus must be held in some sort of memory until the third stimulus occurs so the listener can decide which of the three is the "odd" one. It makes sense to argue that the longer the listener must "hold" these stimuli in some sort of storage, the more likely it is that he will remember a stimulus label rather than its absolute acoustic properties. In contrast to these procedures, a same-different procedure involves only two stimuli and therefore takes less time, but also does not require the listener to depend on stimulus labels. Procedures in which a standard stimulus is constantly repeated and the listener monitors the signal for a change provide even fewer memory constraints, because the repeating standard allows the listener to focus his attention on the stimulus configuration, and therefore to form a better composite description of that standard.

Sinnott et al. (1976) demonstrated that human subjects are capable of discriminating pairs of stimuli that are labeled similarly when a repeating standard procedure is used. She synthesized a nine-step continuum ranging from /ba/ to /da/ by changing the starting frequency to the F2 and F3 transitions, and used standard labeling procedures to identify the phoneme boundary. The repeating-standard technique was used to test discrimination; the standard was either the /ba/ or /da/"endpoint" stimulus and it was repeated once per second, 7 to 12 times, before a "comparison" stimulus (all other stimuli on the continuum) was presented. The listener had to report a stimulus change by lifting a response key. The results were not categorical in nature. The adult listener's ability to discriminate stimulus pairs changed gradually rather then abruptly as the standard stimulus and comparison stimulus were spaced farther apart on the continuum. Carney, Widin, and Viemiester (1977) used a training technique and produced similar results for a VOT continuum ranging in 10-msec steps from /ba/ to /pa/. Their data demonstrate that performance on many within-category discriminations was as accurate as that for between-category discriminations, and, with feedback, discrimination performance for some subjects was 100% correct for all test stimuli.

There is one other important difference between the repeating standard procedure and others. In addition to the changes in discrimination performance brought about by reducing memory constraints, Watson (1976) has pointed out the effect of reducing "stimulus uncertainty,"—reducing the size of the catalogue of patterns from which stimuli are randomly chosen, in optimizing discrimination performance. Using permutations of ten 40-msec tones in which changes in the frequency or duration of one of the tones was tested, Watson and his colleagues demonstrated that when uncertainty is reduced to a minimum, that is, when one particular permutation of the tones serves as the standard stimulus and a single component is changed in the comparison stimulus, performance reaches a level that is only slightly worse than that obtained when the tones are presented in isolation. Watson (1976) argues that listeners learn to "hear out" the various components and to selectively attend to them. In ABX, oddity, and same-different procedures uncertainty is high; the pairs of stimuli are drawn randomly from the continuum, usually with the single restriction that all pairs of stimuli be separated by a constant distance on the continuum. In contrast, the repeating-standard procedure involves the presentation of a single standard to which all other stimuli are compared. Both the reduction of memory constraint and the reduction of stimulus uncertainty play a role in optimizing discrimination performance under these conditions. The picture of a listener's auditory "capability," therefore, depends on the psychophysical task employed. Given the appropriate stimulus continuum, categorical perception is likely to obtain under conditions of maximum memory constraint and high levels of stimulus uncertainty—that is, when the listener must remember what he heard, and when he does not know in advance exactly what aspects of the stimulus he should focus on. These conditions reflect true listening situations to a greater degree than repeating-standard procedures do. Listeners typically get one "look at an auditory event before having to classify it, not multiple repetitions that maximize their chances of detecting a change." The results using a repeating standard, therefore, serve to clarify theoretical postures rather than to reflect the ongoing process more accurately.

One other point should not be overlooked. Although the 10-msec step comparisons made by Carney et al. (1977) demonstrate a listener's ability to make within-category discriminations, the use of such a large step size obscures the possibility that, using smaller VOT step sizes and a minimal uncertainty repeating-background technique, one could demonstrate that discrimination performance improves overall, that is, the baseline level is raised, but that performance might still be enhanced for stimulus pairs that straddle the phoneme boundary when compared to those that fall on the same side of the phoneme boundary.

SPEECH-SOUND PERCEPTION BY ANIMALS

Categorical Perception

The ideal animal for comparative experiments using speech sounds would have identical auditory capabilities as man without any of the productive or linguistic predispositions of man. In essence, the animal would provide identical psychoacoustic processing in the absence of any phonetic or linguistic processing.

The auditory capabilities of mammals as a group are distinguished from those of reptiles and birds by enhanced auditory sensitivity over an extended frequency range. There are phyletic trends toward extension of the range of optimum sensitivity to lower frequencies (below 1 kHz) and a reduction of the range of optimum sensitivity in the high frequency region (above 20 kHz) as one progresses toward man (Masterton, Heffner, and Ravizza, 1968). To date, only the monkey and the chinchilla have been extensively used in speech perception experiments. Both these animals have audibility curves that are very similar to man's (see Stebbins, 1970, 1973, for the monkey data, and Miller, 1970, for the chinchilla data).

The ideal animal, however, should not only have similar audibility curves, but similar acuity for temporal, intensity, and frequency variations in the signal. Here data are far less complete. It is known that the ability of the monkey and the chinchilla to resolve differences in frequency are inferior to those of man. In the 1–2 kHz frequency region, man's difference limen for frequency is approximately 3–5 kHz, but it is about 10 Hz for the monkey (Stebbins, 1970), and it is estimated to be about 4–6 times poorer than man for the chinchilla (Miller, 1970; Nelson and Keister, 1976). Detection thresholds for complex sounds are similar for chinchillas and humans (Luz, 1969) and the effects of temporal summation are similar for those two species (Henderson, 1969).

Kuhl and Miller (1975a; 1978) demonstrated that chinchillas "label" a synthetic-speech continuum the way an English-speaking adult does; that is, an abrupt change in the labeling gradient occurs at the point in the function at which English listeners hear a change from /da/ to /ta/. We trained the animals subjects, using a conditioned-avoidance paradigm, to respond differentially to good synthetic exemplars of /da/ (0 msec VOT) and /ta/ (+80 msec VOT). When performance on these "endpoint" stimuli was near perfect, the stimuli between O VOT and +80 VOT (in 10-msec steps) were presented as generalization stimuli; that is, the animal was given feedback to suggest that his response was "correct" regardless of what he did, and shock was never presented. This result was not contingent upon prior exposure to naturally produced speech; no difference in the labeling functions was obtained for animals trained to discriminate natural-speech categories (/d/-initial syllables versus /t/-initial syllables) and those not previously trained. In addition, the exact location of the perceptual boundary was found to depend on the place of articulation of the voiced-voiceless pair, exactly as it does for human listeners. The location of the bilabial (/ba-pa/) boundary occurred at lower VOT values than the location of the alveolar (/da-ta/) boundary, which in turn occurred at lower VOT values than the velar (/ga-ka/) boundary. This was true for all animal and human subjects (Kuhl and Miller, 1978).

The author has recently obtained discrimination data for chinchillas on the da/ ta continuum (Kuhl, 1976b). The basic procedure involves the detection of a change in a repeating "standard" stimulus. The animal reports the change in the stimulus by crossing a midline barrier to avoid the presentation of a mild shock. The standard stimuli were 0, +10, +20, +30, +40, +50, +60, +70, and +80 msec VOT. For a given standard, for instance +20 msec, the animal's "threshold" for detection of a change (Δt) was determined, both for increments and decrements in VOT, using a modified method-of-limits technique. That is, the "comparison" stimulus was gradually changed until it approached the VOT value of the standard stimulus. Threshold was defined as the minimum Δt detected 75% of the time. The data obtained to date demonstrate that the chinchilla is most sensitive to a change in the stimulus at +30 msec VOT—in the region of the /da-ta/ phoneme boundary. The discrimination functions agree perfectly with the identification functions in the sense that the peak in performance occurs at the phoneme boundary and the poorest performance occurs for within-category pairs. The advantage of this threshold type of procedure for cross-species comparisons is that one can compare the absolute sensitivity of the two species independently of a comparison in the location of the peak in sensitivity. Although not as yet complete, the plan of the experiment is to test discrimination with the three sets of stimuli differing only with respect to place of articulation. The hypothesis predicts that the region of enhanced sensitivity will depend on place of articulation and will correlate with the location of the perceptual boundary determined in the labeling experiments.

Although there are no other data on animals in which both labeling and discrimination functions have been obtained, what data we do have, usually just discrimination, supports the general findings reported above. Morse and Snowdon (1975) used a heart-rate procedure to examine discrimination of stimuli from a synthetic /bæ - dæ -gæ / continuum in rhesus monkeys. The procedure involved 20 presentations of one stimulus followed by 20 presentations of a second stimulus. Heart rate typically habituates to the first stimulus and dishabituates when the stimulus is changed. This stimulus presentation format resembles the repeating-standard procedure, and predictably, the rhesus monkey discriminated both within- and between-category stimulus pairs; both were significantly different from the control subjects who heard a single stimulus repeated 40 times. However, the degree of recovery or dishabituation was significantly greater for those subjects presented with between-category comparisons—those stimuli falling on opposite sides of the adult-defined phoneme boundary than for those subjects presented with the within-category comparisons. In other words, rhesus monkeys discriminate between-category pairs more readily than they discriminate within-category pairs.

Sinnott et al. (1976) tested human and monkey listeners in a discrimination task in which one of the endpoints of a synthetic /ba-da/ continuum was used as the standard stimulus in a repeating-standard format and all other stimuli were used as comparison stimuli. The starting frequencies of the F2 and F3 transitions were manipulated in nine steps to achieve the continuum. The psychometric functions did not show abrupt changes in discriminability at the phoneme boundary for either group of subjects; the percent-correct detection of a change gradually improved for both groups as the comparison stimulus was farther removed from the standard stimulus. The difference-limen (DL) for a transition change was larger for monkey listeners (320 Hz) than for human listeners (160 Hz), which is in keeping with the difference-limens for pure-tone frequency changes for these two groups of subjects. In summary, then, neither group behaved categorically, and because each stimulus on the continuum was not used as a standard stimulus, one cannot compare the relative sensitivity across the continuum, as we have done with the chinchilla.

Sinnott's data are interesting from another point of view. She obtained latency measures for each comparison and demonstrated that humans are uniformly slower in making their responses than are monkeys, and also that the human latency functions show an abrupt increase for stimulus pairs that were members of the same phonemic category. The monkey latency functions show no abrupt increase and, in fact, change very little as the comparison stimulus becomes acoustically more similar to the standard stimulus. In comparison with other psychophysical tasks, both auditory and visual with human and nonhuman subjects, the human latency functions are more typical. That is, it is not uncommon to see an abrupt change in the latency function as the perceptual task (particularly when it involves stimulus detection) becomes more difficult (Moody, 1970; Stebbins, 1966). In this case, however, when the task is more difficult for the monkey listener than it is for the human (the monkey never achieves 100% correct for any comparison stimulus and his DL for frequency is twice as large), the monkey latencies change by only 90 msec as their percent-correct detection changes from 10% correct to 90% correct. Why this should be the case is not precisely clear.

Sinnott argues that the abrupt change in latency for humans is attributable to the fact that stimulus pairs are first processed by a "phoneme discriminator," and subsequent analysis by a "timbre discriminator" occurs only if the two sounds are phonetically identical. This model accounts for the data obtained, that is, uniformly short latencies for phonetically dissimilar pairs and uniformly long latencies for phonetically similar pairs. On the other hand, the model does not account for the data obtained by Pisoni and Tash (1974). These authors measured latency in a same-different task using pairs of stimuli differing in VOT by 20, 40, or 60 msec, some of which were phonetically similar and others than were phonetically dissimilar. Their data show that latency varies most directly as a function of the difference in VOT—stimulus pairs differing by 20-msec VOT resulted in latencies that were nearly comparable, regardless of whether the stimuli were phonetically similar or dissimilar. Pairs that differed by 40- or 60-msec VOT produced very short latencies. The Pisoni and Tash reaction-time data are not categorical in nature, and thus resemble more closely those produced by Sinnott's monkeys. Exactly what reaction time analysis reveals in these experiments is obviously a matter of continued deliberation.

Waters and Wilson (1976) do not examine either labeling or discrimination directly, nor do they test human subjects using their method, which makes their data on the rhesus monkey difficult to interpret. They used a paired-comparison method and scaling procedures to estimate the location of a perceptual boundary for labial VOT stimuli ranging from −140 to +140. Monkeys were trained to cross a midline barrier in a shuttle box to avoid shock when the positive stimulus (+140 VOT) was presented, and to inhibit the avoidance response to avoid shock when the negative stimulus (−140 VOT) was presented. After reaching criterion (90% correct), the animals were given 40 test trials made up of all possible pairs of the following VOT stimuli (−140, −70, 0, +70, +140). During the test trials, the positive stimulus was the one closest to the +140 endpoint. The results of the paired-comparison test trials were analyzed using Thurstone's Case V scaling procedure, allowing the estimation (by interpolation) of a "boundary" between the two categories. All animal boundaries fell between +18 and +28 msec, with a mean value of +21.7 msec—in good agreement with the Kuhl and Miller (1975a) phonetic boundary data obtained for chinchillas and English-speaking adults using standard "labeling" procedures and these same stimuli. Waters and Wilson (1976) also examined the change in boundary location with changes in the endpoint training stimuli. In two other phases of the experiment, +100 and −100 msec VOT and 0 and +140 msec VOT were endpoint stimuli. The authors report shifts in the location of the boundary, although all boundaries were still located in the short voicing-lag region of the VOT continuum. However, the demonstrated "boundary shifts" may well be within the error of repeated measurement using this interpolation procedure and only 40 trials for each VOT pair; no test-retest reliability data were obtained, so that changes in the estimated boundary over time cannot be unequivocally attributed to a change in the endpoint training stimuli.

The boundary-shift issue is at least partially answered by the Kuhl and Miller (1978) study, although not in exactly the same way. With the same endpoint values, 0 msec VOT and +80 msec VOT, and stimulus continua that varied in place of articulation, different crossover points were obtained. Because the location of the crossover depends on the place of articulation of the stimulus set, one cannot argue that the animal simply places the boundary "in the middle" of any nine-point continuum. Secondly, the placement of the boundary can hardly be thought to be circumstantial, because the discrimination data now available supports the notion that the animal is responding to an abrupt change in stimulus quality in the boundary region. A more likely explanation is that this perceptual change underlies both the labeling and discrimination data obtained.

Perceptual Constancy

Experiments that test an animal's ability to form phonetic categories have only recently been undertaken. The general plan of the experiments in our laboratory has been to train animals (chinchillas) to respond differently to single items from two different phoneme categories, and then to systematically increase the number of exemplars from the category when criterion performance (>90% correct) is maintained. Conditioned avoidance is the testing paradigm and mild shock is the punishing stimulus. The animals are trained to lick at a drinking tube for their daily ration of water. Discrimination trials consist of the random presentation with equal probability of a stimulus from the *negative* category or the *positive* category. On positive trials, the animal must flee the drinking tube and cross the midline barrier within the test interval to avoid a mild shock and the sounding of a door buzzer. On negative trials, the animal is rewarded with "free" water if he successfully inhibits the crossing response during the test interval. Once trained on a large number of exemplars from the category, animals can be tested in a generalization paradigm (Kuhl and Miller, 1975a) in which novel stimuli are presented, and the animal is given feedback to suggest that his response is correct, regardless of what he does. In this way, his "rules" for including an item in a particular category can be examined.

Using this method, Burdick and Miller (1975) demonstrated that chinchillas can differentiate the sustained vowels /a/ and /i/ produced by four different talkers at three different pitch levels. This learning generalizes to the /a/ and /i/ tokens of 24 new talkers (male and female) and synthetic /a/ and /i/ tokens. These general results for the synthetic vowels /a/ and /i/ were independently demonstrated by Baru (1975) with dogs. Kuhl and Miller (1975a) demonstrated that chinchillas can correctly classify CV syllables whose initial consonants differ with respect to voicing (/t/ versus /d/). They were trained with the tokens produced by four talkers (two male, two female), that included three vowel contexts (/i/, /a/, /u/). This training generalized to the tokens produced by four different talkers (two male, two female) and three new vowel contexts (/e/, /æ/, /ɔ/) and computer synthesized /da/ (0 msec VOT) and /ta/ (+80 msec VOT). Finally, Miller and Kuhl (1976) demonstrated that chinchillas correctly classify CV syllables whose initial consonants differ with respect to the place of articulation of the voiced-plosive pair (/b/ versus /d/). These latter experiments involving small differences in the starting frequencies and trajectories of the formant transitions seem to be considerably more difficult than discriminations that depend on temporal cues, and we have not succeeded in teaching these animals to differentiate /d/ from /g/ in category experiments. It is important to note that the difficulty these animals experience in the voiced-stop tasks do not seem to be particularly aggravated by phonetic context or talker manipulations. Invariance is not the major problem. If the animal succeeds in one vowel context with multiple repetitions by a single talker (so that we can be sure that the acoustic idiosyncrasies of one particular token are not providing the cue), he tends to succeed across vowel context and talker. This success contrasts sharply with the difficulties (and failures) experienced in trying to specify the invariant acoustic attributes of these sounds.

SUMMARY

In the aggregate, the data gathered from animal subjects both on tasks related to "categorical perception" and on the perception of "constancy" are very similar to those gathered on human infants. They have implications for the evolution of language in general, for theories of speech perception in particular, and for interpretations of the perceptual behaviors of young infants.

Evolutionary Considerations

These data can be viewed as a kind of line drawing of the evolution of a speech-sound repertoire. Let us accept the notion that categorical perception is not a direct result of phonetic categorization, but is instead a function of psychoacoustic processing in general. That is, certain acoustic continua produce what might be called "natural" categories, where small acoustic changes are not detected until they cross a kind of "threshold." Sounds that could be contrasted in this way were specifically selected for a speech-sound repertoire, in the evolutionary scheme of things, because they were ideally suited to the auditory system. If this hypothesized account were correct, one would expect the animals whose psychoacoustic capabilities are at least grossly similar to our own would also provide evidence of the perception of these "natural" categories—one would expect to see the underpinnings of speech-sound perception in animals whose evolutionary histories resemble one's own history. Among phonetic contrasts, those that are widely used in the languages of the world (phonetic universals) would be ideal candidates for testing these predictions. In fact, data to date are not inconsistent with this notion. One would also predict that human infants, regardless of the linguistic environment in which they are being raised and before any extensive linguistic exposure, would discriminate these universals. If so, their accomplishments, although "linguistically relevant," might reflect processing in a "linguistic mode," or might simply reflect psychoacoustic predispositions that are, because of this selection process, favorable to speech-sound perception.

Although the arguments that have been put forth herein emphasize psychoacoustic considerations in the selection of candidates for a speech-sound repertoire, they are not meant to underplay the articulatory considerations that formed another kind of selective pressure on the process. Recently, Stevens (1973; 1975) has elegantly synthesized these ideas. He has identified for particular vowels a kind of quantal relationship between articulatory maneuvers and their resulting acoustic dimensions by demonstrating that certain formant frequency configurations, like the spectrum envelopes of the vowels /i/, /a/, and /u/, are relatively insensitive to a wide range of articulatory perturbations. He believes that "all phonetic features occurring in language have their roots in acoustic attributes with these characteristics. Language seeks out these regions, as it were, and from them assembles an inventory of phonetic elements that are used to form the code for communication by language" (1972, p. 64). Stevens mentions another idea that has been emphasized here—that the selection of preferred regions of articulation must have been guided not only by the relative stability of *acoustic* dimensions (such as F1 and F2), but by the relative stability of their *psychoacoustic* attributes, that is, after the signal has been processed by the auditory mechanism. In essence, that is what categorical perception is; perturbations in articulatory maneuvers produce observable changes in the acoustic dimensions of those signals, but the psychoacoustic or perceptual attributes of the signals are quantal in nature. Changes in the acoustic dimension are not perceived until a kind of "threshold" is reached, and perception changes abruptly to reach another plateau. The data presented here fill out this general scheme in the following way. They suggest that at least some of the perceptual discontinuities that underlie speech-sound contrasts are a natural result of the mammalian auditory system. Speech-sound contrasts were selected to exploit these perceptual discontinuities.

These data tend to support the evolutionary scheme described by Lieberman et al. (1972). If language is viewed as a biological process that evolved gradually, rather than one that apparently "emerged" in a discontinuous evolutionary jump, then the cognitive, physiological, and perceptual substrates underlying language skills might exist as "bits and pieces" of the whole in more "primitive" mammals (Lieberman et al., 1972). In certain cases, like the hemispheric asymmetry in songbirds, what seems to be a substrate for human language is involved in the communication of biologically relevant signals for that animal. Perhaps this will be a general principle. In any event, the continued investigation of the perception of biologically relevant and biologically irrelevant sounds in mammals seems particularly pertinent to present theoretical concerns.

Theories of Speech Perception

Much of the work over the last 20 years has been an attempt to solve the problem of stimulus constancy. Most solutions involved theories that accounted for constancy by "mediation" of some kind. Motor Theory (Liberman et al., 1967) was originally masterminded to solve the problem created by the apparent lack of correspondence between the acoustic representation of the signal and its percept. That is, the relation between articulation at some abstract level and perception was presumed to be more straightforward than that between the acoustic representation and perception (Liberman, 1970). In addition, the fact that until recently, categorical perception was thought to be unique to speech-sound continua, was interpreted to mean that perception, which was discontinuous, was more closely related to articulation, also discontinuous, than it was to the continuously varying acoustic signal. A number of findings have tempered these claims. First, we have recently been more successful at identifying the "invariant" or prototypical acoustic characteristics of particular phonetic categories. They seem to be neither absolute nor static properties of the signal (Fant, 1973; Stevens, 1975; Stevens and Blumstein, 1976), and more complex analyses have been required to identify them. Nevertheless, they seem to *be* there, at least for citation syllables. Second, the fact that animals give evidence of perceptual constancy by forming acoustic categories that conform to phonetic classes traditionally thought to be highly variant (like consonant-vowel syllables beginning with /d/ as opposed to /b/ regardless of talker or vowel context), suggests that some set of acoustic dimensions must characterize these phonetic classes, although we cannot as yet specify exactly what they are. Third, we now know that categorical perception is not a result of articulatory mediation, but is rather a general psychophysical phenomenon that was probably exploited in the selection of good candidates for speech-sound contrasts. Articulation guided this selection process by providing articulatory configurations in which large perturbations resulted in minimal perceptual changes. Although an active model of articulatory mediation cannot be supported, some argue (Liberman, 1975) that listeners have a tacit and abstract "knowledge" of the capabilities of vocal tracts, which accounts for certain perceptual phenomena. The use of animals in speech experiments should help to explicate which perceptual behaviors should be attributed to a listener's tacit "knowledge" of the vocal tract and which can be attributed to complex psychoacoustic processing.

The Perceptual Predispositions of Young Infants

Just as Lorenz's (1957) "innate releasing mechanism" was used to symbolize the relationship between a particular stimulus and its response, the phrase "linguistic mode" has come to symbolize the apparently unique way in which speech sounds are processed. It is tempting, then, given only the data provided by infant listeners, to interpret the infant's apparent sophistication in response to speech as a sign that the infant processes speech in a special way, one indicative of a linguistic mode (Eimas, 1974b; Morse, 1974). Recently, notions such as the "innate releasing mechanism" have come under criticism (Hinde, 1970); some of these criticisms are applicable both to the interpretation of infant and adult behavior with respect to speech-sound perception. Hinde makes the simple point that a particular stimulus-response configuration cannot be attributed to a special mechanism when the sole evidence for the mechanism is based on the study of that particular stimulus-response configuration. Other stimuli, other responses, and in the case of species-specificity arguments, other perceivers must be tested. Both adults and infants have been tested with nonspeech stimuli, and we have now examined the data for animals listeners when the stimulus is speech. The end result is that we have no evidence that the perceptual constraints demonstrated by very young infants have anything to do with the fact that the stimulus is speech or that the perceivers are human. In fact, we are without a definition of "linguistic mode." Categorical perception will not suffice; nor will the perception of constancy, if our current data prove indicative of the general case.

Nevertheless, we do not hear the six-month-old imitating doorslams, birdsongs, or the music made by mobiles, even though the infant is certainly exposed to them. One is tempted to argue that there must be some guidelines afforded the child to at least point him in the proper direction. As Marler (1973) argues, it is hard to believe that the grand design left ontogeny purely to chance. Another example from animal behavior can be used to illustrate the point. Hailman (1969) has recently reexamined the innateness issue using one of the classic "sign stimuli" originally identified by Tinbergen (1951). His set of careful experiments suggests a reinterpretation of this supposedly unlearned "instinctual" behavior. The behavioral routine is the feeding behavior of newly hatched herring gull chicks. Newly hatched chicks peck at the parent's bill to beg for food. Tinbergen identified the critical features of the mother's head by using models and examining an infant's proclivity to peck at them. The red spot on the mother's bill, as well as the shape, orientation, and movement of the bill, proved to be critical features. Tinbergen emphasized the highly configurational aspects of the infant's perception, largely because models in which the red spot was moved to the forehead received very few pecks. Hailman replicated these experiments correcting for the distance the chick had to reach to peck the spot on the forehead, and the extent of the arc through which the spot traveled when it was on the forehead, as opposed to when the head was moved in a pendulum manner. This new forehead-spot model was equally effective in eliciting pecks from the newborns. In another experiment, Hailman examined the pecking responses of newly hatched laughing-gull chicks to the herring-gull models, and found that these infants did not differentiate between models of their real parents and those of the other species. This is interesting because the parents of the two species differ markedly, except for the presence of a prominent red area on each parent's head. The laughing gull has a black head with a red bill; the herring gull has a white head and a yellow bill with a red spot on the lower mandible. Hailman interpreted both of the studies to indicate that the infant is innately predisposed to respond to relatively simple stimulus features, and only with experience does the infant develop a schema of the configurational properties of his parent's head. His experiments bear out these suggestions. By examining the infant's proclivities after three and seven days in the nest, he showed that the infant's pecking became increasingly more selective. By one week of age, both species preferred to peck the models that best exemplified their conspecies. The herring gull chicks preferred the bill-spot model to either Tinbergen's or Hailman's forehead-spot model. The infant's behavior may be similarly described: an infant's innate predispositions with regard to the perception of speech should simply be viewed as proof that infants possess the basic auditory acuity to discern the acoustic differences that differentiate single tokens from two different categories. These sensitivities constitute the infant's "guidelines." These skills are relatively simple, however, and may not reflect an ability to recognize the configurational properties that differentiate speech-sound categories. Although the infant has the basic sensitivites to discriminate individual tokens, perhaps he does not recognize the similarity between the /b/ in /ba/ and /ab/; we simply do not know, but experiments utilizing Kuhl's (1976c) constancy format should provide answers to some of these questions.

We do know, however, that whatever guidelines or predispositions the infant begins with, and regardless of whether their origins are linguistic in nature or more generally psychoacoustic, the constraints they produce are malleable. Linguistic exposure modifies them. For example, the American infant discriminates the /ra-la/ continuum categorically (Eimas, 1975a), and although they have not been tested, we have no reason to suspect that Japanese infants would not do so as well. However, Japanese adults do not discriminate these same stimuli categorically (Miyawaki, Strange, Verbrugge, Liberman, Jenkins, and Fujimura, 1975); their discrimination functions do not show a peak in performance at the English phoneme boundary, at least when an oddity task is used. The time-course and the precise nature of the changes produced by linguistic exposure are largely a puzzle. Whether these changes in discrimination functions between infancy and adulthood reflect changes in sensory capability or in one's ability to code and remember stimuli have yet to be resolved using more sensory-based psychophysical techniques.

Perhaps we will find evidence for special treatment of communicatively relevant sounds in some of the experiments involving perceptual constancy. There seem to be two major thrusts in this research: first, an infant's ability to recognize phonetic similarity regardless of its phonetic context, its position in a word, and the talker who utters it and second, the relative salience of particular dimensions. The ease with which particular kinds of segmental and nonsegmental dimensions can be used as acoustic cues for category formation may tell us what acoustic dimensions an infant attends to, just as the visual fixation measurements tell us what an infant is looking at (Fantz, 1966). There will be interest in experiments in which a variety of acoustic cues are competing for the infant's attention and how his attention to particular dimensions changes with age. These experiments may well demonstrate that both human and nonhuman infants are somehow more efficient, rather than more capable, at forming acoustic categories when they are based on acoustic cues that have potential communicative relevance. "Efficiency" in this context may mean that communicatively relevant signals are more readily discriminable, that they are more effective elicitors of the organism's auditory attention, or that they are more easily remembered. In the interim, judgment must be reserved as to the precise nature and origins of the perceptual constraints evidenced by very young infants, in spite of their obvious "linguistic relevance."

ACKNOWLEDGMENTS

The author wishes to thank colleagues who provided critical comments of this manuscript: J. D. Miller, D. H. Eldredge, I. J. Hirsh, D. W. Sparks, C. S. Watson, and B. S. Scott.

REFERENCES

Barclay, J. R. 1972. Noncategorical perception of a voiced stop: A replication. Percept. Psychophys. 11: 269–273.

Baru, A. V. 1975. Discrimination of synthesized vowels /a/ and /i/ with varying parameters in dog. In G. Fant and M. A. A. Tatham (eds.), Auditory Analysis and Perception of Speech, pp. 91–102. Academic Press, New York.

Burdick, C. K., and Miller, J. D. 1975. Speech perception by the chinchilla: Discrimination of sustained /a/ and /i/. J. Acoust. Soc. Am. 58: 415–427.

Carney, A. E., Widin, G. P., and Viemiester, N. F. 1977. Noncategorical perception of stop consonants differing in VOT. J. Acoust. Soc. Am. 62: 960–970.

Crystal, D. 1973. Non-segmental phonology in language acquisition: A review of the issues. Lingua 32: 1–45.

Cutting, J. E., and Rosner, B. S. 1974. Categories and boundaries in speech and music. Percept. Psychophys. 16: 564–570.

Dewson, J. H., Burlingame, A., Kizer, K., Dewson, S., Kenny, P., and Pribram, K. H. 1975. Hemispheric asymmetry of auditory function in monkeys. J. Acoust. Soc. Am. 58 (suppl. 1): S66(A).

Eilers, R. E. 1977. Context sensitive perception of naturally produced stop and fricative consonants. J. Acoust. Soc. Am. 61: 1321–1336.

Eilers, R. E., and Minifie, F. D. 1975. Fricative discrimination in early infancy. J. Speech Hear. Res. 18: 158–167.

Eilers, R. E., Wilson, W. R., and Moore, J. M. 1977. Developmental changes in speech discrimination in infants. J. Sp. Hear. Res. 20: 766–780.

Eimas, P. D. 1974a. Auditory and linguistic processing of cues for place of articulation by infants. Percept. Psychophys. 16: 513–521.

Eimas, P. D. 1974b. Linguistic processing of speech by young infants. In R. L. Schiefelbusch and L. L. Lloyd (eds.), Language Perspectives—Acquisition, Retardation, and Intervention, pp. 55–74. University Park Press, Baltimore.

Eimas, P. D. 1975a. Auditory and phonetic coding of the cues for speech: Discrimination of the [r-1] distinction by young infants. Percept. Psychophys. 18: 341–347.

Eimas, P. D. 1975b. Developmental studies of speech perception. In L. B. Cohen and P. Salapetek (eds.), Infant Perception. Academic Press, New York.

Eimas, P. D., Siqueland, E. R., Jusczyk, P., and Vigorito, J. 1971. Speech perception in infants. Science 171: 303–306.

Fant, G. 1973. Speech Sounds and Features. MIT Press, Cambridge.

Fantz, R. L. 1966. Pattern discrimination and selective attention as determinants of perceptual development from birth. In A. H. Kidd and J. L. Rivoire (eds.), Perceptual Development in Children. Int. University Press, New York.

Fodor, J. A., Garrett, M. F., and Brill, S. L. 1975. Pi ka pu. The perception of speech sounds by pre-linguistic infants. Percept. Psychophys. 18: 74–78.

Fry, D. B., Abramson, A. S., Eimas, P. D., and Liberman, A. M. 1962. The identification and discrimination of synthetic vowels. Lang. Speech 5: 171–189.

Fujisaki, H., and Kawashima, T. 1969. On the modes and mechanisms of speech perception. Sogoshikenjo-Nenpo 28: 67–73.

Fujisaki, H., and Kawashima, T. 1970. Some experiments on speech perception and a model for the perceptual mechanism. Ann. Rep. Engineer. Res. Inst., Fac. Engineer., U. Tokyo 29: 207–214.

Gardner, R. A., and Gardner, B. T. 1969. Teaching sign language to a chimpanzee. Science 165: 664–672.

Hailman, J. P. 1969. How an instinct is learned. Sci. Am. 221: 98–106.

Hayes, C. 1951. The Ape in Our House. Harper, New York.

Henderson, D. 1969. Temporal summation of acoustic signals by the chinchilla. J. Acoust. Soc. Am. 46: 474–475.

Hinde, R. A. 1970. Animal Behaviour. McGraw-Hill, New York.

Hirsh, I. J. 1959. Auditory perception of temporal order. J. Acoust. Soc. Am. 31: 759–767.

Jackson, J. H. 1884. Evolution and Dissolution of the Nervous System: Selected Papers, Vol. 2. Basic Books, New York.

Jakobson, R.. 1941. Kindersprache, Aphasia, und Allegemeine Lautgesetze. Almquist and Wiksell, Uppsala.

Jusczyk, P., Rosner, B., Cutting, J., Foard, C., and Smith, L. 1977. Categorical perception of nonspeech sounds by 2-month-old infants. Percept. Psychophys. 21: 50–54.

Kellogg, W. N., and Kellogg, L. A. 1933. The Ape and the Child. McGraw-Hill, New York.

Kuhl, P. K. 1976a. Speech perception in early infancy: The acquisition of speech-sound categories. In S. K. Hirsh, D. H. Eldredge, I. J. Hirsh, and S. R. Silverman (eds.), Hearing and Davis: Essays Honoring Hallowell Davis, pp. 265–280. Washington University Press, St. Louis.

Kuhl, P. K. 1976b. Speech perception by the chinchilla: Categorical perception of synthetic alveolar plosive consonants. J. Acoust. Soc. Am. 60(suppl. 1): S81(A).

Kuhl, P. K. 1976c. Speech perception in early infancy: Perceptual constancy for vowel categories. J. Acoust. Soc. Am 60 (Suppl. 1): S90(A).

Kuhl, P. K., and Miller, J. D. 1975a. Speech perception by the chinchilla: Voiced-voiceless distinction in alveolar plosive consonants. Science 190: 69–72.

Kuhl, P. K., and Miller, J. D. 1975b. Speech perception in early infancy: Discrimination of speech-sound categories. J. Acoust. Soc. Am. 58 (Suppl. 1): S56(A).

Kuhl, P. K., and Miller, J. D. 1978. Speech perception by the chinchilla: Identification functions for synthetic VOT stimuli. J. Acoust. Soc. Am. 63: 905–917.

Lane, H. 1965. The motor theory of speech perception: A critical review. Psychol. Rev. 72: 275–309.

Lasky, R. E., Syrdal-Lasky, A., and Klein, R. E. 1975. VOT discrimination by four-to-six-and-a-half month old infants from Spanish environments. J. Exper. Child Psych. 20: 215–225.

Lenneberg, E. H. 1967. Biological Foundations of Language. Wiley, New York.

Leopold, W. F. 1949. Patterning in children language learning. Speech Development of a Bilingual Child. Vols. 1–4. Northwestern University Press, Chicago.

Lewis, M. M. 1936. Infant Speech: A Study of the Beginnings of Language. Harcourt, Brace, and World, New York.

Liberman, A. M. 1957. Some results of research on speech perception. J. Acoust. Soc. Am. 29: 117–123.

Liberman, A. M. 1970. The grammars of speech and language. Cog. Psychol. 1: 301–323.

Liberman, A. M. 1975. How abstract must a motor theory of speech perception be? Haskins Laboratories Status Report on Speech Research, SR-44, pp. 1–15.

Liberman, A. M., Cooper, F. S., Shankweiler, D. P., and Studdert-Kennedy, M. 1967. Perception of the speech code. Psychol. Rev. 74: 431–461.

Liberman, A. M., Harris, K. S., Hoffman, H. S., and Griffith, B. C. 1957. The discrimination of speech sounds within and across phoneme boundaries. J. Exp. Psychol. 54: 358–368.

Liberman, A. M., Mattingly, I. G., and Turvey, M. T. 1972. Language codes and memory codes. In A. W. Melton and E. Martin (eds.), Coding Processes in Human Memory, pp. 307–334. Winston and Wiley, New York.

Lieberman, P., Crelin, E. S., and Klatt, D. H. 1972. Phonetic ability and related anatomy of the newborn and adult human, Neanderthal man, and the chimpanzee. Am. Anthropol. 74: 287–307.

Lorenz, K. 1957. Der Kumpan in der umwelt des vogels. In C. H. Schiller (Eds.), Instinctive Behaviour. Methuen, London.

Luz, G. A. 1969. Conditioning the chinchilla to make avoidance responses to novel sounds. J. Comp. Physiol. Psychol. 68: 348–354.

Marler, P. 1973. Constraints on learning: Development of bird song. In W. F. Norman (ed.), The Clarence M. Hicks Memorial Lectures for 1970. University of Toronto Press, Toronto.

Masterton, B., Heffner, H., and Ravizza, R. 1968. The evolution of human hearing. J. Acoust. Soc. Am. 45: 966–985.

Mattingly, I. G., Liberman, A. M., Syrdal, A. K., and Halwes, T. 1971. Discrimination in speech and nonspeech modes. Cog. Psychol. 2: 131–157.

Miller, J. D. 1970. Audibility curve of the chinchilla. J. Acoust. Soc. Am. 48: 513–523.

Miller, J. D., and Kuhl, P. K. 1976. Speech perception by the chinchilla: A progress report on syllable-initial voiced-plosive consonants. J. Acoust. Soc. Am. 59 (suppl. 1): S54(A).

Miller, J. D., Pastore, R. E., Wier, C. C., Kelly, W. J., and Dooling, R. J. 1976. Discrimination and labeling of noise-buzz sequences with varying noise-lead times: An example of categorical perception. J. Acoust. Soc. Am. 60: 410–417.

Miyawaki, K., Strange, W., Verbrugge, R., Liberman, A., Jenkins, J., and Fijimura, O. 1975. An effect of linguistic experience: The discrimination of /r/ and /l/ by native speakers of Japanese and English. Percept. Psychophys. 18: 331–340.

Molfese, D. L., Nunez, V., Siebert, S. M., and Ramanajah, N. V. 1976. Cerebral asymmetry: Changes in factors affecting its development. In S. R. Harnad, H. D. Steklis, and J. Lancaster (eds.), Origins and Evolution of Language and Speech, pp. 821–833. Academy of Sciences, New York.

Moody, D. B. 1970. Reaction time as an index of sensory function. In W. C. Stebbins (ed.), Animal Psychophysics: The Design and Conduct of Sensory Experiments. pp. 277–302. Plenum Press, New York.

Morse, P. A. 1972. The discrimination of speech and nonspeech stimuli in early infancy. J. Exp. Child Psychol. 14: 477–492.

Morse, P. A. 1974. Infant speech perception: A preliminary model and review of the literature. In R. L. Schiefelbusch and L. L. Lloyd (eds.), Language Perspectives—Acquisition, Retardation, and Intervention, pp. 19–54. University Park Press, Baltimore.

Morse, P. A., and Snowdon, C. T. 1975. An investigation of categorical speech discrimination by rhesus monkeys. Percept. Psychophys. 17: 9–16.

Nelson, D. A., and Keister, T. E. 1976. Frequency-difference thresholds in chinchilla using conditioned avoidance techniques. J. Acoust. Soc. Am. 59 (suppl. 1): S54(A).

Nottebohm, F., Stokes, T. M., and Leonard, C. M. 1976. Central control of song in the Canary, Serinus canarius. J. of Comp. Neurol. 165: 457–486.

Pastore, R. E. 1976. Categorical perception: A critical re-evaluation. In S. K. Hirsh, D. H. Eldredge, I. J. Hirsh, and S. R. Silverman (eds.), Hearing and Davis: Essays Honoring Hallowell Davis, pp. 253–264. Washington University Press, St. Louis.

Peterson, G. E., and Barney, H. L. 1952. Control methods used in a study of the vowels. J. Acoust. Soc. Am. 24: 175–184.

Pisoni, D. B. 1977. Identification and discrimination of the relative onset time of two-component tones: Implications for voicing perception in stops. J. Acoust. Soc. Am. 61: 1352–1361.

Pisoni, D. B., and Lazarus, J. H. 1974. Categorical and noncategorical modes of speech perception along the voicing continuum. J. Acoust. Soc. Am. 55: 328–333.

Pisoni, D. B., and Tash, J. 1974. Reaction times to comparisons within and across phonetic categories. Percept. Psychophys. 15: 285–290.

Premack, D. 1971. Language in Chimpanzee? Science 172: 808–822.

Rumbaugh, D., and Gill, V. 1976. The mastery of language-type skills by the chimpanzee. In S. R. Harnad, H. D. Steklis, and J. Lancaster (eds.), Origins and Evolution of Language and Speech, pp. 562–578. Academy of Sciences, New York.

Sinnott, J. M., Beecher, M. D., Moody, D. B., and Stebbins, W. C. 1976. Speech sound Discrimination by monkeys and humans. J. Acoust. Soc. Am. 60: 687–695.

Stebbins, W. C. 1966. Auditory reaction time and the derivation of equal loudness contours on the monkey. J. Exp. Anal. Behav. 9: 135–142.

Stebbins, W. C. 1970. Studies of hearing and hearing loss in the monkey. In W. C. Stebbins (ed.), Animal Psychophysics: The Design and Conduct of Sensory Experiments, pp. 41–66. Plenum Press, New York.

Stebbins, W. C. 1973. Hearing of Old World Monkeys (Cercopitheimae). Am. J. Phys. Anthropol. 38: 357–364.

Stevens, K. N. 1972. The quantal nature of speech: Evidence from articulatory-acoustic data. In E. E. David, Jr. and P. B. Denes (eds.), Human Communication: A Unified View, pp. 51–66. McGraw-Hill, New York.

Stevens, K. N. 1973. Further theoretical and experimental bases for quantal places of articulation for consonants. Quarterly Progress Report No. 108, pp. 247–252. Research Laboratory of Electronics, MIT, Cambridge.

Stevens, K. N. 1975. The potential role of property detectors in the perception of consonants. In G. Fant and M. A. A. Tatham (eds.), Auditory Analysis and Perception of Speech, pp. 191–196. Academic Press, London.

Stevens, K. N., and Blumstein, S. E. 1976. Context-independent properties for place of articulation in stop consonants. J. Acoust. Soc. Am. 59 (suppl. 1): S40(A).

Streeter, L. A. 1976. Language perception of 2-month-old infants shows effects of both innate mechanisms and experience. Nature 259: 39–41.

Studdert-Kennedy, M., Liberman, A. M., Harris, K., and Cooper, F. S. 1970. The motor theory of speech perception: A reply to Lane's critical review. Psychol. Rev. 77: 234–249.

Swoboda, P., Morse, P., and Leavitt, L. 1976. Continuous vowel discrimination in normal and at-risk infants. Child Dev. 47: 459–465.

Tinbergen, N. 1951. The Study of Instinct. Clarendon Press, Oxford.

Waters, R. A., and Wilson, W. A., Jr. 1976. Speech perception by rhesus monkeys: The voicing distinction in synthesized labial and velar stop consonants. Percept. Psychophys. 19: 285–289.

Watson, C. S. 1976. Factors in the discrimination of word-length auditory patterns. In S. K. Hirsh, D. H. Eldredge, I. J. Hirsh, and S. R. Silverman (eds.), Hearing and Davis: Essays Honoring Hollowell Davis, pp. 175–190. Washington University Press, St. Louis.

Williams, L. 1977a. The perception of stop consonant voicing by Spanish-English bilinguals. Percept. Psychophys. 21: 289–297.

Williams, L. 1977b. The cue for voicing cue in Spanish. J. Phonetics 5: 169–184.

Wilson, W. R., Moore, J. M., and Thompson, G. 1976. Sound-field auditory thresholds of infants utilizing Visual Reinforcement Audiometry (VRA). Paper presented at ASHA, November, Houston.

Wroton, H. W., and Watson, C. B. 1974. An anomolous influence of tonal context on frequency discrimination. J. Acoust. Soc. Am. 56 (suppl. 2): S44(A).

The Analysis
of Intonation
in Young Children

David Crystal

INTONATION IN ADULTS

It may seem paradoxical to begin an account of the development of intonation in children by discussing the findings of adult studies of the subject. Unlike most other areas of linguistic inquiry, however, the theoretical, methodological, and empirical issues surrounding intonational study are too ill-defined to permit the investigator to take much as axiomatic. Even in relation to the adult, the topic has received far less general linguistic investigation than any other, for reasons that are now well recognized (primarily, the lack of discreteness in the phonetic and semantic data of nonsegmental phonology; see Bolinger, 1949; Crystal, 1969). To the child language scholar, of course, this neglect might well seem to be a blessing in disguise. At least this way, it might be argued, one will avoid falling into the various traps that have ensnared workers in syntax and semantics, such as the assignment of conversational abilities and cognitive/semantic relations to the young child, that more reflect the analyst's or parent's belief patterns than any demonstrable linguistic behavior on the child's part (see, for example, the critique in Howe, 1976). To argue thus is not to deny the potential value of working with adult models as heuristic devices, but it is to affirm the dangers of uncritically imposing such models on the young child, or of setting up hypotheses about language ability that are in principle incapable of falsification (as in much of the discussion so far about speech acts in the first year of life). To begin empirically, then, by examining early child data, using as a framework of reference only the most general considerations of phonetic and phonological theory, and by attempting to see the intonational system of the child in its own terms, would seem to constitute a promising and well-grounded (albeit vast) enterprise.

Unfortunately, it is already too late to proceed along these lines. Several fundamental misconceptions about the nature of nonsegmental phonology, and about intonation in particular, are already widespread in the language acquisition literature. Two of these are central to any developmental discussion. The first is the view that units of intonational form represent in a one-to-one manner units of syntactic

257

or semantic function. A common example of this way of thinking is the claim that the change from a falling to a rising tone corresponds to a grammatical or speech-act distinction between statement and question. It may even be believed that the rising tone "expresses" the meaning of question. However, there is no isomorphism between such variables. Several adult language studies have shown that rising intonations signal a great deal more than questions, and questions are expounded by a great deal more than rising intonations (e.g., Crystal, 1969; Fries, 1964). Interpretation depends on several factors, of which the lexical, grammatical, non-verbal (especially kinesic), and situational contexts are most relevant. One also has to be extremely careful about the use of such terms as "question." If the term is already being used in a formal syntactic sense (covering the use of question-words and subject-verb inversion in English, for example), then it would be misleading to use it for the semantic effect produced by an intonational change. To say that *He's còming → He's cóming* is a change from "statement" to "question" may seem plausible at first, but when one considers the identical intonational substitution on the following pair of sentences, the usage becomes confusing: *What's he dòing? → What's he dóing?* One could hardly say that the "question" has become a "question." Rather, one needs to talk in terms of the addition of "questioning, puzzled, surprised," etc. elements of attitudinal meaning. The problem is not a grammatical one; it is one of identifying and delimiting the emotional nuances involved. An identical problem would affect any analysis involving speech-act terminology.

Another reason why a one-to-one analysis of intonational form and meaning is unjustified stems from an overconcentration on intonation at the expense of other areas of nonsegmental phonology. To a certain extent, intonation (in its usual definition as "the linguistic use of pitch") can be studied as an autonomous prosodic system, but ultimately one has to adopt an integrated view, seeing pitch as one exponent of meaning, along with the other prosodic variables (loudness and duration) and paralinguistic features of language (the "tones of voice" based on variations in tension, labialization, nasalization, etc.). From a formal point of view, the distinction between intonation and these other features is fairly clear; from a semantic point of view, it is often irrelevant: a given "meaning" (such as sarcasm) is usually signalled by a range of prosodic and paralinguistic features, pitch being but one. Over the first two years of life, in fact, nonintonational features (such as variations in loudness, duration, rhythmicality, and muscular tension) are of considerable importance in the expression of meaning. This is so not only for attitudes, but also for grammatical patterning, where any adequate phonological discovery procedure for sentences at around 18 months (see below) has to refer to far more than sequences of pitch contour and pause. Two lexical items could be linked in several ways, e.g., both being pronounced with extra pitch height, loudness, longer duration, marked rhythm, or with some shared paralinguistic feature—all of which would make the use of pitch contour and pause less significant. Only these last two features are ever given systematic attention in the literature on early syntax, however.

The second central misconception concerning the nature of intonation referred to above is the view that it is a single, homogeneous phenomenon, formally and functionally, as is implied by such phrases as "the intonation shows . . . ," "intonation is an early development," and the enormous (and hardly classified) coverage of the term "dysprosody" in the clinical literature. The oversimplification on the formal side is evident if one briefly characterizes the primary distinctions that almost all theories of intonation provide (terminology varies), namely:

1.   The basic distinction between pitch *direction* and pitch *range*. A pitch may fall, rise, stay level, or perform some combination of these things in a given unit (e.g., falling-rising on a syllable), and these directional *tones* provide one system of intonational contrastivity. Any of these tones may be varied in terms of range, however, which is seen as a quite separate system of contrasts, viz. at an average pitch level for a speaker, or higher/lower (to various degrees), or widened/narrowed (to various degrees—the ultimate degree of narrowing being, of course, monotone).

2.   The intonation contrasts perceived in connected speech are not all of the same kind, and some carry more linguistic information about the organization and interpretation of the utterance than others. Four types of contrast are central.

a.   The primary organizational distinction is the analysis of speech into *tone-units* ("sense groups," "primary contours"), namely, a finite set of pitch movements, formally identifiable as a coherent configuration, and used systematically with reference to other levels of language (segmental phonology, syntax, semantics). For example, the normal tone-unit segmentation of the utterance

John came at three/ Mary came at four/ and Mark came at five/

is as indicated by the slant lines. The assignment of tone-unit boundaries seems generally to have a syntactic function (see Crystal, 1975, Chapter 1, for a classification in English).

b.   Given the analysis of an utterance into tone-units, the next decision is the placement of the primary pitch movement, or *tonic* syllable, as in

It was a very *nice party* versus
It was a very nice *party* versus
It was *a very nice party.*

This is the focus of most of the discussion on intonation in the context of generative grammar, where the aim was to demonstrate that tonicity had a syntactic function (see Bresnan, 1971). This author's view basically agrees with Bolinger's (1972), that the factors governing tonic placement are primarily semantic, although it is possible to find cases where tonic placement is obligatory or disallowed for syntactic reasons, e.g.,

*it *was a nice party/*
**he's going/isn't* he/*

c.   Given an analysis of an utterance into tone-units and tonic syllables, one may then decide on the tone for those syllables—if rising, falling, or whatever, along with a specific pitch range. These features seem to signal primarily attitudinal information, although certain tonal contrasts can expound grammatical contrasts, e.g., utterance end versus continuation, as in

would you like bèer/ or whiskey/ or tèa/

compared with

would you like bèer/ or whiskey/ or tèa/

In written English, the former would be concluded with a period, the latter probably with a dash or dots (. . .).

d. Other pitch features of the tone-unit may then be decided, the most important being the height of the first prominent syllable, the change-points within the overall contour, and the height of any unstressed syllables.

Roles of Intonation

The homogeneity view of intonation also produces an oversimplified account of the function of this feature of language. It is possible to distinguish at least four roles for intonation in English.

Grammatical   In the grammatical role, pitch is being used to signal a contrast, the terms of which would be conventionally recognized as morphological or syntactic in the rest of a grammar, e.g., singular/plural, present/past, positive/negative. These contrasts are common in tone languages, but they may also be found in English, where tone-units, tonic syllables, and tones can perform a grammatical role, as in the distinction between restrictive and nonrestrictive relative clauses:

> *my bróther/ who's abróad/ wrote me a letter/*   (= one brother)
> *my brother who's abróad/ wrote me a letter/*   (= 1+ brothers).

In a secondary sense, pitch may also be used to reinforce a grammatical distinction already overt in word order or morphology, as in the obligatory tone pattern on parallel coordinations such as

> *I liked the green dress/ and she liked the red one/.*

Semantic   The semantic role subsumes both the organization of meaning in a discourse, and the reflection of the speaker's presuppositions about subject-matter or context. Under the first heading, the highlighting of certain parts of an utterance is often carried out by intonational means (and analyzed in terms of such distinctions as "given" versus "new" information, or the "focus" on marked patterns of word order—see Quirk, Greenbaum, Leech, and Svartvik, 1972, Chapter 14). This includes the use of intonation to emphasize the relatively unfamiliar item in a sequence, as Bolinger argues in his critique of the generative account of tonicity (1972), e.g., *clòthes to wash* versus *clothes to làunder.* Under the second heading is included the interactional use of intonation, as when the focus on a specific lexical item presupposes a specific context immediately preceding, e.g.,

> *there were thrèe books on the table/*

implying a context in which the number of books was in doubt (cf. Chomsky, 1970).

Attitudinal   The attitudinal role is the traditionally recognized function of intonation, whereby personal emotions are signaled concerning the subject matter or context of an utterance, e.g., anger, sarcasm, puzzlement, emphasis.

Social   In the social function, intonation signals information about the sociolinguistic characteristics of the speaker, such as his sex, class, professional status, and so on (see Crystal, 1975, Chapter 5). In language acquisition, the importance of this function is beginning to be recognized in relation to such notions as role play (cf. Sachs and Devin, 1976), but of all the functions of intonation, it is the least well studied, either for child or adult language use.

In short, there are evident grounds for a more sophisticated awareness of the form and function of intonation patterns when commencing the analysis of early child utterances. In particular, being aware of the main issues of theoretical debate in the adult literature (such as the relevance of "emic" models of analysis, or the relationship between intonation and syntax) would provide a perspective that might forestall the premature construction of theories of acquisition where intonation is made to take a weight it cannot legitimately bear (see below).

ACQUISITION OF INTONATION

Contrastivity of Intonation

Remarks about the acquisition of intonation are scattered, selective, and largely impressionistic, as one well-known conference discussion displays very clearly. This author has reviewed the relevant literature elsewhere (Crystal, 1973). On the basis of the very limited empirical study that has taken place, it seems premature to talk in terms of stages of development in this area. On the other hand, the available evidence is suggestive of a general developmental progress that can provide a useful working hypothesis for application to clinical problems.

Awareness of Voice Tone   Awareness of tone of voice involving pitch direction and range has long been known to be present in children from around two to three months (the tradition is well summarized in Lewis, 1936), but experimental studies are lacking that: a) systematically distinguish pitch from other prosodic variables, and b) distinguish between phonetic and phonological contrastivity. The kind of contrast in pitch that Kaplan (1970) demonstrated could be discriminated from around four months (emphatic falling and rising tones) is of considerable interest, but it is a fact of unclear linguistic (i.e., phonological) significance. Likewise, there are problems in evaluating the nature of the language-specific contrastivity in the productive use of pitch that Jakobson, Tervoort, and others have claimed to be apparent in children's vocalizations from around six months (see Huxley and Ingram, 1971, pp. 162–3; Crystal, 1973). It is fairly clear that the pitch patterns detectable in the crying and babbling of children in the first six months are nonlinguistic in character, but how and how soon phonological contrasts in pitch emerge is controversial (cf. Olney and Scholnick, 1976). Recognition of language-specificity involves both phonetic notions of "community voice quality" (e.g., the characteristic "twang" of a language) and phonological notions of accent, and distinguishing these aspects in early vocalization is inevitably a problem.

Learned Patterns   Evidence of "learned" patterns of intonational behavior in the second half of the first year can be interpreted both semantically and syntactically. Under the former heading, one would argue for an interactional function of intonation as a means of signaling participation in an action sequence shared by parent and child. This point, emphasized by Bruner (1975a,b) and several ethologically-orientated studies (reflected in Richards, 1974), reflects a theory of development wherein vocalization is seen as playing a role in communication that is also performed by nonvocal behavior, such as reaching or eye contact. That there is institutionalized variation in interactional behavior using vocalization is evident from several studies in which cultural and social factors have been shown to affect the quantity as well as the quality of the utterance (e.g. Blount, 1970; Tomlinson-Keasey, 1972), pitch being a salient differential indicator. The development of "turn-taking" also involves prosodic delimitation, as Bruner points out in his studies of the joint behavior of parent and child in "peep-bo" routines, and action sequences involving a prosodic climax (see Bruner, 1975a). It is as yet unclear how far the intonational component in such vocalization patterns is an independently functioning variable (as opposed to being a subordinate element within a gestalt), but this way of viewing it seems the more plausible, given the tradition summarized in Lewis (1936), the evidence of perceptual studies on the early development of pitch, music, etc. (Friedlander, 1970; Fridman, 1974), the greater stability of intonation patterns compared with segments (e.g. Lenneberg, 1967, p. 279), and so on. In one child studied at Reading, the phrase *all gone,* regularly said by the parent after each meal, was rehearsed by the child using the prosodic component only: the child hummed the intonation of the phrase first, viz.

and then attempted the whole, producing an accurate intonation but only approximate segments ([∧ʔd∧]).

Prosodic Patterns   The delimitation of units of communication in dialogue provides the basis for the development of prosodic patterns whose systematic status becomes gradually more determinate during the second half of the first year. What is unclear is whether the best way of explaining the use of these patterns is to use syntactic, semantic, or sociolinguistic metalanguage. There is general agreement as to the formal features involved: the organization that comes to be imposed upon early vocalization and babble is prosodic—primarily an intonation-cum-rhythm unit followed by a pause. This unit has been labeled a prosodic "envelope" or "matrix" (Bruner, 1975a, p. 10), a prosodic "frame" (Dore, 1975), and a "primitive prosodic unit" (Crystal, 1971); Weir (1966) had earlier talked about the splitting up of utterances into "sentence-like chunks" at this stage. Bruner sees the function of these prosodic units as "place-holders." A mode of communication (such as a demand, or a question) is established using prosody, and primitive lexical items are then added. Dore refers to the formally isolable, repeated, and situationally specific patterns observed at this stage as "phonetically consistent forms," whose "proto-phonemic" segmental character is complemented by a distinctive prosody. It is the prosodic marker that is the more stable. In one child studied at Reading, the end of any jargon sequence was marked with a predictable pitch movement

within which, there was, however, considerable segmental phonetic variation. By the end of the first year, formal features of this general kind seem well established.

This stage has attracted much recent attention under the heading of the "prag-matics" of language development. The main viewpoint seems to be that various speech acts can be postulated based on the formal features of these early utterances, and intonation is usually cited as primary evidence. Dore, for example (1975, p. 31 ff.), argues that intonation patterns are crucial. Primitive speech acts are said to contain a "rudimentary referring expression" (lexical items) and a "primitive force indicating device" ("typically an intonation pattern," p. 31), as in labeling, request-ing, and calling. The distinction between referent and intention is pivotal: "whereas the child's one word communicates the notion he has in mind, his prosodic pattern indicates his intention with regard to that notion" (p. 32). The point is taken up by Bruner (1975a, p. 19), among others. The approach is attractive, especially because it suggests a way around the intractable problems raised by the notion of holophrasis, but it raises its own problems. The trouble, of course, is empirical verification. The fact that parents interpret their children's intonation systematically is no evidence for ascribing their belief patterns to the child's intuition. Therefore, how, in principle, can one know that a child at this age intends a distinction between *calling* and *greeting* (two of Dore's categories)? Searching for 1-1 correlations between intonation and the child's own behavior is unlikely to be successful, partly because of the indeterminacy of the situations in which the language is used, and because there are fewer pitch patterns available than there are situations to be dif-ferentiated (cf. the comment on isomorphism above). It is possible that more detailed behavioral analyses will give grounds for optimism, but for the present such approaches seem to be in great danger of being determined as unfalsifiable.

Tonicity and Tonal Contrastivity   Within these prosodic frames, it is unclear if tonicity or tonal contrastivity develops first, or if they emerge simultaneously. Evi-dence is mixed, and largely anecdotal. The suggestion about parallel development is based on the observation that tonicity contrasts are more in evidence in jargon sequences (in which sequences of rhythms are built up that reflect the intonational norms of connected speech), whereas tone contrasts are early heard in the use of such lexical items as single-word sentences. If one ignores the jargon, however, as being a less central communicative "style," then it would seem that tone develops before tonicity. Polysyllabic lexical items at this stage tend to have fixed tonic place-ment, although they may vary in terms of pitch direction and range, e.g., *dàda* (said as daddy enters the room), ↑*dáda* (said when a noise was heard outside). Based on samples taken from five British children between 9 and 15 months, early tonal contrasts seemed to develop as follows:

` versus ↑´	(the latter especially for query)
` versus ↑`	(the latter for surprise, insistence, etc.)
↑´ versus ´	(especially in playful, anticipatory contexts)
` versus ↑^	(especially for "aren't you good" contexts, e.g., *clever bôy/*, or for being impressed, e.g. *bûs/* versus *bùs/*
´ versus ˘	(especially in warning contexts, e.g., *be cǎreful/*)
↑^ versus ^	(especially in play contexts)

These features appear on isolated lexical items to begin with, and later come to be used in sequences—the "contrastive syntagmas" and intonational "substitution games" reported by Carlson and Anisfeld (1969, p. 118), Eisenson, Auer, and Irwin, (1963), Keenan (1974, p. 178), Weir (1962), and others, noticeable from around 18 months. Halliday (1975) reports several sequences of this kind, from around 15 months, e.g., the distinction between seeking and finding a person, signaled in his child by high versus mid-low pitch range (p. 154).

An important theoretical question here is how far these formal distinctions are genuinely semantically contrastive for the child. It is insufficient to show that adults can differentiate these patterns and give them consistent interpretations (cf. Dore, 1975, p. 29, Menyuk, 1971, pp. 61–62, Menyuk and Bernholtz, 1969). As Bloom points out (1973, p. 19), this is not evidence of contrastivity for the *children*. On the other hand, it does not necessarily follow that there is no contrastivity at all at this stage. In the absence of detailed behavioral analyses, and given certain fundamental limitations of the descriptive apparatus used (see below), such a conclusion would be premature. There are two main theoretical positions taken up. One argues that intonation by itself is evidence of grammatical structure (Brown, 1973; Menyuk, 1971). The other argues that intonation comes after the development of syntax, especially word-order (Bloom, 1973). The former position is clearly found in Brown (1973), who argues for the sequence "intonation" → "meaning relations" → "syntax":

> It is the use of intonation contours to mark word sequences as in construction, rather than word order, that is the single universal syntactic device of Stage I. And it is ultimately the relational interpretability of these constructions, heard in context, that justifies attributing relational semantic intentions to the child (p. 43).

The point is also made by Clark, in her review of Bloom (1975, p. 178). The trouble is that Brown's views are not wholly empirically based. As was argued in this author's review of Brown's recent book (Crystal, 1974, p. 296), he seems to have analyzed only one of the children intonationally (see Brown, 1973, p. 52), and hardly any of the data provided to illustrate his work are given an intonational transcription. Bloom's arguments, on the other hand, seem at first sight more well-founded empirically. She represents the second theoretical position, arguing for the sequence "meaning relations" → "syntax" → "intonation." She cites the evidence that in her data, early utterances (at 16 months) apparently had what she refers to as sentence prosody (single contour, no pause), whereas later utterances (around 19–22 months) did not, and only much later still (around 28 months) did sentence prosody clearly emerge. On the basis of this, she (citing work by Lahey) argues that the early prosodic patterns could have had no contrastive force, and that the "unified" patterns observed must have been attributable to a process of mimicry of adult contours (the way babbling is often said to be a mimicry of segmental features, or the use of "unanalysed wholes" in syntax, whose role in development seems to have been much underestimated, cf. Clark, 1974). Intonation, as a productive linguistic system, has to be "re-learned" phonologically after the development of the word order contrasts that constitute syntax proper.

Any attempt to resolve this debate will have to recognize three possible views about the status of early pitch movements: 1) they are in free variation, 2) they are phonologically contrastive, and 3) they are invariant with reference to the segmental features of utterance (i.e., prosodic "idioms"—a not infrequent phenomenon, as Halliday, 1975, argues). The first two positions, unfortunately, depend totally on a prior specification of the notion of situational context, within which concepts of variation or contrastivity can be defined. The trouble is, as adult intonation studies have repeatedly shown over the past twenty years, that this notion of context cannot readily be specified in clear behavioral terms. Moreover, as this author has argued elsewhere (Crystal, 1975, p. 31 ff.), this notion cannot be explicated without reference to other kinds of "context" (of a lexical, syntactic, intonational, and semiotic kind), most of which information is simply not available at the stage of child development with which we are dealing. It may be a theoretical impossibility to resolve the issue at this stage. On the other hand, it would be premature to conclude this without carrying out the same procedures as have characterized the progress of ideas in adult work, in the first instance making a narrow auditory phonetic analysis of early vocal behavior. The surprising thing is that this has not been done for either position. There has been a tendency to use acoustic specifications of events, at one extreme, and vaguely defined constructs, such as "falling" and "rising," at the other. What is lacking is a reasonably comprehensive account of the whole range of nonsegmental variables that characterize vocalization during this period—in much the same way as increasingly detailed descriptions of early infant vocalization have come to be made (e.g., Stark, Rose, and McLagen, 1975). This would show, for instance, that a specification of intonational contrastivity in terms of direction alone is not enough; range of pitch is equally crucial. This can be seen from Halliday's excellent attempt at a phonetically accurate account. For his analysis, he needs eight pitch range variations (very high, high, mid-high, mid, mid-low, low, wide, narrow), as well as four directions (level, fall, rise, rise-fall), and other prosodic and paralinguistic features (slow, short, long, loud, sung, squeak, frictional, glottalized). Range is particularly important in his study, this (mid versus low, later high) being used far more often in the identification of early items than is direction. Given these kinds of variability, it is therefore very much an open question as to what different scholars are thinking of phonetically when they talk about "falling" versus "rising" contours and the like. The notion of "sentence prosody," pivotal in the above debate, cannot be taken as a primitive term.

Likewise, the situational concepts introduced into the debate cannot be taken as self evident. In much the same way as has been argued for syntax and segmental phonology (Howe, 1976; Lenneberg, 1967), it is necessary to free the mind from the constraints of adult language studies, where situational notions such as "question," "command," and "statement" are normal. Given some precise notion of "rise" versus "fall," it will not always (ever?) be the case that the semantic specifications of this contrast will be identical to those required for the analysis of the contrast in the adult language. Halliday, once again, provides cases where it is evident that the child's use of the pitch contrast is not the same (e.g., 1975, pp. 29, 52). For a while, his child used rising tones for all "pragmatic" utterances (those requiring a response, in his terms), and falling tones for all "mathetic" utterances (those not requiring a response). In a child studied at Reading, the falling-rising tone was initially used only in smiling-face contexts, with a generally "playful" meaning, and never to express doubt or opposition with a frowning or neutral face, as it frequently does in adults. In another case (see Crystal, 1971), a child began to use English as if it were a tone language, in certain limited respects, e.g., he referred consistently to any vehicles that made an engine noise as "bus," with a low falling tone, but when a *real,* big, red, double-decker bus went by, he would say "bus" with a wide rising-falling tone. It would seem, on the basis of examples such as these, that we are but at the beginning of seeing the child "in his own terms" with respect to the tonal features of his intonation system.

Tonicity and Two-Word Utterance   Tonicity (or "contrastive stress," as it is often misleadingly called) becomes apparent around 18 months, as two-word utterances appear (Bloom, 1973; Brown, 1973; Clark, Hutcheson, and Van Buren, 1974, p. 49). There seems to be general agreement about the developmental process, at least in outline. First, lexical items that have appeared independently as single-element utterances, marked thus by pitch and pause, are brought into collocational relationship. At first, the lexical items retain their prosodic autonomy, with the pause between them becoming reduced, e.g., /teddy/ chair/. Often, long sequences of these items appear, especially repetitively, e.g., /man/ there/ man/ there/. Such sequences are unanalyzable into conventional grammatical/semantic relations. There is no nonarbitrary way of demarcating pairs or triples of these items to fit in with contemporary models of meaning-relations, etc. Word order, at this point, seems to be far more random than was expected in the early linguistic studies of syntactic acquisition (cf. the summary in Brown, 1973).

The next step is the intonational integration of sequences of items, usually two, into a single tone-unit. The empirical evidence for this step is extremely limited, but it is a common subjective impression among those working in this field. One item is made more prominent than the other(s); it is the only one to have an identifiable pitch movement—there is a rhythmic (isochronous, for English) relationship between the items, and intervening pauses become less likely in repeated versions of lexical sequences. This step is considered to be of central theoretical importance, either for the notion of meaning-relation or grammatical sentence, e.g., Brown (1973, p. 182):

> What expressive means does the child employ in talking about the relations he understands? Most generally the simple concatenation under one utterance contour of the words which interact to create a compositional meaning that is different from the meanings of the two words in sequence.

There are problems here, however: "There is no problem ordinarily in distinguishing a two-word utterance from two single-word utterances because the child ordinarily controls prosodic features which make the difference obvious even to the phonetically untrained" (Brown, p. 148). If only this were so. The awkward fact is, however, that samples of data regularly produce sequences like the following:

1. /gírl/   /slèeping/   (picture of girl sleeping)
2. /gírl/   /pìano/   (picture of girl at a piano)
3. /gírl/   /bòy/   (picture of a girl and a boy)
4. /gírl/   /nò/   (picture of a girl-like thing)
5. /gírl/   /gìrl/   (picture of a girl)

The intonation and pause patterns may be identical in each case—for the sake of argument, let us say the more prominent item is the second—so if one is being consistent, the reasoning that would lead one to set up a compositional meaning for the first sentence (plausibly subject + verb, or some such specification) has to be used for the others. One cannot bring in intonation as a discovery procedure at one place, and then leave it out whenever the compositional meanings that as a result would appear do not seem to be permitted by one's a priori views as to what meaning relations can be. However, this seems to be what happens in the literature. Everyone would accept the legitimacy of the analysis of the first "sentence," but as one proceeds down the list, decisions become more and more uncertain—(2) locative?, (3) coordinative??, (4) corrective???, (5) repetitive??? Indeed, there will be a point at which situational factors will intervene and suggest the absurdity of searching for a single sentential interpretation, when all that is happening is that there are two sentences being said in a hurry. The adult language provides countless cases: /yes I'm hère/, /I'm terribly sorry I'm late the bùs was late/, etc. In the case of the child, where syntactic controls are lacking, the whole argument is thrown back onto the criteria of situation ± parental interpretation, which are notorious in their indeterminacy, as has been observed.

Despite these problems, several scholars have gone on to analyze data at this stage within some kind of contrastive semantic framework. Brown, for example, claims that one can distinguish *that book* as being Determiner + Noun as opposed to Subject + Complement on suprasegmental grounds, the first being ` ı, the second ıı. Wieman (1976), following up reports by Bowerman (1973) and others, observes that certain syntagmas tend to have predictable stress (e.g., Possessive + Noun has the possessive stressed, Subject + Object has the object stressed). In her data, again, she found that Verb + Locative always had the locative element stressed, whatever the syntactic category (e.g., *coming* up, *play* museum, and that this was a more consistent feature than word order (e.g., rug *jumped,* said as the child jumped from a box onto a rug). There are considerable difficulties in working in this way, however. For instance, Wieman (1976) reports that Agent + Verb combinations always had stress on the verb, but adds, "an agent was never stressed by any of the children in a non-contrastive, non-emphatic utterance." How is this to be determined? How is the notion of personal emphasis to be verified? The same point applies to Wieman's general theory, that new information in a sentence affects the stress placement, whereas old information does not, e.g., *One marble missing. See*

marble breaks the expected Verb + Object pattern, because *marble* is old information the second time. How does one know that what is new to the observer, interpreting the situation in terms of adult expectancies, is also going to be new to the
child? Wieman's theory predicts that having been told to wash hands, the child will
say, e.g., /*my hànds*/ *dírty hand*/, but this author has several examples of the type
/*nòt wanna wash hands*/ *not clean my hànds*/. Wieman would presumably say that
this was therefore contrastive, but this would only be so by definition, and the
dangers of circularity are evident.

   There are, of course, several well-recognized difficulties in working with any
theory of the "given-new" type (cf. other informational dichotomies, such as topic/
comment, rheme/theme), all of which emerge with force in the case of intonation.
For instance, after one makes the initial distinction (assuming this to be possible),
then what? How does one analyze types or degrees of newness or oldness, and thus
make the theory fruitful in hypotheses? What does one do with compound tones,
such as /*I mìght kíck that ball*/? It seems to me that there is a great deal of detailed
analytic work that needs to be done before we can proceed to the stage of utilizing
theories of this kind in the analysis of intonation. There are, on the other hand, some
extremely specific hypotheses that need to be investigated, e.g., that tonicity
contrasts signal the development of the child's awareness of lexical sets (e.g., color
terms, as in /*I gotta réd brick*/ *you gotta grèen one*/) or grammatical systems (as
with possessive pronouns in /*mý brick*/ *yòur brick*/). Certainly such uses develop
long before the use of tonicity to mark personal emphasis or other affective states,
as in the adult /*yóu*/ *múst*/ *gó*/ *nòw*/.

   To trace the subsequent development of the relationships between tone-units,
tonicity, and tone is a major task that the literature largely ignores. To an appreci-
able extent, it largely depends on the prior understanding of the acquisition of grammatical and social awareness—e.g., one can discuss the intonation of relative clauses
at that point in development when the corresponding syntactic patterns emerge.
What perhaps needs emphasizing is that full learning of the various functions of
intonation takes several years. Cruttenden (1974), for example, has recently pointed
out that the more subtle contrasts involved in the use of pitch range and direction
are still being acquired at around age nine, and work on the later development of
syntax and semantics is continually referring to the role of intonation in marking
such things as person reference and contrastive order, e.g., /*John gave a book to
Jím*/ *and hĕ*/ *gave one to hìm*/, /*it was in Woòlworth's I said I'd meet you*/.

IMPLICATIONS FOR STUDIES OF DISABILITY

It is not usually appreciated how pervasive intonation is in the study of language
disability. The notion of *dysprosody* is widely recognized, but little classification of
dysprosodic types has taken place, and the specific problems caused by intonation in
the analysis and remediation of speech and language disorders have been little investigated. The main reason for this is a failure to distinguish clearly, within the clinical
literature, between the linguistic and the nonlinguistic functions of pitch. It is
generally assumed that a pitch disability (e.g., excessive height, monotone,

repetitiousness) will be the result of a more general pathological condition, such as hearing loss or voice disorder. Apart from such phonetic disorders of pitch, however, one must allow for phonological disorders, where the use of pitch is abnormal (but with no evident anatomical, physiological, or neurological malfunction to account for it), and where contrasts normally available in the language are unable to be expressed.

In addition to the conceptual confusion that exists, there is also the regrettable fact that negligible descriptive work has been carried out. It is rare to find samples of data transcribed intonationally—where an impressionistic, ambiguous, punctuation is used instead (e.g., words in capitals, the use of triple dots, exclamation marks). The field, in other words, reflects the situation as it existed in general linguistics several years ago, and improvements are likely only with the development of more systematic courses of training for clinical practitioners than are normally available. Enough anecdotal information is available, however, to see the general directions in which research in this field should move.

The formal and functional frameworks proposed in the earlier part of this paper can be used in order to suggest a preliminary classification of the main types of intonational disability. All four functional types are affected—grammatical, semantic, attitudinal, and social—although the most noticeable problems, affecting the intelligibility of the utterance, relate to the first two. Specific abnormal patterns relating to each of the formal intonational categories can be found. In relation to the use of tone-units, for example, disordered speech may display two very different tendencies: a patient (P) may overuse tone-units, giving the impression of speaking a word at a time, or tone-units may be underused, giving the impression of speaking without paying attention to punctuation. A sequence of tone-units may also be abnormal if it introduces inappropriate contrasts in pitch range, such as giving a main clause (containing the central "information" of an utterance) a low pitch range relative to the surrounding level, and thus giving an impression of parenthesis. Under the heading of tonicity, it is common to find structures in which the wrong item is stressed (e.g., *one* egg *or two, it* was *nice*), as well as patterns that show that P has not taken into account the linguistic context of his utterance (e.g., *Who's got a ball?* P: *The man's got a* ball.). Under the heading of tone, one may find confusion of both pitch direction and pitch range, e.g., using a falling tone instead of a rising one, thus losing the contrast between continuity and finality (and making it difficult, for instance, to know whether an utterance is finished). A further example from one child was *me got ŏne,* where the falling-rising tone replaced the negative element in expressing the meaning *I haven't got one.*

In remediation, the role of the teacher or therapist (T) in maintaining controlled intonation patterns is crucial. T needs to avoid varying intonation tunes too much, especially with a P in the early stages of language development. Bearing in mind the tendency of children at these stages to respond to the intonational rather than the verbal aspects of utterances, altering the intonation of a set of stimulus sentences is often tantamount to presenting quite different utterances to the child. The intonational profile of /the ˈman's ˈkicking the bàll/ and /the màn's ˈkicking the ˈball/, to a child, especially one with restricted perceptual and comprehension skills, would be very different. An illustration of the way in which a varied stimulus can condition an abnormal response is, T: *There's a càt. It's a lìttle cat.* P: *There lìttle.* Another example came from a drill sequence being used by T: *It's a Nòun. What is it?* P: *It's a Nòun.* After several of these, T switched to *It's an Àdjective Noun,* and P, instead of following the syntax/semantics, followed the intonation, producing *It's an Àdjective.*

Several other examples of the use and treatment of abnormal intonation patterns can be found in Crystal, Fletcher, and Garman, 1976, Chapters 7 and 8. However, the role of intonation in facilitating the development and use of lexicon and grammar in the various clinical conditions has received hardly any systematic study, and it is difficult to generalize on the basis of examples such as these. The function of intonation in developing sequencing, recall, memory, and other abilities has also attracted some attention (e.g., Goodglass, Fodor, and Schulhoff, 1967; Stark, Poppen, and May, 1967), but the studies are again very restricted. It is to be hoped that, with further descriptive and experimental studies, a proper empirical perspective for discussing the theoretical issues raised in this paper will emerge.

REFERENCES

Bloom, L. 1973. One Word at a Time. Mouton, The Hague.
Blount, B. G. 1970. The pre-linguistic system of Luo children. Anth. Ling. 12: 326–42.
Bolinger, D. L. 1949. Intonation and analysis. Word 5: 248–54.
Bolinger, D. L. 1972. Accent is predictable (if you're a mind-reader). Lg 48: 633–44.
Bowerman, M. 1973. Early syntactic development. C.U.P., London.
Bresnan, J. W. 1971. Sentence stress and syntactic transformations. Lg 47: 257–81.
Brown, R. 1973. A First Language. Harvard University Press, Cambridge.
Bruner, J. S. 1975a. The ontogenesis of speech acts. J. Child Lang. 2: 1–19.
Bruner, J. S. 1975b. From communication to language: A psychological perspective. Mimeographed.
Carlson, P., and Anisfeld, M. 1969. Some observations on the linguistic competence of a two-year-old child. Child Dev. 40: 569–75.
Chomsky, N. 1970. Deep structure, surface structure and semantic interpretation. In R. Jakobson and S. Kawamoto (eds.), Studies in General and Oriental Linguistics, pp. 52–91. Tokyo.
Clark, R. 1974. Performing without competence. J. Child Lang. 1: 1–10.
Clark, R. 1975. Review of L. Bloom (1973). J. Child Lang. 2: 169–83.
Clark, R., Hutcheson, S., and Van Buren, P. 1974. Comprehension and production in language acquisition. J. Linguist. 10: 39–54.
Cruttenden, A. 1974. An experiment involving comprehension of intonation in children from 7 to 10. J. Child Lang., 1: 221–31.
Crystal, D. 1969. Prosodic Systems and Intonation in English. C.U.P., London.
Crystal, D. 1971. Prosodic systems and language acquisition. In P. Léon (ed.), Prosodic Feature Analysis pp. 77–90. Didier, Montreal.
Crystal, D. 1973. Non-segmental phonology in language acquisition: A review of the issues. Lingua 32: 1–45.
Crystal, D. Review of R. Brown (1973). J. Child Lang. 1: 289–307.
Crystal, D. 1975. The English Tone of Voice. Edward Arnold, London.
Crystal, D., Fletcher, P., and Garman, M. 1976. The Grammatical Analysis of Language Disability. Edward Arnold, London.

Dore, J. 1975. Holophrases, speech acts and language universals. J. Child Lang. 2: 21–40.

Eisenson, J., Auer, T., and Irwin, J. 1963. The Psychology of Communication. New York.

Fridman, R. 1974. Los comienzos de la conducta musical. Paidos, Buenos Aires.

Friedlander, B. Z. 1970. Receptive language development in infancy: Issues and problems. Merrill Palmer Quart. 16: 7–51.

Fries, C. C. 1964. On the intonation of 'yes-no' questions in English. In D. Abercrombie, (eds.), In Honour of Daniel Jones, pp. 242–54. Longman, London.

Goodglass, H., Fodor, I. G., and Schulhoff, C. 1967. Prosodic factors in grammar—evidence from aphasia. J. Speech Hear. Res. 10: 5–20.

Halliday, M. A. K. 1975. Learning How to Mean. Edward Arnold, London.

Howe, C. J. 1976. The meanings of two-word utterances in the speech of young children. J. Child Lang. 3: 29–47.

Kaplan, E. L. 1970. Intonation and language acquisition. Papers and Reports on Child Lang. Dev. 1: 1–21.

Keenan, E. O. 1974. Conversational competence in children. J. Child Lang. 1: 163–83.

Kopczynski, G. 1975. Contribution à l'étude des structures prosodiques chez les enfants de 1 à 2 ans. Proc. VIII. Cong. Phon. Sci. Leeds.

Lenneberg, E. H. 1967. Biological Foundations of Language. Wiley, New York.

Lewis, M. M. 1936. Infant speech. Routledge and Kegan Paul, London.

Menyuk, P. 1971. The acquisition and development of language. Prentice-Hall, Englewood Cliffs.

Menyuk, P., and Bernholtz, N. 1969. Prosodic features and children's language production. MIT QPR 93: 216–19.

Olney, R. L., and Scholnick, E. K. 1976. Adult judgments of age and linguistic differences in infant vocalization. J. Child Lang., 3.

Quirk, R., and Crystal, D. 1966. On scales of contrast in English connected speech. In C. E. Bazell, (eds.), In Memory of J. R. Firth, pp. 359–69. Longman, London.

Quirk, R., Greenbaum, S., Leech, G., and Svartvik, J. 1972. A Grammar of Contemporary English. Longman, London.

Richards, M. (ed.). 1974. The Integration of a Child into a Social World. C.U.P., London.

Sachs, J., and Devin, J. 1976. Young children's use of age-appropriate speech styles in social interaction and role-playing. J. Child Lang. 3: 81–98.

Stark, J., Poppen, R., and May, M. Z. 1967. Effects of alterations of prosodic features on the sequencing performance of aphasic children. J. Speech Hear. Res. 10: 844–48.

Stark, R. E., Rose, S. N., and McLagen, M. 1975. Features of infant sounds: The first eight weeks of life. J. Child Lang. 2: 205–21.

Weir, R. 1962. Language in the Crib. Mouton, The Hague.

Weir, R. 1966. Some questions on the child's learning of phonology. In F. Smith and G. Miller (eds.), The Genesis of Language, pp. 153–168. MIT Cambridge.

Wieman, L. A. 1976. Stress patterns of early child language. J. Child Lang. 3.

Learning to Pronounce:
The Earliest Stages
of Phonological Development
in the Child

Charles A. Ferguson

The human child learns the language or languages of the speech community in which he grows up. This is the fact to be explained, as many linguistic and psycho-linguistic investigators of child language see it. How does the child manage to acquire mastery of the incredibly complex phenomena of natural human language? Whether or not this feat is, as Jespersen (1922) once claimed, the greatest intellectual achievement of every individual's life, it is certainly impressive, and no current linguistic theory is capable of adequately specifying the nature of language, just as no psychological theory is capable of adequately accouting for the processes of acquisition. During the decade 1960–1970, most of the psycholinguistic research on language development focused on the development of syntax and, to a lesser extent, phonology—often in relation to explicit theories of grammar and notions of innate language universals. The empirical results led investigators increasingly to question the centrality of syntax in development, the correctness of the grammatical theories, and the specifically linguistic nature of the child's innate capabilities for language acquisition. The key words in psycholinguistic study of child language now are semantics, pragmatics, speech acts, communicative competence, cognition, interaction, and individual differences, and the new approaches are proving fruit-ful—children, after all, are essentially "learning to mean," as Halliday (1975) puts it, rather than acquiring syntax and phonology. What is sometimes overlooked, however, in the euphoria of the apparent success in our research, is that the acquisi-tion of syntax and phonology has become even more mysterious. If the child could learn to *mean* without all the intricacies of adult syntax and phonology, why (and how) does he acquire them, and how does it happen that natural languages exhibit substantive universals of syntax and phonology (cf. Greenberg, 1966)? This paper explores at least the early stages in the acquisition of phonology with the goal that such tentative conclusions as are reached will aid both the specification of

273

phonological systems and the understanding of processes of language development (i.e., linguistic and psycholinguistic theory). The explorations may also be suggestive for the question of assessment, which is the ultimate concern of this volume.

First, let it be made clear that no explicit theory of phonological development is being endorsed or proposed. In another paper (Ferguson and Garnica, 1975), current theories were examined and found wanting, and the recommendation was made that researchers should work on concrete hypotheses and narrowly focused empirical studies before attempting to construct comprehensive theories. If the present paper is going against the letter of that recommendation with the generality of its approach, it is following the spirit of the recommendation by offering only a description, an "account," of early phonological development as a stimulus to further empirical studies and eventually to more ambitious theorizing.

Phonological development has been surveyed from a linguistic point of view on a number of occasions, and it will help to explain the orientation and biases of the present paper if it is noted that this author finds Leopold's second volume still the most comprehensive study of phonological development (Leopold, 1947), Menyuk's phonology chapter the most convenient review of research since Leopold (Menyuk, 1971, Chapter 3), and Ingram's summary of normal acquisition the most congenial recent statement (Ingram, 1976, Chapter 2); Ferguson and Farwell (1975) come nearest to the author's present views on early stages of acquisition. Macken (1974) is a good selective list of readings, and the references in Ferguson and Garnica (1975) constitute a basic bibliography in the field up to 1974.

GETTING THE IDEA

During the first 18 months to two years of his life, the normal child lays the foundation for the amazingly rapid and sure development toward mastery of his mother tongue that takes place during the next several years, and continues at a less dramatic pace throughout the rest of his life. The foundations laid during the first period are so basic and universal that it is hard to see in them much of the linguistic structure that characterizes the particular language of the community in which the child is growing up. However, this early period is correspondingly important because it is during this time that universal human capabilities and the range of possible individual variation are exemplified—both to a considerable extent independently of the particular phonological and grammatical structure of the input language. Unfortunately, this early language development is even more difficult to study and analyze than the following stage, which itself offers the practicing linguist or psycholinguist problems enough. The account given here is of necessity based on scattered sources of varying merits, and not on a broad base of established research findings.

Development of Perception

One problem in the study of early phonological development is the special difficulty of investigating the perception side, as opposed to the production side, which is so much more accessible. Many linguist observers of child language tend to ignore the early development of perception altogether. Jakobson (1968), whose important linguistic work on phonological development has stimulated and inspired so many subsequent studies, hardly discusses perception at all, except in a single important paragraph (pp. 22–23). Halliday, in a highly original and noteworthy recent linguistic treatment of language development, writes of this early period: "The language that is learnt at this stage owes nothing at all to the adult language that the child hears around him, [although] the child *may* use imitations of the adult phonology as part of the resources for expressing meaning" (Halliday 1975, p. 9). Halliday has in mind the vocables of his own son at this stage, which in general have no adult models, and ignores the fact that a child in this period "understands" (i.e., responds consistently to) many words of the adult language and distinguishes between phonetically similar adult expressions. In this attempt to follow both perception and production and the relations between them, we must depend largely on earlier accounts such as Lewis (1963) for our longitudinal material on perception. In order to follow the development with one child and avoid the complications of different languages and nonrelated examples, the illustrative examples are cited, to the extent feasible, from Lindner (1898), one of the most informative of the older diary studies; it follows the boy Hans from birth to age four as he acquires German as his mother tongue.

During the early period of the child's language development, his linguistic perception, as inferred from naturalistic observation, develops from the ability to distinguish between speech and nonspeech to a capability of perceiving subtle differences in the prosodic and segmental phonetics of the language around him. The child's auditory discrimination abilities are already impressive shortly after birth (for a review of the growing literature on neonate speech-sound discrimination, cf. Eimas 1974; Morse, 1974; and Morse, this volume), but the child must learn to perceive linguistically, i.e., to use sound differences consistently to identify and store words so that they can be recognized later and eventually be called up for production.

The first steps in this development are the perception of speech versus nonspeech, and the identification of "tones of voice," nonsegmental complexes that identify calling to the child, soothing him, singing, or the like. Hans Lindner, from the ninth day, responded in special ways to speech addressed to him. He stopped crying when spoken to, and not just at the coming of a caregiver; he opened his eyes when spoken to, but he kept them closed when his father clapped his hands in his presence. He reacted to a call by directing his eyes to the speaker, but it was the "tone of voice," not his name that prompted the reaction: even several months later he still reacted identically to his own name and to his sister's name (Olga) when said in the same calling tone.

The next step is the recognition of a particular phonetic shape and the appropriate occasion for its use, i.e., the connection between sound and meaning that is the basis of the lexical aspect of language. Hans's first clear instance of this was *ticktack,* in reference to a loudly ticking wall clock that his parents lifted him up to hear every day as they carefully enunciated the German equivalent of *tick-tock.* At 20th weeks, he first responded to the stimulus *ticktack* by turning his eyes toward the clock when he was lying in his crib; in four weeks time he was regularly responding correctly in this way to *ticktack.* Many speech communities have game routines for infants that consist of a verbal cue expression and a simple hand or hand and head action, such as our *pat-a-cake, bye-bye,* and *peek-a-boo.* The next step after recognizing items like *ticktack* is learning to respond to one or more of these game cues with the appropriate motions. A week after Hans was regularly reacting to *ticktack* by directing his gaze to the clock, he had learned to do the motion for *Händchengeben—give handie*. At first, the identification of the phonetic shape in these early recognized signs is in terms of such gross features as length, number of syllables, intonation, and place of accent, but it develops toward greater use of the finer segmental features (Fradkina, 1955; Lewis, 1936, pp. 114–116). Lewis cites a nice example of the transition from Schäfer (1922): at 0;9,7 his son responded to *mache bitte bitte, make please-please* (i.e., clap your hands to get something), when said with exaggerated baby-talk intonation, at 0;10,0 he responded to *bitte bitte* said in ordinary tone of voice, and at 0;10,9 clapped at the nonsense stimulus *kippe kippe* in baby-talk intonation, but not at *lala lala* in the same rhythm and intonation, giving evidence of his recognition of the phonetic similarity of *bitte* and *kippe* as opposed to *lala*.

The question of how fine the linguistic perception is at this stage remains open. At least it is clear that the child can notice a familiar phonetic shape embedded in a larger utterance and respond to it. Hans Lindner, in his 11th month, responded with pat-a-cake motions not only to *backe Kuchen, bake cake,* but to *backe doch einmal Kuchen, bake then once cake* (that is, come on do pat-a-cake), in which the two elements were separated, and to *backe* or *Kuchen* alone. This ability varies greatly in older second language learners, and there may be important individual differences here that are related to success in language acquisition. In an incident about five months later, Hans gave striking evidence of this ability to attend to a familiar item in the midst of unintelligible material. He was familiar with the word *butter,* and was accustomed to bringing the butter to his mother when she sliced bread. One day his father was peeling a pear for him, and he said, "Das ist eine Napoleonsbutterbirne," "That's a Napoleon butter-pear"—and Hans ran off to get the butter. It is also clear that even at this early stage the child can distinguish two meaningful parts of an utterance. Thus Hans could respond appropriately to *Wo ist die Mieze?—Where's the kitty?—*and *Wie macht es die Mieze?—How does the kitty go?* The former is one of a set of "where is?" questions (e.g., *Wo ist die Ticktack?*) to which he responded by looking at the right place. The other is one of a set of "how does X go?" questions, (e.g., *Wie macht es die Fabrik?—How does the factory go?—*referring to its noontime whistle), to which he responded by making an appropriate noise. Even if some of the burden of the distinction was on the tone of voice or paralinguistic aspects of the utterance, clearly two meaningful elements are recognized.

Very few studies throw much light on this question of the degree of phonetic difference that children utilize linguistically at this period. Shvachkin, and others who use his minimal-pair nonsense-word research technique (Barton, 1976; Edwards, 1974; Garnica, 1973; Shvachkin, 1948), hardly reaches down to this age, and the research method itself has many problems. Once again we must depend on anecdotal evidence. Hans offers one interesting case of phonetic confusion, but the phonetic similarity is accompanied by strong semantic similarity, and the case may not do justice to the question. In the 49th week, Hans was asked at the table to *bete auch mit, pray also with*—i.e., to (fold his hands and) join the others in table prayer, but to his father's surprise he clapped his hands as though he had been asked to make *bitte-bitte*. The confusion is evident, but the phonetic similarity of *bete : bitte*, the similarity of the hand motions, and the fact that *bitte-bitte* is usually done before getting a piece of cake or other food and the table-prayer is said just before getting food, may all be factors in the confusion. One useful way of getting evidence on his question would be to encourage phonetically sophisticated parents and caregivers to try to evoke revealing incidents based on their knowledge of the linguistic repertoires of particular children. (Two of the best accounts, by Deville and Lewis, are reported in Lewis, 1936, pp. 106–109, 300–301; Vihman, 1976 also gives valuable examples).

As mentioned above, it is not easy to determine the young child's linguistic repertoire in the sense of those sound-meaning correspondences of the input language that he has identified and stored and can utilize for recognition. The parent's fond belief that "he understands every word we say to him," and the speech scientist's skepticism about the child's linguistic perception in the absence of evidence from production are equally unhelpful. Some rough idea of the extent of such repertoires may come from several of the diary studies that have acknowledged this question, but the information is much more fragmentary than the production data they provide. At Hans's 30th week, his father reported that he definitely recognized *ticktack*, his own name as distinct from the names of others around him, the names of his doll and the cat, and the word *gingein, glug-glug* (drink). The last item is an example of the well-known phenomenon of a word created by the family on the basis of a sound made by the child, in this case in connection with drinking; the "word" was then learned and recognized by Hans from the family's use of it. This list is probably incomplete, because at least *Händchengeben* (*gib Händchen!*) is also attested. A few weeks later, his father reported that Hans definitely recognized the word for teeth (he had just had a painful two weeks of teething problems), but that he kept learning for the moment and forgetting a number of other body parts (nose, eye, ear, mouth). At the beginning of the 15th month, when the father recorded a current inventory of recognized command, the list was : go, come, stand up, listen, smell, give, speak, and say, and the questions: where is? how does X go? how does it taste? (*wie schmeckt's*? answered by a special click sound). At that time he doubtless also had names of objects and people, game-cues, and other items in his recognition vocabulary. This was at a time when Hans's total active lexicon consisted of only a handful of items (*mamam, m̄, ā, da,* see below). At the beginning of the 18th month, when the father attempted another inventory, he reported that Hans knew the names of most of the objects in his room and the kitchen, i.e., he could either point to them or bring them on request. He also recognized these verbs: come, go, be (in a place), fetch, bring, catch, eat, drink, sleep, close eyes, lift up, hold, wash, go in the water (*eintauchen*), dry off, put (*legen*), stand up, give, take, laugh, cry, hear, listen, want, "and many others." He knew hot, wet, dirty, tired, away (absent); and who, what, where, where to (*wohin*), and how. This inventory is undoubtedly only partial, but it gives some notion of Hans's ability to make linguistic use of phonetic differences in perception and memory. At that time he had an active vocabulary of about a dozen items, discussed below.

Intonation and Speech Rhythm

Before moving to a discussion of the phonological development of production in the young child, the important questions of intonation and speech rhythm should be mentioned. It is widely accepted that the development of the infant's use of intonation starts earlier and proceeds more rapidly than the development of his "segmental" phonology, but no studies seriously pursue this question on the perception side. Existing studies either tap the child's auditory discrimination ability (e.g., Kaplan, 1969), or his phonetic differences in production (e.g., Menyuk and Bernholtz, 1969; Tonkova-Yampol´skaya, 1968). Crystal's thorough review of the literature on intonation and related phenomena in first language acquisition offers very little on early perception (Crystal, 1975, pp. 125–138), and his chapter in this volume, although helpful as a frame of reference, offers few examples. This whole prosodic issue—both perception and production—is likely to be crucial in our understanding of language development, and now that the lack of a suitable descriptive and analytic framework is being remedied (cf. e.g., Crystal, 1969; 1975; Lehiste, 1970, Vanderslice and Ladefoged, 1972), perhaps the problem of adequate research techniques can be solved. The area of timing and rhythm, also likely to be important and perhaps assessable and diagnostic, is even less well treated (Allen, 1976).

Development of Production

During the early period, the child's linguistic production, as described by a variety of observational, analytical, and experimental techniques, develops from the early "cooing" or "comfort sounds" (Lewis, 1936, pp. 30–33) through an extensive period of babbling to the active control of a small set of meaningful vocables with incipient phonological organization. If we disregard the crying and "fussing" vocalizations because their relevance to phonological development is questionable and at best indirect, the first vocalizations on the way to phonologically organized speech are presumably the back sounds (e.g., velar fricatives and continuants, central and back vowels), called "cooing," that typically appear in the second month. In many speech communities, this kind of vocalization is conventionalized as the baby's "first word" or "first sound." Thus, in a large part of the Arabic-speaking world, the baby's first sound is expected to be [nkɨɣ]. The Arab mother often playfully says this "word" to her child and "recognizes" it when the child says something like it (Ferguson, 1956). In the English-speaking world, there is some tendency to expect *goo* or *coo* as an early sound (cf. the term "cooing"), and among German speakers there is a fairly widespread expectation that the first baby sound will be *ärrä* or *arra*. Accordingly, it is not surprising that Lindner recorded the first cooing of Hans on his 59th day as *ärrä* or *arra* (the Sterns report *erre* for their children, Preyer reports *örro, arra* for his son). All these conventionalized "first sounds" contain velar or postvelar voiced consonants and non-high-front vowels; they provide a convenient normalization of the infant's varied productions, and may even serve as an imitation facilitator in the early months' vocalizations.

Two explanations have been given for the early predominance of back sounds. The older, traditional view is that the pleasurable vocalizations usually occur after feeding when the infant is lying on his back, and are produced by swallowing and air-expelling movements associated with feeding, involving the back of the tongue and velum, which are also favored by the reclining position (Lewis, 1936, pp. 30–32). The newer view is that the progression of myelination in the primary motor cortex proceeds from back of the mouth to front in the "homunculus," and as a consequence the child's neuromuscular control of the vocal tract progresses from the back parts of the mouth to the front (Salus and Salus, 1974; Whitaker 1973).

Babbling   The next step is babbling. The cooing sounds diversify, and a wide range of sounds are produced, often apparently as a kind of oral play. The baby may produce clicks, grunts, and sounds hard to identify phonetically, as well as more vowel-like and consonant-like sounds alone and in sequences. The sounds of the child's babbling often differ strikingly from the speech sounds of the surrounding language because of at least three reasons: 1) the child's vocal tract differs considerably in size and configuration from the adult's, 2) the child has not yet acquired the basic motor control of articulation (breathiness, voicing, fundamental frequency, timing, nasality, etc.), and 3) the child has not yet acquired the phonological patterns of the language. During the typical six to eight months of the babbling period the child makes great progress on (2), and indeed this may be regarded as one of the accomplishments of the child's babbling "practice": by the end of the period, for example, spectrograms of the child's vowel sounds are beginning to look like recognizable vowels. The role of babbling in phonological development is often seen in either of two extreme views: a) the continuity view, which holds that the varied sounds of babbling are gradually shaped toward the sounds of the input language by selective reinforcement on the part of the parents and other speakers in the environment, and b) the discontinuity view, which holds that babbling is of little or no significance for phonological development and there is a sharp break between the random vocalizations of babbling and the more limited but highly structured productions of "true speech." Neither of these positions is tenable. On the one hand, the child may make sounds frequently and easily in his babbling that he is unable to make later in speech and must acquire slowly and with effort, and there is no convincing evidence of the kind of selective reinforcement for adult sounds that would be required. On the other hand, the child's babbling develops in the direction of adult speech, at least in terms of syllable structure and intonation, and there are often similarities between the syllable repetitions of late babbling and the reduplicated early words of the child (see Ferguson and Garnica, 1975; Oller, Wieman, Doyle, and Ross, 1976).

The development of Hans's babbling is a typical example of the progress in production during this period. In the third month, Hans's father noted that his babbling monologues became more frequent and the sounds in them more varied. Some sounds were produced "accidentally," and occurred only once (e.g., *bewe*), and others were frequently used favorites (e.g., *nging, ärre*); some were impossible for the father to identify or pronounce (e.g., *hrngl*). His progression in the use of babbling responses to speech addressed to him was typical: in the 30th week he would respond by repeating his babble sound when his mother or sister imitated it after him, in the 33rd week he would regularly respond with his own babbling when someone spoke to him, and in the 40th week he could imitate an adult *a* addressed to him. By the first month of his second year he was babbling strings of clear CV syllables with occasional V or CVC syllables (*mammam, papap, dadada, nanana, anna, dedededei*), the C's in all cases being labial or apical stops or nasals.

Early Vocables   The study of child language development usually moves from a consideration of babbling to a consideration of the "first word," or the earliest words in the child's active lexicon and the holophrastic period of one-word sentences. To make that jump, however, is to miss one of the most revealing periods in the development. At some point in the babbling period, the child typically begins to make active use of sound-meaning correspondences of his own, i.e., he produces a set of vocables that function communicatively much like the later "first words," but that are not based on words of the adult language. Although some investigators have commented on how difficult it is to recognize the true "first word," the significance of these linguistic creations of the child is generally missed. The active lexicon of the child at around the end of the first year, between 10 months and one year, two months depending on the child, typically consists of a dozen or so vocables of which only one or two are clearly based on adult words; most of the rest are apparently based on a nonspeech noise in the environment or a babbling sound originally uttered by the child in a certain context and used by him when the context recurs, or when he wants to allude to it. Halliday's son at about the 10th month is reported to have had 11 or 12 expressions in more or less consistent use, and only one of them, [bø], meaning roughly "give me my bird," had an obvious source in the adult language. See Dore, Franklin, Miller, and Ramer, 1976 (pp. 15–21) for a discussion of such vocables, which they call PCFs (phonetically consistent forms).

Hans Lindner at the 42nd week began saying a loud clear [ha] after he finished each mouthful of solid food; a few weeks later he was making various noises in response to *How does the* X *go?* and a click for *How does it taste?* In the first month of the second year, he had the clearest example of a vocable without adult model: a long *m̄* that meant in effect something like *Here comes a wagon* or *I hear a wagon coming.* At this same time, Hans used a series of short *ä*'s when pretending to read aloud from the newspaper his father had just put down, and also would say *mamam* (one of his babbling sequences) when someone said to him either *mama* or *papa.* This last is of special interest, because Hans definitely recognized the difference between *mama* and *papa* as referring to his mother and his father, but did not use them himself to call his parents, and had only the one form for both in his response to the adult elicitations. A month later *mamam* became *mama,* and he used it on his own initiative.

The early non-adult modeled vocables of the child tend to be of four phonetic types, in addition to clicks or other "nonspeech" sounds: 1) single or repeated vowel, 2) syllabic nasal, 3) syllabic fricative, and 4) single or repeated CV syllable, in which the C is a stop or nasal. Examples of these may be found in the detailed lists of Lewis (1936, pp. 302–303) and Halliday (1975, pp. 148–150). Many other examples are scattered throughout the literature, e.g., Roberto's *m* (von Raffler-Engel, 1964), and Hildegard's palatal click and ʃ (Leopold, 1947). Jakobson, in his *Kindersprache* (1968), regarded such examples as marginal, noting that marginal sounds may play a larger role in child phonology than adult phonology and may sometimes be the starting point for sounds of true speech.

The normal emergence of a small active lexicon of sound-meaning correspondences, largely without adult models, at a time when the child has a much larger passive lexicon of sound-meaning correspondences almost entirely with adult models, suggests three important characteristics of early phonological development:

1.   The child plays a highly active, creative role in the acquisition process. He "gets the idea" of having particular sound sequences "mean," i.e., that they should have appropriate occasions of use. He creates his own sound sequences from surrounding sounds (e.g., animal cries, sounds of wagons) or sources other than adult models. It cannot be assumed that this is always because the adult expression is too hard to remember or produce or because no adult model has come to his attention.
2.   The child's early vocables constitute a connecting link between babbling and adult-modeled speech. The early vocables are more limited and more structured than babbling and they only partly fit the constraints of the child's emergent phonological system. They are not babbling sounds being shaped toward adult sounds, but babbling-like sounds used meaningfully. Their use begins during the babbling period and continues into the stage of predominantly adult-modeled lexicon.
3.   At least in the early stages, the child's phonological systems for perception and production are relatively independent. At least as early as the sixth month, the child gives evidence of a phonological system for perception by distinguishing different words of the input language. Although the extent to which the differentiation may be whole word-shapes, intonation contours, word prosodies, syllables, or phoneme-length segments is not clear, it must be directly related to the phonetic characteristics of the adult words. The child's first meaningful vocables, however, typically consist of repeated vowels, syllabic consonants, and other sounds that are marginal or nonexistent in the adult phonology and that do not reflect systematic substitution processes in relation to the adult words. For a discussion of the plausibility of two phonological systems connected by a network of transduction relations that becomes denser as the child's language develops, see Ferguson, Peizer, and Weeks, 1973. A somewhat similar view is proposed for syntax in Bever, 1974, although with a different rationale.

EARLY WORDS

Beginning late in the nineteenth century and reaching a peak of activity in the 1920s and 1930s, students of child language development devoted critical attention to the characteristics of the child's "first words." This material is summarized in Bateman, 1917; Lewis, 1936; McCarthy, 1954; and a number of other places. The literature tends to disregard the early vocables not based on adult models, but it is valuable for the study of phonological development because these early words are the beginnings of control, on the production side, of the phonology the child is acquiring. It was to a considerable extent this literature that Jakobson utilized for examples in his *Kindersprache* (1968).

Because different observers have used different criteria for identifying the "first word" and generally each case is decided by a single observer, and because observers also differ greatly in the exactness of their phonetic descriptions, it is unwise to calculate precise statistics on the date of appearance and phonetic characteristics of the first words. It is probably safe to estimate, however, that the majority of children produce their first adult-modeled words between the 10th and 13th months, and that the majority of the first words are CV or reduplicated CVCV, in which the consonants are labial or apical stops or nasals. Lewis (1936), in his summary of the first words of 26 children as reported by various observers (using a maximum of six different words per child), figures that 75% of the words contain front consonants and 85% are either monosyllables or reduplicated.

Jakobson's impressive theory of phonological development claims that "the relative chronological order of phonological acquisitions remains everywhere and at all times the same" (Jakobson, 1968, p. 46). He specifies the very first word as "ordinarily" having the phonological structure /pa/, i.e., some kind of labial stop followed by some kind of low vowel. This structure is followed in succession by the opposition between oral and nasal stop and the opposition between labial and apical stop: 1) *pa*, 2) *mama : papa*, 3) *papa : tata, mama : nana*. This consonantal differentiation is then followed by the opposition between lower and higher vowel *a : i*. Jakobson's predictions of these early stages in phonological development are useful as a kind of idealized progression justified by underlying linguistic or psycholinguistic principles, but they are not borne out in the numerous diary studies available. At the present time, it is not even possible to give a statistical validation of his predicted order as the most frequent, partly because of the incomparability of the published studies. Certainly many children do not follow Jakobson's "universal order" at this early stage, if the observers' accounts are to be trusted. Even Velten (1943), one of the classic descriptions in terms of the Jakobson paradigm, requires an alternative possible order at this earliest stage to allow for his subject's acquisition of a stop-spirant opposition before stop-nasal.

Jakobson's contributions to the understanding of phonological development at the earliest stages are his insistence on the different phonological status of babbling and meaningful speech, on the orderliness of phonological development, and on the relationship between patterns of acquisition and the essential characteristics of the sound systems of human languages (cf. Ferguson, 1975c).

The Moskowitz view of early phonological development, which is a revision of the Jakobson theory, incorporates the reduplication phenomena in the universal order of acquisition (Moskowitz, 1973). She claims that the child's first phonological units of opposition are syllables, not phoneme-type segments as Jakobson suggests. The child first produces $\widehat{CV}$ and reduplicated $\widehat{CVCV}$ words, then produces $\widehat{CVCV}$ words with only consonant harmony or only vowel harmony

$C_i\widehat{VC_i}V$ or $\widehat{CV_i}\widehat{CV_i}$, and only arrives at phonemic segmentation when he can produce CVCV words without harmony of either kind. This predicted order of acquisition accounts for some behavior that Jakobson's theory does not explicitly predict, but it is also an idealized progression justified by underlying principles that is not borne out in the diary studies. Even Burling (1959), which Moskowitz cites as evidence for her theory, includes data that do not fit. The Moskowitz contributions are her insistence on the active role of the child in discovering contrastive units and on the gradual progression from larger word and syllable units to smaller cluster and phoneme units.

At the stage of the first words, the normal patterns of development can be summarized in terms of semantic and phonological probabilities as follows. Over a period of several months, the child acquires a small active lexicon of adult-modeled words appropriate to situations in the semantic fields of food, caregivers, sleep, deixis, animals, moving/noise-producing objects, toilet functions, pleasure, absence/departure. These words are most commonly CV or CVCV, less commonly VCV, CVC, CVCVC; they most commonly exhibit full reduplication, or syllable harmony (same syllables), or partial reduplication—either consonant harmony (same consonants) or vowel harmony (same vowels). A word may fluctuate considerably in pronunciation, most often in the following ways: final consonant present or absent, monosyllable or reduplication, or stop or spirant consonant articulation, voiced or voiceless, low central or mid-front vowel.

The semantic/pragmatic side is left to those such as Halliday, who describes his own son's development in English (Halliday, 1975), or Bates (1974), who follows the "gradual passage from vocalization, to vocalization-as-signal, to word-as-signal, to word as proposition with referential value" (p. 73) in two Italian children. The phonological side calls for discussion of the structural limitations and the variability of pronunciation.

Structural Limitations

The structural limitations are striking. Presumably, the child has in his long-term memory scores of adult expressions that are sufficiently identified phonetically for him to be able to recognize them when he hears them again. He also presumably has the ability to make a wide range of sound sequences in his babbling. His first adult-modeled vocables are severely constrained in phonetic shape, however. We may acknowledge that the stored representations are probably fuzzy and indeterminate in part and sometimes even wrong, i.e., misheard or misremembered. We must also acknowledge that there are structural constraints on babbling, e.g., consonant clusters and fricatives are rare, as are polysyllabic sequences with varied consonants. Even so, the production constraints suggest that the child, in building up a stock of lexical representations for production, is proceeding to develop step by step a phonological system structurally independent of the other two.

As the child begins to realize, as it were, the enormousness of the task of constructing his own production capacity the words of the adult vocabulary, he selects a few word types as a basis and avoids attempting other kinds of words, even if they are familiar items in his recognition store. The fact of selection and

avoidance, although sometimes noted earlier (e.g., Engel, 1965), has been largely ignored until fairly recently, but a succession of studies in the 1970s have documented
it and underlined its importance (Ferguson et al., 1973; Ferguson and Farwell 1975;
Kiparsky and Menn, 1977; Macken 1976, Vihman, 1976). The selection is in terms
of two parameters: 1) size and complexity of structure, and 2) segmental sound
types. On the first parameter, for example, one child may choose to attempt only
adult models of the shape CVCV ending in -ie/-y, such as *doggie, mommy, pat-a* (-
cake), *daddy* (Leslie, reported in Ferguson et al., 1973); another child may choose
only CV(C) words such as *see, that/there, juice, no, hi* (Jonathan, reported in
Braine, 1971). Many children probably select CVCV models in which the consonants are either identical or at least agree in place or in manner of articulation
(e.g., J, reported in Macken, 1976). On the parameter of sound types, for example,
children may choose only words beginning with labial or apical stops or nasals, i.e.,
they may avoid words beginning with fricatives or velars (Leopold, 1947). A
particular child, however, may choose to avoid adult words with nasals (Vihman,
1976) or even to prefer words with velars (Menn, 1971) or with fricatives (T, Ferguson and Farwell, 1975). The phenomenon of selection and avoidance continues
past the period of the very first words, and it is discussed below; the important point
here is the evidence it gives for the construction of the child's own production
phonology.

The word selection patterns are only part of the process; the other part is the
construction of word production patterns, and these may well be logically prior in
the sense that the selection patterns may be based on them. A child may, for
example, set up as his "canonical shape" a full reduplicated CVCV: Leslie, at 0;11
(Ferguson, et al 1973), generalized one of the consonants in the model and the first
vowel *doggie* → [gaga], *pat-a(-cake)* → [bæ bæ]. Another child may set up a CV
monosyllable of one sort or another: Jonathan (Braine, 1971) had *d*V as his pattern,
substituting *d* for the initial consonant of the model, copying the vowel
approximately, and dropping the final consonant *see* → [di:], *no* → [do]. Many
children have both CV and CVCV as production patterns, with internal constraints
on phonetic qualities. The use of CVC is probably more common as an early pattern
among children whose input language has such syllables (e.g., German as opposed to
Spanish learners). It is important to note that the production patterns appear also in
words without adult models, as in Leslie's [gæ gæ].

Hans Lindner's active lexicon in the 17th month had six adult-modeled words,
in chronological order of observed use, and appears in Table 1.

Hans's selection patterns were (C)V(C), reduplicated CVCV and CVC(C)ə; his
production patterns were (C)V, reduplicated CVCV and CVC. His first word, whose
CVC model ends in *s*, fluctuates among all three production patterns, finally settling
on *da~dat*. The reduplication models are copied, and the other disyllables are
produced as CVC, in which the consonantal onset and coda are the same stop,
voiced and voiceless respectively. All three of these production patterns are frequent
in children's early words.

The construction of favorite production patterns and the child's insistence on
fitting his selected models into them continue past this earliest period and are discussed, along with the increasing diversification of the patterns, below. For the

Table 1.   Hans Lindner's earliest words.

Age	Model	Gloss	Child's word	Gloss
1;2	*das*	"that"	da~de~ded~dada~dat	"look at that, I want that"
	Mama	"mommy"	mama	"mommy, daddy"
	Papa	"daddy"		
1;3	*ah*	"ah"	ā	"oh, mommy's all gone"
1;4	*Birne*	"pear"	bap	"pear, fruit, something good to eat"
	Gasse	"street"	gack = [gak]	"going out of the house"
1;5	*Wewe*	"weewee"	wēwē	"I've wet my diaper"
	Papa	"daddy"	papa	"daddy"

Data from Lindner, 1898.

moment, it suffices to note the separateness of the perception and production systems. The *mama:papa* mismatch of Hans is a good example and it is not an isolated, idiosyncratic instance. This pair of words, found in so many of the world's languages (Jakobson, 1967), is frequently combined in production even though the two words are distinct in perception, and initial m- and b-/p- occur in other patterns and in babbling.

Variability of Pronunciation

The words in the child's active lexicon vary in pronunciation. Some may be relatively constant and others may show extensive fluctuation, but the general fact of variation is important (see Ferguson and Farwell, 1975, for discussion and examples). Some variant pronunciations are "natural" in that they reflect the same kind of processes found in historical sound change and in the language interference of borrowing and second language learning, e.g., the dropping of final consonants and the substitution of stops for spirants, as in *dat~da* from model *das*. Other variation is less typical of sound change in general and is more clearly related to the child's perception and production skills and strategies. The two best documented types are reduplication of a monosyllable (e.g., *das* → *da~dada*) and segmental "migration," as when a final nasal in the model appears as an initial nasal in the child's pronunciation. Jakobson (1971, pp. 25–26) explains reduplication as a means of marking structured true speech as opposed to babbling; Moskowitz (1973) explains it as a framework within which segmental differentiation can take place. Waterson (1971 and elsewhere) explains the "migration" by the hypothesis of prosodic as opposed to segmental perception and production. Both phenomena need further study.

A final feature of the pronunciation of the earliest words must be noted; particular words or parts of words may not conform wholly to the child's characteristic production patterns. Thus, one word may be pronounced with an exactness quite out of line with the general level of phonological development (e.g., the classic example of Hildegard's *pretty*) or may be quite aberrant, as in Hans's *jjj* "sugar" (18th month, model *Zucker?*). This phenomenon is familiar to the foreign language teacher who has observed learners pronouncing particular words strikingly better than their general level of pronunciation or quite outside the system of the languages. In children's development, such "phonological idioms" (Moskowitz, 1973) sometimes seem to regress in that they may be temporarily brought into line with the child's current phonological system before finally returning to the more accurate pronunciation. For discussion of this phenomenon from different points of view, cf. Ferguson and Farwell, 1975; Kiparsky and Menn, 1977; Moskowitz, 1973.

Baby Talk

The child's earliest active lexicon, as characterized above by semantic fields and phonological constraints, has a counterpart in adult speech addressed to young children. Every speech community has special ways of talking to young children, including such modifications as higher pitch, shorter and simpler sentences, repetitions, hypocoristics, and attentionals (Ferguson, 1964; Snow and Ferguson, forthcoming), and "baby talk" (BT) of this kind includes a special lexicon of words that is regarded by the community as primarily appropriate for use to and by children. The semantic fields and phonological structure of these BT words tend to match those of the children's first words. Most BT words are conventionalized, i.e., are part of the total word stock of the community, transmitted by historical processes and diffusing from one speech community to another (e.g., BT *pap(p)a* "food" is attested in languages around the Mediterranean for 2000 years). For discussion and examples, cf. Ferguson, 1964. Apart from any functions BT words may have in the cognitive/semantic development of the child or in general socialization processes (Ferguson, 1975b), they may serve as appropriately simplified phonological models for early child vocabulary, and as such may play a useful (although presumably not a necessary) role in early phonological development.

The phenomena of selection/avoidance, production patterns, variability, and BT counterparts suggest the following additional important characteristics of early phonological development.

In the child's construction of a phonological system for production, he begins with structural constraints in selecting adult model words and in producing his own words. The constraints are typically in syllable structure and degree of phonetic diversity within the word. Although at this stage the constraints do not operate in phonemic terms (i.e., by contrastive segments composed of distinctive features), they foreshadow the complex regularities and constraints of adult phonological organization.

The baby talk lexicon of the child's speech community provides a reservoir of phonologically simplified models from which the child can draw for his early words. Although the child may select other adult models or fix on word-shapes of other origins, the BT lexicon is a major source of early words.

BUILDING A PHONOLOGY

The acquisition of the first fifty words has been selected, more or less arbitrarily, as a period in which to study phonological development by Ferguson and Farwell (1975), Pačesova (1968), and others. Ingram, however, in recent treatments of child phonology (1975, 1976), suggests that this period up to about the fiftieth word constitutes a natural stage in phonological development that is significantly different from what follows. In making this judgment, he relates phonological development to

Piagetian stages and, like a number of other recent studies of language development (e.g., Halliday, 1975, Nelson 1973), finds important linguistic phenomena that coincide roughly with the onset of symbolic representation at the end of Piaget's sensorimotor period of cognitive development. The insistence on differences between earlier and later phonological development is a healthy reaction. Some of the most impressive modern studies of phonological development (e.g., Moskowitz, 1970, Smith, 1973) have focused on the two- to four-year-old period, when it is possible to make statements about inventories, representations, and rules that are similar in kind to those made for adult phonologies, and the linguists' natural inclination has been to retroject the machinery of phonological analysis as far back as they can. Some linguists, for example, assume that the child's lexical representations (i.e., the form in which words are identified and stored) are at an early age essentially identical with the adult's, and that the improvement in pronunciation is caused either by gradually learning to produce distinctive features in various combinations and environments (e.g., Smith, 1973) or by gradually suppressing, limiting, or reordering innate natural phonological processes (Stampe, 1969). These approaches take phonetic segmentation, phonological organization, and linguistic perception for granted and leave little or no room for phonetic word-shapes, constraints on phonetic diversity within words, and individual differences in development, all of which are striking characteristics of phonological development in the early period of "the first fifty words."

Words and Sounds

Linguists' attempts to analyze the child's earliest utterances in terms of phonemic segments, oppositions, features, and rules have been useful in providing a framework for statements about phonological development, but recent longitudinal studies have given evidence that these units of analysis cannot have their adult value at this stage, and that other units are more basic. In particular, the total word seems to function as a phonetic unit, i.e., the child remembers and recognizes the phonetic shapes of whole words and articulates in terms of phonetic word-shapes. Thus, the "oppositions" in the child's system are at first in terms of words, and only gradually do the partial similarities and differences between words and within words come to be in terms of segmental identities and oppositions.

The evidence for the primacy of the word is of several kinds. First there is the obvious fact that individual words vary greatly in their stability of pronunciation. One word may be pronounced almost the same way for a long time while another word may show great fluctuation in pronunciation, even being pronounced in a number of different ways on the same occasion. Sometimes the more stable words have simpler and easier-to-pronounce adult models and the more variable words have more difficult models, but this is not always the case, and other factors are at work. For example, Hildegard's *Carolyn* was a stable [dada] for months, but *ball* fluctuated quite widely. Second, the phonetic ranges of word pronunciations make the establishment of phonemic oppositions very problematic. For example, the girl K during an eight-week period (Ferguson and Farwell, 1975) had one word, *no*, that was always pronounced with [n-], several words beginning with *m* or *n* in the adult models that she pronounced with [m-] (sometimes varying with [n-] regardless of the model), and several words beginning with *m* in the model that were regularly pronounced with [b-] similarly to a number of other words with adult *b*. During that period, K did not have clear-cut *b* : *m* : *n* oppositions; she had word oppositions with only incipient identification of *b, m,* and *n* segments.

Another kind of evidence for the word as phonetic unit is prosodic interchange within the word, as when the child perceives nasality or some other phonetic characteristic in the model and then locates it in the wrong place, or spreads it through the word. Ferguson and Farwell (1975) offer an extreme example of this phenomenon, when K is attempting a new word *pen* and has trouble sorting out the features of nasality, bilabial closure, alveolar closure, and voicelessness. In a single half-hour session, K pronounced the word ten different ways, including [mãᵊ], [dɛᵈⁿ], [pʰin], and [buã]. This certainly does not suggest a representation consisting of an ordered sequence of phonemic segments. Waterson (1971 and elsewhere) emphasizes this kind of word prosodic perception and production and the child's construction of perception "schemas" and production "patterns" for sets of phonetically similar words.

Overgeneralization   Perhaps the most striking evidence for the child's early word-shape representations is the existence of the "phonological idioms" mentioned above, i.e., words that are pronounced better ("progressive idioms") or worse ("regressive idioms") than other words that are more typical of the child's current phonological system. The notion that the child learns words as whole phonetic shapes and constructs his own phonological segments, rules, and systems allows us to see these phonological idioms as natural, not aberrant, phenomena, but any theory of phonological development must account also for the instances when a child changes his pronunciation of a word (e.g., a "progressive idiom") to a version that seems farther from the adult model.

This phenomenon of going backward or changing for the worse is the counterpart in phonology to the child's extensions and overgeneralizations in other aspects of language development, first documented for inflectional morphology (Ervin, 1964), but now recognized in lexical semantics (Clark, 1973) and syntax (Bowerman, 1974), as well. For the overgeneralization interpretation in phonology, cf. Kiparsky and Menn (1977). When the child's pronunciation of a word apparently regresses to a less accurate one, this often reflects the operation of a newly acquired rule affecting a number of words of similar phonetic shape, and the change represents a step forward in the development.

This kind of apparent regression in phonological development is now well attested for the later stage of rapidly increasing vocabulary and the development of phonological organization. A widely cited example is the succession of pronunciations of the words *side* and *light* by Smith's son, Amahl (Smith, 1973, p. 80). After learning to distinguish the two words in pronunciation, Amahl a little later merged them again as part of a lateralization rule applying to /s/ and /ʃ/ under certain conditions, a step toward his mastery of the sibilants. The facts are given in Table 2.

The apparent regression is comparable to the appearance of overgeneralized forms, such as *comed* when the child has previously used the correct *came*; the "error" reflects the operation of a newly acquired general rule affecting many verbs, and it represents an advance over the word-by-word learning of past tense forms.

Table 2.   Development of *s*- and *l*- in A's speech
(data from Smith, 1973).

Stage	Side	Light
I	[dait]	[dait]
II	[dait]	[lait]
III	[lait]	[lait]

The exceptions and incorrect formulations of the rule must then be corrected by the child.

At the later stage of Smith's child, a phonological overgeneralization often reflects the replacement of one phonological rule by another one that is in some respects better. At the early stage under discussion here, the overgeneralization often represents a basic step in moving from a whole word shape toward a segmental phonological structure of the word. The most frequently cited example is Hildegard Leopold's "first permanent word," *pretty*. She pronounced it almost perfectly for about a year (1;10–1;9) until she reduced it to [pIti], bringing it into line with the phonological structure of other words. A month later, as she was beginning to master the voicing distinction in production, she overgeneralized her initial voicing rule (cf. Ingram, 1974) to this word, make it [bIdi], still further from her early phonetically accurate pronunciation. Leopold noted in the first two years nine such words that started just about perfectly and changed in the course of development.

Hans Lindner provides a nice example of an early change in the pronunciation of a word in which part of the change is phonetic improvement by the addition of a previously omitted segment, and part is phonetic regression by overgeneralization. In the 22nd month, Hans at first said *dake, thank you* for adult *danke*, but later in the same month changed to *ganke*. He added the nasal segment and at the same time assimilated the initial dental stop to the following velar in accordance with a velar-dominant consonant harmony rule. This rule affected his version of adult *gut, good,* and *Stock, stick/cane,* transcribed by his father as *gug* and *gock*, and was consistent with his early C_iVC_i canonical form (e.g., *Gasse* → *gack*, cf. Table 1.).

Thus, the phonological development of the child at the early stages proceeds by changes in the pronunciation of individual words. These changes may in some instances result from improved identification of the phonetic shape or phonological structure of the word, i.e., by "restructuring" its input representation, as when a child discovers that the word begins with *s*-, not *f*- as he had supposed (Smith, 1973, pp. 145–146). In some instances, the changes show improved ability to produce particular segments or sequences, as when a child learns to pronounce the sound complex [ŋk], which he had previously not been able to do, e.g., Hans's *ganke*. The most interesting cases, however, for our understanding of the processes of acquisition, are when the child makes a hypothesis about phonology that he applies to words that meet the conditions for its application, as when a child tries out a rule of initial voicing, e.g., Hildegard's [bIdi]. Ferguson and Farwell (1975) treat such a hypothesis or rule application as similar in nature to a sound change in progress: it may spread from one word to another, it may fluctuate in application, it may eliminate an existing contrast. The example cited there of the early development of Hildegard's /l/ illustrates her word-by-word struggle to acquire /l/ as a phonological segment and to apply her rule of replacing liquids by [j]. See Table 3.

Changes that represent the relaxing of constraints on complexity, whether as additions to inventory or application of rules, are discussed below; here we may summarize the main point of this section by listing another important characteristic of early phonological development: the child invents and applies to his repertoire of phonetic word shapes a succession of phonological rules that regularize the pronunciation of phonetically similar words. The rules may be straightforwardly facilitative of pronunciation or they may be steps in the increasing phonological organization superimposed on the word shapes; in either case they reveal the problem-solving, hypothesis-forming capacity of the child.

Permitted Complexity

The earliest words of the child tend to be severely restricted in their structural complexity (e.g., number and type of syllables) and in the amount of phonetic diversity within them (e.g., phonetic similarity of consonants). A large part of the development during the "50-word" period is the successive loosening of these restrictions. For example, if a child has the early limitation on production that words of the shape CVC begin and end with the same consonantal articulation except that the onset tends to be voiced but the final is unvoiced, the limitation may first be loosened to allow only one difference (place, manner, or voicing), and later two differences. In fact, this was the case with Hans. His early CVC words were *dat, bap~pap, gak, pip, mem~möm*; in the 22nd month he added *bet* and *wap* to his active vocabulary, the former illustrating a place difference, the latter a manner difference.

Macken (1976) gives a detailed report on J, a Spanish-learning child whose early phonological development gradually relaxed the structural and phonetic similarity restrictions in an extremely orderly way, showing a "strength hierarchy" of stops, nasals, and fricatives. For example, his rendition of adult *tasa, cup,* went successively *ta, tata, tasa* (with difficulty), *sasa, tasa* (transcriptions simplified) over a period of five months. His production of final nasals began in monosyllables with initial stops and was extended gradually to longer words and words with fricatives. Similarly, his production of fricatives began in words that had no other consonants

Table 3.   Development of the lateral /l/ in H's speech during the 2nd year.

Age	Hello	Alle	Bottle	Lie	Loch	Löscher
1;5	ʔələ					
1;6			ba:ı			
1;7		ʔalə	ba:ı			
1;8		ʔajə	baıu			
1;9			balu			
1;10	jojo	ʔalə	baju		lokʻ/jokʻ	
1;11	jojo		balu	jaı		loko/joke

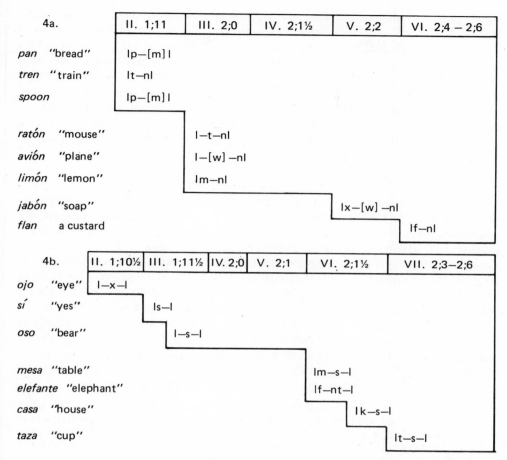

Figure 1.   Development of "permitted complexity" adapted from J. Macken (1976). 4a summarizes acquisition of final nasals; 4b summarizes acquisition of fricatives.

and was extended gradually to words with nasals or fricatives, and finally to words with stops. Figure 1 reproduces a summary chart prepared for Macken (1976) but not included in the published version.

Not all children show such an orderly progression as J in the relaxation of limitations on complexity, but presumably every child, as a part of the acquisition of his vocabulary and the construction of his phonological system, struggles through these processing problems with structural complexity and phonetic diversity. The notion of "permitted complexity" is equally valid for adult users of language, as the universal existence of phonotactic constraints, the language-specific phonotactic patterns shared by users of particular language varieties, and individual profiles of difficulty in processing phonological complexity demonstrate. Its significance at the early stages of phonological development lies in the fact that the child's struggle with complexity is one of the principal means by which he achieves phonological segmentation and the identification of allophonic and morphophonemic relationships in the ambient language. Early phonological development includes (along with the mastery of particular articulations and the testing of rule-hypotheses) development of the ability to cope with increasing phonological complexity. This may be summarized as another important characteristic of phonological development. The child gradually relaxes his constraints of selection and production to allow greater structural complexity and phonetic diversity within words. Further analyses of individual children's early phonological development should be instructive on the role of words, syllables, and other prosodic domains of phonotactic constraints in the development process, and in phonology in general.

Individual Strategies

Linguists have traditionally been interested in characterizing human language in general, particular human languages, and dialect variation within a language, but not individual differences in language. Similarly, linguists studying child language development have generally been more interested in finding a universal order of acquisition, or universal processes operating in acquisition, than in examining the different routes children follow in acquiring language. It has long been this author's conviction, however, that the study of individual linguistic "profiles" is of value for general linguistic theory because it shows the nature and extent of variability within overall universal constraints, and that it is of immediate value for "applications of linguistics"—i.e., the use of linguistic findings by linguists, or others interested in dealing with individual pathologies or social problems involving language (Ferguson, 1975a, p. 68). This view is becoming more acceptable in psycholinguistic research on child language. A quotation from a recent paper by Nelson expresses it well:

> It is becoming clearer . . . that there is a wide variety of strategies or styles with which children approach the language learning task . . . Even if there is only one language to be learned, there is more than one way to learn it. At the least, this should cause us to ask, "What are the possible ways of learning language?" in order both to build better theories and to understand better the developing child (1975, p. 138).

Individual differences in phonological development have been discussed from a linguistic point of view for "deviant" phonologies in a series of publications beginning with Haas (1963). This literature is reviewed, synthesized, and extended by Ingram in his recent book (1976) and represents an important advance in the understanding of phonological deviance and therapy. Most of this work deals with older, deviant children, however, and apart from comments in diary studies, discussions of individual strategies in normal phonological development are few (Farwell 1976; Ferguson and Farwell 1975, pp. 435–437; Ferguson et al., 1973, pp. 61–62). Here are a few examples of well-documented individual strategies that can be given as an indication of the possibilities.

1. *Favorite sounds or variations.* It frequently happens that a child treats one sound type or set of related sound types as "favorite." He chooses adult models containing it, he produces words with it more often than other words, he "plays" with the sound. T., reported in Farwell (1976), chose [s ʃ tʃ dʒ] as favorite sounds almost from the beginning of language production, welcoming

words like *ice, eyes, shoes, keys, cheese,* and *juice* into her vocabulary, and pronouncing them variably; the sounds themselves seemed more important to her (or more fun) than using them to make lexical contrasts. It may also happen that a child treats one sound or set of sounds as something to be avoided. Another child reported in Farwell (1976) avoided almost all adult words containing fricatives for several months.

2. *Reduplications.* Although all children show some tendency to reduplication, individual children vary greatly in the extent to which they use it. Leslie (Ferguson et al., 1973) used reduplication for all her early words and persisted in reduplication as a major strategy for months, whereas Daniel (Menn, 1971) preferred to reduce everything to monosyllables. The reduplication strategist prefers to choose adult models closer to reduplication, and will even reduplicate monosyllabic models; the monosyllabist prefers monosyllabic models and reduces polysyllabic ones.

3. *Unique reduction devices.* At the end of the "50-word" period, or in the following period, some children adopt a special strategy for coping with words of greater complexity than their production system can handle. They construct a unique reduction device (URD) that allows parts of different adult models to be produced the same way (cf. Menn, 1971, pp. 241–242; Smith, 1973, p. 172). The URD typically persists for several months until the child finally "gives in," and starts acquiring the correct adult forms. A striking example is one child's URD that made adult disyllables into CV*j*VC (Priestly, 1975).

4. *Phonological differentiation versus lexical expansion.* As an example of a broad "style" of phonological development, as opposed to specific strategies, some children prefer to build their phonological system slowly and carefully and limit their active lexicon to words they can say pretty accurately; others prefer to build vocabulary more rapidly, pronouncing many of the words inaccurately and without much evident phonological organization. In the former category are, for example, Hildegard, Macken's J, and Vihman's daughter. Hildegard's sister Carla and Macken's Si have the latter learning style.

There has been no attempt to date to examine the range of individual variation in phonological development or to classify main types, but research of this kind is necessary if any useful sort of early assessment is to be developed. In the present state of knowledge, clinical experience and personal hunches are the only basis for assessment at the early stages. On the basis of a handful of cases, Ferguson et al. (1973) hazarded the guess that a child who uses reduplication as his principal strategy, other things being equal (e.g., the amount of reduplication in the input), will be slower in phonological development than one who does not. Such hunches are nearly useless in the absence of confirmatory data, but there is a good chance that assessments of that kind, based on sufficient research, could be of diagnostic value. In any case, the basic point of individual difference may be listed as another important characteristic of phonological development: Each child follows his own distinctive route in phonological development. "Universals" in order of acquisition and "natural processes" in the child's rules are statistical outcomes of the interaction of various factors rather than the inevitable features of development.

SUMMARY

This paper has dealt with only selected aspects of early phonological development. It has not dealt with such topics as intonation or semantic function, which would be necessary for any comprehensive treatment of the subject, and it has deemphasized the "naturalness" and "universality" of specific facts of inventory and process. Although the paper has discussed the connections between babbling and the period of early phonological development, it has not treated the transition from that period to the following stages of more complex and more adult-like phonological organizations. Finally, it has neither accepted nor proposed any general theoretical framework. Its value is intended to lie in calling attention to aspects of early phonological development that are neglected or not accounted for in much of the current literature, and in providing an informative account of the general course of events. The account of development offered has been summarized in eight important characteristics that may be collected in a summary paragraph:

The child plays a highly active, creative role in the acquisition process. The child's early vocables constitute a connecting link between babbling and adult-modeled speech; the child's phonological systems for perception and production are relatively independent. In the child's construction of a phonological system for production, he begins with structural constraints in selecting adult model words and in producing his own words. (The baby talk lexicon of the child's speech community provides a reservoir of phonologically simplified models from which the child can draw for his early words.) The child invents and applies to his repertoire of phonetic word shapes a succession of phonological rules that regularize the pronunciation of phonetically similar words. The child gradually relaxes his constraints of selection and production to allow greater structural complexity and phonetic diversity within words. Each child follows his own distinctive route in phonological development.

REFERENCES

Allen, G. D. 1976. Development of rhythm in early phonology. Paper presented at Eighth Annual Child Language Research Forum, April 3, Stanford.

Bar-Adon, A., and Leopold, W. F. (eds). 1971. Child Language: A Book of Readings. Prentice-Hall, Englewood Cliffs, N.J.

Barton, D. 1976. Phonemic discrimination and the knowledge of words in children. Papers and Reports on Child Language Development, 11: 61–68.

Bateman, W. G. 1917. Papers on language development I. The first word. Pedagog. Sem. 24: 391–398.

Bates, E. 1974. Language and context: Studies in the acquisition of pragmatics. Unpublished Ph.D. dissertation, University of Chicago.

Bever, T. G. 1974. Psychologically real grammar emerges because of its role in language acquisition. Georgetown Univ. Round Table Lang. Linguist. 63–75.

Bowerman, M. 1974. Learning the structure of causative verbs: A study in the relationship of cognitive, semantic, and syntactic development. Pap. Rep. Child. Lang. Dev. 8: 142–178.

Braine, M. D. S. 1971. The acquisition of language in infant and child. In C. E. Reed (ed.), The Learning of Language, pp. 7–95. Appleton-Century Crofts, New York.

Burling, R. 1959. Language development of a Garo and English speaking child. Word 15: 45–68.

Clark, E. V. 1973. What's in a word? On the child's acquisition of semantics in his first language. In T. Moore (ed.), Cognitive Development and the Acquisition of Language. Academic Press, New York.

Crystal, D. 1969. Prosodic Systems and Intonation in English. Cambridge University Press, London.

Crystal, D. 1975. The English Tone of Voice. Edward Arnold, London.

Dore, J., Franklin, M. B., Miller, R. T., and Ramer, A. L. H. 1976. Transitional phenomena in early language acquisition. J. Child Lang. 3: 13–28.

Edwards, M. L. 1974. Perception and production in child phonology; the testing of four hypotheses. J. Child Lang. 1: 205–219.

Eimas, P. 1974. Linguistic processing of speech by young infants. In R. Schiefelbusch and L. Lloyd (eds.), Language Perspectives—Acquisition, Retardation, and Intervention, pp. 55–73. University Park Press, Baltimore.

Engel, W. von Raffler. 1965. Un esempio di "linguistic consciousness" nel bambino piccolo. Orientamenti Ped. 12: 631–633.

Engel, W. von Raffler. 1973. The development from sound to phoneme in child language. In Ferguson and Slobin (eds.), Studies in Child Language Development, pp. 9–12. Holt, Rinehart and Winston, New York.

Ervin, S. 1964. Imitation and structural change in children's language. In E. H. Lenneberg (ed.), New Directions in the Study of Language, pp. 163–189. MIT Press, Cambridge.

Farwell, C. G. 1976. Some ways to learn about fricatives. Paper read at the 8th Child Language Research Forum, April, Stanford University.

Ferguson, C. A. 1956. Arabic baby talk. In M. Halle (ed.), For Roman Jakobson, pp. 121–128. Mouton, The Hague.

Ferguson, C. A. 1964. Baby talk in six languages. Am. Anthropol. 66.6 Pt. 2: 103–114.

Ferguson, C. A. 1975a. Applications of linguistics. In R. Austerlitz (ed.), The Scope of American Linguistics, pp. 63–75. De Ridder Press, Lisse, Belgium.

Ferguson, C. A. 1975b. Baby talk as a simplified register. Pap. Rep. Child Lang. Dev. 9: 1–27. To appear in Snow and Ferguson (eds), Talking To Children. In press.

Ferguson, C. A. 1975c. Sound patterns in language acquisition. Georgetown Univ. Round Table Lang. Linguist. 1–16.

Ferguson, C. A., and Farwell, C. B. 1975. Words and sounds in early language acquisition: English initial consonants in the first fifty words. Language 51: 419–439.

Ferguson, C. A., and Garnica, O. 1975. Theories of phonological development. In E. and E. Lenneberg (eds), Foundations of Language Development, Vol. II, pp. 153–180. Academic Press, New York.

Ferguson, C. A., Peizer, D. B., and Weeks, T. 1973. Model and replica phonological grammar of a child's first words. Lingua 31: 35–65.

Ferguson, C. A., and Slobin, D. L. (eds.). Studies of Child Language Development. Holt, Rinehart and Winston, New York.

Fradkina, F. I. 1955. Voznikovenie rechi u rebenka [The emergence of speech in children]. Uch. zap. LGPI im. A. I. Gertseva 12. English abstract in F. Smith and G. A. Miller (eds.), The Genesis of Language, p. 367. MIT Press, Cambridge.

Garnica, O. 1973. The development of phonemic speech perception. In T. E. Moore (ed.), Cognitive Development and the Acquisition of Language, pp. 215–222. Academic Press, New York.

Greenberg, J. H. (ed.). 1966. Universals of Language 2nd ed. MIT Press, Cambridge.

Haas, W. 1963. Phonological analysis of a case of dyslalia. J. Speech Hear. Disord. 28: 239–249.

Halliday, M. A. K. 1975. Learning How to Mean—Explorations in the Development of Language. Edward Arnold. London.

Ingram, D. 1974. Phonological rules in young children. J. Child Lang. 1: 49–64.

Ingram, D. 1975. Surface contrast in children's speech. J. Child Lang. 2: 287–292.

Ingram, D. 1976. Phonological Disability in Children. Edward Arnold, London.

Jakobson, R. 1960. Why "Mama" and "Papa"? Studies on Child Language and Aphasia, pp. 21–30. Mouton, The Hague.

Jakobson, R. 1968. Child Language, Aphasia and Phonological Universals. Translation of original 1941 edition in German. Mouton, The Hague.

Jespersen, O. 1922. Language: Its Nature, Development and Origin. Holt, New York.

Kaplan, E. 1969. The role of intonation in the acquisition of language. Unpublished Ph.D. dissertation, Cornell University.

Kiparsky, P., and Menn, L. 1977. On the acquisition of phonology. In J. MacNamara (ed.), Language Learning and Thought. Academic Press, New York.

Lehiste, I. 1970. Suprasegmentals. MIT Press, Cambridge.

Leopold, W. F. 1947. Speech Development of a Bilingual child: A Linguist's Record, Vol II. Northwestern Univ. Press, Chicago.

Lewis, M. M. 1936. Infant Speech; A Study of the Beginnings of Language. Routledge and Kegan Paul, London. 3rd ed., Basic Books, New York.

Lindner, G. 1898. Aus dem Naturgarten der Kindersprache. Th. Grieben's Verlag, Leipzig.

McCarthy, D. 1954. Language development in children. In L. Carmichael (ed.), Manual of Child Psychology, pp. 492–630. John Wiley and Sons, New York.

Macken, M. A. 1974. Readers, books and articles on child phonology. Linguist. Rep. 16(10): 9–12.

Macken, M. A. 1976. Permitted complexity in phonological development: One child's acquisition of Spanish consonants. Pap. Rep. Child Lang. Dev. 11: 28–60.

Menn, L. 1971. Phonotactic rules in beginning speech. Lingua 26: 225–251.

Menyuk, P. 1971. The Acquisition and Development of Language. Prentice-Hall, Englewood Cliffs, N.J.

Menyuk, P., and Bernholtz, N. 1969. Prosodic features and children's language production. MIT Res. Lab. Electron. Quart. Progr. Rep. 93: 216–219.

Morse, P. A. 1974. Infant speech perception: A preliminary model and review of the literature. In R. Schiefelbusch, and L. Lloyd (eds.), Language Perspectives—Acquisition, Retardation, and Intervention, pp. 19–53. University Park Press, Baltimore.

Moskowitz, A. I. 1970. The two-year-old stage in the acquisition of English phonology. Language 46: 426–441.

Moskowitz, A. I. 1973. Acquisition of phonology and syntax: A preliminary study. In Hintikka G., Moravcsik, J., and Suppes, P. (eds.), Approaches to Natural Language, pp. 48–84. Reidel Publishing Co., Dordrecht, Holland.

Nelson, K. 1973. Structure and strategy in learning to talk. Monogr. Soc. Res. Child Dev. 38, no. 149.

Nelson, K. 1975. Individual differences in early semantic and syntactic development. Ann. N. Y. Acad. Sci. 263: 132–139.

Oller, D. K., Wieman, L. A., Doyle, W. J., and Ross, C. 1976. Infant babbling and speech. J. Child Lang. 3: 1–12.

Pačesova, J. 1968. The Development of Vocabulary in the Child. Universita J. E. Purkyne, Brno.

Priestly, T. 1975. One 'idiosyncratic strategy' in the acquisition of phonology. Paper read at the International Symposium on Child Language, September, London.

Salus, P. H., and Salus, M. W. 1974. Developmental neurophysiology and phonological acquisition order. Language 50: 151–160.

Schäfer, P. 1922. Beobachtungen und Versuche an einem Kind. Z. Pädagog. Psychol. 23.

Shvachkin, N. Kh. 1948. Razvitie fonematičeskogo vosprijatija reči v rannem vozraste. [The development of phonemic speech perception in early childhood]. Izy. Akad. Pedagog. Nauk RSFSR 13: 101–132. English translation in Ferguson and Slobin (eds.), Studies in Child Language Development, 1973, pp. 91–127.

Smith, N. V. 1973. The Acquisition of Phonology: A Case Study. Cambridge University Press, Cambridge.

Stampe, D. 1969. The acquisition of phonetic representation. Papers from the 5th Regional Meeting, Chicago Linguistics Society 433–444.

Snow, C. E., and Ferguson, C. A. Talking to Children. Cambridge University Press, London. In press.

Tonkava-Yampol´skaya, R. V. 1968. Razvitie rečevoj intonacii u detej pervyx dvux let žizni [The development of intonation in children of the first two years of life]. Vopr. Psixol, 14: 94–101.

Vanderslice, R., and Ladefoged, P. 1972. Binary suprasegmental features and transformational word-accentuation rules. Language 48: 819–838.

Velten, H. V. 1943. The growth of phonemic and lexical patterns in infant language. Language 19: 281–292.

Vihman, M. 1976. From pre-speech to speech: On early phonology. Paper read at the 8th Child Language Research Forum, April, Stanford University.

Waterson, N. 1971. Child phonology: A prosodic view. J. Linguist. 7: 179–211.

Whitaker, H. A. 1973. Comments on the innateness of language. In R. W. Shuy (ed.), Some New Directions in Linguistics. Georgetown University Press, Washington, D.C.

Discussion Summary: Development of Phonology

Rebecca E. Eilers

Philip Morse began the discussion on infant phonological development with a series of observations that were directed toward speech perception, but that had equal application to productive phonology, including both its segmental and nonsegmental aspects. The general discussion of the Morse paper and the other phonology papers centered on the basic question of the origins of the abilities of infants. In the area of speech perception, this question led to a discussion of the meaning and role of categorical perception in infants, adults, and animals, a discussion of cross-cultural data, and a discussion of developmental change in speech perception. In the area of segmental phonological development, discussion was focused on origins of infant abilities, including the meaning of individual differences in order of acquisiton, phonological "universals" in language acquisition, continuity in learning to produce sounds, and the need for instrumental approaches to data acquisition. George Allen led a discussion that centered on the paucity of intuitively pleasing theories of prosody and the importance of the role of sequential behavior in language acquisition, and its relationship to universal motor and perceptual constraints.

It would obviously be difficult to reproduce the hours of discussion of phonological development. The intent here instead is to highlight which, in this author's opinion, were the most salient points, and to relate them to the written versions of the papers as well as to the open discussion that followed paper presentations. The discussion reflects the focus of the papers in that it centers almost exclusively on normal development and the assessment of normally developing skills in infancy.

INFANT CATEGORICAL PERCEPTION AND CROSS-LANGUAGE STUDIES

Both the papers of Kuhl and Morse addressed themselves, at least in part, to the issue of the status of the "innateness" model of infant speech perception. This model proposed by Eimas, Siqueland, Jusczyk, and Vigorito (1971) and Eimas (1974) suggests that infants are preprogrammed to perceive major speech contrast categories at or shortly after birth. The phenomenon of categorical perception (see

Morse and Kuhl, this volume, for definition) by infants has frequently been cited as evidence for the innateness view. In addition, because infants cannot predict in advance of linguistic experience which voice onset time (VOT) boundary or boundaries will be relevant to their native language, infants (according to the innateness model) must be able to discriminate across all major VOT boundaries used in the world's languages. Morse, in this volume, makes the case for attributing categorical perception to infants in both the lead (prevoiced) and lag (aspirated) regions of the VOT continuum, and concludes that: 1) experience is unnecessary for the emergence of discrimination at major boundaries (lag and lead), and that 2) the role of experience may be to make discrimination "*more* categorical;" conversely, lack of experience may lead to loss of discrimination skill. These conclusions are based upon a body of data that can be interpreted differently.

Much of this difference of opinion centers on Eimas's et al. (1971) assumption that the stimulus pair 0 versus -20 represents a within-category pair. This assumption led them to believe that lack of evidence of discrimination would provide further evidence for the innateness view. However, Morse (this volume) acknowledged that the value of the common prevoiced (lead) boundary has not been clearly established, even for adults. Judging from Williams's (1974) work with monolingual Puerto Rican Spanish speakers and the author's own work (Eilers, 1977) with Cuban Spanish speakers, the VOT boundary for Spanish should be between 0 and -20 (based on judgments of Lisker and Abramson's synthetic VOT stimuli), precisely the value suggested by Eimas et al. as a within-category pair. Eimas et al. (1971) reported that infants at four months showed no evidence of discriminating the 0 versus -20 pair, a finding at odds with the innateness position, given that it seems actually to be a between-category pair. Similarly, no evidence of discrimination of prevoiced contrasts was reported by Butterfield and Cairns (1974) for the stimuli 0 versus -40, -30 versus $+20$, -60 versus -20, and Eimas (1975) reports no evidence of discrimination for -40 versus $+20$ and -40 versus -100. Eimas (1975) does report evidence of discrimination for the pair $+10$ versus -70. However, the 80 msec voice onset difference is so great that this pair may be discriminable on the basis of auditory cues such as perceived loudness, and thus it provides little relevant information about categorical perception of VOT.

Recent work with six-month-old English-learning infants (Eilers, Wilson, and Moore, 1977) using the visually reinforced infant speech discrimination (VRISD) paradigm has also failed to yield persuasive evidence that infants discriminate prevoiced labial stops. In studies of the VOT pairs $+40$ versus $+70$, $+40$ versus $+10$, $+10$ versus -20, -20 versus -50, -20 versus -60, and -30 versus -60, English-learning infants only provided evidence for the discrimination of $+10$ versus $+40$, the English lag boundary. Data are currently being collected on these same stimulus pairs with Spanish-learning infants. Already available cross-cultural data are illuminating. Streeter (1976) reports Kikuyu (Bantu language) infants and their parents discriminate the pair 0 versus -30. Lasky, Syrdal-Lasky, and Klein (1975) report that Guatemalan infants (Spanish-learning) discriminate the pair -20 versus -60 rather than the pair $+20$ versus -20 that their parents discriminate. (It should be noted that the +20 versus −20 parental value fits well with the Puerto Rican and Cuban boundaries described by Williams, 1974, and Eilers, 1977.) The −20 versus −60 discrimination evidenced by the Guatemalan babies would seem to be a within-category discrimination for Spanish-learning infants. It is unclear why these infants discriminate across a value that their parents do not recognize as linguistically relevant.

Where does all this leave us? There seems to be very little evidence to support the notion that English-learning infants discriminate at any VOT lead boundary. Furthermore, there is no evidence whatsoever to indicate (as the innateness model predicts) that English-learning infants discriminate the prevoiced stimuli categorically. There is some evidence to suggest that infants whose target language includes a lead contrast discriminate that contrast. The Lasky et al. (1975) data cloud this issue, because the infants and adults do not seem to agree on the relevant boundary values. Even so, these data *do* suggest, contrary to predictions of the innateness theory, that experience may be an important determiner of the discrimination of at least some major speech contrasts, the lead category contrast being one of these. Naturally, further cross-cultural work will be necessary to evaluate the nature and extent of linguistic experience in speech perception.

Morse's second major point is that experience with a language has two potential effects on development. On the one hand, it leads to "more categorical" perception of target language contrasts and, on the other hand, lack of experience with foreign language contrasts leads to suppression of perceptual skills. Although it may be true that speech discrimination shows developmental trends in that older infants discriminate stimuli that younger infants may not, there is little evidence that English-learning infants discriminate either within-category or between-category lead boundary contrasts. In order to suggest that perception becomes "more categorical," one would have to obtain evidence of both "between" and "within" discrimination, in addition to developmental data suggesting a shift toward "between" responding with age. Otherwise, it is more parsimonious to simply suggest that some perceptual target contrasts are learned during the first year of life.

Furthermore, Morse's suggestion about suppression of innate skills is not consistent with the adult data. Although categorical perception may be demonstrated with adults, when paradigms are used with repeating standards as in infant research, adults demonstrate excellent "within-category" discrimination. Several recent studies (Barclay, 1972; Carney, Widen, and Viemeister, 1977; Eilers, 1977; Eilers, Wilson, and Moore, 1977; Sinnott, 1974) have demonstrated consistent and pervasive within-category discrimination of stop consonants for adults. The author's own data demonstrate that adults are able to discriminate many VOT contrasts that are not phonemic in their native language. In summary, given the nature of the animal data concerning categorical perception (excellently reviewed by Kuhl in this volume), new insights into conditions contributing to categorical perception in infant paradigms, and infant data that conflict with predictions of the innateness hypothesis, future research will be directed at the role of experience in linguistic perceptual development.

DEVELOPMENTAL STUDIES IN PERCEPTION

Not all of our data concerning the role of linguistic experience stem from studies of categorical perception. Recent methodological advances have made it possible to test the same infants at several ages, between birth and about 18 months. Whereas the high amplitude sucking procedure (HAS) and heart rate habituation procedure (HR) are only applicable to infants younger than four to six months, the visually reinforced head turn procedure (VRISD) (see Eilers et al., in press a for details of paradigm) allows testing of individual infants across a 12-month age span starting at six months. In addition, this procedure is both clinically and scientifically more useful, in that individual rather than group data can be obtained.

When six-month-old infants were tested in the author's laboratory using VRISD with a variety of speech contrasts (including CV and VC syllables with both stop and fricative consonants), all infants presented evidence of discriminating [va-sa], [sa-ʃa], [sa-za], [as-a:z], [a:s-a:z], and eight of nine infants discriminated [at-a:d]. Only one of these same infants showed evidence of being able to discriminate [a:t-a:d] or [fi-θi], and none of the infants were able to discriminate [fa-θa]. When a similar group of infants was tested with the same procedure and the same stimuli at 12 months, several changes were noted. Half of the 12-month-old babies could discriminate the pairs [a:t-a:d] and [a:t-at], contrasts with which the six-month-olds did not succeed. Similarly, seven of eight babies discriminated [fi-θi] at 12 months, even though only one of eight had succeeded at six months. In summary, at least three contrasts showed improved discrimination scores with older infants, despite the fact that the older infants were *more* difficult to test. Furthermore, because all of the infants were tested on all of the contrasts, these results could not be attributed to subject variables across pairs.

Further evidence of developmental change can be found if data from HAS and VRISD are compared. One- to four-month-old infants gave evidence of discriminating [va-sa], [sa-ʃa], [as-a:z], [at-a:d], and [a:t-a:d]. They did not present evidence of discriminating [sa-za] or [a:s-a:z], although the six-month-old VRISD infants did. At the same time, the data for the youngest babies were consistent with the six-month-old VRISD data for [at-a:t], [fa-θa], and [fi-θi], i.e., no evidence of discrimination was found in either group. One apparent reversal of the trend for greater experience to result in greater discrimination was found: six-month-old babies showed no evidence of discriminating the pair [a:t-a:d], even though younger babies did discriminate it (see Eilers et al., 1977, for a discussion of this point).

With VRISD, as with any infant discrimination paradigm, we are left with the problem of interpreting a negative result when an infant's performance fails to reach statistical significance. Using VRISD we have tried to minimize error by testing each infant on each contrast twice. If both testing sessions fail to yield evidence of infant discrimination we still *may not* conclude that the infant cannot discriminate. Instead, we must conclude only that evidence of discrimination was not obtained. It may be that given a different paradigm, a greater amount of practice or experience, and/or a different physiological state, evidence of discrimination might eventually be obtained. However, when groups of individual infants fail to yield evidence of discrimination on a given contrast while they succeed on others, it may be safe to conclude that there is a hierarchy of difficulty among the stimuli: i.e., that some speech sounds are easily discriminable by infants and others are more difficult. Our data for the CV and VC stimuli, discussed above, indicate that this is the case. There seems to be a hierarchy of difficulty for perception of linguistic acoustic features of speech stimuli. These findings have, of course, important implications for developmental assessment.

Although all the studies discussed at the conference in the area of infant perception are theoretically useful, only the work described by Kuhl on category formation addresses a crucial question in perceptual language development: are infants able to mobilize their perceptual skills in tasks that are linguistically relevant? There are some very limited data (Eilers, 1976) that suggest that although infants may be able to discriminate phonemes in isolation in tasks with repeating background stimuli, they may not be able to discriminate these same phonemes in a labeling task at about two-years of age. It is time to begin investigating the perceptual capacity of infants in more language-oriented tasks such as those suggested by Kuhl (e.g., by studying discrimination of multiple tokens of phonemic speech stimuli one can ask, how do infants categorize speech stimuli, how do they learn to recognize irrelevant variation and separate it from defining characteristics, etc.). In general, researchers in infant perception at the conference and elsewhere seem to be reorienting themselves toward study of the perception of more complex phonological structures in meaningful linguistic contexts.

UNIFYING THREADS: SEGMENTAL AND NONSEGMENTAL PHONOLOGY

A unifying thread emerged during discussion that may not have been evident in the content of the individual papers. A number of suggestions were made that clarified the notion that it may not be reasonsable to study phonology as if it consisted of separable segmental and nonsegmental (prosodic) units. For instance, Minifie reiterated that phonetic context influences prosodic patterning in lawful and reproducible ways. The vowel [a] will have different timing characteristics before a voiced rather than voiceless stop consonant and will influence durational features of the final consonant as well. In addition, prosodic programming has a direct influence on segmental phonology—a highly stressed vowel may have a more wide open vocal tract, and thus a different segmental quality than a less stressed vowel of the same "phonemic" category. It is clear that perceptual mechanisms in the infant and young child must "adjust" for allophonic variants in segmental elements that are dictated by nonsegmental programming. What is not clear is how (or if) the infant recognizes that a stressed and unstressed vowel [i] represent a general class, [i]. The work of Kuhl and Miller (1975) suggests that infants successfully ignore some kinds of suprasegmental variation (primarily pitch contours) while selectively attending to vowel quality distinctions. Highnam and Beykirch (1976) find some evidence that the process of vowel indentification is not complete as late as three years, i.e., children have difficulty normalizing speaker variation.

This theme also emerged in discussions of the development of perception. It has long been suggested that "suprasegmentals are discriminated earlier" than segmentals. This belief is widely held, although there does not seem to be any empirical evidence to justify it. The existing infant speech perception literature is persuasive in demonstrating that infants can discriminate at a very early age (at least by one month) subtle phonetic segmental contrasts (Eimas, et al. 1971). Similarly, Spring and Dale (1977) have demonstrated that young infants can discriminate stress contrasts based on minimal suprasegmental cues (changes in amplitude and F_o) at a similarly early age. However, the relationship between the child's ability to discriminate segmental and nonsegmental information in little understood. Trehub (1976) has demonstrated that duration of segments is crucial in infant discrimination studies. Infants did not show evidence of discriminating consonants embedded in the second syllable of two-syllable CVCV utterances when the duration of the final syllable was less than 500 msec. Discrimination problems were not alleviated when the final syllable was "stressed" (4 dB louder than the initial syllable). Trehub's work suggests an intricate relationship between the perception of factors normally thought of as segmental and those factors normally thought of as suprasegmental by very young infants.

If infants can discriminate both segmental and nonsegmental phonetic information from the beginning, then what does the claim that segmental perception follows suprasegmental perception mean? With regard to Ferguson's paper, the claim did not seem to be directed at peripheral discrimination, but rather at the issue of meaningful discrimination. Roughly translated, the question becomes, "Do infants invest meaning in suprasegmental contrasts before they associate meanings with segmentals?" Ferguson cites examples from diary studies that might be interpreted to suggest that, in fact, children first attend to suprasegmentals. There is not any experimental evidence to provide systematic support for these anecdotal data. In order to provide adequate support it would be necessary to systematically vary prosodic features, segmental features, and at least the situational context within which the child is addressed. In fact, in all of the diary study anecdotes, the situational context may have cued the child to respond as if the suprasegmental information carried the message. It would seem important to know what kinds of alterations in either segmental or nonsegmental phonological shape would lead the child to misinterpret a linguistic message. To date, these factors have not been successfully or meaningfully dissected.

Finally, if the early babbling data alluded to by Ferguson and amplified by Oller (in press) are examined, it becomes clear that it is unreasonable to talk about phonology as if segmental and nonsegmental systems were developing independently. Both segmental and suprasegmental contrasts are founded in a common set of metaphonological parameters (timing of opening and closing gestures, manipulations of signal amplitude, pitch, etc.) that are developing throughout the first year of life.

Consider, for example, that most normal infants begin producing reduplicated babbling at six to nine months of age. Reduplicated babbling consists of sequential, nearly identical syllables ([bababa], [dadada], [mamama], etc.). If one wishes to emphasize the development of a *suprasegmental* feature, one can describe this new vocalization type as a syllable-timing achievement. Vocalizations before this stage rarely have the regular syllable pattern associated with reduplicated babbling. On the other hand, if one wishes to emphasize the *segmental* characteristics of the development, one can focus on the fact that in reduplicated babbling the timing relationships of openings and closures, for the first time, result in well-formed consonant-vowel transitions. Indeed, during the last half of the first year, a whole series of segmental factors like place of articulation and voice onset time can be manipulated by the infant. Both views are consistent with the data and serve to further highlight the fact that separation of segmental and nonsegmental features, although convenient in some contexts, should not be allowed to lead to spurious conclusions about segmental or nonsegmental factors appearing earlier in development.

THE RELATIONSHIP BETWEEN PERCEPTION AND PRODUCTION

Given the state of knowledge of infant perception and production, it is reasonable to ask what relationship exists between the two domains. Unfortunately, at present there is little in depth research focused on the development of both the perceptual and productive phonological systems of individual children. Little is known about the interaction between ease of perception and ease of production and how this interaction contributes either to order of acquisition or individual differences in the acquisiton of language in infants and children. Although the available research suggests that few developmental errors are perceptually motivated by two years of age, some production rules seem nevertheless to be influenced by perceptual constraints (Eilers and Oller, 1976). It is probable that perceptually motivated phonological "errors" are more common in younger children. This question remains to be addressed in future research.

REFERENCES

Barclay, J. R. 1972. Non categorical perception of a voiced stop—a replication. Percept. Psychophys. 11 (4): 269–273.

Butterfield, E., and Cairns, G. 1974. Whether infants perceive linguistically is uncertain, and if they did, its practical importance would be equivocal. In R. Schiefelbusch and L. Lloyd (eds.), Language Perspectives—Acquisition, Retardation, and Intervention. University Park Press, Baltimore.

Carney, A., Widen, G., and Viemeister, N. Non categorical perception of stop consonants differing in VOT. J. Acoustic. Soc. Am. 62(4): 961–970.

Eilers, R. E. 1976. On tracing the development of speech perception. Paper presented at the Society for Research in Child Development, March, New Orleans.

Eilers, R. E. 1977. Perception of voice onset time by Spanish-learning infants. Paper presented at the 94th meeting of the Acoustical Society of America, December, Miami.

Eilers, R. E., and Oller, D. K. 1976. The role of speech discrimination in developmental sound substitutions. J. Child Lang. 3: 319–329.

Eilers, R. E., Wilson, W. R., and Moore, J. M. 1977. Developmental changes in speech discrimination in infants. J. Speech Hear. Res. 20: 766–780.

Eilers, R. E., Wilson, W. R., and Moore, J. M. Speech discrimination in the language-innocent and the language-wise: A study in the perception of voice-onset-time. J. Child Lang. In press.

Eimas, P. 1974. Linguistic processing of speech by young infants. In R. Schiefelbusch and L. Lloyd (eds.), Language Perspectives—Acquisition, Retardation, and Intervention. University Park Press, Baltimore.

Eimas, P. 1975. Speech perception in early infancy. In L. Cohen and P. Salapatek (eds.), Infant Perception: From Sensation to Cognition, Volume II. Academic Press, New York.

Eimas, P. D., Siqueland, E., Jusczyk, P., and Vigorito, J. 1971. Speech perception in infants. Science 171: 303–306.

Highnam, C. L., and Beykirch, H. L. 1976. Normalization in vowel recognition by children: A developmental study. Paper presented at the Asha Convention, November, Houston.

Kuhl, P., and Miller, J. 1975. Speech perception in early infancy: Discrimination of speech-sound categories. J. Acoustic. Soc. Am. 58 (suppl. 1): S56(A).

Lasky, R., Syrdal-Lasky, A., and Klein, D. 1975. VOT discrimination by four-to-six-month-old infants from Spanish environments. J. Exp. Child Psychol. 20: 215–225.

Oller, D. K. Infant vocalizations and the development of speech. J. Allied Health Behav. Sci. In press.

Sinnott, J. M. 1974. A comparison of speech sound discrimination in humans and monkeys. Ph.D. dissertation, University of Michigan.

Spring, D. R., and Dale, P. S. 1977. The discrimination of linguistic stress in early infancy. J. Speech Hear. Res. 20: 224.

Streeter, L. 1976. Language perception of 2-month-old infants show effects of both innate mechanisms and experience. Nature 259: 39–41.

Trehub, S. 1976. Infants discrimination of two-syllable stimuli: The role of temporal factors. Paper presented at Asha, November, Houston.

Williams, L. 1974. Speech perception and production as a function of exposure to a second language. Ph.D. dissertation, Harvard University, Cambridge.

ORIGINS OF SYNTAX, SEMANTICS, AND PRAGMATICS

Semantics and Syntax in the First Two Years: The Output of Form and Function and the Form and Function of the Input

Jill G. de Villiers and Peter A. de Villiers

SYNTAX

Learning the grammar of a human language is an extraordinarily complex task, especially considering that it begins at such an early age. It was this phenomenon that first excited the interest of psychologists and linguists alike, particularly in the early 1960s. Several large scale studies of early child speech were undertaken (Braine, 1963; Brown and Bellugi, 1964; Miller and Ervin, 1964), and the method of data collection was to tape record and to transcribe large samples of speech from children. The corpora were then submitted to a structural analysis for the purpose of writing grammars for different stages of development. The investigators used techniques borrowed from anthropological linguists, although they did not have the advantage of a cooperative native "informant" to offer interpretations!

Braine (1963) described the results of a distributional analysis of three boys in the early stages of language development. He proposed that grammar initially took the form of a *pivot grammar* , in which certain high frequency words, "pivots," were learned in fixed positions in the simple sentences, and they combined with other less frequent "open" words. It was the first attempt to describe child language in terms of rules that were *not* borrowed from adult language, but that emerged from a careful formal analysis. The rules were defined without reference to meaning at all. It was clear even at this point that something was amiss with pivot grammar, because it predicted certain combinations that simply never appeared, for example, *night-night vitamins*. However, McNeill (1970) was confident that this was attributable to

Preparation of this manuscript was supported in part by NSF grant no. GS 3971X to Professor Roger Brown.

sampling limitations, and that eventually such combinations would be "generated" by the children as well as by the grammar. There was no principled reason to exclude them.

These techniques revealed the formal rules of early child speech; for example, the co-occurrence relations between various parts of speech, the ways in which new phrases were composed and expanded (Brown and Bellugi, 1964), and the order in which complex structures appeared (Menyuk, 1969). In addition, several elegant descriptions emerged of particular grammatical structures like the negative (Bellugi, 1967), the interrogative (Brown, 1968; Klima and Bellugi, 1966), and tag questions (Brown and Hanlon, 1970) traced throughout the first few years. Investigators such as McNeill (1970) and Brown and Hanlon (1970) were particularly gratified that the insights into grammar provided by the transformational linguists also proved so illuminating for the study of child grammar.

McNeill was the major interpreter of Chomsky's (1957, 1965) theory as it applied to language acquisition. He expanded on the notion that the child possessed a "language acquisition device," equipped with certain hypotheses about the nature of universal grammar, that guided his search for regularities in the language input. Part of the postulated universal grammar was the notion of grammatical relations such as subject and predicate. It was convenient to equip the child with these notions, because it is difficult to account for his abstracting them from the language he hears. The other major guiding hypothesis in the language acquisition device was the separation between deep and surface structure of language. This was also a putative universal, and it was stressed by transformational linguists that the *deep structure* had to be accessed by the child, yet there was no isomorphism between it and the surface structure the child actually heard. McNeill (1966, 1970) proposed that the child began by producing *deep structures,* and that language aquisition was essentially a matter of learning the transformations that resulted in an adult-like surface structure.

SEMANTIC APPROACHES

The Under-Representation Issue

What led to dissatisfaction with the above approach? One major consideration was the idea that a pivot grammar under-represented the child's actual knowledge. Reports were also appearing that cast doubts on the universality of pivot grammar as a first step in language acquisition (Bowerman, 1973a). However, the strongest criticism of the whole approach derived from Bloom (1970). She argued that an analysis based on distributional grounds at the level of surface structure seriously underestimated what the child was trying to express. She presented several examples of structural homonyms, that is, utterances with apparently the same superficial *form* but very different *meanings* when considered in context. The best-known example is from the child Kathryn, who said *Mommy sock* on two distinct occasions: once when she found her mother's stocking, and once when her mother was putting Kathryn's sock on Kathryn. It was clear to Bloom and to the mother that Kathryn meant two different things on these occasions, and therefore a pivot grammar approach would underestimate the child's linguistic knowledge in giving each utterance an identical reading. Bloom went on to claim that the two utterances should be generated from two distinct deep structures, much in the same way a sentence in adult grammar, like *flying planes can be dangerous,* is disambiguated in deep structure (Chomsky, 1965). Of course, if one is to attribute that knowledge to the child, it is necessary to explain why he does not express it in his utterances and resolve the ambiguity himself. Bloom introduced the idea of *deletion transformations,* rules that would operate on the differentiated deep structure of the utterance to reduce it to the surface form that we hear from the child. These rules were postulated to act automatically, because of a length constraint at this stage of child speech. That is, the child exercised no choice over the constituents that were deleted and those that were retained. The motivation for this "rich interpretation" approach was similar to that which led to transformational linguistics: regularities could be captured in a more elegant and simple way by allowing for two distinct levels of formal representation, rather than trying to account for them at the level of surface forms.

At this point, the model for child speech was still fairly orthodox transformational syntax. However, the focus had shifted from distributional evidence compiled from a written transcript to an increased attention to the context of utterances to clarify their meaning. Bellugi (1967), for example, in her study of negation, had found an early stage at which children merely appended a negative marker to the statement, as in *No the sun shining.* Bloom (1970) discovered that such utterances can convey very different propositions if they are seen in context. One of the children she studied produced both *no dirty soap* and *no pocket,* but on the first occasion the child was pushing away a worn piece of soap, and on the second occasion she made the statement after searching her mother's skirt in vain for a pocket. The *no* in the first instance seems to be an example of *rejection,* in the second, an expression of *nonexistence,* yet both would receive the same treatment in a grammar that restricted its evidence to the forms themselves.

Some investigators, however, were not terribly happy with the idea of a rich deep structure that spelled out the full meaning, plus deletion rules. As Braine (1971) noted, development should not consist of the "unlearning" of deletion rules! Schlesinger's solution (1971) was to say that the surface forms derived from distinct *intention* or *input* (I) *markers* that were directly semantic, rather than formal, deep structures. The child perceives his environment in terms of such categories as agent and action, possessor and possessed, location and object, etc., and learns to map these concepts directly onto the forms available in his language, without a *linguistic* deep structure as intermediary. To illustrate with a simple example, suppose a child is watching his mother eat an apple, and says *Mommy eat.* The pivot grammar approach might note that he frequently came up with utterances in which *mommy* was in first position, and that word could attach to a variety of other less frequent words, as in *mommy drink, mommy look, mommy come,* etc. The utterance would thus qualify as an instance of Pivot + Open.

In Bloom's approach, the context would be taken into account, from which one might guess that the child had in mind a proposition such as *"Mommy is eating the apple."* The deep structure would contain that information, and deletion transformations would reduce the form by deleting one of the major constituents—in this case, the direct object.

According to Schlesinger (1971), the child knows that *mommy* is the agent of the action *eat,* and he has a formula, called a *realization rule,* by which he orders the words to express that relation in his speech.

Universals

It was noted earlier that pivot grammar was proposed as a universal first step in syntax acquisition. The increasing focus on meaning revealed even more similarity among children from diverse language backgrounds (Bowerman, 1973a; Brown, 1973). It seems on the available evidence that children in the first stage of word-combination express a fairly limited set of basic semantic relations, no matter what their language background. Included in such a set are the relations: agent and action, action and object, action and locative, entity and locative, possessor and possession, entity and attribute, and demonstrative and entity. Brown (1973) found that these relations accounted for some 70% of the utterances produced by children in the early stages of language acquisition.

Continuity in Development

From the assumption that children must acquire the rules and structures of transformational syntax, two major conclusions have been drawn. The first arises from the idea that the syntactic categories such as "subject," "object" are not exhibited in the surface structure, but are defined in terms of deep structure configurations. It is argued that any theory of language learning then has to admit a substantial innate mechanism already equipped with knowledge of deep structure aspects (Fodor, Bever, and Garrett, 1974; McNeill, 1970). The second consequence is that this mechanism must be language-specific; hence there is little continuity proposed between cognitive and language development.

In contrast, the semantic relations approach stresses the continuity of language learning with conceptual development in general. Schlesinger's input-markers are seen as a subset of the conceptual distinctions that humans are capable of making; that subset being those that make a difference in the language. It did not escape notice that the particular semantic relations that are so prevalent in Stage I speech are cognitive distinctions that the preverbal child has mastered in the period of sensorimotor development (Piaget, 1963). The distinctions between agents and actions, agents and objects, etc., are the culmination of this stage in infancy, and it is interesting that such groupings were also posited to be the contents of the first propositions in the symbolic mode (Brown, 1973; Sinclair-de Zwart, 1971). Bowerman (1976) notes that although this is an important insight, it is still necessary to give an account of how a child's mastery of object permanence, causality, or other general achievements could give rise to the specific semantic categories proposed for Schlesinger's input-markers. This issue is discussed more thoroughly in the next section.

Veneziano (1973) has attempted to trace the development of particular schemas involving agents and actions through to new expression in the one-word stage. Part of the problem is a methodological one: no one would want to say that the concepts somehow lie fallow in the one-word stage; however, there is considerable disagreement about how much meaning one can infer from a single word in context, rather than a two-word relation. The kinds of evidence accrued for inferring knowledge of agent categories in behavior differ from that used for assigning semantic relations to two-word utterances. Until the gap is bridged, it will be difficult to ascertain whether the continuity is real or imposed by the adult investigators.

Inferring Intentions

In trying to capture more of the meaning than is expressed by the words themselves, investigators opened up a new methodological issue. Just what kind of evidence may be taken into account in inferring the intention behind an utterance? To take an extreme example: what of the dog who wags his tail excitedly at a door, makes eye contact with his owner, and barks? Do we impute a proposition such as "open the door" to the animal? Perhaps not, but why are we so much more confident in the case of a child who utters a word in a similar situation?

Greenfield and Smith (1976) wish to extend the "rich interpretation" of child utterances to the one-word level. These authors believe that even a single word can express a semantic *relation* rather than just label an aspect of the situation. How can a single word be in relation to anything? They argue that contextual features can be considered part of linguistic structure. The child is structuring the environment into categories such as Agent, Object, Location, etc., and into this rich conceptual framework he inserts single words. Therefore, both the child and the listener interpret the word and context as a richer meaning than the word alone. Ingram (1971) also claimed that one-word utterances have propositional value, and that crying, gestures, and intonation could be considered linguistic elements in combination with the single word.

In contrast, Schlesinger (1974) argued strongly for distinguishing knowledge of the world from knowledge of the language. He wanted to retain a distinction between those relations that are expressed in speech, namely the I-markers, and the "infinitely richer" cognitive structures. "A relation in an I-marker is one which makes a difference linguistically" (1973, p. 144). Dore (1975) feels similarly that the "semantic approaches have often tended to attribute too much linguistic significance to nonlinguistic features" (p. 32).

All this has not had much effect on the ingenious students of the child's first words. There are several types of evidence that suggest that it would be an error to close off investigation prematurely by too much theoretical scolding, although the evidence is not completely convincing. Interesting data are provided by Greenfield and Smith (1976), who posit a progression in the holophrastic period in the relational meanings expressed. For example, they report that there is a roughly invariant order of emergence of such relations as the vocative, action by an agent, experiencer, etc. Of course, as Brown (1973) pointed out, the relations themselves heavily depend on interpretation by the mother or investigator, given the contextual support. It could be that the child is merely labeling different aspects of the situation over time rather than expressing new relations. One important consideration is whether the child knew the words for more than one aspect of the situation, because only then could he be said to be exercising some choice of expression. It is hard to achieve the necessary degree of control in observational research, but one would like to see the child several times in an identical context, with full records of the vocabulary at his command. Brown (1973) quoted an example from Bloom (1973) of a child who used names such as *Mama* and *Dada* in connection with the persons and also with their *possessions*. Later she acquired the names of the possessions themselves, but still occasionally used the proper names in their connection. This might be one case where the conceptual knowledge, in this instance "possession," has a linguistic effect, namely in the *choice* of words in connection with an object.

Parisi (1974) replied to Schlesinger's (1974) criticism that Antinucci and Parisi (1973) fail to distinguish cognitive from semantic knowledge. He presents four types of evidence in support of the postulated semantic structure:

1. The interpretation of a child's utterance by the adult, in particular the mother, who is "continually and successfully going beyond the child's utterances to reconstruct their underlying meanings" (p. 98).
2. An indirect test of (1) is if the adult deliberately misinterprets the utterance—for example, if the child asks for a ball by saying *Mommy give,* and the mother gives it to a third party.

We do not find that (1) constitutes *evidence,* because it is what is in dispute. (2) has neither been systematically tested, nor does it seem to bear on the issue of *cognitive* versus *semantic* structures. The next two arguments are more relevant:

3. A verb like *da* in Italian, that has three arguments, is never used by very young children with all three. However, it appears with each of the three arguments in different utterances. Such use demonstrates that the child *can* express these aspects in his speech, although not all at one time.
4. In dialogue, the elements of the semantic structure are expressed sequentially by the child. Parisi gives as an example the following:

Claudia	Mother
Etto ("here is")	*Dove'è la pupa?* ("where is the doll?")
Bamboa ("doll")	*Come si chiana questa?* ("what is this called?")
Totto ("cookie")	*Cosa le dai alla bambola?* ("what are you giving your doll?")

Parisi, like Greenfield and Smith argues that to answer a question appropriately involves knowing the structure of the question. Hence, underlying the single word answer is a more elaborate structure of relations. He gives further examples where the adult, by prompting the child, gets him to express further aspects of the situation in later utterances. Here, then, is a further claim extending the limits of evidence: words strung out over time, and words in relation to the utterances of another person, reveal that the cognitive structures "make a difference, linguistically."

Other investigators have been more restrictive in their definitions of a linguistic difference. For example, Bloom (1973) found that at the end of the one-word period, children produced successive single word utterances that are *not* syntactic. By this she meant that they occurred in free order, and each word was in its own prosodic envelope. The lack of syntax was not because of lack of vocabulary. Nor was it a result of an inability to string phonemes, because Bloom's own daughter used to construct utterances with one recognizable word and a meaningless form /widə/. Therefore, Bloom concluded that the child's developing conceptual knowledge in the one-word stage is not yet linguistic in nature.

Another very important source of inference about meaning in the holophrase is intonation. However, this literature is more pertinent to inferring communicative intent than to interpretation of the semantic relations, it is deferred to the equivalent section entitled "Pragmatic Approaches."

At the two-word stage, there are two additional kinds of evidence. The first is the use of the dominant word order to encode a semantic relation. If the child consistently chooses one order in expressing two words, one can be more certain that he is not just successively naming aspects of the situation as they occur to him. Second, the two words have a single prosodic contour without a pause, suggesting they are conjoined to express a relation. Brown (1973), along with most other researchers, feels comfortable about attributing semantic relations to the child based on the convergence of: 1) interpretation in context, 2) prosody, and 3) word order.

The Psychologically Real Categories

It is evident that we can impose multiple descriptions on any particular complex stimulus, and the problem is to decide which is functional for the person or creature we are studying. Suppose we trained an animal to push a lever in the presence of a slide of a Ming vase. Think of the alternative descriptions we could provide for that stimulus: a) a slide, b) a blue slide, c) a blue patch on a black background, d) a three-dimensional object, e) a container, f) a particular orientation of a container, or g) a Ming vase in a particular orientation. The list is potentially infinite. The traditional means of determining the appropriate level of description is to perform a generalization test with different slides and objects fitting each category to see what the organism regards as similar to the original.

This is exactly the procedure used to determine the meaning of single words in the child's lexicon: we look for extensions of the word to new objects or events to see if the child's meaning coincides with ours (Clark, 1973). The problem is slightly more complex for utterances, however. Any given two-word utterance can be described in multiple ways: as Pivot + Open, Subject + Predicate, Agent + Action, Animate + Event, Thing + Process, Topic + Comment, Kitty + Hit—which is the appropriate level? Schlesinger (1974) proposed two criteria for this decision: 1) if utterances from two subclasses enter the child's speech at the same time, there is reason to believe that they are from the same class, and 2) if utterances from the two subclasses use the same syntactic device, e.g., word order, then they belong to the same class. To give a concrete illustration, a child studied by Braine (1976) constructed sentences with *big* and *little* in constant sentence position at around the same time in development. There was thus reason to class them together as *size* to predict the construction of new utterances on the model Size + x, rather than two distinct rules Big + x and Little + x. At around the same time, this child produced utterances with other modifiers such as Hot + x, Old + x, etc. Could he possess a linguistic rule at an even more general level, such as Property + x? Braine argued that that was too abstract, because the child produced other utterances with *wet* that showed unstable word order: either Wet + x or X + wet. Hence, a superordinate category like *property* was not functional for the child.

Similarly, both Bowerman (1973a) and de Villiers and de Villiers (1974) noticed that in the early sentences of the children they studied, the agents were almost always animate nouns. Therefore, a superordinate concept such as *agent* was inappropriate at first for these children, because they did not extend the word order rule to inanimate nouns. This was, however, much weaker evidence than Braine's because there were very limited opportunities for them to observe and talk about inanimate agents. It is interesting, however, that these same children failed on a comprehension task where agent-hood could not be identified consistently with animacy (de Villiers and de Villiers, 1973).

Another apt example comes from Bowerman (1973b). She reported that a Russian child studied by Ghozdev had apparently a more restricted notion of *object* than is usual for adult speech. In Russian, the accusative form is marked by an inflection rather than word order, and this child at first did not mark any nouns at all. When he began to use the inflection, he marked only those nouns in a semantically restricted role: as objects of direct movements such as *give, carry, throw.* He did not use the inflection on direct objects of such actions as *read* or *draw* until much later.

As Bowerman (1976) and Brown (1973) point out, the child could proceed by learning the position associated with the individual semantic roles of a verb; e.g., he could learn that the one that *eats* goes first, the one that *is eaten* goes last. Then he could generate *Mommy eat* and *Daddy eat, kitty eat,* and also *eat lunch, eat apple,* and so forth. He could repeat the process for a verb such as *hit,* and for *throw,* and for *kiss.* They point out that it would, however, be more economical to learn to categorize these as *actions,* and to learn a rule such that the name of the one who performs the action goes in first position. The rule for any new verb does not have to be learned anew: if it qualifies as an *action,* the general rule applies.

The question remaining is how abstract do these classifications get? Bloom, Miller, and Hood (1975) present some evidence that children in the two-word stage know more than an order defined by semantic roles; they also possess syntactic information. They argue that a word like *lamb* serves the same semantic function in the case where the child moves it around and says either *lamb go here* or *put lamb here*. Yet the child puts the word appropriately in either preverb or postverb position, and does not produce *go lamb here* or *lamb put here*. These positions are obviously not defined by the noun's semantic function. Why could they not be defined by the verb's semantic role? Bloom et al., after all, present other evidence in support of three distinct verb categories: agent-locative action, mover-locative action, and patient-locative action, each of which has different lexical membership. *Go* and *put* fall in distinct semantic categories in Bloom et al.'s own scheme; therefore there is reason to regard this as another example of a semantically-based rule in which the semantic category is more narrow than the syntactic categories employed in the adult language.

The Emergence of Syntax

The claim has been made that the categories used by children in the first stages of language development are more restricted than grammatical categories, more semantically unified, and more tied to cognitive categories useful in the sensorimotor period. How does the child proceed from here to an adult-like grammar? There are two classes of solution to this problem:

1. The child's semantic categories incorporate wider and wider instances until there is no difference between, e.g., *agent* and *subject*
2. The adult model of syntax is not psychologically real: even adult grammar is semantically based.

The grammatical category *subject* can not be consistently identified with a semantic notion such as *agent*. Subjects play many different semantic roles such as *experiencer* (e.g., John *heard a cry*), agent (e.g. The boy *hit the ball*), and instrument (e.g., the key *opened the door*). However, there are certain linguistic operations that show the equivalence of these disparate semantic forms, e.g., *clefting* and *passivization*. One can treat all these sentences in the same way in clefting and retain the meaning:

> *It was John who heard a cry*
> *It was the boy who hit the ball*

and in passivization:

> *The cry was heard by John*
> *The door was opened by the key.*

Therefore, Bowerman (1973b) proposed that just as there is an economy in classing various events together as one *action* category, there is a similar advantage to collapsing semantic distinctions such as *agent, beneficiary,* and *experiencer,* and subsuming them under the notion *subject* for these complex aspects of syntax. These syntactic operations are not mastered for several years in child speech, so the evidence for an over-riding concept like *subject* is missing at the beginning.

Schlesinger (1974) had a different solution. His idea was that agents and the like are not *subsumed* under a grammatical category, but that the child comes to believe that cases like the instrumental, the experiencer, etc., are agents when he notices that such relations have the same word order in English. This predicted that instruments in subject position should be seen as instigators of action, and in support, Schlesinger noted the peculiarity of the sentence *The brush paints the picture.* Thus he wanted to propose that syntactic categories are semantically defined even for adults.

In response to this, Bowerman (1974) argued that many subjects can not be easily interpreted as extended agent concepts, for example in the sentences:

The situation justifies taking drastic measures.
The boat trip resulted in several deaths.

She concluded that a semantic specification of structural relations was inadequate for adult grammar, as was in fact stated by Chomsky (1957, p. 101): "We cannot, apparently, find semantic absolutes, known in advance of grammar, that can be used to determine the objects of grammar in any way." Chomsky was referring to the linguist's task, but the arguments he advanced should be equally considered in assessing the claim that syntax derives from semantics in the language acquisition process. It remains a matter of dispute whether we can trace the emergence of syntactic categories from semantic categories (e.g., Bowerman, 1973b), or whether we should adopt a semantically based grammar for adults, also (see Fillmore, 1968, for an example of this approach).

PRAGMATIC APPROACHES

Work on the development of language in its social context falls into two categories. There are some researchers who study discourse, dialogue, and the like as yet another aspect of language that the child has to learn, and there are others who treat language first and foremost as a social act, and who try to derive semantic and syntactic forms from these pragmatic functions.

It is the second group whom we consider in this paper, although the interested reader is referred to the research in the first category by Garvey (1975) Gelman and Shatz (1975) Keenan (1974), and Keenan and Klein (1975) for some current findings.

Several investigators have afforded a more central role to the functions of language in a theory of language acquisition. In particular, Antinucci and Parisi (1975), Bates (1976), and Halliday (1975) have spelled out their own models of acquisition and the way in which pragmatics or function is central to their concerns. In much the same way that semantics was initially considered irrelevant, then recognized as a help to further specify the grammar (Bloom, 1970), and finally became the cornerstone of a model (Schlesinger, 1971), pragmatics has moved to the center of attention from similar considerations.

The Under-Representation Issue

Investigators such as Bloom had noticed that careful attention to context could disambiguate the syntactic form of utterances like *Mommy sock* into two deep structures with distinct propositional content. Antinucci and Parisi (1973) focused not only on the nonverbal context, but also on the nature of the interaction between child and adult. They used additional information over and above the propositional content, namely the *use* to which the form is put. For example, a child might say, *Mommy give* on two occasions, one with the intention of *describing* an event and the other as a *request* to the mother. The two utterances cannot be described only as *agent action,*—their *function* must also be included in a full description. They argue that any representation must be made up of these two parts: the proposition representing the semantic content of the sentence, and the performative or illocutionary force, which specifies how the content is to be taken by the listener. These features are proposed as obligatory and present from the start in children's utterances.

Universals

The work on early-appearing performatives does not yet have the same cross-linguistic base as the work on semantics, because most of the available literature is on Italian (e.g., Antinucci and Parisi, 1973, 1975; Bates, 1974), English (e.g., Halliday, 1975), or American English (e.g., Dore, 1975). One would expect even more convergence here than in the area of semantic relations, because nothing seems more universally similar than the social interactions in which parents and children engage. Dore (1975) quotes Slobin (1971, p. 302): "Everywhere language consists of utterances performing a universal set of communicative functions (such as asserting, denying, requesting, ordering, and so forth)." Nevertheless, the initial functions served by language may be a restricted set, because some functions seem to emerge *after* language is syntactically complex (e.g., *promise,* see Searle, 1971). Greenfield and Smith (1976) found that the very first words of their subjects were "pure performatives" with no propositional content, such as *hi* and *bye-bye.* Shortly after, they could identify a division into imperative and declarative functions, as could Antinucci and Parisi (1973) for Italian. Gruber (1973) found all of the early utterances of his subject to be performatives, with reportatives developing subsequently.

Halliday (1969, 1975) suggested a tentative system of developmental functions appearing very roughly in the order listed below. These are proposed as universals of human culture, and mastery of all of them is said to be a necessary and sufficient condition for the transition to the adult system.

Instrumental	(I want)
Regulatory	(Do as I tell you)
Interactional	(Me and you)
Personal	(Here I come)
Heuristic	(Tell me why)
Imaginative	(Let's pretend)
Informative	(I've got something to tell you)

Halliday has collected data for only one English child so far (1975), but the hypothesis has the strongest implications for universals of all the current accounts.

Continuity in Development

Researchers in the present framework have endeavored to show the continuity between nonlinguistic and linguistic communication in early infancy. For example, Bateson (1975) and Bruner (1975a,b) saw the roots of dialogue in the reciprocal turn-taking in nonverbal interaction between mother and infant. Scaife and Bruner (1975) demonstrated that the very young infant is in the process of learning to coordinate reference to an object or event with his caregiver, and they point to the importance of this as the basis for all later communication.

Bates, Camaioni, and Volterra (1973) traced the development of performatives in the period before speech. They found three stages in this development. Between birth and about 10 months, the infants were apparently unaware of the communicative value of their signals. Thus they would not look imploringly at an adult while reaching for an object, nor would they use objects to attract the adult's attention.

Between about 10 and 15 months, the infants used adults as the means to get an object they desired. Similarly, they used objects to gain the adults' attention. The authors called these "proto-imperatives" and "proto-declaratives," because they regarded them as the precursors to verbal expressions of these functions. In the final stage, the infants began to use words with referential value in these same performative schemes, for the purposes of either gaining objects or attention. It is necessary to turn now to the question of how these intentions are inferred.

Inferring Intentions

The purpose of this section is to clarify the grounds on which different researchers have classified the child's intentions. Notice that "intention" is here used in a broader sense than Schlesinger's "intention-markers." It refers to "the deliberate pursuit of a goal by means of instrumental behaviors subordinated to that goal" (Dore, 1975, p. 36), so it is more concerned with function than propositional content.

The debate is once again: to what extent must the inferred intention have linguistic effect to be counted. Some investigators (Antinucci and Parisi, 1975; Greenfield and Smith, 1976) are content to judge from context alone, and to observe the child's persistence in pursuit of a goal or his reaction to consequences as confirmatory evidence. Of course, then any behavior can be classified in this scheme, not just verbal behavior. These authors are interested in the very early stages of language development, so perhaps there is more to be gained by loosening the criteria and observing the transition from nonverbal to verbal communicative behavior.

Halliday (1975) also uses context as the main indication of the function of the speech act, although he is gratified when, on occasion, his subject began using different intonation patterns with the two general functions he had classified on contextual grounds alone. This was seen as evidence that the scheme was psychologically real to the child, too.

Dore (1975) was much stricter in his classification of primitive speech acts. These were defined as containing a rudimentary referring expression and a primitive force-indicating device, "typically an intonation pattern" (p. 31). The word *mama* was used by his subject in three different ways: with a rising terminal contour to ask if an object belonged to his mother; with a falling terminal contour where the child merely labeled; and with an abrupt rising-falling contour to call his mother when she was some distance away. Thus, the child's "prosodic pattern indicates his intention with regard to that notion." Dore advocated treating contextual features merely as clues to the child's intentions rather than as part of his linguistic knowledge, and assigning linguistic status only to the two actual manifestations of language: single words and minimal prosodic patterns.

It should be pointed out, however, that there is by no means full agreement concerning the reliability of intonation as an indicator of illocutionary force. Dore (1975) reported that his scheme of classification had reasonable reliability. The strongest evidence comes from Menyuk and Bernholtz (1969), who studied an 18–20-month-old child in whose speech they identified five words judged in context to be intended in three different ways: statement, question, and emphasis. They found adults could classify the tape-recording of these sounds out of context with more than 80% agreement. In addition, a spectrographic analysis revealed a typical fundamental frequency contour for each utterance type.

Unfortunately, this was a single child (although Dore reports it as "children"!) and there is conflicting evidence from other investigators. Bloom (1973) observed that the intonation of single-word utterances was *not* consistently correlated with semantic intentions. For example, a rising terminal contour did not always signal a question. Weir's (1966) evidence agrees with this, as does that of Miller and Ervin (1964), who reported: "Susan was over 2 years old before the rising intonation consistently indicated a question. It may be that she learned the intonation by noting which sentences drew a response from the adult." Such a progression might also account for Halliday's (1975) observation that his subject, Nigel, began to differentiate pragmatic intentions (interrogatives, imperatives, and the like) by applying a rising intonation on that whole class at the age of 19 months, in order to contrast it with a class of "mathetic" (referential) functions. Halliday believed that Nigel made systematic use of intonation from the start "like all children" (p. 258), but he denies that Nigel was using intonation as in adult English. Instead, the child adapted the distinction between rising and falling tones to a functional system within his own limitations, not isomorphic with the adult system.

This suggests that children may, in fact, use intonational contrasts to signal different intentions, but individuals may have quite idiosyncratic systems and it could be a serious error for investigators to map adult functional categories onto these intonational devices. This is an area desperately in need of systematic research.

Another area of research in pragmatics concerns *presuppositions*. Bates (1976) divides these into three types: logical, pragmatic, and psychological, which have in common that an utterance in a discourse context has implications beyond the proposition it encodes. In any dialogue, some information is taken for granted and other information is asserted. Obviously, the question of how and when children acquire these skills is a most interesting one from social, cognitive, and linguistic perspectives. Unfortunately it creates a serious methodological difficulty: how can one determine whether a child *intended* to presuppose something, rather than just not asserting it?

Greenfield and Smith (1976) and Veneziano (cited in Bates, 1976) claim that children in the one-word stage of development almost always encode that element undergoing greatest change or emphasis. For example, if the child is placing toys in a bucket, he tends to name them individually rather than saying *put* or *bucket,* which remains constant in the situation. Bates (1976) studied Italian children in the two-word stage, and found they adopted a heuristic for expressing new information in first place, followed by old information. She believed this to be the next step from the "new only" expressions at the one-word stage.

This is intriguing data: what could be the explanation? For Parisi (1974, p. 102), it is clear: "He is also able to select for encoding precisely that element of his semantic structure which is the most informative." This sounds rather sophisticated for the child in the one-word stage of language development. There is a wealth of other evidence (Flavell, Botkin, Fry, Wright, and Jarvis, 1968) suggesting that children at a much later age are notoriously poor at taking into account their listener's needs. In a communication situation, seven-year-olds seem unable to extract the relevant dimensions to delimit a referent precisely enough for their listener to choose it from an array. How can these findings be reconciled?

Bates (1976) does not want to grant linguistic knowledge of presuppositions to the child until he can use recognizable signals to demonstrate his control. She argues that salient, new information gets labeled because of the focusing properites of the perceptual system, and the early acts of presupposing reflect only this. The child takes much longer to recognize that his listener's needs might differ from his own, and that he may have to assert information that *he* knows, but that his listener does not know.

There exist other data on comprehension of presuppositions that may illuminate the ontogeny of this process in communication. These techniques generally point to gradually developing understanding of presuppositions (Maratsos, 1972, 1973), although in some cases, such as the negative, the appropriate conditions for use may be known surprisingly early (Antinucci and Volterra, 1973; de Villiers and Tager-Flusberg, 1975).

The Psychologically Real Categories

Just as any number of *semantic* classifications can be imposed on a given utterance, there is a great deal of freedom about the *functional* categories we can impose. Surprisingly, this has received no systematic treatment in the current literature. The dilemma is thus: because there is possibly only one (disputed) linguistic device correlated with function, namely prosody, the child has no way of demonstrating *his* classification to us. Investigators are then free to slice the functions as finely or as broadly as they choose, depending on *their* perception of similarity of acts-in-context.

Unexpectedly, the various researchers have converged on a similar broad categorization of function, although they label the functions differently (see Table 1). This suggests that they are using some implicit criterion in common. It seems to consist of one of Schlesinger's (1974) criteria for classifying semantic relations as equivalent: coincident emergence. Gruber (1973) found all the early utterances of his subject to be *performatives,* which then subdivided into *reportatives* and *performatives.* There seems to be a pattern in development, with pragmatic functions emerging before the more referential uses. However, part of the difficulty in assessing the generality of this finding comes from the use of different starting points for investigation. Some researchers, such as Gruber and Halliday, begin with words and the functions they serve. Others, such as Bates et al., search for the roots of various communicative functions in the child's earlier prelinguistic behavior, with the words being slotted into preexisting schemas.

Halliday (1975) is one of the few writers to subdivide the functions more finely (see Table 1). Yet in fact, the first four functions came in roughly together in his subject's speech, so if one applies the weak criterion of coincident emergence they would be considered one "real" category. The next two functions also emerged at around the same time and might constitute a second category for the child. Schlesinger's second criterion, of sharing a linguistic device, also partially fits these data, because it will be remembered that the child imposed a rising intonation on utterances expressing the *pragmatic* functions and a falling intonation on *mathetic* functions, the latter being roughly isomorphic with *referential.* The exception in this scheme is Halliday's *personal* function, which emerges early but is considered non-pragmatic. It forms the basis for the mathetic class when it is combined with the heuristic function at a later point.

Interestingly, Halliday believes the early *referential* utterances are not intended to *inform* the listener who did not share the experience, but rather to consolidate the child's learning experiences in his explorations of the world.

Table 1.   Some representative descriptions of the development of language functions

Gruber (1967)		Performative	Performative	
			Reportative	
Greenfield and Smith (1976)		"Pure" performative	Imperative	
			Declarative	
Halliday (1975)		Instrumental Regulatory Interactional	Heuristic Imaginative	Informative
		Pragmatic Personal	Mathetic	
Bates, Camaioni, and Volterra (1973)	Perlocutionary Acts	Proto imperatives	Imperatives	
		Proto declaratives	Declaratives	

The Emergence of Syntax

A parallel can be made between the solutions offered for the emergence of syntax from semantics and for the emergence of form from pragmatic function. The solutions proposed are either: 1) linguistic devices become increasingly free of specific functions, or 2) linguistic characterizations of adult language should make no distinction between form and function, because every utterance is a pragmatic *act*.

The first approach is that of Halliday (1975). He found that the early words and phrases of his subject Nigel were highly function-specific. For example, Nigel had words such as *syrup* meaning only *I want my syrup*, or *cat* meaning *Hullo, cat*. His first phrases, too, had this quality: *more omelet, more bread* were only pragmatic, whereas *two train, green peg*, etc., were only mathetic, i.e., never used as request forms. There are many similar reports, summarized in Bates (1976). Svachkin (1973) cites the case of a child who used the word *kat* only for a game in which she threw her toy out of the crib and waited for an adult to return it. Bates et al. (1973) report that their subject used *da* (Italian for "give") in all acts of giving and taking objects, but never as a request or as a description of giving. Skinner (1957), in *Verbal Behavior*, proposed that *mands* and *tacts* might be learned in distinct ways: the child does not learn a word that can be used in various ways, but having learned *milk* as a mand, may have to re-learn it as a tact. This suggestion could be true in two ways: 1) words are highly function-specific at first, and 2) the referential use may emerge subsequent to the pragmatic use.

Halliday suggests that a major change occurs when words become *pluri-functional*, i.e., available for use in more than one way. He offers one possibility: in a pragmatic form such as *more meat* the request element, *more*, is noticed as a comparative quantifier, and becomes used in a mathetic sense as in *look here's some more meat*. Halliday offers no reason why this should occur, but one can think of a plausible case. The child will presumably be more successful at his pragmatic goals if his linguistic forms specify correctly what it is he refers to, so the properties of the object or attributes become more precisely linked to the words he uses. In Skinner's sense, the attribute or object becomes a discriminative stimulus for the verbal response. What is interesting is that this act of tacting or making reference is governed by a different kind of *purpose* than that for which the form evolved, namely *manding*.

It seems that this secondary or derived activity becomes motivating in its own right, either because the listener praises or shows increased attention to these forms, or because the forms are somehow helpful to the child in exploring his environment. It may be that children who use words primarily for pragmatic purposes tend also to believe that new words have a similar function. At a later time, when a more referential function has emerged, the same child might mistakenly *seek* a referent for a "pure performative." Two isolated observations may make this possibility clearer. Piaget's daughter Jacqueline used the word *panama* (grandfather) as a request for actions, objects, and the like—an all-purpose pragmatic function—rather than as a name for her grandfather (as is often the case with grandparents, her grandfather was frequently associated with indulgence) (Piaget, 1962). In contrast,

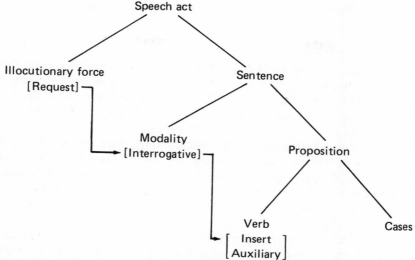

Figure 1. Dore's (1975) model for the formation of a request. (Reprinted from *Journal of Child Language 2:* 36 by permission.)

Bowerman's daughter Christy used the word *hi!* to *refer* to any object covering a limb. Apparently this odd use derived from her mother using it in a game in which a finger puppet approached and said "hi!" (Bowerman, 1976). Both children made errors of generalization, but along different dimensions: in the first case, a proper name used as a request, in the second, a greeting used as a description. An interesting direction for future research would be to clarify the relationship between the predominance of certain functions and the acquisition of new words.

It may be a fundamental property of human language that most words are not tied to specific communicative functions. Thus, understanding the process by which the range of functions of a word expands in development is of the utmost importance, yet there has been little theoretical interest in the question.

Like other accounts (Antinucci and Parisi, 1975; Ross, 1970), Dore (1975) analyzed a speech act into two parts: an illocutionary force and a proposition. In addition, he provided an account of speech act development that did allow for some interaction between the two components. Unless they are seen as autonomous developments, it is clearly desirable to specify how one might derive from or influence the course of the other. Dore proposed that the propositional elements became grammaticized, whereas the illocutionary force finds conventional expression via the *modality* component of the sentence, that in turn influences elements of the proposition. Figure 1 is an example from Dore (1975) on the formation of a request. This would be an interesting way to proceed; however, certain cases would soon require revisions. In particular, indirect speech acts (Searle, 1975a) would cause trouble for this simple account. These cases provide one of the primary motivations for the *separation* of illocutionary force from the sentence modality component, e.g., the sentences:

How many times must I tell you to close the door?

or

Can you tie my shoe?

in which the intention of the speaker is not directly interrogative in nature. They are in fact directives to perform the action. It is nevertheless possible that the initial process of acquisition proceeds as Dore has outlined, and that the indirect exceptions are treated in a different manner at a later age (see Bates, 1971; Ervin-Tripp, 1974; Shatz, 1974a on the development of polite forms).

Despite the interaction allowed in the above model, there seems to be a separate development of the referring expression and the illocutionary component. Hence, such a model would qualify as an instance of the genre "pragmatics is something else the child has to learn, in addition to syntax and semantics." In that case, it is hard to reason that "form emerges out of function." There are stronger claims made by other researchers in pragmatics.

Bates (1976) takes a more radical position on the relations among pragmatics, semantics, and syntax. She believes, like Searle (1971, 1975b), that pragmatics should occupy center stage in our accounts of language in both children *and* adults. Searle (1975b) argued that a speech act analysis was more informative with regard to communication and the psychology of language than an approach resting on models in linguistics. He criticized recent movements in linguistics to incorporate performatives as part of linguistic deep structure (cf. Ross, 1970) on the grounds that speech act theory already accounts for the same facts independently. Ross had proposed that all English sentences have a performative main verb in their deep structure, this being designed to account for certain facts about reflexives in English. It is permissible to use a reflexive pronoun in a subordinate clause if the main clause includes a noun phrase to which the pronoun has an anaphoric relationship (Searle, 1975b), e.g., *Tom believed that the paper had been written by Ann and himself,* but not: *The paper had been written by Ann and himself.* However, with the first person reflexive, the equivalent sentence is acceptable: *The paper had been written by Ann and myself.* Therefore, Ross proposed that in all these cases the sentence S is embedded in a structure of the form *I say to you that S,* in which case *myself* is anaphoric, *himself* is not. This performative hypersentence is then deleted in the surface form of the sentence. Notice that such a treatment is the one adopted by many of the writers on pragmatics in child speech (e.g., Antinucci and Parisi, 1975; Dore, 1975).

It is Searle's (1975b) contention that this theory is unnecessarily complex and counterintuitive. "Since we already know that a speech situation contains a hearer, a speaker, and a speech act, it is an unnecessary complexity to introduce deleted syntactic elements corresponding to these entities" (p. 31). He especially objects to the elevation of established facts about speech acts to the status of "rules" and "objects" to be incorporated into a linguistic theory. He regards them as possessing "no explanatory power, since they are mere reformulations of the material we need to explain" (p. 37). The task of theories of language is, in Searle's view, that of relating the sounds we make to the illocutionary acts we perform. Pragmatics is then not an adjunct to linguistic theory, but the central question. Bates (1976) holds an essentially similar view when she says, "we have just proposed that, logically and ontogenetically, all of semantics and syntactics are derived ultimately from pragmatics, from 'language games' that consist in the use of signals in contexts, to carry out some function" (p. 426).

Although a focus on communication provides insights into the continuity with cognitive and social development that are missed by the syntactic approach, many of the problems addressed by traditional approaches to child language are *not* easily solved by the pragmatic approach. Bates admits that there is a difference between acquisition of a performative function and acquisition of the conventional means for expressing that function in any particular language.

Whereas the syntactic and semantic approaches had difficulty accounting for the *motivation* to learn language, the pragmatic approach stresses this aspect. On the other hand, a transition to propositional, referential, or mathetic language is reported by many investigators, yet no good theory of its emergence has been put forward. It is possible that the initial lexicon is acquired for very specific functional purposes, but that these purposes broaden to include commenting on the world and its events. The latter purposes might be based in general cognitive development, and be manifested in other behaviors such as nonverbal play. The authors propose, then, that *all* language may not be oriented toward communication, although ontogenically its roots are there. Instead, certain forms, such as the basic semantic relations, may have Halliday's "mathetic" function, designed to incorporate, organize, and experiment with events occurring in the world.

At a later point, the child becomes increasingly free to use language in the absence of immediate referents, and perhaps at this time the language that he hears reveals to him its structural possibilities. Schlesinger (1974) proposed that the influence of cognition on language is not one-way, but that language has a role in shaping the cognitive repertoire. This occurs not only in learning individual concepts and their referents. The learning of sentence structures also has consequences for the way the child comes to "slice up" his experience. In this way, the forms of language affect the way functions and concepts get classed together. All of this is what it means to acquire the conventional means for expressing a variety of illocutionary intentions, and it seems that no single approach has a privileged role in explanations of the process of language acquisition.

The conclusion is thus: at a certain point in development, the child's semantic encodings are liberated from serving particular performative functions. At a later point, syntactic forms gain independence from particular semantic roles. The motivation for these reorganizations is something of a mystery. We turn now to a consideration of the other side of the communication, namely the mother or caregiver, and what she says and does that might influence the child's progress toward adult communicative competence.

THE CONTEXT OF SEMANTIC AND SYNTACTIC DEVELOPMENT

As early as 1964, Brown and Bellugi pointed out that the utterances of parents to young children were short, semantically and syntactically simple, well-formed, and repetitive—quite unlike the "defective" and "degenerate" speech of adults, as

Chomsky (1965) characterized it. Yet it was not until the late 1960s and early 1970s that researchers in the area of language acquisition began to study the linguistic input to the child in any detail. In fact, most developmental psycholinguists took Chomsky's characterization of adult speech as incomplete, full of false starts, grammatical errors, and disfluencies, as an adequate description of the linguistic input from which the child extracts the semantic and syntactic rules of his language. Thus, Fodor described the input to the child as "a sample of the kinds of utterances fluent speakers of his language typically use," and suggested the working assumption "that the language environment of a child does not differ in any useful way from that of an adult" (cited in Smith and Miller, 1966, pp. 108, 126). Given this assumption, it is not too surprising that psycholinguists were caught up with wonder at the accomplishment of the child in ever learning language at all and were readily prepared to attribute much of the grammatical structure of language to an innate language acquisition device (McNeill, 1966; 1970). In our wonder at the "creation of language" by the child in a mere two years, the commonsense fact that children acquire language in communicative interaction with parents or other adults, although it was acknowledged as true, was not sufficient to direct attention toward specification of the details of that interaction.

However, over the past six years, several comprehensive studies of adults' (usually the mother's) speech to children have been conducted, comparing several grammatical and semantic aspects of adults' speech to children of different ages with their speech to other adults. Increasing emphasis on the pragmatic, communicative features of early child language has enhanced the interest in adult-child verbal interaction. We here consider the findings of several such studies in so far as they illuminate the possible processes by which mature semantic and syntactic forms emerge from the pragmatic use to which the child first puts language.

General Features of Adult-Child Speech

Table 2 summarizes the major relevant differences between adult-child and adult-adult speech revealed by these studies. They are classified as phonological, syntactic, semantic, or pragmatic differences, but it should be noted that some aspects could fall into more than one category. Differences in the relative frequency of commands, requests, and queries are probably based on pragmatic considerations in adult-child speech, but they clearly lead to differences in the relative frequency of syntactic forms.

The tabled results indicate that subsequent studies have confirmed and extended Brown and Bellugi's qualitative impressions of parents' speech to their children. Almost all of them have measured the mean length of utterance (MLU) of adult-child speech in either words or morphemes and have found that it is considerably shorter than adult-adult speech (Drach, 1969; Lord, 1975; Newport, 1977; Phillips, 1973; Sachs, Brown, and Salerno, 1972; Snow, 1972). In fact, the mothers' utterances become even shorter when the child first begins to produce intelligible words (Lord, 1975; Phillips, 1973). Mothers' speech to 18-month-olds is significantly shorter than that to 28-month-old children, but speech to 8-month-olds is the same

Table 2.   Review of the general characteristics of adult-child speech

Phonological differences	
Higher pitch and exaggerated intonation	Drach, 1969; Phillips, 1970; Remick, 1971; Sachs, Brown, and Salerno, 1972.
Clear enunciation, slower speech, and distinct pauses between utterances	Drach, 1969; Newport, 1977; Sachs et al., 1972.
Phonological simplification, distinct consonant-vowel combinations, and frequent syllable reduplication	DePaulo and Bonvillian, 1975; Ferguson, 1974.
Syntactic differences	
Shorter and less varied utterance length (MLU), shorter mean preverb length	Brown and Bellugi, 1964; Cross, in press; Drach, 1969; Lord, 1975; Moerk, 1972; Nelson, 1973; Newport, 1977; Phillips, 1970, 1973; Sachs et al., 1972; Shatz and Gelman, 1973; Snow, 1971, 1972; Vorster, 1974.
Almost all sentences well-formed and intelligible	Broen, 1972; Brown and Bellugi, 1964; Cross, in press; Drach, 1969; Newport, 1977; Phillips, 1970, 1973; Remick, 1971; Snow, 1971, 1972.
Many partial or complete repetitions of own or child's utterances, sometimes with expansion	Brown, Cazden, and Bellugi, 1969; Kobashigawa, 1969; Newport, 1977; Snow, 1971, 1972.
Fewer disfluencies or broken sentences	Broen, 1972; Newport, 1977; Snow, 1972.
Many constituents uttered in isolation	Broen, 1972; Newport, 1977; Snow, 1971, 1972.
Transformationally less complex	Drach, 1969; Pfuderer, 1969.
Fewer verbs per utterance, fewer coordinate or subordinate clauses, fewer embeddings	Drach, 1969; Newport, 1977; Phillips, 1970, 1973; Shatz and Gelman, 1973; Snow, 1971, 1972; Vorster, 1974.
Rarity of modifiers and pronouns, more content words and fewer functors	Newport, 1977; Phillips, 1970.
Subject nouns or pronouns and auxiliary in yes/no questions often deleted	Newport, 1977; Remick, 1971.
More imperatives and questions to young children, particularly occasional questions	Blount, 1972; Brown et al., 1969; Drach, 1969; Gelman and Shatz, 1975; Newport, 1977.
Increasing number of declaratives with increasing age of child	Brown and Hanlon, 1970; Newport, 1977.
Semantic differences	
More limited vocabulary use, but with unique words for objects and many diminutives	Blount, 1972; Drach, 1969; Ferguson, 1974: Phillips, 1970.

Reference invariably to the here and now; words have concrete referents and there are few references to the past	Cross, in press; Phillips, 1970; Remick, 1971; Shatz and Gelman, 1973; Snow, 1971.
Different level of generality in naming objects	Anglin, 1976.
More limited range of semantic relations	Snow, 1974.
Pragmatic differences	
More directives, imperatives, and questions	Blount, 1972; Gelman and Shatz, 1975; Newport, 1977; Shatz and Gelman, 1973.
More deictic utterances	Newport, 1977.

length as that to the older children (Phillips, 1973). Lord (1975) observed a similar reduction in MLU in a longitudinal study of mothers' speech to their children from 8 to 18 months. The mothers' speech to their 8-month-old infants seems to be more concerned with catching and maintaining the child's attention, or for the mothers' own entertainment. Once the child begins to respond with a word or two, much of the mother's speech is concerned with eliciting a verbal response from the child. There are more single-word and language-teaching utterances either naming objects or asking "What's that?", and this decreases the average MLU.

Several investigators have demonstrated that adult-child speech contains remarkably few ungrammatical or unintelligible utterances (Broen, 1972: Drach, 1969; Newport, 1977; Phillips, 1970, 1973; Remick, 1971; Snow, 1972), but contains many partial or complete repetitions of the child's or the adult's own sentences (Kobashigawa, 1969; Newport, 1977; Snow, 1972). In Newport's study of the speech of 15 mothers to their children, only one in 1500 utterances was ungrammatical in the sense of being syntactically garbled, and fully 34% of the mothers' sentences were full or partial repetitions of one of their previous utterances, or imitations of one of the children's utterances.

Many different measures of grammatical complexity indicate that adult-child speech is syntactically simple. If an index of derivational complexity based on the number of transformations required to generate the adults' utterances from their deep structure is taken (Brown and Hanlon, 1970), adult-adult speech is transformationally more varied and contains more transformations than adult-child speech (Drach, 1969). Considering only the complete utterances of the parents to the children studied by Brown and co-workers (Brown et al., 1969), Pfuderer (1969) demonstrated that the parents' speech became transformationally more complex as the children went from an "early" stage to a "late" stage of linguistic development (as measured by MLU). Subordination and coordination, measured as number of verbs or number of connectives per utterance, or as the number of complex and/or compound sentences, occurs significantly more frequently in adult-adult speech (Vorster, 1974). In Newport's (1977) sample, fully 84% of the mothers' grammatical sentences to children contained only one clause, a finding typical of all the studies.

Newport points out that some 20% of the mothers' utterances were grammatically simple in the sense of being unanalyzable routines like "thank you," "yes," "no," "uh-oh," and so on; another 20% are single sentence constituents, usually nouns or noun-phrases, uttered in isolation. Mothers use few noun modifiers (Phillips, 1970), and maintain syntactic simplicity by using verb qualifiers as catenative modal auxiliaries (e.g., *Do you* wanna *play?*) rather than as more complex main verbs (e.g., *Do you want me to play?*) (Newport, 1977).

Finally, clear semantic and lexical differences show up between adult-child and adult-adult speech. In addition to being "very much in the here and now," as Brown and Bellugi suggested, adult-child speech is lexically less variable (as revealed by type-token ratios from most studies), restricting itself largely to concrete referents. In adult-adult speech most impersonal pronouns have nonphysical referents, whereas in adult-child speech their referents are predominantly present physical objects (Remick, 1971).

Extensive analysis of the general properties of adult-child speech therefore reveals that considerable simplification and other modifications take place in the speech of adults when they talk to young children. Similar findings come from studies of black (Drach, 1969) or white (Snow, 1972) mothers, different social classes (Snow, Arlman-Rupp, Hassing, Jobse, Joosken and Vorster, 1974), and even different language communities and cultures (Blount, 1972). Furthermore, parents perform similarly to non-parents (Sachs et al., 1972), mothers being only slightly better at predicting the linguistic needs of their children than women without children (Snow, 1971). Even four-year-old children produce simpler speech to two-year-olds than to adults, whether they themselves have two-year-old siblings or not (Shatz and Gelman, 1973), and they can switch to the appropriate speech mode if told that a doll is a "baby" or "a grown-up" (Sachs and Devin, 1973). These findings with four-year-olds gain further importance from the fact that, particularly in non-Western cultures, the primary caregivers of young children are often their older siblings (Slobin, 1968). Vorster (1974) puts it best when he writes: "In the spirit of Cole Porter one may say that women do it, men do it, adults do it, children do it, parents and non-parents do it; and the recent investigation mentioned above shows that indeed 'the Dutch in old Amsterdam do it'—in essentially the same way at various socioeconomic levels (Snow et al., 1974)."

Determinants of Speech Modification to Children

The Sachs and Devin (1973) study suggests that both adults and children have a general conception of what constitutes appropriate speech to a linguistically incompetent baby, but it is unlikely that adults automatically switch to just the correct degree of semantic and syntactic complexity for any given child. This finer adjustment seems to be attributable at least in part to the verbal or nonverbal feedback from the child. Shipley, Smith, and Gleitman (1969) and Snow (1971) found that children's attention and understanding drop sharply with more complex adult speech. Snow (1971) further demonstrated that adults' modification of their speech to a two-year-old child is greater if the child is actually present. Together with the adjustment of mean length of utterance and syntactic complexity by mothers when their children first began to provide verbal responses to their utterances (Lord, 1975; Phillips, 1973), these results indicate that the ongoing verbal interaction with the child constitutes a major determinant of the modulations of adult-child speech. On the other hand, in pointing out that the semantic relations underlying children's speech in the early stages of language development make up over two-thirds of the semantic relations in mother-child speech, Snow (1974) suggests that these semantic constraints might produce the syntactic differences noted above.

Blount (1972), Gelman and Shatz (1974), and Newport (1977) stress the role of nonsyntactic conversational constraints in producing the syntactic and semantic simplicity of maternal speech. For example, Blount (1972) argues that the frequencies of various sentence types in the speech of Luo and Samoan parents to their young children depend on the social status of the interactors in the conversation. Very young Luo and Samoan children are considered social inferiors, and as such are not expected to initiate any activities. Instead, they characteristically have many imperatives and wh-questions addressed to them, directing their behavior and verbal responses. Blount suggests that middle-class American children are considered more social equals by their mothers, able to make their own decisions, so they are asked more yes/no questions, and are addressed by fewer direct commands.

Gelman and Shatz (1974) propose a similar, although more comprehensive, account of the pragmatic determinants of speech to children. They suggest that in any conversation, the speaker selects a particular syntactic form on the basis of particular conversational rules that reflect the context and conversational agreements existing between the participants (Searle, 1969). They cite examples from their own study of four-year-olds' speech to adults and two-year-olds (Shatz and Gelman, 1973), showing that the syntax of the speech to the two-year-olds is simpler even when the topic of conversation remains the same (how to use a complicated toy). The four-year-old child typically directs the behavior of the younger child, but would not attempt to do so for the adult. Because there were several instances when the speech to the two-year-old was grammatically complex yet conversationally simple, but never instances in which the reverse was true, Gelman and Shatz conclude that the syntactic simplicity found in speech to young children is probably an artifact of conversational constraints.

An example of such a conversational constraint operating to determine the syntactic form of speech to the child is provided by the requirement of politeness. Politeness determines whether directives are expressed as imperatives or as questions and declaratives. Parents spend much of their time directing their children's activities, but the way in which they do it is governed by the children's age and by culturally determined attitudes toward children. The prevalence of imperatives in Luo and Samoan parents' speech to their children, and their attitudes toward them, have already been mentioned. Holzman (1972) and Shatz (1974b) pointed out that many yes/no and wh-questions, as well as some declaratives, function in the interaction between American middle-class mothers and their children to direct the child's actions. Newport (1977) found that the frequency of imperatives declines and the frequency of declaratives increases with the age and linguistic maturity of the child.

The present authors are only too well aware of the constraints that politeness places on the form of one's directives to another person's child. A short while ago, the authors were engaged in a study of the language of a group of 30-month-old children that involved a two-hour play session with the child. During these interactions it was noticeable that the experimenters were even more likely than the mother to use the polite form of the directive, often beginning with *Why don't we/you . . .* or *Let's . . .* However, during one of these interactions, one of the authors noticed the 30-month-old smearing Play-Doh onto the clothes of her little sister, who happened to be present. Unable to restrain himself, he blurted out: "Don't do that! . . . . I wouldn't . . . should you?", switching the form in midutterance as he remembered his proper social role.

The modifications found in the speech of parents, other adults, and even children when it is addressed to young children therefore seem to have multiple determinants, some reflecting social factors, some the pragmatic considerations of the mother, and others the cognitive and linguistic capacities of the child. Newport (1977) considered which aspects of mothers' speech to their children are age-determined and which are tied to the child's linguistic development. She correlated various semantic and syntactic features of the mothers' speech with the age and several measures of linguistic development of the children.

Neither well-formedness nor sentence complexity (number of S nodes in deep structure) correlated significantly with the children's age or any measure of linguistic development. This suggests that these features are grossly adjusted only to children versus adults, although it should be noted that Newport investigated only a limited age range (one to two years). The mean utterance length of the mothers was significantly correlated with the age, although not the linguistic capacity of the children, but Newport suggests that this results from the fact that constituents are less frequently deleted in speech to the older children, rather than from an increase in the complexity of the sentences. The constituents that are typically deleted from speech to the younger children are the underlying subject (*you*) in imperatives, and AUX + *you* in yes/no questions. On the other hand, verb ellipsis (e.g., *He is, John can*) increases with the age *and* linguistic maturity of the child. The possible role of deleted constituents in the facilitation of language acquisition is discussed later in the chapter.

Newport observed that the frequency of sentence types in mothers' speech correlated with several aspects of the children's development. The frequency of declaratives increased with age, MLU, and noun phrase length; and the frequency of imperatives declined with age and all of the measures of linguistic development. The frequency of deictic expressions, drawing the child's attention to or naming an object or action, correlated significantly with vocabulary size as measured by the number of word types used by the child, but not with age or any other measure. Finally, the number of repetitions by the mother of her own utterances correlated negatively with age and several linguistic measures of the children, but the number of partial imitations by the mother of the child's utterances, especially when coupled with an addition of more information, increased significantly with age and linguistic sophistication.

Newport concludes that the changing functional basis of mother-child conversations as the child gets older and cognitively more mature leads to several changes in maternal speech. Imperatives decrease in frequency, while information-exchanging declaratives increase in frequency as the mother directs the child's behavior less, although some of the declaratives may still serve to direct action—e.g., "the car goes in that garage." Questions do not change in frequency over the age range she investigated, but they may still change in type. The earliest questions do not require a response from the child, but more polite directives or motivational questions and questions requiring a response begin to be asked as the child gets older (Remick, 1971). Newport suggests that "deictic utterances increase with the vocabulary of the child as mothers adjust the frequency of their object naming quite specifically to the child's interest in naming" (p. 207). What grounds are there for deciding that the directions of influence is from the child's interest to the mother's practice? It seems just as possible that the increasing deictic use by the mother as the child gets cognitively more mature leads to the vocabulary growth of the child, or that the influence is bidirectional. The difficulty of determining the direction of effect of the mother and the child's speech recurs frequently in this literature.

Newport attributes all of the above effects on maternal speech to one factor, the function of the conversation. She distinguishes it from two other factors. The first of these is the changing processing abilities of the child (Factor 2), which leads to a decrease in the frequency of maternal self-repetitions and imitations, as well as less frequent constituent deletion. The third factor is a direct effort toward formal simplicity by the mother, which leads to well-formedness of utterances, but this does not change with age or listener ability in Newport's sample. Newport therefore suggests that "those features of maternal speech hypothesized to arise directly from conversational constraints on maternal speech (Factors 1 and 2) are adjusted in a continuous way to aspects of the listeners, while those features hypothesized to arise directly from syntactic constraints (Factor 3) are adjusted only grossly, to adults vs. children" (p. 208).

However, there are several problems with Newport's interpretation of her correlational data. In particular, the grounds for classifying the various aspects of child speech as arising from the different factors are not well-specified. Why should well-formedness and clear articulation not be classified with self-repetitions as attempts to be understood by the child simply because they do not correlate with the age range and the variables Newport happened to measure? The basis for classification becomes still more obscure when Newport goes on to state: "In fact the details of the correlational analysis lend support to the further distinction between conversational features relating to listener status and function of the interaction (Factor 1) vs. those relating to listener processing limitations (Factor 2). The former (e.g., distribution of surface sentence type and associated deformations, as well as the frequency of maternal self-repetition) are adjusted to a wide variety of characteristics of the child listener, including his age as well as linguistic competence. The latter (e.g., utterance-shortening deletions and contractions, expansion, and deixis) are adjusted only to the listener's age (and its cognitive concomitants) or vocabulary size" (p. 208). Newport here reclassifies mothers' self-repetitions as the outcome of Factor 1 and the increase in deictic expressions as the outcome of Factor 2.

Recent correlational data from Cross (in press) suggest that the major determinant of much of the mother's modification of her speech to her child is the child's ability to comprehend speech, a measure that Newport did not take. Cross found highly significant correlations between a wide range of measures of parental speech and the children's performance on a substantial test of language comprehension. For example, the total number of expansions (partial, complete, and elaborated) and imitations of the children's utterances by the mothers correlated -0.77, maternal repetitions correlated -0.81, and reference to nonimmediate events correlated $+0.72$ with the children's comprehension scores. The correlations for these variables with measures of the children's production like MLU, although still significant, were not as impressively high.

It is concluded, therefore, that although there are plausible arguments for multiple determinants of the special properties of mothers' speech to children, the respective contributions of pragmatic factors and feedback from the cognitive and linguistic development of the child remain to be firmly established. Because knowledge of the degree to which adults' speech is specifically tailored to the child's development should prove invaluable to understanding the way in which the child's acquisition of syntactic and semantic forms proceeds, this will continue to be a fruitful area of research.

Adults' Speech to Children and Language Acquisiton

We now consider the way in which the special aspects of adult-child speech discussed earlier might assist the child in acquiring the conventional forms of his language. Several recent investigators have suggested that the corpus of speech provided by adults to the child represents an input well-suited for the learning of linguistic structure and form; an input carefully graded in complexity to the child's capacities and containing many teaching devices (Snow, 1972, 1974; Vorster, 1974).

Of the phonological aspects mentioned in Table 2, several might play a role in facilitating language acquisition, but others seem to be more a reflection of the adults' conception of the way babies talk. The adults' utterances are clearly pronounced and have distinct pauses between them, so the child can easily tell where they begin and stop. The exaggerated, sing-song intonation could also be important, because du Preez (1974) has shown that children in the holophrastic period typically imitate the tonic word in an intonation grouping, i.e., the word on which the major stress falls. That stress is greatly exaggerated in adults' speech to children. The tonic word often falls at the end of the utterance, but when it appears earlier in the utterance, the child tends to imitate that word plus some of the words following it. In fact, du Preez's children only imitated clauses or phrases if the tonic stress was placed early in the utterance. Recently, Bloom, Hood, and Lightbown (1974) have shown that imitation of words and semantic relations may play a role in the acquisition of lexical items and semantic relations by some children.

With respect to the intonation patterns of adults when speaking to young children, researchers have reported that the fundamental frequency is typically higher and the contour more exaggerated than it is in adult-adult speech, but no one has studied whether particular patterns are also more consistently tied to particular pragmatic functions. Although rising and falling intonation patterns in adult-adult speech do not always signal queries and statements or imperatives respectively, they may do so in adult-child speech. This would be a considerable help to the child in learning to use intonation to signal his communicative intent.

The role of the phonological simplification and reduplication that is typical of adult-child speech, other than providing a clearly enunciated model for phonological development, is not obvious, and these factors may simply reflect imitation of the child's own forms by the adult (Moerk, 1972; Weir, 1962).

The most general of the syntactic features of parental speech, well-formedness and short utterance length, are likely to be helpful to the language-learning child. Glanzer and Dodd (1975) observed that mothers are more likely to elicit a response from their children when they modify the length of their utterances. Shipley et al. (1969) reported that children were most likely to respond to short, well-formed instructions, and may simply not respond at all when the input becomes too complex. However, the effects of other syntactic aspects of adult-child speech on language acquisition remain in dispute.

Mothers' speech to young children is generally simpler in derivational complexity (Pfuderer, 1969) and modifiers tend to be absent (Phillips, 1973), so the surface forms of utterances are a clearer reflection of the deep structure semantic and syntactic relationships. On the other hand, Newport argues that in some respects mothers' speech to very young children can be considered more complex in terms of a standard transformational grammar, because mothers delete many deep structure constituents. The speech to young children contains many imperatives that, in the conventional transformational grammar, delete the deep structure subject "you." There are also a large number of yes/no questions in which the mothers delete the AUX + pronoun "you," thus: *want a cookie?* Newport's correlations revealed that the AUX + pronoun are more frequently supplied by the mothers in their speech to older children, when they also use fewer imperatives. Furthermore, Newport found that wh-questions were fairly frequent and declaratives less frequent with the younger children (less than two years old), suggesting that the higher frequency of declaratives in Brown and Hanlon's (1970) data (the same samples used by Pfuderer, 1969) could be attributable at least in part to the fact that their subjects were somewhat older. She concludes that because the underlying propositional form is syntactically much deformed in wh-questions and they are transformationally quite complex in adult terms, mothers' speech provides a somewhat more complex input to younger than to older children. It then becomes difficult to see how the mothers' speech provides an appropriate input for the acquisition of syntactic categories in young children.

Several arguments can be raised against this conclusion. First, consideration of the pragmatic context of utterances suggests that the subject "you" in imperatives is in fact part of the communicative context. The child need not learn its syntactic role in underlying linguistic structure in order to understand or produce imperatives correctly. Second, deletion of AUX + "you" in yes/no questions makes them shorter and perhaps easier to process for the young child. Again, the subject of the question is apparent from the conversational context and such nonlinguistic factors as direction of regard. In the case of wh-questions, one must consider whether the child need possess the knowledge of linguistic structure that we attribute to adults when they understand such questions. There is so much redundancy in the situational context that the child can interpret the question with knowledge of only a few key words. Such wh-questions as *What's that?* are clearly unanalyzed routines for young children, and they begin by using them as routines (Brown, 1973). Other questions may be interpreted on the basis of the wh-word and other stressed words in the utterance.

In fact, some question forms do seem to provide an important learning experience for the child. Brown et al. (1969) pointed out that a common type of question to young children is the *occasional question,* a request for the child to supply a missing answer or repeat a word or phrase. Thus, in the interaction:

> Child: I want milk.
> Mother: You want what?
> Child: Milk.

the child is asked to repeat a constituent. Similarly, the child is prompted in the following interaction:

> Mother: What do you want?
> Child: (no answer)
> Mother: You want what? (Brown et al; 1969, p. 71)

Such promptings and recasting of wh-questions might assist the child in inferring the constituent structure of the question. Both Brown et al. (1969) and Moerk (1972) report that the child is more likely to answer an occasional question than the regular form, and use of occasional questions by parents correlates positively with the syntactic development of the child.

The above arguments raise two important considerations: the relationship between a syntactic description of the language input to the child and the child's actual understanding of that input, and the need to determine what linguistic knowledge the child is actually acquiring at a particular stage. The first of these concerns the importance of examining the mother's speech in relation to its pragmatic function and how well it fulfills that function. The deletions of constituents mentioned by Newport probably plays a practical role in the mother communicating with the child, even though it may make the utterances more complex in terms of a transformational grammar. The second consideration is no less important. As we have seen in the previous sections of this chapter, it is difficult to determine just what linguistic knowledge the child possesses at any one stage, and what formal aspects of language he is acquiring at that stage. However, such a determination is crucial in interpreting the role of the input at any period of development. For example, the deletion of the underlying subject "you" in imperatives should be of little importance if the child does not begin to acquire such abstract syntactic categories as underlying subject until quite late in development. It is not needed for communication, so is not present. Similarly, the child does not acquire the full yes/no question form in his own speech until roughly two and one-half to three and one-half years of age, much later than the period in which Newport notes that AUX + "you" is deleted. As we have mentioned, the deletion probably facilitates communication by shortening the utterance and stressing the more critical action and object aspects of the question; the agent is already specified by the context. By the time the child is acquiring the full form, the mother no longer deletes the AUX + "you" (Newport, 1977).

Newport and several other investigators analyzed mother-child speech in terms of its syntactic complexity for an adult, but that neglects both the way in which the child might process the input (i.e., the complexity for the child) and what formal aspects are relevant to the child's own linguistic knowledge at the time.

Snow (1971, 1972) emphasized the importance of sentence constituents uttered in isolation by mothers in making the grammatical structure of sentences transparent to the child. These incomplete sentences must be clearly distinguished from the "broken sentences" present in adult-adult speech. In the incomplete sentences of mothers, complete constituent units, usually noun phrases or prepositional phrases, are repeated following the full utterance. For example, the mother says: "Put the red truck in the box now. The red truck. No, the red truck. In the box. The red truck in the box." (Snow, 1972, p. 562). Snow suggests that these are tailor-made lessons in phrase structure.

Although the repetitions of separate constituents of an utterance, as in the example above, may make the structure of that utterance clearer, Newport (1977) questions whether self-repetition by the mother assists the growth of the child's comprehension of such utterances. She examined the probability of a response by three two-year-old children (presumably indicating comprehension) across exact and partial self-repetitions by the three mothers. The overall probability of the child responding to the utterance increased with number of repetitions, but the conditional probability of a response remained fairly constant. This suggests that repetitions did not improve comprehension, but just increased the *overall* likelihood of the mother eliciting a response from the child. On the other hand, Newport, for reasons she does not specify, only examined repetition sequences in which the child *did* respond. It is very possible that including *all* instances of the mothers' commands, the conditional probability of a response would increase with repetitions. Nevertheless, Newport is correct in arguing that if repetition improves comprehension, more responses, even considering only successful sequences of utterances, should be elicited by later repetitions. Because this is not the case, she suggests that maternal self-repetition serves only the function of getting the child to do what the mother wants him to do, and has no effect on the growth of language comprehension.

Another type of repetition in mother-child speech whose importance for language acquisition has been disputed is the partial, complete, or supplemental repetition by the mother of the child's utterances. In particular, the importance of supplemented repetitions or expansions has been studied quite extensively. Cazden (1965) found that systematic expansion of every possible utterance of four two- to three-year-old children for a short period of time each day did not enhance the grammatical development of those children relative to a control group who received no treatment. In fact, Cazden found that a third group of children (a modeling group), who received a varied input of well-formed sentences that added comments to what the child said for roughly the same time per day, showed the greatest gain on six measures of grammatical development. In general, the differences between the groups did not reach statistical significance, but the groups were ordered in overall growth: modeling best, then expansion, and last control. On one task, sentence imitation, the modeling and control groups showed significantly more improvement than the expansion group. Feldman (1971) found no differences in sentence imitation between treatment and control groups in a study that was similar to Cazden's, but added a group in which only the children's utterances with clear meanings were expanded. This counteracts arguments that Cazden's experimenters may have misinterpreted several of the children's utterances, and may have confused rather than helped the children by expanding them. One weakness in both the Cazden and Feldman studies concerns the use of lower-class black children as subjects. The expansions provided by the white student experimenters probably did not take into account differences between so-called Standard English and the Black English dialect spoken in the homes of the children (DePaulo and Bonvillian, 1975). On the other hand, DePaulo and Bonvillian point out that a study by Gonzales, in which the utterances of two Mexican-American children were expanded by their mothers, also failed to find differences between these children and two controls on four measures of language development.

Cazden (1965) and Brown et al. (1969) suggest two reasons for the failure of expansions to enhance acquisition in Cazden's study. First, richness and variety of the linguistic input may be the most important determinant of rate of language acquisition. Cazden's modeling group received a syntactically more varied and semantically richer input from the experimenters than the expansion group. Second, the function of occasional expansions for the child may be to confirm for the child the relationship between his utterance and the situational context. However, the continued expansion of each utterance by the experimenters may have led to the loss of effectiveness of that confirmation, and the children may have ceased to pay attention to them.

These two explanations are supported by the results of an experiment by Nelson, Carskaddon, and Bonvillian (1973). In this study, the experimenters expanded the children's incomplete sentences, but they also recast their complete utterances into a sentence with a different syntactic form, but the same semantic reference. For example, a declarative uttered by the child could be followed by a question concerning the same semantic information. This recast-sentence group later performed significantly better than a control group on a sentence imitation test and also produced more complex predicate forms. On two measures of verb phrase complexity they were also more advanced than a group who heard new sentences modeled by the experimenter, but did not have their own sentences recast. In this study, when the child commented on some aspect of the verbal or nonverbal context of the interaction, the experimenter kept that shared aspect of the context constant, but provided the child with an alternative syntactic means of encoding it. As Brown et al. (1969) and DePaulo and Bonvillian (1975) note, this type of moderate degree of novelty for the child commands his greatest attention (see Kagan, 1970), and might be expected to facilitate his language acquisition by enhancing his attention to the adult's utterance. As Bloom et al. (1974) demonstrated, imitation of adult utterances seems to take place and assist in the acquisiton of grammatical forms and semantic relations when the adult's utterance is moderately discrepant from the child's productive linguistic knowledge, i.e., when the child understands but does not yet use the imitated form productively in his own speech. Analysis of the relationship between mother-child speech and the child's own growing linguistic knowledge in these terms makes contact with work on the role of moderate discrepancy in other areas of cognitive development (Kagan, 1970), and could be a fruitful approach.

Yet another aspect of mothers' speech to children that has been considered in relation to acquisition is the frequency with which particular grammatical forms are modeled in the parental speech. Brown (1973) found that the overall frequency of several grammatical morphemes in parent speech to the child did not predict their order of acquisition in the child's own speech. In the case of complex grammatical forms like questions, negatives, negative questions, and tag questions, frequency might have been a determinant of acquisiton order, although it was confounded with cumulative derivational complexity (Brown and Hanlon, 1970). Whitehurst, Ironsmith, and Goldfein (1974) demonstrated that four-year-old children who had received modeled passive sentences to describe pictures (a very rare form in adult speech) subsequently used those forms significantly more frequently and were better able to comprehend passives than children who had not received the modeling. However, because there was no pretest of the children's comprehension or production of passives, it is uncertain whether the modeling enhanced acquisition. Nelson (1975) provided such a pretest and posttest comparison of the effects of recasting and modeling of complex questions and verb forms on acquisition of those forms in 28- to 29-month-olds. Children who had no cases of productive use of such complex question forms as tag questions and negative questions, or verb forms like future or conditional tense or two verbs in a sentence, were exposed to one of two intervention conditions. In both conditions the experimenter attempted to recast the child's sentences, but in one the recastings were in the form of complex questions and in the other they were complex verb forms. At the end of the treatment period, Nelson found that significantly more of the children exposed to the complex questions showed use of those forms in their own speech than did children exposed to complex verbs. Similarly, significantly more children in the latter group had begun to use complex verb forms. On more general measures of language development, MLU and number of elements per noun phrase, the two groups of children showed the same advances. The effects of increased exposure through recasting on syntactic progress thus seem to be selective. Nelson suggests that the recastings attract the child's attention to the comparison between his own utterance and that of the adult. Because the mothers did use these forms, although infrequently, in speech to the child, the experimenter's recastings did not introduce altogether new forms, but did tend to draw the child's attention to the form. In this sense, frequency of modeling may only be effective when it is tied to what the child produces.

Certain semantic and pragmatic features of parental speech may also influence the course of acquisition. Although it is unclear what role the unique lexical features of baby talk may play in language acquisition, Anglin (1976) demonstrated that some of the naming practices of mothers may affect the acquisition of category names. Mothers name objects for their children at a more general level than they do for adults, but not at the most general level (e.g., "dog" instead of "collie" or "animal"). Children acquire terms of reference at that same intermediate level earlier than those at the more specific or more general level. With respect to semantic relations, Snow (1974) showed that the same basic relations account for roughly the same percent of utterances in mother-child speech and in the speech of the children themselves. Glanzer and Dodd (1975) found that the relative frequencies with which mothers and children used verbs classified according to semantic types (e.g., action verbs or motion verbs) correlated +0.91. However, in these studies, as in others in the mother-child speech literature, the direction of effect is difficult to determine.

Finally, the functional constraints on mothers' speech to children possibly affect not only the relative frequency of syntactic forms in the input, but also the development of pragmatic and syntactic features of language by the child. The acquisition of such features as polite request forms has been studied in child language (Bates, 1971; Ervin-Tripp, 1974; Shatz, 1974a), but the relationship between this acquisition and the use of these forms by the mother has not been systematically investigated. Nelson (1973) reported that functional aspects of mother's speech, namely, the degree to which the mother attempted to direct the child's behavior as opposed to commenting on the world, was correlated with several pragmatic and syntactic aspects of language acquisition in their children. For example, the proportion of directives in the mother's speech was negatively related to the acquisition of vocabulary, the MLU, and to comprehension of commands in the child's second year. The number of questions the mother addressed to the child at 24 months was positively correlated with linguistic development at 30 months. Similarly, the degree to which the mother used language in a social or directive way, as opposed to naming and describing objects, sometimes predicted corresponding functions of language ("expressive" versus "referential") in her child's early words. This was true only of some children and mothers, however; in others there seemed to be a mismatch between the functions of language in mother and child. Moerk (1974) pointed out that the types of activities engaged in by mothers in verbal interaction with children varied with their ages and was related to what the children spoke about at each age. This area should prove an important one for future research, especially with respect to possible changes in the functional aspects of mothers' speech related to changes in the age or linguistic development of their children.

DIRECTIONS FOR FUTURE RESEARCH

Most of the above studies of adult-child speech have concerned themselves with a phonological, syntactic, semantic, or pragmatic description of speech to children of different ages or general cognitive and linguistic development. Very few studies have attempted a closer study of how aspects of maternal speech mesh with those same aspects in the child's language acquisition (see Nelson, 1973). Newport's correlational study, although it provided some interesting data, suffered not only from the difficulty of determining which features of maternal speech arise from which conversational or other constraints, but also used different measures of complexity for adult and child speech. Newport provided no answer to the question of how the mother's speech relates to those aspects of language the child is acquiring at different stages. Longitudinal studies in progress might correct this lack of data (Lord, 1975), but the detailed interaction between the acquisition of certain forms by the child and the input and responses to him by the mother must be examined in any such study. Carter (1975) provided an informative example of such a detailed analysis of the acquisition of two semantic relations, recurrence and possession, and the corresponding development of "mine" and "more" as separate phonological forms in one child, but she did not supply as much detail of the mother's or other adults' verbal and nonverbal responses to those forms as one would like. Vorster (1974) mentioned a tantalizing piece of evidence for such a close interaction between the mother's speech and the child's acquisition of past tense forms. For one child, three samples of speech complete with maternal input were collected at roughly six-month intervals from the age of 32 months. Uses of the past tense by the mother were very infrequent in the first sample (5 instances in 200 utterances), when the child did not use the past tense either. In the second sample, the child only used two past tenses, but the mother used past tense forms much more frequently (21 instances). By the third sample, both child and mother used the past tense fairly frequently, 12 and 17 instances respectively. One wonders whether the child demonstrated comprehension of the past tense, or began to provide the obligatory contexts for past tense morphemes just before the increase in the use of the past tense by the mother. In this way, the mother would provide the correct syntactic form just as the child was beginning to master its use. More analyses of mother-child speech of this form are clearly needed to confirm such a relation.

Another factor that needs further study is the relationship between the linguistic input to the child and the strategies, linguistic or cognitive, that the child might apply to the task of language acquisition. Several such strategies have been stressed in recent years (Bever, 1970; Ervin-Tripp, 1973; Sinclair and Bronckhart, 1972; Slobin, 1973). The question is: to what extent does adult-child speech support or even facilitate such strategies? For example, young children typically show restricted range of word orders early in acquisition, even when the language they are learning has a fairly free word order, e.g., in Russian (Slobin, 1973). This has been held to indicate a strategy on the part of the child, but Snow (1974) cites a study by Klein (1974) showing that the child's adoption of different orders for subject, verb, and object in Dutch corresponded closely to his mother's relative frequency of usage of the various orders to him. Buium (1974) found that a Hebrew-speaking father's use of word orders in declaratives, imperatives, questions, and negative addressed to his child was limited almost exclusively to SVO, although Hebrew possesses a high degree of flexibility of word order. His word order was much more varied in the same forms when they were addressed to another adult. Again, the direction of effect is difficult to determine and further investigation is needed, but such a process would greatly simplify the child's acquisition of language.

In conclusion, similar considerations as those that led to changes in the investigation of language acquisition in the child must be applied to the research on adult-child speech. Most of the studies mentioned here have analyzed the mother's speech in isolation from her interaction with the child, and therefore have missed a great deal of important data. It may well not prove possible to distinguish between the modifications in the mother's speech that are attributable to social or conversational constraints and those that are specifically tailored to the cognitive or linguistic maturity of the child. However, the effects that such modifications, whatever their determinants, have on the child's acquisition of syntactic or semantic forms, or on the development of pragmatic functions, requires a closer analysis of the mother-child interaction, verbal and nonverbal. What is needed is an analysis similar to that provided by Bloom et al. (1974) for imitations, in terms of what the child has in his own speech and what he is capable of understanding at the time that specific modifications take place in the parent's speech. It is also apparent that the linguistic knowledge we attribute to the child, or that the child is considered to be acquiring, will partially determine our interpretation of the importance and effectiveness of the parental input.

IMPLICATIONS FOR WORK WITH THE DEVELOPMENTALLY DISABLED

It is evident from this review that language researchers cannot afford to focus on any one aspect—not syntax, semantics, or pragmatics—at the expense of the others. Although the effort to interrelate these concerns has only now begun, there are some suggestions for work with handicapped children:

1. A characterization of the motivational shifts during normal language acquisition should aid in the design of training programs for the retarded and other populations with language difficulties. Many of the current programs incorporate highly artificial motivation such as candy or praise, inappropriately tied to the function for which the form is designed in normal communication. Researchers have acknowledged the requirement that the language form be appropriate to the *referential* context, but have paid relatively little attention to the natural *functions* it should serve.
2. Interestingly, current models of language learning highlight areas in which the blind child might have difficulties unsuspected by earlier accounts. For example, how does the blind child recognize shared attention, in the absence of eye contact and information about direction of gaze? Is his acquisition of semantic relations delayed by the requirement that events be experienced through tactile exploration?
3. Our final point is this: how do mothers or caregivers of handicapped children compensate for their disability? It becomes even more critical to ascertain the importance of feedback from the child in controlling the mother's speech modifications. If many of the important simplifying devices are tied to age rather than continuously adjusted to the child's developmental level, this could create a serious imbalance in the appropriateness of the input to the retarded or handicapped child (for a reverse case, i.e., a hearing child of deaf parents, see Sachs and Johnson, 1972). Again, the mother of the blind child faces unsuspected difficulties, because she must continually recognize that certain environmental

information is not shared, that contextual support is reduced, that presuppositions may not be shared by her listener. It is hard for the average speaker to remember to take this into account on the telephone to another adult; how much more difficult is it in communicating with a child who does not yet know language?

ACKNOWLEDGMENT

We are indebted to Virginia Koster for her secretarial assistance.

REFERENCES

Anglin, J. M. 1976. Les premiers termes de reference de l'enfant. In J. Erlich and E. Tulving (eds.), La Memoire Semantique, Special Annuel Bull. Psychol. 232–241.

Antinucci, F., and Parisi, D. 1973. Early language acquisition: A model and some data. In C. A. Ferguson and D. I. Slobin (eds.), Studies of Child Language Development. Holt, Rinehart and Winston, New York.

Antinucci, F., and Parisi, D. 1975. Early semantic development in child language. In E. H. Lenneberg and E. Lenneberg (eds.). Foundations of Language Development: A Multidisciplinary Approach, Vol. 1. Academic Press, New York.

Antinucci, F., and Volterra, V. 1973. Lo sviluppo della negazione nel linguaggio infantile: Uno studio pragmatico. In Studi per un Modello del Linguaggio, Quaderni della Ricerca Scientifica. CNR, Rome.

Bates, E. 1971. The development of conversational skills in 2, 3 and 4 year olds. Unpublished master's thesis, University of Chicago.

Bates, E. 1974. Acquisition of pragmatic competence. J. Child Lang. 1: 277–281.

Bates, E. 1976. Pragmatics and sociolinguistics in child language. In D. Morehead and A. Morehead (eds.), Directions in Normal and Deficient Child Language. University Park Press, Baltimore.

Bates, E., Camaioni, L., and Volterra, V. 1973. The acquisition of performatives prior to speech. CNR Laboratory Technical Report #129, Rome.

Bateson, M. C. 1975. Mother-infant exchanges: The epigenesis of conversational interaction. In D. Aaronson and R. W. Rieber (eds.), Developmental Psycholinguistics and Communication Disorders. Ann. N.Y. Acad. Sci., Vol. 263.

Bellugi, U. 1967. The acquisition of negation. Unpublished doctoral dissertation, Harvard University, Cambridge.

Bever, T. G. 1970. The cognitive bases for linguistic structures. In J. R. Hayes (ed.), Cognition and the Development of Language. John Wiley and Sons, New York.

Bloom, L. 1970. Language Development: Form and Function in Emerging Grammars. MIT Press, Cambridge.

Bloom, L. 1973. One Word at a Time: The Use of Single-Word Utterances before Syntax. Mouton, The Hague.

Bloom, L., Hood, L., and Lightbown, P. 1974. Imitation in language development: If, when and why. Cog. Psychol. 6: 380–420.

Bloom, L., Miller, P., and Hood, L. 1975. Variation and reduction as aspects of competence in language. In A. D. Pick (ed.), Minnesota Symposia on Child Psychology, Vol. 9. University of Minnesota Press, Minneapolis (1975).

Blount, B. G. 1972. Parental speech and language acquisition: Some Luo and Samoan examples. Anthropol. Ling. 14: 119–130.

Bowerman, M. F. 1973a. Learning to Talk: A Cross-Linguistic Study of Early Syntactic Development, with Special Reference to Finnish. Cambridge University Press, Cambridge, England.

Bowerman, M. F. 1973b. Structural relationships in children's utterances: Syntactic or semantic? In T. E. Moore (ed.), Cognitive Development and the Acquisition of Language. Academic Press, New York.

Bowerman, M. F. 1974. Discussion summary—Development of concepts underlying language. In R. L. Schiefelbusch and L. L. Lloyd (eds.), Language Perspectives—Acquisition, Retardation and Intervention. University Park Press, Baltimore.

Bowerman, M. F. 1976. Semantic factors in the acquisition of rules for word use and sentence construction. In D. Morehead and A. Morehead (eds.), Directions in Normal and Deficient Child Language. University Park Press, Baltimore.

Braine, M. D. S. 1963. The ontogeny of English phrase structure: The first phase. Language 39: 1–13.

Braine, M. D. S. 1971. On two types of models of the internalization of grammars. In D. I. Slobin (ed.), the Ontogenesis of Grammar. Academic Press, New York.

Braine, M. D. S. 1976. Children's first word combinations. Monogr. Soc. Res. Child Dev. 164.

Broen, P. A. 1972. The verbal environment of the language-learning child. Asha Monogr. No. 17.

Brown, R. W. 1968. The development of Wh questions in child speech. J. Verb. Learn. Verb. Behav. 7: 279–290.

Brown, R. W. 1973. A First Language: The Early Stages. Harvard University Press, Cambridge.

Brown, R., and Bellugi, U. 1964. Three processes in the child's acquisition of syntax. Harvard Educ. Rev. 34: 133–151.

Brown, R., Cazden, C. B., and Bellugi, U. 1969. The child's grammar from I to III. In J. P. Hill (ed.), Minnesota Symposium on Child Psychology, Vol. 2. Univ. of Minnesota Press, Minneapolis.

Brown, R., and Hanlon, C. 1970. Derivational complexity and order of acquisition in child speech. In J. R. Hayes (ed.), Cognition and the Development of Language. John Wiley and Sons, New York.

Bruner, J. S. 1975a. The ontogenesis of speech acts. J. Child Lang. 2: 1–19.

Bruner, J. S. 1975b. From communication to language—A psychological perspective. Cognition 3: 255–287.

Buium, N. 1974. An investigation of the word order parameter of a parent-child verbal interaction in a relatively free order language. Lang. Speech 17: 182–186.

Carter, A. 1975. The transformation of sensorimotor morphemes into words: A case study of the development of 'more' and 'mine'. J. Child Lang. 2: 233–250.

Cazden, C. B. 1965. Environmental assistance to the child's acquisition of grammar. Unpublished doctoral dissertation, Harvard University, Cambridge.

Chomsky, N. 1957. Syntactic Structures. Mouton, The Hague.

Chomsky, N. 1965. Aspects of the Theory of Syntax. MIT Press, Cambridge.

Clark, E. 1973. What's in a word? On the child's acquisition of semantics in his first language. In T. E. Moore (ed.), Cognitive Development and the Acquisition of Language. Academic Press, New York.

Cross, T. G. Mother's speech adjustments; The contributions of selected child listener variables. In C. Ferguson and C. Snow (eds.), Talking to Children: Language Input and Acquisition. Cambridge University Press, Cambridge, England. In press.

DePaulo, B. M., and Bonvillian, J. D. 1975. The effect on language development of the special characteristics of speech addressed to children. Unpublished manuscript, Harvard University, Cambridge.

de Villiers, J. G., and de Villiers, P. A. 1973. Development of the use of word order in comprehension. J. Psycholinguist. Res. 2: 331–341.

de Villiers, J. G., and de Villiers, P. A. 1974. Competence and performance in child language: Are children really competent to judge? J. Child Lang. 1: 11–22.

de Villiers, J. G., and Tager-Flusberg, H. B. 1975. Some facts one simply cannot deny. J. Child Lang. 2: 279–286.

Dore, J. 1975. Holophrases, speech acts, and language universals. J. Child Lang. 2: 21–40.

Drach, K. M. 1969. The language of the parent: A pilot study. Working Paper No. 14, University of California, Berkeley.

du Preez, P. 1974. Units of information in the acquisition of language. Lang. Speech 17: 369–376.

Ervin-Tripp, S. 1973. Some strategies for the first two years. In T. E. Moore (ed.), Cognitive development and the acquisition of language. Academic Press, New York.

Ervin-Tripp, S. 1974. The comprehension and production of requests by children. Papers and Reports on Child Language Development, no. 8, Stanford University.

Feldman, C. 1971. The effects of various types of adult responses in the syntactic acquisition of two to three year-olds. Unpublished paper, University of Chicago.

Ferguson, C. A. 1974. Baby talk as a simplified register. Paper presented at the conference on language input and acquisition, September, Boston.

Fillmore, C. 1968. The case for case. In E. Bach and R. T. Harms (eds.), Universals in Linguistic Theory. Holt, Rinehart and Winston, New York.

Flavell, J. M., Botkin, P., Fry, C., Wright, J., and Jarvis, P. 1968. The Development of Role-Taking and Communicative Skills in Children. John Wiley and Sons, New York.

Fodor, J. A., Bever, T. G., and Garrett, M. F. 1974. The Psychology of Language: An Introduction to Psycholinguistics and Generative Grammar. McGraw-Hill Book Company, New York.

Garvey, C. 1975. Requests and responses in children's speech. J. Child Lang. 2: 41–63.

Gelman, R., and Shatz, M. 1975. Rule governed variation in children's conversations. Unpublished manuscript, University of Pennsylvania.

Glanzer, P. D., and Dodd, D. H. 1975. Developmental changes in the language spoken to children. Unpublished paper presented to the Society for Research in Child Development, Denver.

Greenfield, P. M., and Smith, J. H. 1976. The Structure of Communication in Early Language Development. Academic Press, New York.

Gruber, J. 1973. Correlations between the syntactic construction of the child and adult. In C. Ferguson and D. Slobin (eds.), Studies in Child Language Development. Holt, Rinehart and Winston, New York.

Halliday, M. A. K. 1969. Relevant models of language. In The State of Language. Educational Review 22.1. University of Birmingham Press, Birmingham, England.

Halliday, M. A. K. 1975. Learning how to mean. In E. H. Lenneberg and E. Lenneberg, (eds.), Foundations of Language Development: A Multidisciplinary Approach, Vol. 1. Academic Press, New York.

Holzman, M. 1972. The use of interrogative forms in verbal interaction of three mothers and their children. J. Psycholinguist. Res. 1: 311–336.

Ingram, D. 1971. Transitivity in child language. Language 47: 888–910.

Kagan, J. 1970. Determinants of attention in the infant. Am. Sci. 58: 289–306.

Keenan, E. O. 1974. Conversational competence in children. J. Child Lang. 2: 163–183.

Keenan, E. O., and Klein, E. 1975. Coherency in children's discourse. J. Psycholinguist. Res. 4: 365–380.

Klein, R. 1974. Word order: Dutch children and their mothers. Unpublished master's thesis, Institute for General Linguistics, University of Amsterdam.

Klima, E. S., and Bellugi, U. 1966. Syntactic regularities in the speech of children. In J. Lyons and R. J. Wales (eds.), Psycholinguistics Papers: The Proceedings of the 1966 Edinburgh Conference. Edinburgh University Press, Edinburgh.

Kobashigawa, B. 1969. Repetitions in a mother's speech to her child. Working Paper No. 14, University of California, Berkeley.

Lord, C. 1975. Is talking to baby more than baby talk? A longitudinal study of the modification of linguistic input to young children. Unpublished paper presented at the Society for Research in Child Development, Denver.

Maratsos, M. P. 1972. The use of definite and indefinite reference in young children. Unpublished doctoral dissertation, Harvard University, Cambridge.

Maratsos, M. P. 1973. The effects of stress on the understanding of proximal co-reference in children. J. Psycholinguist. Res. 2: 1–8.

McNeill, D. 1966. Developmental psycholinguistics. In F. Smith and G. A. Miller (eds.), The Genesis of Language: A Psycholinguistic Approach. MIT Press, Cambridge.

McNeill, D. 1970. The Acquisition of Language: The study of Developmental Psycholinguistics. Harper and Row, New York.

Menyuk, P. 1969. Sentences Children Use. MIT Press, Cambridge.

Menyuk, P., and Bernholtz, N. 1969. Prosodic features and children's language productions. Quart. Prog. Rep. No. 93, pp. 216–219 MIT Research Laboratory of Electronics, Cambridge.

Miller, W., and Ervin, S. 1964. The development of grammar in child language. In U. Bellugi and R. Brown (eds.), The Acquisition of Language. Monogr. Soc. Res. Child Dev. 29(92): 9–34.

Moerk, E. 1972. Principles of interaction in language learning. Merrill-Palmer Quart. 18: 229–257.

Moerk, E. 1974. Change in verbal child-mother interactions with increasing language skills of the child. J. Psycholinguist. Res. 3: 101–116.

Nelson, K. 1973. Structure and strategy in learning to talk. Monogr. Soc. Res. Child Devel. 38(149).

Nelson, K. E. 1975. Facilitating syntax acquisition. Paper presented to the Eastern Psychological Association, April, New York.

Nelson, K. E., Carskaddon, G., and Bonvillian, J. D. 1973. Syntax acquisition: Impact of experimental variation in adult verbal interaction with the child. Child Dev. 44: 497–504.

Newport, E. L. 1976. Motherese: The speech of mothers to young children. In N. J. Castellan, D. B. Pisoni, and G. R. Potts (eds.), Cognitive Theory: Vol 2. Lawrence Erlbaum Associates, Hillsdale.

Parisi, D. 1974. What is behind child utterances? J. Child Lang. 1: 97–105.

Pfuderer, C. 1969. Some suggestions for a syntactic characterization of baby talk style. Working paper No. 14. University of California, Berkeley.

Phillips, J. R. 1970. Formal characteristics of speech which mothers address to their young children. Unpublished doctoral dissertation, Johns Hopkins University, Baltimore.

Phillips, J. R. 1973. Syntax and vocabulary of mother's speech to young children: Age and sex comparisons. Child Dev. 44: 182–185.

Piaget, J. 1962. Play, dreams and imitation in childhood. W. W. Norton, New York.

Piaget, J. 1963. The origins of intelligence in children. W. W. Norton, New York.

Remick, J. 1971. The maternal environment of linguistic development. Unpublished doctoral dissertation, University of California, Davis.

Ross, J. R. 1970. On declarative sentences. In R. A. Jacobs and P. S. Rosenbaum (eds.), Readings in English Transformational Grammar. Ginn and Co., Waltham, Ma.

Sachs, J., Brown, R., and Salerno, R. A. 1972. Adults' speech to children. Unpublished paper presented at the International Symposium on First Language Acquisition, Florence, Italy.

Sachs, J., and Devin, J. 1973. Young children's knowledge of age-appropriate speech styles. Paper presented at Linguistic Society of America, December.

Sachs, J., and Johnson, M. L. 1972. Language development in a hearing child of deaf parents. Unpublished paper presented to the International Symposium on First Language Acquisition, Florence, Italy.

Scaife, M., and Bruner, J. S. 1975. The capacity for joint visual attention in the infant. Nature 253(5489) 265–266.

Schlesinger, I. M. 1971. Production of utterances and language acquisition. In D. I. Slobin (ed.), The Ontogenesis of Grammar. Academic Press, New York.

Schlesinger, I. M. 1974. Relational concepts underlying language. In R. L. Schiefelbusch and L. L. Lloyd (eds.), Language Perspectives—Acquisition, Retardation, and Intervention. University Park Press, Baltimore.

Searle, J. R. 1969. Speech Acts: An essay in the Philosophy of Language. Cambridge University Press, Cambridge, England.

Searle, J. 1971. What is a speech act? In J. F. Rosenberg and C. Travis (eds.), Readings in the Philosophy of Language. Prentice-Hall, Englewood Cliffs, N.J.

Searle, J. R. 1975a. Indirect speech acts. In J. Morgan and P. Cole (eds.), Studies in Syntax and Semantics. Vol. 3: Speech Acts. Seminar Press, New York.

Searle, J. R. 1975b. Speech acts and recent linguistics. In D. Aaronson and R. W. Rieber (eds.), Developmental Psycholinguistics and Communication Disorders. Ann. N.Y. Acad. Sci., Vol. 263, pp. 23–38.

Shatz, M. 1974a. The comprehension of indirect directives: Can two-year-olds shut the door? Paper presented at the Linguistic Society of America.

Shatz, M. 1974b. Beyond syntax: The influence of conversational rules on speech modifications. Paper presented at SSRC conference on language input and acquisition.

Shatz, M., and Gelman, R. 1973. The development of communication skills: Modifications in the speech of young children as a function of listener. Monogr. Soc. Res. Child. Devel. 38: (152).

Shipley, E. S., Smith, C. S., and Gleitman, L. R. 1969. A study in the acquisition of language: Free responses to commands. Language 45: 322–342.

Sinclair, H., and Bronckhart, J. P. 1972. S.V.O.: A linguistic universal? A study in developmental psycholinguistics. J. Exp. Child Psychol. 14: 329–348.

Sinclair-de Zwart, H. 1971. Sensori-motor action patterns as a condition for the acquisition of syntax. In R. Huxley and E. Ingram (eds.), Language Acquisition: Models and Methods. Academic Press, New York.

Skinner, B. F. 1957. Verbal Behavior. Appleton-Century-Crofts, New York.

Slobin, D. I. 1968. Questions of language development in cross-cultural perspective. Working paper No. 14, University of California, Berkeley.

Slobin, D. 1971. Developmental psycholinguistics. In W. O. Dingwall (ed.), A Survey of Linguistic Science. University of Maryland, Maryland.

Slobin, D. I. 1973. Cognitive prerequisites for the development of grammar. In C. Ferguson and D. Slobin (eds.), Studies of Child Language Development. Holt, Rinehart, and Winston, New York.

Smith, F., and Miller, G. A. (eds.). 1966. The Genesis of Language: A Psycholinguistic Approach. MIT Press, Cambridge.

Snow, C. E. 1971. Language acquisition and mothers' speech to children. Unpublished doctoral dissertation, McGill University, Montreal.

Snow, C. E. 1972. Mothers' speech to children learning language. Child Dev. 43: 549–565.

Snow, C. E. 1974. Mothers' speech research: An overview. Paper presented at the Conference on Language Input and Acquisition, September, Boston.

Snow, C. E., Arlman-Rupp, A., Hassing, Y., Jobse, J., Joosken, J., and Vorster, J. 1974. Mothers' speech in three social classes. Unpublished paper, University of Amsterdam.

Svachkin, N. 1973. The development of phonemic speech perception in early childhood. In C. Ferguson and D. Slobin (eds.), Studies in Child Language Development. Holt, Rinehart and Winston, New York.

Veneziano, E. 1973. Analysis of wish sentences in the one-word stage of language acquisition: A cognitive approach. Unpublished master's thesis, Tufts University, Boston.

Vorster, J. 1974. Mothers' speech to children: Some methodological considerations. Publications of the Institute for General Linguistics, August, no. 8. University of Amsterdam.

Weir, R. H. 1962. Language in the Crib. Mouton, The Hague.

Weir, R. H. 1966. Some questions on the child's learning of phonology. In F. Smith and G. A. Miller (eds.), The Genesis of Language. MIT Press, Cambridge.

Whitehurst, G. J., Ironsmith, E. M., and Goldfein, M. R. 1974. Selective imitation of the passive construction through modeling. J. Exp. Child Psychol. 17: 288–302.

Words and Sentences: Uniformity, Individual Variation, and Shifts Over Time in Patterns of Acquisition

Melissa Bowerman

Do all children learn to talk in the same way, or are there significant differences among them in the paths they follow toward an adult knowledge of language? Is a child's gradual attainment of greater linguistic knowledge always marked by a steady increase in the apparent maturity of his utterances and patterns of comprehension, or is inner progress sometimes accompanied by an outward decrease in accuracy? Answers to both of these questions are of critical importance to the design of more accurate and sensitive ways to assess the level of linguistic ability of children known or suspected to have language disturbances, and to determine whether and in what ways their language is improving under a particular course of therapy.

The present paper explores questions of interchild uniformity and variability, and the nature of developmental changes across time. The period of development that receives primary attention extends from the beginning of word production, at about 12 months, through the first few months of word combining; later stages are touched on only selectively.

Most child language research over the last decade and a half has been directed primarily at discovering developmental *uniformities* among children, or ways in which all children are similar to each other at any given stage of development and as they progress over time. Efforts of the 1960s concentrated mainly on syntactic development, or how children learn to handle the formal aspects of sentence structure. Toward the end of the 1960s and at the start of the 1970s, there occurred a shift in research focus from concern with the acquisition of sentence structure per se

This research was supported in part by Grant No. HD 00870 from the National Institutes of Child Health and Human Development.

to investigations of the role played in language development by semantic, cognitive, and—somewhat later—pragmatic factors. Although methods of data analysis and the specific questions asked of the data altered as a result of this shift, the desire to discover in what ways all children are alike continued to guide most research efforts. The search for "universals" of language development took on added impetus with the introduction of new data from children learning languages other than English (e.g., Bowerman, 1973a, 1975b; Brown, 1973; Slobin, 1970, 1973).

The persistent concern for discovering uniform principles of language development is now being joined by a rapidly growing interest in sources of diversity or variation among children, a healthy trend—foreshadowed by Bloom (1970)—that not only directs attention to important new problems but also adds a needed perspective to the study of universals. Recent studies have suggested that there may be considerable variability among normal children, even to the extent that they may follow rather different paths to adult knowledge. Information about variability—about its range or extent among normally developing children and about what aspects of language may be involved—should greatly enrich efforts both to determine the type and degree of language deficit a given child may have and to provide him with a therapeutic program optimally suited to his individual needs.

A second kind of information that is indispensible not only to the initial assessment of language problems, but also, even more, to the evaluation of a child's progress over time, addresses the question of how advances in linguistic knowledge are manifested in the child's outward performance. Although steady improvement in the ability to produce or comprehend is to be expected for many aspects of language, there is the problem of how to construe apparent *regression,* when the child begins to make errors in producing or interpreting words, sentence patterns, etc., that he already seemed to have mastered. There is increasing evidence that apparent backsliding is not only frequent in normal development and affects a number of different aspects of language, but also that, far from signaling loss of knowledge, it is usually a sign of an important advance. Initial "correctness" may mask an underlying lack of understanding. Thus, errors with respect to given language forms and structures are often associated with a more mature level of development than is correctness.

The following discussion of the issues raised above is divided into four main sections. The first examines hypotheses and conflicting evidence concerning the nature of the *relationship between language development and level of cognitive ability* during the sensorimotor period of development. The second section explores the question of uniformity, variation, and change over time with respect to the acquisition of *word meaning.* The third section discusses hypotheses about similarities and differences among children during the early period of *word combining.* The final section considers some types of *errors* in children's speech that are indicative of progress.

COGNITIVE DEVELOPMENT AND THE EMERGENCE OF LANGUAGE

Are developmental milestones in language acquisition linked to the achievement of particular cognitive abilities? This question has received increasing attention in recent years. Many investigators are convinced that there is a close relationship between cognitive and linguistic growth, but as yet there is little agreement about its exact nature. In this section, some studies bearing on the relationship of cognitive development to the emergence of single-word utterances and syntax during the child's second year are considered. (For arguments concerning relationships between later cognitive developments and more complex syntactic and semantic structures, the reader is referred to Beilin, 1975; Cromer, 1974; Ingram, 1975a; and Sinclair-de Zwart, 1969.) Two major issues are reviewed: 1) the role played by the child's achievement of the ability to form *mental representations* of objects and events, and 2) whether there are individual differences among children in the first few months of word production that can be attributed to difference in "cognitive style."

Mental Representation, Word Use, and Syntax

The cognitive development most often proposed as the primary prerequisite to language acquisition is the capacity for mental representation or, more generally, the representation of one thing, in its absence, by another that is distinct from it (e.g., Morehead and Morehead, 1974; Sinclair-de Zwart, 1969, 1971, 1975). The representational ability is the crowning achievement of the sensorimotor period of development, and emerges during its sixth and final stage, at about 18–24 months, as outlined by Piaget (1952, 1954, 1962). The capacity for representation is manifested in symbolic play (e.g., pretending to sleep, pretending that one object is another), deferred imitation, the ability to reconstruct invisible displacements of an object (the final test of the concept of object permanence), and other signs of memory for absent objects and events.

What language behaviors depend on mental representation? Relationships affecting a number of different aspects of language have been proposed. However, some of these are mutually conflicting, or have been challenged with counter-evidence. The issues involved are of the greatest importance for designing more accurate ways to pinpoint the source of children's language deficits and constructing appropriate compensatory programs; they are therefore discussed in some detail. Certain proposed relationships between language and mental representation are first reviewed, followed by some counterevidence and alternate proposals. The lack of consensus among investigators may reflect methodological differences (e.g., in decisions as to what nonlinguistic behaviors will be accepted as evidence for the achievement of mental representation) and/or important gaps in our understanding of how the onset of specific behaviors are related to each other (are they indeed merely reflections of broad underlying shifts in "stage" of cognitive growth, or does each skill have its own ontogenetic history to a large degree?) (cf. Fischer, in press). An additional possibility is that there are systematic but as yet unexplored differences among children in the relationship between what they can do linguistically and their level of cognitive ability.

According to several recent studies, much or all of the "holophrastic" period (time during which the child says only one word at a time) takes place before Stage 6, that is, before the child acquires the ability to entertain mental representations of objects and events. The onset of mental representation, in this view, is thus not associated with the beginnings of language, but rather with certain changes in the use of language that are said to take place at about 18 months, shortly before the child begins to construct multiword utterances.

The most detailed arguments for a relationship between Stage 6 cognitive level and certain linguistic developments occurring at this time have been made by Bloom (1973) and Ingram (1974, 1975a). Bloom's proposals are based on a study of her daughter Allison's speech during the one-word period, which extended from 9 to 21 months. She documents several types of changes in Allison's use of one-word utterances during the second half of her second year, and hypothesizes that these changes derived from and depended on Allison's emerging capacity for mental representation.

Substantive versus Function Forms   Some of the changes reported by Bloom involved Allison's use over time of words for objects ("substantive forms") versus words for relationships or behaviors in which diverse objects can participate ("function forms"). Bloom observed that even though Allison produced a number of different words for objects in the early months of word use, "it was fairly clear that she was not acquiring a vocabulary of substantive words" (p. 110). She based this conclusion on the relative frequency and persistence of different kinds of words in Allison's speech. Until about 17 months, words for objects were used relatively infrequently and had a high mortality rate, tending to drop out of usage after their initial debut. (Names for people and very familiar objects were an exception.) In contrast, function forms were frequent and persistent from the start of word production: "The words 'more,' 'there,' 'gone,' 'away,' 'stop,' 'up,' and 'uh oh' were the dominant words in [Allison's] speech before and at 16 months" (Bloom, 1973, p. 110).

Bloom attributed the relative infrequency and high mortality rate of object words (compared to function forms like "more") in Allison's speech to lack of the concept of object permanence and the concomitant capacity for mental representation. Specifically, she argued that the ability to form mental representations of objects is a prerequisite to learning stable meanings for object words. Learning stable meanings for words encoding the *behavior* of objects does not require this ability, hypothesized Bloom, and so can be achieved earlier (1973, p. 111). At about the age at which Stage 6 typically begins, according to Piaget's norms, Allison's vocabulary of object words increased markedly and became cumulative—i.e., the words persisted over time—and she began to *use* object words much more frequently.

Successive Single-Word Utterances   Bloom documented a second change in Allison's language behavior during the one-word period and related it, like the increased stability of Allison's object words, to the emergence of mental representation. This involved the child's beginning to produce two or more different single-word utterances in close succession in reference to the same nonlinguistic situation.

Bloom outlined Allison's developmental progression as follows: during the first few months of the one-word period, Allison generally produced only *one* word in any particular speech context, often repeating it several times. For example, she would say either "more" or "cookie" while picking up a second cookie, "chair" or "up" while climbing into a chair, but not both. Bloom noted that the failure to express more than one aspect of the nonlinguistic context was not because of lack of vocabulary. The child often knew the relevant words, but simply did not use them together either in a sentence or sequentially.

During the second half of her second year, Allison began increasingly often to produce strings of "successive," or different, single-word utterances within a particular speech context. Initially, these sequences were predominantly of a variety Bloom termed "chained": they were linked to successive movements by Allison, or movements and/or utterances by someone else. While topic was thus held relatively constant, the production of each new word seemed to be "occasioned by a shift in context, . . . as Allison noticed, remembered, or did something 'new'" (p. 48). For example, "Allison picked up [a] cow, saying 'cow,' tried to put it on the chair, saying 'chair,' then turned to [her mother] for help, saying 'Mama'" (p. 48).

Gradually, a second type of successive single-word utterance sequence came to predominate, in which "Allison seemed to have an entire event in mind at the outset. Her successive utterances were related to one another by virtue of their relation to the total event to which they referred" (p. 49). For example, after Allison's mother suggested taking off Allison's coat, Allison produced a number of utterances involving the words "up," "neck," and "zip," indicating that she wanted her coat zipped up. Bloom termed sequences like this "holistic," noting that unlike "chained" successive single-word utterances, they were not linked to particular motions or attentional shifts.

Bloom proposed that the onset of holistic successive single-word utterances is tied to the development of mental representation—in particular, to the capacity to mentally represent *relationships* between objects and events. She argued that this ability to "coordinate and hold in mind at once the several notions underlying [the child's] separate utterances" (p. 52) is one major prerequisite for syntax. A second is learning the syntactic code, discussed below in connection with related arguments.

The Transition to Syntax   Why does the child finally move from successive single-word utterances to multiword utterances? Two major types of explanations for the emergence of syntax have been proposed. According to one, the child is in essence learning more during the one-word period about the structure of sentences than he can demonstrate. He is prevented from actualizing his knowledge of sentence structure in speech by limitations of short-term memory and/or of the physiological capacity to program more than one word at a time. According to proposals of this type, the child's one-word utterances are actually propositional or sentential in underlying structure. That is, the child's one uttered word contracts a relationship with one or more unspoken elements of the nonlinguistic context or of the child's cognitive representation of the context (see Parisi, 1974, for the distinction). For example, "gone" might express an action in relation to the mother as the implicit agent of the action (Greenfield and Smith, 1976; see Antinucci and Parisi, 1973; Ingram, 1971, 1974; McNeill, 1970, for related proposals).

According to Greenfield and Smith (1976), progress during the one-word stage consists in part of the child's gradually adding to the repertoire of semantic relationships that he can communicate by embedding one word into a situational context. Greenfield and Smith propose, on the basis of intensive studies of two children during the one-word stage, that relational semantic notions such as agent of action, location, object of action, etc. emerge in a fixed temporal order.

These arguments about the relational nature of one-word utterances may at first seem similar to Bloom's description of the relationships holding between holistic successive single-word utterances. However, Bloom (1973) explicitly challenges the proposal that one-word utterances are sentential in underlying structure, and hence that the onset of syntax may reflect no more than a relaxing of physiological constraints or limitations of short-term memory (see also Brown, 1973, p. 151 ff.; Dore, 1975; Schlesinger, 1974, for critiques of this hypothesis). Bloom argues that although children producing holistic successive single-word utterances have a good *cognitive* understanding of the relationship between objects and events within a context, their conceptual representations of these relationships should not be construed in *linguistic* terms. Thus, Bloom complements her first prerequisite to syntax—that children must attain the capacity for mental representation—with a second: they must learn "the code for mapping . . . mental representations of the intersecting relations among objects and people onto the semantic-syntactic relations among words" (pp. 52–53).

The Role of Mental Representation Reconsidered: Some Counterevidence

Bloom's arguments linking changes in word use shortly before syntax to the emergence of the capacity for mental representation have been accepted and expanded upon by Morehead and Morehead (1974). Ingram (1974) comes to similar conclusions using data both from Bloom and other parent diarists, and McNeill (1974) presents related arguments linking the onset of syntax to the gradual "interiorization of action schemas."

The various proposals are plausible, but the language data discussed by these investigators are rarely accompanied by language-independent evidence as to the child's stage of cognitive development. Confirmation of the hypothesis that the onset of holistic successive single-word utterances, an increase in the vocabulary of words for objects and in the stability of these words, etc., are temporally linked to the emergence of mental representation and, by inference, that they depend on it, requires the assessment of both linguistic *and* cognitive data from the same children.

Fortunately, some recent and ongoing studies attempting to get at just this sort of information have been reported. The evidence is mixed, but on the whole it is not strongly supportive of the proposed relationship between the onset of mental representation and the specific language behaviors outlined by Bloom, Ingram, and others. Counterevidence is of several types. First, it has been reported that many children exhibit a well developed notion of object permanence and/or other behaviors assumed to reflect a Stage 6 capacity for mental representation early in the one-word period, months *before* they begin to produce successive single word utterances, much less combine words. Second, at least some children seem to be capable of syntax *before* there is evidence from nonlinguistic behaviors that they have entered Stage 6, although it is not yet clear whether this syntax is productive, i.e., rule-governed. Third, not all children—perhaps not even many—exhibit the differential use of substantive versus function forms that, according to Bloom (1973) and Morehead and Morehead (1974), should typically characterize the earliest period of word production as a natural consequence of the child's failure to have yet established object permanence.

Evidence for Stage 6 Long Before Syntax   Evidence to the effect that many children show proof of mental representation early in the one-word stage, or even before word production begins at all, comes primarily from Huttenlocher (1974) and Bates and her colleagues (Bates, 1976a, Bates, Benigni, Bretherton, Camaioni, and Volterra, 1975; Bates, Camaioni, and Volterra, 1975).

Huttenlocher (1974) studied word comprehension in four infants followed longitudinally from about 12 months of age. She found behaviors that she construed as evidence for considerable capacity for the mental representation of object properties and the location of out-of-sight objects long before the age (18 months) at which Piaget has argued that a firm notion of object permanence is typically established. For example, children at 10 to 11 months of age would look for objects on the basis of the objects' names. By 13 and 14 months, respectively, two of the subjects could respond to "where is X?", when X was an object currently out of sight but with a permanent location in the house, by going to the spot. By 14 and 16 months, they could also retrieve, without trial-and-error search, a requested object that was temporarily out of sight. These indications of mental representation occurred when the children's active vocabularies were either nonexistent or limited to one or two words.

Bates and her colleagues also have reported evidence for mental representation much earlier in the one-word period than the theories of Bloom (1973), Ingram (1974), and McNeill (1974) would predict. These investigators studied three Italian children longitudinally in an effort to discover cognitive prerequisites to communicative behavior (Bates, 1976a; Bates, Camaioni, and Volterra, 1975); they then followed up their original findings with a study of 13 American and 12 Italian children who were visited four times in their homes at monthly intervals between the ages of nine and one-half and twelve and one-half months (Bates et al., 1977). Sessions 2 and 4 were videotaped, the complete set of Uzgiris and Hunt (1975) scales of cognitive development were administered at each visit, and the mothers were interviewed to obtain anecdotal evidence about their children's behaviors between visits. Bates et al. (1977) found that over half of the children showed at least two manifestations of Stage 6 cognitive ability by 12 months of age. For example, approximately 65% of the children passed the object permanence task at the Stage 6 level at about twelve and one-half months. Other Stage 6 reported or observed behaviors included symbolic play, deferred imitation, and memory for absent objects or people.

As one would expect on the basis of the children's ages at this time, they were not far into the one-word period and were not beginning to produce successive single-word utterances. Rather, they were barely beginning to use recognizable words of the adult language. However, Bates et al. do report several interesting relationships between language and level of cognitive development, both before and at the time of attaining of Stage 6, although these relationships are for the most part different from those hypothesized by Bloom (1973), Ingram (1974), and McNeill (1974).

Bates et al. (1975, 1977) found that the use of vocal signals (mostly idiosyncratic syllables to communicate intentions such as desire for an object) emerged at nearly the same time as the use of nonverbal signals such as gestures for the same purposes, and that both coincided with typical Piagetian Stage 5 noncommunicative behaviors, particularly the use of tools to achieve ends (e.g., pulling on a cushion to get a toy resting on its farther side). Bates et al. interpret these early "words" not as symbols standing for or referring to objects or events, but rather as integral parts of given sensorimotor action schemas, equivalent to gestures. They interpret both vocal signals and communicative gestures such as showing, giving, and eye contact coupled with reaching and pointing as manifestations of the capacity for tool use. Thus, they propose, the child's vocal and gestural efforts to use an adult to obtain an object or an object to obtain an adult's attention are cognitively equivalent to the use of an object to obtain another object.

The possible importance of the cognitive capacity for tool use to the development of language has been suggested in the past (e.g., de Laguna, 1927), but little elaborated before the work of Bates et al.; the attainment of mental representation has received far more attention in recent years and has figured importantly in efforts to assess whether delayed or deviant language development might result from cognitive disturbances (e.g., Morehead and Morehead, 1974). However, the proposals of Bates et al. are strengthened by a recent study that links language delay to disturbances of the tool using capacity. Snyder (1975) reports that of the six Uzgiris-Hunt cognitive development scales, only the means-end scale distinguished language delayed, but otherwise nonexceptional, children from normally developing children matched by mean length of utterance and socioeconomic status. Snyder concludes that language delayed children may have a cognitive deficit that is "specifically linked to the dynamic aspects of cognition (i.e., the development of tool use as a means to an end) rather than the static aspects of representation such as object permanence and the construction of objects in space" (1975, p. 158).

Despite their primary emphasis on the cognitive capacity for tool use as a prerequisite for the development of language and other forms of communication, Bates et al. (1975, 1977) do report an important change in language at about the time that their subjects gave nonlinguistic evidence of mental representation: the use of words *referentially,* to stand for or represent objects or events. Word use that was judged "referential" included the naming of animals in picture books, the extension of words for known objects or pictures to novel-but-similar items, appropriate responses to "what's this?" questions, etc. Bates et al. stress that the onset of referential speech was gradual rather than abrupt, with many words used in ways that seemed transitional between the earlier request forms and other pragmatic signals, and the later more clearly referential usages. Dore, Franklin, Miller, and Ramer (1976) and Carter (1975a, b) have also described the gradual evolution of referential speech. They report that the earliest "words" of their subjects were idiosyncratic syllables used nonreferentially in connection with various desires for service as well as in less clearly "communicative" situations, such as registering pleasure or recognition or while engaged in play with certain toys.

If considerable representational capacity exists in many children from early in the one-word stage, as the studies described above by Huttenlocher (1974) and Bates et al. (1975, 1977) indicate, then at least for these children the later onset of successive single-word utterances and subsequent transition to syntax cannot be accounted for in terms of the child's attainment, after several months of word production, of a qualitatively different stage of cognitive development. In considering discrepancies between her theory and that of Ingram (1974), Bates (1976) proposes that the emergence of syntax indeed does not reflect a mental capacity transformed by the emergence of the representational ability; rather, she suggests, it results from a gradual increase in the *span* of the child's already achieved representational capacity. In other words, the child must progress from the ability to represent one object or event at a time, which coincides with the earlier use of words referentially, to the ability to "internally represent and operate upon an entire group" of related objects and events, which coincides with the emergence of syntax (1976a, p. 83). Bloom too, of course, has argued that syntax depends on the capacity to mentally represent "intersecting relations among objects and people" (1973, p. 53), but, unlike Bates, she does not explicitly distinguish this ability from the ability to represent objects, etc., one at a time.

Evidence for Syntax Before Stage 6   The theories of Bates and her colleagues on the one hand, and Bloom, Ingram, and McNeill on the other, differ in many respects, but they are alike in postulating that the capacity for representation should be well established before the onset of syntax. Both theories therefore run into trouble with recent data indicating that some children may begin sentence construction *before* they achieve a Stage 6 level of object permanence or give other signs of the capacity for mental representation (Corrigan, 1976; Ingram, 1975b).

Corrigan videotaped three infants every three weeks for a period of 18 months, starting at about 10 months of age. At each session she administered a modified version of the Uzgiris-Hunt object permanence scale. She found that although two of the children did not begin to combine words until after exhibiting object permanence behavior, the third child began to combine words many weeks before he at the final level of Stage 6 attained this level.

Ingram's (1975b) findings are similar to those of Corrigan. He followed four infants from 7 to 19 months, collecting language data and administering various Piagetian tasks. Three of the children followed the developmental schedule he had predicted (i.e., showing certain linguistic developments, including the onset of sequences of single-word utterances followed within a few weeks by multiword utterances, at the same time as independent cognitive evidence indicated they had entered Stage 6). The fourth child, however, began to produce multiword utterances while still in Stage 5, and by Stage 6 many of her utterances consisted of more than one word. This finding is particularly interesting given Ingram's initial expectation that syntax would not appear until after clear evidence that a Stage 6 cognitive level had been attained. In attempting to account for this child's linguistic achievements, Ingram notes that, compared to the other children in the study, she was very advanced in her *imitative* skills relative to her other cognitive abilities. He speculates that the child's imitative ability, coupled with her mother's concern with language development and intense teaching efforts, may have led to the relatively precocious acquisition of a "large vocabulary and advanced syntax."

To fully assess the significance of Corrigan's and Ingram's respective subjects for a theory of the relationship between cognitive and linguistic development, it would be necessary to know the nature of their earliest multiword utterances. Such utterances could differ from "typical" Stage 6 combinations in at least two ways. First, they might be produced as unanalyzed units, and hence not "count" as syntax; Nelson (1973) has reported that some children produce some phrases of this sort virtually from the start of word production. However, both Corrigan's and Ingram's subjects went through a clear-cut period of single-word utterances before they began to produce multiword utterances, so it is not clear whether this interpretation is applicable. Assuming that pre-Stage 6 or early Stage 6 syntax is found to be productive, i.e., rule-governed rather than consisting only of unanalyzed phrases, it is possible that it is qualitatively different from later syntax in terms, e.g., of the kinds of semantic relationships expressed or the uses to which it is put.

Substantive versus Function Words: Evidence Against a Link to Cognitive Development   Difficulties involved in trying to place the onset of the capacity for mental representation relative to particular stages of linguistic development have been discussed in the above sections. The argument that children initially use words for objects versus words for relationships and behaviors differentially as a function of lack of mental representation (Bloom, 1973; Morehead and Morehead, 1974) must also be called into question on the basis of recent findings.

In her study of word comprehension, Huttenlocher (1974) found evidence for mental representation of objects and for good *comprehension* of object words at a time when her subjects' vocabularies were limited to one or two words. Huttenlocher suggests on the basis of these data that if object words are initially typically produced less often and less consistently than relational words, the reason lies not in the child's lack of ability to mentally represent objects, but in other factors such as the relative difficulty of retrieving known words for objects versus words for events, differences in the maturation of the child's communicative need to talk about objects versus events, etc. She observes in addition that the phenomenon of words dropping out of use may be attributable to decreases in the salience or interest value of their referents for the child—not to inadequate mental representation.

Further counterevidence comes from Corrigan's (1976) study of the relationship of object permanence to level of language development. Corrigan found no difference in the relative frequency with which function forms and substantive forms occurred in samples preceding and following her three subjects' attainment of the final Stage 6 level on an object permanence task. In addition, Corrigan did not observe any difference between substantive forms and function forms with respect to their relative persistence over time, although she concedes that this phenomenon was difficult to measure with her data. A similar failure to find differential use of substantive versus function words has been reported in Bowerman (1976b, 1978a) in a study of two children, Christy and Eva, during the one-word stage and beyond. Most of the children's earliest words for objects, including many class names (e.g., "ball") as well as words for familiar people and special objects, were used frequently and with consistent meanings from their first appearance at 13 to 14 months; in addition, loss of object words was very rare. Although function words like "more" and "off" were common too, they were neither more frequent nor stabler than object words. Bloom (1973) speculates that the tendency to *imitate* may explain why some children's vocabularies are reported as being cumulative rather than marked by losses: "Their using a word with apparent persistence may simply reflect this propensity to repeat a word heard in a previous utterance" (p. 67n). This explanation does not account for the cumulative quality of the vocabularies of Christy and Eva. Although both children imitated relatively often, unlike Bloom's daughter Allison, only words that occurred completely spontaneously were considered for purposes of this analysis.

An interesting finding reported by Corrigan is that her subjects did not use function forms to request the recurrence of objects ("more") or to comment on their disappearance ("all gone") until after they had passed the object permanence task at the final level of Stage 6.. This finding is incompatible with Bloom's (1973) hypothesis, based on her daughter Allison's development, that the acquisition of stable meanings for such words does *not* require a concept of object permanence, unlike words for objects. If, in fact, the opposite is true, then Allison had achieved this concept before the second half of the second year and before the onset of holistic successive single-word utterances, as the studies by Bates et al. (1975, 1977) and Huttenlocher (1974) indicate is possible. In this case, the relative instability of Allison's object words could not be attributed to the immaturity of her representational capacity.

These various findings suggest that a child's emphasis on function forms over object words at the start of word production may stem not so much from lack of the concept of object permanence as from personal cognitive style—a particular bent either toward *conceptualizing* certain kinds of experiences earlier than others, or toward *communicating* certain conceptions rather than others that are also present.

Studies relating the child's language to individual *cognitive style* (as opposed to level of cognitive development) are still scarce, but evidence is accumulating that significant differences among children do exist. This issue is reviewed below.

Cognitive Bases for Individual Differences in the Use of Words

Recent studies have reported that children differ with respect to the kinds of early words they initially "specialize" in acquiring and in the typical communicative purposes to which they put these words.

In a study of how 18 children acquired their first fifty words, Nelson (1973) found evidence that some children tend to concentrate on learning names for categories of objects ("ball," "shoe," "doggie," etc.) while others focus more on the acquisition of names for people and on verbs, adjectives, and "personal-social" words or "expressive" phrases like "no," "yes," "want," "please," "stop it," "go away," "hi," and "ouch." For purposes of analysis, Nelson divided her subjects into two groups on the basis of whether more or less than half of their first 50 words were "general nominals" (i.e., class names for objects as opposed to proper names). She termed the former group "Referential" and the latter group "Expressive." She found that children in the Referential group acquired words more rapidly than those in the Expressive group, and differed from them in other ways even during the early period of word combination.

Nelson (1973) hypothesized that the difference between "Referential" and "Expressive" children is a function of differences in children's initial perception of the function of language. She proposed that some children regard language primarily as a tool for reference, while others see it as a means of expressing feelings and needs and regulating social interactions. Nelson suggested further that such differences in language use can be traced ultimately to differences in children's prelinguistic cognitive styles—that is, to the ways in which they typically organize their experiences.

The way in which Nelson's data were collected causes certain difficulties in assessing the meaning of her findings. First, Nelson classified words as "general nominals," "personal-social," etc. on the basis of how they were first used, and did not take account of possible changes in the way they were used over time. However, usage can shift such that words initially used "expressively" (or "referentially") are later used primarily "referentially" (or "expressively"), instead (cf. Bates, 1976b; Bowerman, 1976b, for examples). Second, Nelson's identification of "Referential" language with the acquisition of "general nominals" may be misleading. A child who is classified as "Expressive" because less than 50% of his first 50 words are "general nominals" could be specializing in the acquisition of verbs, adjectives, and function forms like "more" and "all gone." Unlike words like "hi" and "please," such words can be, and often are, used referentially by children. A child whose early vocabulary contains many of these words may therefore be just as "referential" and as disinterested in social interactions (relative, of course, to "Expressive" children with many social words like "hi," etc.) as a child who specializes in words for objects. A third difficulty with interpreting Nelson's results has been pointed out by Bloom (1976): "There is no way of knowing . . . how the different forms were used by the children—whether, for example, referential speech or expressive speech really dominated in terms of relative frequency of the different words, and were, therefore, more or less important to the child." Finally, as Bloom (1976) also notes, Nelson's reliance on parents' reports of the words their children had used may have allowed the data to be biased by differences in what kind of language the parents happened to notice and report on.

Despite these difficulties of interpretation, evidence is accumulating that Nelson's Referential versus Expressive distinction may reflect the effects of genuine differences of cognitive style on children's language acquisition. For example, Rosenblatt (1975) reports that her subjects (a group of English children), like Nelson's, could be divided on the basis of whether they seemed to be learning a "reference" language or an "expressive," "person-oriented" language, and, moreover, that the children's tendency to learn words of one type or the other was related to the way they played with toys. The Referential style was correlated positively with "shorter latency to touch toys, high visual attention to toys, [and] high task persistence," and negatively with "social attention and interaction." The

Expressive style, in contrast, was related to "adult-oriented behaviour, and greater time spent 'not playing (pp. 9–10).'"

An intensive study of two children by Dore (1974) also suggests that, as Nelson hypothesized, children may differ in the uses to which they put language. One of Dore's subjects had what he termed a "code-oriented style": she used language "primarily to declare things about her environment." The other subject's style, in contrast, was "message-oriented": he used language "mainly to manipulate other people" (p. 350). The linguistic distinction between these two children did not inhere in the *kinds* of words they used, as in Nelson's study, so much as in their differential use of *intonation* versus words: The code-oriented child produced far more words, whereas the message-oriented child used fewer words but controlled a larger repertoire of intonation patterns that he used to influence other people's behavior in utterances designed to summon, protest, or request.

In conclusion, two possible cognitively based sources of variation among normally developing children have been suggested in this section. The subsection above reviewed some proposals concerning the effects of differences in "cognitive style" on the child's "selection" of particular vocabulary items to acquire and on his relative emphasis on acquiring words versus contrastive intonation patterns. The second possible source of variation lies in the relationship, discussed earlier, between changes in the child's language behavior and his passage from one level or stage of cognitive growth to the next. While most investigators exploring this issue have looked for "universal" phenomena (e.g., "linguistic development X cannot take place until cognitive level Y has been achieved"), the differences in the relationships they have proposed and in the particulars of their reported findings suggest that any such universals may lie at a somewhat more abstract level than we have as yet envisioned. As for the specific issues under current investigation (e.g., at what point in the one-word period does the child achieve the concept of object permanence? for what specific linguistic behaviors is mental representation an immediate prerequisite?), it is possible that no clear-cut answers applicable to all children will be forthcoming.

THE ACQUISITION OF WORD MEANING

What kinds of meanings do children initially attach to their words? How do they go about modifying these meanings until they coincide with those of mature speakers? These questions have been receiving increasing attention in the last few years. Some proposals, evidence, and areas of theoretical conflict are the next topics of review.

Overextensions and Related Phenomena

Most words of the adult language, aside from proper nouns, are labels not for particular items but for categories of nonidentical, yet similar in some way, objects, events, relationships, etc. (Lenneberg, 1967). An important task for the child acquiring words is to determine the nature and boundaries of the categories or concepts to which they refer. He must learn to identify the members of a given concept in some way and to distinguish them from things that are not members. This is a task of enormous complexity. It cannot be solved simply by attending to "ostensive defini-tions" (someone pointing out a referent while uttering a word), because this does not tell the child which attributes of the referent are critical for identifying new referents for that word, which are only characteristic but not critical, and which are irrele-vant. For example, as Clark (1974) observes, the mother's labeling of an object as "doggie" tells the child nothing about what features of the object he should attend to in order to be able to recognize another object as a member of the category "dog-gie." Should he "pay . . . attention to the dog's shape, the dog's size, the texture of its coat, the way it moves, all of these, or only one or two of them"? (p. 107). If the problem is complex even for words with referents that can be pointed to, consider the child's dilemma when faced with the task of determining what features of the nonlinguistic context are critical to the meanings of action, relational, or "experience" words like "open," "off," "big," "need," and so on.

   Overextensions   The fact that children do not acquire the adult meanings of words all at once—that the meanings they initially assign to words often differ from the meanings at which they will ultimately arrive—is evidenced in discrepancies between the ways children and adults use or understand particular words. The most easily spotted symptom of a child's misinterpretation of a word is his use of it for an object or event that an adult would refer to with a different word: for example, "doggie" for a cow or other animal, or "close" for pushing a chair up to a table. This phenomenon has been termed "overextension" (Clark, 1973b).

   Clark (1973b, 1974b) attributes overextensions to the child's having assigned a meaning to the word that is *incomplete* from the adult's point of view. She proposes that children start out by "identifying the meaning of the word with only one or two of its semantic components or features of meaning, rather than with the complete combination of components used by the adult" (1974, p. 108). Because the child has fewer features associated with the word than an adult does, he uses it in a broader range of contexts than the adult. The child's use of the same word for objects as diverse as dogs and cows does not mean that the child cannot *discriminate* between these objects, stresses Clark, but only that he does not yet know that the distinction is relevant to the meaning of the word in question. As the child adds other features to the word, his overextensions of it gradually diminish until the word is used for the same range of referents as in adult speech. The addition of features is primarily occasioned by the child's acquisition of other words in the same semantic domain. For example, when "cow" and "horse" are acquired, something more is learned about the meaning of "doggie" (e.g., "relatively small") that allows the child to keep the words separate.

   Underextension, Overlap   Various difficulties with details of Clark's account of how word meaning is acquired have been discussed by several researchers. For example, Anglin (1977), Bloom (1973), and Nelson (1974) have all noted that overextension is only one of several ways in which children use words differently from adults. For example, children sometimes *underextend* words from the adult viewpoint—i.e., use them only for a subset of the items to which an adult would apply them (see Anglin, 1977; Bloom, 1973, p. 72; Bowerman, 1976b; for some examples). This indicates that they have identified the word with too many semantic features, or with some that are too specific. Alternatively, children sometimes use a word in a way that *overlaps* with adult usage—i.e., they apply the word to only a subset of the items that are included in the corresponding adult concept, as well as to some other items that are outside that concept (Anglin, in press; Schlesinger, 1974).

Overextension in Production but not in Comprehension   Another source of difficulty with Clark's hypothesis as it was originally formulated is that, as recent research has shown, children who overextend a word in production can often pick out the correct referent for the word from a competing array of stimuli when asked to do so (Labov and Labov, 1974; Thomson and Chapman, 1975). In other words, they seem to know more about the meanings of some of their overextended words than their productions indicate.

This phenomenon is open to alternative interpretations, and probably not all instances of the phenomenon should be accounted for in the same way. An explanation offered by Huttenlocher (1974) is that errors in production stem not from incomplete knowledge of the meaning of a word, but from problems in *retrieving* a word when that word is semantically similar to other words that the child understands: "In a domain with many words of closely related meaning, the child may tend to retrieve the most frequent word [in the mother's speech], thus leading to overgeneralization in production" (p. 367).

Clark (1975) has advanced a different explanation for overgeneralization in production but not in comprehension. Revising her original account of overextensions, she now suggests that some overextensions are "partial" rather than "full"—that is, the child has more features associated with the word than his spontaneous use suggests, but he sometimes applies the word to referents that have only one or some of these features.

Prototypical Referents   Some recent analyses of spontaneous speech data provide support for Clark's claim that overextensions may result from the child's use of only a subset of the semantic features he associates with a word. For example, Labov and Labov's (1974) daughter used "cat," one of her first two words, in connection with a range of animals that were characterized by *one or more* of a small set of features such as "pointed ears."

In a study of the way words were used by the author's two daughters, Christy and Eva, during the single-word stage and beyond, many similar examples were found (Bowerman, 1978a). For most of these examples there was evidence that the particular set of features that had come to be identified with a word were derived from the child's association of the word with one or more original or "prototypical" referents and her subsequent analysis of this (these) referent(s) into a small set of attributes or features. These prototypical referents were almost always the child's *first* referents for the words, and they also were the referents for which the words had been most frequently or exclusively modeled in parental speech.

The use of the word "open" provides a good example. "Open" was most frequently modeled by parents and first produced by both children in connection with the opening of doors, boxes, drawers, jars, and the like. All of these referents involve at least two features, which may be termed the "separation of parts" and the "revealing of something within." After a while, the children began to overextend the word to referents that were similar to these original referents in that they either involved the separation of parts *without* the revealing of something (e.g., taking the stem off an apple, pulling pop beads apart, taking a leg off a doll), *or* the revealing of something *without* the separation of parts (e.g., turning on water, lights, the TV, an electric typewriter), or both (e.g., pulling up a sofa cushion to look under it).

A similar example is provided by Eva's use of "moon." Eva applied this first to the real moon and subsequently to such diverse referents as a half-grapefruit seen from below, flat shiny green leaves, lemon slices, a ball of spinach, mounted steer horns, a chrome dishwasher dial, hangnails, and so on. These referents all shared *shape* with the various phases of the real moon (round, half-moon, crescent) and in addition were characterized by one or some combination of several other attributes of the moon, including flatness, shininess, yellowness, being seen at an angle from below, and having a broad expanse as a background (see Bowerman, 1978a, for details and further examples).

Overextensions in which the child's referents for a word share various combinations of attributes with a prototypical referent are interesting in part because they demonstrate the existence of a link between the child's development of word meaning and an *adult* mode of organizing and storing word meaning that has received much attention in the recent literature. Work by Rosch (1973a,b), for example, indicates that the meanings of many words as they are understood by adults have an internal structure describable in terms of a set of variations around "good" or "prototypical" representatives of the semantic category. Rosch and Mervis (1975) have demonstrated experimentally that the degree to which items are viewed as prototypical members of a category labeled by a particular word is, for many categories, a function of the number of attributes they share with other referents for the word. Referents seen as prototypical tend to share many attributes with each other and increasingly fewer with less prototypical referents, and poor exemplars of the category share few features with each other and with prototypical referents. The spontaneous speech data described above indicate that the formulation of word meaning based on a set of variations around central or prototypical exemplars is a process available to young children as well as to adults. The particular *words* that are initially treated in this way may later receive a more constrained interpretation, but the process itself continues to be available as one way of organizing word meaning. (The organization of word meaning around prototypical referents results in "complexive" word use—i.e., the use of words for referents that may have no single feature or set of features in common. Complexive word use has often been considered a primitive stage in the acquisition of word meaning, e.g., Brown, 1965; Vygotsky, 1962. However, the recent work by Rosch and her colleagues indicates that complexive word use—at least of a certain type—is typical of adult speech, as Wittgenstein, 1953, argued earlier, and thus cannot be considered inherently "primitive.")

Cues Used in Categorizing Objects

In extending a word to a novel referent—i.e., a referent to which he has never heard the word applied—the child must disregard discriminable differences between the new referent and familiar ones in favor of attending to some kind of similarity. Investigators differ on the question of what kinds of similarities very young children attend to in categorizing objects as equivalent for purposes of word use. (The question of how children create nonobject concepts to which words like "more," "all gone," "aha!" and "heavy" can be attached has received less attention, but see Bloom, 1973, and Bowerman, 1976b, 1978a.)

After analyzing diary study reports of the overextension of words for objects, Clark (1973b) proposed that most overextensions are based on the child's recognition of *perceptual* similarities of some kind between novel objects and known referents for a word. The perceptual property most often involved is shape; others that account for some overextensions are size, sound, movement, texture, and, to a very limited extent, taste (sweetness). Color is notable for its absence as a basis for overextension. Clark (1976) has hypothesized that many of the perceptual categories on which children's overextensions are based are formed before the learning of the words and reflect nonlinguistic, universal modes of organizing experience.

The hypothesis that the child's early word meanings involve categories based on perceptual similarities has been criticized by Morehead and Morehead (1974) and Nelson (1974). Drawing upon Piagetian theory, these investigators argue that perception is secondary in the young child's concept formation. More important than perception is *function*: objects are considered equivalent—as members of the same category—on the basis of similarities in their behaviors (if they are animate), and/or similarities in the actions upon them and the relationships into which they enter. According to this view, perceptual cues are used not as a basis for classification but simply to identify an object as a probable instance of a concept even when the object is experienced apart from the relationships and actions that are concept-defining.

Nelson's arguments are based in part on her observation that children are selective with regard to which parental words they initially "choose" to learn. In her study (1973) of the acquisition by 18 children of their first 50 words, she found that "the one outstanding general characteristic of the early words is their reference to objects and events that are perceived in dynamic relationships: that is, actions, sounds, transformations—in short, variation of all kinds" (Nelson, 1974, p. 269). Names for objects or places that are "just there" and do not do anything, like tables, trees, cribs, and rooms, are overlooked in favor of names for objects that move or change in some way, or that the child can manipulate, such as food, animals, people, and shoes (Nelson, 1973). Other investigators have also noted that words for moving, changing, or manipulatable objects are learned earlier than names for static objects (Anglin, 1977; Huttenlocher, 1974).

Despite this evidence that dynamic objects are more salient to children than static ones, data on how children generalize words to novel referents do not support the hypothesis that shared function is primary in the formation of the concepts to which children's early object words are attached, and that perceptual characteristics play a purely secondary, predictive role. Specifically, many of children's overextensions involve the application of a given word to objects that are *perceptually similar,* but that the child knows from experience have *different functions* (Bowerman, 1976b, 1978a; Clark, 1975). For example, one child, as noted above, applied the word "moon" to leaves she had just picked, a half-Cheerio she had dropped during breakfast, a ball of spinach she was about to eat, a magnetic capital D she was putting on the refrigerator, lemon wedges she was taking off ice tea glasses, and hangnails she was pulling off. Such overextensions are incompatible with the view that perceptual cues are used only to *predict* that a given object belongs in a particular function-based category, rather than as bases of classification in their own right.

Can the function-based and perception-based theories of how children formulate and name classes of objects be reconciled? Bates and her colleagues suggest that the conflict between the two theories may stem from failure to take into account the difference between the child's initial nonreferential use of words in connection with various sensorimotor action schemata, before his attainment of the capacity for mental representation, and his subsequent ability to use words *referentially,* to stand for or represent objects and actions (Volterra, Camaioni, and Bates, 1975). In other words, shared function may be the primary determinant of the contexts in which a child will utter a word before he achieves mental representation and the capacity to refer, but perceptual similarity may come to predominate following this achievement. It is important to recall that Bates et al. (1975, in press) place the onset of mental representation and the concomitant emergence of referential speech relatively *early* in the one-word period, coinciding with the child's first use of "real" words as opposed to relatively stable but idiosyncratic forms like *na-na*. According to this view, then, virtually the entire period during which children are acquiring their first conventional words for objects takes place after the onset of mental representation, and thus after the child is capable of using perceptual similarities to classify objects. Further detailed work on individual children will clearly be required to determine the generality of this proposed developmental sequence.

Strategies Used in Comprehending Words

The focus in the foregoing discussions has been on what a child's spontaneous production of words can teach us about the process of acquiring words and word meanings. Studies of the way in which words are *comprehended* offer important additional information, particularly about systematic differences in approach by children at the same stage and about changes in the interpretive strategies used at successive stages of development.

Comprehension studies typically investigate the way children interpret words by asking them to answer questions about actions or configurations of objects, or to act out commands. Several semantically related words are often investigated at the same time to determine whether the child distinguishes among them—for example *before* and *after, more* and *less, same* and *different, big, little, thick, thin, long, short,* and so on. Although the results are in one sense specific to the words under investigation, many of the studies conducted thus far have suggested that children's nonlinguistic knowledge of the world significantly influences their responses. Determining how strategies based on nonlinguistic knowledge are related to the development of knowledge of word meaning has proved difficult, however.

Partial Knowledge Supplemented by Nonlinguistic Strategies According to one line of theorizing, children's responses to word comprehension tests are often based on *partial knowledge* of the words' meanings, supplemented by nonlinguistic strategies derived from deepseated cognitive/perceptual organizational predisposi-tions (Clark, 1973a, 1975; Klatzky, Clark, and Maken, 1973; Donaldson and McGarrigle, 1974). An early study exploring this possibility was Clark's (1973a, 1974) investigation of the acquisition of *in, on,* and *under.* Clark asked children ranging in age from 18 months to five years to "put X in/on/under Y." She found that if Y, the reference point (a box, tunnel, crib, truck, table, or bridge), could serve as a container, the youngest children always put X into it, regardless of whether the instruction involved *in, on,* or *under.* If the reference point had a flat surface but was not a container, the child always put X onto it, whether the instruc-tion was *on* or *under.* Thus, *in* was always interpreted correctly, *on* was only interpreted correctly if there was no possibility for putting something into a container and *under* was almost never interpreted correctly. From this and related evidence, Clark concluded that when a child has no knowledge or only partial knowledge of the meanings of *in, on,* and *under,* he bases his interpretations on his perception of "normal or canonical spatial relations" between objects (1974, p. 118).

Further evidence for the "partial knowledge plus nonlinguistic strategies" hypothesis comes from studies of antonymic word pairs. Early investigations of *more* and *less* and of *long* and *short* and other dimensional adjectives indicated that children consistently respond correctly to the "unmarked" or "positive" member of these pairs (*more, long,* etc.) and tend to treat the marked or negative member as if it is synonymous with the positive member (Clark, 1972, 1973b; Donaldson and Wales, 1970). At first this outcome was taken at face value to indicate that children learn the meaning of the positive member first. Subsequently, however, Clark and her colleagues (Clark, 1975; Klatzky, Clark, and Macken, 1973) hypothesized that children initially know the same about both members of the pair—e.g., that they refer generally to amount, length, etc. They attributed children's greater accuracy with positive terms to a nonlinguistic cognitive bias toward the positive pole of a dimension—that is, a preference for choosing the greater of two amounts, the item with the most extent on a dimension, etc.

A study by Donaldson and McGarrigle (1974) showed further evidence for the role of nonlingluistic biases. These investigators found that the way in which the quantifiers *more* and *all* are interpreted varies according to the particular physical context of the questioning. For example, many children used relative fullness as a criterion for judging *more* when cars were arranged in garages, such that they judged four cars in four garages to be "more" than five cars in six garages. However, they often shifted to using the criterion of length of a row or number of cars in the row when fullness was excluded (by the removal of the garages) as a possible criterion, such that they judged five cars to be "more" than four cars.

Donaldson and McGarrigle concluded that in addition to whatever children may know about the actual meaning of a word (e.g., for *more,* perhaps that a "dif-ference in magnitude" is involved), the specific context or "the circumstances locally obtaining" when the word is presented exert an important influence on their interpretation. Such influences of context (which the investigators termed "local rules") may result in the child's interpreting the same word differently at different times. Donaldson and McGarrigle hypothesized that "local rules" derive from "predispositions to structure or interpret the world in particular ways" (p. 194), and suggest that such rules are hierarchically ordered—e.g., for *more,* fullness takes precedence over length, length over density, etc. Their proposal that nonlinguistic predispositions exert a *systematic* influence on comprehension accords well with Clark's hypotheses.

As children mature, according to Clark and to Donaldson and McGarrigle, they depend less and less on nonlinguistic interpretive strategies. The role played by these strategies in the acquisition of a more complete knowledge of word meaning is unclear. However, one interesting possibility has been raised by Clark: "the degree of coincidence between responses based on a nonlinguistic strategy and responses based on semantic knowledge may determine the relative cognitive complexity of different linguistic forms and hence determine their order of acquisition" (1973a, p. 181). Thus, according to Clark, *in* should be learned before *on, on* before *under, more* before *less,* and so on.

Effects of Task Variables   Aspects of these proposals have been questioned by a number of investigators. For example, studies by Wilcox and Palermo (1974) and Grieve, Hoogenraad, and Murray (1977) suggest that the *in* before *on* before *under* response pattern found by Clark is attributable more to the particular stimulus items she used than to a stable predisposition in the child. Varying the items in certain ways and even varying the *names* used to refer to the items led to completely different response patterns. Similarly, several studies have indicated that children either do not necessarily respond more accurately to positive members of antonymic pairs than to negative ones or do not treat negative terms as if they were synonymous with positive terms (e.g., Bartlett, 1976; Carey, in press; Eilers, Oller, and Ellington, 1974; Townsend, 1976). These findings cast doubt on the hypothesis that nonlinguistic response strategies play a *systematic* role in the acquisition of word meaning and focus attention instead on the effect on children of the demand characteristics of the particular tasks used to test word comprehension.

Individual Differences and Changes Over Time   Even when confronted with the same task, not all children of a given age respond in the same way. For example, Clark and Sengul (in press) found that young children who did not yet understand that there is a difference in meaning between *here* and *there* and between *this* and *that* initially interpreted the words in one of four different but consistent ways: they always either chose the object near themselves, the object near the speaker, the object away from themselves, or the object away from the speaker (the first two strategies predominated). The child's initial starting point also had an effect on the pattern of later stages of acquisition.

Other studies that present evidence for children's choice between alternative strategies of interpretation include those by Eilers et al. on dimensional adjective pairs, and Kuczaj (unpublished data cited in Clark, 1975) on *never* and *always.* Eilers et al. found that in responding to questions about *long* and *short,* etc., their subjects used consistent interpretive strategies, but some favored the negative, marked meaning rather than the positive, unmarked meaning. They concluded that possibly "the child makes a choice at some stage between the marked and unmarked meaning and attributes the chosen meaning to both members of the pair" (1974, p. 203).

As children get older, their patterns of responding on word comprehension tests may change in surprising ways. Added linguistic knowledge does not always manifest itself directly in an overall improved pattern of responding. As Clark (1975) observed, "At the earliest stage . . . the child's strategy might lead him to make one kind of mistake in his responses; at a later stage, however, his strategy might change as a result of what he now knows about the word meaning, so that the kind of error he makes also changes" (pp. 89–90).

Alterations in patterns of response that result in children's making errors on words that they seemed to understand at an earlier age are particularly interesting, and must be taken into consideration in any comprehensive plan for evaluating a child's linguistic progress under a particular course of therapy. A number of such changes over time have been identified.

In some cases, children may initially seem to have an adult-like understanding of a word only because the interpretive strategies they use in particular experimental contexts happen to coincide with the word's meaning. This was noted above in connection with the discussions of *in, on,* and *under* and antonymic pairs. Clark and Garnica (1974) furnish a further example in their study of *come, go, bring,* and *take.* These investigators set up play situations with animals on a farm and asked children from five and one-half to nine and one-half years to identify the speaker or the addressee of sentences like *can I come (go) into the garden?* and *can I bring (take) X into the house?* They found that children at different ages use different but systematic rules for selecting speakers and addressees (e.g., the animal at the goal of motion is initially identified with both speaker and addressee; later it is identified only with the addressee and the speaker is taken to be an animal outside the goal). This results in complex and shifting error patterns such that *come* and *bring* are at first consistently interpreted correctly for both speaker and addressee, and later interpreted correctly only for addressee, and incorrectly for speaker.

In this study and those cited earlier, apparent knowledge of word meaning may be illusory. In other cases, the initial knowledge may be real, but "changes in the system of analysis" that the child uses may cause a drop in performance (Maratsos, 1974, p. 69). Maratsos (1973) conducted a study that seems to illustrate a genuine loss of some original knowledge. He found that three-year-olds were considerably better than four- and five-year-olds at deciding which of two cardboard rectangles or animals was the "big" one. The judgments of three-year-olds, like those of adults, were based on gross overall size as a function of both height and width. Four- and five-year-olds, however, began to concentrate exclusively on the vertical dimension, with the result that they treated *big* exactly as if it meant *tall.* After experimentally ruling out conceptual problems in determining size as a possible explanation, Maratsos concluded that the errors were attributable to the children's having arrived at an incorrect semantic definition for *big.*

Decreases in performance accuracy that apparently result from shifts in interpretive strategy are not limited to word comprehension. Such drops have also been observed in the way children interpret sentence structures, particularly passives (e.g., Bever, 1970; see Maratsos, 1974, for replication and discussion). It therefore may be a very general phenomenon in language acquisition.

Discrepancies Between Comprehension and Production

Tests of word comprehension may sometimes credit children with more knowledge than they actually possess, as discussed above. However, the reverse assessment error, *underestimating* their knowledge, is also a danger. Specifically, there is reason to suspect that in responding to comprehension tasks children sometimes fail to display knowledge that they do have, as demonstrated in their own spontaneous speech. (See Bloom, 1974, for a discussion of how the different processes involved in understanding and speaking can lead to complex and shifting discrepancies between comprehension and production.)

For example, in a study of the spontaneous use of deictic verbs in contrived play situations, Richards (1976) found that the acquisition of *come* and *go* was essentially complete by age four, contrary to what Clark and Garnica's (1974) study of the comprehension of these terms would lead one to expect. Performance on *bring* and *take* was less accurate than on *come* and *go,* but still better than that of the much older children studied by Clark and Garnica. Richards concluded that success in Clark and Garnica's task demanded a highly developed ability at perspective-taking, such that true linguistic competence among the cognitively less mature children may have been obscured.

There is also reason to question whether children are as slow to learn the meanings of *in, on,* and *under* as experimental studies have suggested. For example, Brown (1973) presents data on the use of *in* and *on* by his subject Eve at approximately 22–23 months—an age at which, according to Clark's (1973a) study of the comprehension of *in, on,* and *under,* one finds children interpreting *on* as if it means *in* when there is a container present. Brown's Eve used *in* productively in connection with objects in or entering containers of various sorts—such as bags, boxes, pockets, mouths, and rooms—and *on* in connection with objects on flat surfaces—such as floors, pages, papers, tables, and trays. Her performance apparently could not be attributed to learned associations between prepositions and nouns, because at least once she correctly used *on* even though the object in question was a container, in the sentence "don't sit on Cromer's coffee." Brown concluded on the basis of these data and materials from his other subjects that *in* and *on* are learned together in a way that suggests the emergence of a pair of distinctive features having to do with containment versus support (1973, p. 330). Data from my two daughters (unpublished materials) are similar to Brown's, in that by the time both *in* and *on* were present (at 18 and 20 months) they were used completely appropriately. When *under* entered (at 22 and 24½ months), it too was used appropriately for location under (the body, the crib, the bed, etc.) or, occasionally, for location beside or behind (but never in or on).

There is parallel evidence in the domain of syntax that tests of comprehension may fail to reveal children's linguistic knowledge. For example, Chapman and Miller (1975) report an experimental study that indicates that "production precedes comprehension" in the acquisition of knowledge of word order for agent-action-object strings. The study compared children's ability to act out agent-action-objects commands, using toys, with their ability to produce such utterances as descriptions of actions. The children were divided into three groups of five each on the basis of mean length of utterance. The groups' average MLU scores were 1.8, 2.4, and 2.9 morphemes, respectively. Correct word order was "observed significantly more often in speaking than in serving as a clue to subject and object in the comprehension task" (p. 362), especially among the less advanced subjects. Similar findings are reported by deVilliers and deVilliers (1973), although details of their study and results differ. There was evidence in the Chapman and Miller study that in the comprehension task the children may have relied on a semantic strategy (e.g., animate noun is agent; inanimate noun is object acted upon) or on expectations about probable events in interpreting sentences. In other words, the knowledge of agent-action-object word order demonstrated in their spontaneous speech was apparently either inaccessible for use in sentence processing or was overridden by the tendency to look for extralinguistic cues to sentence meaning.

How far these data take us from the era in which it was assumed that comprehension always precedes production, and therefore provides a better clue to children's underlying linguistic knowledge! Information on how children's ability to understand particular words under experimental conditions is related to their ability to produce them appropriately in natural circumstances is still sparse, but judging from the rising tide of interest in the developmental relationship between comprehension and production, it seems likely that we are due for a spate of studies specifically designed to evaluate this.

STRATEGIES FOR SENTENCE CONSTRUCTION

The early period of word combining has been the subject of intensive study and theorizing for well over a decade, with attention first devoted to the formal syntactic properties of children's sentences, and then shifting to the semantic and cognitive correlates of formal structure. An important outgrowth of the research of the early 1970s was the realization that the early sentences of children in a variety of different language communities express closely similar meanings (e.g., Bloom, 1970; Bowerman, 1973a, 1975b; Brown, 1973; Slobin, 1970). For example, there are utterances that point out or name (e.g., *this/that/here/there/see* X), others that express recurrence or addition (*more/'nother* X) or nonexistence, disappearance, or rejection (*no/no more* X, X *all gone/away*), and still others that encode relationships among agents, actions, and objects acted upon, or between objects and their possessors, their locations, or their attributes.

Investigations that have followed the initial identification of the semantic characteristics of children's early sentences have taken a number of different paths. For example, many researchers have focused on the correspondence between the semantic content of the early sentences and the child's level of cognitive development at the time word combination starts (e.g., Brown, 1973; Edwards, 1974; Morehead and Morehead, 1974; Sinclair-de Zwart, 1971; 1973a, b; Wells, 1974). A second line of research has been aimed at identifying the relational semantic or syntactic categories that are "psychologically real" for the child—i.e., functional within his system of rules for producing sentences (Bloom, Lightbown, and Hood,

1975a; Bowerman, 1973a, b, 1974a, 1975a, 1976a,b; Braine, 1976; Schlesinger, 1971, 1974).

A third research emphasis has been on clarifying the relationship between what a child *says*—the outward form of his sentences—and his *underlying knowledge* of sentence structure (e.g., Antinucci and Parisi, 1973; Bloom, 1970, 1973; Bloom, Miller, and Hood, 1975b; Braine, 1974, 1976; Parisi, 1974; Schlesinger, 1974; see Bowerman, 1976a, 1978b, for discussion). Still other investigators have attempted to determine the influence of *pragmatic* factors on early word combinations—i.e., the interaction between formal structure or semantic content and the specific contexts in which sentences are used, or the communicative purposes toward which they are put (e.g., Bates, 1976, a,b; Braine, 1976; MacWhinney, 1975).

The present discussion of the early period of word combining concentrates on two additional important research questions that have recently received concentrated attention: 1) Is there a consistent temporal order in which children acquire the ability to construct sentences expressing various semantic relationships? and 2) Do different children approach the structure of language with qualitatively different strategies that persist across time? Despite certain areas of agreement, there are still significant differences of opinion on the answers to these questions. Some relevant studies are reviewed and compared below.

Order of Emergence of Semantic Categories: Uniform or Variable?

Bloom, Lightbown, and Hood's Study   Bloom et al. (1975a) report an investigation of the order in which children acquire the ability to combine words to express various kinds of relational meanings. The data analyzed were drawn from three to five samples of spontaneous speech from each of four children, collected at intervals during the developmental period when mean length of utterance (MLU) increased from under 1.4 morphemes to about 2.5 morphemes. The multiword utterances in each sample were classified according to a system of "semantic-syntactic" categories that the investigators had devised on the basis of repeated passes through the data in search of developmental trends. When five or more utterances belonging to a given category were observed in a sample, the child was credited with a productive (i.e., rule-governed) ability to construct such utterances. The order in which utterances in the various categories became productive was established for each child and compared across the four children.

According to Bloom et al.'s findings, the ability to make sentences in the various categories emerged as follows: The first productive constructions were those expressing existence ("pointing out or naming an object"), *recurrence* ("reference to 'more' or another instance of an object or event"), and *negation* ("nonexistence, disappearance, or rejection of objects or events").

These were followed by a variety of categories involving *verb relations*. For all four children, verb relation constructions encoding *action events* preceded those encoding *state events*. *Action events* included both *actions* (e.g., *my open that, Gia ride bike, I made, Kathryn jumps, tape go round*) and *locative actions* (*put in box, tape on there, you put ə finger, Mommy stand up ə chair, I get down*). *State events* included a) *locative states*, referring to "the relationship between a person or object and its location," where no movement was involved (e.g., *I sitting, light hall*), b) *notice* utterances (with verbs of attention like "see," "hear," "watch," "look at"), and c) *state* utterances (with verbs like "want," "need," "like," "sick," and "have").

Constructions expressing possession (e.g., *dolly hat, my blanket, dis ə mines)* and attribution (e.g., *new hat, baby elephant, big bottle, that too big, ə dirty sock, two doll)* emerged in variable order for the four children.

Finally, last to emerge were constructions involving *instruments* ("specifying the inanimate object that was used in an action to affect another object"), *datives* ("specifying the recipient of an action that also involved an affected object"), *wh-questions, place of action* (e.g., *baby swim bath, buy more grocery store*), and *intention* (e.g., *I want go park, I want wear it*).

Bloom et al. concluded that the order in which the four subjects of their study acquired knowledge of how to express various kinds of meanings was very similar. The important differences among the children did not involve semantic knowledge, according to their analyses, but, rather, knowledge of the syntactic devices by which semantic concepts can be expressed—a topic returned to shortly.

Braine's Study   Braine (in press) has recently presented an analysis of the semantic relationships expressed in early child speech that contrasts strikingly with Bloom et al.'s study in its conclusion that there are important *differences* in children's semantic knowledge, both in the initial stages of word combination and in the order of emergence or utterances in various semantic categories.

Braine analyzed 16 corpora of speech from 11 children learning either English (six children), Samoan (two children), Finnish, Hebrew, or Swedish (one each) to determine (among other things) the nature of the relational categories represented in the children's earliest utterances, and whether the order in which additional categories emerged was consistent or variable. Data came from published sources or his own files. The MLUs of the samples ranged from 1.1 morphemes or below up to 1.7 morphemes. Thus, the period of development represented was comparable to the first segment of the period examined by Bloom et al.

Braine's method of analysis was to examine and compare the multiword utterances present in each sample in minute detail, considering a) which ones seemed to be semantically related to each other (e.g., all utterances with *more* that expressed recurrence, all those with *want* that expressed desire for an object, all those expressing concepts of possession or location or of a relationship between actor and action, etc.), b) whether utterances that were similar enough on semantic grounds to have been governed by a single pattern for sentence production were also characterized by the same word order, c) whether there were enough utterances potentially derived from the same pattern to permit the inference that the pattern was *productive* for the child, and so on. On the basis of these analyses, Braine first arrived at conclusions about each child's knowledge of how to produce sentences at one (or more, where possible) point in time, and then compared the children to determine how they were similar and different.

Braine's overall conclusion was that children's "first productive structures are formulae of limited scope for realizing specific kinds of meanings. They define how a meaning is to be expressed by specifying where in the utterance the words expressing the components of meaning should be placed (p. 4)." With regard to interchild consistency, Braine observed that:

> Children differ considerably in the kinds of contents expressed by their productive patterns, and in the order in which they acquire them. . . . at any point, the range of individual differences appears to be circumscribed by the fact that the meanings expressed by each child's productive patterns are a sample from a probably open-ended set of possible conceptual relations, with formulae expressing certain relations more likely to have been acquired than others (1976, pp. 57–58).

Among the more common formulas were patterns that draw attention to something (e.g., *see* + X, *here/there* + X), patterns that remark on specific properties of objects (*big/little* + X), note plurality or iteration (*two* + X, *and* + X) or recurrence or alternate exemplars (*more/other* + X), patterns that express motion toward or position at a location (X + *here/there*, X + Y), and patterns encoding possession or actor-action relationships.

The children in Braine's study apparently began with a selection from among these and other less popular patterns. The extent of possible diversity among children is suggested by the fact that there was no overlap at all between the patterns represented in the early samples of two of the English-speaking children, Andrew and Kendall. Braine proposed that "as English-speaking children develop, they acquire more and more patterns and thus become more similar to each other in their output and tend to, converge on a common 'simplified' English (p. 57)". This gradual convergence gives the impression of considerable similarity among children and obscures important differences in developmental history.

Interpreting Discrepant Findings Although the conclusions of Braine and Bloom et al. (1975a) differ in many respects, some of the discrepancies can be attributed to methodological differences in their studies. Bloom et al. applied a single system of semantic categories to all their subjects, many of the categories used were relatively broad (i.e., disregarded finer semantic distinctions that might have been made), and the exact composition of sentences (in terms of which constituents were present and how they were ordered relative to one another) did not affect the way the sentences were classified. Braine's analyses, in contrast, were based on the individual characteristics of each child corpus, and relatively subtle semantic distinctions were often drawn on the basis of differences in the child's handling of word order and the like (see Bowerman, 1976b).

Individual variation in order of emergence would be compatible with a uniform developmental sequence such as that described by Bloom et al. as long as it takes place on a rather molecular level, within limits imposed by certain broader consistencies. Some of the consistencies reported by Bloom et al. (and by other investigators such as Brown, 1973, and Bowerman, 1973a, 1975b) were indeed respected in the samples analyzed by Braine: for example, the initial absence of productive patterns for talking about instruments (e.g., *cut knife*) and recipients of actions (*give Mommy, show Daddy*).

However, even when methodological factors are taken into account, there are still some major differences between Bloom et al.'s and Braine's conclusions (see Bowerman, 1976a,b for more detailed discussion). For example, Bloom et al. found that constructions expressing *locative actions* (X goes to Y; X moves Y to Z) preceded those expressing *locative states* (X is located at Y); they argue that this is because of the cognitive salience of dynamic over static events for young children. Yet Braine's analyses showed individual differences with respect to this distinction. Some of his subjects developed productive formulas for expressing locative actions before formulas for locative states, but others began to produce utterances of both kinds at about the same time.

The picture becomes complicated even further when we take into account a study by Wells (1974). Like Bloom et al., Wells classified his subjects' utterances from successive spontaneous speech samples according to a uniform system of semantic categories. Some of his results accord well with their conclusions. For example, he found that children talk about *actions* and *locations* before they talk about *states* involving feelings and perceptions (sentences with "want" and "see" were an exception: they emerged early, as was also true for several of Braine's subjects), and that utterances expressing *changes of location* emerge before those expressing *locative states*. However, some types of utterances that were classified together in Bloom et al.'s study, and were therefore judged to emerge at the same time, were distinguished by Wells and found to enter separately. For example, Wells found that utterances encoding *functions of people* (e.g., with "eat," "play," "sing," "kiss," etc.) came in later than those encoding *changes of attributive state* (e.g., with "break," "cut," "open," "close"), but Bloom et al. classified all such utterances as *actions* and judged the category to emerge early. Oddly, although Braine (1976), like Wells, reported that functions of people and changes of state apparently do not become productive at the same time, he found them to emerge in the reverse order!

To summarize, there are major discrepancies in the findings reported in different studies designed to extract similar sorts of information about the order of emergence of semantic categories. These discrepancies make it clear that, even though we have by now achieved a general view of what to expect in early samples of multiword combinations, we are still far from an accurate understanding of ways in which children are similar and ways in which they may differ with respect to the semantic characteristics of their early utterances and to the way in which their semantic knowledge builds over time.

Cracking the Syntactic Code

At this point we turn from the semantic content of early sentences to a consideration of their formal properties—i.e., the *structure* by which given semantic intentions are expressed. As is true for the other aspects of language acquisition previously discussed, there is increasing evidence for important differences in children's approaches to structure.

Formal Markers versus Grammatical Categories   In studies published in 1970 and 1973, Bloom discussed differences in the formal structure of children's early sentences that she interpreted as evidence for two alternative strategies for learning syntax. She labeled the strategies "pivotal" and "categorical."

Children who primarily follow the "pivotal" strategy (named after Braine's (1963) notion of "pivot words" for which a position is learned) seem to be searching for consistencies between surface form and semantic or syntactic function. Their speech is characterized by the presence of large numbers of utterances in which *constant forms* have *constant relational meanings* in the sentences in which they appear: e.g., "more _____" to express the recurrence of the object or event with whose label it is combined, "my _____" to encode possession, "this _____" to point out an object, etc.

In the categorical strategy, the semantic or syntactic relationships that hold between the words of a sentence are independent of the lexical meaning of either of the words. That is, the particular words that can function in a given relational role vary: e.g., "baby," "Mommy," "Daddy," etc. can all function as *agents* relative to words for actions or for objects acted upon, and as *possessors* relative to words for objects possessed. Similarly, "ball," "book," etc. can all function as *objects affected* (by an action) or as *objects possessed* relative to words for agents or possessors, and so on.

Bloom et al. (1975a) elaborate on the distinction between the two approaches to syntax with evidence that the strategies continue to operate well beyond the two-word stage. Their arguments are based on differences among their four subjects with respect to the use of nouns and pronouns in major semantic roles such as "agent," "possessor," "object affected," and "place" (location to which something is conveyed or at which an object or event is located). Three of their subjects—Kathryn, Eric, and Gia—were the same children studied in the work in which Bloom (1970) originally made the distinction between two strategies.

In the sentences of Peter—a new subject—and Eric, who both initially followed the "pivotal strategy," pronouns predominated heavily in the early months: e.g., "I" or "my" as agent or mover, "it," "this one," or "that" as object affected, "my" as possessor, and "here" or "there" as place. However, both Eric and Peter knew many names for objects and people and used them in single-word utterances or in combination with words like "more" or "no." Bloom et al. conclude that Peter and Eric were learning a grammatical system that "consisted of relations between different verb forms and a number of constant functional forms" (p. 19). Gia and Kathryn (the original "categorical" strategists) differed from Eric and Peter in that their early speech contained very few pronouns. Major semantic roles like agent, possessor, etc. were filled not by constant forms but by a variety of different nouns.

Bloom et al. found that the children were consistent over time with regard to their strategies. When sentences involving new verb relationships (e.g., "locative action," "locative state") entered their speech, they continued to use the same method (either pronouns or nouns) as they had in earlier sentences to represent the objects or animate beings involved in the relationships.

Over time, Gia and Kathryn began to use more pronouns and Peter and Eric began to use more nouns, until gradually their speech became similar in the proportion of nouns to pronouns. This shift took from about 12 to 20 weeks, and was essentially completed by the time MLU reached about 2.5 morphemes and the children were about two years old.

Bloom et al. concluded on the basis of these analyses that "children can break into the adult linguistic code in one of (at least) two ways: with a system of formal markers, or with a system of rules for deriving grammatical categories" (p. 35). They observed that both strategies "provide the child with a means for representing the same semantic information in his speech, with greater or lesser lexical specification, and both are aspects of the adult code" (p. 35).

Are the two strategies mutually exclusive? In describing the difference between the "pivotal" and the "categorical" strategies for the earliest utterances, Bloom (1970) stressed that they were not: all the children incorporated elements of both, but tended to lean more heavily in one direction or the other. However, in discussing children's treatment of pronouns over time, Bloom et al. did propose that the two systems are initially incompatible: "It appears that an individual child's first sentences are either nominal or pronominal, and the two systems of reference are not mutually substitutable in the beginning" (p. 34). Similarly, the children "were learning two different systems of semantic-syntactic structure that were virtually mutually exclusive in the beginning" (p. 20). Bloom et al. speculate that "it was apparently necessary to learn one system of reference (either nominal or pronominal) before learning the other" (p. 33).

In reviewing Bloom et al.'s data, Maratsos (1975) agrees that the children were clearly different with respect to their treatment of the formal structure of language, but he concludes that the evidence does not support such strong claims as the authors make. He notes that the period of "'impressive consistency' for preference of one linguistic system over the other" seems to end well before MLU 2.0. For example, Eric, at MLU 1.69, used pronouns for affected objects (e.g., *get it*) 32 times, and nouns (e.g., *get ball*) 33 times. Kathryn's sample at MLU 1.89 contained 81 nouns and 41 pronouns as affected objects, "which seems like a preference, not the exclusive use of one system" (p. 92). Maratsos concludes with regard to Eric's and Peter's data that "the periods where pronominal dominance is really marked are ones where expression of the relevant relations is often barely or marginally productive" (p. 92).

Nelson (1975) has recently reported a study that bears upon the question of whether the two systems are initially mutually exclusive, and that relates preference for one system over the other to characteristics of the child's speech at a considerably earlier stage. The study compared speech samples from children who had been classified as "Referential" or "Expressive" speakers on the basis of their earlier speech with respect to a number of measures of noun and pronoun use in multiword utterances. Speech samples from the two sets of children were subdivided according to mean length of utterances, such that altogether there were four groups, each consisting of six samples: two designated as "low MLU" (1–2.5 morphemes) and two as "high MLU" (2.5–4.5 morphemes).

Nelson found that the Referential children's multiword utterances contained a high proportion of nouns to pronouns at the lower MLU level. As MLU increased, the use of nouns declined and the use of pronouns rose. The Expressive speakers, in contrast, began "with a balance of noun-pronoun use, within and out of sentences ["sentences" were defined as multiword utterances containing an implicit or explicit verb relation]. Their use of pronouns changes very little with development. However, there is a striking increase in their use of nouns" (p. 476).

Nelson's finding that some children use few pronouns in their early constructions accords well with Bloom et al.'s (1975a) analyses of Kathryn's and Gia's speech; it is interesting that this noun use is consistent with an emphasis on the acquisition of common nouns (the feature that distinguished Referential from Expressive speakers) at a much earlier stage. However, Nelson's study contrasts with that of Bloom et al. in that it does not reveal an opposite strategy marked by the virtually exclusive use of pronouns in major semantic roles in early sentences. Rather, the children who initially used many pronouns also used many nouns. Unlike Bloom et al., Nelson stressed that the use of nouns versus pronouns and, more generally, the Referential versus Expressive developmental patterns are not discrete strategies, "but rather represent different points along a continuum" (p. 478) of greater or lesser tendency to use particular lexical items versus syntactic "dummy terms" (pronouns) to express major semantic roles.

Because Nelson's study compared pronoun and noun use averaged across samples from six children in each group, it is theoretically possible that the individual Expressive children used either the noun or the pronoun strategy and that the apparent balance of noun-pronoun usage was an artifact produced by averaging (although Nelson's informal discussion of the characteristics of the Expressive children's speech seems to preclude this possibility). Alternatively, it is possible that the Expressive children used the pronoun system exclusively or almost exclusively at lower MLUs, but gradually began to use nouns in their sentences as well. Nelson's grouping of samples might have obscured a developmental trend like this, because the MLUs of the samples in her "low MLU" groups ranged from 1 to 2.5 morphemes—the latter figure representing precisely the developmental point at which Bloom et al. (1975a) found that children who initially adopt either the pronoun or the noun system become indistinguishable.

In sum, although Nelson's study is suggestive, it does not allow one to conclude with assurance that the use of pronouns versus nouns need not be mutually exclusive systems in the early period of sentence production. However, clear-cut evidence to this effect *is* available from at least one child, the author's daughter Eva. Eva's data (collected by periodic taping plus extensive daily note-taking) demonstrate vividly the difficulty of categorizing individual children according to "type" of developmental pattern. Eva was a "Referential" speaker as determined by a classification of her first 50 words (more than 50% "general nominals"), and by the lack of "expressive phrases" and other unanalyzed multimorphemic utterances in her early speech. However, unlike Referential speakers and like Expressive speakers in Nelson's analysis, she used both nouns and pronouns extensively in her early speech.

Similarly, Eva did not observe the link proposed by Bloom et al. between the use of the "pivotal strategy" for early sentence construction and a subsequent dependence on fixed syntactic frames with semantic-syntactic roles expressed almost exclusively by pronouns. Her earliest sentences were patently "pivotal": the first several weeks of sentence construction were marked by the successive emergence of individual patterns such as *want* + X (17 1/2 months), *more* + X (18 months, 1st week), *no* + X, *here* + X (18 months, 2nd week), etc. (see Bowerman, in press c, for details). Moreover, she had a clear liking for certain "fixed syntactic frames" at a slightly later time: e.g., almost all of her subject-verb-object constructions for the first month (starting at 19 months) were of the form *I* (or, occasionally, *Daddy, baby, man,* etc.) *do it.*

Despite this "pivotal strategy" beginning, Eva did not continue to insist on constant forms for constant semantic-syntactic functions, with a concomitant emphasis on pronominal forms, as Bloom et al.'s analyses would predict. Rather, her approach was mixed: nouns predominated in some types of constructions and both nouns and pronouns were common in others. For example, almost all verb-object constructions, from their emergence at 18 months, 2nd week for the next two months, involved noun objects: e.g., *open salt, drop grapes, cut bottle, get book, find soap, close ring, fix doggie.* By 20 months, 3rd week, *it* began to substitute for the name of the object occasionally. Similarly, in almost all utterances expressing position at or movement toward a location, the location was specified by a noun rather than *here* or *there*, from the first occasional use of the construction pattern at about 18 months, 3rd week to real productivity at about the 20th month, 3rd week and beyond: e.g., *salt hand, chalk shirt, tape horsie, doggie stairs,* and *beans table.*

The patterns for subject-verb and possessive constructions involved both nouns and pronouns from the very beginning. S-V constructions began to occur occasionally at 18 months, 2nd week, but at the rate of only a few a week until 19 months, 3rd week, at which time they became frequent. Both *I* and noun subjects such as *Mommy, man, bear, Christy,* and *baby* occurred in these early constructions, and both were frequent when the sentence pattern became established. Possessives began to occur in some numbers at 19 months, 2nd week, and within two weeks both noun + noun and *my* + noun possessive constructions were plentiful.

To summarize, Eva's pattern of development indicates clearly that it is not necessarily the case, as Bloom et al. (1975a) propose, that the use of pronouns in major semantic-syntactic roles is initially incompatible with the use of pronouns, and vice versa—i.e., that it is "necessary to learn one system of reference (either nominal or pronominal) before learning the other" (p. 33). Rather, it seems more likely that, as Nelson has hypothesized, children's preference for noun versus pronoun encoding ranges along a continuum, with perhaps a majority of the children who have thus far been studied in any detail showing a marked initial preference for nouns, a minority showing preference for pronouns, and the rest sprinkled somewhere in between.

Word Order   Until recently it has been generally reported and widely accepted that children acquiring English observe constraints on word order virtually from the start of word combination, and make very few word order errors (e.g., Bloom, 1970, 1973; Bloom et al., 1975a; Brown, 1973; Brown and Bellugi, 1964). There have been occasional reports of children who in fact did not exhibit this consistency (e.g., Braine, 1971; Burling, 1959) but few attempts have been made to reconcile these data with the assumed norm for English-speaking children.

Recent work by Braine (1976) and Ramer (1976) now indicates that our assessment of English-speaking children's early knowledge of word order has been too simplistic: not only may deviations from normal order be more common than has been supposed, but also there may be systematic differences both in the frequency with which a given child misorders sentences of different types, and in the extent to which different children make ordering errors.

A major conclusion of Braine's (1976) study is that children establish "positional patterns"—i.e., consistent word orders—for expressing given semantic contents quite early. However, Braine notes that the establishment of a particular positional pattern is sometimes preceded by a short period in which the word order in utterances expressing that semantic content is relatively flexible. Braine terms this phenomenon a "groping pattern," to indicate that the child has not yet discovered the appropriate order.

Groping patterns in the data analyzed by Braine often involved specific semantic relations. For example, Braine's son Jonathan used consistent word orders for sentences with the modifiers *big, little, hot, old,* etc., paired with nouns, but sentences with *wet* or *all wet* plus a noun were variably ordered for a time. Data from the author's daughter Eva also indicate that the kinds of sentence patterns for which a child does or does not know a consistent word order at a particular time can be quite specific. As noted above, Eva's subject-verb and possessive constructions involved both pronoun and noun subjects and possessors from their earliest appearances at about 18 1/2 months and 19 1/2 months, respectively. However, for many weeks, consistent word order was observed *only* for those strings involving pronominal subjects (*I*) and possessors (*my*); in contrast, strings involving nouns in these roles were ordered variably: e.g., *I wash, I play, I spill, I bite, I get, I walk,* etc., versus *Daddy close, drive Daddy, beary drive, wait beary* (bear will wait), *beary stay, grandma go, sing man, cry boy, lying down birdie,* etc.; and *my baby, my bottle, my salt, my sweater, my cookie,* etc. versus *bottle Christy's, knee baby, Christy's place, Christy's shoes, boat Andrea's,* etc. (all from the 21st month).

Braine found that groping patterns were particularly common for verb-object constructions. He suggests that this may be attributable to children's confusion over the semantic role played by words referring to objects that undergo a change of location or state as a result of an action (e.g., *drive, break*): these words function as "objects affected" with respect to the action upon them, but as "actors" with respect to the specified change or movement they undergo.

What determines the order in which a child arranges the words of a particular utterance belonging to a pattern for which he does not yet know a consistent order? One possibility is that ordering before knowledge of word order constraints may be determined by pragmatic factors such as saliency—e.g., whatever element is most important to the child at the moment is mentioned first (Bates, 1976a; MacWhinney, 1975; Schlesinger, 1972).

The possibility that English-speaking children may differ from each other systematically with respect to their treatment of word order has recently been raised by Ramer (1976). Ramer studied seven children from before they began to combine words until 20% of their multiword constructions consisted of subject-verb-complement strings (an arbitrarily established cutoff point). She found that whether or not the children made word order errors was associated with the *speed* with which they traversed the distance from the onset of syntax to the cutoff point: the three slower children in her group made extremely few errors, while the four faster children made errors on between 3.3 and 3.8% of their total multiword output (e.g., *fast run, cry Mona*). Ramer suggested that these differences "may signal a difference in risk-taking behaviour related to speed" (p. 58). Interestingly, there seem to be parallel differences in phonological accuracy as a function of rate of vocabulary acquisition—see Ferguson, this volume. Ramer also reports several other differences in the "syntactic styles" of the fast versus the slow learners, and hypothesizes that the styles may be sex-linked, with boys typically exhibiting the "slow" style and girls the "fast" style.

It is possible that a more comprehensive account of the acquisition of word order constraints could be achieved by integrating Ramer's observations on the effects of speed with Braine's on the existence of "groping patterns." That is, perhaps "groping patterns" occur primarily among children who are in a hurry to achieve syntactic facility, whereas relative slowness in acquiring syntax may be associated with an unwillingness to combine at random and a tendency to wait until the needed positional patterns have been worked out. Assessing this hypothesis would require determining whether the word order errors made by "speedy" children like those in Ramer's study are—as the hypothesis would predict—typically concentrated in particular construction patterns, while other patterns are relatively error-free, or whether they instead involve only occasional deviations, across a variety of patterns, from ordering constraints that are usually observed.

"REGRESSION" AS A SIGN OF LINGUISTIC PROGRESS

Advances in a child's linguistic knowledge can be manifested in a variety of ways. For some aspects of language, increased knowledge results in a gradual but smooth "improvement" in overall performance. For example, as time passes, the child learns how to encode more and more different semantic relationships in his sentences (Bloom et al., 1975a; Braine, 1976). He uses inflections, prepositions, and other functors in an increasing proportion of the sentential contexts that require them (Brown, 1973), and so on. Sometimes, however, progress involves apparent regression on the child's part—that is, his commission of errors in aspects of language that he seemed to control at an earlier time.

Apparent regression as a consequence of progress has been reported in the realms of phonology (Ferguson, this volume; Smith, 1973), morphology (Ervin, 1964), syntax (Bever, 1970; Bowerman, 1974b; Brown, 1973; Cromer, 1970; Maratsos, 1974; Palermo and Molfese, 1972) and semantics (Bowerman, in press; Clark and Garnica, 1974; Maratsos, 1973). Drops in the accuracy with which children interpret the meanings of particular words were considered in an earlier section. The errors discussed there seem to result from shifts in the child's interpretive strategies. In this section we look at certain "late" errors in the child's spontaneous speech that can be interpreted as signs that the child has arrived at a deeper appreciation of underlying relationships and regularities in the structure of language than he had achieved before.

Comparing, Analyzing, and Relating

Regularity or systematicity in linguistic structure occurs throughout every level of language. The child's progress in acquiring the language to which he is exposed can be conceptualized in terms of which of these regularities he has become aware of receptively or has established control over in his own speech. Acquiring knowledge of systematicity in language, as in any other organized system, requires the ability to implicitly compare and see relationships or similarities among diverse individual products of the system—morphemes, sentence patterns, intonations, semantic structures, etc., in the case of language. A child who could not perform such comparisons could scarcely progress beyond the acquisition of memorized phrases.

For example, consider what it takes to learn inflections such as plural -*s* or past tense -*ed*. To be able to use such forms productively and appropriately, the child must have heard, remembered, and considered *in relation to each other and to their referents* some minimal number of words, all bearing the inflection (in one or another of its allomorphs). For example, to grasp the semantic significance of -*s*—it refers to a notion of plurality independent of its embodiment in any particular array of objects—the child must realize that 1) the -*s* on *dogs* in the context of more than one dog (for example) is the *same* -*s* (i.e., has the same semantic import) as the -*s* on *cups* in the context of more than one cup, and 2) despite the perceptual and functional differences between an array of dogs and an array of cups, they share an abstract similarity, i.e., plurality. To give another example, learning the significance of rising intonation also requires the child to compare diverse input sentences, because he must notice both that *Did Daddy go to work?* and *Is this your bear?* involve the "same" intonation, distinct from others, and that although the utterances for the most part have different semantic contents, they share one important element of meaning: they both encode a "questioning" intent on the part of the interlocutor.

The child's production of a particular form under appropriate circumstances cannot be taken as clear evidence that he understands the regularities that underlie it, because individual forms such as "dogs," "dropped," or "what's this?" can be easily memorized. The best evidence that the child has achieved an understanding of the composition of a given form is his creation of novel forms that are constructed according to the same design (see Bowerman, 1974b). Whenever the system in question contains irregularities—i.e., forms that are not treated according to the general rule—the creation of novel forms results in the *regularization* of irregular forms: for example "camed," "breaked," and "foots." Regularization often follows a period in which the child uses irregular forms appropriately, but—as the subsequent regularization demonstrates—without an understanding of their internal structure. For example, children use forms like "came," "broke," and "feet" in a referentially appropriate way *before* they begin to say "comed," "breaked," and "foots," but these correct forms drop out because the child has not understood them as consisting of "come" + past, "break" + past, and "foot" + plural (Ervin, 1964). It is well recognized that the onset of errors like "comed," although superficially "regressive" if the child had been saying "came" before, are actually "progressive" in the sense that they signal a newly achieved understanding of a patterned way of doing things.

Three types of progressive errors that seem to be common among children at given stages of development are discussed below. The first two involve regularizations that result in the child's apparent disregard of part-of-speech constraints. The third reflects the child's increasing awareness of networks of semantic features that relate lexical items to and contrast them from each other within a semantic domain.

Causative Verb Errors

Table 1 presents some representative examples of a type of error that is common in child speech starting at two or three years.

At first glance, one might be tempted to assume that children who make such errors are confused about part-of-speech classifications, for example, that they don't fully distinguish adjectives from verbs (e.g., "full it up") and don't realize that some verbs are intransitive and so cannot take direct objects. This explanation can be easily ruled out, however. In the case of Christy, the errors did not start to occur until after the forms in question had been accorded an entirely correct syntactic treatment for several months or longer (Bowerman, 1974b). Other children for whom the errors have been reported are relatively old (27 months up to 11 years), suggesting that they are advanced well beyond any initial problems they might have had in identifying the class membership of words.

In Bowerman (1974b) it is argued that, rather than stemming from confusion about part-of-speech, these errors reflect the child's having achieved an awareness of one important device the English language offers for expressing causal relationships among events. This is the use, without modification, of an intransitive verb or an adjective as a transitive verb with a causal sense that is paraphrasable as "cause the event or state of affairs specified by the word to come about." Compare, for example, "the door *opened*" with "John *opened* the door;" "the stick *broke*" with "John *broke* the stick," and "the baby is *dry*" with "Mommy *dried* the baby.

Although this syntactic device can be widely applied in English, there are important restrictions on its usage. For example, many adjectives require the addition of an affix, e.g., "flat/flat*en*," "rich/*en*rich," "legal/legal*ize*." For many verbs, there are one or more special causative forms that are "suppletive," (i.e., that bear no morphological relation to their intransitive counterparts), e.g., "die/kill," "fall/drop *or* knock down," "stay/keep *or* leave," "come/bring," etc. Finally, many verbs and adjectives have no one-word causative counterparts. Specifying causative acts involving these words requires the use of complex sentences with "make" or "get," e.g., "I *made/got* him *to sing*," not *"I *sang* him;" "I *made* it *disappear*," not *"I *disappeared* it." (An asterisk preceding an utterance indicates that it is not grammatical.)

Children's production of sentences like those in Table 1 can be regarded as regularizations, analogous to "comed" and "foots," in that they involve the blanket application of a rule that has wide use in adult speech but is not applicable everywhere. Just as "came" and "feet" drop out in favor of "comed" and "foots" when the child achieves a rule-governed way of marking past time and plurality, irregular causative verbs forms that the child used earlier may temporarily drop out. For example, in Christy's case, the irregular causative verbs "bring" ("make *come*"), "keep" ("make *stay*"), and "leave" ("let *stay*") had all been used correctly before the onset of the operation for turning noncausative verbs and adjectives into

Table 1.   Errors involving the causative use of noncausative verbs and adjectives

Christy

1) 2;3:	*Full* it up. (Make it full/fill it. Re: a bottle.)
2) 2;3:	I *come* it closer so it won't fall. (Make it come/bring it closer. Pulling a bowl on a counter towards her.)
3) 2;6:	Mommy, can you stay *this open?* (Make it stay/keep. Re: a door.)
4) 2;11:	How would you *flat* it? (Make it flat/flatten. Re: a carton.)
5) 2;9:	I'm just gonna *fall* this on her. (Make fall/drop.)
6) 3;3:	But I can't *eat* her! (Make her eat/feed. Re: a doll.)

Stevie

7) 2;2:	Tommy *fall* Stevie truck down. (Make fall/knock down.)

Hilary

8) 4;+:	Let's *take* mama a ride. (Make her take/give her a ride.)
9) 4;+:	He's gonna *die* you, David. (Make you die/kill.)

Marcy

10) 5;10:	I'm gonna flip it so I *go* it up to my nose. (Make it go. Re: a noodle.)

Jennifer

11) 6;11:	Do you want to see us *disappear* our heads? (Make our heads disappear.)

Aletha

12) 6;10:	You want me to *higher* it up this time? (Make it higher/raise it.)

Robert

13) 11;+:	We *took* him a bath yesterday and we *took* him one this morning. (Made him take/gave him. Re: baby brother.)

Most of these examples are selected from a fuller set reported in Bowerman (1974b); the author has added a few other examples collected more recently from other children. Age in years, months.

transitive causative verbs, but these disappeared for some time, being replaced by causative "come" and "stay."

The evidence from Christy indicates, and limited data from other children corroborate, that acquiring a productive method of turning noncausative words into causative verbs, as signaled by the production of "deviant" sentences like those in Table 1, is an achievement that depends on the child's having already mastered certain syntactic prerequisites: for example, the ability to produce explicitly causative constructions like *I can't* get *door* open and *I* made *it* full, and, more generally, the ability to relate two propositions causally or in some other way, as in *Christy fall down hurt self* and *watch me swinging* ("you watch X" and "I am swinging") (Bowerman, 1974b). Thus, far from being "primitive" mistakes, errors with causative verbs indicate the attainment of relatively sophisticated methods of processing language in search of regularities relating a number of superficially diverse types of utterances.

Nouns Used as Verbs

How should one interpret the behavior of a child who, after several years of using nouns in a syntactically appropriate way, begins to say things like "I am crackering my soup" (as she crumbles a cracker into it), "it can blade your finger if you do it real fast" (as she rotates a toy airplane's propeller), and "barrette my hair back" (wanting to have a barrette put in her hair) (all examples from the author's daughter Christy at about four years of age or beyond). Is the child simply "stretching" her use of nouns a little because she has no better way of expressing these ideas? Clearly not. In every case, prior knowledge of more "appropriate" forms had been extensively demonstrated. Relevant for these particular examples, for instance, is that the child had on innumerable similar past occasions used words like "put in," "cut," and "fasten . . . with." If she knew the more appropriate forms and had communicated effectively with them in the past, why did she suddenly begin to make errors like these?

Clark and Clark (1978) observe that one of the major sources of innovation in the use of English is the creation of novel "denominal" verbs—that is, verbs made from nouns. There are large numbers of existing denominal verbs in standard English usage that can serve as a guide for producing new ones. These existing denominal verbs can be classified into several large semantic categories on the basis of the way the object referred to by the verb is involved in the action (Clark and Clark, 1978). Most of the errors that Christy and other children reported in the literature have made in using a noun as a verb fall into one or another of these classes, as illustrated in Table 2. Thus, although the sentences are deviant from the adult point of view, they conform closely to certain regular patterns of English.

In one large class of denominal verbs, a noun referring to an *instrument* by means of which an action is carried out is converted to a verb. There are two major subclasses of instrumental denominals. In one, the denominal verb is paraphrasable as "to travel by means of [vehicle name]": e.g., "to bicycle/scooter/bus/jet/truck/helicopter," etc. Notice that there are gaps in this set: the vehicle names "car" and "airplane" cannot be used in this way (*"I carred/airplaned home"). Clark and Clark suggest that the verbs "drive" and "fly" fill in these gaps, meaning "travel by car" and "travel by airplane," respectively. It is interesting, therefore, to note that two of Christy's incorrect denominal verbs (Table 2, example 1) involve these very words, and that in the case of "car," she showed very clearly her awareness that "to car" and "to drive" were equivalent. Because these errors involved the substitution of "regularized" forms for the existing "irregular" forms "drive" and "fly," they are analogous to inflectional errors like "comed" and "foots" and to the causative use of "come," "stay," "die," etc. in place of "bring," "keep," "leave," "kill," etc., in that they represent the overgeneralization of a rule that happens not to apply in a particular instance.

A second important subclass of instrumental denominal verbs of adult English include the verbs "to saw/knife/nail/glue/buckle/pin/hammer/stone/whip/club" etc. These are paraphrasable as "to use a saw/knife/nail" (etc.) to carry out an action such as cutting, fastening, hitting, etc. For example, "to saw/knife" means

Table 2.   Nouns used as verbs

To travel by means of [vehicle name]:

---

    1) 4;0:   We're all going to *airplane* to Mexico. Not *car* to Mexico. Not drive to Mexico. *Airplane* to Mexico. (Planning an imaginary trip.)

To carry out an action (cut/fasten/etc.) with [object name]:

---

cut
    2) 3;11:   It can *blade* your finger if you do it real fast. (Rotating propeller of toy airplane.)
    3) 4;0:   I don't think I'll have it 'cause it *papers* me. (Refusing a piece of paper because she'd gotten a cut from it.)
    4) 4;7:   I was just about to *scissor* it. (About to cut something she hadn't intended to cut.)
fasten
    5) 4;3:   *Barrette* my hair back. (Wants M to fasten her hair out of her face with a barrette.)
    6) 4;3:   How was it *shoelaced*? (Struggling to lace up boot.)
    7) 4;4:   I can't *zipper* it. (Trying to zip sweatshirt. "Zip" was standard in C's speech, so this was an overregularization of an existing irregular form, as in 1.)
miscellaneous
    8) 4;8:   C: I'm gonna horn—I'm gonna tie you up with that horn. (Waving a party horn around E.)
             E: No!
             C: Then I'm gonna *horn* you up.
    9) 4;10: Now can I *sieve* it? (Wanting to use a sieve to strain juice with.)
   10) 4;9:   Can I *typewriter* with your typewriter or Daddy's? (To M.)

To put [object/substance] into/onto [a location].

---

   11) 3;11: I am *crackering* my soup. (Crumbling a cracker into her soup.)
   12) 3;11: I think I'll *bead* it. I think I'll *rubber band* it. (Putting a bead, then a rubber band, into a lump of Play-Doh.)
   13) 4;11: All I have to do to *milk* her is to put her up to my chest. (Demonstrating how she could nurse her doll.)
   14) 5;6:   You're *germing* it all up. (After E, who has a cold, licks a kitchen spoon.)

Data from Christy. C = Christy, E = Eva (younger sister), M = Mother. Age in years, months.

"to cut with a saw/knife." "To nail/glue/buckle," etc. means "to fasten with nails/ glue/a buckle," etc. "To hammer/stone," etc. means "to hit with a hammer/stone, etc. Examples 2 through 10 in Table 2 are analogous to these.

Still another large class of denominal verbs in English involves the use of a word for an object or substance with the meaning "to put [the object/substance] into/onto [a location]": e.g., "to *sugar* (your tea)," "to *powder* (your face)," "to *water* (the plants)." Christy produced a number of errors of this type, as illustrated by examples 11 through 14 in Table 2.

This list of Christy's errors involving the use of a noun as a verb is by no means exhaustive, nor are all the semantic classes of denominal verbs represented, but it serves to illustrate the point: that a child's use of nouns as verbs, following a period in which such errors did not occur, results neither from a loss of knowledge of part-of-speech classifications nor from a random attempt to encode some concept that the child has no other way to express. Quite to the contrary, it marks a decided step forward in the child's understanding of an important network of regularities underlying large numbers of verbs in English. Working out where the denominalizing operation can and cannot apply takes time, of course, as does learning which nouns and verbs do not take regular inflections. However, these are small details compared with the child's major advance of recognizing regularities linking diverse sentences that were scattered randomly across time in the linguistic input to him, and of extrapolating rules from these regularities for the production of novel but analogous sentences.

Relating and Contrasting Semantically Similar Words

Lee (1975) has done a cross-sectional study of the spontaneous use of "give," "get," "put," "take," and "have" by normal, language delayed, and retarded children. Although the data are limited, they indicate that the kinds of errors that children make with these words change over time. The younger normal children in Lee's study (the normal children ranged in age from approximately two years, one month to four years, four months) tended to have difficulties with the syntactic requirements of the words, either making errors of word order ("me this take"), preposition ("policeman take those guys *in* jail"), or omission ("put this one"). These problems were infrequent or absent in the speech of older normal children, although certain errors involving the *semantic* requirements of the words were on the rise. An increase in semantic errors was also observed among the older language delayed children, but such errors were virtually absent from the speech of the mentally retarded children, whose use of the words was correct but stereotyped. Lee (1975) concludes that "problems with the semantic components of verbs are a natural and healthy stage in semantic development. Children show by their problem sentences that they are experimenting with the different meanings of verbs."

In this section we consider some longitudinally collected data (see Bowerman, in press, for fuller data presentation and analysis) that support Lee's tentative conclusion that semantic problems with certain words are a late rather than an early phenomenon, and that they represent an advance in the child's linguistic knowledge. The words to be considered are "put," "take," "give," and "bring"—the same set that Lee looked at, except for the addition of "bring" and the deletion of "have" and "get."

These words are members of a large set of lexical items that are semantically related in that they all specify acts resulting in the *change of location* of an object. They differ from each other and from other words in the set (e.g., "get," "drop," "knock down," "pour," "pick up") with respect to many nuances of meaning. These nuances include *intentionality* (e.g., "put" implies deliberateness whereas "drop" and "get" need not), *accompaniment* to the goal of motion by the agent, subsequent *release* of the object (e.g., "take" and "bring" contrast with "put" in many contexts in that they imply bodily accompaniment but not necessarily release, whereas "put" implies the extension only of the hand or arm followed by release), *deixis* (e.g., "bring" and "take" specify the *direction* of motion relative to the speaker and listener, whereas "put" and "get," for instance, do not), degree of *effort* (e.g., the choice of "get" over "put" or "take" in many contexts is determined by whether or not effort was involved; cf. "I *got* this off" versus "I *took* this off"), and whether or not the goal of motion is *animate* (the selection between "put" and "give" depends on this distinction; see Lyons, 1967).

Table 3 lists a representative group of errors involving these verbs that occurred in the spontaneous speech of the author's two daughters. (Christy is two and one-half years older than Eva. The period during which the kinds of errors shown in Table 3 were common in her speech was well before Eva had even acquired the words in question. Thus, it is unlikely that Eva's later production of similar errors was attributable to Christy's modeling of them. The inference that the errors were a spontaneous result of Eva's own language processing rather than directly learned from Christy is supported by the fact that Eva used the words appropriately for some period of time before making errors, just as Christy had. By the time she started making particular types of errors, those errors had long since disappeared from Christy's speech.) The errors can be conceptualized as involving incorrect substitutions of one word where another word (or, occasionally, short phrase) is required or would be far more acceptable. For example, "take" was substituted for "put" or "bring," "put" for "take," "bring," "give," "make go," etc., "give" for "put," and so on.

These errors are intriguing in that they do not seem to represent an initial confusion over the semantic domain to which a word should be applied, as is true for the kinds of overextensions that Clark (1973b) analyzed. It is striking that all of the words involved had been used frequently and appropriately for variable lengths of time (ranging, in Christy's case, from about three weeks for "bring" to over two years for "give;" a few months was average) before any errors were observed, and they were always used correctly more frequently than they were used incorrectly. Moreover, the errors were not committed for lack of knowledge of a more appropriate word: they did not begin to occur until after a number of candidate "change of location" verbs were already in frequent use.

What process can account for the sudden commission of errors in word choice after weeks, months, or even years of accurate use of the words in question? A plausible explanation is that the onset of the errors coincides with the child's having come to recognize *semantic similarities* among the words involved.

The implicit awareness that adult speakers have of semantic similarities among various words is revealed in a number of ways. For example, adults who are asked to give word associations generally produce words that are from the same part of speech as the stimulus words and that are closely related to them in meaning, often differing by only one semantic feature, e.g., "hot-cold," "on-off," etc. (Woodrow and Lowell, 1916). A more subtle clue to adults' appreciation of semantic similarities among words is found in their spontaneous speech errors involving word substitutions, e.g., "I really *like* to—*hate* to get up in the morning," "The *oral—written* part of the exam," etc. (Fromkin, 1971). Adults also have an *explicit* awareness of abstract semantic features shared by groups of words, as is evidenced, for example,

Table 3.   Some substitutions of "put," "take," "bring," and "give" for one another and for related words

---

"Put" for "take," "give," "bring," "drop," "make go," "pour," "get"

---

1) C, 2;2:   I haffa *put* these off so me can do it better. (Trying to *take* rings off her fingers.)

2) C, 3;1:   I wanta *put* it off. (Taking coat off.)

3) E, 2;1:   I'll go *put* rubber band off. (Starting to *take* rubber band off deck of cards.)

4) C, 3;3:   You *put* me just bread and butter. (Wants M to *give* her bread and butter.)

5) C, 3;4:   You *put* the pink one to me. (Wants M to *give* her pink cup.)

6) E, 2;4:   Can I go *put* it to her? (Then takes juice and *gives* it to C.)

7) E, 2;3:   M: Did you leave a book over there?
             E: Yeah, and I didn't *put* it home. (About a book she didn't *bring* home from sitter's house.)

8) E, 2;1:   I *put* those way down there. (After *drops* 2 Kleenexes on the floor from her high chair.)

9) C, 3;8:   You *put* me forward a little bit. (To M, after M jerks car while driving, *making* C *go forward*.)

10) E, 2;10: *Put* it back in that container. (Wants M to *pour* juice back into glass bottle.)

11) E, 2;9:   Look what you did to my crayon. You *put* BM on it. (After M accidentally brushes by E's crayon with soiled diaper: *got* BM on it.)

"Bring" for "take," "put," "give"

---

12) C, 2;1:   Let *bring* this out. (Wants to *take* cooked bacon out of pan on stove.)

13) C, 3;4:   She *brought* it over there. (Watching dog *take* food into adjacent room.)

14) E, 2;9:   I'm gonna *bring* this outside. (Planning to *take* a toy outside. To M, who is inside with her.)

15) E, 2;9:   I'm *bringing* it back to my pocket. (*Putting* a piece of gum back in her pocket.)

16) E, 2;2:   I will *bring* you one. (Getting cookie out of bag to *give* to M, who is standing next to her.)

"Take" for "bring," "put"

---

17) C, 2;2:   Hey, I *take* this at home. (Finding doll she'd *brought* home earlier.)

18) C, 3;7:   *Take* it to me. (Wants E to *bring* a toy to her from across the room.)

19) C, 2;1:   Daddy *take* his pants on. (Put.)

20) C, 2;3:   I haffa *take* this in. (*Putting* doll's dress into pocket of doll's apron.)

21) E, 2;0:   I *take* it up. (*Putting* bowl up onto shelf in cupboard.)

22) E, 2;3:   I'm gonna *take* your nose on. (Pretending to *put* M's nose back on.)

"Give" for "put"

---

23) C, 4;1:   Whenever Eva doesn't need her towel she *gives* it on my table and when I'm done with it I give it back to her.

24) E, 2;10: Don't *give* those next to me. (As C *puts* toys on couch next to her.)

Data from Christy (C) and Eva (E). M = Mother. Age in years, months.

in their ability to sort words into semantic categories (Fillenbaum and Rapoport, 1971; Miller, 1972).

A number of researchers have postulated that an important process in language development is the learner's gradually increasing awareness of ways in which words are similar to each other and ways in which they contrast with each other—in other words, how they are organized into *systems* by virtue of networks of semantic features that transcend particular words (e.g., Anglin, 1970; Miller, 1972).

Studies that have explicitly looked for children's sense of semantic relationships among words, by analyses of word associations or of word sorting and the like, have generally placed the time at which such knowledge is acquired or has begun to be acquired relatively late—beyond the age of six or seven (e.g., Anglin, 1970; Francis, 1972; McNeill, 1966).

The present data on word substitutions provide evidence for considerable growth before that time in the child's implicit awareness of semantic relationships among words (Bowerman, in press). Like adult substitution errors, the present errors do not involve random selections from the child's vocabulary; rather, they involve words that according to both lay adult intuition and formal linguistic analyses are closely related in meaning. The fact that the children's initial uses of these words were semantically appropriate, with the errors beginning to occur only later, suggests that the words had begun to move into semantic proximity after a period in which they had led relatively independent lives.

Adult speakers who make substitution errors often recognize them and correct them on the spot. In contrast, Christy and Eva almost never indicated any awareness that their word choice was erroneous. Explicit self corrections were virtually never made for the put-bring-take-give, etc. set, although they did occur for speech errors of other sorts, including word substitutions. Occasionally a sentence was repeated with the correct word substituted for the original error, but apparently only as a sort of casual paraphrase, never with urgency.

This lack of awareness of having made an error suggests that despite their generally correct treatment of the words in question, and unlike adults who make substitution errors, the children had not yet fully worked out the meanings of the words. How can one reconcile the fact of generally correct usage with evidence that the child does not yet quite grasp how a particular word differs from other related words within a given semantic domain? As a starting hypothesis, I would speculate that children's early use of particular words may have—for lack of a better term—a rather "habitual" aspect to it: that is, the child can select "put," for example, appropriately in a given setting without necessarily being aware that "put," unlike, e.g., "drop," implies a certain deliberateness, that unlike "bring" and "take" it is deictically neutral, implies release of the object transported, does not imply bodily accompaniment, and so on (see Miller, 1972, for a similar suggestion regarding the possibility of referentially appropriate use in the absence of a full understanding of a word's relationship to other words).

Correct but "habitual" application of "put," etc. is perhaps made possible by the fact that (judging from the Christy and Eva data) children initially use the words in relatively specific, and different, contexts. In other words, the semantic ranges across which the words are initially applied are not nearly so broad nor so closely related as in adult speech (where the choice between two words often hangs on a single, relatively subtle distinction such as whether or not effort is involved). For example, in Christy's and Eva's speech, "put" was initially used in the contexts of donning clothing, placing small objects onto surfaces or into containers ("put on," "put in"), returning things to an original location ("put back"), or storing things out of sight ("put away"). "Take," in contrast, was used for the removal of clothing from the body or small objects from surfaces or containers ("take off," "take out"), for requests to be taken outside ("take outside"), and for requesting that something be removed or protesting its removal ("take away").

Perhaps it is only as children begin to apply words like "put," "take," "bring," etc. over an increasingly wide and varied semantic terrain that the words begin to bump up against each others' territories and to compete for selection in particular speech contexts. When this competition begins to occur, errors are made. At this point the child must start to sort out the details of which words imply deliberateness and which do not, which imply accompaniment and which do not, etc., so that when a choice must be made in future situations, it can be made in a semantically principled way.

CONCLUSIONS

Almost every study of language acquisition contributes, directly or indirectly, to our knowledge of the issues that have been emphasized in this paper: how children are similar to and different from each other, and how linguistic progress is reflected in changes in a child's performance over time. Therefore, the studies discussed above necessarily represent only a sampling of those that are relevant. They were selected because they introduce important viewpoints on a variety of currently provocative topics that are particularly pertinent to the themes of uniformity, variation, and change.

On a number of general issues there seems to be a fair amount of consensus. For example, many investigators agree that the level of cognitive development a child has attained has important implications for what he can do linguistically; that the way in which children produce and comprehend words and sentences at successive stages of development is regular and systematic enough to be describable, often, in terms of "strategies" for acquiring language; that nonlinguistic factors, including both the child's knowledge of "usual" relationships and events in his environment and the characteristics of particular settings, have an important influence on how the child interprets various language forms; that there are important differences in children's approaches to language learning; and that despite these differences, the range of possible variation is limited by certain more general constraints on how language can be acquired.

Consensus tends to dwindle when we come to more specific questions about how children acquire given aspects of language, how particular cognitive achievements are related to language ability, whether interchild differences can be described in terms of discrete "strategies" or consist instead of variations along continua, and so on. The range of variation represented in different investigators' findings and hypotheses is at least as broad as the variability among the children whose development they have studied. This diversity of opinion is a sign of the inherent complexity of the processes under investigation. Future research should help to resolve some of these conflicts—as well, of course, as firing a number of new controversies on matters that we have not yet even begun to consider.

REFERENCES

Anglin, J. 1970. The Growth of Word Meaning. MIT Press, Cambridge.

Anglin, J. Word, Object, and Conceptual Development. W. W. Norton, New York.

Antinucci, F., and Parisi, D. 1973. Early language acquisition: A model and some data. In C. A. Ferguson and D. I. Slobin (eds.), Studies of Child Language Development. Holt, Rinehart and Winston, New York.

Bartlett, E. J. 1976. Sizing things up: The acquisition of the meaning of dimensional adjectives. J. Child Lang. 3: 205–219.

Bates, E. 1976a. Language and Context: The Acquisition of Pragmatics. Academic Press, New York.

Bates, E. 1976b. Pragmatics and sociolinguistics in child language. In D. Morehead and A. Morehead (eds.), Directions in Normal and Deficient Child Language. University Park Press, Baltimore.

Bates, E., Benigni, L., Bretherton, I., Camaioni, L., and Volterra, V. 1977. From gesture to the first word: On cognitive and social prerequisites. In M. Lewis and L. Rosenblum (eds.), Interaction, Conversation, and the Development of Language. John Wiley, New York.

Bates, E., Camaioni, L., and Volterra, V. 1975. The acquisition of performatives prior to speech. Merrill-Palmer Quart. 21(3): 205–226.

Beilin, H. 1975. Studies in the Cognitive Basis of Language Development. Academic Press, New York.

Bever, T. 1970. The cognitive basis for linguistic structures. In J. R. Hayes (ed.), Cognition and the Development of Language. John Wiley, New York.

Bloom, L. 1970. Language Development: Form and Function in Emerging Grammars. MIT Press, Cambridge.

Bloom, L. 1973. One Word at a Time: The Use of Single-Word Utterances Before Syntax. Mouton, The Hague.

Bloom, L. 1974. Talking, understanding, and thinking. In R. L. Schiefelbusch and L. L. Lloyd (eds.), Language Perspectives: Acquisition, Retardation, and Intervention. University Park Press, Baltimore.

Bloom, L. 1976. The integration of form, content and use in language development. Paper prepared for conference on the Implications of Basic Speech and Language Research for the School and Clinic, May, Washington, D.C.

Bloom, L., Lightbown, P., and Hood, L. 1975a. Structure and variation in child language. Monogr. Soc. Res. Child Dev. Vol. 40(2), Serial no. 160.

Bloom, L., Miller, P., and Hood, L. 1975b. Variation and reduction as aspects of competence in language development. In A. Pick (ed.), The 1974 Minnesota Symposium on Child Psychology. University of Minnesota Press, Minneapolis.

Bowerman, M. 1973a. Early Syntactic Development: A Cross-Linguistic Study with Special Reference to Finnish. Cambridge University Press, London.

Bowerman, M. 1973b. Structural relationships in children's utterances: Syntactic or semantic? In T. E. Moore (ed.), Cognitive Development and the Acquisition of Language. Academic Press, New York.

Bowerman, M. 1974a. Discussion summary: Development of concepts underlying language. In R. L. Schiefelbusch and L. L. Lloyd (eds.), Language Perspectives—Acquisition, Retardation, and Intervention. University Park Press, Baltimore.

Bowerman, M. 1974b. Learning the structure of causative verbs: A study in the relationship of cognitive, semantic, and syntactic development. Papers and Reports on Child Language Development, Stanford University Committee on Linguistics, 8: 142–178.

Bowerman, M. 1975a. Commentary on "Structure and variation in child language" by L. Bloom, P. Lightbown, and L. Hood. Monogr. Soc. Res. Child Dev. 40(2), Serial no. 160.

Bowerman, M. 1975b. Cross-linguistic similarities at two stages of syntactic development. In E. H. Lenneberg and E. E. Lenneberg (eds.), Foundations of Language: A Multidisciplinary Approach, Vol 1. Academic Press, New York.

Bowerman, M. 1976a. Commentary on "Children's first word combinations," by M. D. S. Braine. Monogr. Soc. Res. Child Dev. 41 (1): serial no. 164.

Bowerman, M. 1976b. Semantic factors in the acquisition of rules for word use and sentence construction. In D. Morehead and A. Morehead (eds.), Directions in normal and deficient child language. University Park Press, Baltimore.

Bowerman, M. 1978a. The acquisition of word meaning: An investigation of some current conflicts. In N. Waterson and C. Snow (eds.), Development of Communication: Social and Pragmatic Factors in Language Acquisition. John Wiley & Sons, New York.

Bowerman, M. 1978b. Semantic and syntactic development: A review of what, when, and how in language acquisition. In R. L. Schiefelbusch (ed.), Bases of Language Intervention, Vol. I. University Park Press, Baltimore.

Bowerman, M. Systematizing semantic knowledge: Changes over time in the child's organization of word meaning. Child Dev. In press.

Braine, M. D. S. 1963. The ontogeny of English phrase structure: The first phase. Language 39(1): 1–14.

Braine, M. D. S. 1971. The acquisition of language in infant and child. In C. Reed (ed.), The Learning of Language. Scribners, New York.

Braine, M. D. S. 1974. Length constraints, reduction rules, and holophrastic processes in children's word combinations. J. Verb. Learn. Verb. Behav. 13: 448–456.

Braine, M. D. S. 1976. Children's first word combinations. Monogr. Soc. Res. Child Dev. 41(1): serial no. 164.

Brown, R. 1965. Social Psychology. The Free Press, New York.

Brown, R. 1973. A First Language: The Early Stages. Harvard University Press, Cambridge.

Brown, R., and Bellugi, U. 1964. Three processes in the child's acquisition of syntax. In E. H. Lenneberg (ed.), New Directions in the Study of Language. MIT Press, Cambridge.

Burling, R. 1959. Language development of a Garo and English speaking child. Word 15: 45–68.

Carey, S. The child as word learner. In M. Halle, J. Bresnan, and G. Miller (eds.), Linguistic Theory and Psycholinguistic Reality. MIT Press, Cambridge, Mass. In press.

Carter, A. 1975a. The development of systematic vocalization prior to words: A case study. Paper presented at the Third International Child Language Symposium, September, London.

Carter, A. 1975b. The transformation of sensorimotor morphemes into words: A case study of the development of 'more' and 'mine.' J. Child Lang. 2(2): 233–250.

Chapman, R. S., and Miller, J. F. 1975. Word order in early two and three word utterances: Does production precede comprehension? J. Speech Hear. Res. 18(2): 355–371.

Clark, E. V. 1972. On the child's acquisition of antonyms in two semantic fields. J. Verb. Learn, Verb. Behav. 11: 750–758.

Clark, E. V. 1973a. Non-linguistic strategies and the acquisition of word meaning. Cognition 2: 161–182.

Clark, E. V. 1973b. What's in a word? On the child's acquisition of semantics in his first language. In T. Moore (ed.), Cognitive Development and the Acquisition of Language. Academic Press, New York.

Clark, E. V. 1976. Universal categories: On the semantics of classifiers and children's early word meanings. In A. Juilland (eds.), Linguistic Studies Offered to Joseph Greenberg on the Occasion of His Sixtieth Birthday. Anma Libri, Saratoga, California.

Clark, E. V. 1974b. Some aspects of the conceptual basis for first language acquisition. In R. L. Schiefelbusch and L. L. Lloyd (eds.), Language Perspectives—Acquisition, Retardation, and Intervention. University Park Press, Baltimore.

Clark, E. V. 1975. Knowledge, context, and strategy in the acquisition of meaning. In D.

Dato (ed.), Developmental Psycholinguistics: Theory and Applications. 26th Annual Georgetown University Round Table. Georgetown University Press, Washington, D.C.

Clark, E. V., and Clark, H. H. 1978. When nouns surface as verbs. Submitted for publication.

Clark, E. V., and Garnica, O. K. 1974. Is he coming or going? On the acquisition of deictic verbs. J. Verb. Learn. Verb. Behav. 13: 559–572.

Clark, E. V., and Sengul, C. J. Strategies in the acquisition of deixis. J. Child Lang. In press.

Corrigan, R. 1976. Relationship between object permanence and language development: How much and how strong? Paper presented at the Eighth Annual Stanford Child Language Forum, April, Stanford.

Cromer, R. 1970. "Children are nice to understand": Surface structure clues for the recovery of a deep structure. Brit. J. Psychol. 61: 397–408.

Cromer, R. 1974. The development of language and cognition: The cognition hypothesis. In B. Foss (ed.), New Perspectives in Child Development. Penguin, Baltimore.

de Laguna, G. 1927. Speech: Its Function and Development. Indiana University Press, Bloomington.

deVilliers, J., and deVilliers, P. 1973. Development of the use of word order in comprehension. J. Psycholing. Res. 2: 331–341.

Donaldson, M., and McGarrigle, J. 1974. Some clues to the nature of semantic development. J. Child Lang. 1(2): 185–194.

Donaldson, M., and Wales, R. J. 1970. On the acquisition of some relational terms. In J. R. Hayes (ed.), Cognition and the Development of Language. John Wiley and Sons, New York.

Dore, J. 1974. A pragmatic description of early language development. J. Psycholing. Res. 3(4): 343–350.

Dore, J. 1975. Holophrases, speech acts, and language universals. J. Child Lang. 2(1): 21–40.

Dore, J., Franklin, M., Miller, R., and Ramer, A. 1976. Transitional phenomena in early language acquisition. J. Child Lang. 3(1): 13–28.

Edwards, D. 1974. Sensory-motor intelligence and semantic relations in early child grammar. Cognition 2(4): 395–434.

Eilers, R. E., Oller, D. K., and Ellington, J. 1974. The acquisition of word-meaning for dimensional adjectives: The long and short of it. J. Child Lang. 1(1): 195–204.

Ervin, S. 1964. Imitation and structural change in children's language. In E. H. Lenneberg (ed.), New Directions in the Study of Language. MIT Press, Cambridge.

Fillenbaum, S., and Rapoport, A. 1971. Structures in the subjective lexicon. Academic Press, New York.

Fischer, K., and Francis, H. 1972. A formal of cognitive development: The control and construction of hierarchies of skills. Psych. Rev. In press.

Fromkin, V. 1971. The non-anomalous nature of anomalous utterances. Language 47(1): 27–52.

Greenfield, P., and Smith, J. H. 1976. The Structure of Communication in Early Language Development. Academic Press, New York.

Grieve, R., Hoogenraad, R., and Murray, D. 1977. On the young child's use of lexis and syntax in understanding locative instructions. Cognition 5: 235–250.

Huttenlocher, J. 1974. The origins of language comprehension. In R. L. Solso (ed.), Theories in Cognitive Psychology: The Loyola Symposium. Lawrence Erlbaum Associates, Potomac, Md.

Ingram, D. 1971. Transitivity in child language. Language 47: 888–909.

Ingram, D. 1974. Stages in the development of one-word utterances. Paper presented at the Sixth Annual Stanford Child Language Research Forum, April, Stanford.

Ingram, D. 1975a. If and when transformations are acquired by children. In D. Dato (ed.), Developmental Psycholinguistics: Theory and Applications. 26th Annual Georgetown University Round Table. Georgetown University Press, Washington, D.C.

Ingram, D. 1975b. Language development during the sensorimotor period. Paper presented at the Third International Child Language Symposium, September, London.

Klatzky, R. L., Clark, E. V., and Macken, M. 1973. Asymmetries in the acquisition of polar adjectives: Linguistic or conceptual? J. Exp. Child Psychol. 16: 32–46.

Labov, W., and Labov, T. 1974. The grammar of *cat* and *mama*. Paper presented at the 49th Annual Meeting of the Linguistic Society of America, New York.

Lee, L. L. 1975. A study of normal and atypical semantic development. Unpublished paper, Northwestern University, Evanston, Ill.

Lenneberg, E. 1967. The Biological Foundations of Language. John Wiley and Sons, New York.

Lyons, J. 1967. A note on possessive, existential, and locative sentences. Found. Lang. 3: 390–396.

Maratsos, M. 1973. Decrease in the understanding of the word "big" in preschool children. Child Dev. 44: 747–752.

Maratsos, M. 1974. Children who get worse at understanding the passive: A replication of Bever. J. Psycholinguist. Res. 3(1): 65–74.

Maratsos, M. 1975. Commentary on "Structure and variation in child language" by L. Bloom, P. Lightbown, and L. Hood. Monogr. Soc. Res. Child Dev. 40(2), no. 160.

MacWhinney, B. 1975. Pragmatic patterns in child syntax. Pap. Rep. Child Lang. Dev. Stanford University Department of Linguistics 10: 153–165.

McNeill, D. 1966. A study of word association. J. Verb. Learn. Verb. Behav. 5: 548–557.

McNeill, D. 1970. The Acquisition of Language: The Study of Developmental Psycholinguistics. Harper and Row, New York.

McNeill, D. 1974. Semiotic extension. Paper presented at the Loyola Symposium on Cognition, April, Chicago.

Miller, G. A. 1972. English verbs of motion: A case study in semantics and lexical memory. In A. W. Melton and E. Martin (eds.), Coding Processes in Human Memory. John Wiley and Sons, New York.

Morehead, D. M., and Morehead, A. 1974. From signal to sign: A Piagetian view of thought and language during the first two years. In R. L. Schiefelbusch and L. L. Lloyd (eds.), Language Perspectives—Acquisition, Retardation, and Intervention. University Park Press, Baltimore.

Nelson, K. 1973. Structure and strategy in learning to talk. Monogr. Soc. Res. Child Dev. 38(1–2), Serial no. 149.

Nelson, K. 1974. Concept, word, and sentence: Interrelations in acquisition and development. Psychol. Rev. 81(4): 267–285.

Nelson, K. 1975. The nominal shift in semantic-syntactic development. Cog. Psychol. 7: 461–479.

Palermo, D. S., and Molfese, D. L. 1972. Language acquisition from age five onward. Psychol. Bull. 78(6): 409–428.

Parisi, D. 1974. What is behind child utterances? J. Child Lang. 1(1): 97–105.

Piaget, J. 1952. The Origins of Intelligence in Children. Norton, New York.

Piaget, J. 1954. The Construction of Reality in the Child. Basic Books, New York.

Piaget, J. 1962. Play, Dreams, and Imitation in Childhood. W. W. Norton and Company, New York.

Ramer, A. 1976. Syntactic styles in emerging language. J. Child Lang. 3(1): 49–62.

Richards, M. M. 1976. *Come* and *go* reconsidered: Children's use of deictic verbs in contrived situations. J. Verb. Learn. Verb. Behav. 15: 655–665.

Rosch, E. H. 1973a. Natural categories. Cog. Psychol. 4: 328–350.

Rosch, E. H. 1973b. On the internal structure of perceptual and semantic categories. In T. E. Moore (ed.), Cognitive Development and the Acquisition of Language. Academic Press, New York.

Rosch, E. H., and Mervis, C. B. 1975. Family resemblances: Studies in the internal structure of categories. Cog. Psychol. 7(4): 573–605.

Rosenblatt, D. 1975. Learning how to mean: The development of representation in play and language. Paper presented at the Conference on the Biology of Play, June, Farnham, England.

Schlesinger, I. M. 1971. The production of utterances and language acquisition. In D. I. Slobin (ed.), The Ontogenesis of Grammar. Academic Press, New York.

Schlesinger, I. M. 1972. Is there a natural word order? Paper presented at the First International Language Acquisition Symposium, September, Florence, Italy.

Schlesinger, I. M. 1974. Relational concepts underlying language. In R. L. Schiefelbusch and L. L. Lloyd (eds.), Language Perspectives—Acquisition, Retardation, and Intervention. University Park Press, Baltimore.

Sinclair-de Zwart, H. 1969. Developmental psycholinguistics. In D. Elkind and J. Flavell (eds.), Studies in Cognitive Development. Oxford University Press, New York.

Sinclair-de Zwart, H. 1971. Sensorimotor action patterns as a condition for the acquisition of syntax. In R. Huxley and E. Ingram (eds.), Language Acquisition: Models and Methods. Academic Press, New York.

Sinclair-de Zwart, H. 1973a. Language acquisition and cognitive development. In T. Moore (ed.), Cognitive Development and the Acquisition of Language. Academic Press, New York.

Sinclair-de Zwart, H. 1973b. Some remarks on the Genevan point of view on learning with special reference to language learning. In L. L. Hinde and H. C. Hinde (eds.), Constraints on Learning. Academic Press, New York.

Sinclair-de Zwart, H. 1975. The role of cognitive structures in language acquisition. In E. H. Lenneberg and E. Lenneberg (eds.), Foundations of Language Development: A Multidisciplinary Approach, Vol. 1. Academic Press, New York.

Slobin, D. I. 1970. Universals of grammatical development in children. In G. B. Flores d'Arcais and W. J. M. Levelt (eds.), Advances in Psycholinguistics. North Holland Publishing Co., Amsterdam.

Slobin, D. I. 1973. Cognitive prerequisites for the development of grammar. In C. A. Ferguson and D. I. Slobin (eds.), Studies of Child Language Development. Holt, Rinehart and Winston, New York.

Smith, N. 1973. The Acquisition of Phonology: A Case Study. Cambridge University Press, London.

Snyder, L. 1975. Pragmatics in language disabled children: Their prelinguistic and early verbal performatives and presuppositions. Unpublished Ph.D. dissertation, University of Colorado.

Thomson, J. R., and Chapman, R. S. 1975. Who is 'Daddy'? Revisited. The status of two-year-olds' overextension in production and comprehension. Papers and Reports on Child Language Development, Stanford University Committee on Linguistics, 10: 59–68.

Townsend, D. J. 1976. Do children interpret 'marked' comparative adjectives as their opposites? J. Child Lang. 3: 385–396.

Uzgiris, I., and Hunt, J. McV. 1975. Assessment in Infancy: Ordinal Scales of Psychological Development. University of Illinois Press, Urbana, Il.

Volterra, V., Camaioni, L., and Bates, E. 1975. Le prime parole: Dagli schemi sensorimotori agli schemi rappresentativi. [The first words: From sensorimotor schemas to representational schemas.] Unpublished paper.

Vygotsky, L. S. 1962. Thought and Language. 1st ed., 1934. MIT Press, Cambridge.

Weiner, S. 1974. On the development of more and less. J. Exp. Child Psychol. 17:271–287.

Wells, G. 1974. Learning to code experience through language. J. Child Lang. 1: 243–269.

Wilcox, S. and Palermo, D. S. 1974. "In," "on" and "under" revisited. Cognition 3: 245–254.

Wittgenstein, L. 1953. Philosophical Investigations. MacMillan, New York.

Woodson, H., and Lowell, F. 1916. Children's association frequency tables. Psychol. Monogr. 22(97).

Observations of Mother-Infant Interactions: Implications for Development

Craig T. Ramey
Dale C. Farran
Frances A. Campbell
Neal W. Finkelstein

Mother-infant interaction is an area of developmental research that is growing rapidly in interest and carefully designed efforts. The focus in the past several years has shifted from an analysis of the implications of early parental behavior for the child's development at a later point in time to microanalyses of specific aspects of the mother-infant interaction as it is ongoing.

Although there is a great deal of research on parent-child interaction generally, this chapter is restricted to studies of parental interactions with infants, from the neonatal period to two years. Where a study of older children is occasionally included, it is included because of its obvious and direct implications for infant development. The chapter is also restricted to studies of interaction between mothers and infants. The original goal was to write a chapter on *parent*-infant interaction; the paucity of research on fathers quickly changed the focus to mothers alone. It is clear that whatever the state of our knowledge is regarding maternal behaviors, it is far superior to anything we know about fathers.

A review of observational research on mother-infant interactions suggests by its title a concentration on method at least as great as the concentration on content. Much of the information currently available on mother-infant interaction derives from observational research. The term "observation" is as broad as the term "test." Observations can be conducted in a variety of settings, with a variety of methods, and the interpretation of the results must be tempered by consideration of the methods employed.

The present chapter includes a section on observational methods that should provide a foundation for interpreting specific studies cited in the several content

This research was funded in part by the National Institute of Child Health and Human Development grants HD03110 and HD09130.

areas following it. The content sections focus on important developmental areas in the infancy period. Reflecting the currently growing interest in mother-neonate interactions, there is a section on the relationship developing between mother and child within the first few days of life. The space devoted to the area of social development focuses on attachment as the major social developmental milestone attained in infancy. There are two sections in the area of intellectual development: the effect of mother-infant interaction on cognitive development, and observations of mother-infant behavior as they pertain to language development. The effect of social-class and handicapping conditions have been combined and covered in the section "Modifying Variables in Mother-Infant Interaction." Finally, there is a summary section addressing the emerging and important area of direction of effects; in any observation of a two-member dyad, one must be concerned with the effects of each member's behavior on the other.

METHODS FOR STUDYING MOTHER-INFANT INTERACTIONS

Generic Methods

The generic ways in which data may be gathered concerning mother-infant social interactions do not differ fundamentally from the methods of studying any other social interactions. These methods include:

Verbal statements gathered from interviews with parents.   These records may be obtained either about the parent's and child's current functioning, or they may be retrospective in nature. Furthermore, these records may be obtained either in an unstructured interview situation, or in a more structured situation that leads toward the completion of some form of rating scale (see Schaefer, 1971; Schaffer and Emerson, 1964; Sears, Maccoby, and Levin, 1957).

Naturalistic observations.   An observer records the ongoing behavior of persons without attempting to alter either the location, form, or frequency of occurrence of the behaviors of interest. Naturalistic observations may employ either an obtrusive or unobtrusive observer. Unobtrusive observations are conducted "in the field." One selects a particular set of behaviors and a site where these behaviors are likely to be found naturally, and makes observations either with or without predetermined codes. For example, one might observe and record behaviors emitted by parents and their children in parks, on playgrounds, in supermarkets, or in any other location in which parents and children are likely to be found. Ideally, the people being observed would be unaware of the observer's presence, or that observations were being made (see Anderson, 1972; Jones and Leach, 1972; Rheingold and Keene, 1965).

Naturalistic observations are also conducted when there is no possibility that the observer can be an unobtrusive presence. Many observations of parent-child interaction occur in the home (see Ainsworth and Bell, 1969; Clarke-Stewart, 1973; Tulkin and Kagan, 1972). It is likely that the presence of an observer will affect parental behavior, particularly if the parent is aware of the behaviors under observation. The extent of such influence and the differential impact it may have on groups of parents is a relatively unexplored, although important, issue.

Standardized observations.   These are utilized when no constraints are placed on the behaviors that may be emitted, and no particular behaviors are requested. The physical context in which the behaviors are to be observed is typically held constant by observing the subjects in a common setting such as a laboratory room. This procedure may also be thought of as a controlled naturalistic observation (see, for example, Bee, Van Egeren, Streissguth, Nyman, and Leckie, 1969; Lewis and Goldberg, 1969; Ramey and Mills, 1975).

Constrained observations.   These are frequently selected when the investigator is limiting his attention to a few prespecified behaviors in which he has a particular theoretical interest. For example, one might be interested in the efficacy of a mother's teaching style when she has been asked to teach her child a particular task. By selecting the task, the relevant behaviors to be coded, and the location in which the observations are to be made, one has manipulated possibly significant factors that influence the form of the parent-infant interaction. By so doing, one has constrained the situation so that he is most likely to observe those behaviors in which he is most interested (see Ainsworth and Bell, 1969; Bee et al., 1969; Stern, 1974).

Each of these four general approaches has advantages and disadvantages. Verbal statements and naturalistic observations are both excellent means primarily of gathering data that can be used to *generate* hypotheses. These methods are frequently most profitably used when a new line of inquiry is being developed. Verbal statements, gathered in an interview context, are frequently less time-consuming and expensive to obtain than naturalistic observations. They are also potentially more subject to intentional or unintentional bias, because of such factors as selective memory for past events and/or the tendency to answer questions in a socially desirable manner.

Standardized observations have, by definition, the advantage of holding the context in which the behaviors are to be observed relatively constant. Thus, one typically would use this approach to examine individual differences on some set of dimensions that had been identified in less structured situations. The main disadvantage of standardized observations lies in the construction of the situation itself. The principal danger is that one will construct a context that is not typical for the dyad to be observed and, hence, generate data that has limited generality to other, and perhaps more appropriate, real-life settings. Finally, the use of constrained situations, in which some aspect of the context is manipulated or systematically altered, tends to allow explicit hypotheses to be brought under experimental test. As with standardized observations, one must constantly be concerned about the issues of external validity and generality of findings. However, with this technique, one is able to move beyond correlational statements about the relationships among variables and can begin to formulate causal inferences.

Standardized and constrained observations are often used for the purpose of determining individual differences; when the situation is held constant and/or behaviors or contextual variables are manipulated, a child's response characteristics may be correlated with other independent variables (e.g., sex, age, social class, mother-infant interactions at home). Comparing individual differences in a constant situation, however, does not remove the possibility that individual dyads are affected by factors unmeasured by the investigator: for example, in a study by Randall (1975), working class mothers' language was more affected by an observer's presence than middle class mothers' language. Although standardized situations allow the possibility of causal inference, they cannot alone explain mother-infant interaction relationships. Observations taken in a variety of situations and utilizing several of the four approaches outlined here provide a more comprehensive, and perhaps accurate, picture of the mother-child relationship.

Observational Techniques

Although the major modes for gathering observational data are well-known, the advantages and limitations of each mode warrant comment.

Live Observations   The observer records behavior as it is occurring in situ. Because there is no possibility of viewing the same sequence of behaviors again after they have occurred, it is necessary to have a well-developed coding scheme before formal observations are begun. Furthermore, because the number of different categories used generally varies inversely with estimates of inter-observer reliability, one frequently is well advised to limit his observations to a relatively small number of behaviors. However, these limitations are offset in part by the observer's ability to alter his physical perspective quickly to maintain the optimal vantage point for ongoing interactions (see Brown, Bakeman, Snyder, Fredrickson, Morgan, and Hepler, 1975; Rheingold, 1969).

Film   Film is an excellent medium in which to preserve complex interactions. Film typically is highly resistant to deterioration over time, thus allowing multiple viewings of particular interchanges. There are, however, several major limitations to the use of film. First, the view through a camera is almost always more restricted than is the view with the naked eye. Second, one must wait for the film to be developed before coding can begin. Third, in general, it is a relatively expensive process. However, film has the advantage of being shot in frames, which make excellent units of analysis, whether one examines every frame or examines samples (see Carr, Dabbs, and Carr, 1975; Condon and Sander, 1974). This capability is particularly advantageous when one is interested in the durations and sequences of behavior that are brief—e.g., less than one second in duration.

Videotape   Videotape shares many of the advantages and disadvantages of film. For instance, one is limited by the field of view of the camera. However, videotape is relatively inexpensive and is available for instantaneous coding. In fact, one can code "live" from a monitor while the behavior is ongoing, and erase the tape if the coding has proceeded satisfactorily—something that obviously cannot be done with film. Good videotape recorders are now equipped with slow-motion and stop-action features. These features, in combination with digital clocks that can be used to superimpose times in almost any units onto the film, allow careful scrutiny of even the most rapidly occurring behaviors (see Kaye, 1975; Ramey and Mills, 1975).

Categorization of Behavior

No matter how thoroughly one attempts to describe behavior in any given setting, the resulting description is an abstraction and summarization of selected aspects of that situation. Thus, the coding system that one constructs or chooses is a matter of critical importance. It is obvious, but worth restating, that there is no single system that is universally best. A coding system must be chosen to fit the particular interests of a given line of inquiry. Observations of a general nature, such as "mother-infant interaction patterns," require the development of a broad coding scheme that will capture all of the interactive behaviors observed. When the questions raised about dyadic interaction are more specific (i.e., sharing behaviors, maternal teaching style, maternal-infant feeding behavior), the categories become more detailed, but are restricted to that subset of behavior in question. The following are some of the more important features to consider in adopting a coding system.

Molar versus Molecular Codes   The terms molar and molecular in this context refer to the level of abstraction or the breadth of a particular category. An example from a child's behavior may serve to illustrate this continuum. A child may be in a room engaged in mouthing, touching, looking at, and manipulating with his hands a small object—a block, for example. To code each of these discrete behavioral acts would be to record behavior at a relatively molecular level as compared with coding that he was "playing with a toy." Although there is no inherent value in either coding approach, it is generally useful to code at the smallest behavioral unit that one might wish to select for analysis. One can usually collapse back to larger units if that has been planned into the coding scheme, whereas a more global category cannot at a later date be subdivided.

In code construction, it is helpful to be aware of the level of behavioral analysis one needs to answer the questions of the study. Molecular codes are most useful in pursuing specific questions dealing with a subset of behaviors (see Jones and Leach, 1972, for an example of molecular coding of greeting and separation behaviors between mothers and children). When one's questions are broad, molecular codes may be less appropriate for these reasons: 1) particular, discrete behaviors may be identical for different molar behaviors, and 2) the number of behaviors to be coded will quickly reach an unrealistic level for high inter-observer reliability to be maintained. Both problems may be resolved to some extent by logical combinations of molar and molecular units. In what is termed a hierarchical code arrangement, molar categories are selected that are then apportioned into finer molecular units. (These "splits" of categories may take place several times until one has developed a hierarchical "tree" with many succeeding levels of detail; see Brown et al., 1975, for an excellent example of a hierarchical code.)

Mutually Exclusive Categories Versus Overlapping Categories   Although this issue is more of a technical one than a major conceptual issue, it nevertheless merits comment. Essentially, the major question is whether the coding scheme should be elaborated to the level in which each behavior or behavioral complex would have its uniquely valid code, or whether one should record behaviors separately while noting their co-occurence in time. Consider the following example, and note the advantages and disadvantages of each approach. Suppose, for the moment, that one is interested in an infant's looking and vocal behavior in the presence of his mother. One could code these two events separately, in which case they would sometimes be occurring independently and at other times at the same instant (i.e., overlapping in time); alternatively one could construct a mutually exclusive coding scheme as follows:

Looking = L
Vocalizing = V
Looking and Vocalizing = LV

In this scheme, it would be assumed that if only L were recorded, V would not also be occurring, otherwise a separate and discrete code LV would be assigned. Such a mutually exclusive system has several advantages, the principal advantage being that it is possible to easily ascertain relative proportions of occurrence of behavioral episodes. The major disadvantage of mutually exclusive codes lies in the added memory load required of the observer when large numbers of behaviors are to be coded at the same time. When large numbers of behaviors are to be coded, one typically suffers a disproportionate cost in reliability if mutually exclusive codes are used. More will is said about reliability in a later section of this chapter.

Criteria for Selecting Behaviors to be Observed

Once an investigator has chosen a particular domain of parent-infant interaction for analysis, several considerations may be of help in selecting particular behaviors to be coded. Chief among these considerations, as Weick (1968) points out, is that any category of behavior be *explicit*. That is, precise definitions should exist for each behavior. Precise definitions of observable behaviors will greatly aid the achievement of acceptable inter-observer reliability. Explicitness includes consideration of the extent to which human observers must interpret the behaviors that occur, in order to assign them to a particular coding category. In general, the less interpretation required, the faster and more reliably human observers can code what is occurring. For example, it is easier to code an infant's "touching" or "manipulating" an object than it is to code "play," which requires more interpretation as to exactly when it begins.

A second consideration is the extent to which naïve observers can master the coding scheme from a set of definitions independent of prolonged formal training in the use of the coding system. Although this consideration is mainly of practical value in that it reduces the amount of time necessary to train observers, it also possesses the additional scientific benefit of allowing immediate determination of the utility of the system by other members of the scientific community.

Methods for Recording Observational Data

In general, there are four major methods for the collection of observational data on parent-infant interactions. The methods are as follows:

1. *Narrative records* may be obtained either by writing a description of ongoing behavior or by dictating a description for later transcription. Although the observer may be interested in particular behaviors, these observations are typically taken without predetermined codes. These records may be either of an *event sequence* nature, in which the order of the events is preserved, but not the times at which they occurred, or by a *time-sequence* method, in which time of occurrence is incorporated into the record. For the written record, one typically puts time lines on a sheet of paper (for example, each line representing a 30 second unit) and moves from line to line at the appropriate interval. For dictated records, the process is basically the same; however, it is helpful to have signals representing time intervals dubbed onto the tape before the beginning of dictation. The person doing the transcribing then has a "real-time" cue for blocking the transcriptions into uniform intervals.

2. *Coded records (nonmechanical),* commonly termed a "paper and pencil" technique, involve the use of a predetermined set of categories that the observer either tallies on a code sheet, or notes by various symbols. Again, these codes may either be event-sequenced, in which case the observer scores the behavior without reference to time of occurrence, or time-sequenced, in which case temporal order, and often the duration of the behaviors, is preserved. In time-sequenced observations, one may either make a continuous record, appropriate when the number of behavioral categories is small or, in utilizing a larger number of codes, one may employ a time-on, time-off method, where the observer watches the interaction for a specified number of seconds and then records the codes in the following time interval. Ordinarily, for purposes of analysis, the latter method assumes that behavior is continuous during the times the observer was recording but not looking. Obviously, the choice of a continuous or observe-record method is determined by the level of question being researched; one cannot investigate contingent relationships between discrete behaviors that begin within the observe interval and end during the record interval with a time-off procedure.

3. *Polygraphic records* require prespecified behavioral categories and, typically, a multichannel event recorder that can be used to note the onset and offset of each behavior. Frequencies and durations of behaviors may be obtained from this record, and these pieces of information can be subjected either to an event-sequence analysis or to a time-sequence analysis. The major disadvantage of this approach is the large amount of time required to transpose the polygraphic records into digital form for computer analysis.

4. *Computer-based acquisition devices* also require a prespecified set of behavioral codes. With this approach, one typically constructs an interface to a computer that can transform numeric or on-off signals into a computer readable format. One can either be linked directly to an online computer system or to a device that will store information about the events for later computer processing. One such system that is currently receiving a great deal of attention is the portable Datamyte system manufactured by the Electrogeneral Corporation. The major

advantage of such a system is that large amounts of data can be processed quickly and with a minimum of research assistant time. However, computer programming skills are necessary to make such a system work efficiently, because the essential "software" is not generally available.

Reliability

The issue of reliability in observational data is one that is particularly important and that has received considerable attention (see Campbell, 1961; Gellert, 1955; Kaplan, 1964; Medley and Mitzel, 1963). Gellert (1955) suggested a general rule about reliability estimates that is still valid. He stated, "the fewer the categories, the more precise their definition, and the less inference required in making classifications, the greater will be the reliability of the data" (p. 194).

Reliability Estimates   Although it is not the intent of this chapter to discuss technical issues in detail, a comment about obtaining reliability estimates for mother-child interactions is warranted. Basically there are two general methods by which one can obtain estimates of inter-observer reliability. These methods are 1) correlational and 2) percent agreement between observers. The issue of which is the more useful and/or appropriate measure is not trivial. When using correlational methods, one typically correlates total scores obtained by two independent observers across a number of observational sessions. Thus, for example, if one were interested in the number of vocalizations emitted by an infant when his mother was present or absent, one might have two observers coding the frequency of vocalization for a number of infants under both of these conditions. The resulting total vocalization frequencies per observation period would then be correlated for the two observers. An alternative to the correlational approach is to calculate the percentage of agreements between the two observers for each incidence of a behavior's occurrence. In general, this is a more rigorous method of estimation. The most rigorous method is to compute the number of agreements over the number of agreements plus disagreements; agreements should be assessed for each behavior as it occurred in time rather than a check of totals per minute, or some other summary procedure. (Summary procedures utilizing percentage agreement can be as questionable as a correlational method.)

In choosing a correlational or a percentage agreement method for reliability estimates, the choice should be governed by the level of analysis that is to be performed. For example, if one chooses to remain at the level of total frequencies or total durations of behaviors, then correlational analyses may be sufficient. However, if one wants to examine the conditional probabilities between several behaviors, then percentage agreement may be mandatory. If one wants to know the probability of a mother touching her infant following an infant's vocalization, then each vocalization and each touch should be examined in determining reliability estimates.

Reliability Checks   Another issue is how often and how obtrusively reliability estimates should be made. The seriousness of this issue for observational studies has recently been emphasized by two studies that determined the unreliability of observational data when the observers did not know they were being checked (Reid, 1970; Taplin and Reid, 1973). A phenomenon that one could term "idiosyncrasy of observations" seemed to occur. In the session immediately following the one in which observers knew their reliability was being checked, regardless of the manner or extent of previous training, observers reverted to a level of agreement at least 20% lower than when they were being checked. Despite training to an 80% or greater agreement level, the only group to maintain percentage agreement at even 70% was one believing their reliability was being randomly checked (Taplin and Reid, 1973).

The implications of these findings are important, particularly for live observations. Observations coded from video tapes can incorporate these results to some extent; video tapes can be randomly assigned to two or more observers with some tapes secretly assigned to both. In this fashion, one creates the illusion of continuous, random check of observer agreement. If Taplin and Reid are correct, however, such a procedure merely assures *less loss* than is obtained with other methods. No similar methods exist for unobtrusive reliability checks on live observations. One must be extremely cautious, therefore, about the reliability of observations taken live. Observational studies often begin with a period of training for observers that continues until some predetermined, acceptable level of reliability is achieved. The observers are then essentially on their own for the period when observations are taken; it is assumed they will remain at the level of reliability obtained initially. That assumption may be unwarranted.

Analysis Strategies for Observational Data

Several recent and excellent summaries of data analysis strategies for dyadic interactions have been published (see Lewis and Lee-Painter, 1974). Although it is a truism that each study of parent-infant interaction has some unique analysis aspects, there are several major strategies that are in general use and that warrant comment.

Correlational Approaches Correlations are frequently used to examine individual differences within groups sharing some common characteristic, such as age, social class, or sex of infant. Generally speaking, these correlations are of two types: 1) contemporaneous correlations, or 2) time lagged correlations. Contemporaneous correlations provide a description of the associative strength of various parent and child behaviors when each is measured at approximately the same point in time. Time-lagged correlations (in which the behaviors of one member of a dyad are used to predict the behaviors of the other member at a later point in time) are frequently used to examine the long-term impact of some existing, and presumably, predisposing demand characteristic of one member of the dyad on the other member. For example, Bell and Ainsworth (1972) found that maternal responsivity to infant crying in the first quarter year of life was related to infant crying in the fourth quarter. Infant crying in the first quarter, on the other hand, was not related to maternal responsivity in the fourth. This finding allowed Bell and Ainsworth to conclude that of the two predisposing factors, infant crying and maternal behavior, maternal behavior was the more potent variable associated with later crying behavior. This research is in contrast to previous time-lagged correlational research. Many studies demonstrate that the behavior of one member of the dyad is related to the behavior of the other at a later point in time (see Clarke-Stewart, 1973; Moss, Robson, and Pedersen, 1969). However, only by including the behaviors of both members of the dyad at each point in time can one begin to address the question of "direction of effects" in social interaction. More is said about the direction of effects issue later in this chapter.

Simple and Conditional Probabilities   Within the past few years these styles of analyses have gained in popularity. To derive simple probability of occurrence estimates, one simply divides an observation session into equal intervals (e.g., 10 sec intervals), and notes whether a given behavior occurred within each interval. From this procedure, one can derive the likelihood of a behavior occurring that can be expressed as a percentage of total observational intervals.

More recently, many investigators have attempted to examine the influence of one behavior upon other behaviors by computing conditional probability estimates. For example, Lewis and Wilson (1972) examined the differences in maternal responses to infant vocalizations as a function of the social class of the mother. For their analyses, they computed the probability of various maternal behaviors (e.g., touching and talking to the infant), *given* that the infant had vocalized. Such analyses typically take the form

$$p(x/y)$$

which is read as the probability of behavior x given the occurrence of behavior y. Although such analyses can be informative, particularly with respect to typological differences in dyadic behaviors as a function of some predisposing characteristic such as context or social class, there is currently much debate about the most appropriate statistical tests to be applied to determine significance of differences.

Other Analysis Strategies   The most widely used group analysis techniques are parametric and nonparametric approaches, such as analysis of variance and Chi Square. These techniques are typically used to assess differences in performance *between* groups that vary on some dimension such as socioeconomic status or age. They are excellent and powerful techniques for these purposes; however, they typically use summative scores from a session or number of subjects possessing some attribute as the unit of analysis. Therefore, these between-groups statistics are of limited use when one wants either to conduct fine-grained sequential analyses of the performance of dyads within a particular session, or to analyze data obtained from a relatively homogeneous group. These two limitations explain, in part, the increasing use of such analyses as simple and conditional probabilities.

A General Model for Parent-Infant Interaction Analyses

Figure 1 is an attempt to summarize in schematic or model form a general approach to the analysis of mother-infant dyadic interactions. No claim for originality is being made for the thoughts that this model represents; rather, it is to be viewed simply as an attempt to summarize concisely the major styles of observational inquiry concerning parent-infant interactions to date.

Figure 1 contains a schematic diagram of a set of dyadic interactions distributed over time. Several major features of this model warrant elaboration. The three large circles in the diagram represent points in time that are not necessarily contiguous. Within each time circle are two rectangles. These rectangles represent

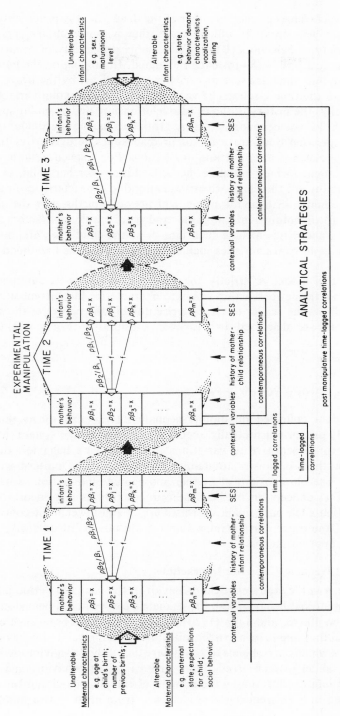

Figure 1. A general model for parent-infant interaction analyses.

the behavioral hierarchies of each member of the dyad (i.e., the probability of occurrence of specific behaviors). It will be noted that within each rectangle (vector), there are a variety of behaviors (B) that have some probability of occurring within that time frame (e.g., pB = X) for each individual. Impinging on the hierarchies of behaviors at any one time are several variables, symbolized by the heavy arrows on the perimeters of the time circles. The variables are: 1) contextual variables such as physical setting, 2) the history of the dyadic relationship, and 3) molar sociocultural influences such as socioeconomic status. Influencing the particular behavioral hierarchies at any one time are a set of predisposing characteristics that can be divided into two classes—alterable and unalterable. For a specific mother, alterable characteristics might include her state, her expectations for her child, or particular social behaviors toward the child, whereas unalterable characteristics might include her age at the child's birth or the number of previous births. For the child in the dyad, a similar dichotomy of alterable and unalterable characteristics exists. Unalterable characteristics include such factors as the child's sex and maturational level. Alterable child characteristics include such behaviors as likelihood of smiling or vocalizing.

Although this model is, strictly speaking, a descriptive or summative model (i.e., it provides a framework within which to characterize the current situation) it is hoped that it allows the reader to characterize quickly the nature of the studies and experiments that are discussed in the later substantive review sections of this chapter.

NEONATE-CAREGIVER INTERACTIONS

Much of the data collected on mother-neonate interactions shows that the two partners quickly organize a mutually accomodating interactive system. Mother and neonate prove to be sensitive to variations in each other's behavior; the partners seem to adjust their behaviors to maintain the interactive pattern within some optimal range. The observations of mother and neonate interaction seem to fit well with Bell's (1971) conception of the dyadic interaction as a homeostatic process. Bell contends that each participant exercises upper and lower limit control to keep the behavior of the other participant within certain bounds of intensity, frequency, and situational appropriateness.

Organization of Neonate-Caregiver Interactions

A major concern in the study of social behavior in the neonatal period has been the integration of maternal behavior into the neonate's preorganized behavioral systems. Sander, Stechler, Burns, and Julia (1970) suggest that one consequence of neonate-caregiver interaction might be a synchronization of biological and behavioral cycles within the infant which corresponds to characteristics of the caregiving environment.

Sander et al. (1970) observed infant and caregiver behavior, and compared three groups of infants, differing in the number of caregivers and number of changes they experienced in the caregiving arrangements, from birth to two months of age.

In the first 10 days of life, little synchrony was observed between the neonates sleep-wake and activity cycles, on the one hand, and occurrences of caregiving interventions on the other. For a child cared for by multiple adults in a nursery situation during the first 10 days of life, increases and decreases in activity were not related to onset and termination of caregiving. Even after these children were given over to the care of a single nurse, the temporal organization of caregiver and infant behavior was delayed. On the other hand, temporal correspondence between the caregiver interventions and the neonate's activity did begin to emerge for a child cared for almost exclusively by his own mother in the same time period.

Sander et al. also reported that group care experience accelerated the development of adult-like sleep-wake patterns. In the first month of life, there was a sharper day/night difference in sleep patterns, with longer periods of sleep at night and briefer daytime naps for group-reared children. The cycle seemed to be more under control of intrinsic cues than extrinsic cues (provided by caregiver). The group-reared child's regulatory system became more autonomous and less capable of accommodating to the organization of the caregiving system.

An interesting example of adult-neonate synchrony was reported by Condon and Sander (1974). They found a relationship between the boundaries of sound segments in an adult's speech and the points in time at which neonates changed in their movement patterns. The synchrony of movement to speech was specific to adult speech, whether live or recorded, and whether American English or Chinese. Disconnected vowel sounds and tapping did not produce interactional synchrony.

Kaye (1975) observed the development of turn-taking between mother and neonate in the feeding situation. At first there was an inherent organization of the neonate's sucking behavior that was independent of the mother's interventions. During pauses in the neonate's sucking, the mother jiggled the infant under the misconception that it would start the infant sucking again. The infant's congenital behavior patterns proved less flexible, and required more accommodation on the part of the caregiving environment. However, there was some evidence of mutual shaping. During the first two weeks after birth, the mother curtailed her jiggling behavior during pauses in sucking, and the infant resumed sucking sooner after the mother stopped the jiggling. Following the phase of mutual accommodation, Kaye conjectured that the dyad entered a phase involving the achievement of mutual "contingency games," where each partner attempted to have effects on the other. At some point, the "contingency games" became a goal in their own right, aside from the goal of providing care. In the final phase, the turn-taking rules were intentionally violated by the partners to confirm the rules' existence and to introduce uncertainty. The uncertainty returned the dyad to the initial phases of achieving a mutual fit and developing contingency games at more sophisticated levels.

Factors Influencing Neonate-Caregiver Interactions

A variety of factors, such as medication during delivery of the newborn, number of pregnancies (parity), and the mother's cultural background, have been shown to alter the course of the organization of mother-neonate interaction patterns. The factors studied are related to differences in both neonate and caregiver behavior. The overall effects of these factors are differences in the kind of compromises reached between the behaviors of mother and neonate.

Sander et al. (1970) have provided some evidence that the effects of prior rearing experience interact with both current caregiving practices and the infant's inherent organization of regulatory systems to determine sleep-wake and activity patterns. As noted above, Kaye (1975) has shown that the neonate's congenital organization of behavioral systems influences interactions with the caregiver.

The Feeding Process   Osofsky and Danzger (1974) observed lower-class mothers and their two- to four-day-old infants during a feeding situation, and rated their behavior on a number of dimensions. For the mother, the quality and quantity of visual, auditory, and tactile stimulation were rated along with general sensitivity to the infant and number of head and facial movements. The infant's responsiveness to auditory stimulation, cuddling, and caregiving activities, as well as to state and eye contact with the mother were rated. In addition, the Brazelton Neonatal Assessment was administered to the infant. The data for the infants indicated marked similarity in corresponding measures of the infant's state and responsiveness to stimulation obtained from the Brazelton assessment and the feeding situation. There was also a strong relation between the mother's frequency and quality of stimulation in a particular sensory modality and the neonate's responsiveness in that modality. It would be of great interest to determine how this match develops. Perhaps mutual shaping processes are involved as in the observations of Kaye (1975) and Stern (1974).

Parity   The effects of maternal parity on mother-neonate interactions has recently been investigated (Thoman, Barnett, and Leiderman, 1971; Thoman, Turner, Leiderman, and Barnett, 1970). Thoman et al. (1970) used an automated apparatus to determine total feeding and nonfeeding time, and number of feeding intervals. Nurses reported amount of formula mothers used. Mothers of first borns (primiparous mothers) were more variable in the time spent feeding their babies. They spent more time feeding their infants than mothers of later borns (multiparous mothers). Primiparous infants consumed formula at a slower rate and consumed less formula than multiparous infants. This gives the impression that the feeding process in primiparous mothers and infants was less efficient.

Separation After Birth   Parity also influences the mother's reaction to separation from her neonate (Salk, 1970). Generally, mothers hold their infant on the left side of their body regardless of the mothers' handedness. Mothers who were separated from their babies for at least 24 hours after birth showed no side preference. In a control group of mother-neonates who had been together in the first 24 hours after birth, there was a distinct preference for the left side. However, multiparous mothers, like control mothers, showed a left side preference even if separated from their newborns after birth. Whether or not the side on which the infant is held has any further consequences for the mother-child social system needs to be determined. The children who were separated from their mothers in this study were either premature (short gestational term) or had other needs for special medical care, whereas control subjects were recruited from well baby clinics. It would be important to determine if mothers separated from their infants were responding to the exceptionality in their child or the separation.

Medication During Delivery   Medication given to the mother near the time of delivery has been observed to affect mother-neonate interactions (Brown et al., 1975; Parke, O'Leary, and West, 1972; Richards and Bernal, 1971). Richards and Bernal (1971) observed mother and infant feeding sessions on a number of occasions in the first 10 days of life. The infant was also observed independently of the mother in a nonnutritive sucking test and in a neurological examination at eight days of age. Infants whose mothers received Pethilorfan injections during labor had lower rates of nonnutritive sucking and were less responsive to removal of the sucking object from their mouth. In feedings with their mothers, these infants were fed for shorter periods and received more maternal stimulation to suck. The lethargic or depressed behavior of the infants resulting from maternal medication seemed to alter the behavior of the mother in a way consistent with Bell's model of "lower limit control." Parke et al. (1972) also found an increase in measures of *maternal behavior* with their one- to two-day-old babies as the amount of medication increased.

Detailed observations of feeding interactions between black inner-city mothers and their newborn infants were reported by Brown et al. (1975). These authors also compared maternal parity and maternal medication during delivery to measures of mother-neonate interaction. The infants were examined using certain of the Graham-Rosenblith Scale items. In this study, neonatal examination measures of the infant were not correlated with measures of infant behavior in the feeding session. This is contrary to the results obtained by Osofsky and Danzger (1974) noted above. Brown et al. (1975) found that primiparous mothers spent more time in the actual feeding process than multiparous mothers. Primiparious infants scored lower on the scale of tactile adaptivity and were motorically weaker than multiparous infants. These results are consistent with the data of Thoman and her colleagues (Thoman, et al., 1970; Thoman, et al. 1971).

Infants whose mothers received more drugs during delivery were more passive, less responsive to auditory stimulation, and more likely to have their eyes closed during the feeding observation. Mothers in turn tended to stimulate passive infants more, hold them more, and feed them more. The drug effects and parity effects, however, were not independent. Primiparous mothers received more medication than multiparous mothers. Thus, the parity effects could be a reflection of the mother's inexperience, or parity effects could be a response to the infant's depressed state. Whether or not amount of medication and maternal parity were confounded in the studies by Parke et al. (1972), Richards and Bernal (1971), Thoman et al. (1970), and Thoman et al. (1971), cannot be determined from the reports as published. Clearly, as Brown et al. (1975) suggest, drug effects need to be considered before any definite statements about effects of parity can be made.

Cultural Background   Brown et al. (1975) found that black inner-city mothers and their infants engaged in little vocal behavior. Mother and neonate behavior seemed temporally unrelated—the likelihood of maternal stimulation was not affected by what the neonate was doing, and the infant's behavior did not seem to depend on what the mother was doing. Among this sample of mothers there was one interesting sex-of-infant result. Mothers spent the most time stimulating the heavy-weight male babies and the least time stimulating lightweight male infants. This difference may be an expression of the kind of infant most valued by black inner-city others. As such, this finding may represent a cultural influence on mother-neonate social interaction.

Brazelton (1972) found a number of interesting differences comparing the patterns of mother-neonate interactions in a remote, isolated Mexican Indian tribe (Zinacanteco) and in western cultures. The Indian neonates receive little social or nonsocial stimulation in the first months of life, even though mother and infant are confined together for the first month. Caregiving is performed with the primary purpose of reducing the infant's restlessness; the babies are fed in response to an increase in their activity before it reaches the level of crying. In turn, the infants seem quieter than the typical American infant. There is also a marked lack of vocalization among the Indian infants. On standardized tests, these infants score about one month below American infants of the same age. Brazelton suggests that the interplay between the passive infants and the reinforcement from the environment for passivity produces the quiet, passive adults of this culture. In turn, the adult passivity provides the adult with behaviors well suited to success in this particular environment.

Summary

The study of neonate-mother interactions has shown that the behavior of each partner is sensitive to the characteristics of the other partner. Mothers match the kind of stimulation they provide to the neonate's responsiveness to different modalities of stimulation (Osofsky and Danzger, 1974). Mothers provide more stimulation to infants whose behaviors are depressed because of medication during delivery (Brown et al. 1975; Parke et al. 1972). Medication during delivery, maternal parity, and separation after birth all have effects on mother-neonate interaction patterns. A question raised by these studies is, what are the long-term implications for social development of factors such as those just mentioned? Assuming the importance of early social interactions for determining subsequent social behavior patterns, there is a clear need for longitudinal research beginning in the neonatal period.

ATTACHMENT AND MOTHER-INFANT INTERACTION

Definition and Background

Attachment is a construct in parent-child interaction that requires by definition the mutual involvement of two people. It has been defined as the "bond" the infant establishes with his mother (or primary caregiver) (Ainsworth, 1973). The relationship between the infant and caregiver is not solely determined by behaviors of each toward the other; over time, Ainsworth (1973) argues, attachment takes on an "intraorganismic," structural characteristic; thus, attachment is thought to be both a relationship between people and gradually an integral part of one of them—the infant. The idea that attachment becomes a structural part of the infant's personality has generated a great deal of research and theoretical controversy about the concept. One is not merely researching an interesting facet of parent-child interaction in focusing on attachment; theoretically, one is addressing an aspect of development crucial for later functioning in all social relationships. This flavor to attachment research originated perhaps in its beginnings in studies of institutionalized infants and its adherence to Freudian principles of development.

Behavioral Evidence of Attachment

Attachment is a term coined in 1958 by Bowlby; it seems pertinent to ask after 20 years of research what we actually know about the concept.

Infants do apparently begin to respond differentially to one adult in their environment, usually the mother, at around seven months of age (Ainsworth, 1963, 1964; Schaffer and Emerson, 1964). The infant will follow the mother if she leaves the room, will remain close to her, will cling to her, and will be distressed when separated from her. Differential responsivity is displayed first to the mother and then gradually to others in the environment: fathers, grandparents, siblings, familiar adults.

The most stable index of attachment is the infant's attempts to seek proximity to the attachment figure (Coates, Anderson, and Hartup, 1972b, Masters and Wellman, 1974). Proximity can be defined as the infant's tendency to remain near or in physical contact with his mother as well as evidence that he desires to be in her visual field. Carr et al. (1975) varied the accessibility of the mother's visual field for the infant by having her either facing or turned away from toys in a novel environment. Children played contentedly with toys—without looking much at the mother—when she was turned toward them. However, when the mother faced away, infants left the toys 50% of the time in order to be in her visual field. Anderson (1972) studied infants in parks with their mothers; infants quickly identified their mothers for the observer by frequent sorties and returns to her side, and by clearly remaining within her sight and sound.

This differential relationship seems to serve many purposes. When the infant is distressed, it is the mother to whom he turns for being picked up and comforted (Tracy, Lamb, and Ainsworth, 1976). In a novel situation, the infant will become distressed without his mother regardless of the presence of toys or another person; if the mother is present, on the other hand, the infant will explore the environment with interest (Rheingold, 1969).

It is apparent that the infant does not like to be separated from his mother unexpectedly. If he is precipitously left by his mother in a strange room with someone he does not know, he often cries and attempts to locate his mother (Ainsworth, Bell, and Stayton, 1971). If a stranger approaches the infant abruptly, signaling possible intrusion between the infant and his mother, the child becomes distressed (Lewis and Brooks-Gunn, 1972; Morgan, 1973). At home, if the mother leaves by an unfamiliar door, the infant displays more upset and greater attempts to find her than if she leaves the room by a familiar door (Littenberg, Tulkin, and Kagan, 1971). The key to the infant's distress seems to be the unexpected aspect of these separations or dealings with strangers. When infants are approached gradually by strangers, they do not become distressed even upon being held by the stranger in the absence of the mother (Rheingold and Eckerman, 1973). Visitations by strangers in the homes are most often greeted with curiosity, interest, and positive approach (Clarke-Stewart, 1975).

Attachment and Attachment Figures

As indicated, preferential behaviors by the infant are not directed solely to the mother. None of the behaviors described above is exclusively the province of the primary caregiver, but will be displayed toward other figures and objects in the child's environment in situations that elicit attachment behaviors, and in situations that are at least mildly stressful, most often novel.

Fleener (1973) provided infants with six and one-half hours contact over three days with someone initially strange to the child. The infant reacted with crying protest when the new acquaintance left the room and reliably chose to approach the new acquaintance rather than a stranger. Feldman and Ingham (1975) varied the departure of mother, father, and an acquaintance, leaving the infant in the company of a stranger; there were no differences in the child's reunion behaviors toward parent or acquaintance when they returned. Passman and Weisberg (1975) found that a child's familiar blanket could serve to alleviate a child's distress and promote exploration in a novel situation.

Several studies have compared attachment behaviors evidenced toward naturally alternative attachment figures in the child's environment. Behaviors displayed toward these attachment figures did not differ qualitatively. In Cohen's and Campos's (1974) comparison of mothers and fathers, children displayed similar attachment behavior toward each when a single parent was present in the room. However, when faced with a choice of mother and father, infants spent 66% of their time in proximity to mother and 33% of the time near their fathers. These figures are remarkably similar to those obtained by Farran and Ramey (1977) when comparing attachment behaviors toward mothers and teachers in infant-day-care reared children; when both figures were present in a room with a stranger, infants spent 68% of their time in proximity to mother. In both Cohen and Campos (1974) and Farran and Ramey (1977), the behaviors evidenced toward the alternate figures were not different; the *amounts* of interaction and time with the figure were.

The comparability of the infant's attachment behaviors toward various figures in his environment suggest that, in times of stress or possible threat, the infant has certain behaviors in his repertoire that are manifested toward a familar person (or object). When an infant is faced with uncertainty or unpredictability, he reacts with distress and a heightened need to be near and in contact with the familiar, whether the familiar person is one of relatively short or long acquaintance. The most predictable, best known figure in his environment is his mother (or primary caregiver). When faced with the choice of people who differ in familiarity, the infant prefers the most familiar: his mother. The concept of preference for the familiar as the key factor in infants' reactions to ambivalent situations alleviates the need to explain infants who prefer mothers with whom they have a negative relationship. (Certainly in all but the most bizarre of mother-child relationships, there are positive aspects to the interaction; the mother does ameliorate uncomfortable, distressing situations, such as hunger, wet diapers, and physical predicaments.)

Maternal Behaviors and Attachment

There are variations in the mother-child relationship; some of these variations may be related to the infant's response to ambivalent situations. It is perhaps misleading to think of these variations as being a function of or resulting in qualitative variance in attachment. When attachment is viewed as a dynamic bond whose force and quality are determined by the interaction of mother and child, one is faced with two problems: 1) attachment moves into the realm of a personality trait, an enduring predisposition relatively unmodifiable by subsequent events, and 2) the relative inaccessibility of the bond for research makes its effects unpredictable and thus not open to scientific inquiry. A more parsimonious, researchable approach is to focus on the *behaviors* of the child in stressful situations and to relate those behaviors to the observed interaction between mother and child over time and in other situations.

Such data exist. It seems that the mother's responsivity to the infant (her predictability) is related to his behavior in a novel situation. The work of Ainsworth and her colleagues on mother-infant interaction in the first year of life suggest that the more smoothly the mother interacts with the child in feeding situations, in face-to-face interactions, and is responding to his distress signals, the more he will explore a strange situation in her presence and the more actively he will seek her when distressed (Ainsworth and Bell, 1969; Bell and Ainsworth, 1972; Blehar, Lieberman, and Ainsworth, 1976; Stayton and Ainsworth, 1973).

Predictability of maternal behavior may be the crucial factor in the infant's reactions to the Ainsworth strange situation series of episodes, where the mother at set intervals leaves the infant in a room with a stranger and then returns. In such a situation the infant could well be confused, not knowing what to expect next. When an infant is in the company of a responsive, previously predictable mother, he responds with active protest when she leaves and with proximity seeking on her return (Ainsworth and Bell, 1969; Stayton and Ainsworth, 1973). However, children whose mothers have not been responsive act strangely when she departs and returns (Ainsworth et al., 1971); prior experience with the mother has not established a system of mutual predictability to their interaction. The ambivalent distressful strange situation is compounded by the infant's also having to deal with an unpredictable mother; it is likely that such infants truly do not know what to do in that situation, and descriptions of their behavior seem to reflect this fact.

A child's placement with others for part of the day, often made necessary by the mother's working, seems to be a separate factor from predictability of the mother's behaviors. Tulkin (1973) compared middle-class and working-class mother-infant pairs in a separation episode (no stranger present); more than one-third of the infants in each group were actively distressed when separated. Protest was unrelated to whether the mother worked outside the home. Rheingold (1969) found that one-third of the children cried *more* after a distressing situation and did not move toward the mother. No independent variable, including whether the mother worked, was related to this variability in the child's reaction to his mother. It is clear that infants do react variably to stressful situations. In an assessment of attachment behaviors of day care infants toward mothers and teachers Farran and Ramey (1977) found that slightly less than one-fourth of the children reacted with distress, choosing to remain near or in physical contact with their mothers throughout the session. This variability was unrelated to being separated from the mother during the day, because all infants observed were in day care. It did seem to be related to the responsivity of the mother to the child in the home; children with less responsive mothers were more distressed in this novel situation.

Blehar (1974) describes day care children's responses to the Ainsworth strange situation as being ambivalent or anxious, indicating a less secure relationship with the mother. There is actually little direct evidence pertaining to the relationship between behavior in a strange situation and interactions between mothers and children in other situations. The evidence that exists (Ainsworth et al., 1971; Farran and Ramey, 1977) suggests that the particular relationship between mother and child may be more important than any global rearing factor such as day care.

Methodological Issues

Much that we know about attachment results from the Ainsworth research on what seems to be a single sample of 26 white middle class infants followed for one year in the late 1960s. Those infants were observed monthly in four-hour visits, during which the observer recorded in narrative form the behaviors of mother and child. The narrations were coded later for a great number of behavioral interactions: feeding (Ainsworth and Bell, 1969); crying and maternal response (Bell and Ainsworth, 1972); maternal departures and infant reactions in the home (Stayton and Ainsworth, 1973); face-to-face interaction (Blehar et al., 1976); maternal responsivity at home and infant behavior in a strange situation (Ainsworth et al., 1971) and infants' approaches to mother and stranger at home (Tracy et al., 1976). Thus, there are a large number of publications resulting from an intense analysis of a small subject pool. In a procedural critique of attachment studies, Masters and Wellman (1974) stress that studies primarily founded on correlations (as most attachment research has been) with fewer than 30 subjects may yield significant results that will not apply to another independent sample.

The results of the Ainsworth research have been highly suggestive of areas to pursue further in studies of attachment. In addition to concern one might have about the size of the sample from which these results were obtained, one must also be cautious about the method of observation. Narrations of the observers were later coded and then rated by presumably the same group involved in the collection of the data. The high correlations between ratings of maternal behavior and ratings of infant behavior could possibly be affected by the theoretical position shared by the raters themselves. As Prechtl observed in a discussion following the presentation of the results of feeding behavior: "It would certainly be better to work with measurements of behavior rather than with ratings of interpretations of behavior" (Ainsworth and Bell, 1969, p. 167).

Research summaries and investigations into attachment behaviors uniformly find that proximity seeking and physical contact are the most reliable attachment behaviors (Coates, Anderson, and Hartup, 1972a, b; Cohen, 1974; Feldman and Ingham, 1975; Masters and Wellman, 1974). Measures of distress, vocalization, visual regard, and following are not reliable either within a session, across situations close in time, or over time (Coates et al., 1972b). It would seem prudent to restrict generalizations about attachment to those behaviors that have some stability in the infant's repertoire, although other behaviors evidenced might seem extremely interesting and suggestive.

Directions for Future Research

In spite of a great deal of work on attachment in the past, it is still not clear what importance attachment has in the infant's overall development. There are no longitudinal studies relating variation in attachment patterns to later development. The concern generated by the studies of institutionalized children regarding maternal deprivation and lack of a stable attachment figure in infancy (see the review of Thompson and Grusec, 1970) have not been addressed by subsequent research. We know a great deal about an infant's reactions to novel situations and to strangers, and we know the mediating effect an attachment figure plays in these situations. We know that the young child's behavior in these situations and toward the attachment figure changes when he is two and three (Feldman and Ingham, 1975; Maccoby and Feldman, 1972), yet we do not have exact information on developmental change after infancy (Maccoby and Masters, 1970). We have some leads concerning the relationship between predictable and responsible mothering and the infant's behavior (Ainsworth et al., 1971; Clarke-Stewart, 1973; Farran and Ramey, 1977; Moss et al., 1969). We do not know, however, the long-term implications of these variations either in the infant's behavior or relationship with his mother. We remain at the level of deducing the importance of these variations in attachment behavior from research done in the 1940s and 1950s on samples of children in atypical situations (see Ainsworth, 1973; Blehar, 1974).

Longitudinal investigations of attachment will be aided by research on attachment addressing the interchangeability of attachment figures for the infant. How is attachment displayed toward alternative attachment figures? Is its development and function comparable across attachment figures, does one attachment figure serve some needs and another serve other needs, or does the infant's response to an attachment figure vary depending on the degree of stress in the situation? These are crucial questions as more and more infants move into early day care or alternative care situations.

In addition, research on attachment must focus more directly on the mother's behaviors with her infant. If responsivity is the key to an adequate, healthy mother-child relationship, as preliminary research suggests, what are the behaviors associated with responsivity? How must those behaviors change over time to fit the needs of the developing infant? Grouping mothers into types may well obscure linear relationships between degrees of maternal behavior and infant response. It is difficult to manipulate maternal at-home behavior experimentally; the alternative is to record with precision the actual behaviors of mothers in their homes, and to focus on mothers who could be expected to display different behaviors toward their infants—mothers who vary by educational level, social class, and/or attitudes about child rearing.

INTELLECTUAL DEVELOPMENT AND MOTHER-INFANT INTERACTION

The Influence of Maternal Behavior on Infant Cognitive Development

It is traditional to begin reviews of the mother's (or environment's) influence on infant cognitive development by citing early studies showing disastrous effects of inadequate institutional care on subsequent intellectual functioning (Caldwell, 1967; Streissguth and Bee, 1972; Yarrow, Rubenstein, and Pedersen, 1975). The fact that social-environmental interventions have been successful in overcoming the harmful effects of the lack of stimulation is further argument for the plasticity and modifiability of infant cognitive structures (Rheingold and Bayley, 1959). The question of how a mother's behavior toward her infant affects his cognitive development is an important one.

Maternal Behavior and Early Learning One study of this question was undertaken by Lewis and Goldberg (1969), who observed mother-infant dyads and coded mother and infant behaviors every 10 seconds in a free-play situation. The observed behaviors were then correlated with a highly technical measure of infant learning-response decrement to a redundant stimulus. Correlations between response decrement in the infants and the amount the mothers held, looked at, and smiled at the infants were found. Lewis and Goldberg's method did not permit a full assessment of maternal responsiveness (contingencies between mother-infant behaviors), but the authors were able to show a relationship between infant response decrement and maternal responsivity to infant crying and vocalizing. Not enough is yet known about the relationship between response decrement in very young children and later cognitive development, but the demonstration of a relationship between maternal behaviors observed in a free play situation and infant performance in an experimental learning task at such a young age is evidence that handling characteristics may make a difference in an infant's "ability" from the earliest ages.

Maternal Behaviors and Standardized Test Results Measurements of maternal behaviors and other environmental parameters from observations in the homes and interviews of the mothers have been correlated with tested developmental levels of infants. Wachs, Uzgiris, and Hunt (1971), in a cross-sectional study of 102 infants, administered the Infant Psychological Development Scale to groups of 7-, 11-, 15-, 18-, and 22-month-old lower- and middle-class infants. They correlated performance on the Scale with measures of the infant's environment. Lower-class infants did less well than middle-class infants on all six subscales, scoring particularly poorly on the language measures at the later ages. The authors drew two conclusions: first, that too much, too intense, and too varied stimulation was deleterious to psychological development, and second, that the opportunity to hear verbal labels for objects, actions, and relationships fostered optimal development.

Longitudinal studies showing the effects of maternal behavior and other environmental parameters on subsequent cognitive development in children were carried out by Elardo, Bradley, and Caldwell (1975) using the Inventory of Home Stimulation, and by Engel and Keane (1975) using extensive blind clinical ratings based on maternal interviews. In both studies, the authors were able to demonstrate significant positive relationships between ratings in such areas as maternal involvement with the child, provision of age-appropriate toys, and awareness of the infant's psychological (as opposed to physical) needs, and concurrent test behavior. Interestingly, these relationships grew stronger over time. In both studies, ratings made during a child's first or second year successfully predicted test behavior in the fourth or sixth year even better than they predicted concurrently tested development.

Beckwith (1971) showed that maternal verbal and physical responsiveness was positively related to Cattell scores in adopted middle-class infants, and that maternal restriction of exploration was negatively correlated with developmental status. Cohen and Beckwith (1975a) found that first born preterm infants received more social attention and more responsiveness from their mothers than did later born preterm infants. This tendency was apparent by three months of age and continued to eight months. At nine months, the first born infants showed superior performance on the Gesell Developmental Schedules.

Predicting later development from maternal behavior *within* a homogeneous, low SES group was demonstrated by Farran, Campbell, and Ramey (1977). The level of predictability and the maternal variables involved depended on whether the child had been enrolled in an early intervention day care. Predictability was greater for an untreated control group.

The Interrelationship of Social and Cognitive Development   Ainsworth and Bell (1974) found that middle-class mothers who are sensitive in responding to their infants and who allow them freedom to explore have infants who are accelerated in development as measured on the Griffiths Scale. Bell has replicated these findings with a sample of black lower-class mothers and infants. These authors are particularly interested in the role that attachment to the mother plays in cognitive development. Bell has shown that infants who develop an early knowledge of "person permanence" subsequently show better development of both person and object permanence. She argues that this reflects a more advanced degree of cognitive development, and that this improvement in cognitive development is evidence that a positive mother-infant attachment affords a foundation for optimal cognitive development. With similar results, Tulkin and Covitz (1975) followed up an earlier observational study of mothers of 10-month-old girls from middle- and working-class homes and found that, particularly for middle-class mothers, the amount of interaction between mother and child at 10 months was positively correlated with the child's test success at age six. Even more pertinent, those laboratory measures that they had described as reflecting attachment to the mother in infants were associated with better tested ability at age six. Those children who did not approach their mothers as infants did less well on all the standardized tests Tulkin and Covitz administered at age six. A causal relationship is not established by any of these studies: one does not know whether infants whose cognitive development is accelerated differentiated their mothers and formed attachment bonds earlier, or whether the formation of a strong attachment bond facilitated later cognitive functioning.

The Effect of Maternal Behaviors Over Time   Yarrow, Klein, Lomonaco, and Morgan (1975), in a detailed look at infant cognitive and motivational variables, found maternal behaviors toward infants at six months of age to be correlated with a measure of environmental mastery that they labeled the "exploratory index" when infants were 19-months-old; the level of social stimulation and contingent response to positive vocalization were predictive of mastery a year later. They also demonstrated consistency in both maternal and infant behaviors over a two-year span. The latter, they believed, argued for long lasting effects of early experience upon cognitive development.

Clarke-Stewart (1973) reported a detailed study of lower-class infants and their mothers covering the age period (9–18 months) that White and Watts (1973) have argued in the most critical for cognitive development. Clarke-Stewart used home observations and laboratory measures of mother and infant behaviors, and submitted her 26 maternal and 23 infant behaviors to a complex series of analyses. She concluded that "children's overall competence was significantly related to maternal care" (p. 92). The overall amount of maternal stimulation was important, more so than the stimulation inherent in the environment. The amount of vocal stimulation directed to the child was critical for intellectual development, especially for receptive and expressive language. Clarke-Stewart factor analyzed the maternal behaviors. One factor that she labeled "Optimal Maternal Care" included verbal and social stimulation, positive emotion to the child, contingent responsiveness to child social behavior, amount of time spent playing with the child, responsiveness to distress, effectiveness with objects, and rejection. A series of cross-lagged correlations showed the first four behaviors listed above to be positively related to the child's overall intellectual development. The last three behaviors were not. Clarke-Stewart concluded that the critical maternal behaviors for optimal intellectual development might best be labeled "social attention."

In longitudinal study of 31 children especially selected because of the likelihood that they would represent extremes of developmental competence, White and Watts (1973) and their colleagues in Harvard Preschool Project have collected extensive data on social, language, and cognitive development. On the basis of these studies, White and Watts have evolved a composite picture of effective caregivers as persons who design an infant's environment for maximum safety and then permit him freedom within it, as "consultants" who provide information and challenge while remaining responsive to the infant's needs, and as providers of firm but consistent limits.

Conclusions   A relationship between maternal behaviors and infant competence or cognitive development is strongly suggested by the studies reviewed. Contradictions and controversy still exist, however. Many feel that standardized tests of infant development are inadequate tools for assessing the outcome of maternal influence upon cognitive development; the Lewis and Goldberg (1969) study represents one of the few attempts to use a different measure of infant cognitive competence. The difficulties inherent in observing, and thereby distorting and changing the very behaviors one wishes to study, have not been fully overcome, and there is a need to learn more about what these distortions may be. Little is yet known about how temperamental characteristics of infants combine with situational variables in affecting cognitive outcomes. The factor of direction of effects, reviewed more extensively later in this chapter, is pertinent to this issue; are bright infants more stimulating and responsive to maternal behavior such that they serve as eliciting stimuli for greater interactive attempts by the mother, or do maternal behaviors serve to stimulate cognitive growth? The interaction of these two variables probably begins very early, making inferences about causation extremely difficult.

Certain consistencies do seem clear, however. Maternal language seems to be a critical factor in infant cognitive development, both as to when and how it is used. Allowing the infant freedom to explore his environment seems to be important, as does sensitivity to the infant's needs and moods. The development of a positive social bond to another person seems to be related to cognitive development. Too much stimulation seems to be harmful. Clarke-Stewart (1973) has suggested possibilities for understanding the dynamic interplay between infant and mother: although the mother's stimulation of the infant seems to be a critical factor in the infant's intellectual development, the infant's stimulation of the mother may be most crucial in maintaining social contact.

Mother-Infant Interaction: Implications for Language Development

Although it is clear that language learning for the infant is a result of an interaction between parent (caregiver) and child, the focus has varied in developmental research between placing primary importance on the child as a language learner (Chomsky, 1965) and the mother as a language teacher (Snow, 1972). As research efforts move more into the area of individual differences in language development, with a concomitant effort to determine causal factors, it is likely that the emphasis will be placed on the *interaction* between the child and the mother. In language development, how do the child's developing skills mesh with the linguistic environment provided by the parent?

Early Vocal Interactions By 24 months of age, the young child understands the rudiments of the structure, content, and function of his language. Most young children understand how to use language and under what circumstances, they understand many of the broad content categories coded by language, and they understand the basic structural relations between words in a sentence (Brown, 1973; McNeill, 1970). This rapid development is evident even in the newborn infant.

The child displays a responsivity to his linguistic environment from infancy. Condon and Sander (1974) propose that well before the infant learns to speak, he has already incorporated the form and structure of the language system of his culture; infants at one to 14 days were found to synchronize their movements with the sound of organized adult speech. At 17 hours of age, infants have displayed, through a sucking response, preference for the speech of a human voice over a like nonspeech signal (Jensen, Williams, and Bzoch, 1975). Other studies have shown similar differential preferences by infants for various auditory signals (Eisenberg, Griffin, Coursin, and Hunter, 1964). By two to five months of age, infants are able to discriminate minimal phonetic contrasts in language (Moffitt, 1968, 1969). By the time the average child is three to four months of age, he is able to discriminate emotional states communicated by voice, and responds both physically and vocally to speech directed to him (Lenneberg, 1967).

Mutual dialogue between mother and child has been described by Stern, Jaffe, Beebe, and Bennett (1975) and by Strain and Vietze (1975), indicating the great responsiveness infants have to a social verbal interchange with their mothers. Bateson (1975) emphasizes the importance of the infant-mother interchange in terms of the infant's developing capacity to understand the functions of language. From the regularities that she has observed in her data, she proposes that infants learn "rudiments of initiation and termination of conversation, alternation and interruption, pacing, and the interspersing of verbal and non-verbal elements" (p. 110). The major function of language for the child at this stage, according to Bateson, is one of social interaction, which provides a basis for the understanding of other functions of language as the infant develops.

Mutual dialogue in face-to-face interactions between mothers and infants seems to peak at about three to four months (Cohen and Beckwith, 1975b). The infant demonstrates his understanding of this social function of language, and mothers obviously find the interaction rewarding, because they tend to attempt to prolong the exchanges when they occur (Stern et al., 1975; Strain and Vietze, 1975).

Influences on Maternal Language Style   From the recent study by Cohen and Beckwith (1975b), it seems that during the infant's first year the amount of language input a mother provides, as well as the amount of contingent vocalization, is more a function of a mother's verbal interactive style than a response to the infant's behavior. Although better educated mothers as a whole seem to talk to their infants more frequently than less educated mothers, marked and consistent individual differences are likely to be obtained within social classes.

Maternal beliefs about what infants can do, and thus what they need for optimal development, may be more potent during the first year in determining maternal verbal style than at later times when the child becomes more verbally interactive. The demand characteristics of infants are not generally verbal, and the infant cannot "understand" the speech directed to him; consequently, that speech—its content and function—may be primarily determined by what the mother believes is important for development.

Support for an alteration in maternal style during the second year, as a consequence of the child's development, can be found in several recent studies that have investigated the extent to which middle-class mothers adjust the overall length and complexity of their utterances in relation to their children's changing linguistic and conceptual abilities. Frazer and Roberts (1975) report a gradual increase in structural complexity of maternal speech to children ranging from one and one-half to six years, with the most marked increase occurring between 18 and 30 months. These results were consistent with those obtained by Phillips (1973), who compared samples of mothers' speech to children 8-, 18-, and 28-months-old. Although Phillips did not obtain an increase in structural complexity between 8 and 18 months, a significant increase on these measures was obtained between 18 and 28 months.

Phillips (1973) reports "qualitative" differences in mothers' speech toward 8 and 18 month olds. The 8-month-olds' activity was not yet directed by the mothers' speech, and mothers seemed to be talking to and for themselves, perhaps consistently with their individual maternal verbal styles. Given early absence of comprehension and attentional cues as feedback for maternal speech, Frazer and Roberts (1975) argue that the structure of speech directed to prelinguistic infants may actually be more complex than that directed to the child who has begun to use and understand language in a rudimentary fashion. If the child has no understanding of language, parents may be less likely to reduce the complexity of their speech. The hypothesis that a curvilinear relation exists between structural complexity of maternal speech and the child's language abilities is a strong possibility.

A recent longitudinal study by Lord (1975) suggests that middle-class mothers may indeed modify the structural complexity of their input to infants between the ages of 6 and 18 months as a response to changing demands of the child. Using a sample of three children, Lord obtained 60-minute tape recordings in the children's homes at monthly intervals, and charted the mean length of the mothers' utterances (MLU) in relation to the children's language level. Three levels were defined: stage 1 (occurrence of first word), stage 2 (occurrence of five single words in a session), and stage 3 (occurrence of first two-word utterances). It was found that the mothers' MLU decreased just before and during stage 2 (at about 12–15 months), but that it subsequently increased as the children approached stage 3. Lord suggests that structural changes reflected by MLU were accounted for by changes in the *functions* of language during this period. At the approach of stage 2, Lord noted that mothers seemed to have altered their language in accord with the children's language abilities, namely by requesting specific labels *That's a* _____) and elicitations (*What's that?*). At stage 3, mothers' imitations of the children's speech began to decrease, but expansions (adding missing words to the children's previous utterances), semantic extensions (adding to the meaning of the children's previous utterances), and corrections began to increase. It seemed that the children were providing the mothers with more feedback as to whether they understood mothers' speech, and mothers adjusted their speech accordingly.

Maternal language styles seem to be influenced by two separate sets of factors. During the infants' first year, when their verbal demands are minimal, mothers seem to display a consistent verbal style that may well be a function of their knowledge about child development and their beliefs about what is important for development. Although, because of the child's lack of verbal response, it may seem that mothers are talking for themselves, infants are active processors of the information that mothers are providing about the functions and structure of language and verbal exchange.

When the child is able to be a more active participant in the verbal interchange, the mother's speech becomes much more a function of the child's specific demands. She ceases talking for herself and begins talking with the child. This alteration in style leading to greater responsivity to the child's language in the second year has, in fact, only been demonstrated in middle-class mothers. We do not know how or even if lower-class mothers alter their language styles over time.

That mothers simplify their speech to young children, especially when the infants are 18 to 24 months old, has been reliably established (Frazer and Roberts, 1975; Lord, 1975; Seitz and Stewart, 1975; Snow, 1972). It seems that this tendency to simplify is found in all adult speech to young children, not only in mothers' speech (Sachs, Brown, and Salerno, 1972), and that it is more influenced by attentional cues provided by the child than it is by the mother's making a concerted language-teaching attempt (Lord, 1975; Newport, 1976). Whether simplification of the language input facilitates the child's learning language is still a very much unresolved question (Newport, 1976).

Facilitative Aspects of Maternal-Infant Verbal Interaction   Research into the developing linguistic ability of young children has tended to focus on small samples of children from relatively homogeneous backgrounds. Consequently, it has been difficult to determine the relationship between linguistic development and particular aspects of maternal speech; the variation in the linguistic environments provided by mothers has been too small.

Nelson (1973) does report that the frequency of mothers' questions was positively related to receptive language scores at 20 months and vocabulary scores at 30 months. In verbal interactions with infants, middle- and lower-class mothers seem to use different sentence types. Lower-class mothers use more imperatives and middle-class mothers use more questions (Snow, Arlman-Rupp, Hassing, Jobse, Joosten, and Vorster, 1974; Streissguth and Bee, 1972). Questions are of concern in relation to the development of language, because they provide a means of eliciting more frequent speech and of encouraging the child to focus on specific cognitive aspects of the environment.

In a recent article, Bloom (1976) established that children were more likely to respond with a contingent vocalization to an adult question; imitation or no response occurred more often after nonquestion adult vocalizations. In a study of residential nurseries, Tizard, Cooperman, Joseph, and Tizard (1972) found that children (aged two to five years) replied more to staff informative talk that included questions) than to supervisory talk, and that, moreover, the amount of staff informative talk was significantly related to children's language comprehension scores.

In addition to a mother's use of questions, maternal vocalizations that serve to expand or elaborate on the child's vocalizations seem to facilitate language development (Cazden, 1966; Feldman and Rogden, 1970). Snow et al. (1974) reported that middle-class mothers use significantly more expansions and exact repetitions than do lower-class mothers. Both these "language-teaching" devices require that the mother attend to those aspects of the referential context to which the child is attending. It may be that such early "tutorial" methods reflect an early dimension of parent-child conversations later manifested in teaching styles that encourage the child to isolate relevant cues.

Summary

Mother and infant are active partners in linguistic exchanges from earliest infancy. Each contributes to the interchange in a fashion consonant with his/her role and skill level. Research has tended to focus first on one half of the dyad and then on the other; with such a strategy, one may lose an essential aspect of language development: the effect each partner in a linguistic interaction has on the other. It seems that the most facilitative verbal interaction for future linguistic ability in the child is one in which the child's developing capabilities are matched by the mother's changing vocal input. Far more research is needed, however, on mother-infant dyads where the mothers are of varying linguistic styles and abilities. Language is a social tool as well as a developing skill for the child; it is a potent means of contact, once removed from physically touching the mother. Linguistic interactions may serve varying roles in different mother-infant pairs. We need more research concerning the social function language plays in the mother-child relationship, particularly because this role may change as the child matures, and because it may be evidenced differently for various mother-infant pairs.

MODIFYING VARIABLES IN MOTHER-INFANT INTERACTION

Several factors may be considered predisposing or modifying characteristics that possibly affect the mother-infant interaction in all aspects of the relationship. One such factor that has been studied in depth is the socioeconomic status of the mother. In general, the research strategy to date has been to study specific components of the mother-child relationship (i.e., the process of attachment, cognitive development) in middle-class children, and then to select a lower-class sample for comparative purposes. This approach often carries with it the assumption that middle-class mother-child behaviors represent what is normal, and that other styles of interaction are therefore deviant.

Although there is less research on the next factor than on social class, the presence of a handicapping condition in the infant is another relatively unalterable and extremely influential variable in the mother-child relationship. One would expect certain handicaps (blindness, physical disability) to alter both the developmental progress of the child and the cues he emits to signal appropriate maternal behaviors. There is a dearth of research in this area; there is even less research into the effects a handicapping condition in the parent has on the infant's behavior.

Socioeconomic Status and Mother-Infant Interaction

Socioeconomic status has proven to be a good predictor of eventual intellectual achievement (Ireton, Thwing, and Gravem, 1970; Willerman, Broman, and Fiedler, 1970); therefore, the description of maternal behaviors occurring within different social classes has provided a useful approach to understanding the mechanisms by which different cognitive styles and behaviors are transmitted to children. Research has focused on the effects of socioeconomic status on mother-infant interaction, despite the fact that most researchers have failed to show social class differences in the first year of life using standardized tests of infant development (Bayley, 1965; Golden and Birns, 1968). Two dimensions of the mother-infant relationship have been studied across social class in an attempt to understand what in the infant's maternal environment is contributing both positively and negatively to infant development. These dimensions are specific maternal behaviors and measured attitudes.

Specific Maternal Behaviors   Lewis and Wilson (1972) studied 32 mothers and their 12-week-old infants, who represented five socioeconomic levels. Mothers of lower socioeconomic status touched, smiled, looked at, and played more with their infants. Although lower- and middle-class mothers vocalized in equal amounts, Lewis and Wilson reported that middle- and lower-class mothers responded to infant vocalizing in significantly different manners. Middle-class mothers were more likely to respond to infant vocalizations with a vocalization of their own, but lower-class mothers were more likely to touch their infants in response to infant vocalizations. The two groups of mothers also differed in their response to a fret or cry by their infants. Middle-class mothers were more likely to hold or touch their infants when they cried, but lower-class mothers were more likely to vocalize to them. Middle-class mothers also looked at their infants more while the infants played. Somewhat in contrast to these findings, Tulkin and Kagan (1972) observed mothers of 10-month-old firstborn girls, and found that middle-class mothers exceeded working-class mothers on every verbal measure they used, including total amount of vocalizing and reciprocal vocalizing. They also found that total interaction was greater in the middle class group of mothers they studied. These mothers were in more face-to-face contact with their infants, entertained them more, and gave more objects to them than working-class mothers. In a recent study by Cohen and Beckwith (1975b), better educated mothers were found to vocalize more to their infants at one, three, and eight months; moreover, they were more likely to address positive comments to their infants.

Ramey and Mills (1975) compared interaction patterns of mothers of six-month-old infants in a group of lower-class mothers contrasted with a random sample of mothers drawn from the same community. The latter were predominantly middle- and upper-middle class. In a 20-minute period of free interaction in a naturalistic laboratory setting, Ramey and Mills found that lower-class mothers talked less to their infants and that their infant vocalized less. Mothers in each group engaged equally in caregiving behaviors by demonstrating toys to their infants and reading to themselves.

Messer and Lewis (1972) studied middle- and lower-class mothers and their 13-month-old infants in a similar naturalistic setting. Concentrating on infant behaviors, they found no social class differences in the amount of time lower- and middle-class infants spent looking at or touching their mothers, but they did find that middle-class infants vocalized much more to their mothers. They did not report mother behaviors in this study, but they inferred that the differences they observed in infant vocal behavior may reflect both an increased attempt to maintain contact with the mother and an enriched linguistic environment for the middle-class child.

Ramey, Mills, Campbell, and O'Brien (1975) compared maternal behavior and home environments in lower-class homes with those in homes drawn from a random sample of all classes from the same community; they reported that the lower-class mothers were observed to be less warm and verbally responsive, more punitive, and less involved with their children (i.e., did not keep them in close proximity, did not make deliberate effort to use toys to teach, did not structure their children's play). The home environments were less well organized, there were fewer appropriate toys and fewer opportunities for variety in daily life, as measured by the Home Observation for Measurement of the Environment (HOME) (Caldwell, Heider, and Kaplan, 1966).

Maternal Attitudes   In an early descriptive study of the attitudes of upper-lower and lower-lower class mothers, Pavenstedt (1965) reported that upper-lower class mothers were more involved in caring for their children and more eager to have them profit from school than were lower-lower-class mothers. Ramey and Campbell (1976) found that lower-class mothers were more external in locus of control and also were more authoritarian, less democratic, and less hostile and rejecting as measured by the Parental Attitude Research Inventory (Emmerich, 1969) than were middle-class mothers. (The hostility-rejection factor included irritability, rejection of the homemaker role, and information about marital conflict, areas about which middle-class mothers might be more candid.)

Tulkin and Cohler (1973) studied the relationship between maternal attitudes measured by a maternal attitude scale and observed behaviors in middle- and working-class mothers. They found that middle-class mothers' attitudes, especially a factor they labeled "encouragement of reciprocity," correlated with such behaviors as time spent in close proximity to infants, face to face vocalization, giving objects to the infants, and total interaction. Encouragement of reciprocity is defined as the mothers' awareness that babies can communicate and seek interaction, and that mothers can respond. There was less correspondence between stated attitudes and behavior in working-class mothers. The authors speculate that working-class mothers might feel somewhat less able to control outcomes in their children's lives, and thus, might make fewer attempts to behave in ways congruent with their attitudes, or perhaps they were less open about their attitudes. An additional factor that may interact with maternal attitudes is the accuracy of the mother's perceptions about infant development. Streissguth and Bee (1972) report that lower socioeconomic status mothers markedly underestimate developmental accomplishments, such as when babies can see and hear. A mother's behaviors may reflect her expectations about infant abilities, as well as her general attitudes.

Cautions and Criticisms of SES Research   Randall (1975) noted the differential effects of obtrusive (observer present) and unobtrusive (observer absent and mother unaware of being observed) observations upon middle- and working-class mothers. He found that working-class mothers' vocal behavior seemed to be powerfully affected when they were aware they were being observed; they talked less to their infants when they believed themselves to be observed. This finding suggests that research based on observations of mothers and their infants may produce a less reliable view of the lower-class mother than of the middle-class mother, a precaution to be noted in all the studies reported above.

Tulkin (1972) cautioned that the entire attempt to explain why children from lower-class homes often show deficits in cognition and behavior may be somewhat misguided. To assume that whatever middle-class mothers do is "right" and whatever lower-class mothers do is "wrong," he argued, is to ignore the fact of cultural relativism. There are strengths and positive aspects inherent in different segments of any culture. Furthermore, the dominant culture may prevent the availability of the full range of behavioral options to minority cultures. For example, a mother's attitude and behavior in regard to the health of her child may be more a reflection of the availability of medical care than it is of a basic predisposition on her part to undervalue health care. Tulkin suggested that social scientists should be more active in seeking social change in cooperation with those they study and attempt to help.

Social class, per se, of course, cannot be considered a causative factor. To look at the relationship between maternal behavior and child performance, it would be better to seek the specific maternal behaviors that foster successful learning stategies in children irrespective of the social milieu in which they occur. Taking this approach would avoid some of the problems Tulkin addressed in his argument, because the focus would be on the behaviors, not on persons who may represent one cultural segment.

Mother-Infant Interactions in Mothers with Handicapped Children "Handicapped" children have been divided into three groups for purposes of this paper. The first group consists of preterm infants, the second of physically disabled children including the blind and paralyzed, and the third group includes intellectually retarded children.

Preterm, low birthrate infants have often been considered to be so physically vulnerable that social stimulation by their mothers was discouraged at first. Scarr and Williams (1971) instituted a program of maternal stimulation that began in the hospital and continued for a year at home. Compared to a group of low birth weight control infants, the infants whose mothers were trained to work with them showed significant gains in developmental status.

Beckwith, Parmelee, and Cohen (1973), in a study of preterm infant boys and girls divided into high risk and non-high risk groups found that mothers held high risk preterm infants more, held high risk boys for longer periods of time, and talked to high risk boys more. The authors concluded that mothers who were more concerned about the vulnerability of their infants held them more. Low risk infants elicited more maternal gazing, but once held, the high and low risk infants were talked to equally.

Fraiberg (1974) described in some detail the responses mothers of blind infants showed toward their children. In a sample of 10 dyads, she found only two mothers who established good communication systems through tactile means without some professional guidance. Blind infants seemed less responsive, vocalized less, and were slower than sighted children in learning to localize objects by sound. By the middle of the second year, however, all blind infants showed definite signs of being attached to their mothers and were fearful of strangers whom they identified by sound and touch.

Kogan and Tyler (1973) found mothers of older physically handicapped children to be more assertive and warm toward their children than were a comparison group of mothers of normal children. Kogan and Tyler also compared the behavior of mothers of mentally retarded children and physically handicapped children. Mothers of retarded and handicapped infants behaved in similar ways toward their children; in contrast, the handicapping conditions affected *children* differently. Physically handicapped children tended to be more assertive and controlling than retarded children; they were less involved with their mothers. Kogan, Wimberger, and Bobbitt (1969), in an earlier study, reported that retarded children and their mothers "did nothing more together than did normal children and their mothers." Mothers of normal children more often adopted a submissive role with their children; retarded children were rarely assertive with their parents. In contrast to mothers of normal children, mothers and their retarded children were more likely to behave in extreme ways when they did adopt assertive behaviors toward one another. Marshall, Hegrenes, and Goldstein (1973) compared the speech patterns of retarded child-mother dyads and nonretarded child-mother dyads. Nonretarded children used more labeling and commands, and were more verbally responsive than retarded children; the retarded children used more echoic speech. Mothers, however, used the same proportions of speech with their children with the exception that mothers of retardates used more commands and requests in talking to their children. Buium, Rynders, and Turnure (1974), on the other hand, found that the language environment of 24-month-old retarded (Down's Syndrome) children differed from that of 24-month-old normal children. Mothers of Down's Syndrome children used more but shorter utterances, composed of less complex forms of speech. Mothers of both nonnormal and normal children seemed to tailor their speech to fit the developmental level of their children. The authors did not make clear, however, the appropriateness of the mothers' speech for the developmental levels of the Down's Syndrome children.

The specific effects that a handicapping condition in the child may have on the behavior of his mother may be influenced both by the handicap's effects on the child's development (his rate of language acquisition, his motoric capabilities) and its effects on maternal response to the fact of the condition, or a combination of the two. When the mother is the handicapped member of the dyad, it may be possible to determine more clearly the effects of the handicap itself on the other member's behavior. Adamson, Als, Tronick, and Brazelton (1975) conducted interesting research in this area, by following the developing interaction patterns between a sighted infant and her blind parents. They concluded that the infant developed behaviors that in some respects compensated for the mother's blindness, but that the quality and intensity of the interaction were unaffected by the condition.

In summary, it seems that mothers of handicapped children are sensitive to the needs of their children and adapt their behavior to fit those needs. The children respond to their mothers in different ways, being less responsive in some ways but more assertive in others. Fraiberg's work with mothers of blind infants underscores the need for special training for mothers of handicapped children to help them meet their children's needs.

DIRECTION OF EFFECTS

In 1968 and again in 1971, Bell reminded researchers studying social development of the lack of careful study concerning the child's effects on adult behavior. Although, as Bell noted in 1971, many investigators had commented on this imbalance, little research had been done to correct the onesided view of adult-child social interactions existing in the literature. Since 1970, more research addressed to the issue of the child's effect on adult behavior has been carried out using many of the strategies suggested by Bell (1968, 1971, 1974).

As research on children's effects on adult behavior increased in frequency, a variety of conceptualizations of the processes involved emerged. The conceptualizations in turn facilitated the development of more sophisticated research methods and strategies. Conceptualizations differ in the extent to which they simultaneously consider both child and adult influences on each other's behavior. A fundamental conceptualization views the child's behavior as a stimulus and the adult's behavior as a response or reaction. This conceptualization is just the reverse of the predominant viewpoint of the adult's behavior as the stimulus and the child's behavior as a response. A first step toward bidirectional analysis is reflected in the consideration of the adult's or child's behavior as both a response to the previous behavior and a stimulus for the next behavior of the interacting partner (Bell, 1968). Another conceptualization views adult-child behavior in the context of turn-taking (Kaye, 1975), and emphasizes mutual control over each member's behavior.

It could be argued that the value of segmenting the pattern of dyadic interaction into sequential events is the simplification of the phenomena so that it can be carefully analyzed. When studied as a whole, the interaction is too complex to determine precise relations between events. It should not be forgotten, however, that the occurrence of any particular behavior in an interaction sequence depends on a wealth of contextual features of both partners, most importantly all of the preceding behaviors, and not only the immediately preceding event. In the end, the worth of any model is judged by how well it explains the behaviors studied.

The Child as a Stimulus for Adult Responses

Research on the child as a stimulus for adult behavior has been a one-sided approach to the study of direction of effects, emphasizing child effects. Bell (1974) argues such a strategy can be justified in light of the imbalance in the previous emphasis on adult effects on child behavior. In actual interactions, of course, the behavior of one participant is often both a response to the other participant's *previous* behavior, and stimulus for the other participant's *next* behavior (Bell, 1971).

Children provide numerous stimuli to adults through their physical appearance and their behaviors that serve as releasing stimuli, unconditioned or conditioned stimuli, discriminative stimuli or, complex combinations of these functions. Bell (1974) asserts that congenital differences in the child's physical appearance and condition might be partly responsible for differences in maternal behavior. Certain characteristics such as handicaps in the child may inhibit social stimulation from adults. Hess (1970) reviewed the ethological literature, which suggested that there are a number of morphological features common to the young of many species. These features, called "babyishness," elicit heightened visual attention from adults, and also presumably serve as innate releasers for other parental behaviors.

Décarie (1969) found that children with physical deformities caused by maternal use of thalidomide suffered most in the area of language development. It was suspected that these children received diminished amounts of social stimulation from the caregivers, whether they were reared in institutional settings or in their own homes. Differences between children in their behaviors elicited different reactions from adult caregivers. Parents seemed to respond to congenital differences in children's personalities in order to maintain the children's behaviors within certain upper and lower limits; parental socializing techniques also depend on whether children are high or low in interest and responsiveness to adults (Bell, 1971).

The Child as a Reinforcing Stimulus

The stimuli children provide not only occasion various adult resonses, but they also maintain or alter adult responses. To maintain both the caregiving and the social interaction behavior of the parent, the child must provide reinforcing feedback that is contingent on the parents' behaviors. Robson and Moss (1970) reported that the development of maternal attachment depended heavily on the infant's responsiveness to the mother's behaviors. The question of the infant's contribution to the mother-child relationship may be examined by comparing normal infants to infants with handicaps that render them unable to respond contingently to the caregiver. Brown (1975) reported that an intervention program to increase the responsivieness of a critically ill newborn infant with a limited behavioral repertoire enhanced both the qualitative and quantitative characteristics of parent-child interactions. Children can increase maternal stimulation by becoming increasingly selective in directing behaviors, such as vocalizing and smiling solely to the mother (Bell, 1974).

Children's reactions to parental behavior might also have negative effects on parental behavior. If a fussy infant fails to be quieted after the mother has tried to comfort him, this might lead to a decline in maternal caregiving (Moss, 1967). Likewise, Ainsworth and Bell (1974) report that mothers of infants who cry for long periods are more reluctant to respond to the infant's crying.

Direction of Effects Over Time   Child behaviors can have immediate or delayed and short-term or long-term effects on adult behaviors. Bell (1974) proposed that previous social interactions, maturation, and other experiences alter the child's behavior in social interactions. The effects on adult behavior of changes in the child's behavior might have to be assessed at a later time. Moss (1967) noted that excessive irritability shown by male infants in the first three months of life was followed by a subsequent decrease in maternal social behaviors toward the infants. Ainsworth and Bell (1974) reported that infants whose mothers responded quickly to their cries early in the first quarter year of life subsequently cried less in the fourth quarter of the first year of life. The less crying an infant does, of course, the more opportunity for playful mother-infant interactions.

Learning to Control Stimulation

One aspect of early adult-infant social interactions is that the interactions provide a context in which the child can learn to control aspects of his environment. The child's effects on adult behavior are part of the process by which the child learns to control and have effects on both the behaviors of other people and the inanimate objects in the environment. There is a good deal of evidence to suggest that the opportunity to control environmental stimulation, regardless of the type of stimulation produced, is a rewarding experience for both young and old, human and non-human organisms (e.g., Kavanau, 1967; Singh, 1970; White, 1959).

According to Watson (1967), very young infants have only a few responses available that can be repeated within the brief span of their short-term memory, interfering with the infants' ability to associate response and outcome, and therefore with their opportunity to experience control over environmental events. The few responses the infant has to control stimulation, such as sucking, smiling, crying, and babbling, usually produce stimulation in the context of social interactions with adults. Thus, social interactions with adults become increasingly important and valuable to the child, because they provide the opportunity to have effects on adult behavior (Watson, 1972). Kaye (1975) notes that in the development of interactional patterns, mothers and infants pass through a phase of mutual "contingency games," and then a phase where contingent stimulation becomes a goal in itself.

There is also data suggesting that prior experience with response-contingent stimulation facilitates subsequent learning to control stimulation (Finkelstein and Ramey, 1977, Watson and Ramey, 1972). Thus, child effects on adult behavior and adult effects on child behavior can be viewed as part of a process in which each participant is becoming increasingly adept at influencing the other's behavior.

Homeostatic Control Model

Bell (1974) has emphasized the homeostatic nature of the processes by which the child and adult control each other's behavior. When the behavior of one partner reaches the upper or lower limit of intensity, frequency, age or situational appropriateness, the other partner reacts to redirect, reduce, or increase the out-of-proper-range behavior.

Brazelton, Koslowski, and Main (1974) posited a cyclical nature to the neonate's duration of visual attention in mother-infant interactions. Interactions gradually build up in terms of intensity of activity of each partner, then the infant gradually decreases his excitement level and turns his attention away from the mother. A homeostatic mechanism is presumed to be operating to control the intensity of visual stimulation to which the infant attends. The mother's task is to learn from the child's cyclic pattern of attention to respond appropriately to the infant's need for non-interaction in order to prolong the overall period of social interaction.

Stern (1974) observed social play of three- and four-month-old infants and their mothers, and concluded that much of the interaction involves mutual regulation of stimulation to maintain an optimal level of stimulation that is affectively positive.

With regard to mutual gaze, according to Stern, 94% of all the occurrences are initiated and terminated by the infant. During the interactions, the mother modifies her behavior in response to cues provided by the infant to maintain the infant's interest and arousal at an optimal level. However, in this interactive process, the infant is in turn influenced by the mother's behavior. Conditional probability analysis of state transitions of mutual gaze patterns indicate bidirectionality. The mother is less likely to look away if the infant is looking at her; the infant is also less likely to look away if the mother is looking at the infant.

Similar kinds of analyses have been carried out on vocal interactions of mothers and infants (Strain and Vietze, 1975). Both mothers and their three-month-old infants were more likely to start vocalizing if the other partner was already vocalizing. As with mutual gazing, there is evidence of mutual regulation of vocal behavior in mother-child interactions.

Turn-taking

The research relevant to the homeostatic model extends the direction of effects analyses to include both partners in a truly bidirectional analysis. Another model that places equal emphasis on the role of both participants in dyadic interaction is a turn-taking conceptualization (Kaye, 1975, 1976).

As noted above, Kaye's (1975) observations of mother-infant feeding behavior revealed that each partner was shaping the feeding behavior of the other partner. Kaye (1976) also provides evidence of turn-taking in a study of maternal teaching strategies. In a detour problem, six-month-old infants signaled the end of their turn by gaze aversion from the task. At that time mothers were likely to respond with an instructional strategy that was related to the infant's skill level and motivational needs. In this turn-taking conceptualization of mutual influence, each partner learned the rules for beginning and ending his turn, from the feedback provided by the other partner. The child becomes more competent at influencing maternal behavior as he both learns and teaches the mother about turn-taking.

Strategies for Studying Direction of Effects

A variety of strategies for studying direction of effects has been described in the literature (Bell, 1968, 1971, 1974; Lewis and Rosenblum, 1974). Unidirectional strategies are capable of identifying either child effects or adult effects on the appropriate partner's behavior, but not both. Examples of unidirectional strategies include assessing differences in adult behavior as a function of variations in child behavior along a defined dimension. One such dimension might be the child's intellectual development as measured by standardized tests or experimental situations. Comparisons of parental behaviors toward their handicapped children with parental behavior toward normal children would be another example of this approach. Fraiberg (1974) found that the blind infant shapes the parent's behavior in different ways from those of normal children. However, if the mothers of blind children learned to read their children's nonvisual signals, the formation of attachment bonds seemed to parallel the development of attachment in sighted children. The Fraiberg intervention strategy can have experimental analogues. It is possible to train older children as confederates and randomly assign adults to interact with these children. Osofsky (1971) trained children to behave either dependently or independently in a structured teaching situation with unrelated adults. Differences were found in adult behavior as a function of the child's behavior role. It is certainly not necessary to use unrelated adult-child pairs, nor is it necessary to use older children. Conditioning and other learning paradigms can be used to modify the child's behavior as a treatment phase. Parent behavior can be monitored concurrently as the child receives the treatment, as well as after the treatment phase. For example, studies at the Frank Porter Graham Child Development Center are examining changes in adult behavior toward children whose rate of vocal responding has been increased by conditioning procedures. Appropriate control groups, including a noncontingent stimulation group and nonstimulation group, have been included with children randomly assigned to groups.

Ramey and Mills (1975) and Ramey, O'Brien, and Finkelstein (1975) compared the behavior of lower-class mothers whose children were randomly assigned to either a day care intervention program or a control group when the children were both 6 and 20 months of age. Some differences in maternal behavior were found and were presumed to be caused by differences in the children's behavior as a function of treatment group assignment. These strategies fit well with the "child as a stimulus" conceptualization of child effects.

Parent behavior can be controlled or manipulated and the child's response can be observed (Bell, 1968). An unrelated adult might be substituted for the child's own parent to achieve greater experimental control. The changes in the child's behavior might include attempts to redirect the adult's behavior to bring behaviors of the child within bounds of preferred or expected frequency, and intensity or situational appropriateness. For example, one could slightly modify the procedures of Brazelton et al. (1974) or Stern (1974) and direct the adult to remain silent and look away from the child, or conversely, to maintain vocalizations, tactile stimulation, or eye contact with the child. The child's strategies to regulate adult behavior could then be examined. This strategy is suited to the homeostatic conceptualization of child and adult effects (see Tronick, Adamson, Wise, Als, and Brazelton, 1975, for an example of this type of manipulation).

Bidirectional strategies are more typically suited to either the homeostatic or turn-taking conceptualization of the direction of effects. These strategies build on those previously mentioned by including observations of both child and adult behavior and by analyzing the interaction sequences. Contingencies are sought between child and adult behavior, often through conditional probability analyses. Microanalyses of second by second changes in adult and child behaviors are used to infer cause and effect relations between adult and child behavior (e.g., Strain and Vietze, 1975).

Summary

Much of the research summarized in the attachment, intellectual, and modifying variables sections of this chapter was conducted without reference to the issue of direction of effects. Although results of studies cited are important, and suggestive of the power of the mother in affecting particular aspects of the infant's development, they cannot be conclusive without consideration of how and by whom interactive behaviors are controlled in the mother-child relationship. A conception of the infant as a plastic, noncontributing member of the mother-child dyad has led to the possibly erroneous and certainly overstated emphasis on the mother's behavior as the determining factor in individual differences in infant behavior and characteristics. Such a conception is beginning to change as research addresses the regulatory behaviors of even very young infants. It is clear that infants do contribute substantially to the mother-infant interaction; it is likely there are individual differences in the extent and type of contribution infants make. Bidirectional models and analyses are necessary in all aspects of mother-infant research in order to reach full understanding of the complicated nature of parent-child relations and their consequences for the child's later development.

ACKNOWLEDGMENT

We wish to thank Susan Jay for her assistance is obtaining the research articles reviewed in this article.

REFERENCES

Adamson, L., Als, H., Tronick, E., and Brazelton, T. B. 1975. Social interaction between a sighted infant and her blind parents. Paper presented at the biennial meeting of the Society for Research in Child Development, April, Denver, Colorado.

Ainsworth, M. D. 1963. The development of infant-mother interaction among the Ganda. In B. M. Foss (ed.), Determinants of Infant Behaviour. Vol. II. Methuen London.

Ainsworth, M. D. 1964. Patterns of attachment behavior shown by the infant in interaction with his mother. Merrill-Palmer Quart. 10: 51–58.

Ainsworth, M. D. 1973. The development of the infant-mother attachment. In B. Caldwell and H. Ricciuti (eds.), Review of Child Development Research. Vol. III. University of Chicago Press, Chicago.

Ainsworth, M. D., and Bell, S. M. 1969. Some contemporary patterns of mother-infant interaction in the feeding situation. In J. A. Ambrose (ed.), Stimulation in Early Infancy. Academic Press, New York.

Ainsworth, M. D., and Bell, S. M. 1974. Mother-infant interaction and the development of competence. In K. Connolly and J. Bruner (eds.), The Growth of Competence. Academic Press, New York.

Ainsworth, M. D., Bell, S. M., and Stayton, D. J. 1971. Individual differences in strange-situation behavior of 1-year-olds. In H. R. Schaffer (ed.), The Origins of Human Social Relations. Academic Press, New York.

Anderson, J. W. 1972. Attachment behaviour out of doors. In N. B. Jones (ed.), Ethological Studies of Child Behavior. Cambridge University Press, London.

Bateson, M. C. 1975. Mother-infant exchanges: The epigenesis of conversational interaction. In D. Aaronson and R. W. Rieber (eds.), Developmental Psycholinguistics and Communication Disorders. The New York Academy of Sciences, New York.

Bayley, N. 1965. Comparisons of mental and motor test scores for ages 1–15 months by sex, birth order, race, geographical location and education of parents. Child Dev. 36: 379–441.

Beckwith, L. 1971. Relationships between attributes of mothers and their infants' IQ scores. Child Dev. 42: 1083–1097.

Beckwith, L., Parmelee, A. H., and Cohen, S. 1973. Infant feeding in relation to infant and mother behaviors during non-feeding. Paper presented at the annual meeting of the American Psychological Association, September, Montreal.

Bee, H. L., Van Egeren, L. F., Streissguth, A. P., Nyman, B. A., and Leckie, M. S. 1969. Social class differences in maternal teaching strategies and speech patterns. Dev. Psychol. 1: 726–734.

Bell, R. Q. 1968. A reinterpretation of the direction of effects in studies of socialization. Psychol. Rev. 75: 81–95.

Bell, R. Q. 1971. Stimulus control of parent or caretaker behavior by offspring. Dev. Psychol. 4: 63–72.

Bell, R. Q. 1974. Contributions of human infants to caregiving and social interaction. In M. Lewis and L. A. Rosenblum (eds.), The Effect of the Infant on Its Caregiver. Wiley-Interscience, New York.

Bell, S. M., and Ainsworth, M. D. 1972. Infant crying and maternal responsiveness. Child Dev. 43: 1171–1190.

Blehar, M. C. 1974. Anxious attachment and defensive reactions associated with day care. Child Dev. 45: 683–692.

Blehar, M. C., Lieberman, A., and Ainsworth, M. D. 1976. Early face to face interaction and its relation to later infant-mother attachment. Manuscript submitted for publication.

Bloom, L. 1976. Adult-child discourse: Developmental interaction between information processing and linguistic knowledge. Paper presented at the Child Language Research Forum, Stanford University.

Bowlby, J. 1958. The nature of the child's tie to his mother. Int. J. Psychoanal. 39: 350–373.

Brazelton, T. B. 1972. Implications of infant development among the Mayan Indians of Mexico. Hum. Dev. 15: 90–111.

Brazelton, T. B., Koslowski, B., and Main, M. 1974. The origins of reciprocity: The early mother-infant interaction. In M. Lewis and L. A. Rosenblum (eds.), The Effect of the Infant on Its Caregiver. Wiley-Interscience, New York.

Brown, J. 1975. Psychological care of critically ill newborn infants. C. T. Ramey (chair), Infant-environment interactions: The effects of responsive and unresponsive environments. Symposium presented at the annual meeting of the Southeastern Psychological Association, March, Atlanta.

Brown, J. V., Bakeman, R., Snyder, P. A., Fredrickson, W. T., Morgan, S. T., and Helper, R. 1975. Interactions of black inner-city mothers with their newborn infants. Child Dev. 46: 677–686.

Brown, R. 1973. A first language: The early stages. Harvard University Press, Cambridge, Massachusetts.

Buium, N., Rynders, J., and Turnure, J. 1974. Early maternal linguistic environment of normal and Down's syndrome language-learning children. Am. J. Ment. Def. 79: 52–58.

Caldwell, B. M. 1967. What is the optimal learning environment for the young child? Am. J. Orthopsychiatry 37: 8–21.

Caldwell, B. M., Heider, J., and Kaplan, B. 1966. The inventory of home stimulation. Paper presented at the annual meeting of the American Psychological Association, September, New York.

Campbell, D. T. 1961. The mutual methodological relevance of anthropology and psychology. In F. L. K. Hsu (ed.), Psychological Anthropology. Dorsey, Homewood, Ill.

Carr, S. J., Dabbs, J. M., and Carr, T. S. 1975. Mother-infant attachment: The importance of the mother's visual field. Child Dev. 46: 331–338.

Cazden, C. B. 1966. Subcultural differences in child language: An interdisciplinary review. Merrill-Palmer Quart. 12: 185–219.

Chomsky, N. 1965. Aspects of the theory of syntax. MIT Press, Cambridge.

Clarke-Stewart, K. A. 1973. Interactions between mothers and their young children: Characteristics and consequences. Monogr. Soc. Res. Child Dev. 38: (6-7, 153).

Clarke-Stewart, A. 1975. Sociability and social sensitivity. Paper presented at the annual meeting of the Eastern Psychological Association, April, New York.

Coates, B., Anderson, E. P., and Hartup, W. W. 1972a. Interrelations in the attachment behavior of human infants. Dev. Psychol. 6: 218–230.

Coates, B., Anderson, E. P., and Hartup, W. W. 1972b. The stability of attachment behaviors in the human infant. Dev. Psychol. 6: 231–237.

Cohen, L. J. 1974. The operational definition of human attachment. Psychol. Bull. 81: 207–217.

Cohen, L. J., and Campos, J. J. 1974. Father, mother, and stranger as elicitors of attachment behaviors in infancy. Dev. Psychol. 10: 146–154.

Cohen, S. E., and Beckwith, L. 1975a. Caregiving behaviors and early cognitive development as related to ordinal position in pre-term infants. Paper presented at the biennial meeting of the Society for Research in Child Development, April, Denver.

Cohen, S. E., and Beckwith, L. 1975b. Maternal language input in infancy. Paper presented at the annual meeting of the American Psychological Association, August, Chicago.

Condon, W. S. and Sander, L. W. 1974. Neonate movement is synchronized with adult speech: Interactional participation and language acquisition. Science 183: 99–101.

Decarie, T. G. 1969. A study of the mental and emotional development of the thalidomide child. In B. M. Foss (ed.), Determinants of Infant Behaviour. Vol. IV. Methuen, London.

Eisenberg, R., Griffin, E. J., Coursin, D. B., and Hunter, M. A. 1964. Auditory behavior in the human neonate: A preliminary report. J. Speech Hear. Res. 7: 245–269.

Elardo, R., Bradley, R., and Caldwell, B. 1975. The relation of infants' home environments to mental test performance from six to thirty-six months: A longitudinal analysis. Child Dev. 46: 71–76.

Emmerich, W. 1969. The parental role: A functional cognitive approach. Monogr. Soc. Res. Child Dev. 34 (8, 132).

Engel, M., and Keane, W. M. 1975. Black mothers and their infant sons: Actecedents, correlates and predictors of cognitive development in the second and sixth year of life. Paper presented at the biennial meeting of the Society for Research in Child Development, April, Denver.

Farran, D., Campbell, F., and Ramey, C. 1972. Social interactions of mothers and young children: Implications for development. Paper presented at the biennial meeting of the Society for Research in Child Development, New Orleans, Louisiana.

Farran, D. C., and Ramey, C. T. 1977. Infant day care and attachment behavior toward mothers and teachers. Child Dev. 48: 1112–1116.

Feldman, C., and Rogden, M. 1970. The effects of various types of adult responses in the syntactic acquisition of two-to-three-year-olds. Unpublished paper, University of Chicago.

Feldman, S. S., and Ingham, M. E. 1975. Attachment behavior: A validation study in two age groups. Child Dev. 46: 319–330.

Finkelstein, N. W., and Ramey, C. T. 1975. Learning to control the environment in infancy. Child Dev. 48: 806–819.

Fleener, D. E. 1973. Experimental production of infant-maternal attachment behaviors. Summary of the Proceedings of the 81st annual convention of the American Psychological Association.

Fraiberg, S. 1974. Blind infants and their mothers: An examination of the sign system. In M. Lewis and L. A. Rosenblum (eds.), The Effect of the Infant on Its Caregiver. Wiley-Interscience, New York.

Frazer, C., and Roberts, N. 1975. Mothers' speech to children of four different ages. J. Psycholinguist. Res. 4: 9–17.

Gellert, E. 1955. Systematic observation: A method in child study. Harvard Educ. Rev. 25: 179–195.

Golden, M., and Birns, B. 1968. Social class and cognitive development in infancy. Merrill-Palmer Quart. 14: 139–149.

Hess, E. H., 1970. Ethology and developmental psychology. In P. H. Mussen (ed.), Carmichael's Manual of Child Psychology. Vol. 1. Wiley, New York.

Ireton, H., Thwing, E., and Gravem, H. 1970. Infant mental development and neurological status, family socioeconomic status, and intelligence at age four. Child Dev. 41: 937–945.

Jensen, P. J., Williams, W. N., and Bzoch, K. R. 1975. Preference of young infants for speech vs. nonspeech stimuli. Paper presented at the annual meeting of ASHA, November, Washington, D.C.

Jones, N. B., and Leach, G. M. 1972. Behaviour of children and their mothers at separation and greeting. In N. B. Jones (ed.), Ethological Studies of Child Behavior. Cambridge University Press, London.

Kaplan, A. 1964. The Conduct of Inquiry.: Methodology for behavioral science. Chandler, San Francisco.

Kaye, K. 1976. Infants' effects upon their mothers' teaching strategies. In J. Glindwell (ed.), The Social Context of Learning and Development. Gardner Press, New York.

Kavanau, J. L. 1967. Behavior of captive white-footed mice. Science 155: 1623–1639.

Kogan, K. L., and Tyler, N. 1973. Mother-child interaction in young physically handicapped children. Am. J. Ment. Def. 77: 492–497.

Kogan, K. L., Wimberger, H. C., and Bobbitt, R. A. 1969. Analysis of mother-child interaction in young mental retardates. Child Dev. 40: 799–812.

Lenneberg, E. H. 1967. Biological Foundations of Language. John Wiley and Sons, New York.

Lewis, M., and Brooks-Gunn, J. 1972. Self, other, and fear: The reaction of infants to people (ETS RB 12–23). Educational Testing Service, Princeton, N.J.

Lewis, M., and Goldberg, S. 1969. Perceptual-cognitive development in infancy: A generalized expectancy model as a function of the mother-infant interaction. Merrill-Palmer Quart. 15: 81–100.

Lewis, M., and Lee-Painter, S. 1974. An interactional approach to the mother-infant dyad. In M. Lewis and L. A. Rosenblum (eds.), The Effect of the Infant on Its Caregiver. Wiley-Interscience, New York.

Lewis, M., and Rosenblum, L. A. 1974. The effect of the infant on its caregiver. Wiley-Interscience, New York.

Lewis, M., and Wilson, C. D. 1972. Infant development in lower-class American families. Hum. Dev. 15: 112–127.

Littenberg, R., Tulkin, S. R., and Kagan, J. 1971. Cognitive components of separation anxiety. Dev. Psychol. 4: 387–388.

Lord, C. 1975. Is talking to baby more than baby talk? A longitudinal study of the modification of linguistic input to young children. Paper presented at the biennial meeting of the Society for Research in Child Development, April, Denver.

McNeill, D. 1970. The Acquisition of Language. Harper and Row, New York.

Maccoby, E. E., and Feldman, S. S. 1972. Mother-attachment and stranger-reactions in the third year of life. Monogr. Soc. Res. Child Dev. 37 (1, 146).

Maccoby, E., and Masters, J. C. 1970. Attachment and dependency. In P. H. Mussen (ed.), Carmichael's Manual of Child Psychology. Vol. 2. John Wiley and Sons, New York.

Marshall, N. R., Hegrenes, J. R., and Goldstein, S. 1973. Verbal interactions: Mothers and their retarded children vs. mothers and their non-retarded children. Am. J. Ment. Def. 77: 415–419.

Masters, J. C., and Wellman, H. M. 1974. The study of human infant attachment: A procedural critique. Psychol. Bull. 81: 218–237.

Medley, D. M., and Mitzel, H. E. 1963. Measuring classroom behavior by systematic observation. In N. L. Gage (ed.), Handbook of Research on Teaching. Rand McNally, Chicago.

Messer, S. B., and Lewis, M. 1972. Social class and sex differences in the attachment and play behavior of the year-old-infant. Merrill-Palmer Quart. 18: 295–307.

Moffitt, A. R. 1968. Speech perception by infants. Unpublished doctoral dissertation, University of Minnesota, Minneapolis.

Moffitt, A. R. 1969. Speech perception by 20–24 week old infants. Paper presented at the biennial meeting of the Society for Research in Child Development, March, Santa Monica.

Morgan, G. A. 1973. Determinants of infant's reactions to strangers. ERIC Document

Reproduction Service No. ED080193. National Institute of Child Health and Human Development, Bethesda, Maryland.

Moss, H. A. 1967. Sex, age and state as determinants of mother-infant interaction. Merrill-Palmer Quart. 13: 19–36.

Moss, H. A., Robson, K. S., and Pedersen, F. 1969. Determinants of maternal stimulation of infants and consequences of treatment for later reactions to strangers. Dev. Psychol. 1: 239–246.

Nelson, K. 1973. Structure and strategy in learning to talk. Monogr. Soc. Res. Child Dev. 38 (1-2, 149).

Newport, E. 1976. Motherese: The speech of mothers to young children. In N. J. Castellan, D. B. Pisoni, and G. R. Potts (eds.), Cognitive Theory. Vol. II. Lawrence Earlbaum Assoc., Hillsdale, N.J.

Osofsky, J. D. 1971. Children's influences upon parental behaviour: An attempt to define the relationship with the use of laboratory tasks. Gen. Psychol. Monogr. 83: 147–169.

Osofsky, J. D., and Danzger, B. 1974. Relationships between neonatal characteristics and mother-infant interaction. Dev. Psychol. 10: 124–130.

Parke, R. D., O'Leary, S. E., and West, S. 1972. Mother-father-newborn interaction: Effects of maternal medication, labor and sex of infant. Summary of the Proceedings of the 80th Annual Convention of the American Psychological Association.

Passman, R. H., and Weisberg, P. 1975. Mothers and blankets as agents for promoting play and exploration by young child in a novel environment: The effects of social and nonsocial attachment objects. Dev. Psychol. 11: 170–177.

Pavenstedt, E. 1965. A comparison of the child rearing environment of upper-lower and very low-lower class families. Am. J. Orthopsychiatry 35: 89–98.

Phillips, J. R. 1973. Syntax and vocabulary of mothers' speech to young children: Age and sex comparisons. Child Dev. 44: 182–185.

Ramey, C. T., and Campbell, F. A. 1976. Parental attitudes and poverty. J. Genet. Psychol. 128: 3–6.

Ramey, C. T., and Mills, P. J. 1975. Mother-infant interaction patterns as a function of rearing conditions. Paper presented at the biennial meeting of the Society for Research in Child Development, April, Denver.

Ramey, C. T., Mills, P., Campbell, F. A., and O'Brien, C. 1975. Infant's home environments: A comparison of high-risk families and families from the general population. Am. J. Ment. Def. 80: 40–42.

Ramey, C. T., O'Brien, C. H., and Finkelstein, N. W. 1975. The influence of day care on mother-child interaction patterns. Paper presented at the annual meeting of the Southeastern Psychological Association, March, Atlanta.

Randall, T. M. 1975. An analysis of observer influence on sex and social class differences in mother-infant interaction. Paper presented at the biennial meeting of the Society for Research in Child Development, April, Denver.

Reid, J. B. 1970. Reliability assessment of observation data: A possible methodological problem. Child Dev. 41: 1143–1150.

Rheingold, H. L. 1969. The effect of a strange environment on the behavior of infants. In B. M. Foss (ed.), Determinants of Infant Behaviour Vol. IV. Methuen, London.

Rheingold, H. L., and Bayley, N. 1959. The later effects of an experimental modification of mothering. Child Dev. 30: 363–372.

Rheingold, H. L., and Eckerman, C. O. 1973. Fear of the stranger: A critical examination. In H. W. Reese (ed.), Advances in child development and behavior. Vol. 8 Academic Press, New York.

Rheingold, H. L., and Keene, G. C. 1965. Transport of the human young. In B. M. Foss, (ed.), Determinants of Infant Behaviour. Vol. III. Methuen, London.

Richards, M. P., and Bernal, J. F. 1971. Social Interaction in the first days of life. In H. R. Schaffer (ed.), The Origins of Human Social Relations. Academic Press, New York.

Robson, K. S., and Moss, H. A. 1970. Patterns and determinants of maternal attachment. J. Pediatr. 77: 976–985.

Ryan, E. B., and Collins, C. 1976. The role of question—answer interactions in language development. Unpublished manuscript, University of Notre Dame.

Sachs, J., Brown, R., and Salerno, R. A. 1972. Adults' speech to children. Paper presented at the International Symposium on First Language Acquisition, September, Florence, Italy.

Salk, L. 1970. The critical nature of the post-partum period in the human for the establishment of the mother-infant bond: A controlled study. Dis. Nerv. Syst. 31: 110–116.

Sander, L. W., Stechler, G., Burns, P., and Julia, H. 1970. Early mother-infant interaction and 24-hour patterns of activity and sleep. J. Am. Acad. Child Psychiatry 9: 103–123.

Scarr, S., and Williams, M. L. 1971. The effects of early stimulation on low birth weight infants. Paper presented to the Maternal and Child Health Section of the American Public Health Association, October, Minneapolis, Minnesota.

Schaefer, E. 1971. Development of hierarchical, configurational models for parent behavior and child behavior. In J. P. Hill (ed.), Minnesota Symposia on Child Psychology. Vol. 5. The University of Minnesota Press, Minneapolis.

Schaffer, H. R., and Emerson, P. E. 1964. The development of social attachments in infancy. Monogr. Soc. Res. Child Dev. 29(3, 94).

Sears, R. R., Maccoby, E. E., and Levin, H. 1957. Patterns of Child Rearing. Row, Peterson and Company, Evanston, Illinois.

Seitz, S., and Stewart, C. 1975. Imitations and expansions: Some developmental aspects of mother-child communications. Dev. Psychol. 11: 763–768.

Singh, D. 1970. Preference for bar pressing to obtain reward over freeloading in rats and children. J. Comp. Physiolog. Psychol. 73: 320–327.

Snow, C. E. 1972. Mothers' speech to children learning language. Child Dev. 43: 549–565.

Snow, C. E., Arlman-Rupp, A., Hassing, Y., Jobse, J., Joosten, J., and Vorster, J. 1974. Mothers' speech in three social classes. Unpublished paper, Institute for General Linguistics, University of Amsterdam.

Stayton, D. J., and Ainsworth, M. D. 1973. Individual differences in infant responses to brief, everyday separations as related to other infant and maternal behaviors. Dev. Psychol. 9: 226–235.

Stern, D. N. 1974. Mother and infant at play: The dyadic interaction involving facial, vocal and gaze behaviors. In M. Lewis and L. A. Rosenblum (eds.), The Effect of the Infant on Its Caregiver. Wiley-Interscience, New York.

Stern, D. N., Jaffe, J., Beebe, B., and Bennett, S. L. 1975. Vocalizing in unison and in alternation: Two modes of communications within the mother-infant dyad. In D. Aaronson and R. W. Rieber (eds.), Developmental Psycholinguistics and Communication Disorders. The New York Academy of Sciences, New York.

Strain, B. A., and Vietze, P. M. 1975. Early dialogues: The structure of reciprocal infant-mother vocalization. Paper presented at the biennial meeting of the Society for Research in Child Development, April, Denver.

Streissguth, A. P., and Bee, H. L. 1972. Mother-child interactions and cognitive development in children. In W. W. Hartup (ed.), The Young Child: Reviews of Research, Vol. 2. National Association for the Education of Young Children, Washington, D.C.

Taplin, P. S., and Reid, J. B. 1973. Effects of instructional set and experimenter influence on observer reliability. Child Dev. 44: 547–554.

Thoman, E. B., Barnett, C. R., and Leiderman, P. H. 1971. Feeding behaviors of newborn infants as a function of parity of the mother. Child Dev. 42: 1471–1483.

Thoman, E. B., Turner, A. M., Leiderman, P. H., and Barnett, C. R. 1970. Neonate-mother interaction: Effects of parity on feeding behavior. Child Dev. 41: 1103–1111.

Thompson, W. R., and Grusec, J. E. 1970. Studies of early experience. In P. H. Mussen (ed.), Carmichael's Manual of Child Psychology, Vol. 1. John Wiley and Sons, New York.

Tizard, B., Cooperman, O., Joseph, A., and Tizard, J. 1972. Environmental effects on language development: A study of young children in long-stay residential nurseries. Child Dev. 43: 337–358.

Tracy, R. L., Lamb, M. E., and Ainsworth, M. D. 1976. Infant approach behavior as related to attachment. Child Dev. 47: 571–578.

Tronick, E., Adamson, L., Wise, S., Als, H., and Brazelton, T. B. 1975. Infant emotions in normal and perturbated interactions. Paper presented at the biennial meeting of the Society for Research in Child Development, April, Denver.

Tulkin, S. R. 1972. An analysis of the concept of cultural deprivation. Dev. Psychol. 6: 326–339.

Tulkin, S. R. 1973. Social class differences in attachment behaviors of ten-month-old infants. Child Dev. 44: 171–174.

Tulkin, S. R., and Cohler, B. J. 1973. Child-rearing attitudes and mother-child interaction in the first year of life. Merrill-Palmer Quart. 19: 95–106.

Tulkin, S. R., and Covitz, F. E. 1975. Mother-infant interaction and intellectual functioning at age six. Paper presented at the biennial meeting of the Society for Research in Child Development, April, Denver.

Tulkin, S. R., and Kagan, J. 1972. Mother-child interaction in the first year of life. Child Dev. 43: 31–41.

Wachs, T. D., Uzgiris, I. C., and Hunt, J. McV. 1971. Cognitive development in infants of different age levels and from different environmental backgrounds: An exploratory investigation. Merrill-Palmer Quart. 17: 283–317.

Watson, J. S. 1967. Memory and "contingency analysis" in infant learning. Merrill-Palmer Quart. 13: 55–76.

Watson, J. S. 1972. Smiling, cooing and "the game." Merrill-Palmer Quart. 18: 323–339.

Watson, J. S., and Ramey, C. T. 1972. Reactions to response-contingent stimulation in early infancy. Merrill-Palmer Quart. 18: 219–227.

Weick, K. E. 1968. Systematic observational methods. In G. Lindzey and E. Aronson (eds.), The Handbook of Social Psychology, Vol. 2. Addison-Wesley Publishing Co., Reading, Pa.

White, B. L., and Watts, J. C. 1973. Experience and environment: Major influences on the development of the young child, Vol. 1. Prentice-Hall, Englewood Cliffs.

White, R. W. 1959. Motivation reconsidered: The concept of competence. Psychol. Rev. 66: 297–333.

Willerman, L., Broman, S., and Fiedler, M. 1970. Infant development, preschool IQ, and social class. Child Dev. 41: 69–77.

Yarrow, L. J., Klein, R. P., Lomonaco, S., and Morgan, G. A. 1975. Cognitive and motivational development in early childhood. In B. Z. Friedlander (ed.), Exceptional Infant: Assessment and Intervention, Vol. 3. Bruner-Mazel, New York.

Yarrow, L. J., Rubenstein, J. L., and Pedersen, F. A. 1975. Infant and Environment: Early Cognitive and Motivational Development. Hemisphere Publishing Corp., Washington, D.C.

Early Speech in
Its Communicative Context

Katherine Nelson

There is a current explosion of work on child language from the perspective of prag-matics and sociolinguistics that is comparable in extent to the earlier outpouring of studies of child syntax in the 1960s and early 1970s. This phenomenon has its roots in at least three directions—philosophy of language, and specifically the speech act analysis (e.g., Austin, 1962; Searle, 1969); sociolinguistics (particularly the work of Bernstein, 1970; Ervin-Tripp, 1973; Halliday, 1973; Hymes, 1974); and the study of child language itself, which increasingly called out for the analysis of the social context of language acquisition (Bloom, 1970; Cazden, 1970; Nelson, 1973).

The current emphasis has two somewhat contradictory effects on our attempts to understand the task of language learning for the young child. First, it enormously complicates that task. What the child has to learn in the course of mastering his native language has gone far beyond the complexities of grammar as explicated by Chomsky in 1965. Today we understand that grammar is only one part of the total communicative competence—to use Hymes's (1974) term—to be achieved. Per-formance rules—for example, rules of address, appropriateness, presuppositions, conversational postulates—turn out to be as complex as any rules conceived by transformational grammarians, and far more problematical. What needs to be explained, therefore, has mushroomed while our understanding of the complexities of language use has grown.

Compensating for this increasing complication is the realization that children may use a great deal of surface information provided by the context of language use as they go about the job of making sense of what is said. That is, they are not confined to the analysis of the grammar of sentences they hear, or even to determin-ing reference or lexical meaning, but they can take advantage of knowledge of shared intentions, and of nonlinguistic context and communication in decoding messages. Thus we see that the language learning puzzle as we understand it has grown in size, but that the strategies for solving it are much more varied, and seem to be more accessible to the young child than we once thought. This accounts for the dual emphasis that is apparent in the research and that is found throughout this paper, first on the analysis of communicative structure, and second on the use of that structure for acquiring knowledge of the language itself.

The new look in language development views the child less as a language learner (or worse, as a language acquisition device, or LAD) than as a partner in a two-way communication system with intentions to be expressed and received through whatever means can be managed. This view is actually much closer to older functional analyses of language in linguistics and psychology than to more recent structural analyses. There is every reason to believe, however, that the current trends will reflect and integrate the knowledge gained from the many sophisticated structural analyses of child language production in recent years.

Rather than attempting a comprehensive review of the literature in a field that is growing so rapidly that any review will be outdated long before it appears in print, this author would like to review selectively examples of the kind of work that has been and is being done and the types of analyses that are being employed, and in the course of so doing, to comment on the appropriateness and applicability of such analyses and their implications for future research. Because dyadic communication in context is such a complex system, and because of the different sources of analytical systems, the great majority of current work has concentrated on only one part of the communication network—that is, on either parent or child. Only a few have as yet tried to put the two together in a meaningful way. Therefore, one of the aims of this paper is to highlight ways in which that task might be accomplished. A final section considers communicative function as a source of individual differences in development.

The discussion throughout is concerned principally with the communicative context and functions of speech for the beginning talker—roughly defined as the age range between 10 months and 30 months, or the proficiency range between response to a few spoken words and the ability to use simple sentences fluently—comparable to Brown's (1973) stage III. The focus is therefore more on what the sociopsycholinguistic context offers the child in the way of support than on the more complex aspects of conversational rules to be learned, which are the focus of recent studies of presupposition and discourse analysis, for example. The reasons for confining the discussion to this age range are both practical and topical, respecting space and time constraints, but also reflecting the central theme of this conference as early assessment of communicative and cognitive abilities. The first two years of language development pose problems to the young child different from those that he faces in using language in more complex situations, after basic language skills have been acquired. Before turning to specific research approaches, the components of the communicative context of the young child are briefly considered, in order to set the framework for later discussion.

ASPECTS OF COMMUNICATIVE CONTEXT

Hymes (1974) has identified 16 different "components of speech," not all of which are equally relevant to the beginnings of speech. The following four general categories include most of those that seem to be crucial to the consideration of early child speech.

Situation

The situation in which communication takes place is of obvious importance in defining what will be said. In discussing the impact of the "neglected situation" on child language, Cazden (1970) identified the *topic,* the *task,* the *listeners,* and the *initiation of interaction* as situational variables that might affect fluency or spontaneity, length and complexity of sentences, and content or style of the language used by the child. Although her analysis was concerned with preschool and school children (where lower-class children have often been found to be at a disadvantage), the same variables could be expected to be equally important—or perhaps more so—to the beginning talker. The relative restriction of settings within which mother-child talk takes place at the outset is probably of considerable importance, to the degree that the child is able to make sense of what is said. At present, however, we do not have any studies that have examined this assumption directly. The *locations*—both spatial and temporal—in which early mother-child exchanges are established seem to be relatively stereotyped, at least in our culture; they are organized around such social events as feeding, dressing, bathing, going out, and sharing social proto-games such as "give and take." The stereotypical nature of these occasions tends to set the *topic* and the *roles* to be played by each speaker, as well as the context. The child language literature in general has tended to assume a common environment within which early language learning takes place. However, considerable variability of situational structure has been found within a small, white middle-class sample by Nelson (1973). In this study, variables such as number of outings, time spent with other children, and time spent watching television were all associated with progress in language development during the second year, outcomes that call into question easy assumptions about the uniformity and invariable utility of mother-child interaction settings. Bruner's (1975a) recent studies also have emphasized that some mothers are very good at establishing stereotyped exchanges within settings such as feeding and bathing, but that other mothers seem not to do so.

One situational factor that has consistently been found to be important is composition of the speaker-listener dyad, and in particular whether the participants are children or adults. Although recent studies (Shatz and Gelman, 1973) have shown that even four-year-olds may adapt their speech to the level of younger children, the research is almost unanimous in showing that peer speech is less conducive to language learning and mature language use than in speech from an adult (see Bates, Camaioni, and Volterna, 1975, for review). Thus twins have been shown to be slow in language acquisition, as have younger siblings, when compared to first or only children. Oddly, however, almost all of our knowledge of the factors influencing the early stage of language learning is based on samples of first-born children, with siblings deliberately screened out of the sample, or at least from the interaction analysis. Sibling to sibling speech may differ in many important ways—stylistically, functionally, conceptually—from that of adult-to-child speech, and the setting in which it takes place may be a less important factor in determining the quality of peer speech. It is not difficult to imagine, however, that some peer defined situations—disputes over property rights, for example—may have their own important implications for how and what language is learned by the younger child. In fact, there is some evidence, albeit indirect, that younger siblings use more possessives than first or only children (Nelson, 1976).

Sooner or later, of course, the child comes to use language in many different situations and contexts, with many different people, in both the speaker and the listener role. He also differentiates between situations in terms of style or code (Ervin-Tripp, 1973; Labov, 1970). One of the first differentiations made, according to Berko-Gleason (1973) is that between stranger-present (no speech) and stranger-absent (speech). At a later point, the situation may direct what things are said and how; in the first period of language development the situation may determine in addition what is *learned*. Thus, we need to know a great deal more than we presently do about situational variables and their effects on language development.

Function of Language

The use of language is the central subject matter of pragmatics, the branch of language study that relates the language to the speaker. Several of the research programs considered later in this review employ functional analyses of child language. It is important to note, however, that a functional analysis can be made from two different directions: the function of the language addressed to the child, and the function of the language used by the child. Although there is a great deal of research to report on the analysis of language addressed to the child, relatively little is focused on function, while a number of researchers have tried to categorize the child's own speech in these terms.

Still a third approach asks what is the function of child language that is not addressed to other people, but this question has seldom been integrated with the previous questions. Self-directed speech can be conceived as practice in the service of learning new forms, as a medium for categorizing the world, as "egocentric" speech in Piaget's terms, or as the prelude for "verbal thought" in Vygotsky's sense. Categorization of infant speech has usually revealed a relatively large proportion that is undirected to other persons, but rarely has this kind of speech been analyzed further. This problem is particularly important because it is not clear that one can analyze speech that is not directed to others in the same terms as one can analyze interpersonal speech. Until the attempt is made to integrate the two, we will know little about similarities and differences of the two forms, or about what part nonsocial speech plays in the language learning task. However, because the focus of this paper is on *social* speech, or interpersonal communication, the intraindividual function is not considered further here.

Content

What the child talks about is integrally related both to the function of speech and to its form. Content may derive from what the child knows and is interested in, or what the parent (or other partner) chooses to talk about. Studies of topic discourse (e.g., Keenan and Schiefflin, 1976) may shed light on these relations, but as yet we have few leads to them.

Here, as in so many areas, what language the child understands must be distinguished from what language he himself uses. The two may in fact be quite different, particularly in such well-studied areas as the differentiation of conceptual categories. The fact that some children can differentiate between members of a class such as vehicles, when these are named for them by others, but when producing names call all examples by the same term (e.g., "car;" see Rescorla, 1976), indicates that we need to take into account not only the child's knowledge of the world, but also his knowledge of language terms. Furthermore, we need to take into account shared knowledge as revealed in the dyadic system—that is, what mother and child both know, and understand each other to know. In this respect, content of the language is intimately tied to situational context, because it is within specific well-defined situations that such shared knowledge is revealed. It is also within such situations that shared knowledge is derived; conceptual content depends in part on situation and context, and therefore ultimately on the sociolinguistic conditions of the language learning situation. Although the child may be able to learn about the categories of the world through his own exploration, he will not be able to name them unless that knowledge is shared with a namer who will supply the needed label. These considerations lie behind Bruner's (1975a, b, 1976) studies of the early communication system.

Structure: Style or Code

Considerable attention has been directed to the question of how the speech of mothers directed to young children differs from adult-to-adult speech. Such factors as length of utterance, complexity of sentence structure, and intonation have all been discussed in the context of the analysis of "motherese" (to use Newport's, 1976, term), the special code that is used in addressing beginning talkers, and these are considered below in more detail. In addition, such speech is supplemented by use of gesture, and it incorporates situational objects and activities as part of the message. The relation of these factors to the acquisition of a style or code by the child has received relatively little, if any, attention, despite its potential importance (e.g., Bernstein, 1970; Labov, 1970).

Together, these factors—situation, function, content, and code—define the communicative context of early child speech, and therefore of language learning. No study has yet succeeded in considering them all at once, and few have concentrated on more than one end of the dyad at a time—either parent or child. First considered in the discussion to follow are studies of parent to child speech, followed by two approaches to the study of child speech in a pragmatic framework, and finally by a consideration of the few attempts that have been made to consider adult and child as a single interactive system. It becomes clear in the course of this discussion that there is as yet no agreed-upon framework for analysis in these studies, but that each approach has revealed different facets of the communication system. In a final section, the question of future directions and implications is considered.

PARENT TO CHILD COMMUNICATION: MOTHERESE

The original impetus for the study of the characteristics of mothers' speech to their young children came from the assumption by a number of students of child syntax that the "primary linguistic data" presented to the child in his parents' speech was unsuited for the extraction of linguistic rules because it was ungrammatical, fragmented, dysfluent, and in other ways inaccessible to analysis. This characterization was based on the analysis of adult speech, particularly of speech transcribed at scholarly conferences, that was indeed filled with garbled and ungrammatical forms. Many students of child language were persuaded, however, that the speech used by mothers in speaking to their young children was simpler and less ill-formed than this characterization suggested, and that therefore the child might be able to extract linguistic structure from the data presented to him much more easily than assumed by Chomsky (1965) and McNeill (1966), among others. Thus, in the late 1960s, a series of studies began to appear that analyzed mother to child speech directly, and compared it to the speech used in adult-adult conversation. (Almost every study has used mothers as the subject of analysis, unless the focus was on the comparison between mothers and other less well—practiced speakers, such as children or nonparents. Few authors have been concerned with the speech of other family members, such as fathers. An exception was the study by Friedlander, Jacobs, Davis, and Wetstone (1972), which time-sampled all conversation directed to the child in the home. Thus, the subject of these studies are characteristically labeled "mother's speech," although this author does not subscribe to the implicit assumption that this is the only speech that counts. This assumption has been reinforced by the invention of "motherese" as a term applied to this code by Newport, Gleitman, and Gleitman (1975). Although it is important to recognize that early speech is a dyadic affair and can only be understood in the context of the interactive situation, it is equally important to recognize that the family structure of the young child includes other speakers besides the mother, whose impact upon his language learning may be equally as important.)

Several reviews of the literature on mothers' speech have recently been published (Bates, 1976; Newport, 1976; Snow, 1974; Vorster, 1975), but a detailed review of the findings is not attempted here. The findings have been remarkably consistent and can be summerized briefly. Child-addressed speech is acoustically differentiable from adult-addressed speech in speed, fundamental frequency (pitch), and variability (intonation), according to studies by Broen (1972) and Phillips (1973). There is, then, a basis on which the child could determine which sentences were addressed to him without understanding the linguistic message at all, and he could presumably filter out all speech not directed to him. In addition, mothers characteristically modify the structure of the message, both lexically (by use of a restricted and concrete vocabulary) and syntactically (Baldwin and Frank, 1969; Broen, 1972; Phillips, 1973; Snow, 1972). Sentences are typically short, well-formed, and simple in structure.

These studies have made it clear that the language that the child hears is radically different from the language that occurs in the interactions of adult speakers. Although this finding supports the notion that the child might be able to discern the underlying linguistic structure of the language more easily because a simplified model is available to him, it has also been pointed out that some of the adjustments that adults typically make in speaking to young children may obscure rather than clarify underlying linguistic relationships (e.g., Newport et al., 1975). For example, much of the adult talk consists of either imperatives with subjects deleted, or of questions employing the relatively complex wh-forms or inverted auxiliary structures. The prevalence of these sentence types makes the Simple Model assumption somewhat shaky, and that the use of particular forms makes it harder or easier for the child to grasp the structure of the language should be proved before concluding that the model provided is indeed beneficial to the child's syntactical progress.

In summary, we know now that motherese is different, we are less sure that it is appropriate to language learning, and we have little information as to why it is used. Why do mothers talk that way? They might do so in order to make themselves understood, they might do so consciously to provide an optimal teaching model, or motherese may simply be a by-product of the kinds of communication in which mother and child engage at this time. Let us consider the appropriateness and the functional questions in turn.

Correlations Between Motherese and Language Learning

Is the motherese style beneficial to the child's language learning? Considerable attention has been given to documenting the fact that the use of motherese is characteristic of mothers of many different social classes and cultures, as well as of nonparents, and even of children (Ferguson, in press; Snow, 1972; Shatz and Gelman, 1973; Snow, Arlman-Rupp, Hassing, Jobse, Joosten, and Vorster, 1976), a finding that tends to downplay the possibility that there might be learning differences associated with its use. If all mothers use it to the same degree, then all children must benefit to the same degree, or at least differences between children could not reflect differences between mothers. There have in fact been few analyses of the association of "motherese" variables with the language progress of the child. Several studies, however, have reported an increase in mean length of utterance (MLU) with language progress of the child (Glanzer and Dodd, 1975; Nelson, 1973; Phillips, 1973). Furthermore, Lord (1975) reported that over the period from 6 to 18 months the length of mothers' sentences first dropped (at the time when the child began to say single words), then gradually rose during the one-word time period, and then dropped again when the child began making short sentences. This indicates a fine adjustment to the language status of the child, directed critically at his acquisition of new abilities. (In contradiction, a recent study by Snow (1976) reports no difference in MLU on several other code variables over the child's age range of 3 to 18 months.)

Newport (1976), however, has claimed that the correlation of mother's MLU with child's language status is an artifact of increase in the child's age and of age-appropriate utterances, and that when age is held constant, the correlation of mother's MLU (and other indices of syntactic complexity) to child's language progress should disappear. Newport's argument is not clearly supported by her own cross-sectional data, and is contradicted by Nelson (1973), in which MLU of mother was correlated to various aspects of the child's language status, including MLU at age two, when age was held constant across children. It is also contradicted by Lord (1975) in the study described above. In fact, the finding that length of mother's sentences tracks the complexity of the child's language production is one of the most reliable of findings from these studies. It may indeed be a reflection of functional communication rather than of formal syntactic factors, as Newport claims, but if so, language status of the child would seem to be one of the prime indicators to the mother of what functional communications are appropriate. This interpretation is supported by the findings of Seitz and Stewart (1975) concerning the mother's use of expansions and complex sentence structures in response to children's imitations and questions, respectively.

One of the problems with drawing conclusions about effects from the studies of motherese thus far is that the samples have been restricted in terms of factors that might be expected to determine variability in mothers' language use. For example, most studies have used middle-class mothers and first-born children. Yet Nelson (1973) showed that there was considerable variation in interaction patterns associated with differences in parental education, age, and sex of children, and presence or absence of siblings. In addition, if one wishes to know whether variations in mother talk influence characteristics of child talk, one must find dimensions along which children differ at a given age as well as across ages, and, preferably using a longitudinal design, test the extent to which the variation among the mothers matches the variation among the children over time. This strategy has not been employed to any significant extent thus far. Although Nelson (1973) used such a design, it was not employed to look at syntactic or style characteristics of mother-child interaction, but rather functional and content characteristics. Interestingly, a partial exception is a study by Newport et al. (1975). They state: "What we have found thus far is that the frequencies of certain kinds of structures in maternal speech [e.g., auxiliary fronted questions] do selectively predict learning of related structures by the child [e.g., verbal auxiliaries], but only when these maternal structures are presented in such a fashion that they interact with the processing strategies (Slobin 1973), or biases, of the child" (p. 112). Although one can only applaud the effort to relate mother talk to child strategies, their data and analyses, unfortunately, would not seem to support unequivocally their further conclusion that simplicity itself and frequency of occurrence of constructions are unimportant to the child's learning. A more recent report based on the same data (Newport, Gleitman, and Gleitman, 1976) claims that language specific features such as auxiliary use may be affected by motherese, but that language universal features such as verb phrase use are not. Both reports rely on an attempt to partial out age and initial language status from the analysis of change scores, but this analysis could only yield relevant conclusions if the language characteristics in question increased linearly over the one to two year age range employed, which is manifestly not the case. A cross-lagged correlational procedure (Campbell and Stanley, 1963) would seem to be a more appropriate analytic tool, although even this would not yield a definitive answer. The question, "Does the 'Motherese' code facilitate children's language learning?" must remain, therefore, basically unanswered at the present time.

Motherese as a Teaching Model

The aspect of mother-talk that has received greatest attention in terms of its possible impact on the child's acquisition of syntactic structure is that of expansions of the child's utterances. Expansions were first identified and defined by Brown and Bellugi (1964). They represent a different characteristic of mothers' speech than the code variables thus far considered in that they are functionally contingent on the child's productions; they are therefore a product of the interaction itself, and cannot be measured independently. Although one could measure the lexical, syntactic, intonational, and phonetic properties—even imitations and repetitions—in mothers' speech to prelinguistic children, one cannot so identify and measure expansions. As is now well-specified, expansions operate on a child's incomplete or ungrammatical construction by repeating the basic structure and filling in the missing parts. For example, the child's production *Daddy shoe* might be responded to with *Yes, that's Daddy's shoe.*

Brown and Bellugi indentified a large proportion of expansions by the mothers in their study—up to 30% of responses to the child—and they believed that such responses must provide a particularly appropriate model for the child's grammatical development. Subsequent research has been disappointing to such beliefs, however, in two ways. First, other investigators (e.g., Friedlander, et al., 1972; Nelson, 1973; Seitz and Stewart, in press) have consistently failed to find as high a level of expansions as appeared in Brown and Bellugi's study. Although age, definitional, and measurement differences might account for some of the discrepancies, it seems probable that Brown's rates were inflated by the situational demands in which the mother was clarifying the child's utterances for the researcher as much as for the child (Newport, 1976, has also suggested this explanation). Thus, the prevalence of expansions in mothers' speech is not as high as previously thought.

In addition, evidence that expansions might facilitate learning for the child has been hard to come by. Early efforts by Cazden (1965) and Feldman (1971; reported by Nelson, Carskaddon, and Bonvillian, 1973) to test the effect experimentally failed to show higher learning for preschool children exposed to expanded models over those exposed to responsive models, or even to a control group. It has generally been concluded that expansions may benefit the mother by clarifying and confirming her understanding of the child's message, but that they do not facilitate the child's syntactical advance. It has been widely suggested that the effect might be more semantic than syntactic. All of the evidence is not yet in, however, and Nelson and his colleagues (Nelson, et al., 1973; Nelson, 1976) have shown specific effects on the acquisition of particular aspects of syntax—for example, verbal auxiliaries and questions—when these were the focus of the experimental intervention. Thus even in the clearest case of expansion of the child's utterance, the evidence as to the effect on the child's language learning of characteristics of mother's speech is equivocal.

Why Mothers Use Motherese

The other question—why do mothers talk that way?—sets the analysis in terms of the communicative function served by this kind of speech. This question in turn focuses on other nonsyntactic characteristics of the mother's typical conversational style. For example, as noted above, mothers tend to use imperatives, questions (Holzman, 1972; Soderbehg, 1974), and repetitions (Benedict, 1975; Snow, 1972) of the message to a markedly greater degree when speaking to young children than when speaking to adults. Do they do this as a direct function of the primitive linguistic status of the young child, because of the conversational function and role of the mother-child relationship (as argued by Newport, 1976, and Snow, 1976), or for purposes of instructing the child (effectively or not) regarding either the language or other aspects of the world? In point of fact, the impetus to use these modes of interaction may derive from all three sources—and variations in their use may be the result of the extent to which each of these purposes is paramount for a particular mother at a particular point in the child's developmental history.

Let us examine the question of repetitions. It has been noted by almost every observer that mothers (and others) who talk to young children repeat themselves, often with variations on a basic message (see Table 1). In fact, it is very difficult for mothers, or any adult, to inhibit repetition to the young child. Benedict (1975) found

Table 1.   Examples of repititions in mothers' speech to young children

Craig (10 months, 14 days)	Michael (10 months, 14 days)
put this in the pumpkin put it in the pumpkin come on put it in the pumpkin	give me some give Mommy some what give me some good? can I have some please

Amy (11 months, 5 days)	Diane (12 months, 14 days)
Amy, can Mommy see are you going to bring it over to Mommy can Mommy see can I see the ball huh	give it to Mommy oh, please can Mommy have it

David (14 months, 2 days)
oh, you have to back it up you have to pull it back, Davey

From Benedict, 1975.

that 43% of the utterances directed to children 12 to 14 months of age were repetitions of a message.

Does repetition function to assure the mother that she is communicating, or does it also have a function for the child in permitting him to decode more of the message? Putting the question this way obscures the multifunctional nature of the language acquisition context. Parents might use a particular form in response to the linguistic deficiencies of their child, and that form in turn might or might not have an important effect on the child's ability to learn. In Benedict's study, repetitions by the mother served both to get the child's attention and to give the child the opportunity to process more of the message. Snow (1972) has suggested also that repetitions model variations in syntax and demonstrate the arbitrariness of the sound-meaning relationship. From the mother's point of view, it would seem likely that attention getting was the important function, and the additional opportunity for processing was a coincidental but beneficial by-product. A similar account was suggested in the case of expansions above. It seems clear that the question of "why" is logically independent of the effect of any particular component of the mother's speaking style on the child. On the other hand, mothers are in most cases interested in having their children learn to talk, and they may consciously adjust their speech, at least to some degree, to make the task easier for the child. The fact that they adjust their speech more when the child is present (Snow, 1972) than absent suggests that they use cues from the child as to current level of understanding.

Because these purposes and outcomes seem to depend on and interact with the child's communicative role, it seems likely that we will not be able to untangle the reasons for them without considering that role. A number of recent studies have attempted to characterize early child speech within a function or act framework. They can be divided into those studies that are derived from or related to traditional concerns in linguistics and psychology with the function of speech—a diverse group—and those derived from the philosphy of language utilizing the Speech Act analysis as a framework for looking at child speech.

DEVELOPMENT OF THE SPEECH ACT

The most formalized approach to the study of pragmatic or communicative competence is embodied in the Speech Act analysis, based on the work of Austin (1962) and Searle (1969). In this analysis, sentences are viewed not simply as propositions, as in traditional linguistic philosophy, but as acts or events in themselves. Indeed, every time a sentence is used, it is claimed, three kinds of speech acts are carried out: a locution, an illocution, and a perlocution. *Locution* refers to the making of speech itself, and especially to the construction of propositions. *Illocution,* in contrast, is the conventional social *act* of questioning, commanding, advising, stating, etc. that is embedded in the speech act. For example, the sentence, "He urged me to shoot her" (to take Searle's example) is a description of the illocutionary act expressed in the locution "shoot her!" The original speech act ("shoot her!") contains in addition a *perlocutionary* act—namely an effect—that can be described as, "He persuaded me to shoot her."

The Speech Act analysis has been extended and utilized by philosophers and linguists (e.g., Fillmore, 1968; Ross, 1970) in the claim that every *sentence* contains two parts: a *propositional* (or constative) component (the locution) and a *performative* component (the illocutionary force). A number of child language studies have incorporated these notions (e.g., Greenfield and Smith, 1976; Gruber, 1973; Ingram, 1971), but two investigators—Bates and her colleagues and Dore—have made it the central focus of major studies, and they have come to somewhat different conclusions about the underlying developments involved.

The assumptions underlying Bates's studies are well-expressed in the following excerpt:

> In terminology that can be applied to child language, a locution requires the uttering of sounds and construction of propositions. Hence, locution requires the onset of verbal speech. An illocution requires the intentional use of a conventional signal to carry out some socially recognized function, e.g. commanding, indicating the presence of objects or events, etc. Hence illocutions might be carried out with conventional gestural signals like pointing. Perlocutions require simply that a signal issued by one person have some effect, intentional or unintentional, on the listener. Hence the hunger cry of a newborn infant can at least be regarded as a perlocution (Bates et al., 1975, p. 206).

Based on this analysis of the problem, the authors go on to propose:

> We decided to undertake a study of the development of performatives during the first year of life, inferring the intention to communicate from its first manifestation in gesture, eye-contact, and prelinguistic vocalizations. In Austin's terms, we proposed to follow the development of communication through three stages: (1) a *perlocutionary* stage, in which the child has a systematic effect on his listener without having an intentional, aware control over that effect; (2) an *illocutionary* stage, in which the child intentionally uses non-verbal signals to convey requests and to direct adult attention to objects and events; (3) a *locutionary* stage in which the child constructs propositions and utters speech sounds within the same performative sequences that he previously expressed non-verbally (p. 207).

Bates and her colleagues also attempted to relate these developments to the child's cognitive development as specified in Piaget's stage theory. They concentrated their attention on the development of two "performatives"—commanding and declaring—that have been distinguished in the one-word utterances of young children. They conceptualized commanding, or the imperative, as the use of the adult as the means to a desired object, and the declarative as the use of an object as the means to obtain adult attention. This enabled them to identify a preverbal or gestural "protodeclarative" and "protoimperative" that appeared before the use of words in similar action contexts. In turn, on the basis of their longitudinal study of three Italian infants of different ages, they tied the illocutionary stage—involving gestural means for achieving these ends—to the attainment of Piaget's Stage 5 of sensorimotor development, and the locutionary stage—when propositions could be expressed—to the attainment of Stage 6, entailing the use of symbols and mental representations. In their more recent study of 25 children between nine and one-half and twelve and one-half months of age, from which only preliminary results have been reported, they have been much more concerned with this relationship between cognitive development and linguistic development than in the development of the speech act itself.

Social, cognitive, and linguistic development must all be considered within a complete model of language development, as their extensive discussion indicates, and as others before them have argued (e.g., Bruner, 1975a, b; Nelson, 1973; Sugarman-Bell, 1978). However, it is not clear that the Speech Act model as employed by Bates et al. (1975) contributes significantly to such a goal.

This is in fact the position argued by Dore (1976b), who has used the same model in a somewhat different way. In commenting on the Bates et al. study he states:

> It seems indisputable that this [early communicative] sequence is accurate. But the value of phrasing it in speech act terminology is questionable; the metaphor, though intriguing, may be misleading. It implies that at stage two the communicative acts children perform non-verbally are essentially illocutionary acts, like 'requesting,' and that the later use of propositions is merely a verbal substitute for the prior behavior. Yet, when one considers what has been described as the content of genuine requests—namely, the communicative intention being an inducement in a listener of the recognition of a complex set of the speaker's internal states (Grice, 1975; Dore, 1976), the proposition containing specifications of the agent, future, act etc. (Searle, 1969) and the use of which involving assumptions about the listener's willingness and ability to perform the future act (Garvey, 1975)—the analogy breaks down. What Bates et al. describe is the pre-speech development of communicative intentions only, not of speech acts; the description overlooks the grammatical contribution to speech acts (p. 9).

Dore, then, prefers to reserve the Speech Act model for *linguistic* acts while recognizing the prelinguistic communicative intent and content of some of the child's acts. He takes a discontinuous position in contradistinction to the continuity position that Bates has pointed out as a common factor among recent studies of communicative development. His position is clear: "knowledge of propositional [i.e., grammatical] structures cannot be explained by any pragmatic inputs this far proposed," and he faults Bates (1976) for conflating grammar with communication in her statement that "*all* of semantics is *essentially* pragmatic in nature" (p. 20).

Dore argues, in essence, that the development of communicative intentions in the social interchanges of infancy (as described by Bruner, 1975, for example) is a necessary, but not sufficient, condition for language development, which requires in addition the development of grammar. Where then does Dore's own speech act analysis fit? He asks the developmental question: "How does the child acquire the linguistic conventions necessary to express his intentions? In other words, how do speech acts develop?" (1975, p. 30). He has described single-word utterances of two children in terms of Primitive Speech Acts (PSA), defined as containing a rudimentary referring expression (e.g., words like *doggie*) and a primitive force indicating device (typically an intonation pattern). The PSAs he identified were labeling, repeating, answering, requesting (action), requesting (answer), calling, greeting, protesting, practicing. He projects the development of the primitive speech act into the complete speech act in terms of Figure 1, in which the principal development is the expansion of the rudimentary referring expression into the complete sentence containing a modality component and a proposition, as in a case grammar. Dore is willing to ascribe primitive force—or intention—to the beginning speaker, but not the conventional means for expressing it as implied in Speech Act theory. Furthermore, he denies that the conventional means—i.e., the grammar—can be derived from the child's nonlinguistic communicative experience. For these reasons, he concentrates on development of the speech act during the holophrastic period in contrast to Bates et al.'s description of communicative development in the preholophrastic period.

An interesting by-product of Dore's analysis was the distinction (Dore, 1974) between two types of speech progress during the presyntactic period: the code-oriented child who seems to elaborate the propositional component, and the message-oriented child who seems to elaborate the performatory component. As he noted these types are "strikingly similar to Nelson's Referential and Expressive speech types" (see following section).

Greenfield and Smith (in press) have suggested that the first words are "pure performatives," an argument which differs from both Dore's analysis (because the PSA contains both a referring expression and a primitive force) and at least one interpretation of Bates et al.'s position (in that the prelinguistic illocutionary stage is succeeded by the linguistic locutionary stage when words are used propositionally). On the other hand, Gruber (1975), in a recent reanalysis of Bullowa's data on a single child, has claimed that the first *sentences* should be classified as performatives and that it is not until week 10 of sentence production that constative (i.e., propositional) sentences appear in the data. This conclusion, however, is based on an extremely obscure analytical procedure that classifies "Dory spoon" as a performative and "Leon sock" as a constative, for example. How the child's *intentions* were identified in these cases is unclear.

Clearly, the Speech Act model has caught the imagination of a number of different investigators, but there is lack of agreement about how to apply it to early language data, and correspondingly lack of agreement concerning the stages in its development, with Bates claiming essentially the same development during the prelinguistic period that Greenfield and Smith claim for the holophrastic period and

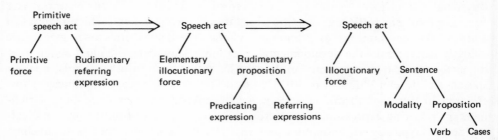

Figure 1.   Evolution of the speech act. (Reprinted from J. Dore, 1975, Holophrases, speech acts and language universals, *Journal of Child Language 2:* 35, by permission.)

that Gruber sees in the two-word sentence period; Dore claims concomitant development of the two essential components during the early linguistic period. This disagreement seems to result from at least three problems inherent in the Speech Act model:

1. It is not a complete and well-specified model as is a generative grammar, but is rather a heuristic framework for viewing communicative acts. Its terms do not have well-defined referents; instead it relies on the analysts' intuitions about the components of communicative situations. Thus, different investigators have interpreted the theory in different ways.

2. It is a model of adult speech without clear developmental implications. Adult speech acts contain all three act components, but, despite Bates's plausible claim, there seems to be no reason why one component should precede another in development. The set of possible performatives is open, as Bates and Dore both recognize. Therefore, although there may be some interest in analyzing the course of acquisition of these, there is no reason to expect a universal course of development independent of some other nonspeech factor, for example the communicative context of early speech.

3. It relies on the interpretation of intentions underlying the speech act, which is clear and verifiable in adult language, but as both Bruner (1976) and Ryan (1974) have pointed out, is extremely problematical for early child speech, and certainly for prelinguistic communication.

Speech Act analysis has contributed significantly to our perspective on the functions of speech in general and on the components of well-formed adult speech acts. It is unlikely to contribute more than heuristically to further analysis of child language, however. If this is true of Speech Act analysis, what is to be said of more traditional kinds of functional analysis? It would seem that they must also be subject to many of the same objections.

Function Analysis

Functional analyses of speech are traditional in psychology (e.g., Skinner, 1957) as well as linguistics (e.g., Jakobson, 1960) and philosophy (e.g., de Laguna, 1963), and have revently been the central focus of sociolinguistics (e.g., Hymes, 1974). In Hymes's view (as well as in the view of many others, including Searle, 1974), language structure is subordinate to function and must be explained in its terms. He has succinctly set forth the appropriateness of this view for the study of child language as follows:

> The potential richness of studies of socialization, enculturation, and child development in this regard is manifest. . . . The importance of concern with the child is partly that it offers a favorable vantage point for discovering the adult system, and that it poses neatly one way in which the ethnography of communication is a distinctive enterprise, i.e., an enterprise concerned with the abilities the child must acquire, beyond those of producing and interpreting grammatical sentences, in order to be a competent member of its community, knowing not only what may possibly be said, but also what should and should not be said (reprinted from *Foundations in Sociolinguistics: An Ethnographic Approach*, p. 26, © 1974 by University of Pennsylvania Press, by permission).

As Bruner (1975a) has pointed out, the analysis of a communicative act in terms of its function does not rely on the specification of the speaker's intention, as does Speech Act Analysis, where intuition was found to pose formidable problems for developmental analyses. Rather, it relies on a specification of result, and is therefore closer to the aim of interactive analysis because it takes into account both speaker and listener. Bruner has utilized this framework most productively in its interactive aspects.

(The relation of the type of functions to be considered here to the perlocutionary component of the speech act that also specifies the result of the act, (e.g., *He persuaded me to shoot her* in the example given above), is unclear. It may be possible to join these into a single productive model.)

Many standard lists of speech functions have been proposed. Hymes (1974) lists expressive, directive, contact, metalinguistic, contextual, poetic, referential, and metacommunicative. Bruner (1975a), relying on Jakobson's (1960) analysis, generates a similar list with the following definitions: *Expressive* "is made up usually of accompaniments to the addressor's feelings." *Poetic* "involves modes of structuring messages to achieve the illuminative or exhibitive effects of an art form." *Conative* "is concerned with forming messages in such a way as to produce desired behavior in the addressee." (Bruner adds: "It encompasses the philosophers' illocutionary force.") *Phatic* "relates to the maintainence of a channel of communication between addresser and addressee." *Metalinguistic* "serves to explicate, usually by reference to a code." *Referential* "make(s) clear the referent of a message by clearing up the context for interpreting an utterance" (pp. 262–3).

As Halliday (1975) makes explicit, such speech functions are not mutually exclusive; a single message typically encodes more than one. Whether or not there are constraints on their combinations has not been determined.

The foremost exponent of the functional analysis of child language in recent years has been Halliday (1973, 1975), whose studies of his own son's speech productions have yielded a rich and provocative analysis. Rather than relying on an analysis of adult functions and applying them to the child productions, Halliday attempted to derive the functions served by the child's speech directly from hypotheses about the emerging speech itself.

The functions so derived can be arranged in a developmental order on the basis of Nigel's use of them. The first four functions appeared in Phase I (from 10 1/2 to 16 1/2 months) and are described as follows:

Instrumental: The child attempts to achieve his ends through speech—this category is used for demands and desires. It is the "I want" function.

Regulatory: The child attempts to regulate the actions of others; this mode therefore goes beyond the instrumental, using language to achieve ends through intermediaries. Its prototypical form is "Do as I tell you" (traditionally conative).

Interactional: The child uses speech to form a bond, or for purely social or affective communication. It expresses the relationship "You and me" (contact or phatic in the above lists).

Personal: The child informs others of his own actions—for example, "Here I come."

Two additional functions appear subsequent to this phase, described in the following terms:

Heuristic: This mode focuses on the explanation behind a statement or event. The child separates the actions and intentions of others from his own. Halliday's example is "Tell me why."

Imaginative: This is the "Let's pretend" function.

Last to appear, and extremely important to Halliday's theory, is the *Informative* function, which uses language to impart information that is not apparent to the listener from his own direct experience. It is thus characterized as the "I've got something to tell you" function.

The first six functions appeared in the protolanguage of the child, that is, forms used consistently to express a meaning but not part of the conventional language system. The last, however, was associated with the transition to "true" language that took place at about 18 months. At this point, according to Halliday, the child's progress was marked by two important steps: the emergence of word combinations or grammar, and the new ability to adopt a communicative role—to engage in dialogue. This ability was prerequisite to acquiring the informative function, he claimed, stating:

> The use of language to inform is a very late stage in the linguistic development of the child, because it is a function which depends on the recognition that *there are functions of language which are solely defined by language itself. All the other functions in the list are extrinsic to language* . . . The informative function . . . is an intrinsic function which the child cannot begin to master until he has grasped the principle of dialogue, which means until he has grasped the fundamental nature of the communication process (p. 31).

Halliday distinguished the first three functions from the last four, terming the former *pragmatic* and the latter *mathetic* (meaning, broadly, related to learning or knowing). He believes that the former are related to what are usually identified as *interpersonal* functions in adult speech, and the latter to *ideational,* although not in any simple equational form. Nigel, according to his observations, used a contrasting intonational pattern to distinguish between the two types of functions in Phase II (between 16 and 18 months). He noted that Nigel adapted the elementary opposition between rising and falling, which is significant in the adult system, "to a functional system that is within his own limitations . . . the distinction . . . between the pragmatic function, or language as doing, Nigel's rising tone, and mathetic function, or language as learning, Nigel's falling tone." This contrast, he observed, leads the child into the meaning potential of the adult system in Phase III, where "the ideational, concerned with the representation of experience," and "the interpersonal, concerned with the communication process as a form and as a channel of social action" are distinguished. However, "pragmatic and mathetic are generalized functional categories of the content, in the developmental system of the child, in which every utterance is, in principle, *either* one *or* the other. Ideational and interpersonal are abstract functional components of the lexico-grammar, in the developed, tristratal system of the adult; here every utterance is, in principle, both one and the other at the same time" (1975, pp. 53–54).

It is easy to criticize Halliday's analysis in terms of the lack of standardized procedures for classifying utterances into functional categories. It is, however, the most completely worked out functional analysis of the child's first language, and it connects at least in principle with the acquisition of intonational patterns, vocabulary, grammar, and even dialogue. It has illuminated the many different functions that the child's first communicative acts can serve at the same time that it has distinguished two general classes of functions in both child and adult language.

It is obvious that further justification of this system in terms of larger samples and other investigators would be helpful. One question that might be raised in light of the concluding discussion of the previous section is: do Halliday's classes depend on interpreting the child's intention to the same degree as the Speech Act analysis does? The answer is probably "yes," in that most uses of language by the child require the interpretation of the adult, and it is for this reason that an interactional analysis, in contrast to one that focuses only on the child, may be most revealing. However, two points are worth emphasizing, based on Halliday's work.

First, Halliday was able to provide for the continuity between the protolanguage of the child and the later conventional language by using this system. This is a goal that has eluded most investigators. Although he discerned a developmental course in which the pragmatic functions all appeared before the mathetic ones (except for the Personal), there was a gradual expansion of function, and later an integration and differentiation, rather than a shift to a different level. It is most important to note, however, that the pragmatic functions can all be expressed in gesture or through other nonlinguistic means, whereas the heuristic and imaginative functions are more language-dependent, and the informative function depends entirely on the use of symbolism. This may provide a clue to some of the individual differences in language development that are discussed below, in that as long as the child is satisfied with communicating pragmatically, there is little need to learn a conventional language system.

The second point to be emphasized is that the emerging duality of the child's system fits well the observed duality of emphasis in studies that have found differences between social (interpersonal) orientation and object (ideational) orientation, or as Dore found, a message versus a code emphasis in early speech. Again, individual differences in patterns of language acquisition may be related to this implicit duality in language function, at first expressed in different forms, later integrated into one.

Several other investigations recently completed or now in progress have utilized functional analyses of the child's early communication (see for example, Carter, 1974, and the review by Bates, Benigni, Bretherton, Camaioni, and Volterna, 1976), derived either from analysis of the child data or from an a priori list of adult language functions, and more can be expected if current estimates are any guide to the emerging Zeitgeist.

One of the earliest was Sugarman's (1973; Sugarman-Bell, in press) study of the development of prelanguage communication during the first year. She was able to classify social interactions in an objective system that did not rely on interpretation of intent. Rather, she focused on orientation toward a person or toward an external object, and found that at first, a given interaction included only one of these, but that at about one year a coordination of person and object orientation in social interactions developed. This development was correlated with the emergence of speech, and Sugarman suggests that person-object integration in social interaction is a necessary but not sufficient condition for language emergence. This is an intriguing suggestion in light of Halliday's notion regarding the integration of the interpersonal and ideational functions in early speech as a prerequisite to development of true language. The disparity in age for the proposed integration (one year in Sugarman's study and 18 months in Halliday's) suggests, however, that the integration of person-object in prelinguistic communication does not lead directly to a similar integration in speech; rather, the development must be re-played at the language level. This is an example of what Piaget would call vertical decalage.

Sugarman's study repeats once more the common finding of alternative emphasis on the interpersonal and the ideational or object orientations in early communicative functions. It seems appropriate at this point, therefore, to mention Nelson's (1973) analysis, although it was primarily based on data quite different from the speech sampling techniques normally (and justifiably) employed in studies of language function. In this longitudinal study of 18 children, one of the central focuses was the vocabulary acquired (that is, used) up to the first 50 words for each child. What emerged from the content and form analyses of these vocabulary data were two emphases that came to be termed Expressive and Referential. That is, on the basis of what words the child learned to say first, one could distinguish related characteristics of language function and structure, not only at the same point in time, but 5 to 12 months later. This is a striking demonstration of two points: First, the interrelations of content, form, and function in the child's acquisition of language is clear. Here the claim is that the difference between children was apparent in the vocabulary data *because of* the difference in their speech functions. That is, what they learned to say was a function of the uses to which they put the language. Second, the robustness of the relationship between function and structure stands out in that structural differences related to the early functional differences were apparent in the children's use of syntax at both two and two and one-half years (Nelson, 1975a, b; 1976).

What is the nature of this relationship? The primary identifying characteristic of Referential children was the high proportion of object-referent words in their early vocabularies, but the Expressive children produced more social-expressive phrases (e.g., "thank you," "stop it") and action words. The contrast and its relation to other factors is probably most apparent in Table 2, which displays the first 10 word combinations produced by two children who represent extremes along the functional emphasis dimension. Here each phrase or sentence is classified according to its *possible* speech function, using Halliday's system. That is, the judgment was made as to whether an utterance of this type could be used for a given function,

Table 2. Comparison of first 10 word combinations between two children who represent different functional emphases.

First 10 word combinations	Possible language functions	Word classes	Semantic Relations
Child R (16 months)			
1. Daddy all gone	Informative or Heuristic	N. adj.	Ob—disappearance
2. Daddy shoe	Informative or Heuristic	N, N	Possessor-Ob possessed
3. Daddy milk	Informative or Heuristic	N, N	Possessn-Ob possessed
4. Mommy bite	Informative, Heuristic, or Regulatory	N, N	Agent-Ob of Action
5. Mommy cookie	Informative, Heuristic, or Regulatory	N, N	Agent-Ob of Action
6. Coat on	Personal, Heuristic, Instrumental, or Regulatory	N, prep.	Ob—Location
7. Meat bite	Informative or Regulatory	N, N	Modifier—Ob
8. Spoon milk	Informative or Heuristic	N, N	Ob—Location
9. Blanket dirt	Informative or Heuristic	N, N	Ob—Modifier
10. Coat wet	Informative or Heuristic	N, adj.	Ob—Modifier
Child E (16 months)			
1. I do	Regulatory or Personal	ProN, V	Agent-action
2. You do	Regulatory	ProN, V	Agent-action
3. I want it	Instrumental	ProN, ProN	Exper-State-Patient
4. I don't want it	Instrumental	ProN, neg-aux, V, ProN	Exper-State-Patient
5. Do it	Regulatory	V, ProN	Action-Ob of Action
6. Don't do it	Regulatory	Neg-aux, V, ProN	Action-Ob of Action
7. I love you	Interactive	ProN, V, ProN	Exper-State-Patient
8. I don't know	Interactive or Personal	ProN, neg-aux, V	Exper-State
9. What d'you want?	Interactive	Int, ProN, V	Exper-State
10. Go away	Regulatory	V, adv	Action-location

regardless of its actual use. As can be seen, Child E is restricted almost entirely to pragmatic functions by her expressions, although Child R could express (and probably is expressing) mathetic ones as well. The related differences between the two in terms of word classes (note particularly the use of pronouns by Child E and nouns by Child R, a difference that was characteristic of the entire group at age two as shown in Nelson, 1975b) and in case relationships in the different sentences is of interest. In particular, it seems that Child E's sentences have a more mature or complete formal structure, a finding that was borne out in the later group analysis, and that they express a wider variety of semantic relationships. Neither type could be termed more mature across all relations; however, the differences in function, content, form, and structure seem to be consistent and interrelated. Analysis of similar differences in the speech of preschool children and their mothers is currently under study by Baron (personal communication).

Analyses of the group data showed that these differences might well be a function of the type of communicative context within which the child's early language was acquired, a context that depends on social factors (for example, the presence of siblings) as well as on the cognitive or personality characteristics of the children and their parents. This finding points to the importance of studying early language in the context of the communication system as a whole.

The studies under review here have focused either on the characteristics of the mother's speech or on the characteristics of the child's speech, more or less independent of its social context. However, these analyses have revealed serious flaws, many of them inherent in the problem of trying to interpret objectively the child's intention. What the Speech Act analysis has shown is that interpreting the intent of the speaker is crucial to interpreting the message, prompting the question: is it possible to interpret the intent of the child speaker from analysis of the utterance and the observer's knowledge of the situation in which it was spoken? As Ryan (1974) has pointed out, an important aspect of the mother-child communicative system is interpretation by the adult of the child's intent, often with little or no support from the message itself. Indeed, one can view the prelinguistic period of mother-child interaction as a time for the establishment of a mutual intent-interpreting system. Something like this view has been proposed by Bruner (1975a, b; see discussion below). Thus, from the viewpoint of either understanding the functional context of the child's early speech, or understanding the child himself, it seems necessary to consider both speaker and listener within the same event frame of the communicative system.

The Communicative System

In her excellent analysis of the communicative context of early language development, Ryan (1974) notes four kinds of difficulty that adults experience when trying to understand young children, as follows:

> (1) difficulty due to the fact that the child makes noises with no speech-like characteristics at all, such that adults would not readily say she was even trying to speak, (2) difficulty due to the fact that the child's noises are not recognisably part of the adult vocabulary, but that she makes (utters) them in such a way that she would be described as

trying to speak, (3) difficulty due to the fact that a child utters a recognisable standard word but what she means by uttering it is unclear, (4) difficulty due to the unconventional reference with which a child uses a standard word. This categorization cuts across the more traditional descriptions of what a child has to learn prior to syntax, namely the sounds (phonology) and meanings (semantics) of words. What it adds are various features pertaining to the intentionality of the act in question: (1) whether the utterance of a particular noise is to count as an instance of communication at all, and what kind of an utterance it is to be understood as; (2) suggests that a child can be counted as speaking in the sense of meaning something even though the noises she makes do not have any conventional meaning; (3) that even when words with conventional meanings are used, there can still be a question as to what the child meant by uttering these words (pp. 206–207).

As Ryan points out, current studies of language development seldom take these problems into account, and she ends by noting:

> How inadequate it is to regard "communicative competence" as the application of linguistic skills to the prevailing social context. Any analysis of human communication must include a description of the structure of inter-subjectivity between participants in a dialogue . . . this intersubjectivity consists, at least in part, of the mutual recognition of certain kinds of intention . . . What is needed next is an analysis of the development of different forms of intentional behaviour in the child, combined with detailed descriptions of the preverbal dialogues and other reciprocal interchanges that adults and children participate in (p. 211).

It is precisely the latter type of exchange that has been the focus of Bruner's (1975a, b, 1976) studies of the development of communicative competence through the establishment of "the regulation of *joint* attention and *joint* activity within the mutuality between mother and infant." Bruner's work is unique in its focus on the establishment of mutual intentions through joint activity. Even those studies that have recognized the necessity of interpreting the child's speech in terms of actions and reactions of others (for example, Moerk, 1972; Nelson, 1973) have failed to see the advantage—indeed the necessity—of viewing the mother-child dyad as a unit. Bruner's analysis of the establishment of meaning within routinized patterns of activity has not yet progressed to the point of providing a taxonomy or a theory of development. Rather, he has shown how, when the child is between six months and a year, mothers "standardize" forms of joint action by "setting up standard action formats by which the child can be helped to interpret the mother's signals, her gestures, her intentions" (p. 12). One common example is what he calls an exchange routine, that leads the child to learn the appropriate order for such early speech forms as "kew" (for "thank you") and "look" or "there."

In concluding a recent discussion (1976) he states:

> Language acquisition occurs in the context of an "action dialogue" in which joint action is being undertaken by infant and adult. The joint enterprise sets the deictic limits that govern joint reference, determines the need for a referential taxonomy, establishes the need for signalling intent, and provides a context for the development of explicit prediction (p. 56).

A stronger version of his emerging theoretical stance is contained in the following passage:

The claim is that the child is grasping initially the requirements of joint action at a pre-linguistic level, learning to differentiate these into components, learning to recognize the function of utterances placed into these socially ordered structures, until finally he comes to substitute elements of a standard lexicon in place of the non-standard ones. The process is, of course, made possible by the presence of an interpreting adult who operates not so much as a corrector or reinforcer but rather as a provider, an expander and idealizer of utterances while interacting with the child. It is not imitation that is going on, but an extension of rules learned in action to the semantic sphere. Grammatical rules are learned by analogy with rules of action and attention (1975 b, pp. 17–18, *Journal of Child Language*. Reprinted by permission.).

In recent paper, Snow (1976) provided a somewhat similar analysis of the development of turn-taking in the "conversations" of two mothers and their babies, beginning at three months of age. She asserts that what mothers teach and children learn in the prelinguistic communication context is the function of their roles as conversational partners. Where Bruner stresses the referential and intentional aspects of these exchanges, Snow stresses the social. It is interesting that her analysis seems to conflict with Halliday's claim that it is not until late in the second year that the child masters the concept of dialogue, which launches him into mature language functioning. However, the implications of the two claims are not entirely clear, and it might be that Halliday's dialogue is but a later and more mature form of Snow's conversation.

In a recent paper, Dore (1976b) took issue with Bruner's interpretation of the relation between action or cognition and language, in which units of language are inserted into slots previously occupied by units of action. Grammar must be viewed as a fundamentally different system from action, Dore argued, and cannot be a simple extension of it. The continuity position has been carried too far, in his view, in the work of Bruner, as well as in that of Bates.

One point on Dore's side is that not all mothers are equally adept at establishing joint action routines, a fact that Bruner also recognized. He stated: "There is, of course, a great deal of variation in the attitudes of mothers toward their children's communicative intent, variation that produces considerable disparity in the manner in which mothers interact and talk with their young children" (1975a, p. 264). However, if mothers vary in their provision of the opportunities to establish interpretable routines, most children between one and two years do nonetheless begin to talk. It might be concluded that there are alternative routes into the language system, and that described by Bruner is one effective route, or it might be concluded that what it essentially provides is the context for establishing mutually interpretable *intent*. What is essential in the language learning context is the interpretation by the child of the intent of others (pointed out by Macnamara, 1972), as well as the interpretation of the child's intent by those with whom he is in communicative contact (the point made by Ryan, 1974). The joint activities described by Bruner are ideal in this regard, because through the establishment of well-understood routines, the intent of the pair is in a sense unitized and undifferentiated. Although the routine may provide for different roles (e.g., giver and taker), both participants share equally in their expectations of role behaviors. Sooner or later the child must begin to build out from this well-understood base to understand intent in less constrained situations and with less familiar persons. He may do this with or without language, but the formal language will obviously help. At the same time, his prelinguistic interpretive system will serve as a building block for his language learning.

Within this framework, we can begin to understand both the precursors of the dual emphasis (social and objective; interpersonal and ideational) so frequently noted in the literature, and the meaning of individual differences among children in their language learning.

INDIVIDUAL DIFFERENCES IN LANGUAGE LEARNING

In describing a language intervention curriculum, which emphasized the use of multiple language functions, Starr (1973) noted: "Some mothers found descriptive referential speech extremely difficult. This was clearly not the type of speech they addressed to a child" (p. 31). Similarly, Nelson (1973) found wide variation in both the content and the form of speech addressed by mothers to their children in a standardized play situation when children were between one and two years, and related these differences to the child's speech at age two. It is, of course, a well known finding that mothers of preschool children employ differential speech styles that have been associated with social class differences (Bernstein, 1970; Hess and Shipman, 1965). It is possible that these differences may operate on the child's language not so much through the model they provide as through the opportunity they give for establishment of the interpretation of intent of various kinds. Thus, mothers who talk primarily about the child's behavior provide a speech context in which pragmatic or expressive messages may be interpreted, and mothers who share activity and talk about objects and events of interest to the child may provide the opportunity to interpret the intent implicit in referential speech. Certainly the growing body of knowledge about pragmatics, when applied to the communicative context and function of both mother and child speech (as Bruner has begun to do with prelinguistic communication), should illuminate the differences found among children in both their rate and pattern of development. This work has hardly begun, although there are some interesting, and potentially relevant, studies beginning to emerge that utilize topic in children's discourse and the Speech Event which encompasses both speaker and listener.

The focus on communicative context and function thus provides a framework within which one can understand the implications of individual differences in language development. What must be learned about the language system is embedded in a communicative system that may be concerned with one or another speech function, but not with others. At the same time, the child may take on one or another role within a Speech Event, and may become proficient at one component of the Speech Act before another, as Dore (1975) has documented. Some communicative functions (e.g., regulatory, interpersonal) may not require linguistic expressions, but others (referential, informative) may require speech or some other symbolic formulation for their realization; this difference may be reflected in the child's rate of language acquisition. In such cases, one should be able to analyze the content and function of the child's linguistic communication to determine the functions that his nonverbal acts are serving and the potential for expanding the system.

Two points are important here. First, one need not take a position as strong as Hymes's in regard to the general dependence of language structure on its function to recognize that the acquisition of knowledge about language structure may in fact depend on the functions for which the beginning language is used. Concretely, a child who uses the language only instrumentally may learn and use the expression "I want it," and little more (Such a child was observed in the author's sample.) The pragmatic functions may be expressed not only nonverbally, but by relatively restricted verbal forms, as Table 2 shows. The full complexity of productive syntax—and even of reference—is necessary only for what Halliday calls the ideational functions. However, there is no logical developmental sequence implied in the functional analysis for language itself (although there may be for communication in general). It is possible for a child to begin using language forms for their mathetic or ideational functions while continuing to express the pragmatic or interpersonal functions nonverbally. In such a case, it is likely that both vocabulary and grammatical development will progress at a rapid rate, being necessary to the expression of the ideational content. This is in the author's opinion the significance of the progress made by the children termed Referential in the author's longitudinal study (Nelson, 1973; 1975a, b). Expressive children, on the other hand, translating their pragmatic functions directly into language forms, needed fewer syntactic expressions and less vocabulary to express what they wanted to say, and therefore took a different course of development.

The second point to be emphasized is implicit in the first. If the course of learning depends on what is present in the communicative context, one may expect to discover a number of different patterns of language development rather than a single developmental sequence of stages as heretofore sought. This may seem to threaten the notion of universals in development, but we merely need to refine that notion. We need to define major stages—for example, lack of productive speech and productive command of simple complete sentence forms—that are clearly identifiable. Rather than search for universal substages along the way from one major stage to the next, however, we need to analyze the component skills required, to determine which are logically precedent to the next, and which are not. For example, the production of single words is *not* logically precedent to word combinations, according to our current understanding of the structure of language, and indeed there are a few children who seem never to go through a "one-word" stage, just as there are children who do not crawl before they walk.

The analogy with walking is a revealing one. Standing logically precedes walking, just as walking logically precedes running. It would be surprising indeed to find the latter in the absence of the former. However, other forms of locomotion—creeping, crawling, sliding all bear a *functional* relation to walking, but are not logically precedent to it. We note the unusualness of the child who does not crawl before walking, but we do not view it as a violation of natural law. Rather we acknowledge that there are a number of possible courses of substages or transitions in motor development that all lead to the same end.

Our description of substages or transitions between major and universally observed points of development must allow for a number of different combinations of components that will be reflected in different patterns of transition. Only when one component is logically necessary to the development of another will an invariant sequence be observed.[1] However, communicative functions do not seem to present such a logical sequence, and therefore one may expect to observe considerable variation among parent-child dyads in their expression and, concomitantly, considerable variation in the acquisition of the linguistic forms to which they are related.

It is of extreme importance to the early detection of communicative deficits to understand the implications of individual differences in communicative expression. The point to be emphasized is that we can only understand those differences in terms of the functional and contextual variations in the social interaction environment.

Implications

The appropriateness of a pragmatic approach to the study of child language learning has led to its rapid and widespread application. Despite the selectiveness and incompleteness of this review, it is apparent that the approach has already been fruitful and promises to become more so. Let us document first the ways in which it has contributed thus far. What has been called "motherese"—the speech code used by mothers and other adults in talking to young children—has been revealed as functional within the speech event in which both mother and child are engaged. That is, its primary function seems to be to interpret and maintain the exchange. Its utility as a teaching mechanism has yet to be demonstrated convincingly, although it seems unwarranted to deny that it may have a facilitative effect on the child's acquisition of syntax, and there is some recent evidence that it does (K. E. Nelson, 1975; Newport et al., 1975). It would seem that the time for studying the characteristics of the code is past, but that its relation both to the maintenance of the communicative interaction and to the child's progress in language development deserve further study.

Analogous forms of the basic components of the Speech Act may be discerned in nonspeech forms in prelinguistic communications, as well as at different points in the development of speech itself. The most reasonable conclusion regarding these developments seems to be that communicative acts before the development of conventional language consist of analogous components that may develop more or less independently and may be transformed into grammatical expressions more or less independently of one another, before their integration into a complete speech act. Because the speech act depends on its interpretation by another of the intent expressed, this development should be viewed within the context of the Speech

---

[1] Brown, 1973, has been attempting to discover invariant sequences and relate them to underlying logical necessities in linguistic or cognitive development. It would seem that the opposite course of discovery—identifying the logical necessities first—would be easier in that it avoids the problems involved in inducing invariant sequences from limited data. This is in fact what Piaget has done so brilliantly. Unfortunately, however, others working from linguistic theory in syntax and semantics have fared less well.

Event, more or less equivalent to the conversation (Hymes, 1974), clearly including both speaker and listener. It will undoubtedly be found that, however degraded the child's first speech acts may seem when viewed alone, they are completed by the interpretation accorded them by the listener.

Relatedly, the functions served by early speech may vary individually, situationally, and developmentally. Because what is learned of linguistic structure depends on the functions expressed in speech, this variation leads to differences among children in the language they acquire. In addition, the kind of functions that will be expressed derive from the opportunities the child has for engaging in social interactive contexts that enable him to interpret the intentions of others. The acquisition of speech forms for expressing intent depends on such situations. Establishment of social games and interactive routines seems to be a particularly helpful route toward such interpretation and subsequent expression.

The major gap in the research surveyed here lies in our lack of an analytical framework for studying the speech event as a unit and relating it to questions of language development as well as to the child's concurrent, prior, and subsequent social and cognitive functioning. What is needed is an application of discourse analysis to the speech interactions of the child with others, beginning with its earliest manifestations. Given the current interest in such analyses for the speech of older children, as well as adults (e.g., Coulthard, 1977; Erving-Tripp and Mitchell-Kernan, 1977), it would seem to be a safe prediction that such studies will not be long in coming, if they are not already under way. It is hoped that they will be helpful in revealing not only the structure and function of the speech events themselves, but will also reveal the relationship of these events to the child's knowledge of the formal language system—that is, its grammar, phonology, and lexicon. The analysis of the acquisition of knowledge about rules governing speech events might well benefit from the application of the Frame Analysis of Goffman (1974) or its computer counterpart (Minsky, 1974). A similar suggestion has been made by Cook-Gumperz and Corsaro (unpublished), but the paucity of studies employing these notions with children of any age makes it difficult to make the suggestion more specific.

One factor that has received little or no attention here is the cognitive development of the child, which plays a large role throughout the period in which language is being acquired, as so many analysts have been at pains recently to point out (e.g., Bates et al., 1976; Bloom, 1973; Brown, 1973; Edwards, 1974; Nelson, 1974). The child's cognitive status undoubtedly interacts in important ways with other features of the communicative system, particularly the content and intent of the message, but quite possibly also the functions that the child wishes to express. These interactions have not been spelled out in the research reviewed, but it is hoped that future efforts will be fruitful in this respect (see Bates et al., 1976).

The implications of this study for knowledge relevant to the early identification of communicative deficits lies in two directions. First, what the child wants to say seems to be so intricately bound up with what he learns about the language, that the latter seems almost automatic given the former (cf. Cazden, 1974, for a similar argument). We must therefore distinguish carefully between specific *language* deficiencies appearing in children who seem to develop normal communicative functions, and more general *communication* deficits. Presumably, the two will have different etiologies and outcomes.

Second, it is important to keep in mind that the communication dyad is a system, and must be analyzed as such. Deficiencies may arise, particularly from the child's inability to interpret the message the other intends, but this in turn depends on the establishment of a system of interaction that makes these intentions clear. Many early deficiencies in learning the formal aspects of language may result from a learning context that lacks the provision for the exercise of different speech functions, which are in turn related to certain forms.

Finally, although the discussion has emphasized the mother-child pair throughout, one should be cautious about confining the analysis of social context in this way. It is a research and terminological convenience to talk about mother-child interaction, but so many others are—and ultimately must be—important to the establishment of the child's communicative competence, that their role should not be overlooked even at the beginning. Certainly the role of fathers and siblings should find more of a place in our analysis of the social interactions of infants than they now do.

REFERENCES

Austin, J. 1962. How to Do Things with Words. Oxford University Press, London.
Baldwin, A. L., and Frank, S. M. 1969. Syntactic complexity in mother-child interactions. Paper presented at the biennial meeting of SRCD, Santa Monica.
Bates, E. 1974. Acquisition of pragmatic competence. J. Child Lang. 1: 277–281.
Bates, E. 1976. Pragmatics and sociolinguistics in child language. In Morehead and Morehead (eds.), Language Deficiency in Children. University Park Press, Baltimore.
Bates, E., Benigni, L., Bretherton, I., Camaioni, L., and Volterna, V. 1976. From gesture to first word: On cognitive and social prerequisities. In M. Lewis and L. Rosenblum (eds.), Origins of Behavior: Communication and Language. Wiley and Sons, New York.
Bates, E., Camaioni, L., and Volterna, V. 1975. The acquisition of performatives prior to speech. Merrill-Palmer Quart. 21: 205–226.
Benedict, H. 1975. The role of repetition in early language comprehension. Paper presented at the biennial meeting of SRCD, Denver.
Berko-Gleason, J. 1973. Code switching in children's language. In T. Moore (ed.), Cognitive Development and the Acquisition of Language. Academic Press, New York.
Bernstein, B. 1970. A sociolinguistic approach to socialization: With some reference to educability. In F. Williams (ed.), Language and Poverty. Markham, Chicago.
Bloom, L. 1970. Language Development. MIT Press, Cambridge, Mass.
Bloom, L. 1973. One Word at a Time. Mouton, The Hague.
Broen, P. 1972. The verbal environment of the language learning child. Asha Monogr. 17.
Brown, R. 1973. A First Language—The Early Stages. Harvard University Press, Cambridge, Mass.
Brown, R., and Bellugi, U. 1964. Three processes in the child's acquisition of syntax. Harvard Educ. Rev. 34: 133–151.
Bruner, J. S. 1975a. From communication to language—a psychological perspective Cognition 3: 255–287.
Bruner, J. S. 1975b. The ontogenesis of speech acts. J. Child Lang. 2: 1–19.
Bruner, J. S. 1976. Learning how to do things with words. Paper presented at the Wolfson Lecture, Wolfson College, Oxford.

Campbell, D. T., and Stanley, J. C. 1963. Experimental and quasi-experimental designs for research in teaching. In N. L. Gage (ed.), Handbook of Research on Teaching. Rand McNally, Chicago.

Carter, A. 1974. Communication in the sensori-motor period. Unpublished doctoral dissertation, University of California, Berkeley.

Cazden, C. 1965. Environmental assistance to the child's acquisition of grammar. Unpublished doctoral dissertation, Harvard University, Cambridge.

Cazden, C. 1970. The neglected situation in child language research and education. In F. Williams (ed.), Language and Poverty. Markham, Chicago.

Cazden, C. 1974. Two paradoxes in the acquisition of language structure and function. In K. Connolly and J. Bruner (eds.), The Growth of Competence. Academic Press, London.

Chomsky, N. 1965. Aspects of a Theory of Syntax. MIT Press, Cambridge, Mass.

Cook-Gumperz, J., and Corsaro, W. A. Social-ecological constraints on children's communicative strategies. Unpublished paper.

Coulthard, M. 1977. An Introduction to Discourse Analysis. Longman Group Ltd., London.

de Laguna, G. 1963. Speech: Its Function and Development. Indiana University Press, Bloomington, Indiana.

Dore, J. 1974. A pragmatic description of early language development. J. Psycholinguist. Res. 3: 343–350.

Dore, J. 1975. Holophrases, speech acts and language universals. J. Child Lang. 2: 21–40.

Dore, J. 1976a. Children's illocutionary acts. In R. Freedle (ed.), Discourse Relations: Comprehension and Production. Lawrence Erlbaum Associates, New York.

Dore, J. 1976b. Conditions on the acquisition of speech acts. In I. Markova (ed.), The Social Context of Language. Wiley and Sons, New York.

Edwards, D. 1974. Sensory-motor intelligence and semantic relations in early child grammar. Cognition.

Ervin-Tripp, S. 1973. The structure of communicative choice. In S. Ervin-Tripp (ed.), Language Acquisition and Communicative Choice. Stanford University Press, Stanford.

Ervin-Tripp, S., and Mitchell-Kernan, C. (eds.). 1977. Child Discourse. Academic Press, New York.

Ferguson, C. A. Baby talking as a simplified register. In C. Snow and C. Ferguson (eds.), Talking to Children: Language Input and Acquisition. Cambridge University Press. Cambridge. In press.

Fillmore, C. 1968. The case for case. In E. Bach and E. T. Harmes (eds.), Universals in Linguistic Theory. Holt, Rinehart and Winston, New York.

Friedlander, B. Z., Jacobs, C. A., Davis, B. B., and Wetstone, H. S. 1972. Time-sampling analysis of infant's natural language environments in the home. Child Dev. 43: 730–740.

Garvey. ., Requests and responses in children's speech. J. Child Lang. 2: 41–63.

Glanzer, P. D., and Dodd, D. H. 1975. Developmental changes in the language spoken to children. Paper presented at the biennial meeting of SRCD, Denver.

Goffman, E. 1974. Frame Analysis. Harper, New York.

Greenfield, P., and Smith, J. H. Language Beyond Syntax: The Development of Semantic Structure. Academic Press, New York. In press.

Grice, H. 1975. Logic and Conversation. In P. Cole and J. Horgan (eds.), Syntax and Semantics. Academic Press, New York.

Gruber, J. 1973. Correlations between syntactic construction of the child and the adult. In C. Ferguson and D. Slobin (eds.), Studies in Child Language Development. Holt, Rinehart and Winston, New York.

Gruber, J. 1975. Performative—constative transition in child language. Found. Lang. 12: 513–521.

Halliday, M. 1973. Explorations in the Functions of Language. Edwin Arnold, London.

Halliday, M. 1975. Learning How to Mean. Edwin Arnold, London.

Hess, R. D., and Shipman, V. 1965. Early experiences and the socialization of cognitive modes in children. Child Dev. 36: 869–886.

Holzman, M. 1972. The use of interrogative forms in the verbal interaction of three mothers and their children. J. Psycholinguist. Res. 1: 311–336.

Hymes, D. 1974. Foundations in Sociolinguistics: An Ethnographic Approach. University of Pennsylvania Press, Philadelphia.

Ingram, D. 1971. Transitivity in child language. Language 47: 888–910.

Keenan, E. O. 1974. Evolving discourse—the next step. In Seventh Child Language Forum. Department of Linguistics, Stanford University, Stanford, California.

Keenan, E., and Schiefflin, B. T. 1976. Topic as a discourse notion: A study of topic in the conversation of children and adults. In C. Li (ed.), Subject and Topic. Academic Press, New York.

Labov, W. 1970. The logic of non-standard English. In F. Williams (ed.), Language and Poverty. Markham, Chicago.

Lord, C. 1975. Is talking to baby more than baby talk? A longitudinal study of the modification of linguistic input to young children. Paper presented at the biennial meeting of SRCD, Denver.

Macnamara, J. 1972. Cognitive basis of language learning in infants. Psychol. Rev. 79(1): 1–13.

McNeill, D. 1966. Developmental psycholinguistics. In F. Smith and G. Miller (eds.), The Genesis of Language. MIT Press, Cambridge, Mass.

Minsky, M. 1974. Frame systems. AI memo, Massachusetts Institute of Technology, Cambridge.

Moerk, E. 1972. Principles of interaction in language learning. Merrill-Palmer Quart. 118: 229–257.

Moerk, E. 1974. Change in verbal child-mother interactions with increasing language skill of the child. J. Psycholinguist. Res. 3: 101–116.

Nelson, K. 1973. Structure and strategy in learning to talk. Monogr. Soc. Res. Child Dev. Vol. 3, no. 149.

Nelson, K. 1974. Concept, word and sentence. Psychol. Rev. 81(4): 267–285.

Nelson, K. 1975a. Individual differences in early semantic and syntactic development. Ann. N.Y. Acad. Sci. 263: 132–139.

Nelson, K. 1975b. The nominal shift in semantic-syntactic development. Cog. Psychol. 7: 461–479.

Nelson, K. 1976. Some attributes of adjectives used by young children. Cognition 4: 13–30.

Nelson, K. E. 1975. Facilitating children's syntax acquisition. Unpublished manuscript.

Nelson, K. E., Carskaddon, G., and Bonvillian, J. D. 1973. Syntax acquisition: Impact of experimental variation in adult verbal interaction with the child. Child Dev. 44: 497–504.

Newport, E. 1976. Motherese: The speech of mothers to young children. In N. J. Castellan, D. B. Pisoni, and G. R. Potts (eds.), Cognitive Theory. Vol. II. Lawrence Earlbaum Associates, Hillsdale, N.J.

Newport, E. L., Gleitman, L. R., and Gleitman, H. 1975. Contributions to the theory of innate ideas from learning: A study of mothers' speech and child language acquisition. Paper presented at the biennial meeting of SRCD, Denver; The Stanford Child Language Forum, Stanford.

Newport, E. L., Gleitman, H., and Gleitman, L. R. 1976. Mother I'd rather do it myself: Some effects and non-effects of maternal speech style. Unpublished manuscript, March.

Phillips, J. R. 1973. Syntax and vocabulary of mothers' speech to young children: Age and sex comparisons. Child Dev. 44: 182–185.

Rescorla, L. 1976. Concept formation in word learning. Doctoral dissertation, Yale University, New Haven, Connecticut.

Ross, J. R. 1970. On declarative sentences. In R. A. Jacobs and P. S. Rosenbaum (eds.), Readings in English Transformational Grammar. Ginn, Waltham, Mass.

Ryan, J. 1974. Early language development: Towards a communicational analysis. In P. M. Richards (ed.), The Integration of a Child into a Social World. Cambridge University Press, Cambridge.

Searle, J. 1969. Speech Acts. Cambridge University Press, Cambridge.

Searle, J. 1974. Chomsky's revolution in linguistics. In G. Harman (ed.), On Noam Chomsky: Critical Essays. Anchor Press, Garden City, New York.

Seitz, S., and Stewart, C. 1975. Imitations and expansions: Some developmental aspects of mother-child communications. Dev. Psychol. 11: 763–768.

Shatz, M., and Gelman, R. 1973. The development of communication skills: Modifications in the speech of young children as a function of listener. Monogr. Soc. Res. Child Dev. Vol. 152(38), no. 5.

Skinner, B. F. 1957. Verbal Thought. Appleton, New York.

Slobin, D. I. 1973. Cognitive prerequisites for the development of grammar. In C. A. Ferguson and D. I. Slobin (eds.), Studies of Child Language Development. Holt, Rinehart and Winston, New York.

Snow, C. 1972. Mothers' speech to children learning language. Child Dev. 43: 549–565.

Snow, C. 1974. Mothers' speech research: An overview. Paper presented at the Conference on Language Input and Acquisition, September, Boston.

Snow, C. E. 1976. The development of conversation between mothers and babies. Unpublished manuscript.

Snow, C. E., Arlman-Rupp, A., Hassing, Y., Jobse, J., Joosten, J., and Vorster, J. 1976. Mothers' speech in three social classes. J. Psycholinguist. Res. 5: 1–20.

Soderbugh, R. 1974. The fruitful dialog, the child's acquisition of his first language: Implications for education at all stages. Project Child Language Syntax, reprint number 2. Institutionen for Nordiska sprak, Stockholms Universitet.

Starr, S. 1973. Language: The formation of discourse. Symposium presented at the biennial meeting of the International Society for the Study of Behavioral Development, August, Ann Arbor, Michigan.

Sugarman, S. 1973. A sequence for communication development in the pre-language child. Hampshire College honors thesis.

Sugarman-Bell, S. Some organizational aspects of preverbal communication. In I. Markova (ed.), The Social Context of Language. Wiley, London. In press.

Tanouye, E., Topic variation in mother-child discourse. Unpublished manuscript, Columbia University Teachers College, New York City.

Vorster, J. 1975. Mommy linguist: The case for motherese. Lingua 37: 281–312.

Discussion Summary: The Role of Pragmatics in Child Language Research

D. Kimbrough Oller

Most of the comments about child language at the conference seemed to center on the role of pragmatics in the study of child syntax and semantics. Linguistic pragmatics is the study of the influences—whether social, psychological, physical or logical—that determine the form language takes or that determine how language is learned. During the 1960s, child language researchers followed transformational linguists in the belief that the study of language should be limited to language structure and should ignore factors related to the "performance" of language events. "Performance," of course, implies pragmatic factors. In the 1970s, however, child language researchers looked outside of the structure of language and outside of the superficial manifestations of language acquisition (namely, the utterances that children produce). Instead, researchers have shifted focus toward the many nonlinguistic factors (or at least nonsyntactic factors) that may influence language acquisition.

This seems a healthy direction for child language research to take, but it is necessary for practical reasons to limit the kinds of pragmatic factors that are to be considered as possible influences on the acquisition of language. At present, linguistic pragmatics seems to be a Pandora's box that has been opened in order to solve certain semantic and generality problems, but that has introduced many new problems of definition and theoretical clarity. The ultimate success of the approach will surely depend on the extent to which pragmatic frameworks can be clearly defined, delimited, and thus brought under interpretive control.

FUNCTIONS OF LANGUAGE

One of the major pragmatic factors influencing the form of language, and its acquisition, concerns the functions that language may serve. Here, especially, there seems to be a need for delimitation and clarification of the theoretical directions that pragmatically oriented studies should take. In the paper by Nelson, a number of approaches to the study of speech acts and functions of language are reviewed. The reader of the paper may have been struck by the extent to which different authors have formulated differing categories of linguistic function. As pointed out in the paper by de Villiers and de Villiers, all of these approaches seem to cover a core of similar kinds of communicative functions. However, the proliferation of terminology and the overlapping of definitions both within and between the various authors is confusing.

Because of the concern that confusion in the various categorization frameworks may be limiting the possibilities of the pragmatic function approach, it is worthwhile to notice that an important feature is missing from all of the frameworks thus far proposed. The authors of the various pragmatic functional approaches have not given sufficient attention to natural, logical relationships between categories of communicative function. Although authors may speak of overlap between categories, there has been little attempt to take into account a natural hierarchy of communicative functions. In fact, Nelson suggests in this volume that communicative functions do not seem to present the sort of "logical sequence" that might entail a necessary order of appearance of functions in development. She claims, on the other hand, that standing, walking, and running do constitute such a logical sequence. Whether or not an individual child may walk or run before standing alone remains an empirical question, even if there is a logical relationship among standing, walking, and running. In a similar, although not identical, way, communicative functions are related to each other in a logical fashion that suggests a possible, but not certain, order of appearance of events in acquisition. The suggested order, if it occurs empirically, might be at least partially explained by the logical relationships. Whatever the empirical results turn out to be, they should interpreted at least partly in the light of these relationships.

Consider the following definitional framework: Among the class of all *acts* there is a subset that could be called *vocal acts*. In its simplest case, a vocal act might be a meaningless babble. Within the class of all vocal acts, there is a subset of *conventional vocal acts* that conform to the linguistic (phonological, syntactic, semantic) restrictions of some language. In other words, a conventional vocal act can be said to be an utterance of a particular language. In some cases, of course, such utterances may not be heard by anyone except the speaker. When, however, they are heard by another speaker of the language, they "communicate" meanings. It can be said, then, that within the class of conventional vocal acts, there is a subset of *communicative conventional vocal acts* (or informally, "communicative" acts). Often what is communicated between a speaker and a listener is not new information. It is possible to tell someone something that they already know. However, in many cases, perhaps in most, a communicative act can be said to be informative and to constitute an *informative communicative conventional vocal act* (or informally, an "informative" act). Although many informative acts do not require any physical response of the listener, there is a subset of informative acts that in fact constitute requests. This subset could be called *requesting informative communicative conventional vocal expressive acts* (or informally, "requests"). The formal definition of any function in this system includes all the underlined terms. The more terms needed to

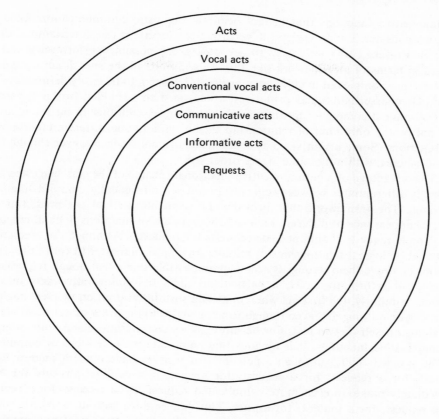

Figure 1.   Set-subset relationships among some functions in a theory of linguistic pragmatics.

define the function, the more embedded it is within sets, and the more steps required to derive it.

This hierarchical picture, represented in Figure 1, implies recursive properties. For example, within the class of requests there are further derivable subsets: requests for acts, requests for vocal acts, requests for conventional vocal acts, requests for communicative acts, requests for informative acts, requests for requests for acts, requests for requests for vocal acts, and so on, indefinitely. The framework, then, specifies an infinite number of different kinds of possible communicative functions of language. Given an ordered set of primitive terms (act, vocal, conventional, communicative, informative, requesting, etc.) and a recursive subset operation that specifies recombination of the primitives, assuming certain restrictions, every communicative function derivable within the system is related in a well-defined way to every other communicative function derivable within the system. Furthermore, a straightforward simplicity metric is implied: the more steps required in the derivation, the more complex the function.

The set of primitives suggested above is far from exhaustive of the kinds of communicative functions that in fact occur in linguistic communication. If, however, we consider a wide variety of performative functions (as, for example, those listed in Fraser, 1974) it is easy to see how every possible performative can be defined in terms of a framework like this. In addition, all the speech act categories that have been employed in child language research seem to be easily defined in such terms. Of course, additional primitives would need to be added to the system in order to make it complete.[1] Furthermore, the set-subset relationship suggested above may not be the only kind of relationship that occurs among different communicative functions. Some primitives may relate at equivalent set levels, even though they are all included within the same higher order sets.

The advantage of a communicative functional scheme of the sort suggested here is that it differentiates between logically primitive and logically complex linguistic functions. The framework thus provides a reasonable method for predicting the order of appearance of different kinds of communicative functions in child language (i.e., simple requests should precede requests for requests). Although the predictions are based on logical relationships, it remains an empirical matter to verify these predictions or prove them wrong. It seems quite possible that even though requests are a subset of informative acts, a particular child's first informative acts may be requests. Similarly, the first act wherein a child sustains himself on two feet could be a running or walking act, even though running and walking are a subset of all acts of sustaining oneself on two feet. Furthermore, as we consider more and more complex communicative functions, it is obvious that some intermediate steps of complexity can be skipped. Thus, although a person X may never have made a request$_1$ for a request$_2$ for a request$_3$ for a request$_4$ for an act, it should be possible for X to immediately make an even more complicated request$_1$ for a request$_2$ for a request$_3$ for a request$_4$ for a request$_5$ for an act. This can be done without going through a stage of producing the simpler request first. The interpretation of any empirical results will necessitate consideration of the logical relationships between different functions. If child language researchers could come to some basic agreement on what functional primitives to consider, it would be possible to largely overcome the problems inherent in proliferation of terminology and overlapping meanings of terms.

SOCIAL INTERACTION

Another kind of pragmatics study that is of current interest was also discussed in some detail at the conference and was treated especially in the papers by Ramey, Farran, Campbell, and Finkelstein and de Villiers and de Villiers. Studies of the interactions between parents and children have revealed a number of consistencies.

---

[1] Some relatively complex communicative functions seem to imply sociocultural markings on primitive functions. For example, a *command* can be reasonably characterized as a more elaborate or marked form of a *request*, i.e., command = request + social marking. The social marking specifies that the speaker bears a relationship to the listener that allows the speaker to require a response to the request. Eventually it may be important to describe in detail the sociocultural (or other) factors that might determine the nature of the set-subset relationship occurring between communicative functions.

Parents seem to speak to children in "simplified" language. In the conference discussion, Philip Dale reiterated that the importance of specialized speech to children is still uncertain. However, he went on to say, it seems a reasonable working assumption that the simplified forms of language presented to children by most parents may provide a basis upon which children can learn more easily. Clinicians may then be well-advised to present delayed learners with relatively simple linguistic inputs. Still, a number of conference participants expressed concern that studies of interactions between parents and children had not yet revealed clear-cut, long-term clinical implications.

Keith Scott pointed out a gap in the papers' reviews of the literature on parent/child interaction. He drew attention to the work of Klaus and Kennell (1976), which has indicated that there may be considerable importance to the interaction of parents and infants even in the first minutes of life. The research focuses, for instance, on the possibility that the communication and bonding processes that may occur when a mother first holds her child may have impact on the child's development. Furthermore, children who are not allowed to relate to their mothers in the first days of life because of medical problems may show detrimental social effects later. Joseph Fagan pointed out that these detrimental effects may actually have to do not so much with the child's lack of access to the mother as with the mother's lack of access to the child. Keith Scott further pointed out that there is a growing body of evidence that children with various physical and emotional handicaps may be treated by parents differently from normal children.

COGNITIVE STATUS

Another possibly important pragmatic influence on language acquisition is cognitive status of the child. The impact of Piaget's theory of cognitive development on studies of language acquisition in the 1970s in this country has been immense (see, for instance, the paper by Bowerman, this volume, for some discussion of studies in this area). However, Keith Moore criticized this literature for its relative lack of treatment of more modern work in child cognition. Students of child language acquisition have tended to accept Piagetian concepts and empirical views without adequately considering new views resulting from recent studies in developmental psychology. For example, our view of the nature of imitation in the first year of life is seriously altered by the very work Moore reports in this volume. Moore's point that the future of child language acquisition research will require a more active participation of developmental cognitive psychologists, in order to bring it up to date, is well taken.

ON SOCIOECONOMIC STATUS

Although there may be many other pragmatic factors that influence the development of language, conference participant Rita Naremore expressed concern that child language researchers may obscure the really important factors by considering correlated but noncausative factors. She expressed particular concern about the use of socioeconomic status as a variable in language acquisition research. Her contention was that even though a correlation between language acquisition and socioeconomic status might be established, such a correlation would not indicate a unique relationship between socioeconomic status and language acquisition. Naremore suggested that a number of other variables (e.g., nutrition, emotional stability, parental communication skills, etc.) were far more likely to explain variations in language acquisition, and that they were perhaps in an indirect way associated with socioeconomic status. Ramey, whose paper with Farran, Campbell, and Finkelstein reviewed a number of articles in which a socioeconomic variable had been correlated with language acquisition, expressed agreement with Naremore's comments.

THE FUTURE OF PRAGMATIC STUDIES IN CHILD LANGUAGE

Participants in the conference expressed considerable optimism that the study of child language will make substantial progress in coming years. Discussants seemed to think that the direction such research will take will be heavily influenced by the pragmatic approach. Jill de Villiers raised what seems to be an important long-term problem that must be dealt with in coming years if child language research is to progress. She pointed out that all of our syntactic, semantic, and pragmatic treatments of child utterances depend on an interpretation of the child's intent and that, unfortunately, there are meager methods available to justify particular interpretations. She argued that development of systematic procedures whereby interpretations of utterances might be given relative justification when compared with possible alternative interpretations should be a major concern for the future.

The study of methods of interpreting child utterances bears a substantial relationship to pragmatic approaches in child language research. For example, in order to interpret a child's utterance, it is necessary to consider information about the interaction in which the utterance occurs, including aspects of the verbal discourse as well as nonverbal communicative factors (e.g., whether or not the child has eye contact with the listener or speaker, whether or not gestures are involved, whether or not the child repeats himself until some satisfaction is given, and so on). In addition, the child's cognitive status should be considered in interpretation of utterances. A systematic treatment of these kinds of pragmatic factors may help us to provide some sort of index that compares the relative plausibility of various possible interpretations for a particular child utterance. The fact that most child utterances have multiple possible interpretations is an inherent problem in studying the acquisition of any communicative system. To fail to deal with that problem is to fail to advance the science.

REFERENCES

Klaus, M. H., and Kennell, J. H. 1976. Maternal-Infant Bonding: The Impact of Early Separation or Loss on Family Development. C. V. Mosby Co., St. Louis.
Fraser, Bruce. 1974. A partial analysis of vernacular performative verbs. In R. Shuy and C. J. Bailey (eds.), Toward Tomorrow's Linguistics. Georgetown University Press, Washington, D.C.

IMPLICATIONS FOR INTERVENTION

Interaction of Assessment and Intervention— Hearing Impairment

Edgar L. Lowell
Marilyn O. Lowell

This chapter considers the interaction of assessment and intervention for the young hearing impaired child. Interaction here refers to the interchange of information between assessors and intervenors with the goal of improving the quality of the intervention. This is a desirable process that reaches its highest form in a "diagnostic teaching" situation, where a multidisciplinary assessment team has continuing interaction with the intervenors until all possible questions concerning evaluation and intervention have been resolved. Understandably, this is an expensive procedure that is rarely available. The more typical situation for the young hearing impaired child (without other major handicaps) is that he is referred to the educator of the deaf with an audiologic assessment, some general medical information, and very little else. Between these two extremes should be a middle ground based on a cost/effectiveness evaluation of both assessment and intervention procedures. Although it is difficult to reduce help for the handicapped to economics, services ultimately must be paid for, and the cost may determine how much is provided. This is a problem that deserves further consideration.

Currently, interaction is most likely to occur when the teacher questions the audiologic findings or encounters some difficulty in dealing with the child and seeks additional assessment information. This may result in valuable interaction, but it depends for its success on the ability of the teacher and the assessors to communicate, and the availability of the necessary additional assessment services. It would be desirable if more comprehensive assessment and more opportunity for interaction could be routinely programmed into our service delivery system before, rather than after, the fact.

Some insights into the climate in which such interaction takes place can be obtained from a survey of audiologists and educators of the deaf conducted by the Joint Committee on Audiology and Education of the Deaf (ASHA-CEASD)

(Ventry, 1965). At that time, 115 of the educational facilities surveyed reported employing no audiologist; there were only 45 that did. There was a general consensus on the part of both educators of the deaf and audiologists that too little emphasis on their field was contained in the other group's training program. That is, both directors of education of the deaf training programs and audiology training programs were in agreement that too little emphasis on education of the deaf was contained in audiology training programs, and that similarly, there was too little emphasis on audiology in education of the deaf training programs. With this background, it was not surprising that when teachers and audiologists were asked their opinion about interprofessional relationships, 75% of the audiologists and 54% of the teachers rated relationships as only fair or poor.

It must be kept in mind that this study was conducted more than 10 years ago, and even at that time both audiologists (74%) and teachers (79%) felt that interprofessional relationships had improved over the years. It may be expected that this trend has continued.

This paper deals with some of the problems that may account for the lack of interaction between assessment and intervention, and suggests some of the research that might improve this situation. The chapter is divided into three sections: Assessment, Early Intervention Procedures, and Research Needs.

ASSESSMENT

Identification

A prior condition to assessment is the identification or location of the potentially hearing impaired child. This selection is necessary because assessment procedures are too time-consuming and costly to be administered to all infants.

There have been two major approaches to identification—Newborn Infant Screening and the High Risk Register. They are described elsewhere in this volume (Wilson). Neither, used alone, has proved entirely satisfactory for widespread use.

Identification seems to be difficult because there are no visible stigmas associated with deafness, and the hearing impaired infant's behavior is apt to be very similar to that of a normal hearing infant. Yet the problem does not lie in the inherent difficulty of the task. For example, a mother who has one hearing impaired child will generally know whether her subsequent newborn has a hearing problem before they leave the hospital. What is needed is a greater awareness on the part of the health and health related service personnel to the importance of early identification. When they are alerted to the possibility of a hearing loss, as was the case following the 1964–1965 rubella epidemic, the age at which infants were referred for testing because of suspected learning loss dropped dramatically. After the epidemic, as the likelihood of rubella related hearing loss decreased, the age of referral increased again. We need a serious and continuing effort to keep early identification concerns on the list of neonatal procedures. Lloyd's (1976) suggestion for including hearing screening along with the infant immunization program is an interesting possibility.

Hearing Assessment

The work on early auditory assessment is also reviewed elsewhere in this volume (Wilson). It is well to keep in mind the lag between research studies and clinical application. As Wilson reports, considerable progress is being made in sophisticated auditory assessment of infants, yet it is unrealistic to expect that these procedures will be rapidly adopted on a widespread clinical basis. This may be in part because the research reports on new hearing assessment procedures generally do not provide sufficient detail to allow the clinician to feel comfortable applying the new procedure. This is clearly an area that deserves attention.

In addition to the behavioral assessment procedures, there are respondent or electrophysiologic techniques for evaluating infant hearing. Although not directly related to the topic of this conference, they are of interest, because when they are used in a battery with behavioral assessment measures, they contribute to the confidence we can place in our evaluations.

One of these is evoked response audiometry (ERA). This procedure includes the computer analysis of electrical activity of the brain (EEG) in response to repeated auditory stimulation (Lowell, 1961; Reneau and Hnatiow, 1975). The computer averages the electrical activity that tends to enhance the response to auditory stimulation and cancels out that which is not. It yields a response that is close to threshold.

In a study of the reliability of this procedure (Lowell, Lowell, and Goodhill, 1975), 129 infants with a median age of 12 months were tested using the ERA, and retested at six-month intervals until they were able to be tested by behavioral audiologic procedures. All children were referred because of suspected hearing problems and difficulty in testing by other means. All test-retest correlations between six-month testings were statistically significant, but tended to be higher as the group became older. The same was true of the correlations between evoked response auditory tests and behavioral tests. The correlation between the behavioral testing and the first ERA test was 0.71, 0.90 for the six-month ERA test, and 0.93 for the 12-month ERA test. Another way of viewing the agreement between the last ERA test and the behavioral results is shown in Figure 1. Although 80% of the cases were within ± 20 dB of the behavioral thresholds, 16 cases differed by more than 20 dB. This is an obvious limitation in planning intervention. The average disagreement between the two test procedures was 13 dB, with a range of 0 to 50 dB. In summary, although the test-retest reliability correlations are satisfactory, the validity of the procedure when evaluated against traditional behavioral audiometry leaves a great deal to be desired.

There are numerous variations on this technique, so that the general field is now frequently referred to by the same initials, ERA, for electrical response audiometry. Among these related techniques are "brain stem electric responses" (BSER), "far field responses," and "electrocochleogram" (ECochG) (Davis, 1976). These vary in detail depending on the placement of the electrodes and the period of the electrical response that the computer analyzes. Some involve invasive procedures (where an incision is made in the tympanic membrane in order to place the electrode in the

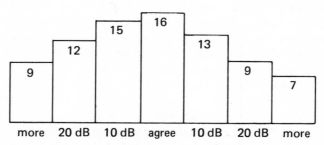

Figure 1.   Agreement between behavioral audiogram and last ERA test (500 Hz).

middle ear). Some involve sedation or anesthesia with children. Still others yield responses only at suprathreshold levels. In general, these newer procedures have not been tried extensively with retarded and other developmentally disabled people. They have some serious limitations, but they do offer considerable promise for the future.

Impedance audiometry is a relatively new clinical test in the audiologic battery (Jerger, 1975). It consists of tympanometry, static compliance, and acoustic reflex tests as revealed by movement of the ear drum. It involves placement of a probe in the external ear with a tight seal. The probe is connected to a bridge that permits measurements of the flexibility of the ear drum, compliance of the middle ear mechanism, and the stapedial reflex during auditory stimulation. These tests as a group provide information regarding the integrity of the peripheral auditory mechanism. They have application to the evaluation of young children, but require that the child be cooperative and not crying. Although this technique has become a useful tool with adult subjects, there has been some controversy over the reliability of its use with infants and children.

Keith (1975) tested 20 babies ranging in age from two and one-half to 20 hours. His results revealed that the impedance data was identical to that obtained on babies over 36 hours of age and similar to older children with normal middle ear function. The babies were examined by an ENT specialist one hour before testing, and ear canals were suctioned. It is Keith's belief that, as a general rule, the middle ear of infants is not completely "filled with mesenchymal tissue at birth and that it does not take a few days for this tissue to be resorbed."

Wilson, Lloyd, Decker, and Moore (1974) found tympanometry to be useful with almost all infants, but they differ from Keith somewhat. Although Keith reported that his tympanogram results could be compared with normative data on older children, these authors have found greater variation in the range of compliance. They suggest a slightly expanded range in translating clinical case results.

Limitation of Auditory Test Results

One of the problems of audiologic assessment of the very young child is that we frequently expect too much from it. We believe that an early hearing loss will lead to impaired communication skills, but it does not follow that we can predict the development of language and speech behavior from the audiologic assessment. Hearing test results alone do not provide enough information to plan a meaningful intervention program, but it is often the major data the clinician has to work with. There are so many other variables, including intelligence, time intervention initiated, amount of intervention, and the language environment the child is raised in, that enter into the determination of language and speech development, but they are often more difficult to quantify.

It is fortunate that the current interest in behavioral assessment of auditory functioning shows promise of providing information on the infant's ability to process and integrate sound that may ultimately be more useful in planning intervention strategies.

Special Problems

The discussion so far has assumed an infant with a hearing impairment and no other major problems. There are many multiply handicapped infants for whom accurate auditory assessment is extremely difficult. For these children, continuing differential diagnostic work is required if a meaningful assessment is ever to be attained. In a volume such as this, and in light of recent judicial and legislative interest in the care of the severely and multiply handicapped, this group would seem to deserve special attention. Perhaps more than any other group, they require continuing interaction between the assessors and the intervenors.

Another group who present special problems in early assessment are those children variously labeled as "problems of selective attention," aphasia, central deafness, hemispheric asymmetry, etc. These terms describe an unresponsiveness to acoustic stimuli, but they may ultimately be determined to involve peripheral auditory dysfunction.

Other Types of Assessment Needed to Facilitate Intervention

Visual Assessment   Because the deaf must rely on vision as a major avenue of communication, their visual functioning assumes unique importance. The difficulties of assessing the hearing of an infant generally result in referral to a center that specializes in the assessment of hearing. Such centers frequently do not have personnel and facilities required for visual assessment.

Studies by Jensema and Mullins (1974), Myklebust and Lawson (1970), and Pollard and Neumaier (1974) have documented the fact that hearing impaired students have more vision defects than hearing students. A review of the literature by Pollard and Neumaier (1974), covering seven studies between 1933 and 1971, indicated "that among deaf school-age students, 40 to 60 percent have ocular defects." Similar studies on hearing students show only 20–30% with ocular defects.

Intellectual Assessment   If assessment reveals that a young child does have a hearing problem, the next consideration in planning an intervention program is whether the child has any intellectual advantages or deficits. The general topic is covered by Horowitz and Dunn (this volume).

The limitations of standardized intellectual assessment instruments with young deaf children is well known. Smith (1960) analyzed the standardization data on instruments most frequently used in the evaluation of preschool children suspected of hearing loss. These include:

Pintner-Paterson Scale of Performance Tests
Arthur Point Scale of Performance Tests, Forms I, II
Randall's Island Performance Series, Schick Lane Alteration
Ontario School Ability Examination
Nebraska Test of Learning Aptitude
Leiter International Performance Scale
Arthur Adaption of the Leiter

Smith found that there are serious gaps in the norming populations. "Extrapolated norms" are the rule. Children, ages two and three, seem to be almost absent from most of the standardizing populations. Only the Randall's Island and Leiter had children under four years of age in the norming group.

Smith (1976) has attempted to overcome some of these problems by selecting performance subtests from the various standardized instruments and renorming them on a large population of hearing impaired children. Mindel and Vernon (1971) have reviewed a number of I.Q. tests used with hearing impaired, although only a few were used with young children.

Assessment of Communication Behavior   It has been anticipated that the great interest on the part of linguists in early language and speech development would begin to have some implications for those concerned with intervention, particularly for the clinician working with the hearing impaired infant. Some estimate of the extent of interaction between assessment and intervention in the language and speech area can be obtained by reading Katherine Nelson's excellent chapter on "Early Speech in its Communicative Context" (this volume). The studies described seem to be concerned more with an understanding of communication development than with the development of assessment tools. This is a true reflection of the state of the art, and it may further explain the low level of interaction between assessment and intervention.

The attempt has been made to use the concept of Performatives (as described in detail by Nelson, this volume) in studying the communicative behavior of young hearing impaired children (Curtiss, 1976; Lowell and Rouin, 1975). Although the children in the author's study were older than infants, they were still in the beginning stages of speech development. The authors' work was originally based on the work of Austin (1962) and Bates, Camaioni, and Volterra (1975). Videotape recorded samples of deaf children's communicative behavior were scored by multiple observers for both pragmatic and semantic categories that have been developed by many other investigators:

Pragmatic categories	Semantic categories
demand	performative
command	locate/name
question	volitional object
labeling	agent
response to a question	action or state of an agent
response to a summons	action or state of an object
response to a command	object
imitation	dative
imitation—repetition	object associated with another
summons	object or location
description	possession
protesting	locative
ritual	aspect (of an event)
request for approval	negation
request for confirmation	
or acknowledgment	
acknowledgment	

Videotaping the context in which the communication takes place and using multiple scorers helps somewhat with the interpretation of the intentions underlying the children's speech acts. Preliminary findings show a consistent increase in the number of communicative acts per minute with age (from two to four). Hearing impaired children in this age range show well-developed pragmatic communicative abilities (according to the categories used in this study), except that the two-year-olds do little "labeling." The three- and four-year-olds show well-developed semantic communicative ability.

Although it is early to judge the ultimate value of this line of inquiry, it seems to offer new insights into the order in which prelinguistic categories are acquired, which in turn has implications for the type of intervention that might ultimately be recommended; that is, it may be appropriate to "teach" the hearing impaired child the linguistic symbols for concepts that he already has rather than those concepts selected by the teacher or parents.

Another type of assessment that may ultimately have implications for intervention in the communication field is the assessment of mother-child interaction. A pilot study (Kenady and Proctor, 1968) analyzed interaction between 220 hearing impaired children with a median age of 4.2 years of age and their mothers, and a control group of 20 normal hearing children with a median age of 3.7 years and their mothers. The interaction was analyzed using Bales's Interaction Process Analysis Categories (Bales, 1951).

Kenady and Proctor's results show that there is a significant difference between the language used by mothers of deaf children and the mothers of hearing children:

It was found that mothers of deaf children do not give praise or show agreement as much as mothers of hearing children. These mothers also were found to give a greater number of suggestions. In addition, mothers of deaf children showed more antagonism than mothers of hearing children.

On the other hand, mothers of hearing children showed more solidarity and agreement than mothers of deaf children. They also asked their hearing children for more information and opinions.

An analysis of the amount of time spent talking showed that there was a significant difference between the two groups, with mothers of deaf children talking less than mothers of hearing children.

These differences might account for some of the variations between deaf and hearing language development and its related unique social outlook. If this is true and these psycho-social variations are undesirable, then these language category differences might be taken into consideration when planning educational programs for parents of the deaf and for their children (Bales, 1951).

It would be highly desirable to replicate this research with even younger children.

EARLY INTERVENTION PROCEDURES

Intervention with Hearing Impaired Children

When one considers the foregoing description of the problems of early assessment of the hearing impaired child, it is not surprising that the interaction between assessment and intervention leaves something to be desired. The problems do not end with assessment. There is no consensus on the most desirable type of intervention. The major difference is over communication methodology; that is, oral versus manual communication, and there is little solid research upon which decisions can be based.

Studies of early intervention with hearing impaired children are limited in number because deafness is not always discovered in infancy. The studies that have been done generally suffer from the fact that it is difficult to evaluate the effect of intervention when the child is still very young because our assessment procedures have been so crude, and we have not always made maximum use of those that were available. The common solution is to test the child when he is older and can complete some of the standardized instruments. The problem here is that there are so many uncontrolled intervening educational experiences that might affect the results (Craig, 1964; Phillips, 1963).

Another problem is that some studies of young deaf children are based on small samples, where the dangers of generalizing are well known. For example, a study by Vernon and Koh (1970) compared oral and manual education for young deaf children. Three groups of 23 students were selected; one group were graduates of the John Tracy Preschool Program, one group had deaf parents and no preschool, and the third group had hearing parents and no preschool. They were matched on age and IQ. When these groups were 18 years of age and attending the California State School for the Deaf at Riverside (CSDR), California, they were administered various subtests of the Stanford Achievement Test. Vernon and Koh concluded that the group of deaf children with early manual communication and no preschool were far ahead of the group who had three years of oral preschool experience at John Tracy Clinic, and whose family had had counseling. Deaf children with no early manual communication and no preschool were far below the early manual group, and not significantly below the Tracy Sample.

The fallacy of dealing with small samples when there are so many intervening variables is demonstrated by a follow-up study by Balow and Brill (1975). Dr. Brill is Superintendent of the California School for the Deaf at Riverside, where Dr. Vernon obtained his data on 23 John Tracy Clinic children. Dr. Brill studied *all* of the Tracy Clinic graduates who attended the California School for the Deaf, not a sample of 23. There were 264 children and their families who had some association with the Clinic. They were compared on the Stanford Achievement Test with other California School for the Deaf graduates who had not received the Clinic's services. Of the 590 students who graduated from CSDR from 1956 through 1970, the 264 who had themselves participated in, or whose parents had participated in, the John Tracy Clinic programs, scored significantly higher on (Wechsler Adult Intelligence Scale), and significantly higher on the total battery Stanford Achievement Test score. An analysis of covariance showed that a significant difference remained when the effects of IQ were controlled.

With these limitations in mind, there are other studies of early intervention that are of interest. In one study (Lowell, 1967), hearing impaired children between the ages of one year, seven months and three years, eight months were followed during an intervention program that involved instruction for the mother and child in a homelike setting, in the belief that such training in language development and auditory training would have greater carry-over to the actual home situation than instruction offered in a classroom. Although this was primarily a demonstration project, modified Boone (1965) scales of linguistic encoding and decoding behavior showed significant gains for two groups of 24 and 28 children over a three and one-half month period. Two control groups that were enrolled in a traditional nursery school program did not show a significant improvement, although these children were older than the experimental groups. Questionnaires designed to assess parent information showed significant increases for parents in both experimental groups and for one of the control groups. Despite the limitations of the research design and measuring instruments used in this demonstration project, it suggests the direction that future research might follow.

Although there is general agreement that early intervention is important for the hearing impaired child, there have been no definitive studies of how early the intervention should begin. Greenstein, Greenstein, McConville, and Stellini (1976) conducted a study to test for a "critical" period at the Lexington School for the Deaf—Infant Center:

> Thirty deaf children admitted to an auditory training program during the first two years of life were studied longitudinally to age 40 months. Those admitted prior to 16 months of age were found to show greater language competence. Children with better language skills looked more at their mothers at age two and their mothers were found to be less coercive and more accepting and sensitive to the child. Affective aspects of mother-infant interaction were more highly correlated with the child's language acquisition than were technical aspects of the mother's language. The results suggest a reciprocal interaction among maternal acceptance of the child, early intervention, and the child's language acquisition. Differences among hearing mothers, and between the deaf and hearing, suggest that there may be a normal flow of verbal and nonverbal communication with the child which is essential to language acquisition. The mother's discovery of her child's handicap may drastically disrupt this flow and the role of early intervention programs should be to facilitate its resumption.

Generalizations concerning the critical period are limited by the sample size. "Collection of more data on children, particularly from hearing homes, who are aided before 16 months of age might isolate the age period, if one exists, during which intervention is maximally effective" (Greenstein et al., 1976).

Jew (1974) reported an intervention program with 90 families of handicapped children over a three-year period. The handicaps included aurally handicapped, orthopedically handicapped, mentally retarded, and environmentally deprived children. Before 18 months, infants were visited weekly in the home by clinicians, who offered supportive help and training to the parents and developmental training for the child. Parents were given suggestions for stimulating their child and were helped to develop realistic expectation. After 18 months, the children were bused five mornings a week to a school where they received individual therapy and participated in small group activities. The children made significant developmental gains in all four areas measured by the Denver Developmental Screening Test (Frankenburg and Dodds, 1967).

McConnell and Liff (1975) describe a study of six hearing impaired children whose parents had been enrolled in an early intervention program before the children were three years of age, compared with a group of five hearing impaired children whose parents had not been enrolled in such a program, and six children with normal hearing who were enrolled in the same regular first grade class as the two experimental groups, when all were approximately seven years, six months of age. Analysis of 50 spontaneous language samples showed that the Early Intervention group was significantly different from the Late Intervention group, but not significantly different from the Normal Hearing group on performance as measured by Lee's Developmental Sentence Types (Lee, 1966).

In addition to the traditional intervention procedures, there is considerable activity in developing devices (in addition to auditory amplification) to assist the hearing impaired. These involve primarily transmission of information by visual and vibro-tactile devices (Lowell, 1973; National Academy on Engineering, 1970; Nickerson, Kalikow and Stevens, 1976; Pickett, 1968). Some indications of the difficulties inherent in substituting visual for auditory information are provided by Liberman, Cooper, Shankweiler, and Studdert-Kennedy (1968).

There are also surgical procedures (House, 1976) that attempt to substitute an electronic device for the damaged cochlea. This involves implanting microelectrodes into the cochlea and stimulating the cochlea electrically from an external device. The problem here is that we are not certain what kind of information should be sent to the cochlea, because we do not completely understand how the ear encodes auditory signals for transmission to the brain. Although this approach offers great hope for the future, it is at present a limited experimental procedure.

Intervention With Hearing Children

In view of the limited number of studies on early intervention with hearing impaired children it may be fruitful to explore some of the studies of infant intervention with hearing children for possible application.

One of the most important aspects of early childhood education is the mother-child relationship. Ringler, Kennell, Jarvella, Novojosky, and Klaus (1975) studied the effect of mother-child postnatal contact on later linguistic behavior. Mothers who had extended contact with their infant in the first three days after delivery, when compared with a control group of mothers who did not have early contact, stated that they:

1. Picked up their babies more frequently in response to crying
2. Had a greater tendency to stay home with their infants
3. Were observed to be more comforting in stressful office visits
4. Showed more fondling and increased eye-to-eye contact during filmed feedings.

The fourth item might be the most important in the event the infant was later diagnosed as hearing impaired.

At age one, the patterns of speech used by the two groups of mothers (extended contact and control) differed in only one respect: the extended contact group used fewer statements than the control group.

At two years, the number of differences increased. The extended contact mothers used fewer content words and more adjectives in communication with their children than did mothers in the control group. They also asked more questions, expressed fewer commands, and used more words per proposition than did the control group mothers. The authors concluded that by allowing a mother a few additional hours after birth with her child, she seems more sensitive to the child's needs, and she attempts to widen the child's external environment as the child matures. For the hearing impaired, developmentally disabled child, this may be of benefit in providing additional assistance in developing communication skills (see also Nelson, this volume).

In an attempt to provide descriptive information about the relationship between interpersonal distances and vocal behavior of mothers and infants, Strain, Vietze, and Dokecki (1975) studied 24 three-month-old infants. Data was collected via an electronic digital recorder. Observations of mother-child interactions were collected in the home situation. Although summed data regarding the amount of infant vocalizations were not significantly different in the mother-present versus the mother-absent condition, there was significantly more infant vocal activity when the mother was out of the infant's room than when the infant was held by the mother.

Second, the infants vocalized more often when mothers were within arm's reach but not holding the baby, than when they were more than three feet from the infant but still in the room. Also, infants vocalized significantly more when mothers were within arm's reach but not holding the baby than when being held by the mother. The authors suggest that "a more detailed, sequential analysis of the infant behaviors immediately antecedent and consequent to being picked up" will help to establish the effect of holding an infant on vocal responsiveness, as well as to determine infant responses which elicit maternal holding.

Lowell (1968) investigated the use of a home language stimulation correspondence course with mothers of young hearing infants. Although this study did not measure effects of the program on the infants, it does suggest something about the wide variety of intervention techniques that are available. The major goals of the program were to:

1. Be supportive and reduce any anxiety or concern the parents might have about their child
2. Provide knowledge of infant and early childhood development
3. Give knowledge of early language and speech development
4. Give knowledge of the expressive and receptive communication process
5. Plan for language enrichment or stimulation.

The service reached 623 mothers of six-month-old infants who had not been diagnosed as handicapped. In analyzing success or failure of the mother to continue twelve monthly installments, the investigators determined that 1) more education of the mother, 2) fewer children in the home, and 3) higher birth weight of the child were associated with successful completion of the program. A test about general child development and language development was administered to a control group, as well as the experimental population. The mothers who participated in the course scored significantly higher than the control group.

Use of Amplification in Early Intervention

Almost all forms of intervention for the hearing impaired involve the use of residual hearing with amplification. It was pointed out earlier that it is difficult to test very young hearing impaired children, and consequently it is difficult to make appropriate hearing aid recommendation. One danger is that excessive amplification may damage the existing residual hearing. The facts relating to noise-induced hearing loss are well established.

Kinney (1961) showed concern about the fitting of "powerful hearing aids" on children. In a study of 126 children fitted with "powerful aids," five showed an increased loss of 10 dB on the average in the ear using the hearing aid, eight showed a 20 dB increase in hearing impairment, four showed an increased loss in the ear not wearing the aid, and 109 showed no change of hearing status. Of the 52 cases who had demonstrated a decrement in hearing, 39 used unilateral amplification—of these, 19 (48.8%) showed an increased loss of 20 dB in the aided ear. Thirteen of the 52 used binaural amplification. Of these, nine showed a 25 dB increased loss bilaterally. Kinney's results raise the question of how much loss of hearing is the result of amplification and how much is the result of degenerative deafness that would have resulted in lost hearing without the use of amplification.

Several case studies have also reported the deterioration of hearing in patients using a hearing aid (see Harford and Markle, 1955; Kasten and Braunlin, 1970; Roberts, 1970).

Other investigators have not been in complete agreement. Naunton (1957) reviewed charts of 120 hearing impaired patients who were fitted monaurally, and compared thresholds of the aided ear versus the nonaided ear. He concluded that the changes caused by hearing aid use were not significant.

Macrae and Farrant (1965), Northern and Downs (1974), and Ross and Lerman (1967) are in agreement that caution should be used in recommending maximal power output hearing aids for children. Regardless of the gain employed, good audiologic management should include periodic reassessment of hearing status and a check on the function of the hearing. The possibility of damage emphasizes the importance of this part of the intervention process. Despite the fact that these studies were not carried out with infants, the question of possible damage from amplification cannot be ignored.

Another problem in providing appropriate amplification is that, until recently, the equipment required to evaluate the performance of an individual hearing aid was so expensive that it was not widely available. This meant that it was difficult to tell whether a hearing aid was functioning appropriately unless there was gross malfunctioning. Fortunately, hearing aid calibration equipment is now much more widely available at a more reasonable cost. This should result in improved use of amplification for the young hearing impaired child.

Still another possible explanation for our failure to provide appropriate amplification may be in the lack of knowledge on the part of educators, and in their attitudes about amplification. For example, in a study by Gaeth and Lounsbury (1966) of 134 hearing impaired children from the public and parochial schools in the Detroit metropolitan area, only 16% were wearing hearing aids that would be considered adequate when fairly stringent requirements on the mechanical condition of the aid were applied. By using the most lenient standards, it was determined that no more than 50% were getting adequate amplification. Interviews with the parents of these children indicated that they were poorly informed about all aspects of hearing aids and their use, and did not know how to judge when a hearing aid was working properly. Similar findings have been reported by Hanners and Sitton (1974), Porter (1973), and Zink (1972).

In summary, despite the importance of amplification in early intervention with the hearing impaired child, there are a number of factors that seem to interfere with maximum use of the child's residual hearing potential through amplifications.

RESEARCH NEEDS

Priorities

One intent of this paper was to highlight some of the areas in which additional research is needed to facilitate improved assessment and intervention. One question that should be raised early in a discussion of research needs is whether we are ready to establish priorities. How should we allocate our research resources to contribute to our understanding of the developmentally disabled child? Are we as a society content to continue supporting a wide spectrum of research efforts dictated primarily by the scientific interest of the investigator, or has the time come for a directed attack through research bearing directly on practical assessment and intervention problems?

Certainly we have had experience with the success of directed research effort, such as the development of the atomic bomb, or our space exploration. There is no doubt that, once convinced of the need, we can marshal the necessary resources, including qualified manpower, to solve many of our problems. The question then becomes whether we are ready to decide on priorities for research relating to the developmentally disabled. Such a question inevitably raises the spectre that establishing priorities would stifle the creativity and freedom of the individual investigator.

Identification

It is clear that improved identification procedures need to be developed. This paper has detailed some of the difficulties with existing procedures, and has also suggested that identification is not a difficult task, given sufficient awareness of the likelihood of deafness. It would seem desirable to develop some way of sensitizing both professionals and paraprofessionals to participate in the identification process. Additional research is needed on improved screening procedures.

Auditory Assessment

Further studies need to be directed to problems of the reliability of early hearing tests, both for behavioral observations and for new instrumentation. The behavioral observations would undoubtedly benefit from consideration of child development information. Increased efforts should be made to develop and evaluate new instrumentation that would improve the reliability and validity of early test results.

A major need is to develop tests that would yield more meaningful results than our current audiograms. It would be extremely helpful to have tests directed to the assessment of the infant's ability to integrate sound rather than merely to sound awareness.

The multiply handicapped deserve special consideration in the development of new assessment procedures. Despite our current efforts, and despite the great surge of interest in children's rights, it is still extremely difficult, if not impossible, to evaluate the potential of many severely multiply handicapped infants. More sophisticated assessment procedures would, it is hoped, provide information on the degree to which intervention might be expected to succeed. Too many developmentally disabled infants, even in this enlightened day, may be doomed by the lack of adequate assessment to a life of total custodial care.

Visual Assessment

If the authors were to establish priorities for additional assessment of the hearing impaired child, visual assessment would rank very high because of the reliance of the hearing impaired child on vision as a major avenue of communication. Although some visual tests are relatively easy to perform, the weight of evidence seems to suggest that an adequate visual assessment has not been performed on the deaf population in our schools, nor does there seem to be any dramatic change in the offing. As in the field of identification of the hearing impaired, it may be that increased sensitization of the professionals and paraprofessionals working with these children, coupled with increasing knowledge of the types of visual assessment that can reasonably be provided, would be a beginning step.

Intellectual Assessment

In their discerning chapter on "Infant Intelligence Testing" (this volume), Horowitz and Dunn suggest: "The basic proposal in this paper is that the traditional approach to infant intelligence testing should be replaced by a research strategy that involves continued illumination of basic infant information processing, individual differences, and the relationship of these factors to environmental stimulation available to the infant."

From the standpoint of the clinicians charged with discussing the interaction between assessment and intervention, our question can only be: What are we to do until this grand research design is completed? We must daily face parents who want desperately to know what, if anything, in addition to deafness is wrong with their infant, and we desperately want to know what we can tell them. Again, there may be a need for establishing some priorities in the allocation of resources, with an objective of obtaining some of this badly needed information in the shortest possible time.

It may be that what is needed for the hearing impaired child is an assessment instrument that would focus more on the child's communication problem rather than on general intellectual development as currently extrapolated from tests designed for older hearing children.

Communication Behavior

Although great strides have been made in the assessment of language development, further effort is needed to develop instruments that would yield information more pertinent to the intervention process. This may not be as theoretically gratifying to the linguist, but it is sorely needed by those concerned with improving current intervention. The study of performatives may be a step in this direction.

Evaluation of Early Intervention Procedures

Those involved in early intervention with hearing impaired children are sharply divided on the issue of methodology. The trend now seems to be running in favor of some form of manual communication. This issue has resulted in much wasted effort on the part of the professionals engaged in the debate, much confusion for parents, and undoubtedly considerable loss in the amount of service delivered to the children. Because intervention cannot be viewed in a vacuum, some far-reaching study is needed that would first, establish the goals of the intervention; second, clarify the terminology, which is currently confused; and last, support a definitive study with enough subjects, adequate control procedures, and of sufficient duration to permit conclusions that might be agreed upon.

What is the goal of early intervention for the hearing impaired? Is it merely the development of communication skill, or should the concern be with more far-reaching life goals? Can the goals be measured in terms of academic achievement in school, employment status as adults, annual income, etc.? Until some of these major issues can be clarified, it is unlikely that any genuine progress will be made in improving our overall intervention procedures with young hearing impaired children.

Application of Intervention Studies with Normal Hearing Infants

Attention should also be paid to the application of early intervention studies with normal hearing infants. A great deal of information currently available may have some direct or tangential implications for our current intervention procedures. The mechanisms for making the translation need to be explored.

Critical Period

One of the underlying assumptions in this discussion is that there is a critical period for language development. That is, there is a period early in life when it is easier to acquire language, and that after that period has passed it becomes more difficult. It would be extremely useful to have definitive studies directed to this issue. Does it really make any difference when we begin? What is the evidence? If we miss the critical period, are their different routes or approaches to the development of communication skill that should be considered?

Amplification

It has been suggested that the information provided by early auditory assessment is not always being used in the most efficient fashion to provide appropriate amplification. An effort is needed to increase the likelihood that the amplification that is provided is consistently and appropriately employed. Research questions in this area would include studies on the possibility of further damage to hearing through inappropriate early amplification.

SUMMARY

This paper has explored the interaction of assessment and intervention for the hearing impaired infant. The overall impression is that there is not as much as might be desired. On the assessment side, there are exciting and promising experimental procedures that have not yet been widely adapted to the clinical firing line. On the intervention side, there are suggestions that early intervention makes a difference, but there is no consensus on the most desirable type of intervention. The age-old controversy over communication methodology is still a central issue.

Although some specific suggestions for further research are offered, it seems that in some cases we desperately need more information, but in others we are not using the information that is available. It is clear that what we need most is some new mechanism to translate and disseminate research findings in a way that would enhance the likelihood of incorporating them into clinical practice more rapidly than is currently the case.

Some of the funding agencies may wish to consider a "follow through" on some of the more promising research findings, so that their potential benefits may be more widely shared. We also need a far-reaching evaluation of intervention procedures that would agree upon the goals of the intervention, agree upon the terminology and procedures, and agree to support a major study with sufficient subjects, adequate controls, and of sufficient duration to permit definitive conclusions.

REFERENCES

Austin, J. L. 1962. How to Do Things with Words. Oxford University Press, New York.

Bales, R. F. 1951. Interaction Process Analysis. Addison-Wesbey Press, Inc. Cambridge, Mass.

Balow, I. H., and Brill, R. G. 1975. An evaluation of reading and academic achievement levels of 16 graduating classes of the California School For the Deaf, Riverside. Volta Rev. 77: 255–266.

Bates, E., Camaioni, L., and Volterra, V. 1975. The acquisition of performatives prior to speech. Merrill-Palmer Quart. 21(3): 205–226.

Bloom, L. 1970. Language Development Form and Function. MIT Press, Cambridge, Mass.

Craig, W. N. 1964. Effects of preschool training on the development of reading and lipreading skills or deaf children. Am. Ann. Deaf 109: 280–296.

Curtiss, S. 1976. A search for performatives in young deaf children. Unpublished Progress Report, John Tracy Clinic, Los Angeles.

Davis, H. 1976. Principles of electric response audiometry. Ann. Otol. Rhinol. Laryngol. 85(suppl. 28).

Frankenburg, W. F., and Dodds, J. B. 1967. The Denver developmental screening test. J. Pediatr. 71(2): 181–191.

Gaeth, J. H., and Lounsbury, E. 1966. Hearing aids and children in elementary schools. J. Speech Hear. Disord. 31: 283–289.

Greenstein, J. J., Greenstein, B. B., McConville, K., and Stellini, L. 1976. Mother-Infant Communication and Language Acquisition in Deaf Infants. Lexington School For the Deaf, New York.

Hanners, B. A., and Sitton, A. B. 1974. Here's to hear—A daily hearing aid monitoring program. Volta Rev. 76: 530–536.

Harford, E. R., and Markle, D. M. 1955. The atypical effect of a hearing aid on one patient with congenital deafness. Laryngoscope 65: 970–972.

House, W. F. 1976. Cochlear implants. Ann. Otol. Rhinol. Laryngol. 85(suppl. 27): 51.

Jensema, C., and Mullins, J. 1974. Onset, cause, and additional handicaps in hearing impaired children. Am. Ann. Deaf 119: 701–705.

Jerger, J. 1975. Handbook of clinical impedance audiometry. American Electromedics Corporation, New York.

Jew, W. 1974. Helping handicapped infants and their families: The delayed development project. Child. Today 3: 7–10.

Kasten, R., and Braunlin, R. 1970. Traumatic hearing aid usage: A case study. Presented at Asha Convention.

Keith, R. W. 1975. Middle ear function in neonates. Arch. Otolaryngol. 101: 376–379.

Kenady, K. E., and Proctor, C. L. 1968. A comparison of the language used by mothers of deaf children and mothers of hearing children. Unpublished master's thesis, University of Southern California.

Kinney, C. E. 1961. The further destruction of partially deafened children's hearing by the use of powerful hearing aids. Ann. Otol. Rhinol. Laryngol. 70: 828–835.

Lee, L. 1966. Developmental sentence types: A method for comparing normal and deviant syntactic development. J. Speech Hear. Disord. 31: 311–330.

Lloyd, L. L. 1976. Discussant's comments: Language and communication aspects. In T. Tjossem, Intervention Strategies for High Risk Infants and Young Children. University Park Press, Baltimore.

Liberman, A. M., Cooper, F. S., Shankweiler, D. P., and Studdert-Kennedy, M. 1968. Why are speech spectrograms hard to read. Am. Ann. Deaf 113: 127–133.

Lowell, E. L. 1967. Home teaching for parents of young deaf children. Final Report, HEW Grant #32-14-0000-1014. John Tracy Clinic, Los Angeles.

Lowell, E. L. 1968. Training program for children with language disorders. Final Report, Children's Bureau Project No. 234. John Tracy Clinic, Los Angeles.

Lowell, E. L., Elinas, V. B., and Phillips, D. T. 1973. SPOT (Special Phoneme Optical Tracker), A visual speech training device. Report of the Proceedings of the Forty-Sixth Meeting of the Convention of the American Instructors of the Deaf, Senate Document 93-65, 93rd Congress, 2nd Session. 725–732.

Lowell, M. O., Lowell, E. L., and Goodhill, V. 1975. Evoked response audiometry with infants: A longitudinal study. Audiol. Hear. Educ. 1: 32–37.

Lowell, E. L., and Rouin, C. 1975. A search for performatives in young deaf children. Unpublished Language Project Report, John Tracy Clinic.

Lowell, E. L., Williams, C., Ballinger, R., and Alvig, D. Measurement of auditory threshold with a special purpose analog computer. J. Speech Hear. Res. 4(2): 105–112.

McConnell, F., and Liff, S. 1975. The rationale for early identification and intervention. Otolaryngol. Clin. North Am. 8: 77–87.

Macrae, J. H., and Farrant, R. H. 1965. The effect of hearing aid use on the residual hearing of children with sensorineural deafness. Ann. Otol. Rhinol. Laryngol. 74: 409–419.

Mindel, E. D., and Vernon, M. 1971. They Grow in Silence. National Association of the Deaf, Maryland.

Myklebust, H., and Lawson, L. 1970. Ophthalmological deficiencies in deaf children. Except. Child. 37: 17–21.

National Academy of Engineering. 1970. Committee on the Interplay of Engineering with Biology and Medicine: Subcommittee on Sensory Aids. In Levitt, H., and Nye, P. W. (eds.), Sensory Training Aids for the Hearing Impaired. Proceedings of a Conference, Easton, Maryland.

Naunton, R. F. 1957. The effect of hearing aid use upon the user's residual hearing. Laryngoscope 67: 564–576.

Nickerson, R. S., Kalikow, D. N., and Stevens, K. N. 1976. Computer-aided speech training for the deaf. J. Speech Hear. Disord. 41: 120–132.

Northern, J., and Downs, M. 1974. Hearing in Children. William and Wilkins Co., Baltimore.

Phillips, W. D. 1963. Influence of preschool training on achievement in language arts, arithmetic concepts and socialization of young deaf children. Unpublished doctoral dissertation, Teachers College, Columbia, New York City.

Pickett, J. M. 1968. Proceedings of the Conference on Speech-Analyzing Aids For the Deaf. Am. Ann. Deaf 113(2): 116–330.

Pollard, G., and Neumaier, R. 1974. Vision characteristics of deaf students. Am. Ann. Deaf 119: 740–745.

Porter, T. A. 1973. Hearing aids in a residential school. Am. Ann. Deaf 118: 31–33.

Reneau, J. P., and Hnatiow, G. Z. 1975. Evoked response audiometry, A topical and historical review. University Park Press, Baltimore.

Ringler, N. M., Kennell, J. H., Jarvella, R. J., Novojosky, B. J., and Klaus, M. H. 1975. Mother-to-child speech at 2 years—effects of early postnatal contact. J. Pediatr. 86(1): 141–144.

Roberts, C. 1970. Can hearing aids damage hearing? Acta Otolaryngol. 69: 123–125.

Ross, M., and Lerman, J. 1967. Hearing aid usage and its effect upon residual hearing: A review of the literature and an investigation. Arch Otolaryngol. 86: 57–62.

Smith, A. J. 1960. Performance of subjects aged two to four on pantomime: A phase in the development of a test. Unpublished doctoral dissertation, Ohio State University.

Smith, A. J. 1976. Smith-Johnson Nonverbal Performance Scale. Western Psychological Services.

Strain, B. A., Vietze, P., and Dokecki, P. R. 1975. Interpersonal proximity and vocal behavior in the mother-infant dyad. Paper presented at the Animal Behavior Society and Human Ethology meetings, May, Wilmington, North Carolina.

Ventry, I. M. 1965. Audiology and education of the deaf: A research project and training manual. Washington, D.C.

Vernon, M., and Koh, S. D. 1970. Effects of early manual communication on achievement of deaf children. Am. Ann. Deaf 115: 527–536.

Wilson, W. R., Lloyd, L. L., Decker, T. N., and Moore, J. M. 1974. The use of behavioral and impedance audiometry in the assessment of hearing of infants. Paper presented at the Alexander Graham Bell Association For the Deaf National Convention, Atlanta.

Zink, G. D. 1972. Hearing aids children wear; a longitudinal study of performance. Volta Rev. 74: 41–52.

Interaction of Assessment and Intervention for Visually Impaired Infants and Preschool Age Children

Edwin K. Hammer

SERVICE AND RESEARCH HISTORY

The past two decades have been productive in research areas concerning visual impairment and in intervention areas concerning persons with visual problems. This productivity is part of a larger progression of efforts to help the person with visual impairments. This discussion cannot, because of space, include the larger progression; however, it traces the thread of progress in context with past changes, and looks toward future needs and directions by reviewing key studies. Emphasis is placed on intervention procedures, assessment practices, and the research activities relating to intervention and assessment of children with visual impairments.

Definitions

The shift that has occurred in the field during the past two decades seems to center on performing assessment and providing intervention in terms of functions or behaviors. This represents a change from prior perspectives, where the emphasis centered on the comparison of visually impaired persons, to a normal population to show deficits. This shift can be illustrated in terms of past efforts to study the "blind personality," that is, to compare visually impaired persons to normal populations in order to indicate the profile of deviance found among blind persons. It is generally held today that there is no blind personality, per se, visual impairments per se do not lead to a similar profile of personality traits among all visually limited persons. Instead, inquiries are now directed more toward the effects of visual impairments that may impede the development of personality traits. The shift, then, is from one of expected deviance from the normal population to one of expecting normal development, perhaps at a different rate, but following the same progression as the nonimpaired person. Underlying this change is the shift away from the previous goal of services to visually impaired persons, which were administered to normalize the person. Normalization in this respect implied that blindness or visual impairments would have such severe effect on function that visually limited persons would require services to ensure that they could be similar to the sighted person in all functions. The underlying implications of services to blind persons at present is to increase function so that, even though visually limited, the person can attain potential abilities.

To better understand this shift, and to offer operational definitions for this discussion, it might serve to review the terms blind, or blindness. The legal definition of blindness reflects the medical influence, and states that blindness is:

> Central visual acuity of 20/200 or less in the better eye, with correcting glasses; or central visual acuity of more than 20/200 if there was a field defect in which the peripheral field had contracted to such an extent that the widest diameter of visual field subtends an angular distance no greater than 20 degrees (Kerbey, 1940, p. 3).

If blindness does not mean the total loss of vision, why was it assumed that visual loss led to certain deficits? It was assumed by ophthalmologists during the first decades of this century, that vision was similar to a commodity. Once it was used, it could not be replenished. Intervention procedures often centered on sight saving. Children with visual problems were restricted in using their sight for fear that it would be damaged with use. Sight was to be saved for use in critical, necessary functions. It was also assumed that visual losses were progressive. If the loss of vision could not be corrected through medical procedures, deterioration was the prognosis. It is little wonder that the deficits of hopelessness, dependency, despair, and isolation could be found among the population of individuals "going blind."

Another aspect of the definition of blindness is that of distance vision. Acuity measured in terms of the eye at rest, that is 20 feet in distance, does not account for near point vision. A measurement of 20/200 in an eye means that a person sees at 20 feet what the "normal" eye sees at 200 feet. It does not, however, indicate what this person sees at close ranges. The eyes are also at rest, that is, require minimal accommodation, at approximately 14–17 inches distance. Children with less than 20/200 vision might have vision at near point to learn to read print and be visual learners, and yet meet the legal definition of blindness.

In terms of this discussion, the word *blind* or *blindness* is used to mean that no residual vision has been observed and that the person uses tactile or auditory channels for primary learning. *Visual impairment* is used to indicate that residual vision is present to the extent that learning through the visual channel is possible to some extent. Also, within operational definitions, the word *children* is used to define preschool and primary age levels (three to eight years). The term *infant* is used to identify birth to two year age levels.

Effects of Vision Loss on Developmental Process

Relationship Between Vision and Reading   Investigations of the effects of loss of vision on the developmental process that emerged in the middle of the twentieth century typically addressed the effects of visual impairment in terms of near point vision. This movement may be shown in three particular studies. Jones (1961), in surveying the relationship of degree of vision to mode of reading among blind school age children, reported that for the first time, in the late 1950s and early 1960s, more visually impaired children were receiving their education in local day school programs than in residential school programs. This seems to be more of a sociological statement than an entirely educational finding. There was no indication that local schools provided a higher quality educational service than did residential schools; in fact, the reverse would seem true. Residential schools could concentrate resources to have a greater impact on the visually impaired child in a local school program more than in the past, either through parental pressures, availability of funds, or other factors. The central finding reported in this study was in terms of mode of reading for visually impaired children. The method of reading, that is, print or braille, did not seem to be as direct a relation to the degree of visual loss as much as it related to the child's placement, the teacher's preference for teaching reading, and the expectancies of the school for reading mode. This study raised the issue that there was more to how a child learned than the definition of blindness revealed. Factors other than distant visual acuity entered into the level of function.

Relationship Between Visual Activity and Visual Efficiency It was this issue, specifically of the use of near point visual function, that Barraga (1964) addressed, in what may be the most important single study in the area of blind and visually impaired children's learning. Barraga studied the relationship of visual acuity and visual efficiency. By developing specific techniques to teach children with visual problems, she was able to increase visual use, although visual acuity did not change. This major breakthrough permitted educators to begin to develop practices that would help visually impaired children to learn to use the remaining vision that they had. This study also allowed terms to be developed to describe visual impairments to indicate visual function rather than visual deficit. Blindness could now be defined in terms of visual function or lack of function. Visual impairment could now be used to indicate some residual vision. For persons who have had functional vision and are losing it, there is a need for aids or devices to help in learning to use remaining vision. For those who have not had adequate visual function—for example, children—there is a need for specific training to help the visually impaired person use his vision. Barraga's study showed that efficient use of vision could be learned, and this, in effect, prompted the emergence of a new perspective in providing assessment and intervention services to visually impaired persons.

Thus, Barraga's study typified the focus of further studies that illustrate that vision was a process that was developmental and learned (Ashcroft, Halliday, and Barraga, 1965). It became important, in the education of visually impaired children, to find out what remaining vision the child had, including both acuity and function. It was important to understand the level of development attained in the visual process, and to stimulate remaining visual function to its highest level of efficiency. This expanded concept of vision from a sensory skill to a perceptual/cognitive/affective process encouraged further investigation along developmental lines. Moreover, from this study, professionals began to consider visual limitations in terms of what effect the loss had on development, rather than the deficit produced by lack of vision.

Patterns of Development   A third study continued this shift in understanding the effects of visual loss on the developmental process. Fraiberg (1968) used a psychoanalytic framework to study patterns of development in blind and sighted infants. She reported that blindness maintained helplessness and dependence into the second and third year of life in congenitally blind infants and children. This continued infantile dependency manifested itself in the blind child not learning to act on the environment at the same rate as the sighted child. The basis of this dependency, according to Fraiberg, was found in the blind child's delay in establishing a mental representation of the mother. Because the congenitally blind infant could not keep in contact with the mother through vision when the mother was out of physical contact, delay was observed in the development of object permanence that in turn led to delay in relation to objects and, thus, to delay in acting on the environment. Fraiberg stated that the congenitally blind infant did not develop a basic notion of space and spatial relations, and that this encouraged the congenitally blind infant to rely on regression rather than aggression in coping with the environment.

This inquiry has proceeded longitudinally. Fraiberg (1975) detailed the gross motor milestones of congenitally blind infants. Delays in creeping and free walking were noted among the blind infants as compared to the sighted infant's motor development. The interesting aspect of this inquiry was the recognition of the use of mobility by the blind infant in a manner similar to the sighted infant's use of vision to discover and explore the environment. For the sighted infant, coordination of the eye and hand led to reaching for objects. According to Fraiberg, the emphasis shifted in the blind infant to coordination of ear and hand. Where the sighted infant learned to move toward an object that was in the visual field, the blind infant learned to move toward an object that was heard. This sound-touch encouragement to find a toy or a person was, therefore, not only important in terms of mobility, but also in terms of development of the cognitive skills of space and spatial relations and, thus, the development of personality components of displacement, or finding objects that are beyond touch. Although Fraiberg studied blind infants, the implications for the effects of visual loss on preschool age children seem to warrant further investigation for children with limited vision.

These studies served to illustrate the critical issues of the field of visually impaired children's development. First of all, there has been some movement in the past few decades in viewing visual impairment in terms of function as well as in terms of acuity. The differences among the population of visually impaired persons led to a recognition that "blindness" was many things to many people. There has been a shift from viewing visual impairments as leading to specific disabilities to viewing visual impairments in terms of degree of vision, onset of loss, and the effects of the limitation on the developmental process rather than the deviance that was assumed to automatically occur.

Recent Advances and Trends

With the changes in understanding of the developmental process in children with visual impairments, it has been possible to undertake further inquiry to enhance services to blind and visually impaired children. This activity has proceeded along several lines of inquiry, and has resulted in changes in assessment and intervention services for visually impaired children.

Medical Advances Prevention and early detection of visual problems has advanced over the past few years. At one time, premature infants placed in pure oxygen incubators were at risk of becoming blind as the result of retrolental fibroplasia. This condition was avoided with the discovery that moist oxygen intake prevented blindness from occurring in premature infants. Some cases of retrolental fibroplasia are reported, but there are not the numbers that were previously found. Current cases of retrolental fibroplasia are generally the result of procedures necessary to save the life of severely impaired infants whose only hope for survival is a high intensity oxygen environment.

Similarly, the rubella immunization program has minimized the numbers of children born with congenital rubella syndrome. This means that the large number of congenital rubella syndrome children born with rubella retinopathy and congenital cataracts are not being born at this time. There are still reported cases of congenital rubella syndrome in the United States; however, with ongoing immunization programs, this should continue to diminish.

Advances in genetics have also broadened the knowledge of such conditions as glaucoma, retinoblastoma, and anophthalmia, that are linked to chromonomal causes. Other conditions, such as retinitis pigmentosa, that are clearly linked to genetic factors, are being prevented through genetic counseling, an emerging field that has immediate impact on preventing visual impairments.

Advances in surgical procedures have contributed to the prevention of physical disorders from affecting visual function, and to the correction of physical disorders. There have been surgical procedures developed to correct imbalances in muscles that control eye movements. Conditions that previously led to progressive loss of visual function, such as strabismus, are being successfully treated in preschool age children to prevent visual dysfunction. Advances in restoration and repair to the retina and the cornea, including corneal transplants, have led to greater probability that previously damaging conditions may be treated and blindness prevented. New treatments of glaucoma in children have minimized the effects this condition has on visual function. Amblyopia, or lazy eye, was once misunderstood as to its contribution to visual loss; it is now being treated early in the child's life to prevent eventual loss of visual function.

One problem in the area of prevention that requires continued surveillance is that of the "crisis population." There seems to be a tendency for certain problems to occur that increase the number of visually impaired children for periods of time. Thus, the retrolental fibroplasia population of the 1940s and 1950s and the congenital rubella syndrome population of the 1960s and 1970s increased the numbers of visually impaired children needing services. Continued monitoring of demographic data, through model reporting systems or better case finding procedures, is needed to prevent future crisis populations of visually impaired children from going unnoticed until severe problems have resulted that affect the entire field of service delivery.

Need for Early Detection   Not only is there a need for continued monitoring of causes of visual problems in newborn infants and preschool age children, but there is also a need to monitor the early detection programs existing in the United States. For example, the Texas Commission for the Blind has a statewide program to find visually impaired children. This program, the Visually Handicapped Children's Caseworkers network, is funded with state monies and is generally charged with casefinding and eye medical services for children, birth to adolescents. The effectiveness of this program may be illustrated by the example that in fiscal year 1971,

> 1,354 children were accepted for services; 800 cases were closed; and 548 no longer had a visual impairment while 252 still had severe visual impairments (Management Services Associates, 1973, p. 8).

From 1971 to 1976 (J. Young, personal correspondence), 65% of all cases referred to the Texas Commission for the Blind's children's program were closed as no longer having visual impairments. For all of these cases, Texas Commission for the Blind provided services to parents to help them understand the child's condition and the treatment procedures available, provided services to help establish local programs for education and habilitation for children by synthesizing local resources into supportive services, and provided information to professionals in home communities to assist local programs in modifying existing services to meet the needs of young visually impaired children. Although this program and similar programs in other states may be admired for the contributions being made to detect eye problems in preschool age children and infants, there is a noticeable inconsistency in the services available to this population. This discrepancy has been noted for the total population of visually impaired persons:

> The range of services provided the Blind vary from state to state. The quality of service provided the Blind vary from state to state. The differences are many and rather extreme. We do not see a trend toward the gathering of data which could assist states to upgrade services. It would seem a small group of states should be set up as model reporting areas and other states gradually tied in. This is especially critical since in many states the Services to the Blind's function is gradually losing its identity (Management Services Associates, 1975, p. 28).

The range of services to preschool age visually impaired children needs to include thorough eye medical examination and treatment to prevent further damage to visual function. Early childhood development experiences are required to ensure that the rate of development is encouraged and that visual loss does not dominate developmental progress. Services need to include support to parents to help them understand the child's problems and the child's progress.

An example of the types of services that are missing, as a result of delayed planning, may be found in the early childhood education programs for visually impaired children. Those programs that do exist are usually not part of a larger effort to habilitate the young visually impaired child. Various factors need further clarification. Existing programs may not be perceived as part of a continuum of services. Standards may be low as far as the quality of services. Even more critical is that the program goals may be diffuse and may not lead to specific actions at the end of the program service. It is not uncommon for the parent to seek an early education placement for a visually impaired child only to find that the next crisis is in finding a placement for the child in an educational setting that will build upon what the child has learned in the early education setting.

There is a need to develop early educational opportunities for visually impaired children based on research, such as the findings of Barraga, Fraiberg, and others. These programs may be part of larger programs for young children with specific experiences designed for the visually impaired child, and emphasis placed on integration of the child into a group of children at a similar developmental level.

The research currently undertaken by Stephens (1975) may help in the development of services to young blind and visually impaired children. This study used a framework based on the work of Jean Piaget to assess the cognitive levels of function in blind students. Preliminary findings from this investigation indicated that blind adolescents were delayed in their development of logical thinking as measured on Piagetian tasks. The study sought to develop remediation techniques to increase logical processes. If these procedures prove to help the blind student in older childhood, there are immediate implications for visually impaired and blind children in early childhood. This study also seemed to provide complimentary information to the results of Fraiberg's investigations of patterns of emotional development in young blind infants. Both studies, for instance, identified the importance of the blind child developing awareness of space and spatial relations. From an affective perspective, this development would lead to seeking objects in space and an understanding of object permanence in ego formation. The same experience would lead the child to explore causality and to act on the child's environment to make things happen, from a cognitive perspective. Research studies such as the one undertaken by Stephens may assist service delivery to young visually impaired children. The importance in applying these findings to younger children seems to be in developing mediation programs rather than remediating the deficit after the fact. These programs would be beneficial in ensuring that opportunities were available for visually impaired and blind children at the time they needed these experiences. The goal would not be to accelerate development, in the sense of advancing cognitive function beyond levels attained through ordinal gains, but to insure against developmental delays hindering progress in young visually impaired children.

Directions in Research   There are other current research efforts that have direct application to preschool age visually impaired children. The American Printing House for the Blind (A.P.H.) has conducted a vigorous research program over the years, and it continues to provide major findings to help young visually impaired children. One recent project was the development of a "Look and Listen" series of taped lessons for very young visually impaired children. To provide listening activities, the series included: parent/teacher guidebooks, taped demonstrations, activity cards, taped activities, and developmental checklists to assess entering behaviors (A.P.H., 1975). This series has three levels aimed at: children who receive sound but do not recognize it, children who have receptive language but little expressive language, and children who have expressive and receptive language with few concepts.

The American Printing House has undertaken the task of developing a sensory experience kit to provide basic sensory experiences in primary modalities: visual, auditory, tactual, gustatory, and olfactory. This type of resource material will assist in providing sensory stimulation to young visually impaired children, especially multiply handicapped children who have visual dysfunction.

A primary braille reading series is also being investigated. This series will consist of children's readers from preprimer to third grade level and will include parallel workbook activities and teacher guidelines. The investigation of relevant factors of general tactual perception, concept development in blind children, and research on reading may serve as an assistance in assessment of readiness levels in young visually impaired children.

The American Printing House maintains a resource center for media and materials for use with visually impaired children. A full listing of materials and media is available upon request to the American Printing House for the Blind, 1839 Frankfort Avenue, Louisville, Kentucky, 40206. Relevant materials for young visually impaired children range widely, from sensory cylinders that provide the child with comparison of weights, colors, and tectures, to slide-cassette programs for parents and teachers of rules for talking to visually impaired and blind children.

Other research efforts center on application of technological discoveries to assist visually impaired persons. Although few of these studies are directly related to young children's learning, they portend future developments that may be available to young children with visual losses. The Atomic Energy Commission (Grunwald, 1975) is involved in the development of braille machines using magnetic tapes to transmit braille rather than the more bulky printed braille sheets. Investigations are underway to utilize laser beams for increased mobility, sonar devices for mobility, optical scanning devices to transfer printed letters into vibrating cells for tactile reception, and use of television on an interactive basis to increase visual learning. Computers have been developed to teach blind children mathematics (Lamon and Threndgill, 1975). Although none of these investigations have been used with visually impaired or blind children under school age, future studies may disclose use of these systems for exploration and learning of the environment by young children with visual losses.

CURRENT PROBLEMS AND ISSUES

Assessment Procedures and Practices

Recent activities in the field of visually impaired children have yielded increased knowledge and new practices. These actions have had a reciprocal effect in the area of assessment of visually impaired children. Assessment procedures have changed and have affected assessment practices. When assessment of visually impaired children was guided by the principle of showing deviance by comparing the sighted population to a visually impaired population, assessment practices did not always relate directly to programming. In fact, there was often a dichotomy of efforts. Assessment was held to be a separate activity from programming. Together, they form a circular process of assessment and programming being conducted in an ongoing manner. There is a common goal to provide the most appropriate services to the child.

Assessment, operationally defined as the collection of information to make decisions, must be conducted in the context of the needs of the child and in terms of the child's levels of function. The person responsible for assessing the visually impaired child can collect these data in the natural setting of the child's familiar environment. Programming, operationally defined as the provision of appropriate services to enhance the child's level of functioning, must also be provided in the child's natural setting. The child's total environment, home, playgrounds, shopping centers, family automobile—wherever the child is—becomes the program site.

It is evident that under these definitions parents are important as part of the assessment and programming effort. They see the child in the total setting more often than any other group of people concerned with assessment and programming for children with visual losses. Communication also becomes a central focus of the assessment and programming effort. It is important for parents to know what to report, what to observe in their child, and to see others working with the child to observe how to assist the child in programming efforts. To assist the parents in becoming part of the habilitation effort, more time may be devoted by professionals to the parent in the initial phase, rather than to working directly with the child. In this manner, a rapport may be established between parent and professional to out-line procedures and areas of mutual need for assistance. Once rapport has been established, the setting for both initial programming and assessment is set in the child's environment. This allows for systematic observation and collection of data from all those concerned with the child's development.

Formal Assessment   Formal assessment may be used in those instances where comparison groups exist to relate the child's behavior to a larger population. In most instances, this type of assessment yields data that must be verified in terms of the unique functions of the child being assessed. Few standardized instruments provide the total range of information needed for appropriate assessment. Certainly, the Hayes-Binet scale (Hayes, 1950), an adaptation of the Binet scales for use with blind children (age range three years and up), and the Maxfeld-Bukholtz adaptation of the Vineland Social Maturity Scale (ages nine months to six years) (Maxfeld and Bukholtz, 1957) may be used for initial information screening in cognitive and social level, respectively. However, these adaptations must be used with caution. The profile of strengths and weaknesses are clues for further investigation. The total scores provide little information to achieve the goal of appropriate services to the child.

The Ipsative Approach   Perhaps the approach more appropriate for children with visual limitations is a comparison of functions over time within the child. This ipsative approach uses the subject as both criterion reference and data source. The results do not necessarily generalize to other children, although the underlying developmental approach allows for use of ipsative data to be used in some groupings where children have common needs. This was the guiding concept in the develop-ment of the Callier-Azusa Scale (Stillman, 1974), which utilized teacher/parent observations to systematically plot the child's progress. The Uzgiris-Hunt Scales (1975) also follow this approach, using a Piagetian framework to observe nonimpaired children's development, and may be used with visually impaired children with caution. There are developmental frameworks, based on the work of Piaget, Gesell, Doll, and others, that provide a structure for assessment. These may be used with visually impaired children if assessment and programming are viewed as ongoing and cyclical, and if the examiner is capable of using data collection to help the child, and not to exclude the child from appropriate services.

The key to assessment and programming is to understand that information collection, whether formal or informal, is conducted to provide appropriate services. This continual observation of behaviors may be undertaken from a variety of approaches that synthesize all types of observations and seek to define 1) learning patterns, 2) learning rates, and 3) the interaction effect between what is learned and how it is used in the environment.

Systems Behavior One approach to assessment and programming may be found in child development practices of observing the child in terms of systems of behavior. There are four component systems that need to be included in observing children with visual losses: physical (including sensory function), emotional, mental, and social. In observing these systems, it is important to observe not only the skill, but also the process that must develop before the skill emerges in the child's repertoire of spontaneous behaviors. These processes are the means by which a child gathers and accumulates information in order to act on the tangible and intangible environment. Processes provide the means for the child to learn of personal needs and requirements as well as environmental needs and requirements. These processes may not be observable; however, the skills that emerge from processes may be observed in the four systems of behavior. Process is therefore indirectly observed. Behavior is directly observed. Assessment and programming centers on observing behaviors, inferring process, and designing strategies for intervention to provide experiences that enhance the rate of development, increase use of learning patterns, and build upon the interaction between the person and the external environment.

Physical The physical system includes sensory as well as motor functions. Motor behaviors may be observed using any of several developmental scales: the Gesell Developmental Appraisal (Gesell and Amatruda, 1974), the Milani-Comparetti Scales (Milani-Comparetti and Gidoni, 1967), the Cerebral Palsy Assessment Chart (Semans, Phillips, Romanoli; Miller, 1965; Miller and Skillen, 1965), the Callier-Azusa Scales (Stillman, 1974), or the Coordination Exercises for Children with Minimal Cerebral Dysfunction (DeHaven and Mordock, 1970). In assessment and programming activities for visually impaired children, this permits observation of how the child occupies space and moves through space. These observations are highly relevant to the development of the visually impaired child. The importance lies in what ways the visual loss has affected the child's integration of motor functions and how well the child has learned to move toward objects in the environment to act upon them. From object manipulation, the child moves into relationships with people, especially the caregiving person and into the permanence that Fraiberg studied. Thus, motor development serves as the basis for primary integration and for investigation of the environment. Motor development is important not only for affective development, but also for cognitive development.

Program activities for the young visually impaired child in motor development, therefore, try to ensure that the visual loss does not delay development because of lack of experiences. The young visually impaired child, for instance, who does not turn his head from side to side, may need to be positioned so that the head is turned. Changes in posture from prone to sitting with support may be necessary to provide the young child with motoric experiences. These experiences are attempts to provide the child with specific attributes in motor developments: body awareness, motor planning, balance, physical fitness, and agility. Body awareness is also important for the visually impaired child to understand where the body is in space. It helps define the physical boundaries, the "me" and the "not me." Stone (1974) stated that this early exploration of boundaries of the body led to imitation of "his own movements in space as with learning to crawl, to finally being able to imitate his mother washing dishes so he pulls up a chair along side her and washes dishes also." For the visually impaired child, this provides the beginning of concepts of space such as up, down, in, out, over, under, around, through, and other spatial relationships.

Motor planning provides experiences for the child to sequence an action. The child learns that the act has a beginning, middle, and end. This sequential ability becomes one of valuing or placing meaning in what had been achieved and leads to a higher level of planning, that of combining motor acts to produce new actions and experiences. Van Dijk (1965) has developed sequential teaching approaches for use with visually impaired/multiply handicapped children to assist them in moving through motor planning. Temporal and spatial relations are viewed by Van Dijk as the basis for language development. This approach permits the child with limited vision to move toward sophisticated movement patterns, such as balance, physical fitness, and agility, and, in turn, toward further cognitive and language development. Balance is needed to maintain the body against gravitational pull, and is particularly important for visually limited children, who may not comprehend the spatial dimensions of gravity pulling down to the floor or ground. Physical fitness develops through exercise and provides the child with endurance and strength in motor actions. It is important for the young visually impaired child to develop this fitness to reduce dependency and to encourage development. Agility is also important for the visually impaired child to provide the precision of movement to perform skilled tasks.

Fine motor activities compose another key part of the motoric development of the visually impaired child. A fundamental achievement in fine motor skills development is the process of reaching-grasping-releasing an object with the hands. This process is initially a reflex grasp, but with maturation in the first months of life, voluntary holding of objects emerges. For the visually impaired child, this is an important development because it permits the child to bring objects closer for more thorough inspection with the mouth, or at near range for visual inspection using remaining vision. Reaching and grasping an object signals the beginning of seeking out information from the physical environment. This behavior also calls upon the child to use hearing or other cues to find objects that are either out of the field of vision or not felt by the child. Transfer of an object from one hand to another indicates that the child is beginning to integrate both sides of the body into a single unit. Crossing the midline is a behavior that signifies that the process of motor integration is progressing. From this, the child may begin to refine hand use, first with palm grasps, then with thumb and finger in opposition. When these activities are achieved, the child is able to act upon the environment with purpose and can begin to place objects into containers, dismiss objects from his presence by throwing or pushing away, or perform the fine motor acts of opening, closing, molding, and other manipulations of objects that are encountered. The accomplishments lead to later academic activities held necessary for the visually impaired child, such as reading, writing, and coordinating visual-motor or auditory-motor actions to acquire information in an efficient manner.

A major component of the physical system for the visually limited child is the development of the visual process. A general rule may be to assume that the child can see until the child proves otherwise. This, however, is broken into components for assessment and programming purposes so that visual function may be explicitly observed. The primary level of observation of visual function may be observed in the child's attending to light. If it can be established that the child can fixate on light, it is then possible to try to assess the child's ability to focus. Focusing is the physiological process of selecting an object out of a range of objects and visually attending that object over others. In this process, the child is stimulating the cells of the retina, which is necessary for the visual process to develop (Reisen, 1951). Such stimulation develops the ability to discriminate form, color, quantity, and movement. This stimulation and discrimination leads to fusion of the visual image in each eye to binocular vision. Binocular vision permits depths to be perceived and dimensions to be comprehended. In this manner, the eyes learn to work in concert with the hands, arms, feet, and legs to form visual-motor acts, and with the ears to perform auditory-motor acts. Focusing, as a primary function, may be observed in the child reaching for a light moved closely toward the eyes. Sheridan (1973) has developed a series of assessment procedures to observe how young children see an object. Seeing was defined as:

> the reception of mobile and static patterns of light, shade, and hue by the eye and transmission of this intake information to the central nervous system, i.e. it is mainly a physiological process and depends upon adequately functioning optical judgment (1973, p. 36).

Sheridan developed the graded balls test as a procedure to observe seeing, or focusing, in young children. Efron and DuBoff (1975, pp. 18–20) described ways in which a teacher may observe visual functions such as attending to light and the near point focusing ability of the child. Both of these procedures underscore the importance of beginning with near point visual activities before attempting to work at distances in the child's visual field.

Once the focusing abilities at near point have been observed, tracking an object in the visual field follows. Tracking an object indicates that the child can attend to movement within the visual field and later leads to use of progressions (left/right, up/down, top/bottom). Tracking is also closely associated with the development of scanning to select objects out of an array of items. It is important for the child to be able to track an object in the visual field before the child is expected (or developmentally able) to select an object out of the visual field. To assess tracking and scanning in young children, Sheridan (1975, pp. 27–29) developed a procedure using white balls on a black background.

From scanning, that is, the ability of the child to sweep the visual field and select stimuli from the environment, it is possible to observe the child's use of vision in terms of hand/eye coordination or eye/foot coordination to see how the eye coordinates motor acts. These visual motor actions are extremely important in terms of the child learning to act on the environment, rather than being under the direction of environmental happenings. What the eye sees, or as Fraiberg noted with blind infants, what the ear hears, the muscles of the body respond to, and movement becomes purposeful.

The visual process, however, has not completed its progression. More sophisticated visual functions are still to be developed. Hull and McCarthy (1973) described programmatic activities that follow the developmental sequence of vision. Visual activities of identification and discrimination, sorting and classifying, reproducing visual patterns, and visual memory follows: Assessment components to this progression as outlined by Hull and McCarthy include the Visual Efficiency Scale (Barraga, 1970), the Slingerland Pre-Reading Screening Procedures (Slingerland, 1968), the Beery-Buktenica Visual Motor Integration Scale (Beery and Buktenica, 1967), and the Body Image of Blind Children Procedure (Cratty and Sams, 1968).

However, in assessment and programming for visually impaired children, it is the discerning interpretation of the observer that differentiates relevant data from mechanical collection of information. Behaviors must be recognized in context. There must be a reason, and behaviors that may be considered atypical in sighted children may be clues to the types of experiences needed by a visually impaired child. These subtleties may make the difference between meaningful assessment and program in being able to establish the needs of the child and the level of development attained.

For instance, it must be remembered that vision and hearing are distant senses. These two modalities permit the human being to bring information that is not in close proximity into the human experience. For the child who is visually limited, there is either a lack of visual experiences or fragmented visual experiences. Thus, assessment and programming concentrates on providing the visually limited child with the specific experiences to bring in information. Behaviors that may be abnormal for the sighted child may be important experiences for visually handicapped children. Rocking, for example, may be an attempt to define space by using the whole body. It permits the visually impaired child to experiment with where the body is in space and the limits of gravitational pull that will tumble the body. Rocking behavior in preschool age visually impaired children is an orientation activity, and need not be considered a deviant behavior. The visually impaired child rocks to stimulate the receptors of the brain, which measure the experiences of pressure of the body in space. For the sighted child, movement in space, such as falling to the floor or sudden shifts in the body plane, is mediated by visual clues of distance, righting the body to the ground, and protective reactions. For the visually impaired child, this stimulation and reaction pattern development may be delayed or missing. Falling, jumping, rolling, or other changes of the body in space may be very threatening to the child with visual limitations. The automatic reactions may be present, but not necessarily experienced in a full range of development. Thus, rocking provides one way of gaining this experience. Instead of a perseverant behavior, it is an attempt by the child to gain an experience. A physical therapist or an occupational therapist can provide assessment and programming to help the visually impaired child experience sensorimotor integration as a part of the developmental process, and thus reduce the need for rocking behaviors to continue. Research is needed in the area of the study of blindisms, not to point out deviance, but to indicate the relationship between atypical behaviors in visually impaired children and the need for experiences of a sensorimotor level of integration.

It is in being able to pick up these subtle behavioral cues that assessment and programming serve to attain their goal. By observing physical development, by calling upon resources to assist in understanding the level of development attained, it is possible to develop meaningful programming for the physical system of development of young children.

Emotional and Mental   The mental system includes knowing as well as acting on the environment. Mental behaviors that are important to observe in visually impaired children include: how a child solves a problem, how a child evaluates incoming information, how a child learns from trial and error, and how a child may bring together many bits of information and arrive at a new answer, or how a child recalls information. This system is closely intertwined with the sensory experiences of the physical system, and the emergence of functions in the emotional system of behavior. It is, therefore, difficult to assess mental functions in isolation. In fact, the newer thinking among those active in defining and measuring mental functions tends to point out the interrelation among systems rather than assessment in isolation Horowitz and Paden, 1973; Wechsler, 1975). It is also becoming more widely recognized that the intelligence of an individual is not a static faculty, but changes because of many factors.

Assessment of mental system functions for visually impaired children must raise questions about behaviors that need to be answered. Some of these may be answered in formal testing. Other questions may be answered in observation of the child and family, interview or observation of the child in a learning situation, or diagnostic teaching to establish the child's rate of learning. In any instance, assessment cannot be separated from programming. There is no dichotomy, even though there may seem to be separate endeavors. This means that a short-term evaluation of a visually impaired child will provide short-term information. If long-term information is necessary, a long-term assessment period is required.

Initial evaluation of the mental abilities of a visually limited child may provide the broad brush strokes of the picture. The Wide Range Achievement Test has been adapted for use with blind or visually limited children by the American Printing

House for the Blind, and is available through them. This instrument assists is assessing reading, spelling, and arithmetic, and may be used with kindergarten age children. For children beyond the third grade level of academic achievement, the Wide Range Vocabulary Test has been made available in special editions for visually impaired persons. The Durrell Listening-Reading Series, Primary Level, is also available for use with visually impaired children, grades one through three. The Boehm Test of Basic Concepts has been adapted for tactile use with blind children (kindergarten through grade two). The Stanford Achievement Test is also available for children who have attained a 2.5 grade level of academic proficiency. All of these instruments have application to the broad sweep of finding ranges. Further assessment is necessary to provide the total picture of the mental abilities of visually impaired children.

To add further detail to the picture of mental abilties in visually impaired children, it is necessary to utilize the learning situation. This inquiry centers on identifying the child's learning style, the rate of learning exhibited in the child, and the measurement of progress in the child. One such approach may be found in the Callier-Azusa Scale (Stillman, 1974). This teacher-generated instrument seeks to identify behaviors that are incorporated into the child's repertoire and to note those behaviors that are emerging or seem to be observed at times in children. The tasks are specifically designed for children who function below the ranges generally found in standard instruments and are based on developmental sequences. Although studies of validity and reliability have been completed (Day and Stillman, 1975), the Callier-Azusa Scale is based on an ipsative approach to assessment that compares the child to himself over time and does not necessarily generalize to a broader population norm.

The most specific assessment approach that may be taken in defining the mental system in visually impaired children is the use of criterion-referenced testing by the teacher to match the child's level of function to specific learning tasks. This approach requires that the teacher identify the developmental sequence and the level of function attained by the visually impaired child. Information may be supplied by psychologists, occupational therapists, or physical therapists that indicates the range of function. From all the data available, experiences are provided to assist the child in moving from one level of mental behavior to the next sequential level of behavior. This approach requires great flexibility on the part of the teacher and the program to ensure that the child will be permitted to advance at his own rate and in his own style of learning, rather than being paced by external criterion. It is also important for the teaching personnel to realize that the developmental sequence is a framework, not an absolute; developmental milestones may be attained in whole or in parts without the child going through all steps. The child may go from point A to point G before achieving points, B, C, D, E, and F. The sequential steps must be altered for individual differences and must be broken into the smallest components to remain relevant to the child's developmental needs.

Social   The social system includes how the child relates to the society in which he lives and how societal rules are incorporated into behaviors. Social behavior of visually impaired children under school age may be observed in play. Play is the child's reflection of society. This reflection of society serves to indicate how the child understands the world in which he lives and where he may function. If the child's play is at a certain level, it is possible to infer what has happened previously in the child's social experiences and to predict what will happen later in the child's system of social behavior. The sequence of socialization, as reflected through play, has three stages: isolated play, parallel play, and interactive play.

The first level of play that is observed in a child is isolated play. Very young children, in cribs to toddler stage, are learning to organize the world about them. This type of play enhances organization; it is egocentric, testing the world through experiences. There is tasting, touching, and bringing in information at a primitive physical level. Toys, people, and other elements of the environment are objects to be manipulated. It is in this manipulation that the child begins to experience which behaviors are permitted and which are not allowed. It is at this time that the child begins to exhibit an understanding of causality; the child can make things happen.

It is difficult for the sighted person to relate to the experiences of the blind child and, to some extent, the visually limited child, in terms of experiencing what is permitted through isolated play. Hands may be experienced by the blind child as existing independent of his body. Toys may be experienced as extensions of the child's body. Caregiving persons may be considered as part of the child, and differentiation may not automatically occur. Careful planning and implementation is needed to assist the visually limited child in organizing the world, to learn to experience the "me" and the "not me," and to become aware of what activities are acceptable in various social settings.

If this organization and learning occurs in isolated play, it is possible to look for the emergence of parallel play. Parallel play may be observed in children who indicate that they are aware of other people but show no overt interest in acknowledging the other person or persons. The child seeks to do the same kinds of activities, but does not necessarily recognize the existence of the other children in a small group. Children at this level of socialization play in groups doing the same things, but not together.

For the visually impaired child, this imitation of others in play is often delayed because there are not opportunities to play in small group settings to learn to observe other children. The child with limited vision may not see well enough to observe what other children are doing. Touching may not be acceptable to the other children in the small group, and the understanding of what others are doing may be unclear. Visually limited children between the toddler stage and approximately three years of age may need special assistance to have physical contact with other children to find out what is happening. A structured series of activities may be provided to ensure this type of experience: sand tables with touching and pouring sand over hands, arms, and feet; crawling through mazes using the next child as a guide; or water play activities that permit the child to experience movement of others by the shift of water. It may be necessary to help the visually impaired child learn how to express feelings in socially acceptable ways. A smile may need to be felt to help the child understand how to express the concept of happy, frowning may be taught to express feelings of unhappy. Games used for nursery school age children are appropriate for visually impaired children to learn how they express themselves to others. These are learned behaviors within the context of social rules, and parallel play provides opportunities for visually limited children to learn these social expressions.

If the child demonstrates parallel play activities, it may be expected that the child will begin to engage in an interactive level of play. Interactive play may be observed as the child begins to seek out other children, adults, and situations to be part of the activities of others. Four-, five-, and six-year-old children often indicate that they are intently interested in having others in their activities and may be very unhappy if denied the companionship of others.

Interactive play is extremely important in assessing the social system of visually impaired children, because it indicates that the child is seeking out others in the environment and is beginning to define himself in terms of personal interactions with others. It is this level of interaction that provides clues to the way in which the visually limited child will act on his environment. Unusual quietness may indicate that the child is not sure of how to relate and how to get what is wanted from a social situation. Often this is considered as shyness or lack of social skills when, in reality, it may mean that the child has not learned to use social settings to express himself, has not learned the permissions and prohibitions of the society, and is unsure of the limits of his person in terms of a larger world.

Programming strategies at this level may include providing activities that the child cannot complete by himself but that require another person to achieve. Table games, such as dominoes or cards, that may be used by the visually limited child, help bring the visually limited child into interactive situations. Games such as "I Hear," an auditory version of "I Spy," create a group activity that includes visually limited children. Activities requiring partners assist the visually impaired child in becoming more a part of a group rather than an observer of activities of peers.

The emotional system of behavior includes the development of feelings, values, and judgments. The developmental sequence seems to follow attachment to a caregiving person, differentiation of self from one person, such as the caregiving person, and integration of self into an autonomous unit to get what is valued or desired from the environment. The Fraiberg studies (1968, 1975) conducted with blind infants have revealed many factors to be considered in assessing and programming for the visually impaired child. Activities are needed to provide the visually impaired child with ways to explore the environment and to begin to develop an understanding of space and distance. An infant is responsive to the person who is feeding, bathing, or dressing him. Infants develop through the actions of the caregiving person, and mirror the concerns and emotions of caregivers. Fraiberg suggests that the development of feelings of permanence is vital in the child beginning to differentiate self from others. Feelings about visual loss from parents and professionals may not be openly discussed, leaving the child with a vague understanding of how others feel toward him. Feelings of visual loss by the child might not be expressed by the child as an integral part of a total personality and might be viewed as emphasizing differences.

The visually impaired child who is kept in a dependent state by others may not experience autonomy, and may never learn that each person must use trial and error to encounter life's challenges.

Programming for the emotional development of the visually impaired child needs to include opportunities for the child to learn to express feelings, needs, and desires. For some children, direct learning experiences may be necessary, such as responding to how a person feels in a certain situation. Discussion of ways to cope with various situations in terms of values may help the visually limited child develop patterns of expression and feelings of competence. Playing roles may assist in experiencing how to interact with other people by initiating behavior and receiving emotional signals and cues.

A caution in assessment and programming for the young visually impaired child is needed: a child needs to be viewed as a total person, greater than the sum of various systems of behavior. If the child is expected to integrate these systems of behavior into an effective functioning, the persons assessing and programming for the child must set the tone by looking at the child as a total person.

SUMMARY AND CONCLUSIONS

From these formal and informal approaches to assessment and programming for visually limited children, it is important to recognize that a dichotomy no longer exists between assessment practices and programming procedures. It is, rather, a cyclical process of assessment in context and programming in terms of individual needs of each child. The lessening of this dichotomous approach to assessment and programming came from research that shifted emphasis from expected deviant behavior to understanding that visually impaired children follow the same sequences of development as nonimpaired children, and that this progress is at the individual child's rate.

Even with the advances that have been made in research, assessment, and programming, there are areas where future efforts are needed. The first of these is in the application of what is currently known about visually impaired children to the population in a quality manner. The inconsistencies among programs for visually impaired children throughout the nation point to the lack of application of current knowledge. Validation of research findings in a variety of settings and approaches is an immediate need.

There is certainly a need to replicate the studies concerning visually impaired children that have been conducted with school age children, to look at the results of these research constructs when applied to visually impaired children, birth to six years of age. Although the research seems to generalize, specific data would be helpful in verifying information and procedures. Within this area of research needs are:

1. Studies of families and of the contributions that can be made by providing services to parents and siblings of visually impaired children, to assure developmental opportunities for the impaired child.

2. Studies to show how to utilize resources in programming for young children with visual impairments. What are the criteria for integration of a visually impaired child into a nursery or day care center with nonimpaired children? What type of support services are needed for visually impaired children in a home setting, in a small group program, or in an infant stimulation program?
3. Studies to investigate the use of technological advances in assisting the visually impaired child. These advances almost seem to be from science fiction as new efforts are discussed to attempt implanting devices to stimulate visual areas of the brain, to develop tactile decoding devices to help the blind child learn to identify objects through symbols, and to refine those devices that have been developed for use with very young children so that mediation occurs, rather than remediation after developmental milestones have become delayed.

Perhaps the most important need is to assure that the momentum of current activities is not lost or slowed. Many changes have occurred in programming and assessment of blind and visually impaired children. These must be encouraged until optimum services are available to all children with visual losses.

REFERENCES

American Printing House for the Blind. 1975. Educational Research, Development, and Reference Group Report on Research and Development Activities. Louisville.

Ashcroft, S., Halliday, C., and Barraga, N. 1965. Effects of Experimental Teaching on the Visual Behavior of Children Educated as Though They Had No Vision. George Peabody College, Nashville.

Barraga, N. C. 1964. Increased Visual Behavior in Low Vision Children. American Foundation for the Blind, New York.

Barraga, N. C. 1970. Visual Efficiency Scale. American Printing House for the Blind, Louisville.

Beery, K., and Buktenica, N. 1967. Developmental Test of Visual-Motor Integration. Follett Corporation, Chicago.

Cratty, D. J., and Sams, T. 1968. The Body Image of Blind Children. American Foundation for the Blind, New York.

Davis, C. J. 1970. New Developments in the Intelligence Testing of Blind Children. In Proceedings of the Conference on New Approaches to the Evaluation of Blind Persons. American Foundation for the Blind, New York.

Day, P., and Stillman, R. 1975. Inter-rated Reliability Studies of the Callier-Azusa Scale. Unpublished report, Dallas.

DeHaven, G. E., and Mordock, J. B. 1970. Coordination exercises for children with minimal cerebral dysfunction. Phys. Ther. 50: 337–342.

Efron, M., and DuBoff, B. 1975. A Vision Guide for Teachers for Deaf-Blind Children. North Carolina Department of Public Instruction, S.E.I.M.C., Winston-Salem.

Fraiberg, S. 1968. Parallel and divergent patterns in blind and sighted infants. Psychoanal. Stud. Child 23: 264–300.

Fraiberg, S. 1975. The development of human attachments in infants blind from birth. Merrill-Palmer Quart. 21: 264–334.

Gesell, A., and Amatruda, C. S. 1974. Developmental Diagnosis (4th). Paul Hoeber, New York.

Grunwald, A. P. 1975. Testing Argonne's Braille Machine. Argonne National Laboratory, Argonne, Il.

Hayes, S. P. 1950. The Interim Binet for use with the Blind. Perkin School for the Blind, Watertown, Ma.

Horowitz, F. D., and Paden, L. Y. 1973. The effectiveness of environmental intervention programs. In B. E. Caldwell and H. N. Ricciuti (eds.), Review of Child Development Research. University of Chicago Press, Chicago.

Hull, W. A., and McCarthy, D. G. 1973. Supplementary program for pre-school visually handicapped children. Educ. Vis. Handi. 5: 97–104.

Jones, J. W. 1961. Blind Children-Degree of Vision, Mode of Reading. U.S. Government Printing Office, Washington, D.C.

Kerbey, C. E. 1940. Manual on the Use of the Standard Classification of Causes of Blindness. American Foundation for the Blind, New York.

Lamon, W. E., and Threndgill, J. 1975. The Papy-Lamon minicomputer for blind children. In New Outlook for the Blind. 69: 289–294. American Foundation for the Blind, New York.

Management Services Associates. 1973. The Education of Visually Handicapped Children In Texas. Austin.

Management Services Associates. 1975. An Evaluation of the Organization of State Programs to Serve the Blind. Vol. I. Austin.

Maxfeld, K. E., and Bukholtz, S. 1957. A Social Maturity Scale for Blind Preschool Children. American Foundation for the Blind, New York.

Milani-Comparetti, A., and Gidoni, E. A. 1967. Routine developmental examination in normal and retarded children. Devel. Med. Child Neurol. 15: 433–346.

Reisen, A. et al. 1951. Chimpanzee vision after four conditions of light deprivation. Am. Psychol. 6: 282.

Semans, S., Phillips, R., Ramanoli, M., Miller, R., and Skillen, A. 1965. A cerebral palsy assessment chart. Phys. Ther. 45: 463–468.

Sheridan, M. D. 1973. Manual for the Stycar Vision Test. NFER Publishing Company, London.

Sheridan, M. D. 1975. The Solo-dot test. 1975. Devel. Med. Child Neurol. 15: 433–436.

Slingerland, B. H. 1968. Pre-Reading Screening Procedures. Educators Publishing Services, Cambridge.

Stephens, W. B. 1975. Cognitive remediation of blind students. Unpublished report of research grant #OEG-0-74-7445, U.S. Office of Education, Bureau of Education for the Handicapped.

Stillman, R. (ed.). 1974. The Callier-Azusa Scale. Callier Center for Communication Disorders, Dallas.

Stone, C. 1974. Observing Gross Motor Performance in Deaf-Blind Children. Callier Center for Communication Disorders, Dallas.

Uzgiris, I. C., and Hunt, J. McV. 1975. Assessment in Infancy. University of Illinois Press, Urbana.

Van Dijk, J. 1965. Motor development in the education of deaf-blind children. In Teaching Deaf-Blind Children. Royal National Institute for the Blind, London.

Wechsler, D. 1975. Intelligence defined and redefined. Am. Psychol.

From Assessment to Intervention: An Elusive Bridge

Barbara K. Keogh
Claire B. Kopp

IDENTIFICATION OF EARLY RISK CONDITIONS

The interaction between assessment and intervention is occasionally direct, frequently inferential, and sometimes nonexistent. Diagnosticians and interveners seem to focus on the same children, but with parallel efforts, so that too often assessment leads to statements that list symptoms or define a category of problems. Intervention, however, is determined primarily by program philosophy, even program availability. However articulated, most intervention programs are based on a presumed link between diagnosis and treatment, with many diagnostic decisions carrying a strong therapeutic implication. Although an assumption of a directional (even "causal") relationship between diagnosis and treatment may be warranted for the physician dealing with certain specific medical conditions, it is often unwarranted when applied to marginal conditions, to developmental problems, or to emotionally, socially, or educationally based conditions of deviance (Keogh and Becker, 1973). In such conditions, the diagnostic and assessment data as well as the therapeutic implications are frequently imprecise. Even in the case of developmental disabilities, where cognitive deficits are a critical part of the diagnosis, there is considerable difference of opinion about symptoms and interventions. Without belaboring the point, the authors wish to emphasize that assessment and intervention for infants and preschoolers at risk vary markedly, and sometimes tell us more about the theoretical backgrounds and views of the assessors and the interveners than they do about the children. At least two aspects of identification and diagnosis of early risk conditions for developmental disabilities may be defined as having significance for intervention. The first involves screening and assessment with standardized instruments, and the second involves risk by inference.

Assessment with Standardized Instruments

Concern for optimizing developmental potential has led to early screening and assessment to detect existing or future problems. Although there is lack of unanimity in the definition of terms, it is broadly assumed that "screening" refers to a large scale, relatively coarse mesh that serves as a quick and inexpensive procedure to determine the presence or absence of developmental problems. Assessment, however, usually implies a more rigorous diagnostic approach—a thorough analysis of detailed information about an individual, involving coordinated analyses by several professional disciplines (Frankenberg and Camp, 1975; Meier, 1973). Both screening and assessment may involve the use of standardized instruments and/or clinical observations to delineate the nature of developmental problems. Theoretically, at least, screening identifies children with problems, but assessment provides differential information that may be used as the basis for planning therapeutic or remedial interventions. Assessment also provides data that could be used to monitor ongoing development and to evaluate intervention effectiveness.

Ideally, screening identifies infants and children at risk, and assessment provides the basis and direction for intervention. In practice, however, screening tests have high error rates, and assessment-diagnostic tests have only limited predictive validity for later development; they penalize both the quiet, less sociable young child and the retarded child (Stephens, 1972), and they deny possible subcultural differences in response styles. Additionally, most standardized assessment approaches ignore adaptive and coping mechanisms that develop over time (Escalona, 1972; Tronick and Brazelton, 1975).

Recognizing the limitations of many widely used assessment techniques for planning intervention, a number of investigators have attempted to develop alternative approaches or measures that might provide more powerful data (Brazelton, 1973; Casati and Lézine, 1968; Corman and Escalona, 1969; Haeussermann, 1958; Uzgiris and Hunt, 1975). Despite their promise, many of these assessment approaches lack careful validity or reliability data, are still research tools, and importantly, require highly selective skills and experience on the part of the assessor. Consequently, practical utility of these tools is limited. Because program demands increase, however, the old standbys—developmental tests, neurological examinations, pre-school motor scales, language samples, and intelligence tests—shakily reside in the assessor's offices, providing comfort to the assessor, but limited information to the intervener.

Assessment by Inference

In addition to definitions of risk based on individual screening and assessment information, individuals are frequently assigned risk status on the basis of category membership. Review of the risk literature reveals that three broad categories or classes of risk are consistently defined. One category includes infants and young children who have organically based physical or sensory conditions that interfere with, and may even preclude, normal development; visual and auditory impairments are examples. A second broad risk category takes into account conditions or characteristics of the infant that, although in themselves are not always damaging, have a documented association with later developmental problems; prematurity and perinatal anoxia are examples. A third category, the largest but the least specifically defined, relates developmental risk to broader environmental, social, and economic conditions. Whereas the first two categories of risk fit the "continuum of reproductive casualty," implicating biosocial factors (Lillienfeld and Parkhurst, 1951), the last set may contain conditions at least partially subsumed by Sameroff and Chandler's (1975) "continuum of care-taking casualty." Consistent and powerful evidence over a number of years (Pasamanick and Knobloch, 1966; Pasamanick, Knobloch, and Lilienfeld, 1956; Werner, Bierman, and French, 1971) confirms that these categories are neither independent nor mutually exclusive.

Category membership carries somewhat differing implications for intervention than does diagnostic evaluation. As noted above, in the first category the intervention is directed at overcoming specific, primary, in-child conditions that disrupt development. In the second category, the intervention involves therapeutic activities focused on the child, but designed to enhance a number of dimensions thought to affect subsequent development. In the last category, intervention is directed at providing experiences that overcome or compensate for extra-child conditions which are viewed as threatening to later development. A critical point of difference is that in the first category, the indicators of risk are present in the infant or young child at the time of diagnosis, whereas in the latter two categories, risk is defined as a probability statement, in large part based on class or category membership.

One of the difficulties of category-based risk decisions is, of course, that the categories themselves tend to be broad band and multidimensional. Furthermore, predicted outcomes of these risk conditions are often nonspecific and heterogeneous. Consider the conditions subsumed under the term "developmental disabilities"— mental retardation, autism, cerebral palsy, sometimes even specific learning disabilities. A cursory review of one of these subgroups reveals that definitional and diagnostic disagreements have characterized the mental retardation field for years (Clausen, 1967; Ellis, 1969; Zigler, 1969). These disagreements have become even more critical as the confounding of biological and environmental risks for mental retardation have been delineated. Mercer's (1970) findings of different incidence rates of mental retardation according to psychometric, social-adaptive, and biological criteria bear out the relativeness of the definition. The point is that in attempting to identify infants and young children at risk for subsequent development, we typically invoke a unitary predictive model that must predict (from a broad band of in- and extra- child conditions) outcomes that vary according to age, socioeconomic status, and cultural setting. Because risk signs vary from specific in-child biological conditions to non-specific generalized social and cultural ones, it is not surprising that our predictive accuracy is not always high.

Given the vagaries of assessment of infants and young children at risk, questions of importance to the intervener are essentially practical ones. Their practicality in no sense minimizes their complexity, but rather serves to determine the selection and weighting given assessment data. Evidence relative to risk in the early years may be organized around three questions of fundamental importance for the intervener:

1) Is there stability and continuity of growth, and thus of risk, over time and across developmental periods? 2) What assessment information at infancy can be used to predict later development? 3) How may diagnostic-assessment information at infancy be utilized in planning interventions with long-term outcomes?

Continuity and Stability

The issue of continuity is, of course, central for developmental theorists and interveners alike. Whether framed in the traditional language of phenotypic-genotypic, homotypic-heterotypic, or isomorphic-metamorphic distinctions (Kagan, 1971), at question are developmental and behavioral stability. Theoretical aspects of the continuity question have been developed by a number of authors (Escalona and Heider, 1959; Kagan and Moss, 1962; Moore, 1967), and the continuity issue has been studied in relation to a variety of developmental dimensions, e.g., personality or temperament (Thomas, Chess, and Birch, 1968; Thomas, Chess, Birch, Hertzig, and Korn, 1963; Yarrow, 1964). The major focus of long-term study has been on cognitive growth, however. Experimental techniques and research designs reflect the historical American preoccupation with quantitative, psychometric methods. A number of reviews deal with issues of infant testing, reliability of scales, and the delineation of possible influences on the validity of tests for prediction of later cognitive attainment (Bayley, 1970; Honzik, 1976; Hunt and Bayley, 1971; McCall, Hogarty, and Hurlburt, 1972; Stott and Ball, 1965; Thomas, 1970); matters of assessment are addressed in a separate paper in this symposium (Horowitz and Dunn, this volume). Although studies of assessment of normal children are of general interest to both developmentalists and educators, it is the findings relative to risk groups that must be considered by the clinician proposing interventions with disabled infants and young children. Examination of the risk literature suggests that there are at least two major data sources from which predictions are made, either separately or in combination. One has to do with the actual physical, biological, and behavioral characteristics of a given infant; another with risk inferred from extra-child, category based membership.

Developmental Delay/Central Nervous System Impairment Considering first the predictive validity of infant behavior and performance, it seems safe to say that findings from clinical or nonnormal samples are somewhat ambiguous and inconclusive. Predictions of later developmental accomplishments from measures at infancy are indeed uncertain. Holden (1972), for example, followed the same children from infancy through ages four or seven, and reported that the group of infants who were at least one month delayed at the eight-month assessment showed below average IQ at the follow-up periods. Holden also noted that most of the children who had IQs below 69 at either four or seven years had performed below average on the Bayley Mental or Motor Scales during infancy. However, when the predictive accuracy of the eight-month Bayley score was examined relative to follow-up criteria, there was such great variability within the infant risk group that Holden was led to conclude that "mental retardation is not predictable in infancy" (p. 30), an interpretation not totally incompatible with that of Nancy Bayley (1949; 1955; 1970) regarding the prediction of later intelligence of children within nonclinic samples. Holden's interpretations are not entirely consistent, however, with the findings from other longitudinal studies cited below.

Based on their work at Childrens Hospital of Los Angeles, Share, Koch, Webb, and Graliker (1964) found significant correlations between Gesell scores at infancy and Stanford Binet IQs at five years for Down's Syndrome children. In a related study, Fishler, Graliker, and Koch (1965) reported differential stability of predictive relationships according to diagnosis, with the Down's Syndrome children the most stable, and the cerebral palsied the most variable. In a major longitudinal study, Werner, Honzik, and Smith (1968) found a correlation of 0.49 between IQ at 20 months and 10 years for the sample as a whole; the magnitude of the correlation substantially increased, however (0.71), when only children with scores below 80 on the infant test were included.

In a follow-up study of children with major congenital malformations of the central nervous system (myelomeningocele, hydrocephalus, encephalocele), Fishman and Palkes (1974) found low correlations between developmental quotients obtained before 18-month testing and later school age intelligence test quotients. The correlation coefficients were 0.81 between 18-month and five-year tests, and 0.75 between two-year and five-year tests. The authors noted a trend in their results indicating the infants who score in the normal range might show considerably better intellectual performance in childhood "when better means of measuring adaptive skills are available." Conversely, of the eight infants who had an 18-month IQ of 83 or less, all but one had a later IQ of 81 or less. In an earlier study of children with cerebral palsy, Hohman and Freedheim (1959) observed that 25% of children tested initially at three years of age or younger shifted 16 or more points at a later testing. Of their total 370-case sample, the smallest percentage of shift was found in the groups scoring 90 and above and below 50.

After a careful analysis of predictive testing, McCall et al. (1972) suggest that prediction from infant tests to childhood IQ is better for clinical than normal groups, and conclude that "infant tests may have temporary as well as predictive utility in identifying pathological and 'suspect' conditions in infancy, and a very low score on an infant test . . . may have diagnostic value" (p. 730). The same authors, however, urge that interpretations be made cautiously, noting that correlations within deviant groups may be spuriously high, because the number of subjects with extremely deficient performance at both assessment periods may influence the magnitude of the correlation coefficient. At the same time, it is clear that more predictive confidence can be placed in diagnostic decisions about children in the extreme ends of the risk distribution than about those in the marginal or borderline areas.

Membership in Groups Hypothesized To Be At Risk   Whereas a good deal of psychological research on early risk has focused on assessment of cognitive behavioral dimensions, investigators in the clinical fields, especially pediatrics, have identified another set of conditions and diagnostic approaches that provide information. A growing body of longitudinal data documents the range of developmental outcomes for infants identified because of particular in-child characteristics or because of membership in particular risk categories, such as prematurity (Sameroff, 1975; Sameroff and Chandler, 1975). However, long-term prediction for individual children is uncertain even when the risk signs are primary, in-child conditions. Developmental prediction is even more tenuous when the indicators are predominantly related to category or class membership. Questions must be raised about the power of these class parameters for decisions about individual children. Several specific examples illustrate the predictive problem. Chess (1974), in examination of 242 infants with serological indication of rubella, a clear risk condition, found that whereas a high proportion of the children sampled evidenced physical, developmental, and/or cognitive defects, approximately 20% had no defects and were "normal" for age. Graham, Ehrhart, Thurston, and Craft (1962) reported differences in development between anoxia babies and a normal comparison group at age three. In subsequent follow-up at age seven, however, Corah, Anthony, Painter, Stern, and Thurston (1965) found few indications that the two groups differed, suggesting that risk defined as perinatal anoxia was not necessarily predictive of later developmental status. In another longitudinal study, Drage, Kennedy, Berendes, Schwab, and Weiss (1966) followed infants with differing 5-minute Apgar scores, noting that at one year the infants with low Apgars (0–5) had significantly more indicators of neurological dysfunction than did infants with high Apgars (7–10). By seven years, however, the differences were few, and less than 5% of the low Apgar children showed signs of gross CNS abnormalities. Relationships between Apgar scores and mild neural dysfunctions were even more tenuous.

A final example comes from the extensive work on prematurity and risk (see Sameroff and Chandler, 1975; Weiner, 1962; for reviews). There is some agreement that prematurity is associated with later slight or mild intellectual deficit as expressed in IQ, in higher numbers of congenital defects, and in overall "less optimal" development (Davies and Stewart, 1975; Drillien, 1964; Harper and Wiener, 1965). The majority of preterm infants develop normally, so that by the age of school entrance they are not discernible from their peers by age. Prematurity as a risk class may well signal possible complications of development, but prematurity alone is not predictive of subsequent cognitive deficits. Parmelee and Haber (1973) have delineated some of the complicating conditions associated with prematurity, including low birth-weight, prolonged hospitalization, disruption of mother-child relationships, etc. They suggest that it is not so much prematurity per se as it is these other conditions, which may account for subsequent developmental problems. The point is important because a more differentiated analysis of prematurity as a risk category should lead to more specific and useful directions for intervention.

Multiple Predictors of Risk   In a recent discussion, Rosenblith (1975) concluded that few specific signs to outcome relations were strong enough to allow prediction of developmental risk from any given sign. She opted, thus, for a combination of behavioral and medical information—an approach compatible with that of Parmelee, Kopp, and Sigman (1976), who argue for a "cumulative risk index" for assessment of infant status. The Cumulative Risk Score combines prenatal, natal, and neonatal information in an additive fashion, taking into account biological events and conditions, as well as behavioral and performance indicators of the infant. Specific measures include scales identifying obstetric and postnatal complications, neonatal neurological and behavioral measures, and data from four- and eight- to nine-month-behavioral and developmental examinations. Parmelee et al. (1976) stress the use of multiple measures, noting that "the strength of the approach . . . is that it will make possible the identification of the contributions made by the various measures independently and in combination. . . . We anticipate that the risk score system will be applicable for infants identified as at risk for developmental disabilities due to environmental and/or biological factors" (p. 24). A major goal in the Parmelee et al. work is to define a cluster of infant characteristics and family-social factors that are predictive of later development.

SOCIAL-CULTURAL INFLUENCES ON RISK

Discussions of risk in infancy and early childhood have traditionally focused on assessment of characteristics of the child, but events over the last 10–15 years have made it increasingly clear that caregiving potentials within the environment are enormous contributors to developmental risk. As caregiving characteristics are influenced by the sociocultural milieu of the family, there is a major link between social class and a "continuum of caretaking casualty" (Sameroff, 1975). The findings on incidence rates for cognitive and/or achievement differences across socioeconomic groups support this link (Coleman, 1968; Uzgiris, 1970; Werner et al., 1971). Sociocultural variables are among the most powerful influences on risk conditions, leading Sameroff and Chandler (1975) to note that "the data from . . . various longitudinal studies of prenatal and perinatal complications have yet to produce a single predictive variable more potent than the familial and socioeconomic characteristics of the caretaking environment. The predictive efficiency of the variable of socioeconomic class is especially pronounced for the low end of the IQ scale" (p. 208). The relationship between social class and risk is so well documented that detailed review would be redundant. Of importance is that recognition of this relationship has influenced strongly the nature and focus of intervention programs aimed at ameliorating risk conditions.

Despite clear and substantive evidence that the environment in which the baby lives is among the most powerful contributors to his early risk and is a continuing influence on his development in the early years, the nature of the interaction between the biological condition of the infant or child and the milieu in which he lives remains unspecified. The extraordinary multiplicity and complexity of variables subsumed under the term "social class" make it nearly impossible to use this categorical term for explanatory purposes. As noted by Zigler (1970), the variability within social class is as great as the variability across social classes, so that although "socioeconomic status" is a neat summarizing term, it is undifferentiated and nonexplanatory. At the same time, the evidence is clear that babies with signs of biological vulnerability have a higher probability of developmental problems if born into poverty than if born into more affluent families. For the interventionist, questions of primary importance concern the delineation of effects inherent in the cultural milieu. Such analyses typically involve determining the relative contributions of a number of possible influences: e.g., poor nutrition, adequacy and consistency of caregiving, the social and cognitive environment in the home, etc. How, and under what circumstances, multiple effects combine to interact with the idiosyncratic characteristics of the infant become the major questions facing developmental theorists and interveners.

IMPLICATIONS FOR INTERVENTION

Evidence relative to questions of continuity and prediction is impressively negative, but from the interventionist's point of view the argument is specious. Programs of intervention are based on the assumption that there are indeed recognizable conditions in early childhood and infancy that, if not dealt with appropriately, will lead to long-term negative consequences for the child. Decisions about when to intervene and the nature of interventions are made with the assumptions that individual behavioral-developmental signs are indicative of broader growth dimensions, that there is continuity of growth over time, and that intervention will have long-term, major effects on future development. These points become particularly important because interventions with the developmentally disabled often go beyond the immediate medical treatment surrounding the neonatal and perinatal periods, and are primarily educational and socially rehabilitative in nature.

The growth of early intervention programs over the past 10 years is extraordinary. As might be expected from the number that exist, intervention programs are characterized by broad variations in focus, emphasis, content, implementation, schemes, and target populations. Despite the number and variety of programs, review of the literature yields several generalizations: 1) in most cases, the programs have an educational rather than a medical focus, 2) there are relatively fewer programs aimed at infancy than at the preschool years (although the direction is for earlier interventions), 3) despite the variety of handicapping conditions and diagnostic data, programs are frequently generalized and nonspecific to a given child, providing instead content aimed at enhancement of cognitive or affective dimensions common to all children. The third point deserves particularly careful attention, because it is likely that some of the confusions about program goals, methods, and outcomes are related to it. Unfortunately, few interveners have provided clear evidence of program outcomes, and evaluations have tended to reflect the program implementor's enthusiasm as much as they have clearly documented program effects. The problem of efficacy is not limited to early intervention programs. It is pertinent to consider Sarason's (1972) admonition that "the concept and act of intervention raises issues too often overlooked or deemphasized precisely because the desire to help tends to overevaluate what one knows and to obscure the extent of one's ignorance" (p. 469). Sarason's caution may be an appropriate note on which to examine early intervention programs, because such an analysis may clarify the extent of our ignorance.

Early Childhood Programs

Sheer numbers and redundancy of early intervention programs preclude an exhaustive and detailed review, but four recent analyses (Karnes and Teska, 1975; Levitt and Cohen, 1975; Miller and Dyer, 1975; Parker and Day, 1972) allow some generalizations about program parameters and program outcomes. Parker and Day compared 14 well known preschool programs on five major dimensions: theoretical foundations, goals and objectives, implementation, motivation, and exportability. Karnes and Teska (1975) reviewed early intervention programs that in their opinion were developed from a research base. Levitt and Cohen (1975) compared selected parent-intervention programs for handicapped and disadvantaged preschool children. Thirteen programs for handicapped children were included in their review, with programs designed to serve blind, deaf, deaf/blind, mentally retarded, cerebral palsied, emotionally disturbed, and multiply handicapped children to age six. Twelve programs serving socioeconomically disadvantaged preschoolers were also reviewed for comparison purposes. Miller and Dyer (1975) reported a detailed follow-up study of children enrolled in four program models for disadvantaged preschoolers.

On the basis of these reviews, it seems reasonable to conclude that most programs have common goals, viz. enhancement of cognitive development and social-affective competence. It is in implementation, or the operational characteristics, that programs differ markedly. Parker and Day (1972) specified differences among programs according to structure, teaching styles and methods, use of intrinsic or extrinsic motivators, degree and kind of parental participation, and training and use of personnel. Karnes and Teska also found that the majority of programs focused on cognitive and language development, and noted that program effects were measured mainly in IQ changes, school readiness indices, and achievement in school. Despite the recognized compounding of biological and sociocultural risk conditions, Karnes and Teska noted that few intervention programs sought to include mentally retarded or handicapped children. On the contrary, in the majority of programs, children with handicapping conditions were excluded. The findings from most preschool programs, thus, provide little insight into the multiple and interactive effects of cultural and biological vulnerability.

Levitt and Cohen (1975) identified some differences in programs for children with biological risk conditions and those at risk for social or cultural reasons. In particular, they noted that programs for the handicapped were less comprehensive than were those for disadvantaged children, and that they were less apt to use paraprofessionals as part of the regular program staff. Parents of handicapped children were found to be more involved in ongoing intervention than were parents of disadvantaged children, but the effects of this involvement, as well as the overall effects of the programs, were not well documented or evaluated. Levitt and Cohen speculated that the Piagetian "process oriented" curriculum often found in programs for disadvantaged pupils might well have appropriate application to handicapped pupils. Consistent with the generalizations of Parker and Day and of Karnes and Teska, Levitt and Cohen could find little evidence to support the effectiveness of one program over others, causing them to conclude: "it is evident that most parent-intervention programs for handicapped children are still being conducted within the context of an informal service-oriented tradition. There is obvious need to explore further a more rigorous approach to these programs" (p. 364).

Preliminary evidence derived from a "more rigorous" approach to program analysis and assessment may be found in Miller and Dyer's (1975) monograph.

Beginning with Head Start children enrolled in four program "models" (Bereiter-Englemann, Darcee, Montessori, and traditional enrichment), these investigators monitored ongoing program activities and assessed children's development and achievement during the preschool period, then conducted follow-up assessments at kindergarten through grade two. Miller and Dyer analyzed the four programs in terms of philosophy, curriculum, methods, classroom atmosphere and teacher's role, and goals for children. Specific variables on which comparisons were made included feedback or reinforcement, modeling and imitation, play, sensory stimulation, language, manipulation of materials, sequencing, and ecological dimensions. Differences among programs varied according to program variables, but overall there were ideological and prescriptive differences evidenced in teacher's roles, behaviors, and instructional techniques, as well as in program structure, grouping, and the like.

Of particular importance for the present paper, Miller and Dyer found differential short- and long-term effects according to programs and according to children's characteristics. It should be remembered that a number of earlier studies of Head Start programs had yielded essentially negative findings (Westinghouse Learning Corporation, 1969) or had suggested that any well planned and organized intervention led to similar generalized changes (Weikart, 1967). In contrast, Miller and Dyer reported that didactic programs had stronger short-term, but weaker long-term, effects than did other program models, noting especially that "fade out" effects were most dramatic for the immediate IQ gains in the didactic programs. In earlier work, Karnes (1973) and Bissell (1973) reported differential as well as generalized program effects relative to the kind of interventions studied. The Miller and Dyer findings are consistent with these, and may be interpreted to suggest further that the differential effects are related to characteristics of both the programs and the children, with males consistently benefiting more than females from intervention, and with the most dramatic differences found in long-term effects of nondidactic programs. In short, although limited to comparisons among four preschool programs and to children with risk presumed to be related to "cultural deficit," the Miller and Dyer study provides a more differentiated analysis of program components and effects, and hints at the complex interactions between intervention programs and children's characteristics. It seems likely and necessary that intervention effectiveness for children at risk requires specification of these interactions. By inference, at least, more differentiated and powerful assessment strategies are implied. In this regard, Sigel, Secrist, and Forman (1973) provide data on preschool children in compensatory education programs that suggest that traditional psychometric assessments are indeed limited. They have broadened the base of assessment, implicating attentional as well as cognitive variables, and noting the importance of the contextual bases of assessment.

Differentiated information concerning children's characteristics and needs is particularly important when planning interventions for preschoolers at risk for developmental problems. The federal requirement of 10% "set-asides" for handicapped children in Head Start programs is to be commended, because it provides official public endorsement of critical, although unmet, needs of young handicapped children. Review of existing programs for preschoolers, however, raises questions about the likely effectiveness of most generalized programs for children with a variety of handicapping conditions. Part of the problem is, of course, that the specific effects of particular handicapping conditions on other growth dimensions is not clear. The issue of continuity and stability of growth has already been touched upon in this paper, but it becomes especially pertinent when attempting to determine what and when developmental abilities can be influenced. Taken together, these considerations have major importance for planning interventions for handicapped young children. Unfortunately, a good deal of assessment data does not lead to differentiated program planning but, rather identifies a generalized category of risk.

Infant Programs

As with programs for preschool children at risk, intervention with infants has proliferated dramatically in the past few years. In the Los Angeles area alone there are over 50 programs that offer services of some nature to disadvantaged, developmentally disabled, or other "at risk" infants (Chasen and Sessions, 1975). The impetus for many of the infant programs derives partially from the view that: 1) early interventions are likely to lead to positive outcomes (Meier, 1975; Neilsen, Collins, Meisel, Lowry, Engh, and Johnson, 1975), 2) any intervention is better than none, and 3) assumptions that some previously collected body of knowledge about interventions with older children could be extrapolated to younger children and infants.

Given that the infant programs were only recently implemented, it is not surprising that there are only fragmentary reports of program goals, techniques, and outcomes. Notwithstanding, it seems evident from the limited available data that relationships between assessment and intervention and between diagnosis and programs remain ill-defined, even speculative. Using the Los Angeles area directory of infant programs (Chasen and Sessions, 1975) as one reference point, it may be noted that approximately one-half of the programs listed provide diagnostic as well as intervention services. The nature of the diagnostic services vary, but most utilize primarily medical and psychological (developmental) assessment data. A single program may provide intervention for infants with developmental delays, infants at risk because of biologically handicapping conditions, and infants at risk because of social and economic reasons. Other programs are more specific to diagnostic entities served, and focus on particular disability conditions, e.g., deaf, blind, cerebral palsy. Many programs provide ongoing medical consultation and social services; some require parent or caregiver involvement. Programs may be highly individualized and home based, or may utilize both individual and group experiences that are essentially school based. The point is that like preschool programs for risk children, interventions tend to be "broad band"—directed at infants with widely differing risk conditions. It is not possible to talk of a single or prototype program model, although review of infant programs (Friedlander, Sterritt, and Kirk, 1975) suggests that the single most common approach to infant intervention is nonspecific enrichment, given both in the home and intervention center, and utilizing parents as program mediators. Either explicit or implicit assumptions are made regarding the influence of early experiences on later development, the use of compensatory mechanisms to overcome possible deficit related to specific handicapping conditions, and broad positive benefits for infants and families.

A few intervention programs have developed because clear clinical evidence has demonstrated the advantage of one approach over others. Over 10 years ago, for example, Stedman and Eichorn (1964) showed the advantage of home rather than institutional rearing for Down's Syndrome children. By inference, if homes are better places for Down's children than are institutions, then the better the home, the better the chance for the infant's development. What comprises "better" is still to be determined empirically. Thus, programs for Down's children vary in content and focus (Bidder, Bryant, and Gray, 1975; Connolly and Russell, 1976; Hayden and Dimitriev, 1975; Rynders and Horrobin, 1975). Furthermore, long-term data are not available to demonstrate the effectiveness of intervention in slowing the decelerated rate of IQ often seen in the early years (Carr, 1970; Dicks-Mireaux, 1972). Programs for infants with cerebral palsy or visual and auditory handicaps also have been established—some of these services offered as part of the downward age extension of rehabilitative facilities, others developed specifically for infants. The focus in these programs is on rehabilitation techniques to remediate sensory and motor impairments. The intervention techniques are presumed to foster cognitive growth. As with older children, the rationale for the program derives not so much from a data base as from the feeling that any intervention will aid in development. Of overriding importance is the assumption that appropriate stimulation and opportunities during infancy will facilitate and enhance cognitive growth, and thus, that enrichment programs are appropriate for a variety of risk conditions (see Moore and Meltzoff, this volume).

It is evident, then, that the rationale for infant programs varies, but so does program content. Questions regarding program content and effectiveness are essentially empirical, but they have important conceptual underpinnings. For example, should there be a structured cognitive curriculum such as that proposed by the Portage group or the Marshalltown team, or should intervention be developed for individual mother-infant dyads (Kass, Sigman, Bromwich, and Parmelee, 1974)? The idea of a tightly structured infant program suggests that infant abilities are teachable in the sense that the older child is taught penmanship or the alphabet. An alternative assumption is "that learning depends on an active interchange between the developing organisms and those constants in the physical and social world" (Wolff, 1969). The issue has relevance not only for defining the behaviors that are "teachable" to the infant, but it also raises questions about the generalizable nature of any infant behavior that *can* be taught, as well as the limitation imposed by applying standardized approaches to individual infant needs.

The content of "rehabilitation" for infants is also an issue. Treatment for motorically disabled infants and young children often consists of motor positioning, fostering of developmental sequences, and facilitation of motor responses utilizing sensory stimuli (Bobath, 1967; Fiorentino, 1975). In the last few years another treatment approach, that of sensory-integrative therapy (Ayres, 1972), has been added to rehabilitative practices. Although utilized primarily with school aged children, it is currently being applied to younger children, even infants. Ayres proposes that learning disorders are a result of dysfunction of the organizing mechanisms of the brain. Intervention for disordered sensory integration is directed at enhancing primitive levels of motoric responses by facilitation of maturational sequences and organization of brain stem functioning. The brain stem, particularly the reticular system, is presumed to be influenced by sensory input via tactile, vestibular, and proprioceptive receptors. A number of specific activities (e.g., spinning a young child in a net) are used to elicit responses that supposedly affect neural integration. There are few data to assess program effects, especially with young children, and although increasingly widely used, the technique lacks empirical test.

In sum, the data base for infant programs is limited, and the theoretical underpinnings are often cloudy. We seem to be repeating the scenario used for preschool programs, too often implementing first and reflecting second. Notwithstanding the inherent appeal of babies, the incredible rush to intervene with infants in view of lack of clearly defined conceptualizations, goals, methodologies, and adequately trained personnel is sobering. The questions belatedly asked post hoc about preschool intervention could, and should, be asked now of infant programs.

Assessment and Program Evaluation

On the basis of review of a variety of programs for infants and young children at risk, programs can be described in terms of age and characteristics of children served, extent and kind of parental involvement, home or facility based delivery of intervention services, and the like. A summary of program characteristics according to biological and sociocultural risk status may be found in Table 1. Examination of this table reveals that, whereas long-term goals for children and families are similar, programs do differ in emphases, specific techniques, and in immediate treatment or intervention outcomes. It is difficult to determine how, and in what ways, programs of intervention are successful. It is equally difficult to make differential statements about which kinds of programs are effective with what kinds of risk children. From a practical point of view, it may be that program efficacy is often determined, at least in part, by feasibility and economy. The data concerning the specific nature of the interactions between program content and children's characteristics are somewhat discouraging.

Entry into a particular intervention program is related more to whether a child fits a broad band risk category and/or because a given program is available than it is to the substance of a diagnostic work-up. As noted earlier, children are selected for the most part on the basis of a common attribute (viz. socioeconomic disadvantage, Down's Syndrome), and are provided with similar types of intervention programs. Such programs frequently are variations of a "general enrichment" model. Escalona (1974) suggests that such an approach typifies interventions based on an epidemiological frame of reference, a kind of "mass innoculation" program in which all children receive essentially the same or similar kind of treatment or innoculation, wherein it is assumed that most will benefit from it. However, the prevention of disease cannot be equated with the prevention or amelioration of a multidimensional entity such as mental retardation. The complexities of human organisms, the diversity of changing and stable features of the environments, and the

Table 1. Characteristics of programs for children at sociocultural and biological risk

Program characteristics	Sociocultural risk	Biological risk
Focus	on assumed inadequacies and/or deficiencies in environment	on identified conditions in infant or child
Timing	begins after infancy	begins in infancy upon diagnosis
Major goals	cognitive-prevention of sociocultural retardation	rehabilitative—minimizes and reduces developmental consequences of child's condition
Content	supplementary, enriching, educational	specific remediation directed at compensatory strategies
Organization	primarily group experiences	primarily individual experiences
Implementation	child, maternal experiences and interventions in parallel	child, maternal experiences interactive
Program outcomes	short-term, school referenced	life long referenced
Professional responsibilities	psychologists, educators, paraprofessionals	physicians, psychologists, therapists
Evaluative criteria	school achievement related	developmental milestones, self-care
Assessment tools	psychiatric, standardized tests, child-norm comparisons	clinical-diagnostic instruments, child-child comparisons

variety of interactions of an individual with others preclude taking such a simplistic approach and expecting it to succeed.

Lack of definitive data to evaluate the effects of infant and preschool programs has been attributed primarily to the weakness of outcome measures. We suggest that inconclusive outcomes are also a function of weak theoretical constructs and assessment techniques at the entry stage of programs, that is, at the time diagnosis and program planning begin. It seems reasonable to speculate that the inadequacies of assessment are in large part related to imprecise and/or incomplete understanding of the expression of pertinent developmental processes. Escalona (1974) notes that for the most part clinical skills and developmental theories have not been sufficient to allow us to predict from given conditions of risk to later outcomes, despite frequent retrospective confirmation of diagnostic signs. However, where assessment provides description and delineation of the developmental sequence of behaviors, and when antecedent and outcome developmental events are identified, there is an increased probability that assessment data will lead to appropriate and selective interventions, and that program outcomes can be objectively evaluated.

In our opinion, the assessment and intervention described by Fraiberg (1971) and her colleagues (Fraiberg, Smith, and Adelson, 1969) with blind infants is an elegant example of a coordinated and discerning approach to assessment and intervention that is directly testable. These clinical researchers analyzed the sequence of development of blind babies, and identified through sensitive and precise observation the components of behavior that were inconsistent with behaviors of seeing children of comparable ages. Before attempting to intervene, the researchers observed, assessed, and tested hypotheses. In Fraiberg's words, they became "hand watchers," noting that failure in adaptive hand behavior (midline hand play at four to five months) led to delay in development of sensorimotor schemas and object constancy. Recognition of the blind baby's delays in localization of sound and the relationship of sound cues to creeping behavior followed from observations of hand play. Thus, the interveners' goal was to find adaptive routes that could be utilized to facilitate both cognitive and affective growth in the absence of vision. Educational interventions involving caregivers were direct and immediate, and focused on "education" of the baby's hands. In essence, Fraiberg and her co-workers analyzed the development of object constancy in blind babies, and identified the effects of lack of vision on object permanence and on a variety of subsequent behaviors. Through assessment by observation, they specified the components and antecedent experiences that underlie particular developmental accomplishments. The assessment information directed, and was coordinated with, the intervention. Both led to objective data with which to evaluate the therapeutic-educational program. Fraiberg's analysis required time, patience, and infinite sensitivity, but the approach may well be viewed as a model for work with infants and young children at risk.

A DEVELOPMENTAL APPROACH TO INTERVENTION

Because many assessment instruments and systems lack power and specificity, it is not surprising that many intervention programs are global and nonspecific, based more on inferred risk than on clearly delineated developmental processes. Some limitations of assessment and intervention are related to the very complexity of risk. It is not possible to conceptualize risk in terms of unitary conditions or as a single set of variables, because early risk is clearly a function of multiple conditions and influences. The precise ways in which these various conditions or events combine to influence development is not known. It seems likely that the interrelationship among variables is not simply additive; some conditions may have more powerful effects than others on particular aspects of development. Even a weighted additive model lacks explanatory or predictive power, because the influence of a given condition may serve to either exacerbate or alleviate other influences under certain conditions and at certain age periods. The biologically vulnerable infant or young child may be especially sensitive to environmental conditions or therapeutic effects, so that interventions may have powerful effects on his development, in essence minimizing biological vulnerability and, fortunately, negating the risk condition. By the same token, the cumulative effects of biological vulnerability and caregiving inadequacies may interact to lead to serious and long-term consequences for a given child.

A number of theorists have proposed models to define and describe early development; most recognize the mutuality of child and environmental influences. Sameroff and Chandler (1975), for example, describe three models: a Main-effect Model, an Interactional Model, and a Transactional Model. They opt for the third because in their opinion, it is the one that best allows understanding of continuities and discontinuities of growth over time, and that provides insight into normal as well as deviant or atypical development. Although the Transactional Model has appeal for delineating the nature of growth across major developmental periods, there is still question about the nature of change within periods. The specific and precise growth processes within developmental periods are sometimes overlooked in the emphasis on long-term outcomes. Importantly, although interventions have long-term goals, the substance of intervention is directed at within-period changes, especially for risk children. Thus, assessors and interveners alike need a model of growth that provides insight into specific, minute sequences of change, that identifies both the nature and the timing of experiences, and that directs adaptive, compensatory routes to a given developmental goal.

A Developmental Sequence Model

Flavell (1972) has proposed a model for cognitive growth that may be used to understand within-period development as well as long-term change on a variety of developmental dimensions. In this model, Flavell identifies five principal processes that allow analysis and classification of cognitive-developmental sequences. These processes are: Addition, Substitution, Modification, Inclusion, and Mediation. Flavell proposes that "any cognitive-developmental change reflects the presence of one or more of these five 'developmental processes'" (p. 286). It is reasonable to expect that these five processes might serve as a unifying scheme for assessment and intervention for infants and young children at risk, because they allow a highly differentiated analysis of status and change in infancy and early childhood.

Following Flavell's terminology, we use X1 and X2 to define and describe a behavior, a skill, ability, structure, concept, operation, bit of knowledge, or any other type of cognitive unity" (p. 281). We are expanding his conceptualization in speculative fashion to account for changes over time, changes in terms of expansion of abilities, organization and reorganization of abilities, and consolidation of skills. In Flavell's model, *Addition* is described in this way. Behavior X1 starts at one time and behavior X2 starts at a later date, the two behaviors coexist permanently, and both become part of the child's repertoire, thus offering diversity in behavior and alternative modes of response. In *Substitution,* on the other hand, behavior X1 is replaced by behavior X2 in a gradual process; both may coexist for a period of time, may alternate, complement, or even compete with each other, but in time X2 fully replaces X1. According to Flavell, *Modification* is a process by which behavior X1 undergoes refinement to become X2. Flavell proposes three principle forms of Modification: differentiation, generalization, and stabilization; all three lead to modification or gradual adaptation of a particular ability or process, such that the basic process changes not in kind but in adaptive quality. In *Inclusion,* X1 becomes a component of X2 so that higher order behaviors develop, integrating one or several lower order behaviors. This process is essentially one of linkage of already developed abilities or units of behavior; in the Inclusion category, each ability maintains its own integrity, is instrumental in producing more integrated behaviors, and can be included in a variety of higher abilities. In contrast to Inclusion, where X1 is a component of X2, the critical characteristic of *Mediation* is that X1 "paves the way" for development of X2. X1 does not remain a component, but is rather a bridge to another behavior, influencing formation of that new behavior, there is thus not a necessary permanent association of X1 and X2, because the mediation relationship may change with time.

Infant behavior yields many specific examples of Flavell's five processes. The extraordinary increase in the very young infant's behavioral repertoire is testimony to the addition process. Ambulation is added to prehension, language is added to gestures, and all remain as part of the child's behavioral pool. In terms of substitution, where immature behaviors are phased out, one observes culturally defined words and terms replacing unspecified vocalization and babbling, or in the realm of play one sees reality testing become more cognitive and less fantasy based. Modification serves such a variety of purposes that it may be identified on many dimensions, e.g., perceptual, cognitive, or motor abilities. Consider the process of change in perception, wherein the infant's innate ability to differentiate grossly between patterned and nonpatterned stimuli becomes the finely honed ability to discriminate the many characteristics of a stimulus, and where meaning is attached to highly differentiated and complex perceptual events. Inclusion is well illustrated by the "combination of schemas" observed in the last quarter of the first year of life. In order to solve simple problems such as pulling a string to get an attached ring, the infant employs and combines visual inspection, reach, grasp, and pull. Certainly language patterns of children in the second and third year demonstrate inclusionary processes, so that even errors are predictable within context. Finally, Flavell has provided a classic illustration of the mediation process when he suggests that infant creeping paves the way for construction of "new sensory-motor programs of action," allowing the child to interact and deal with new stimuli and experiences. Importantly, as Flavell notes, creeping is not in itself an integral part of these new schema, but it is utilized in the service of their development.

If we view growth as utilizing and requiring these various processes, and if we assume that these processes are differentially important for certain kinds of accomplishments and at certain times in the developmental spectrum, then the task for the developmental theorist is to delineate the timing and the influenceability of the processes, the task for the assessor is to specify relevant behavioral indicators of these processes, and the task for the intervener is to determine the nature of the environmental experiences that can facilitate and enhance them. The translation of this process analysis to the practicalities of programs is the main challenge. However, it holds promise for a differentiated approach to both assessment and intervention.

To tease out varying effects or influences on growth requires analysis of the content of intervention in terms of what process is targeted and what process is required for given developmental accomplishments. It is likely that some processes are more susceptible to intervention than are others. In this regard, Flavell has suggested that addition and mediation are less amenable to environmental influence than are substitution, modification, and inclusion. It is likely that addition is a particularly important process in the first half-year of life. Review of infant data suggests that there are relatively few behaviors that are directly influenceable (i.e., teachable) in the first half-year of life. Thus, it is consistent with Flavell's model to suggest that the major developmental accomplishments of those early months are probably more a function of the basic biologic substrate (Piaget, 1971) than they are of externally induced events. For this period, environmental or intervention influences can be properly conceived as affecting rate of development and decalage, as for example, the ability to attend to many dimensions of the milieu or to explore relevant parts of the environment. By inference, the necessary environmental conditions and stimulation to induce this growth are part of the advantaged, biologically intact infant's surroundings. For the disadvantaged or atypical infant, such planned conditions may become the substance of early intervention.

In the latter part of the first year and in the second year, the substitution, modification, and inclusion growth processes assume more powerful roles. An expanded and broader repertoire allows and supports the influence of experience, leading to increasing importance of mediation in more complex organizations of abilities. Hypothetically, at least, these processes are more susceptible to direct environmental influence than is the biologically flavored addition. Thus, the stage may be set for a more active and comprehensive program of intervention. It is likely that the preschool child's expanded language abilities, his differentiated and organized attentional skills, and his social development all reflect and express aspects of inclusion, substitution, and modification, and that these accomplishments are indeed directly affected by the nature of the child's experiences.

IMPLICATIONS

Viewed within the context of a developmental sequence model, it is possible to draw inferences and implications concerning more powerful approaches to assessment and intervention with infants and children at risk. It is worthwhile to reiterate that few standard assessment scales are sensitive enough to identify or provide understanding of fundamental developmental processes. Most assessment data are therefore of limited use in planning and implementing intervention. Assessment which specifies antecedent and outcome developmental events, and which takes into account changing effects of biologic and experiential influences as a function of time and condition, should allow differentiated intervention efforts. Broadening the base of assessment information to include indicators of attention, social responsiveness, temperament, and affective and motivational characteristics seems promising. Effective assessment cannot focus exclusively on the infant or child, because extra-child conditions have been shown both to be extraordinarily powerful influences, and to provide integral diagnostic data. The issue of continuity as a fundamental concern for the assessor has been identified. Specification of behavioral indicators of continuity, and delineation of the experiential influences on specific continuities deserve extensive research effort, because, theoretically and practically, questions of continuity and "influenceability" are the bases for intervention.

The recent literature on research with infants abounds with hints of promising variables to add to existing developmental assessments, viz. measures of attention and of information processing (Honzik, 1976; Lewis, 1976). These directions are consistent with earlier work of Kagan (1971), who demonstrated that ability to attend is an important ongoing, adaptive behavior that shows consistency. Furthermore, techniques already developed in the habituation paradigm provide tentative direction for assessing capabilities of severely involved handicapped infants and young children. With the exception of the Case Western group (Miranda and Fantz, 1973; 1974), these techniques have not been explored extensively with atypical infants, but they may well deserve attention.

Other adaptive or coping responses, currently excluded from formal developmental examinations, warrant study. Using a component analysis, McCall (1972, 1976) has shown that changing trends in the way infants responded to their milieu was predictive of later development at 12 months for females and 18 months for males. In a comprehensive recent review of infant tests, Honzik (1976) suggests that diagnostic predictions could be improved by use of maternal reports, measurement of cognitive style, and infant attention. In a similar view, Yarrow, Rubenstein, and Pederson (1975) have suggested that cognitive-motivational variables related to goal directedness and object orientation may enrich our understanding of infant abilities. Finally, item analysis and clustering are methodological techniques that have proved useful for hypothesizing or determining prominent behavior groups, such as sensorimotor alertness, preschool persistence (Meyers and Dingman, 1969), or vocalization of females (Cameron, Livson, and Bayley, 1967). Such techniques may well allow demonstration of continuities in longitudinal data, and could lead to more powerful and precise screening and assessment techniques.

Both the content and techniques of intervention must vary relative to the age and condition of the risk child. It is not enough to provide generalized enrichment experiences or a single program model for all children within a given risk category. In early infancy, it seems that promising interventions have 1) involved attention to individual parent-infant interactions, 2) have focused heavily on the caregiving quality of the home, and 3) have been essentially nondidactic. In a sense, intervention in the early months may be primarily supportive, rather than active, so that the biologically influenced developmental processes may be facilitated. Intervention may focus as much on the caregiver as on the infant, bringing about changes that improve the nature of the caregiver-infant relationship. For infants with biological risk conditions, early intervention may well involve both informational and affective changes on the part of the caregiver; this complex aspect of intervention needs assessment and analysis. An essential aspect of intervention in the first few months of infancy may be to provide biological stability to set the stage for more active and directed intervention efforts in later developmental periods.

Intervention in the second year may more appropriately be active, because it is likely that the prepotent developmental processes for older infants and young children are influenceable and effected by the nature of experience. Assessment thus involves recognition of subtle changes in timing and in rate of developmental expression, so that the intervener may modify intervention strategies as appropriate. Possible differences in intervention content and emphasis raise questions about training of professionals, use of multiple interveners, and the like. It seems likely that variation in child characteristics in early infancy and preschool periods may require different caregiving climates and caregiver skills, so that the effectiveness of intervention must be assessed in terms of both child and caregiver.

Conditions of biological risk and sociocultural risk may require, at least in part, different content, techniques, and implementation of intervention, which raises questions about whether children with widely varied risk conditions can be most effectively helped in a single program. Children at risk for developmental disabilities may require intense, long-term, rehabilitative programs, and the training and intervention skills for professionals and paraprofessionals may be specialized. On the other hand, children from sociocultural risk conditions, at least in the preschool years, may profit from broader, educationally-oriented programs. For those older children, the nature of the child-intervener interaction may be less focused or intense than is the interaction for the child with biological risk conditions. Clear benefits of placement in "least restrictive environments" must be enhanced with differentiated within-program interventions.

Despite the enthusiasm for and proliferation of intervention programs for infants and young children, assessors and intervener too often seem to work in isolation with programs and techniques reflecting limited, even parochial points of view. There is a strong aura of advocacy surrounding most programs—an understandable attitude given the desire to provide services and the pressures of funding and support. However, isolation of clinical or educational personnel may occur at the program level and can lead to continued application of sometimes inappropriate, possibly ineffective, interventions—not because of unwillingness to change, but because of lack of availability of information and new ideas. The literature relative to infant and preschool programs is diverse, fragmented, and inconsistent. To gain a representative, to say nothing of a comprehensive, overview of the state of the art requires continued search of medical, psychological, rehabilitative, educational, and social service literature. A substantial number of important articles appear in unpublished or privately circulated materials, others are in specialty library collections, unavailable to the worker at the program level. Dissemination and communication continue to be problems that affect delay of service.

It seems reasonable that several directions may change this aspect of early intervention. One concerns recognition of the importance and value of continuing substantive research within the context of clinical-educational programs. Such a direction has obvious implications for funding patterns, for review and evaluation of researchers' activities, and for changes in the conceptual frames of reference that generate specific research projects. Closely related, there is need for commitment to dissemination of applied program research on the part of journal editors and publication review boards. It may well be that a clearing house for assessment and intervention information is needed, or that major prestigious journals devote space on a regular basis.

Finally, and perhaps most importantly, the enthusiasm for early identification and early intervention for children at risk must not lead to premature and pejorative classification, so that category placement, rather than individual characteristics, becomes overriding when decisions are made about programs and interventions. Assessment approaches have tended to focus on problems and deficiencies in development, and interventions have developed in response to these disabilities. Yet clinicians can recount case histories of children with definitive risk signs who developed to become healthy, normal individuals. Tronick and Brazelton (1975) commented upon the neonates—"marvelous capacity to orient to and organize a response to a 'positive' or social stimulus." The authors would carry the observation further and suggest that both assessment and interventions are most beneficial when the positive, compensatory aspects of child and setting are identified and strengthened.

REFERENCES

Ayres, A. J. 1972. Sensory Integration and Learning Disorders. Western Psychological Services, Los Angeles.

Bayley, N. 1955. On regrowth of intelligence. Am. Psychol. 10: 805–818.

Bayley, N. 1949. Consistency and variability in the growth of intelligence from birth to 18 years. J. Genet. Psychol. 75: 165–196.

Bayley, N. 1970. Development of mental abilities. In P. H. Mussen (ed.), Carmichael's Manual of Child Psychology (Vol. 1). John Wiley and Sons, New York.

Bidder, R. T., Bryant, G., and Gray, O. P. 1975. Benefits of Down's Syndrome Children through training their mothers. Arch. Dis. Child. 50: 383–386.

Bissell, J. S. 1973. Planned variation in Head Start and follow through. In J. C. Stanley (ed.), Compensatory Education for Children, Age 2–8. Johns Hopkins Press, Baltimore.

Bobath, B. 1967. The very early treatment of cerebral palsy. Dev. Med. Child Neurol. 9: 373–390.

Brazelton, T. B. 1973. Neonatal Behavioral Assessment Scale. J. B. Lippincott Co., Philadelphia.

Cameron, J., Livson, N., and Bayley, N. 1967. Infant vocalizations and their relationship to mature intelligence. Science 157: 331–333.

Carr, J. 1970. Mental and motor development in young mongol children. J. Ment. Def. Res. 14: 205–220.

Casati, E., and Lézine, I. 1968. Les Etapes de l'Intelligence Sensori-Motrice. Les Editions du Centre de Psychologie Applique, Paris.

Chasen, F., and Sessions, R. 1975. Infant Program Directory: The Los Angeles Area. Exceptional Children's Foundation, Los Angeles.

Chess, S. 1974. The influence of defect on development in children with congenital rubella. Merrill-Palmer Quart. 20(1): 255–274.

Clausen, J. 1967. Mental deficiency—Development of a concept. Am. J. Ment. Def. 71(5): 727–795.

Coleman, J. 1968. The concept of equality of educated opportunity. Harv. Educ. Rev. 38: 7–21.

Connolly, B., and Russell, F. 1976. Interdisciplinary early intervention program. Phys. Ther. 56(2): 155–158.

Corah, N. L., Anthony, E. J., Painter, P., Stern, J. A., and Thurston, D. L. 1965. Effects of perinatal anoxia after seven years. Psychol. Monogr. 79,(3), no. 596.

Corman, H., and Escalona, S. 1969. Stages of sensorimotor development: A replication study. Merrill-Palmer Quart. 15: 351.

Davies, P. A., and Stewart, A. L. 1975. Low-birth-weight infants: Neurological sequelae and later intelligence. Brit. Med. Bull. 31(1): 85–91.

Dicks-Mireaux, M. J. 1972. Mental development of infants with Down's Syndrome. Am. J. Ment. Def. 77(1): 26–32.

Drage, J. S., Kennedy, C., Berendes, H., Schwab, K., and Weiss, W. A. 1966. 5-minute Apgar scores and 4-year psychological performance. Dev. Med. Child Neurol. 8: 141.

Drillien, C. M. 1964. The Growth and Development of the Prematurely Born Infant. Williams and Wilkins, Baltimore.

Ellis, N. R. 1969. A behavioral research strategy in mental retardation: Defense and critique. Am. J. Ment. Def. 73: 557–566.

Escalona, S. K. 1972. Socio/emotional. In background papers of the Boston Conference Screening and Assessment of young children at developmental risk. DHEW Publication (OS): 73–91.

Escalona, S. K. 1974. Intervention programs for children at psychiatric risk; The contribution of child psychiatry and developmental theory. In E. J. Anthony and C. Koupernik (eds.), The Child in His Family, John Wiley and Sons, New York.

Escalona, S. K., and Heider, G. M. 1959. Prediction and Outcome. Basic Books, New York.

Fiorentino, M. 1975. Occupational therapy: Realization to activation. Am. J. Occup. Ther. 29(1): 15–2.

Fishler, K., Graliker, B. V., and Koch, R. 1965. The predictability of intelligence with Gesell Developmental Scales in mentally retarded infants and young children. Am. J. Ment. Def. 69: 515–525.

Fishman, M. A., and Palkes, H. S. 1974. The validity of psychometric testing in children with congenital malformations of the central nervous system. Dev. Med. Child Neurol. 16(2): 180–185.

Flavell, J. 1972. An analysis of cognitive-developmental sequences. Genet. Psychol. Monogr. 86: 279–350.

Fraiberg, S. 1971. Intervention in infancy: A program for blind infants. J. Am. Acad. Child Psychiatry 10: 381–405.

Fraiberg, S., Smith, M., and Adelson, E. 1969. An educational program for blind infants. J. Spec. Educ. 3(2): 121–139.

Frankenburg, W. K., and Camp, B. W. 1975. Pediatric Screening Tests. Charles C Thomas Publisher, Springfield.

Friedlander, B. Z., Sterritt, G. M., and Kirk, G. E. 1975. Exceptional Infant. Vol. 3: Assessment and Intervention. Brunner/Mazel, New York.

Graham, F. K., Ehrhart, C. B., Thurston, D., and Craft, M. 1962. Development three years after perinatal anoxia and other potentially damaging newborn experiences. Psychol. Monogr. 76(3), no. 522.

Haeussermann, E. 1958. Developmental Potential of Preschool Children. Grune and Stratton, New York.

Harper, P. A., and Wiener, G. 1965. Sequelae of low birth weight. Annu. Rev. Med. 16: 405–420.

Hayden, A. H., and Dimitriev, U. 1975. The multidisciplinary preschool program for Down's Syndrome children at the University of Washington model preschool center. In B. Z. Friedlander, G. M. Sterritt, and G. E. Kirk (eds.), Exceptional Infant. Vol. 3: Assessment and Intervention. Brunner/Mazel, New York.

Hohman, L. B., and Freedheim, D. K. 1959. A study of IQ retest evaluations on 370 cerebral palsied children. Am. J. Phys. Med. 38: 180–187.

Holden, R. H. 1972. Prediction of mental retardation in infancy. Ment. Retard. 10: 28–30.

Honzik, M. P. 1976. Value and limitations of infant tests: An overview. In M. Lewis (ed.), Origins of Intelligence: Infancy and Early Childhood. Plenum, New York.

Hunt, J. V., and Bayley, W. 1971. Explanations into patterns of mental development from the Bayley scales of infant development. In J. G. Hill (ed.), Minnesota Symposia of Child Psychology, Vol. J. The University of Minnesota Press, Minneapolis.

Kagan, J., and Moss, H. A. 1962. Birth and Maturity. John Wiley and Sons, New York.

Kagan, J. 1971. Change and Continuity in Infancy. John Wiley and Sons, New York.

Karnes, M. B. 1973. Evaluation and implications of research with young handicapped and low-income children. In J. C. Stanley (ed.), Compensatory Education for Children, Ages 2–8. Johns Hopkins Press, Baltimore.

Karnes, M. B., and Teska, J. A. 1975. Children's response to intervention programs. In J. Gallagher (ed.), The Application of Child Development Research to Exceptional Children. The Council for Exceptional Children, Reston, Va.

Kass, E. R., Sigman, M., Bromwich, R. M., and Parmelee, A. H. 1974. Educational intervention with high-risk infants. Paper presented at the Conference on Early Intervention for High-Risk Infants and Young Children, May, Chapel Hill, N.C.

Keogh, B. K., and Becker, L. D. 1973. Early detection of learning problems: Questions, cautions, guidelines. Except. Child. 40: 5–11.

Levitt, E., and Cohen, S. 1975. An analysis of selected parent-intervention programs for handicapped and disadvantaged children. J. Spec. Educ. 9(4): 345–374.

Lewis, M. 1976. Origins of Intelligence: Infancy and Early Childhood. Plenum, New York.

Lillienfeld, A. M., and Parkhurst, E. 1951. A study of the association of factors of pregnancy and parturition with the development of cerebral palsy: A preliminary report. Am. J. Hyg. 53: 262–282.

McCall, R. B. 1976. Toward an epigenetic conception of mental development in the first three years of life. In M. Lewis (ed.), Origins of Intelligence: Infancy and Early Childhood. Plenum, New York.

McCall, R. B., Hogarty, P. S., and Hurlburt, N. 1972. Transition in infant sensorimotor development and the prediction of childhood IQ. Am. Psychol. 27: 728–798.

Meier, J. H. 1973. Screening and assessment of young children at developmental risk. DHEW Publication (OS): 73–90.

Meier, J. H. 1975. Early intervention in the prevention of mental retardation. In A. Milunsky (ed.), The Prevention of Genetic Disease and Mental Retardation. Saunders, Philadelphia.

Mercer, J. R. 1970. Sociological perspectives on mild retardation. In H. C. Haywood (ed.), Socio-Cultural Aspects of Mental Retardation. Appleton-Century-Crofts, New York.

Meyers, C. E., and Dingman, H. F. 1969. The structure of abilities at the preschool ages: Hypothesized domains. Psychol. Bull. 57(6): 514–532.

Miller, L. B., and Dyer, J. L. 1975. Four preschool programs: Their dimensions and effects. Monogr. Soc. Res. Child Dev. 40(162): 5–6.

Miranda, S. B., and Fantz, R. L. 1973. Visual preferences of Down's Syndrome and normal infants. Child Dev. 44: 555–561.

Miranda, S. B., and Fantz, R. L. 1974. Recognition memory in Down's Syndrome and normal infants. Child Dev. 45: 651–660.

Moore, T. 1967. Language and intelligence: A longitudinal study of the first eight years. Hum. Dev. 10: 88–106.

Nielsen, G., Collins, S., Meisel, J., Lowry, M., Engh, H., and Johnson, D. 1975. An intervention program for atypical infants. In B. L. Friedlander, G. M. Sterritt, and G. E. Kirk (eds.), Exceptional Infant. Vol. 3: Assessment and Intervention. Brunner/Mazel, New York.

Parker, R. K., and Day, M. D. 1972. Comparisons of preschool curricula. In R. K. Parker (ed.), The Preschool in Action: Exploring Early Childhood Programs. Allyn & Bacon, Boston.

Parmelee, A. H., and Haber, A. 1973. Who is the "risk infant"? Clin. Obstetr. Gynecol. 16: 376–387.

Parmelee, A. H., Kopp, C. B., and Sigman, M. 1976. Selection of developmental assessment techniques for infants at risk. Merrill-Palmer Quart. 22(3): 177–199.

Pasamanick, B., and Knobloch, H. 1966. Retrospective studies on the epidemiology of reproductive casualty: Old and new. Merrill-Palmer Quart. 12: 7–26.

Pasamanick, B., Knobloch, H., and Lillienfeld, A. M. 1956. Socioeconomic status and some precursors of neuropsychiatric disorders. Am. J. Orthopsychiatry 26: 594–601.

Piaget, J. 1971. Biology and Knowledge. University of Chicago Press, Chicago.

Rosenblith, J. F. 1975. Prognostic value of neonatal behavior tests. In B. Z. Friedlander, J. M. Sterritt, and G. E. Kirk (eds.), Exceptional Infant. Brunner/Mazel, New York.

Rynders, J. E., and Horrobin, J. M. 1975. Project Edge: The University of Minnesota's Communication Program for Down's Syndrome Infants. In B. L. Friedlander, G. M. Sterritt, and G. E. Kirk (eds.), Exceptional Infant. Vol. 3: Assessment and Intervention. Brunner/Mazel, New York.

Sameroff, A. 1975. Early influences on development: Fact or fancy? Merrill-Palmer Quart. 21(4): 267–293.

Sameroff, A. J., and Chandler, M. J. 1975. Reproductive risk and the continuum of caretaking casualty. In F. D. Horowitz, M. Hetherington, S. Scarr-Salapatek, and G. Siegel (eds.), Review of Child Development Research, Vol. 4. University of Chicago, Chicago.

Sarason, S. B. 1972. Anxiety, intervention and the culture of the school. In C. D. Spielberger (ed.), Anxiety—Current Trends in Theory and Research, Vol. II. Academic Press, New York.

Share, J., Koch, R., Webb, A., and Graliker, B. 1964. The Longitudinal development of infants and young children with Down's syndrome. Am. J. Ment. Def. 68: 689–692.

Sigel, I. E., Secrist, A., and Forman, G. 1973. Psycho-educational intervention beginning at age two: Reflections and outcomes. In J. C. Stanley (ed.), Compensatory Education for Children Ages 2–8. The Johns Hopkins Press, Baltimore.

Stedman, D., and Eichorn, D. 1964. A comparison of the growth and development of institutionalized and home reared mongoloids during infancy and early childhood. Am. J. Ment. Def. 69: 391–401.

Stephens, W. 1972. Screening and assessment of young children at developmental risk. In Background Papers of the Boston Conference. DHEW Publications (OS): 73–91.

Stott, L. H., and Ball, R. J. 1965. Infant and preschool mental tests: Review and evaluation. Monogr. Soc. Res. Child Dev. 30: no. 101.

Thomas, H. 1970. Psychological assessment instructions for use with human infants. Merrill-Palmer Quart. 16: 179–224.

Thomas, A., Chess, S., and Birch, H. S. 1968. Temperament and Behavioral Disabilities in Children. New York University Press, New York.

Thomas, A., Chess, S., Birch, H. S., Hertzig, M. E., and Korn, S. 1963. Behavioral Individuality in Early Childhood. University Press, New York.

Tronick, E., and Brazelton, T. B. 1975. Clinical uses of the Brazelton neonatal behavioral assessment. In B. Z. Friedlander, J. M. Sterritt, and J. E. Kirk (eds.), Exceptional Infant, Vol. 3. Brunner/Mazel, New York.

Uzgiris, I. C. 1970. Sociocultural factors in cognitive development. In H. C. Haywood (ed.), Socio-Cultural Aspects of Mental Retardation. Appleton-Century-Crofts, New York.

Uzgiris, I. C., and Hunt, J. McV. 1975. Assessment in Infancy. University of Illinois Press, Urbana.

Weikart, D. P. 1967. Preschool programs: Preliminary findings. J. Spec. Educ. 1: 163–181.

Werner, E. E., Honzik, M. P., and Smith, R. S. 1968. Prediction of intelligence and achievement at ten years from twenty months pediatric and psychologic examinations. Child Dev. 39: 1063–1075.

Werner, E. E., Bierman, J. M., and French, F. E. 1971. The Children of Kauai. University of Hawaii, Honolulu.

Westinghouse Learning Corporation. 1969. The Impact of Head Start; An Evaluation of the Effects of Head Start on Children's Cognitive and Affective Development: Volume 1, text, and appendixes A–E. Clearinghouse for Federal Scientific and Technical Information, Dept. of Commerce, National Bureau of Standards, Ohio University.

Wiener, C. 1962. Psychologic correlates of premature birth: A review. J. Nerv. Ment. Dis. 134: 129–144.

Wolff, P. H. 1969. What we must and must not teach our young children from what we know about early cognitive development. In Wolff, P. H. and MacKeith, R. (eds.), Planning for Better Learning in Clinics in Developmental Medicine. Spastics International Medical Publications, London.

Yarrow, L. J. 1964. Personality consistency and change: An overview of some conceptional and methodological issues. Vita Hum. 7: 67–72.

Yarrow, L. J., Rubenstein, J. L., and Pedersen, F. A. 1975. Infant and Environment: Early Cognitive and Motivational Development. Halsted Press (Wiley), New York.

Zigler, E. 1969. Development versus different theories of mental retardation and the problem of motivation. Am. J. Ment. Def. 13: 536–556.

Zigler, E. 1970. Social class and the socialization process. Rev. Educ. Res. 40: 87–110.

Children with Autistic Behaviors

Linda Doherty and Linda Swisher

WHAT IS AUTISM?

This paper was written to share information concerning autistic children's behaviors with those interested on the early behavioral assessment of developmental factors affecting communication and cognitive skills. The literature concerning autistic children no longer emphasizes psychogenic mechanisms, socioeconomic status, or the personalities of the parents. Instead, there is now a consensus that the disorder has a neurological basis. There is also widespread agreement on the pattern of behavioral characteristics that describe this group. Recent attention has focused on social behavior, intellectual status, and disorders of language development. Much remains to be learned, but the areas of dispute are narrowing as research findings replace anecdotal reports.

The features that Kanner (1943) used when first describing the syndrome were primarily behavioral. The 11 children described in that paper were characterized by "an inability to relate to [themselves], to people and to situations," a delay in the acquisition of speech, and an apparently obsessive insistence on the maintenance of sameness. Abnormal development was evident in infancy, which was a major characteristic distinguishing this group from previously described varieties of schizophrenia or childhood psychoses. Other accounts have subsequently confirmed the existence of the syndrome that Kanner described. Rutter (1966) and Rutter and Lockyer (1967) found those features present in nearly all autistic children, but infrequently in other children, to be: a profound failure to develop social relationships, language retardation with impaired comprehension, and ritualistic behaviors reflecting an "insistence on sameness." These symptoms group together and are different from those found in other psychiatric conditions (Rutter, 1966). Thus, these recent reports agree with Kanner's initial report describing the essential features of the disorder. In addition, it has become clear that autism may or may not be associated with mental retardation or obvious neurological impairment.

The preparation of this manuscript was supported by Biomedical Science Support Grant 5 S05 RR07028 from the National Institutes of Health.

549

The neurological status of children diagnosed as autistic has been of interest to many investigators. For example, out of the nine children in Kanner's original diagnostic group seen again as adults, two had developed seizures (Kanner, 1971). Other investigators have reported similar findings (Creak, 1963; Lotter, 1974). Because it is now accepted that many, if not all, children diagnosed as autistic are found to have neurological signs at some stage in their development, it is essential that the neurological status of each child be carefully documented at periodic intervals.

Swisher, Drzewiecki, and Swisher (1976) suggest that autism is a behavioral response to a pattern of encephalopathy that has a wide variety of etiological antecedents. This is in line with Schopler and Reichler's (1971b) statements regarding etiology for this area of childhood disorders: 1) in individual cases the primary cause is usually unknown, 2) the void in knowledge of primary causes has been filled by different theories that have little supporting evidence, 3) it is most likely that the primary causes involve some sort of brain abnormality, and 4) it is unlikely that the parents caused the autistic behavior.

Prevalence figures are difficult to compare because differing criteria were used in different studies. Rimland (1964) reported that infantile autism was rare, as did Kanner and Lesser (1958). Lotter (1966) surveyed an English county using the behavioral criteria described by Creak (1961) to determine the incidence during the first few years of life. A prevalence of 4.5 per 10,000 was found. Although these criteria may not have been strictly comparable to those used by Rimland or Kanner and Lesser, this study of an entire county suggests that infantile autism may be more prevalent than earlier workers suspected.

COURSE OF GENERAL DEVELOPMENT

Prenatal

Evidence is conflicting concerning the association of complications during pregnancy and delivery with autistic development. Schain and Yannet (1960) reported no unusual degree of prenatal complications. Taft and Goldfarb (1964), however, reviewed hospital charts and found a significantly greater incidence of both prenatal and perinatal difficulties for autistic children as compared to their siblings and to normal controls.

Chess (1971) has emphasized the high frequency of autistic behaviors noted in a group of children who had contracted intrauterine rubella. Other prenatal, genetic bases for autistic behaviors are suggested by the developmental patterns of some children with phenylketonuria and tuberous sclerosis. Why these metabolic and structural effects on the brain result in autistic behaviors is still to be elucidated.

Several behaviors suggested to represent the development of autism have been observed at different stages from zero to three years of age.

Zero to Six Months

Some children with autistic behaviors have been described as unusually "good" babies, and others have been described as unusually irritable. Ornitz and Ritvo

(1968) have noted that descriptions of an autistic infant frequently include statements such as "a good baby," "he never cried," "he seemed not to need companionship or stimulation," or "he did not want to be held."

During the first six months, signs of deviant development may include: gaze aversion, failure to orient to the sound of someone coming to the crib, lack of anticipating response to being picked up, underactivity, and, paradoxically, overreaction to stimulation such as a telephone ringing. Delayed or deviant prelanguage vocalization might also be noted.

Six Months to One Year

Ornitz and Ritvo (1968) point out that some autistic infants who drink milk and eat strained foods will spit out or gag on—not chew—rough textured foods. They also note that some infants are disinterested in toys and may drop those placed in their hands, or the opposite may occur—the child may hold on to a particular object for an inordinately long time.

During this period, parents often describe the child as unaffectionate, and disinclined to play imitative games such as "peek-a-boo." Unusual responses to sensory input become obvious in some children. Sudden light, sounds, touch, or being moved may cause signs of fear. At around nine months, behaviors referred to as "self-stimulatory" or "repetitive" may occur. For example, a child may flutter his arms, stare at his fingers, spin toys, or flick lights off and on. Continuous body rocking may be observed, especially in those with greater degrees of retardation.

Motor and language development may seem retarded, aberrant, or show a regression.[1] A careful review of case reports describing autistic children indicates that parents reported a developmental regression in approximately 50% of the children. In a retrospective study (Swisher, Reichler, and Short, 1976) of the clinic records of 20 autistic children, the age at which parents reported a regression for 10 autistic children varied from 6 to 51 months, with an average of 19 months, two weeks. No history of regression was reported for the other ten, all of whom had delayed language milestones.

Two to Three Years

The autistic behaviors usually are recognized between two and three years of age. Around age two, the child may be observed to use other people as though they were objects: e.g., taking a taller person's arm and lifting it up to turn on a light switch. At this age, the language difficulties become quite noticeable, and the question of mental retardation may be raised. It is the authors' experience that half of the children with autistic behaviors at or before age three no longer have noticeable

---

[1] Ornitz and Ritvo (1968) suggest that detailed history taking sometimes can reveal evidence of deviant development that had gone unreported. A series of home movies was shown to a pediatric neurologist (Swisher, personal communication). The films had been taken of a child before the age at which onset of behavioral regression was noted by the parents. The neurologist was not provided with any history and did not know that the child was currently considered autistic. He noted the onset of atypical, stereotyped motor activity early in the second year of life, quite dissimilar to the normal acquisition of motor skills noted in the earlier films of the series. This appearance of atypical motor activity preceded by several months the time of regression reported by the parents.

problems at age five. At least three factors seem to be important in this remission: evidence of normal intellectual development, a structured intervention, and the rate at which language skills improve. The other half seem to contain a large percentage of children who are also mentally retarded, but who do progress with structured intervention.

Four to Five Years

There are few results to aid us in counseling parents with regard to the outcome for their child before age five. Clinical experience suggests that there may be many happy surprises when the child is first diagnosed under five years of age. Several studies are reviewed later that indicate intelligence test results become highly predictive of later functioning if obtained when the child is age six. It is important to point out that these are studies of children who did not, in most cases, receive special schooling. Generally, intervention was directed at changing the parents rather than improving the developmental level of the child. We do not yet know how much structured intervention based on a developmental assessment of the child's level of functioning can change the course of development.

LANGUAGE

The language impairment of most autistic children is generally regarded as reflecting aberrant development: i.e., semantics and syntax not observed in normally developing children. This view of the language impairment of autistic children contrasts with the evidence suggesting that language impairment in retarded children seems similar to a developmental delay or deceleration. The degree to which the rate and quality of language acquisition by autistic children parallels that of retarded children needs to be explored.

There are three identifiable courses for language development in autistic children: early speech and language retardation (Bradley, 1941; Pronovost, 1961; Shervanian, 1967; Swisher, Reichler, and Short, 1976), apparently normally developing speech and language, then a regression (Despert, 1947; Swisher, Reichler, and Short, 1976), and an accelerated development of speech and language with precocious use (Kanner, 1951).

Those with a delay in language development seem to have a better prognosis overall, and for language development in particular (Swisher, Reichler, and Short, 1976). The presence of accelerated language development has yet to be documented. It is possible that the development is aberrant: e.g., use of sentences without the accompanying usual use of single or two-word phrases.

The children with a history of regression are initially observed to have normal development by parents. On reflection, the parents realize that around 18 to 24 months, as an average, regression occurred in many areas of development, including language (Swisher, Reichler, and Short, 1976). For example, one child, who spoke no words at age eight years, had said "ball," "my bottle," and "I want to be like my daddy," before he regressed to vowel-like sounds around 26 months. At age seven years he spoke infrequently, primarily in simple, active, declarative sentences.

By age six, three general groups can be identified in terms of both the quality and quantity of language development. In Table 1 they are referred to as the mute, intermittent, and fluent language users. The "mute" children have already been labeled as such in the literature. It is our experience that they have the poorest prognosis and lowest level of comprehension and expression of language. They speak, but do so possibly only once or twice a week, and sometimes only once or twice a year. They do not readily initiate speech or other activities, and give few observable responses to sound. It is possible that the course of early language developments as reported by parents will include regression in skills.

The intermittent language users speak at a higher developmental level than those referred to in the literature as mute. Their infrequent output has little or no echolalia, flat intonation, and articulation errors.

They sometimes use a linguistic complexity that is considered noteworthy by most who know the child well. The higher level output usually occurs when the child is under stress or desires to fulfill a primary need such as getting food. For example, one child who used approximately ten, two-word phrases during the day, said, "I want *you* to stay!" to his mother, when left at camp for the first time. Another sentence like this was not heard during the next six months. This discrepancy between typical and occasional output presents the language clinician with a difficult task. These children attempt imitation more than the mute children. They seem to more readily imitate whole words or sentences rather than single sounds, e.g., /p/. Their hearing is seldom questioned. It is likely that their parents will report an early history of regression in language development. Ruttenburg and Wolf (1967) emphasized that one of the major problems in dealing with children labeled as autistic is their extreme inability or disinclination to communicate effectively, especially through verbal-language. This statement most likely refers primarily to the mute and intermittant language users.

Many of the fluent speakers use jargon and elaborate intonation patterns. As they improve in their understanding of language, their expressive language more closely approximates normal intonation. The parents usually report language development was always delayed, with no history of regression. We have found that language intervention is quite successful with this group. This is in line with the

Table 1.   Three subgroups of children with relating and language problems

	Mute	Intermittent	Fluent
Comprehension	−	±	+
Expression			
amount	−	±	+
level	−	±	+
jargon	−	−	+
imitation	−	+	+
intonation	−	flat	+
regression	?	+	−
Retardation	profound	moderate	mild

experience of Lovaas (1966) who reports, "we do not know why the echolalic children proceed faster in our program than the previously mute ones, even though the latter are given imitation vocabularies." Echolalic children seem to be at a higher overall developmental level than mute or intermittent speakers.

THE USEFULNESS OF INTELLIGENCE TEST RESULTS

There is little information to aid in counseling parents with regard to the outcome before their child reaches five or six years of age. After the age of six, intelligence tests become highly predictive of later functioning. Contrary to earlier, anecdotal reports, it is now clear that reliable and consistent performance can be obtained from even the most severely impaired autistic child (Churchill, 1971; Hingtgen and Churchill, 1969). Alpern (1967) was one of the first to suggest that valid psychometric evaluations can be obtained if diagnostic measurements are at low enough developmental levels for autistic children to demonstrate their typical range of functioning abilities. In fact, once an appropriate level is found, most autistic children seem pleased to have successfully completed a task.

Clinical testing used in the diagnostic evaluations of autistic children includes the Leiter-International, Merrill-Palmer, Bayley Infant Intelligence Scale, WISC, Stanford-Binet, Alpern-Boll Communication Scale, Cattell-Binet, and two checklists usually filled out while interviewing the mother: Vineland Social Maturity Scale and Alpern-Boll Self-Help Scale.

Rutter and Lockyer (1967a) reported that the IQ score obtained for an autistic child differs widely according to the type of task examined. The same child might be average on some tasks and severely subnormal on others. They found that most of the autistic children did very poorly on verbal tasks and those that required abstract thought or logic, but did relatively well on nonlanguage tasks such as block design and object assembly subtasks on the Wechsler Scale. Not surprisingly, the pattern of results is found to be significantly more common among the children with what Rutter (1966) referred to as "retarded development of speech." Rutter (1968) suggested that to "some underlying extent the autistic child's poor level of attainment is related to specific defects in language rather than to a global deficiency in intellect."

Marked scatter between and within sections of tests is a characteristic result (Ornitz and Ritvo, 1968). Because the intelligence quotient obtained can differ vastly according to the tasks (i.e., autistic children do poorly on "verbal" tasks and do better on "performance" tasks), it must be remembered that low intelligence quotients can be the result of language deficits. Thus, the estimates of intelligence are incomplete unless scores for both performance and verbal items are obtained.

PROGNOSIS

The literature relating "speech development" to prognosis is useful, but the reader must be alert to the particular meaning of this term as it is used by varying authors. Although the terminology used by specific authors varies, it is assumed that when DeMeyer, Barton, DeMeyer, Norton, Allen, and Steele (1973) and other authors referred to speech, they were concerned with expressive language development rather than articulation of speech. In line with this interpretation, Rutter (1976) recently pointed out that he used "speech" as the term for "expressive language" in some of his earlier writings.

The literature supports at least four conclusions: 1) those with a history of regression in language development have a poor prognosis, 2) lack of speech is a poor sign and becomes increasingly a matter of concern as age increases beyond age four to six years, 3) overall IQ is the best single predictor of functioning in adulthood, and 4) level of language development influences social functioning in adulthood, especially when the IQ is over 60.

Although test results on children less than five- to six-years-old have little predictive value, language development histories are important for children under six years of age. Behavioral regression, including language regression occurring late in infancy, is apparently related to more serious consequences than the absence of regression (Swisher, Reichler, and Short, 1976). Overall intellectual development, and especially expressive and receptive language skills, are severely impaired.

Kanner and Eisenberg (1956), Kanner (1973), and Rutter (1968), Shapiro, Chiarandini, and Fish (1974) all agreed that a child without speech at five years has a poorer outcome than a child with speech. In a study by Treffert, McAndrew, and Dreifuerst (1973), it was noted that the rate of institutional discharge highly correlated with development of speech by five years of age and completion of bowel and bladder training at the time of admission, which ranged from 4 to 12 years, with a median of 7.4 years. The autistic child who is not speaking by the age of five is also frequently the same child who had or has a profound lack of response to sounds. He may improve considerably in relation to his initial level of impairment, but it is unlikely that he will achieve a near normal level of social adjustment or of language development at adolescence.

Rutter and Lockyer (1967b) reported a hierarchy of variables that predict social adjustment. These variables from highest to lowest predictive values are: IQ, severity of speech disorder, and amount of schooling, IQ below 60 on the WISC predicted a poor outcome. For children with an IQ over 60, level of speech development distinguished between children with a good social adjustment at follow-up and those with a fair or poorer outcome. Thus, language development is of greater importance in predicting social adjustment for children with IQs of 60 and above.

The more unusual behaviors of autistic children have been shown to decrease significantly during treatment, with social and affective contact increasing, leaving children with residual language deficits (Churchill, 1972; Cunningham, 1966; Rutter, 1968; Wing, 1969).

According to DeMeyer et al. (1973), the best single predictor for educational functioning in a work/school setting at an average of 12 years of age was how well the child was rated as functioning in this respect at the initial evaluation, which occurred at an average of five and one-half years of age. The greatest percentage of cases remained in the same category. Five other parameters from the highest predictor to the lowest were: IQ, severity of illness as reflected in the psychiatric diagnostic subcategories, social rating, speech rating, and estimate of brain dysfunction.

In DeMeyer et al.'s study (1973), most autistic children showed some progress in social and conversational skills. Those with higher skills initially improved most in speech and the ability to relate to others. Of the small percentage whose speech improved significantly, most had residual deficits in dealing with abstract ideas. They were noted to repeat questions, perseverate on details or on a single topic, and to have disordered speech rhythm, inflection, and intonation.

DeMeyer et al. (1973) rated occupational and educational functioning in the same group of children at 12 years of age. They reported: 1–2% recovery to normal, 5–15% borderline, 16–25% fair, and 60–75% poor. Rutter and Lockyer (1967b) report that only 2–3% of children with autistic behaviors who were over 16 years of age held paying jobs. Thus, it seems that children who are autistic past preschool age have a poor outcome.

LANGUAGE INTERVENTION

It is important to point out that available follow-up studies involve children who did not, in most cases, receive special schooling. In the past, intervention was generally directed at changing the parents, who were thought to be the primary factor influencing their child's aberrant behavior, rather than at improving the developmental level of the child. We do not yet know how much structured intervention based on a developmental assessment of the child's level of functioning can change the course of development.

The following section describes procedures that may prove useful in improving the autistic child's language behavior. These procedures are generally based on individual case reports that suggest some success for language intervention. The less retarded, more freely speaking autistic child has received little specialized attention because the intervention procedures for nonautistic language delayed children seem to serve these autistic children as well. Most of the procedures developed have been intended for use with the severely retarded, nonspeaking autistic child who has the poorest overall prognosis, as was seen above.

Evidence suggests that educational progress is affected by the type of treatment provided. It is clear that most autistic children respond better to teaching in a structured situation, (Rutter and Bartak, 1973; Schopler, Brehm, Kinsbourne, and Reichler, 1971), i.e., a situation in which the adult determines what tasks the child should be engaged in, rather than the child determining the course of events. It also seems that progress is enhanced by a small staff-child ratio, and by active involvement of the staff, i.e., high levels of intrusion on and interaction with the child. Other considerations, such as choosing appropriate rewards and dealing with self-stimulatory behaviors (e.g., Hargrave and Swisher, 1975), require considerable additional attention by the staff on a child-by-child basis.

Rutter and Bartak (1973) found that autistic children who made progress in a residential environment did not exhibit improved behaviors at home. This report highlights the need of some autistic children for continued interaction with others in order to maintain gains, and the importance of including experiences to aid generalization.

Tanguay (1973) and Kanner (1973) reported that children placed in a custodial-type institution quickly regressed to an essentially nonfunctioning state. The autistic child's poor generalization skills and the need for repeated trials to learn suggest the need for remediation in the home, with the parents as primary therapists. This has been done successfully by many, including Lovaas, Koegel, Simmons, Long, and Stevens (1972). In the home, remediation can be an ongoing process of guiding the child to successfully manage the activities and interactions that he will encounter daily.

Contrary to Bettelheim's (1967) point of view, most clinicians, investigators, and parents agree that parents are essential to the carry-over of whatever progress is made at school (Lovaas et al., 1972; Rutter and Bartak, 1973). In fact, the involvement of parents in the training program itself is highly recommended in the literature (Creedan, 1973; Hawlin, Marchant, Rutter, Berger, Hersov, and Yule, 1973; Kozloff, 1973; Nordquist and Wahler, 1973; Schopler and Reichler 1971a). Schopler and Reichler (1971) summarize the rationale for the inclusion of parents in their "developmental" language remediation program:

> Our experience suggests that it is not only expedient to use parents to supplement the shortage in manpower, but that they are frequently the most important developmental agents for their children.

Most language remediation procedures for autistic children are based on operant principles (Swisher et al., 1976). The two major characteristics of these procedures are the use of a structured program of imitation to elicit language responses and the subsequent rewarding of these responses. The language remediation procedures themselves can be divided into three groups depending on the mode of response required of the child: oral response, signed responses, or responses determined by selected alternate systems of communication.

Oral Response Program

Oral language conditioning programs (Gray and Ryan, 1973; Hartung, 1970; Lovaas, Schriebman, and Koegel, 1974; Marshall and Hegrenes, 1970, 1972) use the clinician's spoken model as the stimulus for the child to orally imitate. The child begins some of these programs with nonlanguage tasks (establishment of eye contact, reduction of disruptive behavior, imitation of motor behavior, etc.) and reaches the language stage through a task of object or picture naming. After a core vocabulary is stabilized, the child progresses through a programmed series of stages during which he is reinforced for the oral imitation of various word combinations.

Mechanical devices may be used to elicit oral language imitation in those autistic children who do not readily respond to live models. (Colby, 1971, 1973; Hargrave and Swisher, 1975).

Modifications in oral language conditioning procedures have been made for the child who echoes part of or all of what is said to him. Risley and Wolf (1967) describe procedures they used with autistic children and that were especially applicable to an echolalic child. First, to increase the probability of appropriate language, they delivered rewards only if the desired response occurred within 5 sec after the model. After a "response class" was established, they trained the child to respond to a question such as *What is it?*. If the child inappropriately repeated the question, the object or picture was withdrawn, and the clinician looked away and was silent for several seconds.

Signed Responses

Several authors (Creedan, 1973; Miller and Miller, 1973) describe the use of simultaneous communication; that is, oral language and manual English at the same time. It seems that progress in the use of signs is usually followed by progress in talking. Up to approximately seven signs may be learned before the child begins to talk, but progress in signing seldom dramatically exceeds progress in talking.

Reports frequently suggest that the success of the signing may be attributable to attention to vision, which is less impaired than the auditory modality. Another interpretation, that the addition of signing makes the task easier, arises from observations of several teachers who use total communication with autistic children. Usually the clinician is learning to sign, or if fluent in sign, is committed to matching each sign to a spoken word. The result is to have a reduced rate of word presentation, a reduced linguistic complexity, and a choice of word presentation, a reduced linguistic complexity, and a choice of very functional words when compared to when the clinician only spoke. In addition, we know that simple signs such as "good-bye" are understood and elicited before words in normally developing children, and that it is easier to move a child's hand to help him gesture than it is to move his mouth to help him talk.

Alternate Modes of Response

Several reports in the literature discuss the use of alternate modes of response in language remediation with autistic children. Two alternative communication systems were designed for autistic children using principles outlined by Premack (deVilliers and Naughton, 1974; McLean and McLean, 1974). Most of these programs continue to employ imitation and reward; however, different demands for responding are made to help the child communicate despite his lack of oral language. Some approaches take advantage of a mode of responding that is already in the child's repertoire. Two examples follow.

Ratusnik and Ratusnik (1974) developed a communication approach based on transformational grammar for a nonspeaking autistic child who could read. Their approach emphasized improving receptive language, and used a communication board for expressive language. Language structures were taught via written words describing pictures available for the child to see. This approach, according to the authors, served to facilitate the development of language in this child, who began to generate sentences spontaneously.

Marshall and Hegrenes (1972) modified their program by using written language for an autistic child. They used flash cards with printed words and first taught recognition of functional vocabulary. They proceeded to teach the child to sequence the cards to form syntactic statements, and finally to transfer concepts to writing.

RESEARCH NEEDS

Two major problems complicate the interpretation of findings regarding autistic children—the frequent presence of a language impairment, and the frequent presence of mental retardation. Kleffner (1973) has pointed out that at present it is difficult to distinguish between skills that are deficient because of an underlying language impairment, and skills that are deficient in addition to language impairment. It is recognized that language skills are used to mediate many skills that are commonly labeled as cognitive. The major problem in studying the differences between normal children and children with language disabilities is to find sufficiently language free tasks, so that there is no advantage to normal children. Too frequently in the study of children with language disorders, the nonverbal tasks have been assumed to be free of language influence, and the results have been interpreted as related to the cause of language impairment, when it may have been more appropriate to consider them as consequences of the language impairment.

Rutter (1976) points out that autism and mental retardation frequently coexist. He summarizes that the results of many studies indicate: "Autistic children with low IQs are just as retarded as anyone else with a low IQ . . ." Studies have revealed that autistic children have stable IQ scores from middle childhood throughout adolescence (Lockyer and Rutter, 1969; Mittler, Gillies, and Jukes, 1966), that their IQ scores predict later educational achievement (DeMeyer et al., 1973; Rutter and Bartak, 1973; Swisher, Reichler, and Short, 1976), and that IQ level remained much the same even when motivation had been increased (Hingtgen and Churchill, 1971) or autistic features decreased (Swisher, Reichler, and Short, 1976). Such findings have important implications for research. Studies comparing autistic and nonautistic children must control for both mental and chronological age. These controls are seldom exercised, yet only these controls permit differences found to be related to autism or to mental retardation. Careful attention must be given to equating groups on verbal and on performance intelligence levels so that developmental factors can be examined.

The primary need in research on autism is for investigators to study large numbers of children in controlled situations. Too often, reports in the literature draw conclusions on the basis of a small number of cases, with little information given concerning individual differences. Children diagnosed as autistic are known to have three broad behavioral characteristics: impaired relating to others, a "fixation on sameness," and a language impairment. Other characteristics of the child not directly related to the diagnosis of autism, such as level of intelligence, are clearly important to both the treatment and prognosis associated with the disorder. A description of other characteristics, such as the presence or absence of regression in language development, may well lead to the identification of subgroups of autistic children.

In their description of research with normal children, several conference participants have described procedures or observations that may be particularly relevant to research with autistic children. Fagan's (this volume) face stimuli and procedure could be used to investigate the one behavior that comes closest to being unique to autism—gaze aversion. In fact, Fagan (personal communication) has seen one child of five months considered by a physician to have gaze aversion. The child responded to the abstract designs more appropriately than to the faces. Thus, he may have an available procedure to use with children as young as 20 weeks.

More information is needed about the autistic child who speaks infrequently at one developmental level and even less frequently at a higher developmental level. The techniques described by Moore (this volume) and by Ramey (this volume) could help determine which environmental variables elicit the higher level of expression.

Bowerman (this volume) suggests that instances of regression in some stages of language development in normal children may be a sign of progress. A history of regression in language development in autistic children is a "red flag" for a poor prognosis, particularly for future language development (Swisher, Reichler, and Short, 1976). Bowerman suggested that the phenomenon of words dropping out of use in normal children may not be because of the lack of adequate mental representation but because of decreases in the salience or interest value of their referents. Possibly this interpretation is relevant to both normal and autistic children.

The current literature on language remediation techniques for autistic children suggests many areas in need of further investigation. The majority of the programs are designed for the autistic child who does not readily speak. Few of these programs deal with communication as opposed to language; few try to incorporate social awareness as a part of language growth. Research needs relevant to remediation include the following:

1. The development of language remediation procedures for the speaking group of autistic children
2. Alternatives to required imitation as a mode of presentation for language
3. Guidelines to help a clinician decide which of the already available language programs are most appropriate for an autistic child who is at a particular developmental level
4. Suggestions on how to maximize "unusual" interests of some autistic children (e.g., machines) to motivate them in therapy
5. Comparative studies to determine which mode of language input and output is most useful for a given child.

REFERENCES

Alpern, G. D. 1967. Measurement of "untestable" autistic children. J Abnorm. Psychol. 72: 478–486.

Bettelheim, B. 1967. The Empty Fortress: Infantile Autism and the Birth of the Self. Collier-Macmillian, London.

Borus, J. F., Greenfield, S., and Daniels, G, 1973. Establishing imitative speech employing operant techniques in a group setting. J. Speech Hear. Disord. 38: 533–541.

Bradley, C. 1941. Schizophrenia in Childhood. MacMillan, New York.

Brown, J. 1960. Prognosis from presenting symptoms of preschool children with atypical development. Am. J. Orthopsychiatry 30: 382–390.

Chess, S. 1971. Autism in children with congenital rubella. J. Autism Child. Schizophren. 1: 33–47.

Churchill, D. W. 1971. Effects of success and failure in psychotic children. Arch. Gen. Psychiatry 25: 208–214.

Churchill, D. W. 1972. The relation of infantile autism with early childhood schizophrenia to developmental language disorders of childhool. J. Autism Child. Schizophren. 22: 182–197.

Colby, K. M. 1973. The rationale for computer based treatment of language difficulties in nonspeaking children. Computer Science Department Report No. STAN-CS-73-346. Available from the National Technical Information Service, Springfield, Virginia 22151.

Colby, K. M., and Smith, D. C. 1971. Computers in the treatment of nonspeaking autistic children. In H. Masserman (ed.), Current Psychiatric Therapies. Grune and Stratton, New York.

Creak, M. 1961. Schizophrenia syndrome in childhood. Progress report of a working party. Cerebr. Palsy Bull. 3: 501–503.

Creak, M. 1963. Childhood psychosis: A review of 100 cases. Brit. J. Psychiatry 109: 84–89.

Creedan, M. P. 1973. Language development in nonverbal autistic children using a simultaneous communication system. Paper presented at Society for Research in Child Development, March, Philadelphia.

Cunningham, M. A. 1966. A five-year study of the language of an autistic child. J. Child Psychol. Psychiatry 7: 143–154.

DeMeyer, M. K., Barton, S., DeMeyer, W. E., Norton, J. A., Allen, J., and Steele, R. 1973. Prognosis in autism: A follow-up study. J. Autism Child. Schizophren. 3: 199–246.

Despert, J. L. 1947. Psychotherapy in child schizophrenia. Am. J. Psychiatry 104: 36–43.

deVilliers, J., and Naughton, J. M. 1974. Teaching a symbol language to autistic children. J. Consult. Clin. Psychol. 42: 111–117.

Gettelmann, M., and Birch, H. G. 1967. Childhood Schizophrenia: Intellect, neurologic status, perinatal risk, prognosis, and family pathology. Arch. Gen. Psychiatry 17: 16–25.

Gray, B., and Ryan, B. 1973. A Language Program for the Nonlanguage Child. Research Press, Champaign.

Hargrave, E., and Swisher, L. 1975. Modifying the verbal expression of a child with autistic behaviors. J. Autism Child. Schizophren. 5: 147–154.

Hartung, J. R. 1970. A review of precedures to increase verbal imitation skills and functional speech in autistic children. J. Speech Hear. Disord. 35: 203–217.

Hawlin, P., Marchant, R., Rutter, M., Berger, M., Hersov, L., and Yule, W. 1973. A home-based approach to the treatment of autistic children. J. Autism Child. Schizophren. 3: 308–336.

Hingtgen, J. N., and Churchill, D. W. 1969. Identification of perceptual limitations in mute autistic children. Arch. Gen. Psychiatry 21: 68–71.

Hingtgen, J. N., and Churchill, D. W. 1971. Differential effects of behavior modification in four mute autistic boys. In D. W. Churchill, C. D. Alpern, M. DeMeyer (eds.), Infantile Autism. Charles C Thomas Publisher, Illinois.

Johnson, R. T. 1975. Hydrocephalus and viral infections. Dev. Med. Child Neurol. 17: 807–816.

Kanner, L. 1943. Austistic disturbances in affective contact. Nerv. Child 2: 217–250.

Kanner, L. 1951. Conception of wholes and parts in early infantile autism. Am. J. Psychiatry 108: 23–26.

Kanner, L. 1971. Follow-up study of eleven autistic children originally reported in 1943. J. Autism Child. Schizophren. 1: 119–145.

Kanner, L. 1973. To what extent is early infantile autism determined by constitutional inadequacies? In L. Kanner (ed.), Childhood Psychosis: Initial Studies and New Insights. John Wiley and Sons, New York.

Kanner, L. 1973. Childhood Psychosis: Initial Studies and New Insights. V. H. Winston and Sons, Washington, D.C.

Kanner, L., and Eisenberg L. 1956. Early infantile autism, 1943–1955. Am. J. Orthopsychiatry 26: 55–65.

Kanner, L., and Lesser, L. I. 1958. Early infantile autism. Pediatr. Clin. N. Am. 5: 711–730.

Kleffner, F. 1973. Language Disorders in Children. The Bobbs-Merrill Company, New York.

Kozloff, M. A. 1973. Reaching the Autistic Child: A parent training program. Research Press. Champaign.

Lockyer, L., and Rutter, M. 1969. A five-to-fifteen year follow-up study of infantile psychosis—III. Psychological aspects. Brit. J. Psychiatry 115: 865–882.

Lotter, V. 1966. Epidemiology of autistic conditions in young children—I. Prevalence. Soc. Psychiatry 1: 124–137.

Lotter, V. 1974. Factors related to outcome in autistic children. J. Autism Child. Schizophren. 4: 263–277.

Lovaas, O. I. 1966. Learning Theory Approach to the Treatment of Childhood Schizophrenia. Paper delivered at Symposium on "Childhood Schizophrenia," American Orthopsychiatric Association, April 13–16, San Francisco.

Lovaas, O. I., Koegel, R., Simmons, J. Q., Long, J., and Stevens, J. 1972. Some generalizations and follow-up measures on autistic children in behavior therapy. J. Appl. Behav. Anal. 6: 131–166.

Lovaas, O. I., Schreibman L., and Koegel, R. L. 1974. A behavior modification approach to the treatment of autistic children. J. Autism Child. Schizophren. 7: 111–129.

McLean, L. P., and McLean, J. E. 1974. Language training program for nonverbal autistic children. J. Speech Hear. Disord. 39: 186–193.

Marshall, N. R., and Hegrenes, J. R. 1970. Programmed communication therapy for autistic mentally retarded children. J. Speech Hear. Disord. 35: 70–83.

Marshall, N. R., and Hegrenes, J. R. 1972. The use of written language as a communication system for an autistic child. J. Speech Hear. Disord. 37: 258–261.

Miller, A., and Miller, E. E. 1973. Cognitive developmental training with elevated boards and sign language. J. Autism Child. Schizophren. 3: 65–85.

Mittler, P., Gillies, S., and Jukes, E. 1966. Prognosis in psychotic children. Report of follow-up study. J. Ment. Def. Res. 10: 73–83.

Nordquist, V. M., and Wahler, R. G. 1973. Naturalistic treatment of an autistic child. J. Appl. Behav. Anal. 6: 79–87.

Ornitz, E. M. and Ritvo, E. R. 1968. Perceptual inconstancy in early infantile autism: The syndrome of early infant autism and its variants including certain cases of childhood schizophrenia. Arch. Gen. Psychiatry 18: 76–98.

Pronovost, W. 1961. The speech behaviors and language comprehension of autistic children. J. Chron. Disord. 13: 228–233.

Ratusnik, C. M., and Ratusnik, D. L. 1974. A comprehensive approach for a ten year old nonverbal autistic child. Am. J. Orthopsychiatry 44: 396–403.

Rimland, B. 1964. Infantile Autism: The Syndrome and Its Implications for a Neural Theory of Behavior. Appleton-Century-Crofts, New York.

Risley, T., and Wolf, M. 1967. Establishing functional speech in echolalic children. In H. Sloane and B. McGulay (eds.), Operant Procedures in Remedial Speech and Language Training. Houghton-Mifflin, Boston.

Ruttenberg, B. A., and Wolf, E. G. 1967. Evaluating the communication of the autistic child. J. Speech Hear. Disord. 32: 314–324.

Rutter, M. L. 1966. Behavioral and cognitive characteristics of a series of psychotic children. In J. Wing (ed.), Early Childhood Autism. Pergamon, London.

Rutter, M. 1968. Concepts of autism: A review of research. Am. J. Child Psychol. Psychiatry 9: 1–25.

Rutter, M. 1976. Autism. Workshop on the Neurobiological Basis of Autism, National Institute of Neurological and Communicative Disorders and Stroke (NINCDS), February, Bethesda, Maryland.

Rutter, M., and Bartak, L. 1973. Special educational treatment of autistic children: A comparative study—II. Follow-up findings and implications for services. J. Child Psychol. Psychiatry 14: 241–270.

Rutter, M., and Lockyer, L. 1967a. A five-to-fifteen year follow-up study of infantile psychosis—I. Description of sample. Brit. J. Psychiatry 113: 1169–1182.

Rutter, M., and Lockyer, L. A. 1967b. A five-to-fifteen year follow-up study of infantile psychosis—II. Social and behavioral outcome. Brit. J. Psychiatry 113: 1183–1199.

Schopler, E., Brehm, S., Kinsbourne, M., and Reichler, R. J. 1971. Effect of treatment structure on development in autistic children. Arch. Gen. Psychiatry 24: 415–421.

Schopler, E., and Reichler, R. 1971a. Parents as cotherapists in the treatment of psychotic children. J. Autism Child. Schizophren. 1: 87–102.

Schopler, E., and Reichler, R. 1971b. Problems in the developmental assessment of psychotic children. Excerpta Medica International Congress Series No. 274, Proceedings of the V World Congress of Psychiatry, Mexico, D.F.

Schain, R. J., and Yannet, H. 1960. Infantile autism: An analysis of 50 cases and a consideration of certain neurophysiologic concepts. J. Pediatrics 57: 560–567.

Shapiro, T., Chiarandini, I., and Fish, B. 1974. Thirty severely disturbed children: Evaluation of their language development for classification and prognosis. Arch. Gen. Psychiatry 30: 819–825.

Shervanian, C. C. 1967. Speech, thought, and communication disorders in childhood psychosis: Theoretical implications. J. Speech Hear. Disord. 32: 303–313.

Swisher, L., Drzewiecki, S., and Swisher, C. N. 1976. Language Impairment of Autistic Children, Workshop on the Neurobiological Basis of Autism, planned by the National Institute of Neurological & Communicative Disorders & Stroke (NINCDS), National Institutes of Health, February, Bethesda, Maryland.

Swisher, L., Reichler, J. R., and Short, A. 1976. Language development history and change in autistic children. In S. K. Hirsh, D. H. Eldredge, I. J. Hirsh, and S. R. Silverman (eds.), Hearing and Davis: Essays Honoring Hallowell Davis. Washington University Press, St. Louis.

Taft, L., and Goldfarb, W. 1964. Prenatal and perinatal factors in childhood schizophrenia. Dev. Med. Child Neurol. 6: 32–43.

Tanguay, P. E. 1973. A pediatrician's guide to the recognition and initial management of early infantile autism. Pediatrics 51: 903.

Treffert, D. A., McAndrew, J. B., and Dreifuerst, P. 1973. An in-patient treatment program and outcome for 57 autistic and schizophrenic children. J. Autism Child. Schizophren. 3: 138–153.

Wing, L. 1969. The handicaps of autistic children—A comparative study. J. Child Psychol. Psychiatry 10: 1–40.

Discussion Summary: Implications for Intervention

Macalyne Fristoe

Research into early behavioral development and its disorders is attracting an increasing proportion of interest among behavioral scientists. Although expansion of knowledge about development and its disorders is a first step, translation of this knowledge into a sound basis for intervention has proved to be difficult to accomplish. It remains a problem that is challenging and often highly resistant to solution. This situation is most widely attributed to the assumed dichotomy between research ("science") and clinical practice ("service"). Unfortunately, academic practices contribute to this. In academic settings, where most behavioral researchers are found, the greatest success and prestige come as a result of doing basic research, not from translating findings into clinically useful applications. Scientists, who have become scientists because they are dedicated to looking for basic knowledge, cannot afford to be diverted to the time-consuming task of translating findings into practical application. Practitioners have chosen their vocations because they are dedicated to working with developmentally disabled individuals. Although they may want to keep aware of the most recent research findings, the demands of providing service frequently manage to overwhelm good intentions. In some cases they may lack the skills and training necessary for evaluating research and for synthesizing findings from a variety of sources into a cohesive approach—or into individualized approaches.

ASSESSMENT AND INTERVENTION

This weakness is forming an interface between research and application is also reflected in a lack of strength in the relationship between assessment and intervention. The separation of assessment from intervention probably had its origin in the disease model and the need for labels for statistical, managerial, and fund-garnering purposes. In the past, many facilities had their "D & E" (diagnosis and evaluation) divisions, and diagnostic centers could be found in most large cities and at

565

universities. It was assumed that treatment could not be undertaken without an adequate differential diagnosis, resulting in a taxonomic decision. Unfortunately, professional time and organizational funds were usually exhausted in the quest for diagnosis. Intervention was recommended, but usually without much in the way of detailed plans. Intervention services were sparse in relationship to need, or else nonexistent.

Another factor has had a detrimental effect on the development of a strong relationship between early assessment and intervention. Because education in this country traditionally began at age six, intervention services provided for developmentally disabled or exceptional children in an educational setting were often aimed at those with a mental age of six and above. Frequently the intervention services provided were simplifications of approaches used with normal children. Extensive assessment of younger children was difficult because few tests were normed on children under school age. Even after attention began to be focused on preschool children, relatively few tests were developed. In fact, obtaining access to an adequate sample of preschool children for norming purposes was difficult. Between birth and entry into school, children were almost inaccessible. Formal tests (standardized and normed) were the only form of assessment that was acceptable, and they were not applicable to preschool children, much less to infants.

Recent interest in the cognitive development theories of Piaget has contributed to a widespread interest in early assessment. Piaget has provided a means by which one can examine—if not measure—the development of cognitive skills in young children. Although knowledge about early development is expanding explosively, the assessment armamentarium is increasing somewhat less rapidly. Intervention techniques are improving, but much more slowly.

Fortunately the dichotomous division between assessment and intervention is breaking down. This change is attributable in part to the careful data gathering and task analysis procedures required by operant intervention procedures. Test . . . train . . . test . . . train . . . At what point does assessment end and intervention begin?

Planning Intervention Programs

Keogh and Kopp (this volume) have eloquently discussed some of the other problems encountered in planning and executing the most effective and efficient intervention program. They have identified two main problems of a general nature: assessment instruments lack power and specificity of the degree necessary to make contributions critical to the success of an intervention program, and, as a result, intervention programs are mostly global and nonspecific. Without the necessary assessment information, tailoring a program to meet the specific needs of a particular child is a goal that remains worthy but unfulfilled.

In the national survey of speech, hearing, and language services for the retarded (Fristoe, 1975), it was found that more facilities for the retarded were offering assessment services than intervention services in both speech and hearing—not an unexpected finding. What was surprising was the discovery that more facilities were offering language intervention services than assessment. This probably reflects a situation in which intervenors realize that children have a problem in this area and want to do something about it even though assessment is unavailable. Unfortunately, this suggests that they are providing a general, unindividualized type of intervention.

Visually Impaired Hammer (this volume) has discussed the need for more information about early cognitive development in blind and visually impaired children for use in planning early intervention (or "mediation" as opposed to remediation or later intervention, in his terms). In this area, much of program planning at present is determined by factors outside the child—teacher preference, child's placement, expectancies of the school. Until more is known about early development, the planning void will continue to be filled by such less vital and less productive considerations.

The area of the visually impaired is an example of how well-intended but misdirected efforts can cause an entire field to get sidetracked into efforts that are nonproductive in terms of intervention. As long as emphasis was on 1) blindness and its associated personality characteristics, 2) assessment of loss of distance vision, and 3) measurement of progression of loss, little resulted that could be used in planning for intervention. Attention was focused on assessment for the purpose of classification. What was to happen after classification was accomplished? Traditional approaches were used because they were available. Now attention has turned to efficient use of vision. The implications of the realization that vision is a process that is developmental and can be learned are beginning to be felt. As a result, more detailed information on early development is being sought for use in intervention planning, along with more specificity in assessment instruments.

Mental Retardation In the area of mental retardation, preoccupation with measuring intelligence formerly narrowed thinking in such a way that one tended to think an intelligence quotient told what a child was like, and that such a number was necessary in order to plan for intervention. Often this meant that the plan was *not* to intervene. For example, speech therapy was not available to children with an IQ of 69 or below but was available to children with an IQ of 70 or above. The intelligence quotient told nothing about the individual child's speech, hearing, or language status and needs. However, the previous conclusions about the reported lack of benefit from therapy for retarded persons were based more on limitations in knowing how to aid them than in their overall limitations in ability. It is hoped that the preoccupation with intelligence quotient is past its peak and that the advisability of detailed individualized assessment for purposes of intervention planning, as discussed by Keogh and Kopp (this volume), is universally accepted.

Language Disorders A major misemphasis that is one more of magnitude of effort than direction of effort has been in language development and language disorders. The compelling works of Chomsky and others in the area of language structure, coupled with our lack of knowledge about other aspects of language, has caused a preoccupation with form while slighting function. For the hearing impaired this goes back far before Chomsky. Deaf children were taught parts of speech and sentence structure in the hope that they would somehow use it spontaneously in speaking and writing. Now there is a rapidly growing interest in the function of language. Pragmatics has joined syntax and semantics as a major area of interest in language development. Lowell and Lowell (this volume) and Nelson (this volume) have discussed the expanding emphasis on performatives (communicative intent)—the function as opposed to the structure or form of language. It is anticipated that the growing interest in this area will result in more effort in research and in the development of appropriate assessment and intervention approach.

Autism   The area of autism is another in which intervention planning was misdirected into nonproductive efforts. As long as autism was felt to be an emotional disorder caused by cold, detached, unresponsive parents, efforts were focused on changing the child's environment, with emphasis on giving much physical contact in an effort to bring the child out of withdrawal. Now that attention is being given to cognitive development in autistic children and to some type of encephalopathy as the probable cause of the behaviors associated with autism, intervention efforts are being concentrated on the child's development. This is particularly true with regard to communication. Doherty and Swisher (this volume) have suggested that most intervention programs for autistic children concentrate on language rather than the broader area of communications, including social awareness. Baltaxe, Elliot, Meyers, Sher, and Yamida (1977) have recently suggested that the basic communication defect in autistic children may be in the area of pragmatic development, the implications being that intervention efforts should be concentrated there before turning to work on linguistic particulars. It seems that we must learn a great deal more about the types of intervention that are most effective with autistic children. (At present, most studies of outcome have been conducted with children who were treated under the assumption that their behaviors were a manifestation of a severe psychogenic emotional disorder. Application of findings concerning intervention outcome and its relationship to other factors may be limited because of the change in understanding of possible causal and contributing factors.)

Risk Registers   Although the theme of this conference was early behavioral assessment of the communicative and cognitive abilities of the developmentally disabled, most presentations have dealt with basic research in normal development. The presentations demonstrate how much more basic research on both normal and developmentally disabled children there is yet to be done before we will be able to design assessment that will in turn lead to effective planning for intervention. There are many problems obvious now that will need to be resolved; this will lead in turn to recognition of new problems that will need to be solved. One of the first is how to locate at a very early stage children who will be developmentally disabled. With regard to developmental disabilities as a whole, use of risk registers may be expensive and inefficient, leading to many Type 1 and Type 2 errors, as pointed out by Scott (this volume), but there are special instances where use of risk registers may be beneficial and more productive. One of these would be in the case of hearing impairment. Risk registers can be used to locate at a very early age children in need of further assessment (which is possible with present knowledge) and institute amplification where needed. This can have a relatively high payoff, as was mentioned by several participants at this conference. This has also been supported by a number of studies reviewed by Northern and Downs (1975) and the recommendation of the AA00, AAP, and ASHA Joint Committee on Infant Hearing Screening (1974). Also, there are disorders that can be diagnosed at birth or shortly after birth, such as Down's Syndrome and cerebral palsy, where the probability of hearing loss is known to be higher than that normally found in the population as a whole.

Need for Earlier Identification   Autism, on the other hand, is a disorder or cluster or disorders about which we still know relatively little, particularly with regard to how to identify its presence in a child at a very early age. Two presentations in this volume have given some ideas that demand further research in this area, both centering around looking behavior (Fagan, visual attention to face versus non-face patterns, and Doherty and Swisher, gaze aversion). Until we can identify autistic children at a much earlier age, we are limited to providing intervention after many valuable years have been lost. Until we have a means for identifying these children earlier, we have no way of establishing the efficacy of early intervention in alleviating or modifying the pattern of deficiency in relating to others in both verbal and nonverbal areas.

Although we recognize that risk registers in general may be of limited value, they may offer a greater benefit in the case of some specific disorders; therefore, they should not be disregarded totally. Also, the means for assessing at risk status can be improved. For example, a cumulative risk register is recommended by Keogh and Kopp (this volume) as a more efficient alternative for general use in locating children who will be developmentally disabled for a variety of reasons.

Training Health Care Personnel

It seems that our greatest potential for very early identification lies in training health care personnel and parents because they can be the best identifiers if they are kept sensitized to the problem. An example of this is the rubella epidemic of 1964–1965. Because the attention of health care personnel was focused on the possible sequelae of this disease when it occurred in pregnant women, hearing evaluations for children who were the victims of maternal rubella were arranged at a very early age. Amplification and training were begun where indicated. Once the epidemic was over, this gradually ceased to be the case. Maternal rubella children were no longer given such immediate attention, and hearing problems went undetected until they were older and valuable time had been lost. Thus, the problem is how to keep health care personnel and parents alert, even in non-crisis times. This is particularly true with regard to hearing loss, which is neither visible nor dramatic—early amplification is critical to ensure maximum opportunity for development in the child with a hearing loss. Doherty and Swisher (this volume) have referred to several reports of a child later found to be autistic that was earlier described as "a good baby" or a baby that "didn't like to be held." If health care personnel could be alert to watch for descriptions like this, combined with observation of gaze aversion and other early symptoms yet to be discovered, children who manifest the syndrome could be identified at a much earlier state for purposes of study and intervention. Unfortunately, some parents are already fairly good identifiers, but they are advised by the health care personnel to whom they first turn for advice not to be concerned and to wait before seeking expert help in ruling out the presence of a developmental problem. A behavioral observation checklist, such as that prepared by NINDS (1969), can help alert parents and health care professionals to potential problems, but both groups must be willing to actively pursue further evaluation, and not "wait and see what happens."

Assessing Development

The next major issue is how to assess the child's development once the child has been identified. We are moving away now from assessment simply to establish needs (head counts) to using assessment to see what is there—to learn the individual child's strengths and weakness and rates of change. This implies that we will also move from emphasis on normative tests, which are most helpful in labeling a child, to ipsative tests, which are more helpful in establishing a particular child's progress, and thus that child's needs. The ipsative type of assessment, unlike the normative, can help determine what to do next for a given child, and this is the type of information that is necessary for effective intervention. Keogh and Kopp (this volume) stated that normed or standardized instruments have very limited value when it comes to intervention planning. They are limited in application, they are limited in the information that they provide, they are limited in terms of the persons who are qualified to use them, and they are limited in the inferences that can be drawn from the results of their use. This is particularly true with regard to prediction of mental retardation in infancy, according to Bayley (1955) and Horowitz and Dunn (this volume), especially when based on class membership. Hammer (this volume) has emphasized, in the case of the visually impaired, how we have progressed from focusing on looking for signs of the disorder in a child to assessing the child's learning ability by looking at styles of learning and rate of learning.

Effective Intervention   Assessment is not an end-product in itself, but should lead to the next question of how to intervene. What will be done in intervention, and who will select the method? Who will carry out the intervention procedures and where will they be done? Planning of effective intervention requires extremely detailed knowledge of developmental sequence and knowledge of what can be taught and learned at any particular stage. Keogh and Kopp (this volume) suggested that there are three major unproved assumptions on which intervention with the developmentally disabled is based at present: that early intervention produces greater progress than delayed or later intervention,[1] that any intervention is better than none ("Do *something* . . . "), and that the knowledge on which intervention with older children is based can be extrapolated down to younger children. They have also directed our attention to other important questions about infant intervention: Can specific skills be taught to infants? If these skills can be taught, when are they best taught and in what way? Are they generalizable? At what point is a structured or an interactive approach more appropriate? To provide the answers, much additional research will be needed. They emphasized that most of the programs that are available at present bear little relationship to assessment. This is attributable both to the shortcomings of the information provided by assessment and to lack of knowledge

---

[1] It should be noted that, although this assumption is still unproved for the developmentally disabled, the benefits of early intervention have been clearly demonstrated for individuals with specific hearing and/or visual disorders.

about how to use specific information in intervention planning even if we had it. At present, most programs are broad and diffuse and based on the justification that we need to "*do something*—it can't hurt and it might help."

In an effort to seek solutions to many of the problems that have been identified, Keogh and Kopp (this volume) have called attention to Flavell's (1972) model for cognitive growth, which seems to have potential for providing a basis for analysis and classification of sequences of cognitive development that can in turn give a basis for developing an effective interface between assessment and intervention. Using such an approach, the task for the developmental theorist would be to delineate timing and influenceability of developmental processes, the task of the assessor would be to specify relevant behavioral indicators of processes, and the task of the intervenor would be to determine the nature of environmental experiences that can facilitate the development of these processes. With such a unified approach, the relationship between research, assessment, and intervention should become far stronger and more productive.

Who will carry out the plans, provide intervention services? This is a task of such magnitude that it seems obvious that representatives of a number of disciplines must be involved. If cognitive development is the basis for intervention, then the person to coordinate the activities of this group should be well versed in cognitive development, as well as being aware of what various specialists can offer. (This often requires knowledge of the capabilities and strengths of individuals as much as the scope of disciplines.)

Some of the day-to-day work must be carried out by professionals, some by parents working under professional supervision, and some by aides working under professional supervision. The choice depends on the developmental stage and the goals of intervention at that stage. For example, some aspects of intervention need to be highly structured and some of the activities involved can be carried out by well supervised aides. Language intervention with severely/profoundly mentally retarded clients using a highly structured approach is an area where this is sometimes appropriate. Parents and other caregivers, trained by professionals, can provide the interactive and supportive contributions that are especially important in the first year of normal development, according to Keogh and Kopp (this volume). In the second year, professionals may be able to contribute more by providing active intervention services (which caregivers can continue to some degree). Children with sociocultural risk situations need attention to interaction with caregivers and a highly structured approach less than a broad, educationally oriented program.

Parent Training   The need to train parents to work with their children at home has been emphasized by Doherty and Swisher (this volume), who suggested that parent training is essential to success in intervention for autistic children. Although a general language stimulation or enrichment program may be helpful for some children, they emphasized that autistic children benefit from systematic teaching in a structured situation and not from a permissive environment. Parents must be instructed and supervised carefully so that they are able to provide such systematic teaching appropriately at home. The critical importance of including parental training in intervention with the hearing impaired has long been recognized. See, for example, Lowell and Lowell (this volume).

Aides   Aides can be very useful in selected programs, but frequently they are used for the wrong reasons. There was an article recently submitted for publication in a national journal that described with great pride a step that the authors had taken in their program for retarded children. Because they could not afford the services of a speech/language pathologist on a regular basis, they hired an aide who was supervised by a speech clinician on what amounted to every tenth therapy session for most of the clients. To compound matters, on the basis of very superficial and questionable diagnostic testing, they had decided that their clients did not need language work so much as articulation therapy, and that was what the aide was providing. Graduate students, who have much more in terms of background information from books and classes in speech, hearing, and language, are not permitted to provide therapy without much closer supervision than this. The upsetting part about this situation is that it is not unusual to see a lack of funds result in no services, or in token and perhaps even detrimental services, in an area as vital as communication development in these children. This is the kind of Band-Aid, corn plaster programming that lulls one into thinking that needs are being met.

Evaluating Intervention Effectiveness   The next question is how to evaluate effectiveness of intervention. This is a problem that perhaps should go back to the researchers. Although it is much easier to evaluate short-term changes than long-term, or "permanent," effects, these also must be included if truly effective intervention is to be planned.

Linking Research to Practice   The last question regards who has responsibility for interfacing research findings with practice. Research findings are important to use as a basis for making intervention decisions, but the lag time between discovery and implementation in intervention programs is immense. In recent years, some funding agencies have attempted to alleviate this perpetual problem in several ways. One attempt was to limit funding only to projects that are applied in nature. Unfortunately, this strategy results in a diminution of basic research, a circumstance that we cannot afford. Another approach has been to insist that projects of an applied nature include validation and dissemination plans, and special funding is made available for such purposes. It is of interest to note that Congress has recently asked research agencies such as NIH to give more attention to showing how the research it funds can be used by practitioners to improve our health care. It is clear that the public will not fund research for basic knowledge at the rate it enjoyed in the 1960s. One participant at the conference suggested that teams be brought together—teams of both clinically oriented and basic research oriented people— people who do not share a common perspective but rather represent the broad range of clinical and research interests. The flow of information and ideas must go both ways, and in this, research and intervention are both facilitated. The practical experience that he has already had with such an arrangement suggests that it is worth emulating. Keogh and Kopp (this volume) suggested the development of a clearinghouse for exchange of information concerning assessment and intervention, a suggestion resulting from recognition that information appears at present in the journals of many disciplines or in materials that are privately circulated.

There is another side to this. The lag between research discoveries and their application in intervention programs is well publicized, but recently a very highly regarded researcher protested that she would like to stop people from taking her findings and translating them into applied usage so quickly. She would like to have more time to investigate newly discovered phenomena in depth before the results and conclusions from her work are put to practical use—a commendable caution, but a rarely heard complaint!

There are two major and sometimes overlapping reasons for doing research in the area of early child development: to gain knowledge and to aid in planning intervention where needed. The subject of the papers presented in this section has been the latter. Although the target population of these papers mainly has been retarded children, children with sensory disabilities—vision and hearing impairments—and children with autistic behaviors have also been examined.

No blanket statement can be made about the status of our current knowledge that will serve as a basis for intervention. Certainly much more is known in the case of children with hearing impairments than is being used in their intervention programs, or even in assessment. For example, procedures that were developed *and published* a decade ago (Fulton, Spradlin, and Lloyd, 1969; Lloyd, 1966; Lloyd, Spradlin, and Reid, 1968) permit establishment of pure tone hearing thresholds for immature and severely/profoundly retarded clients that are generally regarded as untestable, yet this procedure is still not widely used on the populations that could profit most from its application. In the national survey of speech, hearing, and language services for the retarded (Fristoe, 1975), it was found that many more facilities for the retarded were offering assessment services for speech and language than for hearing, even though this population is known to have higher incidence of hearing loss than the population as a whole, and even though it is particularly hard to make significant developmental progress under the double burden of mental retardation and hearing loss, especially when the hearing loss is undetected.

Just as we cannot make a sweeping statement about our state of knowledge and use of present knowledge in assessment and intervention, neither can we make broad statements about all children with a given disability as though they are in some way turned from the same mold. We still sometimes overlook the fact that individual differences may have more impact on the outcome of intervention than group similarities. Lowell and Lowell (this volume) have presented a discussion of this aspect with regard to the outcome of intervention for hearing impaired children.

Talk about assessment for intervention seems premature at this time, especially in light of some of the cautions expressed by Horowitz and Dunn (this volume), Pick (this volume), and Keogh and Kopp (this volume), but intervention must go on because the need is there, imperfect though the present state of the art may be. Perhaps it is the wisest course at this moment to *"do something"* —*perhaps* it won't hurt and it might help—but only if researchers, assessors, and intervenors realize that they must actively work to blend their research findings, assessment information, and intervention planning for future use. Research, assessment, and intervention are not consecutive links of a chain but strands of a rope; maximum strength is present when these strands are intertwined. Meanwhile, intervention, with or without an adequate basis, will go on. Developmentally disabled children cannot afford to wait, and intervenors will be trying to *"do something,"* because they—and to a growing degree, parents—are convinced of the importance of early intervention. We must work together to make certain they are doing *something of value.*

REFERENCES

AAOO, AAP, and Asha. 1974. Supplementary statement of joint committee on infant hearing screening. ASHA/16: 160.

Baltaxe, C., Elliot, D., Meyers, L., Sher, A., and Yamida, J. 1977. An overview of the study of pragmatics with specific presentations on various clinical aspects and their theoretical implications. Panel discussion, Annual Meeting of the American Association on Mental Deficiency, New Orleans

Bayley, N. 1955. On the growth of intelligence. Am. Psychol. 10: 805.

Flavell, J. 1972. An analysis of cognitive-developmental sequences. Genet. Psychol. Monogr. 86: 279–350.

Fristoe, M. 1975. Language intervention systems for the retarded. State of Alabama Department of Education, Montgomery.

Fulton, R. T., Spradlin, J. E., and Lloyd, L. L. 1969. Operant Audiometry with Severely Retarded Children (16 mm sound, color, 16 min). Produced by the Bureau of Child Research, University of Kansas and Parsons State Hospital and Training Center, Lawrence.

Lloyd, L. L. 1966. Behavioral audiometry viewed as an operant procedure. J. Speech Hear. Disord. 31: 128–136.

Lloyd, L. L., Spradlin, J. E., and Reid, M. J. 1968. An operant audiometric procedure for difficult-to-test patients. J. Speech Hear. Disord. 33: 236–245.

NINDS (National Institute of Neurological Disease and Stroke). 1969. Learning to talk: Speech, hearing, and language problems in preschool children. U.S. Government Printing Office, Washington, D.C.

Northern, J. L., and Downs, M. P. 1975. Hearing in Children. Williams and Wilkins, Baltimore.

Conference Summary: Behavioral Assessment of Infants—From Research to Practice

Earl C. Butterfield

Conference summarizers, like the readers of proceedings, inevitably lament the participants' diversity of approaches to the conference theme. Our job would be so much easier if conferees were of a collective mind and would relentlessly address a single issue. However, the nature of conferences is to address issues that cannot be cast simply nor answered finally. A theme becomes many themes, which is for the better. The inevitable lament is misguided. Who would have the patience to read two score answers to any question framed so that 20 thoughtful conferees could agree that it was *the* question?

The reward for summarizing or reading a conference proceedings lies not in being told the question and given the answer, but in refining our views of various problems and perceiving possible solutions. The compensation comes from stretching our minds to encompass themes selected by conferees—from the seeking, not from finding a collective mind. The purpose of a conference theme is to announce the general environs of the search, not to give a map of the territory. If the theme is actually followed by the conferees, so that it can guide us, that is so much gravy, not our just dessert.

TOWARD IMPROVED ASSESSMENT TECHNOLOGY

Before reading the contributed papers, I imagined a technological theme: How can early assessment be made maximally valid and readily affordable? Had that been it, we would have missed some of the liveliest discussion. There would have been no debate about the ethics of early assessment. The very first paper, by Keith Scott, triggered the fray with arguments to indict the idea of nationwide infant screening:

1. Large-scale screening would be terribly expensive, because our ignorance of precisely what to measure would require the use of many ungainly tests with almost all children
2. The long-range benefits of screening would be minimal, because the treatment implications of early diagnoses are unknown
3. Therefore, screening for clinical purposes is unethical. It invades privacy and it carries unacceptable risks of creating self-fulfilling prophecies about who will do poorly. Screening should be used only as a research tool.

In the second paper, Horowitz and Dunn took up the cudgel. They wielded it against infant intelligence testing, which they characterized as misguided. They advocated the abandonment of presently used tests of infant intelligence. Later in the conference, others broadened the attack. Keogh and Kopp derogated nearly all early assessment, arguing especially that current cognitive assessments *cannot* (by reason of irrelevance) or *do not* (by reason of poor communication among professionals) inform the treatments children are given to remedy the conditions revealed by assessment. Lowell and Lowell spoke of the irrelevance of auditory assessments to language training; within the hearing impaired population, response to language training related more closely to motivation and intelligence than to residual hearing sensitivity.

By the end of the conference, a consensus had developed: Problems of prevailing assessment procedures (excepting some sensory assessments) make their clinical use ethically questionable, but those problems need not endure. Indeed, it seemed in retrospect that one purpose of the conferees had been to move infant assessment from what it is (a collection of crude procedures of dubious utility with occasionally evil consequences) to what it might be (ways of specifying which children need what sorts of treatment in order to develop fully). The "might be" of early assessment was fostered in different ways by different conferees, and it is possible to infer from their contributions eight procedures that will have to be performed more generally in order to importantly improve early assessment. Professionals who work directly with infants and who know clinical techniques must:

1. Identify reasons why current assessment procedures fail to contribute to effective health care
2. Pinpoint the characteristics of useful early assessments and the characteristics of important advances in the technology of infant assessment
3. Identify behavioral domains that need to be assessed
4. Suggest feasible alternatives to current assessment devices.

Professionals who conduct research with infants and young children must:

5. Describe their data collection procedures clearly and fully enough to allow judgment of their clinical feasability and cost effectiveness
6. Document the reliability of their procedures for individual children
7. Make empirical (long-term predictive) or compelling theoretical cases, not just intuitive appeals, for the clinical importance of the behavioral domains they study

8. Show that the processes they might assess are amenable to environmental modi-
    fication. (We need no more diagnosable defects for which neglect is the
    indicated treatment.)

These are eight ways to improve the technology of early assessment. It follows
from the fact that only some of the participants took improvement of assessment
technology as their purpose, that some of them did none of these things, and none
did all.

Keith Scott's paper is mainly a consideration of reasons that current infant
assessment procedures are ineffective. The list is long. Too few efforts to differentiate infants from one another provide follow-up to see whether the early differentiations predict later ones. When follow-up has been made, the predictive
validity of the early measures has been discouragingly small. Our understanding of
normal development is too rudimentary to allow disciplined selection of assessment
domains and procedures. When we have a seemingly worthy candidate for early
assessment, the narrowness of infants' response repertoires frequently leave us at a
loss for how to assess our promising process. The cost of intensive assessment is
obviously prohibitive, which makes screening procedures seem appealing, but even
these are yet too costly. It is in the estimation of screening costs that Scott's paper is
most informative. He offers a reasoned realism to temper the usually wishful evaluation of the potential value of screening. For example, he points out that the relevant
figure is not what it costs to screen an individual infant, but what it costs to screen
the number of infants required to identify one who needs special care. The less
frequent a disabling condition, the greater the cost of screening, regardless of the
cost of screening one infant. Screening for rare conditions will probably remain well
beyond our nation's willingness to pay, no matter how simple the test, and simple
tests are very hard to come by. Moreover, if many effective screening procedures
were devised, the more that were already adopted, the less likely the nation would be
to adopt a new one. Such dilemmas have no resolution, but Scott's paper serves an
invaluable function by focusing our attention on them. Like it or not, screening and
assessment tools that identify the more common sources of disability will more
likely be used. Epidemiology will be important to all of us as long as health dollars
are limited.

Like Scott, Horowitz and Dunn forcefully reject medical criteria as useful
indices of subsequent behavioral development. They correctly portray physical
distress during the neonatal period as valueless for predicting developmental problems of behavior. Also like Scott, Horowitz and Dunn see no valid alternatives for
early identification of children who are at developmental risk, and they vigorously
reject the possibility that infant intelligence tests will ever be useful infant assessment devices. They too believe the solution lies in further research on normal human
development. They emphasize especially research that focuses upon individual differences among infants and upon how the infant determines what happens to him.
Despite the inability of developmental psychology to establish the point, Horowitz
and Dunn argue that there are important individual differences early in life.
Moreover, they build this article of faith into the argument that infants elicit dif-

ferential reactions from the environment, and that these differential reactions feed back upon and magnify the original differences among infants, thereby potentiating ultimate differences in intellectual competence. In order to verify this possibility, Horowitz and Dunn call for more discerning analyses of the processes that underlie infant performance, and they argue that the direction to be taken in these analyses in exemplified by the Brazelton Neonatal Scale. This scale seems to reveal a wide range of individual differences, and it focuses especially upon differences in response to enviromental variations of the sorts actually encountered by infants. Whether this kind of assessment is different enough from infant intelligence tests remains to be seen, but there is no doubt that the possibility will be pursued. It is perhaps the most promising general neonatal assessment procedure on the horizon. Some conferees doubted that any general assessment could ever be useful, but none questioned the importance of trying to find out, as Horowitz and Dunn advocate.

Like many of the conferees, Wesley Wilson ignored in his written remarks the question of whether general behavioral assessments will ever be useful. Instead, he assumed that assessment in particular domains will be necessary regardless of whether general assessments are made. He considered early assessment of auditory functions. Among his reasons why present procedures do not work well are audiologists' implicit assumption that the infant is too reflexive to participate in procedures that require the voluntary control of behavior, too exclusive an emphasis upon peripheral sensitivity and not enough concern with complex central functions, and insufficient appreciation of the differing requirements of experimental and clinical procedures. Most procedures for the study of infant's audition have been designed for research rather than for clinical purposes, so they have neglected, for example, the clinician's need for procedures that can be used for multiple assessments of the same infant. Wilson argues that conditioning techniques offer more clinically useful ways to assess auditory sensitivity, and that they can be used for assessing higher order auditory functions as well. The bulk of his paper is a report of procedural experimentation designed to extend downward the age at which conditioning procedures can provide information about children's auditory thresholds. The experimentation is convincing: visual reinforcement and head-turning localization responses yield very nearly adult thresholds for infants as young as five months of age. Variations on the same procedures allow assessment of an infant's perception of speech cues. The work described by Wilson is a major advance in our abilities to assess early differences in auditory functions. It remains only to show directly the clinical relevance of this work to language impairment, to demonstrate that environmental manipulations can alleviate auditory deficits identified with Wilson's procedures, and to extend his procedures farther down the age scale. There is plenty of reason to be optimistic that all of these unmet goals are achievable. Wilson's approach is a model for many sorts of early assessment research. It deserves emulation.

Whereas Wesley Wilson's paper illustrates the value of detailed work on one sort of procedure, Salapatek and Banks demonstrate the great variety of techniques for which procedural experimentation might pay dividends. Salapatek and Banks devote most of their effort to identifying sorts of visual function that should be assessed early. Also, they provide general descriptions and archival references to procedures with which the visual functions have been assessed and that might be greatly refined. Their paper is a treasure house of leads that might be built into valuable clinical research programs. It suggests a score of alternative techniques that might be refined for clinical assessment of infant visual functions. Each suggested technique has demonstrated or highly probable relevance to later visual disability.

Anne Pick's discussion of the papers by Scott, by Horowitz and Dunn, by Wilson, and by Salapatek and Banks is not listed in Table 1, nor are any of the other Discussion Summaries. Each of these is a valuable document, providing as they do more general and integrative views than any of the individual chapters. Pick's stands out too for its treatment of intersensory relations, for which there is no separate chapter in this volume.

Among all of the cognitive functions that have been studied experimentally, memory has been researched the most. Fagan provided this conference's consideration of memory assessment of infants. He provided a detailed view of the procedures required to assess infants' recognition memory, he showed that such assessments were relevant to subsequent development status, and he demonstrated that infants' recognition memory can be improved. Beyond these contributions, Fagan identified criteria for deciding if a research program is relevant to clinical practice in mental retardation: it shows developmental trends and IQ effects in the cognitive domain studied, it produces coherent theory, and it shows that its target cognition is modifiable. Fagan's research shows that all of these criteria can be met, even when infants are studied. His paper is a well worked out example of what a clinically relevant, scientifically sound, basic research program looks like. It is worth seeing. His work sets a standard for socially concerned scientists to strive for.

Ronald Wilson worked to integrate the psychometric and Piagetian approaches to intelligence. His measurement device was the Bayley Scale, administered repeatedly across the first three years of life. These longitudinal data were subjected to correlational analyses, which showed relationships from testing to testing only after 18 months of age. The items that predicted later test scores were analyzed, and a rational effort was made to show that Piaget's analysis of mental stages was supported by the findings. Few people realize that Piaget worked early in his career in Binet's laboratory. The realization is made more difficult by the difference between Piaget's subsequent approach and the directions taken by Binet's descendants. Ronald Wilson's is an interesting effort to bring the two approaches back together, but the current trend away from measurement scales such as Bayley's argues against his succeeding.

Morse's paper contains as one of its parts a consideration of the methodological details of measurement procedures used most frequently to study infants' speech perception: the high amplitude suck procedure and habituation of heart rate. His purpose was to explain the strengths and weaknesses of these techniques for basic science purposes, but his treatment also shows how much must usually be done to make an experimental procedure clinically useful. For example, neither of these scientifically important procedures meets the most basic requirement of a clinical assessment device: Neither gives individually reliable results. Also, neither allows ready measurement of more than one speech contrast discrimination, yet a clinician would need to assess many aspects of speech discrimination in order to make a comprehensive statement about a child's speech discrimination. Morse's paper thus shows reasons why two current assessment procedures cannot yet be used clinically. I say they cannot yet be used because programs of research such as the one by Wesley Wilson show that it is possible to adapt experimental procedures for clinical procedures, if one accepts that as his goal.

It used to be argued that infants respond to the prosodic features of language before they respond to its segmental features, which seems impossible in view of the research described by Morse on early perception of speech segments. Nevertheless, the older arguments seems to suggest that there are well-developed procedures for the study of intonation and prosody. Crystal shows that there are not yet experimental procedures that might be adopted for the clinical examination of infants' mastery of suprasegmental aspects of language. Moreover, Crystal shows why it would be premature in the extreme to seek to assess infants' appreciation and production of the prosodic aspects of language. The prematurity stems from conceptual difficulties. One problem is that prosody and intonation serve many language and communication functions, and there are yet no adequate ways to verify which function is being served by any prosodic feature. Moreover, it will be difficult to devise adequate verification techniques, because they will depend upon the measurement of meanings and situational factors that other conferees show are excruciatingly difficult to tease from infants and their environments. Crystal clarifies such difficulties, which is an important prerequisite for resolving them. Ferguson serves much the same function for the field of developmental phonology, which is even farther from contributing useful clinical procedures, since its main method is the language diary, which is best viewed as a semi-systematic anecdotal record. Language diaries are not only expensive, they are fearfully unreliable and difficult to validate externally.

The chapters by Lowell and Lowell, by Hammer, and by Keogh and Kopp argue the necessity for assessment to inform treatment; otherwise the assessments are useless. All three offer reasons why assessments do not now inform treatment. Speaking of the failure of audiologic assessments to inform the teaching of deaf children, Lowell and Lowell stress the professional separation of audiologists and deaf educators and the failure of audiologic assessments to specify functional capabilities in terms that educators can act upon. They stress to the long-standing disagreement among educators as to whether manual or oral teaching of the deaf is preferable.

Speaking of the failure of visual assessment to inform education of the blind, Hammer notes the failure of visual testing to describe functional capabilities upon which educators of the blind might capitalize. Although Hammer sees some reason for optimism that a more functional diagnostic approach to vision will be adopted, his message is basically the same as that of Lowell and Lowell with respect to the deaf: present diagnostic statements seldom allow the drawing of clear treatment implications. Like Scott, Hammer argues that assessment and treatment must feed back upon one another, probably by being applied by the same professionals. Thus, Hammer speaks strongly for criterion-referenced testing, according to which teaching objectives are stated in measurable terms and measurements are used regularly to evaluate educational progress.

Keogh and Kopp focus on infant and preschool intervention programs designed to enhance general intellectual development. They note that intellectual assessment devices do not inform those programs, nor even establish that early developmental status relates to later status. This failure of child assessments to verify the continuity of development is logically a blow to the underlying rationale for intervention efforts. The rationale is that what happens early to a child influences what he becomes, and interveners hold to this as an article of faith, despite the failure of general assessment devices to provide evidence that early developmental status relates to later developmental status in the absence of special intervention. Keogh and Kopp note that many professionals have argued that the lack of definitive data on the effects of early intervention programs stems from the lack of reliable outcome measures. They deny this as a basic reason, claiming instead that neither intervention nor assessment are based strongly enough in theory. As they see it, neither a consistent treatment program nor pertinent measurement devices can be devised without the help of strong developmental theory. Their argument deserves a hearing, and it received one at this conference: considerations of developmental fact and theory occupied the conferees whenever they were not speaking of how to improve assessment technology.

MATTERS OF FACT AND THEORY

When the conferees were not speaking of how to improve assessment technology, they discussed matters of fact and theory of development. Moore and Meltzoff acknowledged it this way: "The charge to the authors was to focus on early behavioral assessment and its special application to the developmentally disabled. Our appraisal of the ferment in infant cognition led us to focus primarily [they might have said "instead"] on theoretical conceptions of the infant and his development. These conceptions promise not only to further our abilities to assess cognitive development in the disabled but also to enrich our hypotheses about the nature of cognitive impairments and our strategies for their amelioration." Likewise, Horowitz and Dunn focused on "how we might best proceed in our attempts to understand how development happens and in our attempts to prevent developmental disabilities." Similarly, Scott concluded: "screening is appropriate only as a research topic in the present situation. An assessment-intervention model of early childhood education that starts with parent training, and with patterns of behavior as criterion referenced by development sequence and by studying children who have received intensive care, is suggested as a research model." Comparable expressions came from a majority of the conferees. Their knowledge of the state of research and theory in developmental psychology and developmental disabilities led most of the conferees to conclude that the drawing of strong infant assessment implications is not yet possible.

I discerned among the conferees' arguments two approaches that might allow the eventual drawing of clinical implications from developmental science. One approach emphasizes the importance of understanding development of particular sorts of behavior. Thus, Fagan focuses on memory and Ramey on mother-infant interactions. The second approach emphasizes the importance of understanding developmental principles and formulating broad theories. Moore and Meltzoff and the deVilliers exemplify this approach, which seems to be what Keogh and Kopp had in mind when they emphasized the need for theory. From the viewpoint of an assessor/intervener, the two approaches have different strengths. If a comprehensive theory of development was created, it could guide rational derivation of complete assessment and intervention routines, but the derivations would always be relatively tenuous, because any given theory can be translated into various specifics of measurement and instruction. If a comprehensive empirical understanding of behavior in any domain were created, it could be readily transformed into the measurement and assessment specifics required for early intervention programs, but it would necessarily apply to only one of the behavioral domains that a comprehensive intervention program would want to effect. Lacking a comprehensive theory, disciplined judgment could not be made about the importance to overall development of any behavioral domain. Both approaches to drawing clinical implications are thus needed, and it is appropriate that both were represented at this conference.

Because the rationale for intervention requires that there be continuity in development, and because developmental theorists have been deeply concerned with whether development is continuous, the fact of failure to demonstrate long-term predictive validity for early infant assessments was returned to over and over again. There was a general reluctance to view development as discontinuous, so there was a felt need to explain why long-term predictive validity has not been demonstrated. The most frequent explanation had to do with the effects of environmental variables. It was argued that developmental outcome would be predictable if appropriate allowance was made for individual differences in life experiences and for the interaction of early characteristics with environmental factors. Horowitz and Dunn were the first participants to make this argument, which was capsulized at the beginning of this summary.

Ramey and his colleagues focused on the possibility that the study of mother-infant interactions will reveal important information about how the environment tempers development. They classify the various methods that have been used to study mother-infant interaction, and they succinctly summarize the advantages and disadvantages of each. This methodological summary should be useful to researchers and clinicians alike. Ramey and his colleagues review and clearly summarize the extensive literature on mother-infant interaction, which makes it a valuable resource and reference. I take their most important contribution to be highlighting the implications of the fact that there are bidirectional effects in the infant-mother interaction. From the very first hours of life, the infant shapes his mother's behavior toward him. That is the fact. Among the implications is this one: correlations between maternal behavior and infant competence cannot be taken as causal. It may be that a competent infant provokes different maternal behaviors than an incompetent one. Ramey suggests that the technique of cross-lagged correlations can be an important aid in sorting out causation. I am not so sure. The problem is to guarantee that you have measured the appropriate precedent behaviors in both the mother and the child. It is also the guarantee that the mother does not respond to child behaviors that your measurement instruments are too crude to detect. Cross-lag correlations alone cannot do these things. The idea of bidirectional effects creates analytic problems, but they cannot be ignored, because until they are solved there can be no adequate test of whether development is continuous.

Like Ramey, the deVilliers concerned themselves with mother-infant interactions, but since they restricted themselves to language interaction, they could provide special emphasis on particular methodological problems. They took as their two chief problems the choosing of an appropriate level of description of child language and the selection of criteria from which to infer communicative intent. These are absolutely basic questions about how to do psycholinguistic science, and one is unlikely to find a better discussion of them anywhere than in the deVillier's chapter. The main contribution of their chapter, however, is to explain the reasons for the several major changes in focus of developmental psycholinguistic research and theory that have occurred in the past decade. It is important for the scientist to understand why his field evolved as it has, and the deVilliers explain that beautifully for child language researchers. Not knowing the intellectual history of one's science keeps him from judging its importance and where his field is headed. It is also important for the clinician who would draw on scientific findings and theory to develop assessment and intervention routines. It can show the clinician when he should react to and when he should ignore changes in a scientific discipline. It is a rare paper that characterizes a field at this metatheoretical level, and it a rarer one still that does it in lucid language. The deVilliers's is one of these rarer papers.

Bowerman's contribution continues the high standard set by the deVilliers. She too addresses matters that are absolutely basic to developmental psycholinguists, and her writing is likewise crisp and lucid. She considers the extent to which it has been shown that language development depends upon cognitive development. The evidence is inconclusive, but Bowerman's analysis of the analytic problems is absolutely definitive. Resolution of this issue must have profound implications for assessment and intervention, because it will determine the extent to which both cognitive and linguistic factors must be assessed separately. Bowerman also considers the evidence concerning the extent to which children follow different developmental paths to language acquisition. Until very recently, students of language development sought to characterize a universal language acquisition pattern. Bowerman documents a recent shift toward a concern with individual differences. Her analysis of the analytic problems created by this focus is sharp and constructive. There is reason for great optimism that the study of language development will eventually provide useful assessment and treatment implications, because that study is now concerned with demonstrating individual differences and studying their developmental consequences.

When students of language acquisition speak of linguistic development being dependent upon cognitive development, they usually mean cognitive development as conceived by Piaget. Thus, Bowerman analyzed the issues involved in deciding whether reaching Piaget's Stage VI, the mental representation of external objects, importantly influences children's movement from the one-word to two-word stage of utterance. According to Piaget, mental representation is the result of a long series of developmental stages culminating sometime during the second year of life. Enter Moore and Meltzoff, who offer convincing evidence that infants represent mental events very near birth. If Moore and Meltzoff are right, then students of language development cannot be correct that coming to represent events mentally is important for moving beyond the holophrastic (one-word) stage of language use. This highlights the need for approaching language from both the psycholinguist's and the cognitive developmentalist's view. The paper by Moore and Meltzoff offers a reinterpretation of early cognitive development, a reinterpretation that is best called neo-Piagetian. More importantly, they draw several testable hypotheses about language acquisition from their reinterpretation, promising a renewed interplay between cognitivists and psycholinguists.

Like the deVilliers and Bowerman, Nelson acknowledges the several conceptual changes that have occurred during the last decade in the study of language development. The field has moved from a focus on syntax to an emphasis upon semantics to an emphasis upon nonlinguistic as well as linguistic meaning, and most recently to an emphasis upon language as a medium for communication. This most recent emphasis complicates the study of language by insisting that nonlinguistic and linguistic behaviors must be studied in concert, but it highlights nonlinguistic factors as a source of valuable information from which the child can learn much about language. Nelson, more than Bowerman or the deVilliers, describes and analyzes the importance of studies that view language as a social act, which brings her paper into close contact with Ramey's on mother-child interaction. Indeed, these four papers should be read as a group along with the one by Moore and Meltzoff. Viewed as a group, these five are the heart of this conference's contributions to the approach that contends that assessment must be based on developmental theory. They show both the promise and the rigors of that approach.

Mixed in with the question of whether development is continuous or discontinuous is the question of the role of experience in modifying behavior. Interventionists believe behavior is modifiable, and few conferees questioned this with respect to the behaviors in which they specialize. However, the question did arise with respect to speech perception. Morse reviewed the evidence suggesting that there is little or no development in speech perception. Lack of development is one of the bases from which to infer lack of modifiability. Eilers presented other evidence that suggests that speech perception does develop, implying that experience may be important. Species specificity is another indirect indication that a behavior is innate, and Kuhl showed that speech perception, especially its categorical aspects, are not specific to the human. Kuhl was almost alone in bringing a biologic and evolutionary perspective to the conference's considerations of human development, but she showed the value of doing so. She also reviewed the evidence showing that categorical perception is not unique to speech stimuli, which argues further against the view that speech perception is unique and innate. All three of these papers contain valuable suggestions for future developmental perceptual research, especially as it applies to speech.

FROM RESEARCH TO PRACTICE?

The premise of looking to developmental research and theory for assessment implications is that clinical practice grows from scientific understanding. Anyone who has found relief from aspirin might doubt this premise, since there is still no theoretical or empirical understanding of how that effective analgesic operates. Keith Moore and Andrew Meltzoff drew the finest focus of the conference on the danger of seeking assessment and intervention procedures in basic research and scientific theory.

Imagine for a minute that Moore and Meltzoff had prepared their paper *before* they discovered that neonates imitate. They would have probably begun as they did, by showing that there are easily observable, marked developmental changes in imitation. Then they would have put a theoretical perspective on the facts, likely the Piagetian one. According to that explanation, coming to imitate invisible gestures near the end of the first year of life is important because it reflects a new cognitive competence. That competence is to internally represent events, and Piagetian theory says it must be achieved before language can develop. Having noted these things, Moore and Meltzoff might reasonably have argued that clinical assessments of different sorts of imitation would provide indices of supremely important cognitive capabilities. Because Moore and Meltzoff wrote *after* they discovered that neonates imitate, they made no such arguments. Instead, they argued that Piaget's interpretation of changes in imitation at about one year is invalid, and they advanced an alternative interpretation. They outlined some research approaches to test their interpretation, which they designated neo-Piagetian, and they deferred the drawing of assessment and intervention implications until those researches are completed.

The paper by Moore and Meltzoff shows how a supremely promising clinical implication of developmental theory can seem to go down the drain as a result of developmental research. The apparent undoing of clinical possibilities by making research advances was noted often during the conference, and with special feeling during the discussions of the child language papers by the deVilliers, Bowerman, and Nelson. Since facts and theories change, the question was posed, how can we justify the time and effort to translate present facts and theories into clinical tools? No direct answer was given, but during the discussion of the papers on child language, Moore observed that it might still be useful to employ measures of imitation for clinical purposes. In his brief comments, Moore crystallized the possibility that research might invalidate a theory without invalidating its clinical implications. The answer to the question is clear: Theory is a tool, and even though it works poorly for one purpose, it might work well for another. The important consideration is not whether a clinical technique is based on the latest theory. It is whether the clinical tool, regardless of the theory on which it is based, serves a socially valued purpose. If a scientifically questionable theory leads to a clinically useful procedure, so be it. The clinician can and should draw on the understandings produced by scientific research, but he need not be at the mercy of the scientist. There is no rule of nature that only the most current or most valid theory can provide important clinical guidance. The rate of which theory changes in some domains, as for example the deVilliers showed it has in the study of language development, might only mean that the domains are fickle, which is a problem for people in the domain, but it need not cripple those who wish only to draw clinical inspiration from research and theory.

This conference illustrates especially well that diverse considerations will determine the future of early assessment. Some of those considerations are theoretical and factual. Others are social, financial, and ethical. As I said at the beginning of this summary, no topic worthy of a conference can be subsumed under a single theme. A worthwhile conference is one that sharpens issues and opens possibilities for progress. This one did that, and it must be judged a success.

Index